ROMANS

ROMANS

The Gospel of God

Gerald L. Stevens

PICKWICK *Publications* · Eugene, Oregon

ROMANS
The Gospel of God

Pickwick Publications
An Imprint of Wipf and Stock Publishers
199 W. 8th Ave., Suite 3
Eugene, OR 97401

PAPERBACK ISBN: 978-1-7252-7899-8
HARDCOVER ISBN: 978-1-7252-7900-1
EBOOK ISBN: 978-1-7252-7901-8

Cataloguing-in-Publication data:

Names: Stevens, Gerald L.
Title: Revelation : The past and future of John's Apocalypse / Gerald L. Stevens.
Description: Eugene, OR: Pickwick Publications, 2021 | Includes bibliographical references and index.
Identifiers: ISBN 978-1-7252-7899-8 (paperback) | ISBN 978-1-7252-7900-1 (hardcover) | ISBN 978-1-7252-7901-8 (ebook)
Subjects: LCSH: Bible, NT Romans—Criticism, interpretation, etc. | Bible, NT Romans—Commentaries | Title
Classification: BS2824.53 S77 2021 (print) | BS2824 (ebook)

Cover Image: Roman Colosseum at night. © 2021 Gerald L. Stevens. All rights reserved.

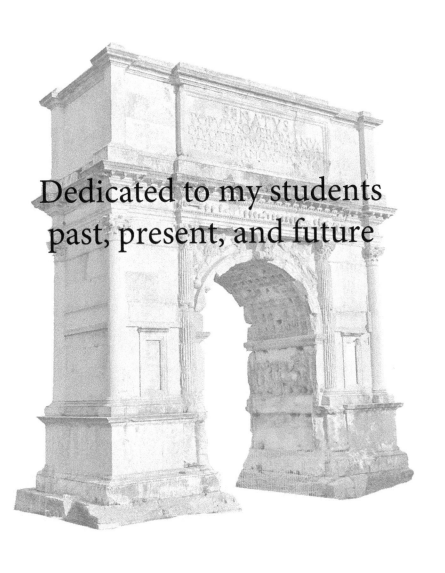

Dedicated to my students
past, present, and future

Credits and Permissions

As I have indicated in other publications, one never walks alone in the pursuit of learning. We always stand on others' shoulders. I obviously am indebted to the extensive commentary tradition on Romans, as well as special studies. I worked to control footnotes, but notated instances of specific debt. I have reconfigured ideas into my own distinctive perspectives, so no one is to blame for such ideas but me. Especially assisting the production of this volume, as in every single one, has been my wife, Jean M. Stevens, and Allyson Presswood Nance.

Contents

Figures

Preface

PAUL'S LETTER TO THE ROMANS has been one of the most studied portions of the Bible, and thereby one of the most intimidating on which to write. So many have said so much for so long. The years have flown by since I first became fascinated with Paul through his incredibly insightful handling of the wrath of God, which I eventually turned into a dissertation.[1] I never have stopped poring over his letters ever since. I have participated in many a learned presentation on Paul, or his letters, or Romans in particular at national and regional conferences of scholars since the late 1970s shortly after Sanders's *Paul and Palestinian Judaism* sent shock waves through the Pauline world. I have read as many books and commentaries on Paul and Romans as I think my brain can handle without exploding. I read four or five recently published volumes just while trying to write this book. I seriously hardly could write for downtime reading. I have taught masters level classes and doctoral seminars on this letter for over thirty years.

I run through this academic reverie only to say that the really depressing news in all this is, I realize I have yet to scratch the surface. So, in defense, I will say that many more books have been read than are in the bibliography. Even so, I am confident some will be keen to note the many more that should have been there as well. I think, however, all those books is my point. Why write this one in the face of so many on Paul and on Romans? As the matter turns out, I have a clear, straightforward thesis about Romans that plays out in unexpected ways that

---

[1] Updated and published as *Divine Wrath in Paul: an Exegetical Study* (Eugene, OR: Pickwick, 2020).

should be of interest even to a veteran Paul reader. The idea is not like wacko in left field or anything like that, but still surprising in interesting and even exciting ways in how one reads Romans. The method in the madness is pretty simple—close reading. I work hard to stay close to the text as written and let the chips fall where they may.

Some just do not have the time for another book on Paul. Believe me, I understand completely. For you I have written the compressed "Cliff's Notes" version in the Epilogue. Just jump over there now and read those few pages. Then you will not have to feel obligated to read one more Pauline volume. For those who hang with me through this volume, thank you for your time. My fondest hope will be that in the process, I have stimulated your thoughts on Paul and Romans in fresh directions.

I have had the privilege of working with many bright and gifted doctoral students over the years, and for that I am so very grateful. I never get over how different they all are in so many ways. Everyone to a person has said, "You have to write a book on Romans." I said no for many years, complaining of the huge mountain we already have. I must say, however, this book never would have been written without one former student in particular, Dr. Allyson Presswood Nance. I told her in a pleasant evening in their home after dinner that my main problem was that all I had to go on with Romans, unlike many other books I had written, was an idea, an intuition, and that was not enough on which to write a book. She reflected for a moment, and then as serious as she could, she responded with acute force, "Dr. Stevens, you just need to trust your intuition more." One cogent comment, and she wiped away all my arguments. As we drove home that evening, I told my wife, "I think I just started writing my commentary on Romans." Well, not a commentary in the technical sense of that genre, of course, but more like a midrash for my students. Well, Dr. Nance—and everyone else who chimed in over the years—here you go!

Gerald L. Stevens
New Orleans, Louisiana
Easter 2021

Abbreviations

AB	Anchor Bible
ANTC	Abingdon New Testament Commentaries
AV	Authorized Version
BEC	The Bible Exposition Commentary
BECNT	Baker Exegetical Commentary on the New Testament
BJS	Brown Judaic Studies
BNTC	Black's New Testament Commentaries
BRLJ	Brill Reference Library of Judaism
BRS	The Biblical Resource Series
CBET	Contributions to Biblical Exegesis and Theology
CCSNS	Cincinnati Classical Studies, New Series
CIS	Copenhagen International Seminar
CJ	The Classical Journal
CRINT	Compendia Rerum Iudaicarum ad Novum Testamentum
ESV	English Standard Version
EGT	The Expositor's Greek Testament
HCSB	Holman Christian Standard Bible
HTR	Harvard Theological Review
HTS	Harvard Theological Studies
ICC	International Critical Commentary
IDB	*Interpreter's Dictionary of the Bible*
INTF	Institute for New Testament Textual Research
IVPNT	InterVarsity Press New Testament
JBL	Journal of Biblical Literature
JSNT	Journal for the Study of the New Testament
JSNTSup	Journal for the Study of the New Testament Supplement
JSPSS	Journal for the Study of the Pseudepigrapha Supplement Series
JTS	Journal of Theological Studies

LBS	Library of Biblical Studies
LCL	Loeb Classical Library
LNTS	Library of New Testament Studies
NA28	*Nestle-Aland Greek New Testament*, 28th Edition
NASB	New American Standard Bible
NBC21	New Bible Commentary: 21st Century Edition
NCBC	New Century Bible Commentary
NET	New English Translation
NICNT	New International Commentary on the New Testament
NIV	New International Version
NIVAC	The NIV Application Commentary
NJB	New Jerusalem Bible
NKJV	New King James Version
NLT	New Living Translation
NRSV	New Revised Standard Version
NT	Novum Testamentum
NTIC	The New Testament in Context
NTL	New Testament Library
NTM	New Testament Message: Biblical-Theological Commentary
NTS	New Testament Studies
OHE	The Oxford History of England
PBTM	Paternoster Biblical and Theological Monographs
PC	Proclamation Commentaries
PCCS	Paul in Critical Contexts Series
RBS	Resources for Biblical Study
SBG	Studies in Biblical Greek
SBLSS	Society of Biblical Literature Semeia Studies
SBLSymS	Society of Biblical Literature Symposium Series
SHBC	Smyth & Helwys Bible Commentary
SNTSMS	Society for New Testament Studies Monograph Series
SPNT	Studies on Personalities of the New Testament.
TCS	TEAMS Commentary Series
TJ	Trinity Journal
UBS5	*United Bible Societies Greek New Testament*, 5th Edition
WBC	Word Biblical Commentary
WGRWSS	Writings from the Greco-Roman World Supplement Series
WTJ	Westminster Theological Journal
WUNT	Wissenschaftliche Untersuchungen zum Neuen Testament

SCRIPTURE

OLD TESTAMENT

Gen	Genesis	Song	Song of Solomon
Exod	Exodus	Isa	Isaiah
Lev	Leviticus	Jer	Jeremiah
Num	Numbers	Lam	Lamentations
Deut	Deuteronomy	Ezek	Ezekiel
Josh	Joshua	Dan	Daniel
Judg	Judges	Hos	Hosea
Ruth	Ruth	Joel	Joel
1–2 Sam	1–2 Samuel	Amos	Amos
1–2 Kgs	1–2 Kings	Obad	Obadiah
1–2 Chr	1–2 Chronicles	Jonah	Jonah
Ezra	Ezra	Mic	Micah
Neh	Nehemiah	Nah	Nahum
Esth	Esther	Hab	Habakkuk
Job	Job	Zeph	Zephaniah
Ps (*pl.* Pss)	Psalm (Psalms)	Hag	Haggai
Prov	Proverbs	Zech	Zechariah
Eccl	Ecclesiastes	Mal	Malachi

NEW TESTAMENT

Matt	Matthew	1–2 Thess	1–2 Thessalonians
Mark	Mark	1–2 Tim	1–2 Timothy
Luke	Luke	Titus	Titus
John	John	Phlm	Philemon
Acts	Acts	Heb	Hebrews
Rom	Romans	Jas	James
1–2 Cor	1–2 Corinthians	1–2 Pet	1–2 Peter
Gal	Galatians	1–2–3 John	1–2–3 John
Eph	Ephesians	Jude	Jude
Phil	Philippians	Rev	Revelation
Col	Colossians		

APOCRYPHA

Tob	Tobit

Jdt	Judith
Wis	Wisdom of Solomon
Sir	Sirach (Ecclesiasticus)
Bar	Baruch
1–2 Macc	1–2 Maccabees
1 Esd	1 Esdras
Pr Man	Prayer of Manasseh
3 Macc	3 Maccabees
2 Esd	2 Esdras
4 Macc	4 Maccabees

PSEUDEPIGRAPHA

Gk Apoc Ezra	Greek Apocalypse of Ezra
Apoc Bar	Apocalypse of Baruch
Apoc Mos	Apocalypse of Moses
As Mos	Assumption of Moses
2 Bar	2 Baruch (Syriac Apocalypse)
1 Enoch	1 Enoch (Ethiopic Apocalypse)
2 Enoch	2 Enoch (Slavonic Apocalypse)
4 Ezra	4 Ezra (= 2 Esdras)
LAE	Life of Adam and Eve
Let Aris	Letter of Aristeas
Ps Sol	Psalms of Solomon
Sib Or	Sibylline Oracles
T Benj	Testament of Benjamin
T Levi	Testament of Levi
T Naph	Testament of Naphtali
T Reu	Testament of Reuben
Jub	Jubilees

APOSTOLIC FATHERS

1–2 Clem.	*1–2 Clement*
Epis. Diog.	*Epistle to Diognetus*
Didache	*The Teachings of the Twelve Apostles*
Epis. Bar.	*Epistle of Barnabas*
Epis. Poly.	*Epistle of Polycarp*
Mart. Poly.	*Martyrdom of Polycarp*

Hermas	*Shepherd of Hermas*

GENERAL SOURCES

AESCHYLUS

Ag.	*Agamemnon*
Prom.	*Prometheus vinctus*

ARISTIDES

To Rome	*Encomium of Rome*

ARISTOTLE

Eth. nic.	*Ethica nicomachea (Nicomechean Ethics)*
Rhet.	*Ars Rhetorica (Rhetoric)*

AUGUSTUS

Res Gestae	*Res Gestae Divi Augusti*

AURELIUS, MARCUS

Com.	*The Communings with Himself (Meditations)*

AURELIUS VICTOR

Caes.	*De Caesaribus (The Caesars)*

CASSIUS DIO

Hist.	*Historia Romana (Roman History)*

CICERO

Flac.	*Pro Flacco*

CHRYSOSTOM, JOHN

Rom.	*In epistolum ad Romanos*

EURIPIDES

Med.   *Medea*

EUSEBIUS

H.E.   *Historia Ecclesiastica (Church History)*

HERODOTUS

Hist.   *The Histories*

HESIOD

Op.   *Opera et dies (Works and Days)*

HOMER

Il.   *Ilias (Iliad)*
Od.   *Odyssea (Odyssey)*

HORACE

Epistles   *Epistularum liber secundus*
Satires   *Satirae (Sermones)*

JEROME

Rom.   *Expositio ep. ad Romanos*

JOSEPHUS

Ant.   *Jewish Antiquities*
Apion   *Against Apion*
J.W.   *The Jewish War*

JUSTIN MARTYR

Apol.   *The First Apology*
Dial.   *Dialogue with Trypho*

Livy

Ab urbe cond.   *Ab urbe condita (History of Rome)*

Menander

Min. Frag.   *Minor Fragments*

Mishnah

Avot   *Avot*
Sukk.   *Sukkah*
Bikk.   *Bikkurim*

Origen

Rom.   *Commentarius in epistolum ad Romanos*

Philo

Embassy   *Embassy to Gaius*
Flacc.   *Against Flaccus*
Free   *Every Man Is Free*
Moses 1, 2   *On the Life of Moses 1, 2*

Pliny the Younger

Letters   *Epistulae*

Plutarch

Ant.   *Antony*

Quintillian

Inst.   *Institutio Oratoria*

Seneca

Ep.   *Epistulae morales ad Lucilim (Moral Epistles to Lucilius)*

Sifre

Piska	*Tannaitic Commentary on Deuteronomy*

Strabo

Geog.	*Geographica*

Suetonius

Claud.	*Claudius, De Vita Caesarum*
Jul.	*Julius, De Vita Caesarum*
Titus	*Titus, De Vita Caesarum*

Tacitus

Ann.	*Annales (The Annals of Tacitus)*
Hist.	*Historiae (The Histories of Tacitus)*

Talmud (Babylonian)

'Abod. Zar.	Nezikin *'Abodah Zarah (Avodah Zarah)*
Ned.	Nashim *Nedarim*
Šabb.	Moed *Šabbat (Shabbat)*
Sanh.	Nezikin *Sanhedrin*
Yeva.	Nashim *Yevamot*
Yoma	Moed *Yoma*
Zebaḥ.	Kodashim *Zebaḥim (Zevahim)*

Talmud (Jerusalem)

Ta'anit	Moed *Ta'anit*

Thucydides

War	*History of the Peloponnesian War*

Virgil

Aen.	*Aeneid*
Ecl.	*Eclogae*

MUSEUMS

AAM	Antalya Archeoloji Müzesi, Antalya, Turkey
AM	Acropolis Museum, Athens, Greece
AMA	Aphrodisias Müzesi, Aphrodisias, Turkey
AMAC	Archeological Museum of Ancient Corinth, Greece
AMD	Archeological Museum of Delphi, Greece
AMR	Archeological Museum of Rhodes, Dodecanese
AMV	Archeological Museum of Veroia (Berea)
ASM	Attalos Stoa Museum, Athens, Greece
ASMK	Ancient Shipwreck Museum, Kyrenia Castle, Girne, Cyprus
BMB	Bergama Müzesi, Bergama, Turkey
BML	British Museum, London, England
CEM	Cairo Egyptian Museum
CM	Cyprus Museum, Nicosia, Cyprus
DIA	Detroit Institute of Arts, Detroit, Michigan
DRM	Domus Romana Museum, Rabat, Malta
EMS	Ephesos Müzesi, Selçuk, Turkey
GPMM	Great Palace Mosaic Museum, Istanbul, Turkey
HAM	Hatay Archeoloji Müzesi, Turkey
HAMH	Hierapolis Archeoloji Müzesi, Hierapolis, Turkey
HAMC	Heraklion Archeological Museum of Crete
HMM	History Museum of Mobile, Alabama
IAM	Istanbul Archeoloji Müzerleri, Istanbul, Turkey
IAMI	Izmir Archeoloji Müzesi, Izmir, Turkey
IHAM	Izmir History and Art Museum, Turkey
IMJ	Israel Museum, Jerusalem, Israel
KAM	Konya Archeoloji Müzesi, Turkey
KMM	Karaman Müze Müdürlügü, Karaman, Turkey
LP	The Louvre, Paris, France
MANRC	Museo Archeologico Nazionale di Reggio Calabria, Italy
MCA	Museo Civico Archeologico, Orvieto, Italy
MCF	Museo Claudio Faina, Orvieto, Italy
MM	Milet Müzesi, Miletus, Turkey
MMM	Manisa Müze, Manisa, Turkey
NAM	Nicosia Archeological Museum, Nicosia, Cyprus
NMB	National Museum of Bargello, Florence, Italy
NAMA	National Archeological Museum of Athens, Greece

NNAM	Naples National Archeological Museum, Italy
OAM	Ostia Antica Museum, Ostia Antica, Italy
PAM	Philippi Archeological Museum, Philippi, Greece
PMB	Pergamon Museum, Berlin, Germany
QNPM	Qumran National Park Museum, Qumran, Israel
ROM	Royal Ontario Museum, Toronto, Canada
SMS	Side Müzesi, Side, Turkey
TAM	Thessaloniki Archeological Museum, Greece
TMT	Tarsus Müze, Tarsus, Turkey
YMY	Yalvaç Müze, Yalvaç, Turkey

PART 1

Preliminary Thoughts

Orientation to Paul and Romans

1

Pauline Polarities

Setting the Stage for Study of Paul

THE STUDY OF PAUL AMONG New Testament scholars can be organized around ten polarities of arguments following the trajectories of four major topics: (1) methodology, (2) worldview, (3) hermeneutic, and (4) theology. Scholars position themselves along a continuum that is circulating around polarities within these topics. Students of Paul can grasp the issues more quickly and where scholars stand in relation to these debates by recognizing these polarities, since they do not really change much from generation to generation. We intend to summarize these topics but not solve the problems.

METHODOLOGY POLARITIES

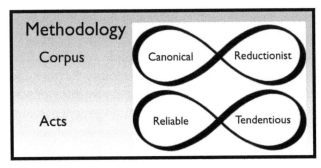

FIGURE 1.1. Pauline Polarities: Methodology.

The first topic is methodology. By this we mean choice of subject matter from a literary and historical point of view. Who is "Paul," and what did he really write?

3

Scholars disagree. Their disagreements are based on assumptions about what constitutes the genuine Pauline literary corpus and what is the Pauline story and its chronology. The question of story and chronology inevitably involves the question of the use of Acts.

Defining the Corpus

Which letters are Paul's? Among scholars, opinions will circulate around two foci, canonical or reductionist, or perhaps somewhere in between leaning one way or the other. Even within the canonical orbit, the question remains as to how the Pastorals in particular should be fitted into the heuristic matrix that can be used to explain "Pauline thought." The reductionist heritage in modern times traces all the way back to F. C. Baur and the Tubingen school in Germany he inspired. Here, the issue of pseudepigraphy looms large over the analytical landscape of Paul.

So, for example, when J. Christiaan Beker wrote his magisterial study of Paul in 1980, he immediately reduced the canonical corpus down to just seven letters (Romans, 1–2 Corinthians, Galatians, Philippians, 1 Thessalonians, Philemon), asserting that 2 Thessalonians, Colossians, Ephesians, 1–2 Timothy, and Titus were "pseudepigraphical," begrudgingly acknowledging that they "transmit Pauline traditions."[1] Beker's reduced corpus is "canonical" in its own way among a host of Pauline scholars. Some may reduce the Pauline corpus more, some less. While exactly where a scholar may circulate on the corpus ellipse may vary, the point is, any such reduction obviously impacts what one is willing to say is "Paul's thought." Hence, one can have significant variances on establishing even an outline of "Pauline theology" tracing directly back to disagreements about the question of the Pauline corpus.

This question in church history traditionally includes the book of Hebrews, but the solution here is much more simple and direct. The book is anonymous, yet Paul did not write anonymously. Further, the author of Hebrews came to faith through the gospel preaching of witnesses of Jesus (Heb 2:1–4), which is foreign to Paul's experience and, in fact, invalidates his argument of independence from Jerusalem (Gal 1:11–17; 1 Cor 15:3–10). The language and style transparently are not

---

[1] *Paul the Apostle*, 3 (note). For a balanced discussion of the issue of pseudepigraphy related to Pauline literature, see deSilva, "Excursus: Pseudepigraphy and the New Testament Canon," *Introduction*: 685–88.

Pauline. The content is not Pauline. The priestly and hieratic thought channel argumentative strategies never employed by Paul elsewhere. The brief mention of Timothy at the end (Heb 13:22) is the only semblance of a Pauline connection and likely the only "hook" to lure any argument to bite on Pauline authorship. One, however, first has to presume the Timothy here is the longtime associate of Paul. One also has to presume that Paul's Timothy was a known and close friend only to Paul among early church leaders. Patristic tradition was mixed on authorship. When Jerome and Augustine threw their weight behind Pauline authorship—more to stack the deck in favor of canonical inclusion than for any literary argument—they sealed the deal for later Catholic tradition. This venerable Catholic tradition of Pauline authorship of Hebrews ironically petrified into the title of the book in the Protestant "authorized" King James Version.

Defining the Biography

How does one establish a biography and chronology of Paul's life? This effort is imperative to establish the sequence and context of his letters for purposes of exegesis. The methodology is not easy. The process involves establishing an "absolute" chronology of fixed dates relative to the story of Paul, such as provided by the Delphi inscription related to Gallio's proconsulship in Corinth, as well as a "relative" chronology of sequences that can be ordered but not precisely dated, such as Paul in Damascus, Arabia, and Jerusalem. Even relative sequences, however, can be argued, such as the sequence of Galatians relative to the Jerusalem Conference of Acts 15, or the sequence of the Thessalonian correspondence (Wanamaker).

Questions of Pauline biography quickly move to the question of Acts. Opinions circulate around the two foci of Acts as historically reliable (Keener) or as so tendentious as to be unusable (Smith and Tyson), or somewhere in between leaning one way or the other. Pauline chronology is crucial because the question of the apostle's theological development depends upon a proposed historical outline of Paul's life and ministry. Thus, the question whether to use Acts and, if so, to what extent necessarily factors into discussion of Pauline chronology. The methodological conundrum is, if we eliminate Acts altogether, we have little historical foundation for Pauline chronology, since his undated letters leave us with biographical pieces from different puzzles all spilled out on the floor. Alternate construals leave little consensus.

WORLDVIEW POLARITIES

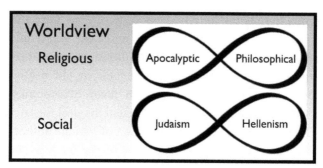

FIGURE 1.2. Pauline Polarities: Worldview.

Another topic is worldview. Two polarities are involved. One is religion and the other society. What ideas were integral to Paul's own religious framework, and how did he integrate centuries of inherited social amalgamation of Judaism and Hellenism into his worldview?

Defining the Religious Worldview

Even the word "religion" is up for grabs. One can argue, for example, that the concept of "religion" itself is a thoroughly post-Enlightenment idea completely foreign to the first-century mind. The idea here is that religion in the first-century world was about duty, moral obligation, or conscience toward anything (family, neighbors, rulers, gods). One might think of Maximus in the movie "Gladiator" performing ritual honorific duties using miniature representations of family members. The post-Enlightenment development turned more toward doctrine, practice, and social structures with prescribed behavior and encoded rituals as definitive of religion. The lesson here is to be circumspect in contemplating "Paul's religion" not to import anachronistically post-Enlightenment concepts.

After clearing the "religion" hurdle, one still has to contemplate apocalyptic thought. This issue in Paul is a spillover from life of Jesus research of the nineteenth and twentieth centuries. We never decided whether Jesus was or was not apocalyptic in worldview in a Shakespearean "to be or not to be, that is the question." We dramatically wavered all the way from a definitive no in Renan and Harnack in the nineteenth century to a resounding yes in Wrede and Schweitzer into the twentieth century. The quest in the west just reversed the tables back to a no (The Jesus Seminar). Yes came again in the Jesus the Jew, new perspective on Paul movements in scholars such as Vermes, Theissen, Sanders, Martyn, Dunn, and Wright. Matlock reverted to no and argued "the king has no clothes" for the entire Schweitzer, Käsemann, Beker circular argument juggernaut in Pauline studies.

Even if Paul's religious thought derives from apocalyptic ideas (e.g., Schweitzer, Käsemann, Beker, Martyn, Wright), how apocalyptic is that framework, and in what way exactly? Would the apocalyptic element be little more than simple imminent expectation (Käsemann), or should this element be conceived more radically as a completely disruptive inbreaking into history (Martyn)? Is Paul framing his theology innovatively on an existing, Jewish, two-age eschatological structure that allows for some continuity between past and present ages (Wright), or is Paul in such a radical frame of mind that he conceives the apocalyptic inbreaking of Christ as rupturing all realities, creating total discontinuity between past and present (de Boer, Martyn)?

On the other side of the equation, one might decide that Paul's religious framework is not apocalyptic at all, but rather, philosophical. This end of the spectrum is a minority opinion, but argued to great length by some (Campbell). If the religious frame of Paul's thought fundamentally issues from a philosophical ground, what are the contours of Paul's philosophical reflections? Are they more distinctly Jewish or Greco-Roman? Or, are his reflections in any particular instance an indeterminate and complex mix (Koester)?

Defining the Social Worldview

Consider the question of Paul's social worldview. Opinions circulate around the two foci of Judaism or Hellenism, or somewhere in between leaning one way or the other. If Paul essentially is Hellenistic (Baur, Bousset, Bultmann), his so-called "Jewishness" is only the husk of his thought to be discarded, and "Judaism" becomes just another example of "self-effort" pagan religion, conveniently castigating any first-century "Jew" as simply the poster child of a prototypical "religious human." If, however, Paul writes exclusively to pagans and not really to Jews (Gager, Gaston, Fredriksen), then could his Jewish categories be only rhetorical devices to persuade a gentile audience? One might argue this "Hellenistic" Paul actually evokes little that is Jewish precisely because he so quickly and easily adapts to Greco-Roman values evident within Greco-Roman philosophy (Stowers, Campbell).

On the other hand, if Paul essentially lives out of a Jewish social matrix (Schweitzer, Stendahl, Davies, Sanders, Dunn, Wright, Watson, Meeks), the question remains, just how Jewish is he, and in what way exactly (apocalyptic, rabbinic, social)? If Jewish, what about Israel? Does Paul's social frame involve an inherent worldview encapsulated in a Jewish metanarrative, the story of Israel (Hayes, Wright)? Further, does Paul conceive continuity with Israel's story (Calvin) or discontinuity (Luther, Stuhlmacher, Martyn, Campbell)? Or, should Paul be interpreted in sociological categories that eschew theological constructs altogether (Judge, Theissen, Malina, Neyrey, Elliott, Esler, Meeks, Jewett)?

HERMENEUTIC POLARITIES

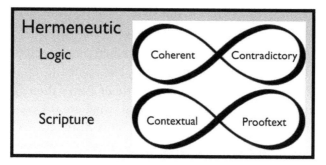

FIGURE 1.3. Pauline Polarities: Hermeneutic.

A third topic is hermeneutic. The polarities in these arguments orbit around issues of Paul's logic and his use of Scripture. Is Paul coherent or incoherent in his logic when he argues so differently about the Jewish law from Galatians to Romans? Further, does Paul incorporate Scripture into his arguments mindful or oblivious to original contexts?

Defining Use of Logic

On the question of logic, opinions circulate around the two foci that Paul internally is coherent or contradictory, or somewhere in between leaning one way or the other. If coherent, what exactly is the organizing center? Is this center apocalyptic thought generally (Beker), apocalyptic crisis specifically (Martyn), justification by faith (Reformers), some nebulous "in Christ" mysticism never precisely defined (Schweitzer, Sanders), or some other idea? If contradictory (Räisänen), at what level is Paul contradicting himself? Does he stumble into simple pragmatic inconsistencies that can be overlooked, or does he egregiously engage in philosophical impossibilities that cannot be ignored? Was Paul aware of the tensions in his thought, and if so, did he successfully or unsuccessfully deal with them, or did he just ignore them?

Defining Use of Scripture

Paul is prolific in quoting Scripture. The high number of quotations in Romans suggests Scripture is crucial in this letter to Paul's hermeneutic. Yet, opinions circulate around the two foci of whether in this process Paul is quoting these passages contextually or simply proof-texting to suit his argument as the occasion arises, or somewhere in between leaning one way or the other. If Paul quotes contextually (Ellis), what text is he quoting (LXX, Masoretic, or other) and what context? Further, was he faithful to the original historical context? If proof-texting (Campbell), was this process purely pragmatic, or was some hermeneutical process applied that was analogical or even historical (Watson)?

THEOLOGY POLARITIES

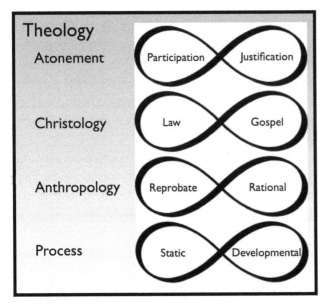

A fourth topic is theology, a mother lode of four sets of polarities at issue for scholars. Is Pauline atonement participationist, that is, bilateral, with a mix of human and divine components, or a unilateral act of justification? Is Paul's Christology law inclu-

FIGURE 1.4. Pauline Polarities: Theology.

sive or gospel exclusive? What is Paul's anthropology? Does he consider the human mind thoroughly reprobate or reasonably rational? Does Paul's theological reflection evolve in traceable, developmental stages (Becker, Hübner), or is his theological system fundamentally in place from the Damascus Road forward (S. Kim)?

Defining Atonement

Consider the question of atonement theory and its fraternal twin, the center of Paul's theology. Opinions circulate around the two foci of participation or justification, or somewhere in between leaning one way or the other. If Paul's atonement is participationist (Schweitzer, Sanders, Campbell), is this rhetorical only in order to distinguish from sanctification (Reformers) or real, but apprehended only existentially (Schweitzer, Bultmann)? Further, on a related issue, does Paul speak sociologically in terms of fictive kinship (Malina), or personally in terms of the essence of being (Schweitzer)? On the other hand, if justification is the center of Paul's thought (Luther, Moo, Longenecker), is this justification a divine, forensic declaration (Augustine) or a co-operative process of dynamic mediation (Käsemann)?

Defining Christology

How do Christ and the gospel relate to Israel and the law? Opinions circulate around the two foci of law inclusive or gospel exclusive, or somewhere in between leaning one way or the other. The problem exposes the exegetical difficulty of synthesizing Galatians into Romans for a coherent theological picture (e.g., Räisänen). Difficulty finding middle ground between the two epistles inevitably inclines the exegete to emphasize one over the other.

Emphasis on Galatians puts more negative opinion on law and tends to provoke "either/or" logic, that is, either law or gospel, but not both. In such a scenario, obviously, the law has to go, so gospel displaces law (Luther, Carson, Gathercole, Das, Westerholm, Longenecker, Catholicism). The consideration of "law" may be impacted by prototyping "Judaism" as a "works religion." The Achilles heel of this view on the law is the question of Israel as the people of God, which inevitably involves a definition of "church." Are gospel and church to be understood as continuous with the story of Israel (Longenecker) or discontinuous (Bock)? Or, do we actually have two, parallel covenants, both in force simultaneously (Rosenzweig)?

Emphasis on Romans puts a more positive spin on the law and tends to generate "both/and" logic on the question, integrating both law and gospel (Calvin, Cranfield, Ridderbos, Wright, Watson). Even if law is viewed as positive, is this law to be understood as a corporate covenant (Wright) or as individual performance (Dunn)?

Defining Anthropology

Bultmann famously organized his 1950s theology of Paul not around the doctrine of God, as was the usual procedure at the time, but around a doctrine of man ("Man Prior to the Revelation of Faith," "Man Under Faith").[2] Using anthropology as the key to Paul's thought was a radical move at that time. Bultmann reopened the question of just what was Paul's anthropology? Opinions circulate around the two foci of humans as reprobate or rational, or somewhere in between leaning one way or the other. If reprobate (Calvin, Barth), then why appeal to human will? How does this appeal make sense logically? If rational (Fitzmyer, Campbell), what role does reason play within the process of human and divine communications and relations?

Defining Process

Consider the process of Paul doing theology, that is, the question of theological development. Opinions circulate around two foci of static or developmental, or somewhere in between leaning one way or the other. Was Paul's theology stable from its inception, that is, fully in place, at least in a nutshell, from the Damascus Road (S. Kim)? The idea would be that Paul's theological reflection as a trained Pharisee already was highly developed and mature. He basically had all the theological ingredients he needed for his reflection on Christ to crystalize immediately.

Or, was Paul's theology in process along the way, impacted by his experiences, constantly in a state of flux, developing, needing to be teased out carefully from a specific chronological sequencing of his epistles (Becker, Hübner)? If developmental, the idea would be that

---

[2] Bultmann, *Theology of the New Testament*, viii–x.

Paul's theological reflection changed and adapted in parallel to mission experience (e.g., Becker's triadic election, cross, justification scheme, or Hübner's Galatians to Romans scheme). The question would be what mission experiences in particular had such impact on Paul, and what theological reflection was provoked by those particular experiences?

CONCLUSION

Pauline scholars can be "typed" on a scholarly continuum circulating around various polarities. Scholars can be positioned relatively along the axis of the two foci controlling each polarity issue. Applying these polarities to any given scholar guides one's grasp more quickly of the arguments offered, as well as how presuppositions function to control the results. In the presentation above, sample scholars have been used simply to be illustrative, not to be exhaustive. Observing this polarity principle hopefully can bring order to the study of Paul in the midst of the chaos of proposals and theories swirling around Pauline scholars and their publications.[3]

---

[3] A helpful summary of what one might call "profiles of Paul," that is, situating Paul within the context of first-century Judasim, with particular focus on the post-Sanders era is Pitre, Barber, and Kincaid, *Paul, A New Covenant Jew*, 28–89. Heuristic categories on the spectrum from discontinuity to continuity are: (1) discontinuous non-Jew, or "former Jew" (Bultmann, Käsemann, Westerholm), (2) discontinuous eschaton Jew, or "eschatological Jew" (Schweitzer, Davies, Sanders, Dunn), (3) continuous same-covenant Jew, or "torah-observant Jew" (Stendahl, Gaster, Gager, Nanos, Eisenbaum, Fredrikson), and (4) continuous, different-covenant Jew, or "new covenant Jew" (Pitre, Barber, Kincaid, inspired by Forman, Hays, Wright, Bird, Fitzmyer, Matera, Hahn).

2

The Righteousness of God

Frontiers of Pauline Research

THE QUEST FOR UNDERSTANDING Paul's language of the righteousness of God and justification never ends.[1] Major proposals have appeared even in just the last few years. The literature not only is voluminous, but individual volumes are exploding in size.[2] In this chapter, we survey three recent proposals on the righteousness of God coming from Watson, Campbell, and Wright.[3] The discussion is guided by what is perceived to be the controlling hermeneutic in each case.

WATSON'S CANONICAL TENSIONS
Introduction

For Watson, Paul in quoting Scripture already is in the middle of an on-going debate of Jewish interpretation. Paul's reading of Abraham, for example, is framed in terms of an appropriation of this patriarch within the structure of the entire Jewish canon that itself is then nego-

---

[1] This chapter is developed with permission substantially from Gerald L. Stevens, "The Righteousness of God: Frontiers of Pauline Research," *CTR* n.s. 12/2 (Spring 2015): 47–69.

[2] The intent for this chapter is not to provide an exhaustive bibliography, which is available in the more recent publications that will be covered in this chapter. A good read for this purpose would be N. T. Wright, *Paul and His Recent Interpreters*.

[3] Francis Watson, *Paul and the Hermeneutics of Faith* (2004); Douglas A. Campbell, *The Deliverance of God* (2009); N. T. Wright, *Paul and the Faithfulness of God* (2013), which inspired a subsequent critique volume in response edited by Christoph Helig, Thomas Hewitt, and Michael F. Bird, *God and the Faithfulness of Paul* (2017).

tiated against other dominant Jewish readings of this "canonical" portrait of Abraham, such as *Jubilees*, Philo, or Josephus. Romans, then, is
infused with scriptural quote and allusion precisely because Paul is in
conversation with alternate readings of canonical Jewish texts within
that canonical framing. Paul, therefore, is reading within the context
of the entire canon, not just looking at solitary texts in isolation. Premier examples would be Hab 2:4 (Rom 1:17) and Gen 15:6 (Rom 4:3).
Watson interprets these quotations deriving their meaning from the
canonical context.

This "canonical reading" of Paul's quotations means his "theology of justification" does not float in an ethereal vacuum. His theology of
justification is a hermeneutic of the Jewish canon as canon. Along the
way to speaking of "justification," that is, Paul actually is engaged in a
larger canonical task, and we need to frame justification language within this larger context. This larger context has inherent tension, and the
canonical tension becomes a key operative concept for Watson. In the
canonical task, Paul is "highlighting and exploiting tensions between
Genesis and Exodus, Leviticus and Deuteronomy" (Watson, 3). Perceived tensions such as with the law are not in Paul, Watson reiterates.
They are tensions inherent in the canonical texts themselves. Any proposed "contradiction" in Paul's "view of the law," in other words, does
not come from Paul's inept attempt at theology but from within the
canonical texts themselves. Paul astutely is exploiting tensions for his
own dynamic reading of the law of Moses in the light of Christ. In this
way, Paul's reading represents an intertextual, inter-Jewish, canonical
hermeneutic.

A study of Ben Sira, for example, reveals a fault line in Sanders's
paradigm-shifting "covenantal nomism."[4] Covenantal nomism itself
levels out inherent canonical tension just as much as older "legalism"
views falsely depicting Judaism that Sanders opposed. Watson thinks
Sanders does not truly get at Paul's understanding of justification,
because he does not work out Paul's intertextual activity in Rom 1:17
in quoting Hab 2:4 in which Paul is resolving the canonical tension of
this prophetic text, correcting, as Paul sees the matter, a reading about
the law in Lev 18:5 ("do these and live"). Sanders fails to see Paul's
quote as exploiting inherent tension in the canon, as canonical texts

---

[4] E. P. Sanders, *Paul and Palestinian Judaism* (1977).

attempt to work out Israel's covenant through Abraham (Gen 15:6) against negative historical results of the intended Law of Life in Moses (Lev 18:5). The tension is resolved, Paul now sees after encountering Christ, by Habakkuk's canonical configuration within The Book of the Twelve prophets "correcting" the inadequate approach to Israel and the law precipitated out of the Pentateuch (Watson, 13).[5] For Watson, two different scriptural soteriologies are in tension, and this tension means that Paul's experience in Christ is not simply trumping Judaism and its Scripture, as Sanders would paint the picture. Christ's coming exposes a hermeneutic within Scripture itself that resolves the conundrum of Israel and the law (Lev 18:5). This alternative soteriology of righteousness by faith (Hab 2:4) obviates the ineptness of the law to save. The coming of Christ revealed to Paul a soteriological reading of canonical literature in a configuration heretofore unperceived by Paul. Paul reads the Christ event in concord with this intertextual dynamic in Scripture, especially seen in Habakkuk.

Paul's hermeneutic of faith exploits two major canonical tensions. These tensions are evident in the Pentateuch: unconditional promise (Genesis) combined with Sinai's legislation (Exodus), versus the law's offer of life (Leviticus) but result of curse (Deuteronomy), which then constantly threatens the unconditional promise. Other Jewish readers perceived the tensions. Paul, however, seized upon them as integral to his hermeneutic of Christ (Watson, 23). This canonical juggling gives Paul's hermeneutic an antithetical structure.

Part 1 ("Antithesis")

Part 1 ("Antithesis") is Watson's presentation of this antithetical hermeneutic. He first sets out the basic contours of the Reformation discourse on justification. In this discourse, justification as derived from Romans 1–4 not only is made the center of Romans, but also the center of Paul, and even the center of the New Testament. The related issue of Paul's "works of the law" was read as salvation by self-effort, a uni-

---

[5] The Twelve are Hosea, Joel, Amos, Obadiah, Jonah, Micah, Nahum, Habakkuk, Zephaniah, Haggai, Zechariah, and Malachi, already seen as a distinct and complete collection several centuries before Christ, as in Ben Sira (Sir 48:17–25; 49:1–7). The Hebrew Old Testament counts them as one book, which meant they usually were studied together. They are "minor" in that they are shorter than the much longer (hence "major") prophets Isaiah, Ezekiel, and Jeremiah.

versal, individualized struggle of the human soul of which Judaism was chief exemplar.

Schweitzer exploded this Protestant non-apocalyptic synthesis of Paul with his "mystical" (i.e., apocalyptic) Paul.[6] The essential Paul is the apocalyptic Paul anticipating the imminent end of all things. This apocalyptic shake up of the universe already had begun in Jesus's resurrection. Believers mystically are immersed into end time realities by being joined with Christ and participating (hence, "participationist") in these realities in Christ. Thus, the real center of Paul's theology is not Romans 1–4 with its forensic justification theme (the conventional reading) but Romans 5–8 with its mystical "in Christ" theme. Schweitzer accused Luther of missing the boat on Romans 1–4, not recognizing that Paul was forced into justification language in those early chapters only as a rhetorical necessity to meet his opponents' justification arguments appropriating texts such as Hab 2:4. Paul then in Romans 5–8 redirected the topic to his "participationist" theme. So Paul incorporates justification rhetoric into Romans 1–4 only to overwhelm his opponents' argument with his core "mystical" union with Christ theme in Romans 5–8. Thus, the traditional "righteousness of God" in Romans 1–4 is as God's righteous judgment, but that idea is not core to Paul.

Käsemann in his momentous commentary on Romans adopted Schweitzer's apocalyptic Paul. Käsemann, however, argued that "the righteousness of God" even in Rom 1:17 could be understood apocalyptically as divine gift. Righteousness is a power, God's saving power that breaks into human experience in Christ. Käsemann was able to join the "power of God" in Rom 1:16 to the "righteousness of God" in Rom 1:17 using this apocalyptic framework.[7] The result was, Schweitzer through Käsemann (and later Beker) permanently let loose an apocalyptic (mystical) Paul upon Pauline scholars.

Watson counterargued Käsemann. Watson read "the righteousness of God" in Rom 1:17 as interpretive gloss more closely connected to the *following* citation of Hab 2:4, "live by faith," not to the previous "power of God" phrasing in 1:16. Thus, the righteousness of God is human righteousness valid before God, which is the righteous status of the believer, exactly as in Habakkuk (Watson, 49). Watson rejected,

---

[6] Schweitzer, *The Mysticism of Paul the Apostle* (1931).

[7] Käsemann, "The 'Righteousness of God' in Paul," 168–82.

therefore, that the (faith) faithfulness described in 1:17 was either God's or Christ's.[8]

Thus, Rom 1:18—3:20 leaves the "shall live" part of the Rom 1:17 quotation in ironic suspension. Paul's demonstration and conclusion, in fact, is presented in an alternate Scripture giving another "voice" to the law ("whatever the law says," 3:19), a contrary voice that declares that "no one is righteous, not even one" (Rom 3:10). So, the righteous person will live (Rom 1:17), but no one is righteous (Rom 3:10), so canonical tension. The tension is clear by reading Rom 1:17 back-to-back with Rom 3:10 or 3:20, and then realizing this same tension is expressed even more compactly in one verse in Gal 3:11. The catena of Scripture in Rom 3:9–20 that gives this "voice" to the law does not come from the law of Moses itself. Watson pointed out that the catena is derived from later canonical writers, David and Isaiah, interpreting the law. Thus, Scripture is interpreting Scripture. Paul adds his own interpretive composition as he himself now modifies and combines the actual texts into one voice. The voice that says "no one" in 3:20 is antithetical to the voice that says "shall live" in 1:17 (Watson, 58–65).

Further, Watson argued that "works of the law" are exactly what comprise Habakkuk's "shall live" statement about Israelite faithfulness to do the law, a distinct rejection of Dunn's new perspective attempt to interpret "works of the law" as nationalistic "boundary markers" of ethnicity and community (Watson 68, n77). The bottom line is a hermeneutical dilemma within Scripture itself that Paul seeks to exploit and resolve.

Paul first established inherent tension in the law's voice on righteousness. Paul then reformulated Rom 1:17 in 3:21–22 to interpret the Habakkuk text further. Paul first interprets "by faith" to mean "apart from the law" to counter the "no one" of the law's voice. Paul then interprets "law and the prophets" not as generic divisions of Jewish Scripture but as distinct voices he now hears that insinuate a new way to the righteousness God requires. The new way is "through faith of Jesus Christ," which, for Watson, is God's saving action in Christ that inspires believing response to Christ. The relationship of this new way of righteousness to the act of Jesus Christ is developed in 3:22–26, and its relationship to the law in 3:27–31. Thus, Watson's handling of Ro-

[8] Obviously targeting both Wright and Hayes; cf. Wright, 79.

mans 1–3 as Paul's exegesis of Hab 2:4 reveals Watson's thesis and book title: "Paul's doctrine of righteousness by faith is an exercise in scriptural interpretation and hermeneutics" (Watson, 76).

Watson then contextualized Paul's Habakkuk interpretation as in dialogue with other Jewish traditions also interpreting the same text. Paul was not the only Jewish interpreter negotiating the felt tensions within the scriptural witness. Paul's doctrine of justification is to be understood as already a part of a scriptural debate Jews were having long before Christ arrived. The Habakkuk quotation was part of the Book of the Twelve. Jewish groups such as the Essenes of the *Damascus Document*, or the pesherist of the Habakkuk commentary at Qumran, demonstrate that Paul was not the only one to use Hab 2:4 as a crucial soteriological text. In these alternate Jewish interpretive efforts, the text was contemporized eschatologically as the "end of days" (like Paul) and "represents a fundamental soteriological statement in which the entire basis of a particular form of communal existence is summed up" (Watson, 120). Further, the Book of the Twelve corporately expresses hope that God will redeem even after the judgment of exile. Non-fulfillment historically, however, conflicts with this canonical hope, creating a fault line within Scripture itself, since this hope is contradicted by Lev 18:5.

Part 2 ("Promise")

Part 2 ("Promise") is used to show Paul exploiting this fault line. Paul starts with Genesis. He innovates a "promise hermeneutic" based on a distinctive reading of Abraham in Genesis. Paul's Abraham motif will demonstrate his reading of Habakkuk is a Torah reading. In contrast to typical Jewish interpretation of Genesis 15, Paul separates promise and performance. Paul's "flesh" and "promise" are not esoteric theological jargon but straightforward readings of the actual story of Abraham's own initiative, characterized literally as "flesh," which is the story of Ishmael, versus God's own initiative, characterized as promise, which is the story of Isaac. So, Genesis 15–21 foreshadows the salvation history summarized in Galatians 3.

Part 3 ("Wilderness")

Part 3 ("Wilderness") continues Paul's exegetical journey through the Pentateuch by taking up Exodus, Leviticus, and Numbers. The main point will be the "wilderness" reality of the law. At this point, Watson eschewed discussion of "Paul's view of the law." He charged that these well-worn problems ignore the fundamental datum that Paul "speaks of the law not as a propounder of dogmatic assertions but as an interpreter of texts" (Watson, 275). Exodus *in context* shows that Israel's story after law is catastrophe. Watson explored other Pauline letters to piece together Paul's hermeneutic of catastrophe. In 2 Corinthians 3, Paul is working the Exodus narrative. In Gal 3:12 and Rom 10:5, Paul pits Lev 18:5 against Lev 19:17–19, to show that whereas the law promises life to the doer of the law, curse always looms on the horizon. Watson rejected Sanders's construct that Second Temple Judaism did not read the commandments as the way to life based on "false dichotomies" essential to Sanders's construct (Watson, 323–29). "Works of the law" would be a globalizing summary of all actions prescribed or proscribed in the law. Watson opted for *telos* in Rom 10:4 as "end," not "goal." What Christ "ends" is a specific hermeneutic of Moses, that is, reading Lev 18:5 as a viable soteriology. Paul contradicts such readings. For Paul, Numbers illustrates a vicious cycle of rebellion and retribution. Numbers tragically shows how the golden calf incident in Exodus is not episodic but paradigmatic of Israel's history (Watson, 355).

For example, take the typically difficult Rom 7:7–12. Watson said this passage best is read as a summary of the Numbers narrative about the nation, not some existential crisis of an individual. Watson shows how other Jewish readings of Numbers, as in the *Wisdom of Solomon*, have to suppress the corporate realities in the canonical text, such as the judgment of Israel, that Paul rather makes center stage. Josephus, for example, so idealized law performance as to claim that the law uniformly and completely was observed among Hebrews. Josephus even claimed that, lived well, the law can provide eternal life.[9]

---

[9] Josephus, *Ant.* 3.223. Relative to the question of eternal life, cf. *Apion* 2.218.

Part 4 ("Last Words")

Part 4 ("Last Words") finishes Paul's exegetical journey through the Pentateuch by taking up Paul's use of Deuteronomy. The construct is Moses's last words to Israel. The theme is Israel's later story of exile. The result is a definitive analysis of Israel's present predicament. The negative result of the law in its curse and consequent dispossession of the promised land is on prominent display in history. Israel's future history anticipated in Deuteronomy 27–29 leaves no impression that, given a second, or third, or fourth chance, Israel would hear Moses's final words of exhortation any better (Watson, 439). Israel's true hope is not in the law with its known tragic consequences but in the promise to Abraham with its absolute certainty as grounded in God. For Paul, the prospect in Deuteronomy 30 of life even after curse does not anticipate a return to the law, as in typical Jewish readings,[10] but a new work of God that transcends the law. Deuteronomy itself insinuates such transcendence in the later Song of Moses (Deut 32:35–43). Yet, to see this interpretive possibility clearly, God will have to act dramatically and decisively to reveal a new initiative, an "apocalypse" of God's new way of righteousness for Israel that suddenly discloses the latent soteriology left in suspension in the scriptural tension in Moses (Rom 1:17). Paul concludes God did act this way in Christ.

Summation

For all this significant work and study of Paul, Watson still winds up reading justification and the righteousness of God in a conventional way (forensic, non-apocalyptic). Yet, by counterarguing Käsemann at the beginning, Watson was clear where he would land. At least Paul is absolved of making "contradictory" statements about the law. However, the price is high. Instead of Paul, Scripture makes contradictory statements about the law. Inevitably, the proposal of canonical tensions means, de facto, every exegete has a tiger by the tail, whether first century or twenty-first century.

---

[10] As in Bar 2:27–35.

CAMPBELL'S FALSE GOSPEL
Introduction

Campbell sets out to demolish forensic justification, not simply as a Reformation construct well past its prime, but as an outright "another gospel" Paul would anathematize. The idea clearly is insinuated in the Gal 1:8 text on the flyleaf opposite the title page when combined with an appraisal of the book's argumentative development. His massive volume has five parts. The first three are only preparatory, but comprise 466 pages. Actual thesis development does not even begin until Part 4.[11]

Part 1 ("Justification Theory")

In Part 1 Campbell analyzed "justification theory," which he presented as a perverse theological program with fatal intrinsic and systematic difficulties, wrong in its concept of God, anthropology, salvation, the human predicament, the process of conversion—basically inadequate on almost any score—and generative of many of the major issues in Pauline study. Campbell's introduction sets the tone. Even scholars whom Campbell will build upon who promote Romans 5–8 as Paul's core (Wrede, Schweitzer, Käsemann, etc.) are charged with not cognizing justification theory's anthropocentric construal of Paul's gospel, derived principally from Romans 1–4, is fundamentally at odds with the Christocentric mysticism of Romans 5–8. They failed to see that salvation construed as individualist, conditional, and contractual (essential components of justification theory) has serious flaws. Even scholars perceiving how justification theory generates a distorted account of Judaism cannot extricate themselves from its fatally flawed analysis of Romans 1–4. Scholars who struggle with the contextualization of Romans have not perceived how justification theory itself is what obfuscates their analysis. After this aggressive argumentation, Campbell spent hundreds of pages unpacking what he considered various wrong construals (false or inadequate) of Paul in previous research.

In dismantling justification theory, Campbell began by outlining its theory of salvation. In this theory, salvation is a paradigmatic story of two stages, a scripted journey of every human being into salvation.

---

[11] This densely argued tome perhaps should have been at least two books: parts 1–3 and 4–5. Part 5, however, is not even essential, no more than a very long addendum to push the thesis onto the rest of Romans and then onto other Pauline letters.

The first stage is gaining specific knowledge about God and behavior he requires. Humans learn that God is a forensically retributive judge, coercive in relationship, prone to violence when not happy, who offers a contractual relationship to humans. His contract demands righteous deeds and strictly punishes non-performance in retributive judgment. Retributive judgment requires humans know the expected behavior. The knowledge is written into human conscience either through natural, unspoken revelation or into scriptural text through supernatural, spoken revelation. Partial performance is unsatisfactory. Perfection is the demand. Against this demand for perfection, inherently sinful humans are thrown into a loop of despair, and, if refusing to despair, are thrown into a loop of delusional foolishness. The second stage of the salvation story is generous, but still strictly satisfies divine contractual demands. Justice is accomplished by the death of Christ as punitive payment of divine demands with a fictive transfer of righteousness to humans (generosity), appropriated by humans by an act of faith.[12]

Campbell concluded by asserting that the construct has intrinsic, systematic, and empirical difficulties. As to intrinsic difficulties, for example, two incompatible epistemologies operate in the two phases. In the first phase, humans are assumed capable of rational knowledge of the divine sufficient to be judged. In the second phase, however, humans require revealed knowledge to be saved. How does a rational person of the first phase subsequently verify the truth of any revelation claim of the second phase? The epistemology is incoherent. Also, ability to perceive rationally specific ethical behavior from natural observation is assumed impossible, but this assumed rational impossibility generates competing criteria with revelation knowledge for establishing just deserts. Humans supposedly able to deduce and fulfill the divine demands rationally in one phase but also characterized as universally sinful and unable to perceive a solution in the second phase proposes both capacity and incapacity simultaneously—inherently incompatible anthropologies.

An example of systematic difficulties would be the deep tensions within Pauline material produced by radically different approaches taken elsewhere by Paul outside Romans 1–4, whether in Romans itself, as in Romans 5–8, or in the rest of Paul's writings. This fundamental

---

[12] Summarized by Campbell in propositional form (Campbell, 28–29).

systematic conflict for the justification construal of Romans 1–4 even in Paul, Campbell asserted, can be documented in at least ten crucial areas: epistemology, anthropology, theology, Christology/atonement, soteriology, faith, ethics, ecclesiology, Judaism, and the related problems of coercion and violent punishment.

Empirical difficulties show up in truth claims made about reality in phase one of justification theory that simply are not true. One such false truth claim is revealed in the fundamental distortions of Judaism, showcased in the impact of the work of Sanders. Another false truth claim is revealed in the fundamental confusion about Paul's conversion, anticipated by Stendahl, but showcased methodically in modern sociological studies based on network theory.

Then, as if that were not enough, Campbell kept charging, like a bull that did not even know he had broken out of the arena. Discussion branched out even more broadly past intrinsic, systematic, and empirical difficulties into areas as diverse as natural theology, post-Holocaust perspectives, homosexual relations, and Constantinianism (coercive violence endorsed by a coercive state justified by justification theory). To demonstrate just how global and pervasive Campbell considers the problems raised by justification theory, he even canvassed internal problems created for Christian doctrine, such as Trinity doctrine, pneumatology, election and assurance, ethics and ecclesiology, and still more.

Such extensive and serious difficulties caused by justification theory in so many major areas simply mean that even the dust up about the "new perspective" on Paul that has preoccupied Pauline scholars is akin to rearranging the deck chairs on the Titanic. Campbell charged that, in the end, even "new perspective" authors—despite their energetic efforts to redress the issue of Paul and Judaism post-Holocaust—wind up acquiescing to justification theory's principal construal of Paul based on Romans 1–4, completely unaware of the iceberg toward which they are steaming ahead at full speed.

Campbell thinks sufficient warnings have been offered in recent scholarship. The alarm was sounded by "apocalyptic" scholars, such as Martyn, who made clear that forensic justification theory just does not square with Paul's "apocalyptic" perspective (i.e., Romans 5–8). Another reality check is Räisänen's protest that Paul read plainly is frankly "inherently contradictory" with no way out. Another ignored warning is tendentiously reading genitive constructions such as "faith of Jesus Christ" as "faith in," as required by justification theory. Such a reading is fundamentally ungrammatical and simply not supported by Pauline genitive syntax elsewhere.

Campbell's argument through hundreds of pages is supposed to have a cumulative force. He ranged far and wide to leave the impression the stakes are stratospheric, and he is blunt: "Hence a solution that could plausibly eliminate Justification theory from Paul would resolve our difficulties. And in fact nothing less than this will resolve them, because of their intrinsic nature. Any purported solution *must* be this comprehensive; it must be this radical" (Campbell, 217). He asserted, "if Paul's coherence is to be saved, *then Justification theory must somehow be eliminated*" (Campbell, 217). Finally, "*The elimination of Justification theory from Paul's interpretation is vital to his fundamental evangelical integrity*" (Campbell, 217).

Part 2 (Hermeneutics)

Campbell regurgitated the complaints of Part 1 in Part 2. The renewed attack this time is chastising justification theory as a hermeneutical process. Justification theory has been constructed as a complex framing discourse, not simply as a single proposition such as "the righteousness of God." Viewed as a framing discourse, one can see that the problem is not Luther. Such a reading is naïve, insisted Campbell, and why he refused to label the view he described as the "Lutheran Paul." The issue of a conflicted reading of Romans 1–4 versus 5–8 goes back before the Reformation. Even church fathers such as Augustine are ambivalent about which Paul they want to emphasize (the justification Paul of Romans 1–4 or the participationist Paul of Romans 5–8). When one does move to the Reformation, the Reformers themselves demonstrate what almost all who use labels like the "Lutheran Paul" must ignore. That is, even in their own writings, Luther and Calvin elicit similar Augustinian ambiguity in trying to decide which Paul is the real Paul.

On the other side of these Reformers, Campbell theorized that justification theory even became integral to the philosophical structure of governments and European nation states. Dangerous implications ensued, such as legitimation of coercive violence to "punish" society's law offenders. Justification theory also is able to play a wicked hand of poker with philosophical individualism (Descartes to Kant to Schleiermacher to Bultmann), or with empiricism (Hobbes to Locke to Hume to Mill), as well as political individualism (John Locke). We are getting into really deep water here.

Part 3 (Rom 1–4)

Part 3 contains the heart of the "conventional reading" (justification theory) in Romans 1–4 spawning this unmitigated disaster (otherwise called western civilization). Paul laid out the justification "problem" in Rom 1:18—3:20. Its "solution" is condensed in Rom 1:16–17 and 3:21–31. Scriptural "attestation" is given in Rom 4:1–25. Students of Paul are not helped at all, asserted Campbell, by the Romans commentary tradition in all this: "In sum, the tradition of advanced scholarly commentary on Romans . . . *almost invariably produces the conventional reading of Romans 1–4*" (Campbell, 334). Even the small minority of revisionist efforts, such as in O'Neil, Wright, Morgan, and Byrne are ultimately unsuccessful, Campbell insisted. The conventional reading then "trickles down," so to speak, everywhere. Avant-garde groups and scholarly colloquia, such as in the annual meetings of the Society of Biblical Literature, wind up simply perpetuating the basic justification theory construal. From here, the tradition trickles down into generalized commentaries, dictionaries, encyclopedias, and study Bible notes.

By now, Campbell has painted the reader into a corner. Justification theory is the theological black hole that sucks up any light of truly understanding Paul—besides completely perverting almost all of western civilization. What all this insinuates is that even the well-intended student of Paul has nowhere to go for the truth about Paul's gospel—except, of course, to Campbell. His own thesis is the supernova of exegetical light bursting forth onto a superdark Pauline universe. Campbell then proceeded to expose what he considered vital exegetical weaknesses in justification theory by using the centerpiece text, Romans 1–4, against itself. The discussion predictably moves along those lines suggested already in the wide-ranging, complex, often redundant analysis of the first three parts of the book. Campbell organized the argument under the categories of what he labeled "textual overdeterminations" and "textual underdeterminations" generated in a justification theory reading. Underdetermination is textual silence, that is, what the theory from major premises of its overall framing discourse needs the text to say, the text does not actually say. Overdetermination is textual noise, that is, the text embarrassingly says precisely what justification theory attempts to deny or is not equipped to handle deftly.

Campbell's proposed solution is predictable. Paul boldly must be reinterpreted radically. Otherwise, he is lost to confusion and contradiction, even as Räisänen so clearly warned. Campbell acknowledged reinterpretation efforts already have been tried. He observed they fall into two basic strategies exemplified most brilliantly, according to Campbell, in the work of four scholars in particular: Watson, Sanders, Dunn, and Stowers.

One reinterpretation strategy is the less ambitious "reframing." "Reframing" the text is explaining the textual features and tensions of Romans 1–4 externally. Some reality underneath the text is bubbling up to generate the lumps on the surface of the text (Watson, Sanders). The failure of this strategy is in leaving the essential justification construal of Romans 1–4 in place and unchallenged.

More ambitious is "rereading" the text. "Rereading" is explaining the textual features and tensions in Romans 1–4 internally. These efforts in some way small or large directly challenge the reading supplied by the conventional approach (Dunn, Stowers). Rereading strategies, according to Campbell, fall into two subcategories, motif and global. "Motif" rereadings challenge only small semantic units, or motifs. They are, therefore, insufficient in and of themselves to engage the global task at hand. These efforts find examples in Käsemann ("righteousness of God"), Dunn and Wright ("works of the law"), and Hayes ("faith of Jesus Christ"). All such efforts fail in the long run, however, because the text surrounding these small, reread units are left to the gravitational pull of the justification moon and the tide simply washes back over the motif rereadings, quickly obliterating their promise to capture Paul's thought.

The other rereading strategy is the more ambitious "global" rereading. Global rereadings inherently hold more promise exegetically because they challenge the broader construct of the text as a whole and are more resilient to the gravitational pull of the justification moon. They are, however, rare in Pauline studies. One of the best is Stowers, a brilliant and valiant effort in Campbell's view. Stowers too fails because of strategic mistakes. For example, Stowers accepts that Rom

1:18—2:16 is Paul's own position, which is all wrong for Campbell. Further, Stowers is forced to reconstruct the role of Christ and God and to suggest judgment by deeds of law even for pagans, all in quite problematic ways—just as problematic as in justification theory (out of the frying pan, into the fire). So, Stowers, according to Campbell, is "so close, yet so far" in a manner of speaking. We learn from Stowers, though, that a global rereading is what is required. One just has to avoid similar strategic mistakes and theologically suspect reconstructions. A global rereading strategy is the ticket, Campbell judged, due to the global hermeneutical task at hand. The problem is, the few that have tried have not succeeded (Stowers).

Part 4 (Radical Rereading)

Part 4 is Campbell's own global, radical rereading of Romans. He styled his rereading "rhetorical" because he applied the rhetoric of speech-in-character in places in Romans no other scholar ever has suspected its presence before,[13] and even then radically inverting the assignment of voices one logically would expect, contrary to the very principles of voice in standard speech-in-character rhetorical analysis, as in 1:18–32, 3:1–8, or 3:27—4:3.[14] The voice in these passages according to Campbell is not Paul's. Rather, the voice is that of a false "Teacher" who is teaching what Paul considers an anathema justification gospel ostensibly based on Jewish Scripture, whom Paul opposes.

This Teacher freshly has arrived in Rome and begun to pervert Roman churches—a biography, Campbell asserted, that is insinuated between the lines in Rom 16:17–20. Thus, "Romans 1:18–32 reproduces compactly the opening rhetorical gambit of the Teacher" (Campbell, 528). This God who is a wrathful, vindictive, demanding, condemning God of absolute justice rendering just deserts to all humanity in Rom 1:18–32 is the Teacher, not Paul. The Teacher's position continues development on into Romans 2. Such a position forces Campbell against all logical procedures with diatribe, to turn the questioner in Rom 3:1–8 into the author (Paul), not the author's opponent (the Teacher). Romans 4 is said to encapsulate the Teacher's position from Scripture

---

[13] Suggesting scholars well versed in rhetorical methodology missed such an obvious point hardly can be read without immediate cautionary suspicion.

[14] Compounding the problem, further reducing the argument's probative force.

that Abraham is a real, literal forefather of a nation, not an Abraham who is Paul's best example in the Scripture of faith for all believers as a "spiritual" forefather. Such a (re)reading of Romans certainly is radical, as this reading turns the Abraham figure of Romans 4 on its head.

Besides rhetorical, Campbell also styled his rereading of Romans as "apocalyptic." By this he is admitting that he has prejudiced the participationist rhetoric of Romans 5–8 as the "real" (read, "only") Paul. His study advances no further than the beginning of the twentieth century as a repristination of Schweitzer's mystical union with Christ as the theological Pauline core. Käsemann's righteousness as God's powerful act in Christ then is tacked on for good measure (Campbell, 678). Righteousness thus as God's power becomes the subject of the verb, so that divine kingship translates into the act of God in Rom 1:17 (Campbell, 704). In Campbell's apocalyptic frame, faith becomes trust in God's faithfulness as redeemer, not belief in theological abstractions about Christ. Atonement is God's singular act of decisive deliverance, not a forensic justification of any person who, using Campbell's perspective, rationally offers faith in making a contract with God. Thus, Rom 1:16–17 and 3:21–26 have been converted by Campbell into an apocalyptic righteousness of God that simply inaugurates participatory faith in the believer, which simultaneously denies all justification theory espoused by the Teacher in Romans 1–4 and shows full concord with the coming argument in Romans 5–8, Paul's "real" voice (Campbell, 750).

So, the real Paul and his real gospel is Romans 5–8. In Campbell's estimation, the "Romans 5–8 Paul" emphasizes sanctification by the Spirit, not justification by legal fiction; law as guide to ethics, not unjust demand for perfect obedience; God as unconditional and gracious in election, not wrathful and conditional in justification; faith as a gift, as union with Christ and regenerative, not as propositional, rational, and believer instigated. Bluntly, Romans 1–4 is a false gospel, not Paul's. Whose gospel? A specific Jewish-Christian Teacher with an alternate "Torah" casting a long shadow over churches in Rome. The purpose of Romans is to expose this false gospel and negate the impact of hostile counter-missionaries—a threat that is concrete, real, imminent, and dangerous to Paul's gospel, mission, and preaching. They appear in the flesh[15] at the end in Rom 16:17–20.

---

[15] OK, yes; pun intended.

Righteousness of God

From his analysis of Rom 3:21–26, Campbell precipitates out the meaning of "righteousness of God" in Rom 1:17. The righteousness of God is an event (story), singular (historical), saving (synonymous with salvation), liberating (from human enslavement, oppression), life giving (results in life), and eschatological (anticipates resurrection). With this theological profile, Paul can pun on the genitive construction: the righteousness of God is Christ disclosing God's offer of this liberating event of atonement, but also this righteousness is a righteousness *from* God, which is Christ himself, who enters the cosmos as sent from God (Campbell, 683).

In discussing the righteousness of God in Romans, Campbell incorporates both Hayes and Wright. He belatedly endorsed Hayes's thesis that Rom 1:16–17 has an intertextual relationship with Ps 98:2–3 (Campbell, 683). Campbell now finds this proposal useful, since Psalm 98 shows Paul is in dialogue with the ancient discourse of kingship, according to Campbell. His argument can utilize a kingship discourse undercurrent in Rom 1:16–17. The king demonstrates the legitimacy of his rule by his "right actions" for his people, whether going to war to defend from enemies or marshaling kingdom resources to respond to famine. This kingship discourse resonated with and therefore affected Jewish expectations of Messiah. To enhance the kingship dialogue undercurrent in Rom 1:16–17, Campbell turned to Wright's emphasis on Jewish framing of the term "Christ" as "Messiah," which centers Jesus's significance on messiahship, bodily resurrection, and exalted lordship, especially as understood in Jewish terms (Campbell, 695).

Campbell integrates the kingship discourse underneath Hayes's echo of Psalm 98 in Rom 1:16–17 into Wright's Jewish emphasis on the significance of Jesus as Messiah. Jesus is King of Israel, not only in that by lineage he is "son of David" but that by resurrection he already has been enthroned royally (Rom 1:3–4). Thus, Israel's king has acted decisively to defeat his enemies and reestablish his rule over creation, and to provide a life of satisfied needs and prosperity for his subjects. He now has sent out his ambassadors (apostles) to engage appropriate submission and fidelity to this inaugurated rule. Thus, the Romans reader should hear in the language Paul uses throughout Romans a resonance with this royal, diplomatic, political ambiance of Jewish kingship discourse, especially in terms such as "reconciliation," "rule," "sonship," "firstborn," "root of Jesse," and "peace." When Jesus as royal representative is resurrected, this event is a deliverance by God of Jesus vindicating his kingship, *not* that Christ in his death is judged punitively by God. Apocalyptic deliverance expresses God's righteousness for both believers and for Christ (hence, Campbell's book title).

What about an emphasis on Israel and covenant as a controlling idea in the concept of the righteousness of God in Rom 1:16–17 so crucial to Wright's framing of Jesus as Messiah? Strangely, Campbell was not keen on the idea. He acknowledged that covenantal resonance is possible in Rom 1:16–17, yet still insisted that the much stronger resonances come from a semantic analysis in the immediate context suggesting kingship discourse within Paul's christological framing (Campbell, 700–701). Along the way, we can go ahead and point out here that Campbell is forced to suppress the clear impression Romans gives that all of Romans 1–8 is simply penultimate rhetorically to Romans 9–11, which is thoroughly focused on Israel and covenant.

Part 5 (Thesis Extension)

In Part 5, Campbell pushes his anathema-gospel Teacher thesis onto other Pauline literature. Campbell is confident the roots of the Teacher's counter-missionary activity go all the way back to Jerusalem, and subsequently show up everywhere, including Antioch, Galatia, Philippi, and Rome (Campbell, 506). Naturally, any analysis of other Pauline material on this radical presupposition is quick and easy. Presuming we can be sure Paul meets this same opponent(s) almost everywhere, Campbell obligingly discovers the activity of the Teacher, or his tribe, and the anathema gospel not only in Galatians, but in Philippians, at Corinth, and well beyond.[16]

WRIGHT'S COVENANT GOD
Worldview Rubric

In his volume on Paul in the "Christian Origins and the Question of God" series, Wright summarized some of the major results of earlier

---

[16] Shades of Robert McL. Wilson finding Gnostics under every rock in the New Testament.

volumes by way of setting the stage for understanding Paul.[17] Wright's approach uses worldview analysis as a rubric for grasping Paul's theology. He first defines worldview as "basic beliefs" driven by a narrative. "Consequent beliefs" flow out of these basic beliefs. Finally, "aims and intentions" illustrate the behavior considered to be consistent with and generated by the worldview's basic beliefs and consequent beliefs.

Worldview fundamentally requires a supporting narrative upon which worldview elements can hang. Wright precipitated out of Scripture the narrative he thought supported a Jewish worldview. Wright offered a vigorous, nuanced defense of the use of narrative analysis of Paul through the lens of worldview (Wright, 456–75). Jewish "basic beliefs" operative in Paul are monotheism as one God, election as one people of God, and eschatology as one future for God's world (Wright, 46).[18] Within these categories, Wright emphasized the thematic function of the faithfulness of Israel's God (Wright, 77). Together these beliefs create a network of interrelated and dynamic associations, such as temple, glory, kingship, creation, exile, rebuilding, and unfulfilled promise. Speak of one, and you invoke a complex resonance of the entire network, like a single breath of wind on a wind chime invoking multiple tones instantly interacting with each other in a sympathetic and cascading series. Wright's point is that, with all these sympathetic vibrations, we already are describing the Jewish mindset (narrative) of Saul of Tarsus.

The Jewish worldview story is a purposeful and faithful God and his purposed creation entrusted to humans. Humans fail their task, so thwart creation from achieving its divinely intended goal, because non-human, evil, destructive powers interfere. God in his faithfulness to creation, however, will triumph over these destructive powers in judgment through God's coming representative king who will effect God's sovereign rule. Creation will be consummated as designed, and justice and peace will reign.

---

[17] Cf. *The New Testament and the People of God* (1992), *Jesus and the Victory of God* (1996), *The Resurrection of the Son of God* (2003), *Paul and the Faithfulness of God* (2013). Wright divided the Paul material into four parts across two books, two parts in each. Wright's monumental volume on Paul invoked thirty-two scholars and essays in response in Heilig, Hewett, and Bird, eds., *God and the Faithfulness of Paul* (2017).

[18] Wright used the disputed Ephesians, Colossians, 2 Thessalonians, and 2 Timothy. Acts is used as illustrative and confirmatory rather than definitive and categorical.

Paul adds three sub-plots to this Jewish worldview narrative. The first is the story of humans and their failure. The second is the story of Israel and its failure. The third is the story of Jesus and his success. Jesus resolves not only the first two sub-plots, but also the main plot's fulfillment. Paul layering composite stories to the worldview model leads Wright to a critique: *"the supposed clash or conflict between two 'models of salvation' in Paul, the 'forensic' or 'juristic' on the one hand and the 'incorporative' on the other, is itself a category mistake, the result of a failure to see how his different stories actually work."*[19] The salient point, Wright said, is that "most Jews of Paul's day perceived themselves at a deep, worldview level, as living in *a story in search of an ending.*"[20] The search for an ending is driven by the intuitive sense that God surely will prove himself faithful to his promises. Jews have returned to their land, and the temple has been rebuilt, but a nagging sense remains that what currently exists could not possibly be what God intended. This perception nurtures an abiding desire for that propitious moment in time when God does act decisively and definitively on behalf of Israel, however conceived. For a zealous Pharisee, perhaps this fulfillment would take the shape of a renewal movement of torah-keeping, and, consequently, temple realization.

Parsing Paul's theology for Wright is revealing Paul's revisions of the Jewish worldview narrative. Within each category (monotheism, election, eschatology), Wright identified and explicated key Pauline texts that best demonstrate the heuristic power of this Jewish narrative approach for understanding Paul's points and argumentative developments. Traditional Jewish categories are "freshly revealed" to Paul through the paradigm-shifting events of the death and resurrection of Messiah and an outpoured Spirit. How does Paul modulate the basic beliefs of this Jewish narrative?

Modulating Monotheism

First, Paul modulates Jewish monotheism. He does this two ways: his revelatory insight on Jesus as Messiah and on Jesus as Spirit. As to the revelation of Jesus as Messiah, Paul resolves the ambiguity of Israel's return from exile in the very person of Jesus, who is himself Israel's

---

[19] Wright, 530; emphasis original.

[20] Wright, 109; emphasis original.

representative and covenant consummator. Jesus inaugurates both the renewed people and the realized return of YHWH. Wright noted, "The long awaited return of YHWH to Zion is, I suggest, the hidden clue to the origin of christology" (Wright, 654). Fully understanding divine identity is the result of the convergence of the return of YHWH theme, Jesus's messiahship validated by resurrection, and the sense of Jesus's continuing presence. This divine identity explains Paul's exploitation of "Lord" passages in Scriptures on behalf of Jesus that feature the name of God (YHWH), culminating in a premier text such as Phil 2:9–11, as well as Rom 9:5. By the time Paul's letters emerge, that is, Paul's new thoughts on divine identity already are fully in place. A crucified but resurrected Messiah becomes the center of a revised monotheism that redefines Paul's Jewish worldview. Christological monotheism simultaneously affirms the Jewish creation narrative and announces its renewal. The pattern is a return to dwell in a restored temple (Ezekiel 43) that resolves the threat of divine absence from Israel after the golden calf (Exodus 32–40) and effects the glory of God diffusing throughout the whole world. A new temple is raised. God's presence on earth is realized. God reigns.

In the new revelation of Jesus as Spirit, Paul develops the idea of the "Spirit of the Son" with divine identity function. This Spirit is the new Shekinah that fulfills the new exodus. While the temple as crux to Jewish theology is well known, Wright charged its role has not been integrated properly into the theme of YHWH's return to Zion. This problem brings into bold relief a text such as 1 Cor 3:16–17, written by a Jew with Paul's pedigree. For Paul, "the founding and building up of the church through the gospel constituted the long-awaited rebuilding of the Temple" (Wright, 712). In similar fashion, Wright saw Paul as fashioning the indwelling Spirit in the church as the return of YHWH to Zion.

Reconfiguration of the Spirit clarifies a single united family, the one people of God, as absolutely essential to the core of a monotheistic worldview. The featured text is Ephesians 4, the church as a new temple, the new humanity. For Paul, Jesus and the Spirit are prime movers establishing the kingdom of God that provide a premier storyline of the Jewish worldview. With this Messiah framing, Wright puts right back into the center of Pauline theology that which was taken out in a previous generation that had no room for Paul the Jew. Wright noted the importance of unity for Paul,

> Once we take into account the overall covenantal framework, then, we see why initial justification is so important. It is not just because of the need for 'assurance', in the terms of classic protestant theology, though that remains important. It is because of the need to be clear that *all* such believers belong to Abraham's single family. Paul never forgot the battles in Antioch and Galatia.[21]

The "dark side" to this new revelation and revised monotheism is a new vision of evil. Stoics denied the reality of evil; Epicureans denied the relevance of the gods; dualists saw an eternal struggle of matched good and evil forces. Paul's second-temple Jewish monotheism rejected such worldviews, but Paul's alternative was revised in the light of Jesus and the Spirit. Evil forces using the subterfuge of idolatry are out to enslave or kill and to cause creation to implode in chaos. The brutal fact is, Messiah was crucified. This stunning development means the human problem was way deeper than anyone ever imagined. Thinking Torah was a solution was simply naïve. Messiah, however, was resurrected. Resurrection reveals God's creative purpose to redeem the entire cosmos, not just to save human souls. God defeats "the powers" thwarting creation's goal. Rejecting Campbell's idea that Paul opposes a false gospel in Rom 1:18—2:16, Wright instead sees Paul accessing an Eden narrative substructure focused on Adam in Rom 1:18–25. This Eden echo shows Israel's golden calf incident to be a primal sin for Israel, like Adam's. In spite of her election, Israel herself is in the same plight as Adam. This conundrum raises the question for Paul of how election serves God's purposes.

Modulating Election

Second, Paul also modulates Jewish election, again on the basis of the new revelation of Jesus as Messiah and Jesus as Spirit. Wright does not intend election to suggest the elaborate schemes of the Reformation and beyond. Wright intended election as simply a useful term to speak of God's choice of Abraham for a particular purpose (Wright, 775). Wright could be charged with trying to circumvent traditional debate

---

[21] Wright, 1032, emphasis original.

on justification, anthropology, in Christ language (incorporation, participation, mysticism), salvation history, apocalyptic, transformation (deification), and covenant, but he argued that covenant, properly nuanced, could integrate most concerns expressed by these contending polarities of Pauline debate.

Election is Wright's code word for Israel and its purpose, which boils down to Abraham. Abraham is the pivotal figure of Israel's story: covenant, progeny, land, slavery, circumcision. This is Israel's identity, the "base text" of Judaism. Paul reads a narrative whose plot is that Adam failed in stewardship over creation, and God has set his task to recover his intended plan for creation. His recovery plan is Abraham, and Abraham helps the worldview story transcend Adam.

Wright acknowledged that the term "righteousness" is complex, hard to translate, with multiple layers. Wright canvassed three layers of meaning: court, covenant, and creation. The court layer is a forensic setting with at least five perspectives on rightness: right relationship, right behavior, right process, right assessment, and right verdict. The judge's own "righteousness" is how he tries the case (process) and decides the verdict (assessment). The defendant's "righteousness" is both the right expected behavior in a covenanted relationship and the court status conferred by the court verdict (court verdict, not moral character). The covenant layer of meaning is the specific covenant relationship of YHWH with Israel and relationship expectations. Here, the emphasis is on God's attribute and action, especially in contexts such as Psalms and Isaiah. Wright here insisted that modern translations obfuscate "righteousness" by translating as "salvation." The actual emphasis is not as much on salvation as on God's prior covenant commitment to Israel. The creation layer of meaning invokes God as creator responsible for putting the world back right in the end. This global level has in view an eschatological, long-term perspective. "God's eschatological judgment will be the ultimate cosmic law court, but it will also be the moment of ultimate covenant vindication" (Wright, 801).

The point would be, no single English word can encompass such diversity and Jewish worldview complexity, including eschatology to boot. More than personal ethics, righteousness for Wright is covenant behavior between Israel and YHWH. The righteousness of God is covenant justice that must exile Israel but also covenant faithfulness that restores Israel. But righteousness does not end with Israel. Israel is the means to a larger goal, the whole world of the creator God. Wright rejected as oxymoronic the charge that recovering a Jewish perspective on the "righteousness of God" is an inverse "Jewish supersessionism" (Wright, 809–11). Paul himself makes clear the larger picture is Israel in Rom 2:25–29 in his analysis of the current status of Israel regarding God's covenant with Israel and its world implications. Paul here is integrating Ezekiel 36 and Isaiah 52. The Jewish narrative indicates that when God does act in a future redemption with a new exodus and return from exile, Israel will keep Torah from the heart, as announced in Deuteronomy 30. God's righteousness is revealed in the faithful death of his Messiah creating a messianic community. In Jesus, God returned in person and redeemed his own. Thus, Wright emphasized a crucified savior *must* be in the form of Israel's Messiah.[22]

Wright gave a vigorous defense of framing *Christos* language in Paul as Jewish, and properly translated "Messiah." His chief evidence is Paul's pervasive use of scriptural texts with messianic import both in Jewish thought and in the New Testament to draw out the meaning of Jesus. That Pauline hermeneutic is one clear sign of what is generative in Paul's thought about Jesus. Further, "wisdom" is associated with the royal house of David in Jewish wisdom literature, and that resonance should not be silenced when scholars are quick to acknowledge that Paul does draw on wisdom literature. Israel's Messiah is the focus of bringing Israel's elective purpose to completion. That focus gives shape to Israel's election and becomes foundational to the meaning of the righteousness of God.

Jesus's messiahship is incorporative, which for Wright not only explains Paul's "in Christ" linguistic world but also integrates the perennially debated "justification Paul" into the "incorporation Paul." Jesus as Messiah both fulfills Israel's covenant destiny through death and resurrection as well as incorporates those who believe in him into a messianic vocation within a community and its mission defined by him. This messianic configuration of Pauline Christology is disputed. The

---

[22] Wright knows he is fighting an uphill battle in contemporary scholarship with his emphasis on the Jewish messiahship of Jesus as crucial to Pauline theology. He noted that even Charlesworth's massive *The Messiah: Developments in Earliest Judaism and Christianity* has only a scant few pages on Paul (Wright, 817, n127).

"incorporative construct" upon which Wright's view is based is not so obviously in evidence in first-century Jewish communities looking for the kingdom of God, such as those of the Dead Sea Scrolls or those following the Bar Kochba revolt. Even so, Wright insisted that Jesus's death and resurrection, core to the story of Jesus as Messiah, forces re-envisioning the entire rubric of Jewish messianic thought.

Jesus as faithful Messiah also clarifies Paul's *pistis Christou* form-ulation. Here too, narrative is key. Israel was chosen to bless the world. Israel failed the task. God, however, ever was faithful to his promise to work through Israel to bless the world. God was faithful to preserve the covenant relationship and its potential for fulfilling the promise to the world through that covenant. The "faithful Israelite" fulfilling the Abrahamic covenant is Jesus (Rom 3:21–26), who is Israel-in-person. Thus, "the faithfulness (*pistis*) of the Messiah is that which marks him out as the true Israelite, the promise-bearer, the one who accomplishes at last the purpose for which the creator called Israel in the first place" (Wright, 839). Jesus then fulfills Abraham's world blessing promised by the creator God. This fulfillment Wright styled as "the faithful justice of the covenant God" (Wright, 841). Jesus's death as "redemption" is a new act of exodus (Rom 3:24). Jesus's death as a "place of atonement" and blood averting death is a new Passover (Rom 3:25). This under-standing of Rom 3:21–26 (covenantal, messianic, redefined in passion realities) Wright thinks holds together juridical and participationist categories of Pauline thought (Wright, 846). This story is a recognize-able "Exodus God" understood in Easter realities. Torah no longer is the boundary definition of Israel. The faithfulness of Messiah defines Israel. God elects Israel specifically to give Israel Torah specifically to neuter sin in its base of power in Adamic flesh (Romans 7). Thus, im-mediately following the story of Torah's effects on Israel in Romans 7 is the summative Rom 8:1–4, which is fully forensic for Wright.

Yet, Romans 8 is supposed to be the heart of so-called "incorpo-rative Christology." Wright asserted the failure to grasp the covenantal basis of Paul's thinking about justification fosters false divisions be-tween "juristic" and "participationist" emphases. In fact, Rom 8:10 is clearly juristic: "the Spirit is life because of righteousness." That right-eousness is the forensic verdict of "righteous" spoken in the present over those who believe grounded in Messiah's already accomplished faithfulness.

Controlling ideas in this construct are climax of the covenant and community incorporation. With these ideas, Paul synthesizes Jewish messianic thought and Jesus realities. That is, if resurrection always was for Israel in Jewish thought, and Jesus was resurrected, then Jesus in some way has to be fulfilling the role of Israel. Again, if YHWH's presence was promised to Israel in the future day of redemption, and Jesus is confessed as "Lord" and experienced as "Spirit" by the church, then YHWH has returned as promised, and the people around Jesus are to be presumed incorporated into God's renewed covenant people. Wright presented three passages illustrating this synthesis in operation in Paul's hermeneutic (Rom 3:1–26; Gal 2:15—4:11; Phil 3:2–11). Thus, Jesus as Israel's Messiah impacts understanding Israel's election and the famous doctrine of justification. However, Wright wanted to be clear, Paul's Jewish concerns in such a narrative are not bound up with surviving a judgment after death to wind up in eternal bliss, the basic frame of justification in western thought. Rather, Paul's question was, when would the one, true God express his sovereignty, come in power, rescue his people, and establish his kingdom?

In his analysis of election and the Spirit, Wright again sought to show the compatibility of juridical and participationist themes in Paul. Justification rooted in a representative Messiah encompasses participationist language without any need to relativize or even eliminate its role, as in Wrede, Schweitzer, Sanders, and Campbell. As well, ethnic Israel is not supplanted but, in fact, comes to fruition in Messiah, even as Messiah reconstitutes Israel to fulfill not only the story of Abraham but even of Adam. Paul uses "gospel" as Isaiah's "good news" of the covenant-keeping God. The power of this spoken gospel is the Spirit. The gospel spoken is the Spirit released as a life-giving, faith-inspiring force. Thus, God's call is effective. The Spirit creates the justified people of Messiah through gospel preaching and faithful hearing. Paul's good news also should be contextualized as counter to the announcement in Roman imperial ideology that the emperor himself is the good news for humanity.

Paul after the Damascus Road sees the coming kingdom of God in the Messiah and the Spirit. The eschatology is inaugurated. Messiah has been resurrected and the Spirit has been poured out. Messiah's resurrection says he was in the right, so functions as a covenant declaration (Wright, 943). Messiah's death means the God of the covenant would not certify Israel in its present condition, and Israel's plight was more desperate than any imagined. The Spirit's arrival signals fulfillment of Deuteronomy 30, reflected also in Jeremiah and Ezekiel. The Spirit creates a "circumcised heart" community in which law finds its true meaning for life and righteousness. The Spirit creates this new badge of faith marking a people without ethnic distinction. God shows fidelity to the covenant with Israel through Messiah and that he also will put all things right, blending a forensic and covenant eschatology into a final eschatology of last judgment that is impartial and just.

Wright can agree that justification is imputation, but he disagrees about what is imputed. Justification is not imputing Messiah's righteous character but rather imputing Messiah's death and resurrection (Wright, 951). Therefore, any believing faith (*pistis*) is only a sign of an already accomplished operation of the Spirit (Rom 10:13–15). Baptism from this perspective anticipates future resurrection, so celebrates the pronounced justification by faith (Wright, 963). To demonstrate how this messianic and Spirit driven Christology can bring coherence to larger Pauline contexts, not just in isolated verses, Wright concluded by analyzing Gal 2:15—4:11 and passages in 1 Corinthians, 2 Corinthians 3, Phil 3:2–11, Colossians 2, Rom 3:21—4:25, and Romans 5–8.

REFLECTION

What a range of thought. Striking differences of approach and results immediately stand out in high relief in contemporary work on Pauline thought among just three scholars. Dramatic differences could be so distracting that commonalities might be overlooked.

Canonical Frame

For example, Watson and Wright agree that, at the hermeneutic level, Paul is working canonically, that is, with a view to the entire compass of Hebrew Scriptures. Paul's quotations and allusions demonstrably are not proof-texting, as assumed so commonly and so easily in a previous generation of Pauline scholars who caricatured Paul as having left "Judaism," as a "works religion" far behind in the dust of his *sola fide*. New canonical sensitivity for understanding Paul's hermeneutical process goes hand in hand with a new appreciation of the Jewishness of Paul.[23] Somehow, we just cannot shake off at least some elements of the "new perspective" on Paul, even as we try to move beyond that construct in more radical approaches, as Martyn's reconfiguration of "apocalyptic" in Paul. In Sanders we still evidence a seismic shift in Pauline studies: Paul is a Jew, and from Sanders's loosening of the snow pack at the top, the avalanche roars down the mountainside to engulf all skiers on the Pauline slopes. In any case, whatever Paul is doing is much more Jewish than previously envisioned by Protestants or Catholics.

Controlling Narrative

Comparing Campbell and Wright, as another example, reveals another commonality. While one might not see much connection between the two positions, they both agree that something dramatically is wrong with the controlling scholarly narratives about Paul's world. Admittedly, neither agrees on what precisely is wrong with the narratives, nor on the manner of proper reframing. Yet, their critique is instructive.

Both Campbell and Wright agree that the supposed overall narrative in which first-century Jews were living as presented in both Catholic and Protestant tradition is fundamentally wrong.[24] Wright judged the Protestant problem to be completely abandoning the Jewish story that culminates in the Jewish hope that the creator God would rescue his entire creation through Israel. For this rich, Jewish narrative, Protestants substituted a reductionist, simplistic picture of little more than disconnected individuals expressing personal faith, but framed in no larger, cohesive story. Wright would judge one cannot correct this individualist narrative egregiously errant in Jewish worldview fundamentals simply by fine tuning details. Wright's worldview rubric seems to grasp the problem more intuitively than Campbell, whose critique slashes away vigorously, like a pirate assaulting a galley laden with theological booty. Part of this slashing away is proposing a discontinuous worldview (redefined as "apocalyptic"), but incongruous with anything Jewish that went before. This worldview frame is unpersuasive, having little concord with the sociology that describes how things worked in

---

[23] Cf. Abasciano, *Paul's Use of the Old Testament in Romans 9.1–9* (2005).

[24] Described by Wright (110–13) with his characteristic penchant for the nexus grid style ever evocative of actantial analysis.

the ancient world. Inadequate worldview analysis is Wright's basic critique of numerous initiatives in Pauline scholarship since World War II, including not only the "new perspective" on Paul with which he himself has been associated, but also most particularly, Campbell.

Framing Faith

What about faith and its place in the scheme of salvation? Even on a matter so fundamental, agreement is illusive. Our three authors have revealed how much one's reading of Rom 1:17 with its appeal to Hab 2:4 is determinative on this question. Both Campbell and Wright insist on a fundamental Jewish frame, so parse *Christos* as "Messiah." They both also interpret *pistis Christou* as "faithfulness of Christ." Watson, in contrast, insists that, in its original context, Hab 2:4 is the faith offered by the individual Israelite. Watson then says this context is assumed by Paul and informs Paul's canonical maneuver to resolve the tension with Torah's aborted promise of life. Paul resolves the problem following Habakkuk's lead, that is, not by "works of the law" (Torah performance), but "by faith." Watson's approach simply winds up conforming to the conventional forensic frame for faith.

In contrast, Campbell and Wright agree that God's righteousness inaugurates faith. Campbell frames righteousness as God's apocalyptic disruption that redeems. Wright frames righteousness as God's forensic declaration now of an eschatological verdict folding back in time from the future judgment. Either way, for both Campbell and Wright, faith is not a believer's contribution that catalyzes salvation. Instead, God creates faith. For Campbell, God creates faith in the event of Messiah's apocalyptic inbreaking. For Wright, God creates faith in the event of gospel preaching of Messiah and consequent vivification of the Spirit.

Stressful Schizophrenia

What about the schizophrenic "personalities" of Romans? What are we to do with the forensic Romans 1–4 in tension with the participationist Romans 5–8? Observing this tension firmly has been in place ever since Schweitzer, so much so that this idea has become a regular assumption among Pauline scholars. Two hermeneutical maneuvers suggest themselves to resolve the tension: separate or synthesize. Separation requires deciding which unit represents the real Paul. Schweitzer casts a long shadow over the landscape of this discussion. Campbell over a century later still is opting predictably for Romans 5–8. Hermeneutically, a choice either way fundamentally is presuppositional, not exegetical. From a presuppositional standpoint, one just as well could prejudice Romans 1–4 as the real Paul. How would one know otherwise?[25] The interpretive conundrums would be no greater than Campbell's move toward Romans 5–8, and the chaos for understanding Paul no less, since Campbell's rhetorical analysis is so thoroughly confused.

Another solution is to attempt to integrate the two disparate personalities exegetically lurking in Romans 1–8. Watson integrates them in a conventional way, which means, for all practical purposes, strongly pivoting to the forensic Paul of Romans 1–4. The Achilles heel of the conventional attempt at integration is unequal integration. Instead of prejudicing Romans 5–8 as the core Paul, Watson subtly prejudices Romans 1–4 as the core Paul. The forensic Paul surreptitiously dominates exegesis of Romans 5–8. Exploring the approach to Romans 7 quickly reveals this domination quite easily, because exegesis here will not have even a hint about Israel. Thus, even in many integration attempts the participationist Paul winds up being only a theological stepchild, subsidiary to forensic Paul. Hence, Romans exposes theological schizophrenia. Will the real Paul please stand up?

Another way sublimation of Romans 5–8 is made clear is simply counting pages in commentaries. Count the number of pages allotted to explication of Romans 1–4 to contrast with the number of pages given to explicating Romans 5–8. They both are four chapters, with Romans 5–8 only ten verses shorter. Yet, the imbalance of exegetical coverage is obvious. From Nygren's older commentary (1958: 282/131) to Longenecker's more recent volume (2016: 392/227) the imbalance is obvious. Subtly by attention alone, forensic Paul is inferred as real Paul.

Almost invariably, resolutions that try to integrate but prejudice Romans 1–4 have the decided deficit also of requiring some staging of salvation (first, justified, then, sanctified). Such staging, however, is only subterfuge for the attempt to validate subordination of participationist material to justification material. Justification effectively becomes the leitmotif of all that is salvation—ergo, the Protestant mantra.

---

[25] If we so easily can turn Romans on its head rhetorically, we most certainly can turn Galatians on its head rhetorically as well, if a presuppositional scheme requires.

Catholics, of course, are not happy with this fictional righteousness and cry foul for sublimating participationist Paul for no better reason than because justification doctrine in Romans conventionally conceived will work only that way. Campbell noted the problem and sounded an alarm.

Wright attempts to integrate Romans 1–4 and Romans 5–8 by his covenant rubric. He reads justification as Messiah's covenant that will have forensic force at the last judgment through the already effected resurrection of Jesus. He reads participation as incorporation into Messiah's covenant community that has mystical force in the present through the already effected outpoured Spirit of Jesus. Justification and participation realities function differently but coherently within the layered stories in the Pauline worldview. That is, both express the same reality of salvation equally. Thus, Wright concludes that subsuming all of Paul's nuanced exegesis of his Jewish worldview in the light of Messiah's death and resurrection into the singular language of justification is reductionist and obscures Paul's covenantal modulations of the Jewish worldview. Wright's understanding of Paul's worldview can accommodate justification in Paul, unlike Campbell, but more integrally than Watson. Campbell's critique of a forensic false gospel is more contrivance than reality missing Paul's covenantal thought (Wright, 40). Wright's justification Paul as a legitimate part of Pauline soteriology is more on target, but Wright does not think Paul intended justification by itself to subsume salvation. Wright thinks balance in understanding Paul and justification is gained by better understanding the work of the Spirit in Paul, because Spirit is integral to participationist language.

Works of the Law

Finally, what about the much disputed "works of the law" concept, new perspective not withstanding? Perhaps we have learned by now that dissecting this phrase never really proves definitive for understanding Paul's thought. The phrase is not definitive because the idea is not determinative. The meaning of the phrase always is hostage to the hermeneutic applied. Efforts focused exclusively on deciphering this phrase alone will not expose light on Paul's thought, because interpretation of the phrase always serves duty to the overarching hermeneutic, always meaning what the chosen hermeneutical solution to the question of righteousness in Paul needs the phrase to mean.

CONCLUSION

Understanding the righteousness of God in Paul turns on Rom 1:17. Literally thousands of published pages on Paul try to decipher this one verse. One item with not enough emphasis in all this Pauline research is the synagogue. If indeed we want to get a new perspective on Paul, Jewish in essence, Pharisee in expression, we need to investigate more seriously the premier institution of the Pharisees that weekly exposed the first-century Judean and Diaspora populations to their worldview frame and hermeneutical trajectories. That institution is the synagogue. One conversation not yet heard sufficiently would be the first-century dialogue between Paul and the synagogue. One avenue to gain some glimpse inside that synagogue dialogue is the Targums. Recent study on Paul, for example, has explored the Aramaic Targums and revealed the promise of investigating this synagogue context for understanding Paul, particularly in Romans.[26] Craig Evans as well has pointed to the Targums for enlightening how Paul's exegesis works. As Evans points out, Paul, of course, did not read the Targums; yet, calculating he was exposed to the exegetical traditions within them through his synagogue life is not a stretch, because on multiple occasions in Romans Paul's exegesis follows Aramaic emphases in the Targums.[27] Evans in this article shows how Paul's hermeneutical horizons follow targumic trajectories in Rom 9–11, particularly in interpreting the prophets. These trajectories help Paul negotiate disturbing Jewish unbelief and stumbling yet gentile belief and righteousness. In an ironic twist, one could say Paul's synagogue life did not fail him as he worked to interpret Israel to Israel.

[26] DelRio, *Paul and the Synagogue*. Perriman (*Future of the People of God*, 16, 92, 102, 127) constantly refers to the synagogue context for exegesis of Romans but never once even alludes to, much less actually uses Targum discussions or traditions.

[27] Evans, "Paul and the Prophets," *passim*, but note especially response to Fitzmyer, 125, n25. Also, McNamara, *The New Testament and the Palestinian Targum to the Pentateuch*, 70–78; see also the updated edition, *Targum and Testament Revisited*. An introduction for the more advanced student is Flesher and Chilton, *The Targums*.

3

The Rhetoric of Romans 7

Romans Is All about Israel

A N ANALYSIS OF PAUL'S first-person rhetoric in the context of his development of authorial ἔθος (*ethos*) and πάθος (*pathos*) in the first
six chapters of Romans is key to exegesis of the *crux interpretum* of Romans 7. Combine this analysis with the structural observation that all of
Romans 1–8 serves the argumentative climax in Romans 9–11, then the
thesis that Romans is all about Israel becomes clear.[1]

One clue to Romans 7 is Jewish lament rhetoric, of which this unit
rhetorically participates. Lament rhetoric is exegetical background for
the emotionally charged expressions in 7:24 and 9:1–5, both of which
usually befuddle commentators. Jewish lament rhetoric, however, can
show how the two passages are tied together. Structurally, this rhetorical
tie means the argument in Romans 7 is fundamental to the development of Romans 9–11. Once the rhetorical "I" of Romans 7 is established, a running paraphrase of Romans 7 with this perspective in view
easily fits into a cohesive Jewish narrative and worldview story. We
start by investigating the opening of Romans for clues to the authorial
rhetoric.

---

[1] Not at all clear to earlier generations of scholars. C. H. Dodd conceived Romans
9–11 as an independent sermon shoehorned into a structure that went fluidly from
8:39 to 12:1; about these chapters he wrote, "They can be read and understood independently, and equally without them the epistle could be read through without any
sense of a gap in the sequence of thought" (*Romans*, xxx). Rudolf Bultmann (*Theologie
des Neuen Testaments*, 484) looked at Rom 11:25–32 as no more than Paul indulging
in some form of "speculative fancy."

AUTHORIAL RHETORIC IN ROMANS

Developing Appropriate Ethos and Pathos

Paul's identification of the sender in Rom 1:1–6 is extraordinary for its length and content and evidences a concern to establish his authorial ἔθος (*ethos*).[2] The later *exordium*[3] reveals that he has not established this church nor ever visited Rome,[4] but this feature is only partial explanation of such careful deliberation in presenting authorial *ethos*. That is, the carefully composed *prescript* evidences rhetorical purpose. No co-senders are mentioned, leaving the authorial *ethos* personally identified with Paul alone.[5]

The Authorial *Ethos*—Jewish

The authorial *ethos* developed in this unique Romans *prescript* is Jewish to the core. Paul's apostleship is consecrated to God's gospel (ἀφω- ρισμένος, "set apart" 1:1). God's gospel is pre-announced in Scripture (διὰ τῶν προφητῶν αὐτοῦ ἐν γραφαῖς ἁγίαις, "through his prophets in the Holy Scriptures," 1:2). God's gospel is about his Son, Jesus, who

---

[2] Aristotle's persuasion through character (ἔθος, *ethos*) presentation is not helpful. His wisdom, virtue, and goodwill categories are too generalized and absent rhetorical examples (*Rhet.* 2.1.5). Still, his comment on πάθος (*pathos*) through ἔθος (*ethos*) in which the hearers are "led to feel emotion by the speech" resonates with various elements of Romans (*Rhet.* 1.2.5).

[3] Generally taken to be Rom 1:8–15. Terms of species analysis in the style of classical Roman school rhetoric, epitomized by Quintilian, are used descriptively, not analytically, for point of reference. Romans is not assumed any particular species. Breakdown, however, into large rhetorical units guides discussion, in as much as macrostructure illustrates needs common to all persuasive speech, including epistolary speech acts.

[4] Rom 1:10; cf. 15:23.

[5] Most of Paul's *prescripts* denote multiple authorship (or association), complicating rhetorical analysis methodologically. Exceptions to multiple authorship are Ephesians, 1 Timothy, 2 Timothy, and Titus. Of these, 1 Timothy, 2 Timothy, and Titus are the only letters ostensibly to individuals, which would impact the rhetorical constraints. In any case, Ephesians, 1 Timothy, and 2 Timothy have expanded identification of the author, but as a simple designation of apostleship by God's will, and for 1 Timothy and 2 Timothy, this expansion does not feature prominently in the letter. Paul's apostleship features in Ephesians 3, but only as a pragmatic παράδειγμα (example) for the readers in Ephesians 4. Thus, of those letters featuring Paul alone, only Titus shows extensive development of the identification of the author. Even here, the expansion, outside of the phrase ἐκλεκτῶν θεοῦ ("called of God") lacks any distinctly Jewish *ethos*, much less any thematic development. We conclude that the thematic development of Jewish *ethos* in the *prescript* of Romans is unique among the letters of Paul.

came as a son of David on Israel's behalf (ἐκ σπέρματος Δαυὶδ κατὰ σάρκα, "from the seed of David according to the flesh," 1:3).[6] God's gospel now empowers messianic Israel[7] toward her eschatological destiny by the power of God's Spirit (τοῦ ὁρισθέντος υἱοῦ θεοῦ ἐν δυνάμει κατὰ πνεῦμα ἁγιωσύνης ἐξ ἀναστάσεως νεκρῶν, "who was declared son of God in power according to the Holy Spirit," 1:4). God's gospel inaugurates messianic Israel's eschatological destiny to bring about the obedience of faith among all the nations (εἰς ὑπακοὴν πίστεως ἐν πᾶσιν τοῖς ἔθνεσιν, "unto the obedience of faith among all the nations," 1:5), a purpose which includes gentiles in Rome (ἐν οἷς ἐστε καὶ ὑμεῖς κλητοὶ, "among whom you also are called," 1:6).[8] So, Paul closely identifies his apostleship with Israel's prophets, Israel's Scriptures, Israel's Messiah, and Israel's destiny. This identification becomes explicit in Rom 11:1. In that passage, Paul asked, Λέγω οὖν, μὴ ἀπώσατο ὁ θεὸς τὸν λαὸν αὐτοῦ; "I ask, therefore, has God cast off his people?" Paul emotionally responded, μὴ γένοιτο· καὶ γὰρ ἐγὼ

---

[6] Hayes's analysis that περὶ τοῦ υἱοῦ αὐτοῦ does not go with the prior εὐαγγέλιον, launches Hayes into this misdirection: "the letter to the Romans does not carry through this implied program of christological exegesis." Hayes, *Echoes of Scripture*, 85. Hayes was attempting to establish an "ecclesiocentric hermeneutics" in Paul. More on target seems to be Wright's argument that Χριστός in Paul has not leveled out to a title (e.g., form) but still retains the Jewish sense of "Messiah" (e.g., function = incorporative). Wright, *Climax of the Covenant*, 41.

[7] Descriptive terminology to capture the theologically loaded emphasis in the creedal σπέρματος Δαυὶδ κατὰ σάρκα of 1:2 when combined with the confessional focus of κυρίου Ἰησοῦ Χριστοῦ in 1:7. As the creedal tradition of Rom 1:3–4 makes clear, resurrection doctrine invests the category of Israel with eschatological nuance, hence, "messianic Israel." In Romans, messianic Israel has as its logical counterpoint what could be labeled descriptively as Mosaic Israel, whose linguistic reference point by *synecdoche* is ἔργων νόμου ("works of the law") and its variations. Cf. Donaldson: "Paul's Christ-Torah antithesis is rooted in a perception that Christ and Torah represent mutually exclusive boundary markers, rival ways of determining the community of salvation," *Paul and the Gentiles*, 172. These categories in Paul probably are not truly "mutually exclusive," even though exclusivity is foundational to Donaldson's remapping.

[8] Nanos pointed to Rom 1:6, 1:13, 11:13, and 15:15 as "quite clear" that Paul "was writing specifically to Christian gentiles in Rome," but the presence of "Christian Jews and Jewish themes" have so monopolized attention that this "has led most if not all scholars to stop short of allowing this observation its full impact on the interpretation of Paul's message," *The Mystery of Romans*, 78–79. Even in the first text Nanos cited, Rom 1:6, the immediate context in the very next verse (πᾶσιν τοῖς οὖσιν ἐν Ῥώμῃ, "to all who are in Rome"), indicates the situation rhetorically is much more nuanced than Nanos has allowed.

Ἰσραηλίτης εἰμί, ἐκ σπέρματος Ἀβραάμ, φυλῆς Βενιαμίν. "By no means! For even I am an Israelite, of Abraham's lineage, of the tribe of Benjamin."[9] Thus, while Paul's letter is addressed inclusively to *all* "who are in Rome beloved of God, called as saints" (πᾶσιν τοῖς οὖσιν ἐν Ῥώμῃ ἀγαπητοῖς θεοῦ, κλητοῖς ἁγίοις, 1:7), he has established a strong *Jewish ethos* as author.

The Authorial *Ethos* —Fluid and Corporate

The *prescript* reveals an even more significant rhetorical observation beyond the Jewish nature of the authorial *ethos*. The moment Paul's apostleship touches on messianic Israel's eschatological destiny to bring about the obedience of faith among the nations in 1:5, *Paul's authorial persona moves to first person plural*: δι᾽ οὗ ἐλάβομεν χάριν καὶ ἀποστολὴν εἰς ὑπακοὴν πίστεως ἐν πᾶσιν τοῖς ἔθνεσιν, "through whom we have received grace and apostleship unto the obedience of faith among all the nations." This authorial number shift from singular to plural descriptively can be called the "pluralizing function" of the authorial *ethos* in Romans. From this shift come two points.

First, Paul already has signaled as early as the *prescript* that he can move fluidly from singular to plural when he functions within the authorial *ethos* of Romans. This observation seems rather obvious and trite, since public discourse easily could default to a plural on the part of the speaker to draw in the audience. The second point, however, establishes the significance of the first.

Second, in this *prescript* Paul explicitly contextualizes this pluralizing function of the authorial *ethos* and his apostleship in messianic-eschatological corporate terms. This connection derives from Paul's foundational sense of call. This call takes Paul's "we" usage far beyond the superficialities of conventional public address. When Paul moves to first person plural within the authorial *ethos* of the *prescript*, he demonstrates his thought functions within a corporate dimension of

---

[9] Of Rom 11:1, Anderson acknowledged that here "Paul is able to use himself as an example of God's selection of a remnant who are saved," *Ancient Rhetorical Theory and Paul*, 237. Note that Kim in his rhetorical study of the letter to Romans also concluded about the opening of Romans, "The most striking feature in the *exordium* is that Paul presents himself as a Jewish apostle in thoroughly Jewish terms" (*God, Israel, and the Gentiles*, 87–88). As we hope to show not only in this chapter but throughout our exposition, Paul's Jewish *ethos* bears the burden of all the rhetoric of Romans.

his call as apostle and his sense of identity with messianic Israel in her eschatological destiny among the gentiles.[10]

Further, the corporate identity of the *prescript's* pluralizing function for the authorial voice remains constant throughout the argumentation in Romans 1–7. Paul's "we," that is, can be read consistently as Paul speaking as a (Jewish) apostle on behalf of messianic Israel moving toward an eschatological destiny to bring the obedience of faith among the gentiles.[11] A sample list of first person plural indicative verbs illustrates:[12]

- 3:9, "are we any better off?": ἐπερώτησις (*eperōtēsis*) for messianic Israel vs. Mosaic Israel (3:1)

- 3:19, "we know that whatever the law says": κεκριμένον (accepted opinion) of messianic Israel in the form of a παρομολογία (non-damaging concession)

- 3:28, "we hold that a person is justified by faith": κεκριμένον of messianic Israel

- 3:31, "we uphold the law": ἀντίθεσις (*antithesis*) on behalf of messianic Israel

- 4:1, "What are we to say was gained by Abraham, our ancestor according to the flesh?": παράδειγμα (*paradeigma*) proleptic of messianic Israel prior to Mosaic Israel couched in diatribe style

- 4:9, "We say, 'Faith was reckoned to Abraham as righteousness'": αἰτιολογία (*aitiologia*) series answered on behalf of messianic Israel.[13]

---

[10] Paul's "we" also tacitly recognizes that he is not the only one laboring in this work, and that his work among the gentiles must show concord in message and strategy with others contributing to this effort (Rom 15:20–21).

[11] Paul's "we" also speaks on behalf of gentiles, *in as much as* gentiles are incorporated into messianic Israel; similarly, Donaldson, *Paul and the Gentiles*, 119.

[12] Robinson, "The Priesthood of Paul in the Gospel of Hope," 236, said that Paul's "we" in Romans 1–8 "reflects Paul's Jewishness," but as a normalization of the individual believer's experience. In contrast, the argument here is that the "we" function is more corporately confessional than individually paradigmatic.

[13] Online glossaries of rhetorical terms are available that can aid students for whom this terminology is unfamiliar.

These examples show that a consistent corporate function attends the rhetoric of the pluralized authorial voice in Romans. This consistency is maintained all the way into Romans 7.

Paul's authorial "we" is matched by a corresponding pluralized "you" in Romans. The second person plural in pronouns and verbs begins in Rom 1:6 of the *prescript* and is used without shifting to the singular throughout the *exordium* into 1:15. Then, a pluralized "you" disappears until 6:3, from which point on, a heavy and exclusive use begins again into 7:4. The singular form does not occur at all until 2:1, directly related to a rhetorical *figure*: ὦ ἄνθρωπε πᾶς ὁ κρίνων, O man, the one who condemns!" This dialogue partner accounts for many of the instances of the second person singular in Romans 2–3. After 4:18, second singular disappears completely until the Decalogue quotation in 7:7, again a rhetorical *figure*. In conclusion, in Romans 1–7, a pluralized "you" consistently parallels the authorial "we." That is, the author discloses the addressee in consistently corporate terms. Singular forms are marked clearly rhetorically as part of the argumentative method.

Only two instances interrupt the flow of this pluralizing rhetoric of the authorial voice from 5:1 to 7:6. Each interruption has clear rhetorical function. The first interruption is the first person *singular* in 6:19. Here, Paul clarifies his own rhetoric (ἀνθρώπινον λέγω, "I am speaking in human terms"). The second interruption includes an explicit rhetorical marker at 7:1: γινώσκουσιν γὰρ νόμον λαλῶ, "I am speaking to those who know the law." One could assume from Paul's prior rhetoric that the personalizing address of "brothers" in 7:1 would be the same as the last reference in the *exordium* at 1:13; in other words, the absolute "brothers" in 7:1 (without qualification) would be heard as a generalized reference to corporate messianic Israel. This impression would be confirmed further by the consistent rhetorical context of the authorial first person plural in 5:1—6:23. Paul in 7:1, however, explicitly establishes a *Jewish* marker for the rhetoric to follow. He does this because his second analogy (7:1–6) is meant to be particularly applicable to the *Jewish* experience of messianic Israel.[14]

---

[14] This distinctive Jewish marker at 7:1 does not change throughout the rest of the chapter. In fact, such an *explicit* marker does not occur again in the authorial voice until 11:13, Ὑμῖν δὲ λέγω τοῖς ἔθνεσιν, "I am speaking to you gentiles."

The Authorial *Pathos* —Thematic

In what functions as the *exordium* to Romans (1:8–15), Paul continues developing his *ethos* by appropriate deployment of *pathos*. Using common religious and social markers, Paul also includes standard *figure*, such as the personalizing address for the reader/hearers in the ἀδελφοί ("brothers") in 1:13.[15] In this development, one obvious linguistic marker of authorial *ethos* is the dominance of first person singular in 1:8–15. Of course, this grammar is to be expected.

What is not expected, however, is how Paul smoothly *continues* first person singular as he shifts out of the *exordium* into the *transitio* in 1:16–17, which functions as the theme statement. While the great majority of commentators find in 1:16–17 Paul's theme statement for the letter, the atypical rhetoric of Paul's theme statement often is unremarked. Two observations seem pertinent to this point. One involves content, the other context.

First, on content, Paul's theme statement shows two particularly striking rhetorical features. One striking feature is the continued use of first person singular into the *transitio*. First person means authorial *ethos* and *pathos* are *integral to the theme statement*. The theme statement is framed in first person. This grammar is the author's deliberate decision and reveals conscious insertion of authorial *ethos* and *pathos* into the very character of the theme statement. The authorial persona, then, is meant to be key to reading the functional development of the theme throughout Romans.[16]

A second striking rhetorical feature of the theme statement is the unexpected negative frame: Οὐ γὰρ ἐπαισχύνομαι τὸ εὐαγγέλιον, "For I am not ashamed of the gospel." The first observation is that this negative is not intended as feigned εἰρωνείαν. (*eirōneian*)[17] The problem,

---

[15] Significantly, this very personal tone will not be heard again until the ἀδελφοί in 7:1.

[16] Kennedy hints at some rhetorical significance to this use of first person within the proposition of the letter as a whole ("it sounds a note which is echoed in the use of the first person singular throughout the letter"), but never develops the idea; Kennedy, *New Testament Interpretation Through Rhetorical Criticism*, 153.

[17] That is, in the *figure* of a *confessio* used as εἰρωνείαν; cf. Quintilian, *Inst.* 9.2.44, 51.

that is, is real. Why is this?[18] Paul clearly has set up a positive *ethos* associated with the gospel through typical methods in the *exordium* of assuming honor through honorable associations.[19] Paul already has styled the gospel as God's gospel.[20] To this honorable characterization Paul adds that the gospel is about God's Son (τῷ εὐαγγελίῳ τοῦ υἱοῦ αὐτοῦ, "the gospel of his Son").[21] In terms of requisite *ethos* development in the *exordium*, if this gospel already in verse one of the epistle is associated with the *ethos* of God and soon in verse nine the *ethos* of God's Son, what possible reason could Paul have for shame when associating his own *ethos* with this gospel just a few verses later? If we frame this question of shame in the theme statement of 1:16–17 as a question of rhetoric, the answer should *not* be based upon arbitrary historical speculation related to Paul's mission preaching, but rather upon rhetorical disclosure within the letter itself.[22]

A first hint at the personal nature of the problem in the theme statement to be resolved surfaces at 2:16. A voice shift to first person slips in as Paul adds a tertiary *ethos* to the characterization of the gospel: κατὰ τὸ εὐαγγέλιόν μου, "according to my gospel." This distinctive shift in characterization is authorial persona resurfacing right at the point of the next mention of the gospel in the letter after the theme statement.[23] Since Paul connects his own *ethos* to the gospel, as revealed in 2:16, then the question of shame in 1:16 is inferred as his own asso-

---

[18] Aristotle's words, simple but perceptive, seem pertinent and worth repeating: "necessarily a person feels shame toward those whose opinion he takes account of," *Rhet.* 2.6.14.

[19] Cf. Quintilian, *Inst.* 3.8.12–13; 6.2.18.

[20] 1:1, εὐαγγέλιον θεοῦ, "gospel of God," genitive of origin, as the following verses make clear.

[21] In 1:9; here, an objective genitive, "concerning His Son"; yet, so soon on the heels of the previous characterization and semantically repetitive, even Dunn acknowledged, "the fact that both phrases are of precisely the same form and are inevitably ambiguous should not be ignored," Dunn, *Romans 1–8*, 29. Rhetorically, the *ethos* of the Son is associated with the gospel.

[22] To this observation of *ethos* associations with the gospel in the epistle opening, one could add that the letter conclusion reintroduces the same two characterizations in a macrostructure *inclusio*: note the τὸ εὐαγγέλιον τοῦ θεοῦ ("the gospel of God") in 15:16 followed by τὸ εὐαγγέλιον τοῦ Χριστοῦ ("the gospel of the Messiah") in 15:19.

[23] Further, εὐαγγέλιον ("gospel") will not come up again until the unit on Israel in 9–11 (in 10:16).

ciation with the gospel. Thus, Paul's association with the gospel generates a question of shame in the theme statement for the character of
God, or Jesus, or both. Paul rejects this shame as a false association.
Consequently, he will be under obligation to show how his gospel does
not shame God.

While the epistolary introduction has a level of *pathos* appropriate
for establishing the good will of the readers toward the author—the typical function of an *exordium*—the theme statement abruptly and unexpectedly injects a higher level of authorial *pathos* associated with the
two issues of shame and the gospel of God.[24] Shame, then, functions as
an authorial *topos* for Paul in Romans related to the theme statement,
negatively nuanced. Unfortunately for Paul, he does not anticipate this
shame to be resolved until the eschaton. This timing becomes clear in
his later comment on the believer's future hope. Part of Christian hope
for Paul personally is that he not be put to shame in that future day,
which seems to infer exoneration as a preacher of messianic Israel's
gospel (καυχώμεθα ἐπ᾽ ἐλπίδι τῆς δόξης τοῦ θεοῦ . . . ἡ δὲ ἐλπὶς οὐ
καταισχύνει, "we boast in hope of the glory of God . . . and hope does
not make ashamed," 5:2, 5). The context for this shame is Israel's hardening in the present time (Rom 11:25).

To these two rhetorical features of the theme statement we may
add a contextual observation. This heightened level of authorial *pathos*
is situated in a context in which a Jewish *ethos* also is prominent. In
1:16, closely following Οὐ γὰρ ἐπαισχύνομαι τὸ εὐαγγέλιον, "For I
am not ashamed of the gospel," comes this amplification: Ἰουδαίῳ τε
πρῶτον, "to the Jew first." Since this phrase is not a traditional Jewish
κεκριμένον (accepted opinion), this phrase apparently is a distinctive
Pauline formulation that will require some rhetorical development for
the reader/hearers' understanding.[25] Regardless the background of the
statement, the encoded Jewish *ethos* and priority is clear and resonates

---

[24] Abrupt because the negative formulation comes at precisely the point a positive
formulation is expected; this is an element of παράδοξαν, which gives an unexpected
turn that is most effective for drawing in the listener. Cf. Quintilian, *Inst.* 9.2.22–24.

[25] Which Paul soon accomplishes in chapter 2 through ἐπιμονή (rhetorical development of a thought through repetition) in 2:9 and 2:10. Paul's artful echo of a notable
element in the theme statement now clarifies that this Pauline formulation is intended
as εἰρωνεία: "to the Jew first" means first not only in salvation but in judgment as well.

with the Jewish character of the authorial *ethos* established in the *pre-script*.

More importantly, we observe how Paul associates by close proximity this shame *topos* with the Jewish *ethos* in the theme statement about faith. Paul continues this close connection between shame and Jewish *ethos* in his chapters bringing the argument to a climax in chapters 9–11. Two of Paul's Old Testament proof texts involve this feature of shame in the context of faith.

The first proof text is Isa 8:14 in Rom 9:33: Ἰδοὺ τίθημι ἐν Σιὼν λίθον προσκόμματος καὶ πέτραν σκανδάλου, καὶ ὁ πιστεύων ἐπ᾽ αὐτῷ οὐ καταισχυνθήσεται. "Behold! I lay in Zion a stone of stumbling and a rock of offense, and the one who believes in him will not be ashamed." In the Old Testament context, Isaiah proclaimed several prophecies to Ahaz of Judah urging fidelity to Yahweh as the only alliance worth trusting during a time when Assyria was on the move through Tiglath-Pileser III. Israel under Pekah already had aligned with Rezin in Syria and was attempting to compel Judah into the confederacy. The promised Emmanuel Child's life would be a marker of God's sovereign judgment on these two kings of Syria and Israel that Ahab dreaded so (Isa 7:14). Further, Isaiah urged that God would become a stone of stumbling that many would fall over because of misplaced trust in human political strategies (Isa 8:14). In 732 BC Syria fell, then Israel fell in 722. Judah later fell to the Babylonians in 586 BC. This misplaced trust brought shame to God's people that ended in the catastrophic judgment of exile.

The other proof text is Isa 28:16 in Rom 10:11: Πᾶς ὁ πιστεύων ἐπ᾽ αὐτῷ οὐ καταισχυνθήσεται, "Everyone who believes in him will not be ashamed." Isaiah's context is prediction of Ephraim's captivity with a warning to Judah and the resultant cornerstone laid in Zion becoming a stone of stumbling. Both of these texts demonstrate that Paul derives his shame *topos* directly from the prophetic speech of the Old Testament, and specifically those related to Israel's fate.

The Authorial *Pathos*—Patterned

Romans 3:1–8 often is identified as a digression in Paul's argument. In as much as this unit functions as πρόληψις (*prolēpsis*), such a characterization is not off track rhetorically. That is, the unit, even as a παράβασις (*parabasis*, brief digression), still contributes to the argument.[26] Significantly for our purposes, this unit shows similar features of rhetoric and content to the theme statement in 1:16–17.

First, in terms of rhetoric, in the unit 2:17–20, Paul has been using ἀποστροφή (*apostrophē*) accusatory rhetorical questions, a special form of ἐπερώτησις (*eperōtēsis*) specifically directed to the Jew (2:17). This shifts in 3:1–8 to the use of αἰτιολογία (*aitiologia*, short questions the speaker answers).[27] Notice that αἰτιολογία involves a voice change (μεταβολή, *metabolē*) from second and third person to first person (cf. ἡμῶν, ἐροῦμεν, "our," "we say," v. 5; ἐμῷ, "my," v. 7). Voice change can trigger expectation for διαφωνία (*diaphōnia*, difference in characterization). This allows the persona of the author directly back into the dialogue but does not change the addressee, the Jew.[28] The point here is that a change in voice also is a change in *ethos*. Correspondingly, along with change in *ethos* is a potential change in the degree of *pathos*. Here in 3:1–8, the element of *pathos* increases, as in the theme statement. Especially is higher *pathos* signaled in Paul's highly stylistic negation, μὴ γένοιτο, "May it not be!" used twice (3:4, 6). Further, Paul labors against a particularly onerous distortion of his message: μὴ καθὼς βλασφημούμεθα καὶ καθώς φασίν τινες ἡμᾶς λέγειν ὅτι Ποιήσωμεν τὰ κακά, ἵνα ἔλθῃ τὰ ἀγαθά; "Why not say just as some slander us as saying, 'Let us do what is evil in order that good may come'" (3:8)? One could assume this damaging calumny would be in relation to Paul's gospel recently mentioned (2:16).

Second, in terms of similarities to 1:16–17, the context for this higher level of authorial *pathos* also involves a question of Jewish *ethos*: Τί οὖν τὸ περισσὸν τοῦ Ἰουδαίου; "Therefore, what advantage is of the Jew?" (3:1). This issue of Jewish advantage in 3:1 ties back directly to the theme assertion, Ἰουδαίῳ τε πρῶτον, "to the Jew first." Thus, in

[26] In agreement with Anderson's analysis, *Ancient Rhetorical Theory in Paul*, 216.

[27] Stowers has analyzed 3:1–9 as a diatribe dialogue and given the μὴ γένοιτο negation to an interlocutor, *A Rereading of Romans*, 165. Anderson, however, is correct to point out that the speaker markers in this text are much too ambiguous to allow for Stowers's discrete analysis (*Ancient Rhetorical Theory in Paul*, 217, n59); more compatible with the text features is a simple conversational style using αἰτιολογία.

[28] Anderson, *Ancient Rhetorical Theory in Paul*, 209, also argued that the use of first person plural in 3:5–9 indicates the πρόληψις (*prolēpsis*) still is directed to the Jew. This conclusion we would also argue for Rom 7:1–6, which rhetorically marks 7:7–25.

both highly *pathetic* contexts, Paul labors with Jewish *ethos* specifically in terms of Jewish identity. This issue of Jewish identity already has asserted itself as part of the theme of Romans. One implicit rhetorical marker that this part of the Romans theme is being harnessed in the argument in Romans is this key element of heightened authorial *pathos*.

Summary Observations

We suggest that early on in the letter of Romans, Paul has established this rhetorical pattern: The closer discussion moves to issues of Jewish identity, the higher the levels of authorial *pathos* in the rhetoric. This increased *pathos* is related directly to the authorial voice in Romans. This voice will be heard with higher than normal levels of *pathos* when the discussion touches upon the burden of the argument as revealed in the problem of the theme statement cued to the reader/hearer by its unusual rhetoric. This pattern of Paul's theme rhetoric can be labeled Paul's *pathetic pattern*. The key observation here is that Paul's pathetic pattern reveals the rhetorical burden of the theme statement. Can this pathetic pattern be established elsewhere in Romans? Yes, of course.[29]

Of several examples, elements of chapters 8 and 9 are perhaps the most obvious. For example, the highly charged emotive content of 8:31–38 often is noted. Paul is concluding the entire movement of Romans 6–8 with a lengthy πολυσύνδετον (*polysyndeton*).[30] This deep *pathos* rhetorically is connected to the theme statement through Paul's pathetic pattern. The elements of this theme rhetoric surface in 8:31–38. First, Paul again reverts to a sustained first person passage with high authorial *pathos*. Second, note that the context of 8:31–38 involves distinct elements of Jewish identity.[31] Anderson concluded that the passage 8:31–39 was "crowned with an Old Testament citation intended to show that the sufferings of God's people are nothing new."[32] He need not stop there: Rom 8:36–37 is the explicit analogue of Rom 7:24–25 and demonstrates the corporate nature of Paul's expression in the earlier

---

[29] Whether formally part of Paul's rhetorical strategy throughout all of Romans would require a global analysis of the text of Romans, which is beyond our scope here. We simply intend to provide other examples of the pattern.

[30] So Anderson, *Ancient Rhetorical Theory in Paul*, 233.

[31] Cf. 8:16, ἐσμὲν τέκνα θεοῦ; 8:17, κληρονόμοι.

[32] Anderson, *Ancient Rhetorical Theory in Paul*, 233.

exclamation in Romans 7. One is spoken from within the context of Mosaic Israel, the other from the context of messianic Israel, but thematically, the two are close. The following bipartite juxtaposition of passages helps illustrate:

7:24 ταλαίπωρος ἐγὼ ἄνθρωπος· τίς με ῥύσεται ἐκ τοῦ σώματος τοῦ θανάτου τούτου;

Wretched man that I am! Who will deliver me from this deadly body?

8:36 καθὼς γέγραπται ὅτι
Ἕνεκεν σοῦ θανατούμεθα ὅλην τὴν ἡμέραν,
ἐλογίσθημεν ὡς πρόβατα σφαγῆς.
Just as it has been written
"For your sake we are being killed the whole day long,
we have been reckoned as sheep for slaughter."

7:25 χάρις δὲ τῷ θεῷ διὰ Ἰησοῦ Χριστοῦ τοῦ κυρίου ἡμῶν.
But thanks be to God through Jesus Messiah, our Lord!

8:37 ἀλλ' ἐν τούτοις πᾶσιν ὑπερνικῶμεν διὰ τοῦ ἀγαπήσαντος ἡμᾶς.
But in all these things we abundantly conquer through the one who loved us.

Another example is Rom 9:1–5. This unit is even higher in *pathos*, universally acknowledged as the most emotionally laden passage in all of Romans. The *ethos* of the authorial persona is transparent. Here the depths of that *pathos* have reached the pitiable. Ancient rhetoricians are agreed that pity is a powerful weapon. Paul's tone in 9:1–5 is similar to the advice given by an ancient rhetorician: "We shall stir Pity in our hearers by . . . revealing what will befall our parents, children, and other kinsmen through our disgrace, and at the same time showing that we grieve not because of our own straits but because of their anxiety and misery; . . ."[33] While the unit 9:1–5 is brief, in conformity with the general advice for evoking pity,[34] the power of the rhetoric still is over-

---

[33] *Ad C. Herennium* 2.31.50.

[34] "Appeals to pity should, however, always be brief." Quintilian, *Inst.* 6.1.27. The advice given, however, should acknowledge that any specific context dictates exactly how to define what may be perceived as "brief."

whelming. This extraordinary *pathos* likely is because the latent burden of the theme statement in 1:16, Ἰουδαίῳ τε πρῶτον, "to the Jew first," now surfaces in its most potent form as revealed in chapters 9–11: characteristic Jewish rejection of Paul's gospel, which here is a source of inestimable grief to Paul, but, as well, potential shame to God. This potential shame to God brought on by Paul's preaching of the gospel and the consequent Jewish rejection of that message is the theological conundrum that Paul labors to work through in Romans 9–11.

The intense *pathos* of 9:1–5, that is, is a clear rhetorical cue to the reader/hearer due to Paul's pathetic pattern in Romans that the unusual negative formulation of the theme statement in the personalizing words of 1:16, Οὐ γὰρ ἐπαισχύνομαι τὸ εὐαγγέλιον, "For I am not ashamed of the gospel," has reached its rhetorical climax in 9:1–5. Paul finally has arrived at the ἐπίλογια (*epilogia*) that should run full circle back to the theme statement and resolve the rhetorical problem latent within. For this reason, the notable mood change at 9:1 is neither sudden nor unexpected, as often asserted.[35] Anderson asserted Paul did not transition well, but was able to achieve his argumentative goal: "In this way he (re)introduces the problem of the Jew's rejection of the Gospel and its Messiah."[36] No, this problem is not being reintroduced. Paul has been unpacking this problem ever since the theme statement.

AUTHORIAL RHETORIC IN ROMANS 7

Notable Features of Romans 7

Can these observations about Paul's *pathetic pattern* in Romans assist in an understanding of Romans 7? We think so. Before providing this analysis, though, helpful here would be to outline the following often noted features of this notoriously difficult passage:

- *Grammar*: First, the passage is subdivided grammatically into two distinct units, 7:7–13 and 7:14–25 based on the tense shift from aorist to present between these two. Second, even though first person *plural*, "we," dominates the illustration in 7:1–6 that introduces the defense of the law in 7:7–25, first person *singular*, "I," is used almost exclusively in 7:7b–25.

---

[35] Even, for example, with Anderson, *Ancient Rhetorical Theory in Paul*, 234.

[36] Anderson, *Ancient Rhetorical Theory in Paul*, 234.

- *Semantics*: The range of meaning of important concepts, such as "death," "life," and "law," seems to drift, causing definitional confusion from verse to verse.[37]

- *Style*: Sin, Death, and Law continue to be personified, as throughout chapters 6–8. However, if the "I" is personification, the reference is not explicit. Proper rhetorical identification, therefore, of Paul's "I" for many seems to be unclear.[38]

- *Theology*: The category of Spirit that plays such a dominant role in the next chapter, and seems fundamental there to Paul's definition of Christian experience (8:14), is completely absent throughout the "I" unit in chapter seven.[39]

- *Context*: Paul has set forth his theme of the gospel as God's righteousness by faith to all who believe in 1:16–17, provided proof in 1:18–3:20, explained its nature in 3:21–31, and, by example, demonstrated scriptural concord in 4:1–25. Paul expanded on the benefits of God's righteousness by faith in 5:1–11 and demonstrated its universal significance in 5:12–21. Paul then seeks to untangle the complicated relationship among Grace, Sin, and Law, as inferred in concluding 5:12–21, in chapters 6–8. Implications for Israel are addressed in 9–11.[40]

---

[37] For example, whether "death" and "life" are encoded with "full theological force" (read "eschatological") or as just referential; whether "law" is Mosaic code only, or can be simply a general "principle" of philosophical thought in some instances.

[38] For this reason, Paul's "I" rhetoric exposes philosophical presuppositions of commentators that are not stated explicitly in the narrative that beg the question by either psychologizing the text existentially, thereby subverting Paul's objective language into subjective evaluation (whether Paul's or general human consciousness), or falsely generalizes the text as if all humankind has been subjected to the Mosaic code.

[39] Generating confusion whether the described experience is either "pre-Christian" or "Christian," including numerous subtle variations, such as whether "pre-Christian human realities seen through Christian reflection" or "pre-conversion Jewish experience as described through post-conversion Christian reflection," and so forth.

[40] Also observed have been both the *internal* and the *external* structural logic of the unit. Internally, the unit itself seems to play out a two-part logical movement in its own immediate literary context in 7:6. In 7:6a we have the logic of being discharged from the law, which seems to be taken up more fully in 7:7–25. In 7:6b we have the logic of the new life of the Spirit, which seems taken up more fully in the next chapter. Externally, the entire unit seems to play out the two-part logical movement in the larger literary context of the *digressio* in the form of πρόληψις (*prolēpsis*) of 3:1–8. Rhe-

What shall we make of these complex phenomena? We focus our energies on two topics that hopefully will advance discussion. These two topics are, first, Paul's use of first person, and, second, authorial ἔθος (*ethos*) credibility.

Ethos Profile of Romans 7

Identity of the First Person

The first topic is Paul's use of first person. Who is represented in the first person in the two units? The major contenders for understanding the first person, whether they are distinguished between the two literary subunits, are Jew, Paul, Adam, humankind, or Israel.[41] However, the list can be narrowed substantially immediately. Distinctions over the Jew, Paul, Adam, or humankind are rather specious, simply minor variations with only slight distinctions on the garden-variety, self-willed, rebellious human being. Romans 7, then, is either about common human experience, typically conceived individualistically, or Israel. The first option, however, no matter how supported through the centuries, is notorious for extraordinary, semantic non sequiturs or logical leaps.

Rhetorical studies hold promise to contribute to these traditional discussions.[42] Some using classical rhetoric have latched on rather hard

---

torically, this fits into a pattern of αὔξησις (*auxēsis*, expansion or development when proof not needed) of one of the two objections raised in the πρόληψις (*prolēpsis*) of 3:1–8. The second objection, whether God is unjust to inflict his wrath, is dealt with first in chapters 6–8. The first objection, whether God is rendered untrustworthy by Jewish disobedience, is dealt with in chapters 9–11. This external logic represents a growing consensus agreeing with the analysis of Campbell, "Romans 3 as a Key to the Structure and Thought of Romans." Cf. Anderson, *Ancient Rhetorical Theory and Paul*, 229; Dodd, *Paul's Paradigmatic "I"*, 227.

[41] Romans 7:7–25, of course, has been contended for centuries. Cf. Dunn, *Romans 1–8*, 378–80; Fitzmyer, *Romans*, 463–65. For a concise summary, cf. Schreiner, *Romans*, 356–94. As illustrative examples: **Jew** (Barnes, Baur, Bengal, Clarke, Greek fathers, Luther); **Paul** (Bruce, Godet, Holman, Hultgren, Morris, Schreiner, Segal); **believer** (Augustine, Delitzsch, Dodd, Hodge, Jerome, Packer); **mixed**, tenses = Paul and believer, (Barrett, Calvin, Cranfield, Murray); **Adam** (Γαρλινγτον, Longenecker, Michel, Stuhlmacher, Theodore of Mopsuestia, Witherington); **humanity** (Bultmann, Dunn, Fitzmyer, Käsemann, Kaylor, Kümmel, Manson, Mounce, Origen, Osborne, Theophilus, Tyndale, Wesley); **Israel** (Black, Chrysostom, Fritzsimmons, Grotius, Karlberg, Kruse, Moo, Seifrid, Stott, Trudinger, Wetstein, Wright).

[42] Besides works already cited, cf. Reid, "Paul's Rhetoric of Mutuality"; Aune, "Romans as a Logos Protreptikos"; Wuellner, "Paul's Rhetoric of Argumentation in Ro-

to the *figure* of προσωποποιΐα (*prosōpopoiia*) as the correct analysis of Paul's rhetoric in Romans 7. Stowers argued Romans 7 was a clear example of *prosōpopoiia* (which he labeled as "speech-in-character") written on behalf of gentiles overwhelmed by the impossibility of personal self-mastery through the law.[43] In contrast, Anderson opted for Romans 7 as personal παράδειγμα (*paradeigma*, example) on Paul's part as illustrative, with which Schreiner and Dodd agreed.[44]

However, these rhetorical approaches have serious weaknesses that render them unsatisfactory. Stowers's reading is flawed for several reasons, but not the one Anderson proposed. First, Stowers's reading was dependent upon Origen's take on Romans 7 from several centuries *later* as indicative of Paul's first-century readers.[45] Such a procedure is flawed methodologically, notwithstanding Stowers's precautions.[46] Second, Stowers falls back on the old Bultmann proposal that Rom 7:15, 19 contain a ubiquitous Greek saying from Ovid's *Medea* central to the self-mastery rhetoric of the Greco-Roman moral world of dramatists and philosophers.[47] Thus, while Paul gives the topic of Romans 7 his own spin, the supposed allusion to *Medea* assures us Paul's topic is gentile self-mastery in the style of Greco-Roman moral tradition.[48]

mans; Jewett, "Following the Argument of Romans"; Elliott, *The Rhetoric of Romans*; Funk, "The Apostolic Parousia"; Manson, "For I Am Not Ashamed of the Gospel (Rom 1:16)"; Porter, "Ancient Rhetorical Analysis and Discourse Analysis of the Pauline Corpus"; Scroggs, "Paul as Rhetorician: Two Homilies in Romans 1–11"; Watson, "The Contributions and Limitations of Greco-Roman Rhetorical Theory for Constructing the Rhetorical and Historical Situations of a Pauline Epistle"; Holland, "The Self against the Self in Romans 7.7–25"; Dodd, *Paul's Paradigmatic "I"*; Kim, *God, Israel, and the Gentiles*. My own soundings exploring classical Roman school rhetoric as background for New Testament authors such as Paul seemed to suggest that Paul's first person rhetoric would yield to easy analysis. The most productive species seemed to be epideictic or deliberative rhetoric. This angle, however, yielded little even close to the particular use of first person within the parameters of Romans 7.

[43] Stowers, *Rereading of Romans*, 264–72, 279; Tobin (*Paul's Rhetoric*, 238) argued "speech-in-character," but immediately fudged on the actual sequence demanded by the rhetorical form ("although not in quite the same order"), invalidating the analysis.

[44] Anderson, *Ancient Rhetorical Theory and Paul*, 232; Schreiner, *Romans*, 365; Dodd, *"Paul's Paradigmatic "I,"* 32.

[45] Stowers, *Rereading of Romans*, 268.

[46] Stowers, *Rereading of Romans*, 269. That Romans 7 strikes Origen as speech-in-character has no *inherent* connection to Paul's usage just because Origen is a "native speaker."

[47] Stowers, *Rereading of Romans*, 260.

[48] Ibid., 264.

Anderson, in contrast, charged that Stowers's proposal of Romans 7 as *prosōpopoiia* was "ruled out, since this requires explicit speaker identification," which the Romans 7 context is distinctly missing.[49] This critique of Stowers, however, is not on target. Correctly, the Romans 7 context is distinctly missing explicit speaker identification. However, the assertion that lack of speaker identification automatically rules out any form of *prosōpopoiia* simply is not correct. This claim is contradicted directly by Quintilian, who identifies a specific mixed *figure* of *impersonation* (Greek: προσωποποιΐα) that, when combined with *ellipse*, is the omission of any indication of who is speaking.[50] Thus, as far as Quintilian is concerned, one *can* have *prosōpopoiia* without the explicit identification of the speaker.

Anderson probably is correct that Romans 7 is not *prosōpopoiia*. We would rather argue the point, though, on the stronger rhetorical basis of *ethos* development, which, above all else, must be credible, consistent, and clear. We already have argued that Romans 7 is crucial to maintenance of credible authorial *ethos*. An additional rhetorical clue to the persona of the Romans 7 "I" is Paul's concluding exclamation in 7:24: ταλαίπωρος ἐγὼ ἄνθρωπος· τίς με ῥύσεται ἐκ τοῦ σώματος τοῦ θανάτου τούτου; "Wretched man that I am! Who will deliver me from this deadly body?" (7:24). While not all agree as to the background of this poignant exclamation,[51] all do agree such an outburst is the highest level of *pathos* to this point in the letter. A rhetorical observation should be added: no other *ethos* in Romans to this point has been disclosed to the recipients with this level of pathos other than the author himself. Thus, 7:24 is another clear instance of Paul's *pathetic pattern* in Romans. The function has changed, but the pattern has not.

---

[49] Anderson, *Ancient Rhetorical Theory and Paul*, 231.

[50] *Inst.* 9.2.36–37.

[51] Stowers, *Rereading of Romans*, 263, for example, would want to make this, too, part of the Greek moral tradition through Ovid *Met.* 7.17–21. But that would involve Paul in an apparent hypocrisy and probable loss of credible *ethos*. A possibility from classical rhetoric might be what Quintilian indicated the Greeks called φαντασίαι (Latin, *visions*), "whereby things absent are presented to our imagination with such extreme vividness that they seem actually to be before our very eyes." *Inst.* 6.2.29. However, in *Inst.* 9.2.27 Quintilian insisted his category for such *figure* must fall under simulation; he would not apply this category to a genuine expression. Paul's expression in 7:24 shows rhetorical complexity: marked as genuine by the authorial *ethos*, yet also as *figure* by ἐπερώτησις (rhetorical question).

Note first that the element of Jewish identity explicitly is present in the context: γινώσκουσιν γὰρ νόμον λαλῶ, "For I am speaking to those who know the law" (7:1). Second, the voice is unmarked first person in 7:7–25. The *prescript* already has established this rhetoric of fluid transition in number without transition in *ethos* as the authorial voice.

Given the unmarked rhetoric of speaker identification in Romans 7 in the context of Paul's *pathetic pattern* in Romans, we conclude, then, that the *ethos* of the "I" in Romans 7 rhetorically must be Paul's. In fact, suddenly to introduce an unnamed, mysterious *ethos*, particularly one so full of *pathos* as 7:24 indicates, at this crucial point in the argument would do rhetorical violence to the audience and generate maximum confusion, a most counterproductive ploy—bluntly, rhetorically incompetent.

Function of the First Person

If the "I" of Romans 7 is Paul, the more crucial question is, what is the rhetorical function of "I"? Many who conclude the "I" is Paul immediately presume—without rhetorical demonstration from within the text in Romans—that this "I" has an *individualizing autobiographical* function.[52] We should resist this presumption, if for nothing else, because the result subjects the text to the abuse of the total subjectivity of the interpreter. That the "I" involved in Romans 7 moves from "life" to "death" in that case invariably must be made to correspond arbitrarily to some life experience of Paul. Usual proposals are:

- Childhood: Paul's childhood "awakening" (whatever that really is)

- Conversion: preliminaries to Paul's own so-called "conversion" experience (ignoring whether the modern notion of "conversion" even is a legitimate category to import into Paul's own self descriptions)

- Confusion: generalized adult confusion with life or "powerlessness"

Clearly, all such suggestions are an exegetical leap of logic. That all this is highly subjective and speculative conveniently is ignored.

---

[52] A good example is: "[on the Antioch incident of Galatians 2] Peter's covetous sin was to bring back discrimination on the basis of circumcision . . . Paul's struggle with sin in Romans 7 was with the similar temptation Paul knew to covet the status of circumcision and the gift of Torah" (Nanos, *Mystery of Romans*, 360). Psychologizing exegesis is evident and unacceptable methodologically.

An autobiographical approach to Romans 7 is indefensible more than simply because Paul's meaning in crucial expressions such as χωρὶς νόμου ("apart from the law") and ἐλθούσης δὲ τῆς ἐντολῆς ("when the commandment came") are rendered virtually incoherent logically.[53] The autobiographical approach is indefensible primarily because rhetorical analysis has shown that the development of the authorial *ethos* from the *prescript* on never has wavered. Paul's "we" speaks from within the context of a Jewish apostle working on behalf of messianic Israel to help Israel reach the prophetic, eschatological destiny to bring about the obedience of faith among the gentiles. This corporate, Jewish *ethos* of the author does not change going into the Romans 7 marriage analogy that continues using first person plural. *With no rhetorical markers for a change in identification of speaker*, Paul's authorial first person plural fluidly shifts to first person singular in 7:7, exactly in reverse mode as in the *prescript* imperceptibly moving from first person singular to first person plural in 1:5.[54] *Thus, our first rhetorical conclusion is that in Romans 7, the function of Paul's first person plural is to speak for, and the first person singular is to identify with, Israel in her present historical and eschatological crisis due to the unexpected coming of Messiah.*[55]

Scriptural Profile of Romans 7

Recent studies on Paul have shown Paul's hermeneutic is grounded in Hebrew Scripture at the canonical level. What is the scriptural profile of the rhetoric of Romans 7? That is, in what contexts do we find both high Jewish *ethos* and *pathos*, and, more importantly, what is the topic?

[53] As Moo already pointed out, "Israel and Paul in Romans 7.7–12," 125.

[54] *Contra* Stowers, *Rereading of Romans*, 269. Authorial voice does *not* change: the author already has indicated fluid shifting between first person singular and first person plural within the authorial *ethos* in the *prescript*. Grammar has to be nuanced with rhetoric: Romans 7 is *not* just a simple a case of μεταβολή (change of voice) triggering an expectation for διαφωνία (difference in characterization from the authorial voice).

[55] On Israel as in view, cf. Moo, "Israel and Paul in Romans 7.7–12," 109; Wright, *Climax of the Covenant*, 197. Added here is a rhetorical argument. The idea that Israel is in view often is denied categorically and without argument, as does Tobin: "He is not describing a typical Jew or a typical Christian or Adam or the history of Israel. . . . The speaker is describing what Paul thinks or imagines is the experience of the typical Gentile Roman Christian" (*Paul's Rhetoric*, 237). Yet, characterizing the *ethos* of the "I" in Romans 7 in this manner is oblivious rhetorically to Paul's careful *ethos* development of the authorial voice to this point in Romans. Tobin argues stylistics, not rhetoric.

Corporate Contexts

First, we find the rhetoric of Romans 7 in corporate contexts. Corporate representations in first person singular on behalf of Jerusalem or Israel in Israel's scriptural traditions seem closest in style to Romans 7.[56] Israel's representatives corporately spoke on behalf of Israel. In the Exodus story, God indicated displeasure with the condition of the Israelites and threatened not to accompany the people into the land. Moses rightly inquired in Exod 33:16: καὶ πῶς γνωστὸν ἔσται ἀληθῶς ὅτι εὕρηκα χάριν παρὰ σοί ἐγώ τε καὶ ὁ λαός σου ἀλλ᾽ ἢ συμπορευ- ομένου σου μεθ᾽ ἡμῶν καὶ ἐνδοξασθήσομαι ἐγώ τε καὶ ὁ λαός σου παρὰ πάντα τὰ ἔθνη ὅσα ἐπὶ τῆς γῆς ἐστιν, "And how will it be genuinely manifest that I have found favor before you, both I and your people, other than you go with us? And I will be glorified, both I and your people, in contrast to all the nations on the face of the earth." The first person singular verb, ἐνδοξασθήσομαι ("I will be glorified"), has a corporate sense, made clear in the epexegetical ἐγώ τε καὶ ὁ λαός σου ("both I and your people").[57] Esther spoke similarly in her response to King Ahasuerus in Esth 7:4: ἐπράθημεν γὰρ ἐγώ τε καὶ ὁ λαός μου εἰς ἀπώλειαν καὶ διαρπαγὴν ("For we have been sold, both I and my people, unto destruction and plunder"). David spoke a blessing over Israel's generous freewill offerings for the temple in 1 Chr 29:14 and confessed: καὶ τίς εἰμι ἐγὼ καὶ τίς ὁ λαός μου ὅτι ἰσχύσαμεν προ- θυμηθῆναί σοι κατὰ ταῦτα; ("But who am I, and what is my people, that we should be able to make this freewill offering?")

Prophetic Contexts

Second, we find the rhetoric of Romans 7 in prophetic contexts. The prophets personified the nation of Israel using various rhetorical strategies. Personification could be accomplished through the prophet's own person, through a characterization, or even through investing another figure from Israel's past with representative status.

---

[56] Texts suggested have included Jer 10:19–22; Mic 7:7–10; and Lam 1:9–22; 2:20–22. See Moo, "Israel and Paul in Romans 7.7–12," 129, also referring to U. Luz, *Das Geschichtsverständnis des Paulus* (BEVT 49; Munich: Kaiser, 1968), 159, n87.

[57] The choice of the LXX translators is curious. The Masoretic text actually has a *plural* verb, נִפְלֵינוּ, from פלה, "to be separate."

Isaiah has several examples. Isaiah 38 incorporates a liturgical song of thanksgiving for deliverance. The conclusion in 38:20 shows a shift from first person singular to first person plural, because the cause for rejoicing is common to the corporate experience of worship:

> The LORD will save me,
>> and we will sing to stringed instruments
> all the days of our lives,
>> at the house of the LORD. (NRSV)

The Servant Songs in Isaiah provide rich context for Romans, as Paul quoted from several Servant passages as he resonates with issues common to the songs as a corpus. Our point, however, mainly is to note the use of voice. The Second Servant Song in Isa 49:1–6 is set in first person singular. Isaiah speaks as the Servant of God. In 49:4, the song contains a complaint about a sense of futility in the Servant's ministry, yet the hope that God will vindicate the Servant's efforts. This vindication theme is common to several Servant songs and resonates with a number of Paul's statements in Romans.

The Third Servant Song occurs in Isa 50:4–11. The Servant is confident he will not be put to shame in 50:7, then indicates trust in God as the judicial defender. When we observe that this Servant song is the context for Paul's quotation in Rom 8:33, then not only does the theme of vindication itself resonate with Romans 8, but the first person of the Servant song also resonates with Paul's first person in his opening defense in Rom 1:16: "For I am not ashamed." Our point, of course, is not that Paul thinks of himself as the Servant. Rather, we emphasize the paradoxical mutuality evoked within the corpus of the Servant songs of both individual and corporate dimensions to the nature of the Servant's mission.

The Fourth Servant Song occurs in Isa 52:13–53:12. Paul quoted Isa 52:15 in Rom 15:21 and Isa 53:1 in Rom 10:16. We observe that the nature of this song is very personalized by the use of first person plural in a confessional mode almost throughout the song. Also, the vindication theme shows up in Isa 53:12.

Isaiah 59 functions as a corporate charge to the nation to repent. The middle third of that charge is a corporate confession couched in an opening first person plural in Isa 59:9–15: διὰ τοῦτο ἀπέστη ἡ κρίσις ἀπ᾽ αὐτῶν καὶ οὐ μὴ καταλάβῃ αὐτοὺς δικαιοσύνη, "For this

reason justice is far from us, and righteousness does not overtake us."
The last portion in Isa 59:15b–21 shifts to third person. This call to repentance is concluded with the assurance that the Redeemer will come
to Zion in 59:20–21, a passage that Paul used to wrap up his ἐπίλογοι
(*epilogoi*, "concluding words") of Romans 9–11 at Rom 11:26.

An extensive psalm of intercession covering almost two chapters
is preserved in Isa 63:7—64:12. The first major section in 63:7–14 is a
resume of Israel's redemptive moment in history in the exodus from
Egypt. Beginning in Isa 63:15 is a petition that God would return Israel
to her former fidelity to God. Note the shift at the beginning from first
person singular[58] to first person plural between 63:15 and 63:16:

> Look down from heaven and see,
>> from your holy and glorious habitation.
> Where are your zeal and your might?
>> The yearning of your heart and your compassion?
>> They are withheld from me.
> For you are our father,
>> though Abraham does not know us
>> and Israel does not acknowledge us;
> you, O LORD, are our father;
>> our Redeemer from of old is your name. (NRSV)

Thereafter, the first person plural is maintained to the end of the chapter.

Isaiah 64 opens with a psalm of confession in 64:1–12. The first
part, 64:1–5a, reveals a longing that God would show himself in the
awesome power once displayed at Sinai. The next part, 64:5a–7, shifts
to first person plural in a confession by the prophet on behalf of God's
people of abject ungodliness. The last part, 64:8–12, maintains the first
person plural in a concluding plea that God not be angry forever.

Jeremiah spoke of a siege that would not be lifted in Jer 10:17–18,
then followed in 10:19–20 with a lament spoken for the character of
mother Zion who loses her children in exile:

---

[58] The Masoretic text has the *singular* form: וְרַחֲמֶיךָ אֵלַי הִתְאַפָּֽקוּ, "and your compassions, have you not restrained from me?" The LXX translators apparently thought
this singular form mistaken: καὶ τῶν οἰκτιρμῶν σου ὅτι ἀνέσχου ἡμῶν, "and your
compassions that you have withheld from us?"

> Woe is me because of my hurt!
>> My wound is severe.
> But I said, "Truly this is my punishment,
>> and I must bear it."
> My tent is destroyed,
>> and all my cords are broken;
> my children have gone from me,
>> and they are no more;
> there is no one to spread my tent again,
>> and to set up my curtains. (NRSV)

Similar in style is Jeremiah's dramatic announcement from God in Jer 31:15:

> Thus says the LORD:
> A voice is heard in Ramah,
>> lamentation and bitter weeping.
> Rachel is weeping for her children;
>> she refuses to be comforted for her children,
>> because they are no more. (NRSV)

The mother of Joseph and Benjamin is invested with representative status for the nation and thus mourns the exile of the northern tribes. Joseph's son Ephraim similarly is given representative status in the following verses (31:18–20).

Ezekiel provides further illustration. He experienced a vision of a valley of dry bones. God enlightened him that the bones represented the whole house of Israel in Eze 37:11: αὐτοὶ λέγουσιν ξηρὰ γέγονεν τὰ ὀστᾶ ἡμῶν, "They say, 'Our bones are dried up, . . .'" Again, first person plural is used in this prophetic rhetoric regarding Israel.

Daniel prayed for his people at the beginning of Daniel 9. In a confessional mode, the prayer begins in first person singular. At Dan 9:5, however, the prayer smoothly shifts into first person plural: ἡμάρτομεν ἠδικήσαμεν ἠσεβήσαμεν καὶ ἀπέστημεν καὶ παρέβημεν τὰς ἐντολάς σου καὶ τὰ κρίματά σου, "we have sinned, acted unjustly, been ungodly, even turned from and transgressed your commandments and decrees." This first person plural continues for a fairly extended period in Dan 9:5–19.

Micah has an extended section in Mic 7:8–10 that generally is understood to be the prophet speaking as Israel:

Do not rejoice over me, O my enemy;
> when I fall, I shall rise;
when I sit in darkness,
> the LORD will be a light to me.
I must bear the indignation of the LORD,
> because I have sinned against him,
until he takes my side
> and executes judgment for me.
He will bring me out to the light;
> I shall see his vindication.
Then my enemy will see,
> and shame will cover her who said to me,
> "Where is the LORD your God?"
My eyes will see her downfall;
> now she will be trodden down
> > like the mire of the streets. (NRSV)

Lament Contexts

Third, and most importantly to understand the element of high *pathos*, we find the rhetoric of Romans 7 in lament contexts.[59] Communal lament psalms portray the transition back and forth from first person singular to first person plural.

Psalm 44 is one such psalm in its prayer for deliverance from national enemies. The first three verses are first person plural; verse 4, however, begins a shifting back and forth between singular and plural for four verses:

> You are my King and my God;
> > you command victories for Jacob.
> Through you we push down our foes;
> > through your name we tread down our assailants.
> For not in my bow do I trust,
> > nor can my sword save me.
> But you have saved us from our foes,
> > and have put to confusion those who hate us. (NRSV)

---

[59] Since this original investigation into Romans 7, lament rhetoric increasingly has figured into Pauline study. Wallace, *Election of the Lesser Son*, demonstrated how Paul integrated the literary form of lament with the exegetical style of midrashic argumentation in Romans 9–11.

One could speculate that this shift in voice could have had liturgical function, such as an antiphonal recitation in which the king or other corporate representative speaks in the first person singular. Even this speculated setting would suggest that such a shifting between singular and plural would have been a familiar *topos* of national lament rhetoric in which *both voices in the psalm rhetorically concern the same ethos: the people of God.* A similar transition also takes place between verses 14 and 15:

> You have made us a byword among the nations,
>> a laughingstock among the peoples.
> All day long my disgrace is before me,
>> and shame has covered my face
> at the words of the taunters and revilers,
>> at the sight of the enemy and the avenger.

We chose this national lament psalm in particular for illustration because Paul quoted verse 22 in the concluding portion of Romans 8 in a section already noted for a highly elevated authorial *ethos* (Rom 8:36).[60]

To be sure, not all first person singular occurrences in national laments should be construed as the voice of an *individual.* A good example is Psalm 129. The opening statement of affliction in first person singular becomes a corporate response at the instruction of a worship leader in 129:1–3:

> "Often have they attacked me from my youth"
> —let Israel now say—
> "often have they attacked me from my youth,
>> yet they have not prevailed against me.
> The plowers plowed on my back;
>> they made their furrows long."

Lamentations, however, offers the most instructive example from lament rhetoric. Jerusalem is a personified maiden and cries out in Lam 1:9: ἰδέ κύριε τὴν ταπείνωσίν μου ὅτι ἐμεγαλύνθη ἐχθρός ("Behold, Lord, my humiliation because my enemy gloats!") The personified lament continues to the end of the chapter, interrupted only by a brief

---

[60] Psalm 85 is another example of shifting between singular and plural in a national lament psalm. Paul does cite an *individual* lament psalm, Ps 69:9 in Rom 15:3, but this rhetorically is marked to the *ethos* of Χρίστος in the context.

descriptive interlude in 1:17. Finally, the author himself directly participates in the lament beginning in 2:11:

> My eyes are spent with weeping;
>> my stomach churns;
> my bile is poured out on the ground
>> because of the destruction of my people,
> because infants and babes faint
>> in the streets of the city. (NRSV)

The *pathos* of this authorial sorrow continues unabated for more than a chapter through 3:24.

A change in voice to third person beginning at Lam 3:25 signals a rhetorical shift in function: this shift facilitates mild exhortation as the readers are addressed indirectly. The readers are exhorted to remember that the Lord does not cast off forever. He still shows his steadfast love even in affliction. That the intent of this voice shift to third person actually is to address the readers becomes clear with a second shift in person that follows close on its heels. Five verses later after the move to third person, an insertion of authorial *ethos* occurs at 3:40, with a transition to first person plural: ἐξηρευνήθη ἡ ὁδὸς ἡμῶν καὶ ἡτάσθη καὶ ἐπιστρέψωμεν ἕως κυρίου ("Let us search out and test our way, and let us return to the Lord"). The exhortation no longer is a subtle third person, but direct and forceful. The first person plural confirms that the previous third person exhortation was, in fact, directed to the readers. The author now includes himself and the readers directly in the exhortation. Further, note that the authorial *pathos* also correspondingly increases in this unit. This plural authorial voice continues another seven verses through 3:47.

Suddenly, however, the voice smoothly shifts from this first person *plural* in Lam 3:47 to first person *singular* in 3:48: φόβος καὶ θυμὸς ἐγενήθη ἡμῖν ἔπαρσις καὶ συντριβή, [3:48] ἀφέσεις ὑδάτων κατάξει ὁ ὀφθαλμός μου ἐπὶ τὸ σύντριμμα τῆς θυγατρὸς τοῦ λαοῦ μου ("panic and tumult have hit us, lifting up and crushing, [3:48] my eye floods down tears because of the destruction of the daughter of my people"). This shift in number *has no rhetorical markers to signal any voice other than the continuation of the authorial first person from plural to singular.* All the salient features of Romans 7 are here:

- authorial ἔθος (*ethos*) augmented with high πάθος (*pathos*)

- *unmarked* voice change from first person *plural* to first person *singular*, or vice versa

- lament rhetoric

Examples from standard Greco-Roman sources that approximate even broadly these lament parameters are hard to find. If one also includes the additional *Jewish* parameters of the text and context, the argument is strengthened even further.[61]

Summary

This brief overview sufficiently establishes the case that Old Testament literature presents a clear rhetorical *topos* in the use of first person in contexts in which issues regarding Israel's current crisis or threatened destiny are involved. In multiple genres and types of material—narrative, confessional, intercessory prayers, lament, psalmic liturgy, prophetic, and others—this literature regularly evidences use of first person, both singular and plural, for Israel, whether as strict personification or as the author more generally functioning simply as a corporate representative of God's people. Even more significantly, in numerous contexts, quickly shifting from first person singular to first person plural (and back again) is a standard feature when high levels of combined *ethos* and *pathos* are present. Further investigation could demonstrate that this *topos* becomes even more pronounced in the non-canonical Jewish writings.[62]

Credibility Profile of Romans 7

Paul's ἔθος (*ethos*) development within the argumentative context of Romans 7 is important. The argumentative context of 7:7–25 is 6:1–

---

[61] As examples, the authorial *ethos* is Jewish. The grief is over slanderous misrepresentations (Lam 3:61–63; cf. Rom 3:8). A deep trust in God as vindicator of the unjustly maligned shines through (Lam 3:64–66; cf. Rom 1:16; 5:5; 9:33). The authorial consternation is over the present cursed condition of Israel (Lam 3:42; Rom 9:1–3; 10:1). Other Jewish paramenters are present, but even this brief list is sufficient to establish the point.

[62] Cf. Wis 5:7, 13; Bar 2:12–26; 3:1–8; 1 Esd 8:82–90; 2 Esd 3:34; 4:23 ("For I did not wish to inquire about the ways above, but about those things that we daily experience: why Israel has been given over to the Gentiles in disgrace"); 7:106; 9:36 ("For we who have received the law and sinned will perish, as well as our hearts that received it").

7:6, in which Paul explains that sin does not magnify grace (6:1–14), nor does grace license sin (6:15—7:6). Paul illustrates this second point by the two analogies of slavery (6:15–23) and marriage (7:1–6). The second analogy infers a changed relationship such that those who have died with Christ no longer sustain their old relationship to the law. Inevitably, Paul's rhetoric about the law has become problematic through his paradoxical usage.

Paul already has responded categorically to the charge of destroying the law in Rom 3:31: νόμον οὖν καταργοῦμεν διὰ τῆς πίστεως; μὴ γένοιτο· ἀλλὰ νόμον ἱστάνομεν, "Therefore, do we destroy the law through faith? May it not be! Rather, we establish the law." He insists he establishes the law. On the other hand, other statements by Paul seem to fly in the face of this asseveration. He has said enough by this point to seem to have slandered the ἔθος (ethos) of the law.[63] Paul's characterization of law has been decidedly negative in the basic units of development up to chapter 6: law simply reveals knowledge of sin (3:20), brings wrath (4:15), and instigates rebellion against God (5:20). Now, in this new unit beginning in chapter 6, Paul has insisted, "You are not under law" (6:14), "you died to the law" (7:4), "our sinful passions, aroused by the law" (7:5), "we have been released from the law" (7:6). The logical inference is that the law is sinful. This inference is false, but stalks Paul's rhetoric and will distract reader/hearers until Paul deals with the falsehood appropriately. If Paul has slandered the law, he has blasphemed God, and the charge he leveled in 2:23 falls on his own head. The connection to preaching the gospel now becomes more manifest. If in order to preach his gospel Paul has resorted to shaming God's law, *as a Jew*, how could he have the hubris to claim his gospel is the gospel of God? How could he be anything but ashamed of such a gospel? Providing an appropriate apology for the law,[64] *from within a Jewish context*, rhetorically is imperative. Paul provides this apology in 7:7–25.

Even more importantly rhetorically, the *putative* problem of law's *ethos* is a *rhetorical* challenge for Paul's own *ethos*. If the author loses

---

[63] Most acknowledge that Paul has personified Sin, Grace, and Law throughout chapters 6–8, such that, rhetorically, one may speak appropriately of the ἔθος (ethos) of the law. Cf. Quintilian, *Inst.* 9.2.31, 58.

[64] Phrasing from Dunn (and others); cf. Dunn, *Romans 1–8*, 377.

credibility in a collapse of his own Jewish *ethos* established immediately in the *prescript* and augmented thereafter in the *exordium*, the persuasive force of his argument is lost even if his logic is flawless. That Paul attempts to reinforce his *Jewish ethos* in 7:7–25 is revealed in the very nature of Paul's argumentative method. Paul inserts a traditional *Jewish* κεκριμένον (*kekrimenon*, accepted opinion) in 7:14: οἴδαμεν γὰρ ὅτι ὁ νόμος πνευματικός ἐστιν ("For we know that the law is spiritual"). This κεκριμένον is a foundational datum of a *Jewish ethos*: the law is *God's* law, and that relationship fundamentally defines law's *ethos*. By inserting this Jewish κεκριμένον, Paul acknowledges and affirms a datum of Jewish belief. Paul then takes the next obligatory step. This first κεκριμένον joins to a second idea that travels in tandem, which Paul states in 7:16: σύμφημι τῷ νόμῳ ὅτι καλός ("I agree with the law, that it is good").[65] After the first κεκριμένον, Paul then is obliged to acknowledge this related κεκριμένον, which he does unequivocally. Through this rhetorical device used within 7:7–25, Paul bolsters his authorial *ethos as a Jew* and continues to work out his theme rhetoric: Οὐ γὰρ ἐπαισχύνομαι τὸ εὐαγγέλιον ("For I am not ashamed of the gospel"). *Our second rhetorical conclusion about Rom 7:7–25, then, is that this passage is crucial to the maintenance of credible authorial ethos, and, hence, to the development of the theme of Romans.*

ISRAEL IN ROMANS 7

Romans 7 always has been considered as a key passage in the argument of Romans 1–8, if not in the larger context of Romans 1–11. Regardless questions of macrostructure, though, this passage is crucial to the assertion that Romans is all about Israel. If that assertion fails here, its viability elsewhere is diminished. The following is a presentation of Romans 7 from a rhetorical point of view for which we have attempted to build a case. We do not intend any detailed exegesis. We simply intend to demonstrate how internally coherent this reading is and, as well, how this reading makes perfect sense of statements that otherwise create considerable consternation and inspire rhetorical gymnastics to derive coherence. We start with the immediate setting.

[65] Cf. 1 Tim 1:8.

The Immediate Setting in 7:1–6

Paul writes Romans laboring under an authorial function as corporate representative of messianic Israel, rhetorically marked in the *prescript* as "we." A pluralized "you" of the addressee consistently tracks parallel to this pluralized authorial "we." This pluralized "you" is the messianic Israel of whom Paul is the corporate representative. Rhetorical *figure* of clearly marked second singular "you" almost completely disappear beginning in chapter 6, as messianic Israel takes center stage. Romans 6–8 is not about the inner life of individual believers, but rather the corporate life of messianic Israel. This corporate life has been inaugurated by the eschatological arrival of God's Messiah.

Prior to Messiah's arrival, the law that was meant for life in the end cursed Mosaic Israel with death. Release from the law is release from the law's curse, which this law was ineffectual to avoid. The law's goal for Mosaic Israel, however, was still in place. This goal Paul made clear with a climactic result clause at the end of his second analogy in 7:6: ὥστε δουλεύειν ἡμᾶς ἐν καινότητι πνεύματος καὶ οὐ παλαιότητι γράμματος ("so that we might serve in newness of Spirit and not in oldness of letter").

Newness of Spirit in 7:6 builds on the concept of resurrection power in the life of Messiah in the creedal formula that Paul affirms in the *prescript* in 1:4: τοῦ ὁρισθέντος υἱοῦ θεοῦ ἐν δυνάμει κατὰ πνεῦμα ἁγιωσύνης ἐξ ἀναστάσεως νεκρῶν ("declared to be the Son of God in power according to the Spirit of holiness by resurrection of the dead"). This newness of Spirit in 7:6 operative in the life of Israel's Messiah is that hidden power that quickens the messianic Israel latent in Mosaic Israel.[66] Finally, this newness of Spirit in 7:6 is the preeminent sign of the benefits of Messiah's redemption in 5:5: ὅτι ἡ ἀγάπη τοῦ θεοῦ ἐκκέχυται ἐν ταῖς καρδίαις ἡμῶν διὰ πνεύματος ἁγίου τοῦ δοθέντος ἡμῖν ("because the love of God has been poured out in our hearts by the Holy Spirit whom he has given to us"). This love is God's steadfast covenant love for his people, especially recognizable in God's acts of redemption in spite of Israel's behavior that has not been commensurate with the covenant obligations expressed in the law. In

---

[66] Perhaps alluded to in Rom 2:27 in the cryptic phrase: ἀλλ᾽ ὁ ἐν τῷ κρυπτῷ Ἰουδαῖος, καὶ περιτομὴ καρδίας ἐν πνεύματι οὐ γράμματι, "but the hidden Jew, even the one circumcised of heart by the Spirit not by the letter."

the present time this redeeming love is God's action in Jesus Christ. The effective operation of this love is in that sphere of Israel's life untouched by the letter of the law: ἐν ταῖς καρδίαις ἡμῶν διὰ πνεύματος ἁγίου ("in our hearts through the Holy Spirit"), which continues to unpack 2:29: καὶ περιτομὴ καρδίας ἐν πνεύματι ("and circumcision is of the heart by the Spirit").

The law effected covenant curse, which decreed death to Mosaic Israel. This reality has threatened Israel's future and her destiny as God's people even more critically now than ever in her history—now, that is, that God has sent his Son. Within the scriptural traditions of Israel, the rhetoric of confession and lament find their essence in this historical context. These corporate laments function as sincere expressions of national grief and repentance. By direct and indirect quotation and allusion, Paul draws upon the background of this lament rhetoric in Rom 7:7–25 to express those paradoxical realities under which messianic Israel has to labor to bring to fruition her eschatological destiny from within the context of Mosaic Israel.

The Past Tense in 7:7–13

The "I" of 7:7–13 starts where Paul starts in the associated passage of 9:1–4. At the beginning of chapter 9, Paul takes up the traditional *ethos* of Moses on behalf of Mosaic Israel in a powerful example of ἠθοποιΐα (*ēthopoiia*, a subcategory of προσωποποιΐα, *prosōpopoiia*, imitation of another person's characteristics).[67] Paul's constitution as a Jew is κατὰ σάρκα ("according to the flesh"), which is fundamental to his Jewish ἔθος (*ethos*), which Paul defines as an᾽ Ἰσραηλῖται ("Israelite," 9:4), further defined in 11:1 as ἐκ σπέρματος Ἀβραάμ ("from the seed of Abraham"). So being a Jew for Paul historically starts with corporate existence that goes back to Abraham.[68] The nation has its historical

---

[67] Quintilian, *Inst.* 9.2.58. Anderson, *Ancient Rhetorical Theory and Paul*, 234, acknowledged that an allusion to Moses was probable in this passage.

[68] This comports with 4:1: Ἀβραὰμ τὸν προπάτορα ἡμῶν κατὰ σάρκα. Paul's parsing of the Adam unit in 5:12–21 is only by way of explaining *Sin's presence in the world*, and with Sin, Death. Sin would not be afforded the privilege of furtively lying in wait throughout all time to inflict Death on humans indiscriminately, all the while leaving humans unaware of its life-threatening presence or remedy. Law enters in to guarantee that Sin is exposed as rebellion against God and to reveal Sin's true nature as the antithesis of all God's purposes in creation. In this line of reasoning, Abraham

roots here and its redemptive roots in Moses and the corresponding covenantal existence that maintained that redemption in the law. Paul could wish ἀνάθεμα εἶναι αὐτὸς ἐγὼ ἀπὸ τοῦ Χριστοῦ, "I myself to be anathema from Messiah" (9:4) because this touches on the fundamental problem of Mosaic Israel at the present time—living under the law's curse and anathema from Messiah.

So Israel's story comes to life with Abraham, whose lineage (ἐκ σπέρματος ᾿Αβραάμ, "from the seed of Abraham") defines the essence of Mosaic Israel prior to Sinai: ἐγὼ δὲ ἔζων χωρὶς νόμου ποτέ, "Now I was alive apart from the law formerly" (7:9).[69] The commandment came, which was meant for life. However, stalking the commandment was (personified) Sin, present since Adam, but not out in the open in its brutal and savage deadliness. Sin, not recognizing God's ultimate purpose for the law, only saw opportunity to work Death extraordinarily through the law's curse. So, Sin came into its full force in the world within Mosaic Israel (ἐλθούσης δὲ τῆς ἐντολῆς ἡ ἁμαρτία ἀνέζησεν, "but when the commandment came, sin came alive," 7:9), robbing the law of its intent for life. Sin produced all manner of rebellion against God in Israel, which was remedied neither by her kings nor her prophets. With Israel's ultimate rebellion came the law's ultimate curse, threatening Israel's very existence by exiling her away from the land that defined her existence as a nation among the nations and gave her a chance to fulfill her destiny in God's purposes for calling Abraham: ἐγὼ δὲ ἀπέθανον καὶ εὑρέθη μοι ἡ ἐντολὴ ἡ εἰς ζωὴν, αὕτη εἰς θάνατον, "So I died and discovered that the very commandment

is not a necessary *topos*, explaining why Paul jumps from Adam to Moses in Rom 5:14. Romans 7 is not about Adam. Romans 7 is about the law. Adam explains Sin's presence but not the law's problem, which is the immediate topic in 7:7. Other Jewish traditions, however, *did* analyze Adam as a prototype of receiving God's commandment; note 2 Esd. 3:7; 7:118.

[69] Schreiner's reading (*Romans*, 364–65) makes subjective Paul's objective language. Schreiner claimed that the voice in this present tense "I" is Paul's "own consciousness before receiving the law." He then conflated rhetorical *topoi* with the assertion that Paul's "I" is a "paradigmatic" Adamic experience. From this rhetorical leap, he finally throws the entire discussion into total logical confusion with the revealing expression, "All through human history the encounter with the law"—a stunning exegesis, as if all humans entered into the covenant at Sinai! On the contrary, law in Romans 7 does not have schizophrenic meaning, jumping around unpredictably from pagan code, to philosophical principle, to patriarchal Israel (at a minimum suggesting serious worldview confusion). Consistently and coherently law in Romans 7 is Israel at Sinai.

that intended life resulted in death" (7:10). Mosaic Israel was deceived tragically about what would turn out as the real outcome.

So the law is God's law—holy, just, and good. Clearly, then, that the good intended resulted in death was not the law's fault but Sin's design. On the other hand, Sin, for the first time since Adam, had to come out from the corners of life to be exposed as exceedingly sinful.

The Present Tense in 7:14–25

Messianic Israel currently understands that the law is spiritual and so ultimately sourced in God (because God has poured out his Spirit "in our hearts"). At the same time, messianic Israel, struggling to realize her destiny, now is burdened with the weight of Mosaic Israel, which, in the absence of the power released in the Messiah, continues to live under the power of Sin, whose sphere of especial effectiveness continues to be corporate, that is, κατὰ σάρκα: ἐγὼ δὲ σάρκινός εἰμι πεπρα-μένος ὑπὸ τὴν ἁμαρτίαν, "but I am fleshly,[70] having been sold over to sin" (7:14). Thus, absent Messiah's redemptive power, Mosaic Israel desires the good the law intends but does the evil the law condemns. This ultimately will prevent messianic Israel from obtaining her goal in Christ.[71]

What really is at work in this vicious cycle of good intent and bad result is Sin. Mosaic Israel corporately remains constituted through Moses only and has no effectual remedy for Sin (τοῦτ᾽ ἔστιν ἐν τῇ σαρκί μου, "that is, in my flesh," 7:18), so no good ultimately can dwell within. The ultimate good here is accomplishing Israel's destiny as the intend-ed instrument through which the promise to Abraham to be a blessing to all families of the earth is fulfilled (Romans 4). The figure of Abra-ham sustains and climaxes the rhetorical argument in all of Romans 1–3. As VanHorn observed,

> Paul utilizes Abraham as a unifying rhetorical warrant for the
> logic of Rom 1–3 even without appealing to the patriarch direct-

---

[70] The corporate existence of Israel encoded in the doubly nuanced κατὰ σάρκα ("according to the flesh") is difficult to bring across in translation when linguistically encoded as an adjective.

[71] In the sense of Rom 10:4, τέλος γὰρ νόμου Χριστὸς εἰς δικαιοσύνην παντὶ τῷ πιστεύοντι, "For Messiah is the goal of the law unto righteousness for everyone who believes."

ly in those chapters. Precisely because the remembrance Abraham was a transtextual phenomenon in early Judaism, the patriarch served as the natural subtextual foundation upon which the apostle could establish his gospel (cf. Rom 3:27–4:25).[72]

Mosaic Israel at the present time encounters the law from a new reality of an unmediated curse (Εὑρίσκω ἄρα τὸν νόμον, "So then I discover the law," 7:21). If Mosaic Israel can apprehend the truth about the law by reflection (τῷ νόμῳ τοῦ νοός μου, "the law my mind appropriates") what messianic Israel already knows by experience, then a meeting of the minds on the law of God seems possible. Mosaic Israel might could see, if she stood back long enough to take a sobering look at her corporate existence now (κατὰ σάρκα, "according to the flesh") in the lives of those who constitute her (ἐν τοῖς μέλεσίν μου, "in my members," 7:23),[73] that the law effectively has become other than what originally had been intended (ἕτερον νόμον, "another law," 7:23).[74] From that angle, under Sin's control, the law could be called "the law of Sin" (τῷ νόμῳ τῆς ἁμαρτίας, 7:23). In effect, law has reduced Israel back to the cursed state of Adam, but this condition, unknown to Sin, sets up the overwhelming redemptive act on behalf of Israel and for the whole world through Messiah (Rom 5:12–21).

Paul then in Rom 7:24–25 concludes this apology for the law with his deepest expression of authorial πάθος (pathos) and representative identity to this point in the letter. The following is a paraphrase that attempts to bring out the essence of this rhetorical climax. Paul first speaks in 7:24 in standard Jewish lamentation rhetoric on behalf of Mosaic Israel. The term ἄνθρωπος ("man," "humanity") encodes the Adamic condition of Israel in rank rebellion against God alluded to in Rom 1:18–32, which uses the same ἄνθρωπος (Adamic) rhetoric for Israel in the opening verse of Rom 1:18. For example, note the following key observations of Skipper,

> In Rom 1, Adam's function is primarily for ecclesiology, for Paul's task of reforming the self-identity of the people of God. Adam

---

[72] VanHorn, "Arguing from Abraham," 187.

[73] Anticipating precisely what Paul does metaphorically in exhortations to believers in Rom 12:4–5 by using the same metaphorical concept of "members" (μέλη).

[74] Very close in sentiment is 2 Esd 3:20: "But you did not take away their wicked heart and enable your law to bear fruit in them . . . although your law was in your peoples' hearts."

as paternal head of both Jews and Gentiles gives Paul leverage for dismantling dividing walls separating Israel from Hellenists and also from the barbarians of Spain. The mingling of Eden and Sinai, of Moses and Adam can be observed in Rom 1:23, where Paul has inserted Adamic language into a subtext describing the idolatry of the golden calf at the foot of Mt. Sinai. The connection between Adam and Israel is reinforced in Rom 5:13, 14, 20, and Rom 7. In Rom 1, Israel is included in the Adamic accusation.[75]

Paul exclaims with deep empathy and strong authorial *pathos,*

ταλαίπωρος ἐγὼ ἄνθρωπος· τίς με ῥύσεται ἐκ τοῦ σώματος τοῦ θανάτου τούτου;

"O wretched man (nation) that I am! Who will deliver me from this deadly body (cursed destiny)?"

Morris asserted such words "are impossibly theatrical if they apply to other people."[76] Such a characterization is nonsense. Morris is totally out of touch with Jewish lament rhetoric as already documented. As to be expected from such a comment, Morris wanted to insist that this statement has to be Paul himself. *Of course this is Paul himself.* But in rhetorical analysis of authorial *ethos* in Romans, what is clear is that Paul himself is not Paul alone, or even Paul paradigmatically. Osborne, though acknowledging interpreting Romans 7 as Israel "is very possible and definitely does fit the centrality of the law in this passage and the Jewish nature of 7:7–25," still objected, "but it does not do justice to the whole passage."[77] What he meant by that was finding Israel in Rom 7:24 exegetically was a bridge too far, and in support quoted with approval the "impossibly theatrical" comment by Morris.[78] These are the typical commentary comments that must be reevaluated and rejected in light of the rhetorical function of authorial *ethos* in Romans when distinctly Jewish issues are on the table, such as the law in Romans 7.

Thus, Rom 7:24 indeed is Paul himself, but Paul prophetically in corporate lament mode over Israel's current eschatological crisis. Paul's experience trying to preach Jesus as Messiah in the synagogue shadows

[75] Skipper, "Echoes of Eden," 184.

[76] Morris, *Romans,* 277.

[77] Osborne, *Romans,* 173–74.

[78] Ibid., 174.

that of the prophet Elijah, who also confronted a hardened Israel over-taken by a strange idolatry that hides the disastrous destiny awaiting the nation—except for a remnant God has left to himself to insure fulfill-ment of the promise to Abraham. Note that this implicit Elijah parallel underneath the rhetoric of Romans 7 surfaces concretely in Rom 11:1–15, where Paul explicitly harnesses the 1 Kings 19 story of Elijah in the cave fleeing Jezebel's wrath and bemoaning he is the only one left loyal to God. Cooper has shown how the Elijah story is the hermeneutical lens for Paul's own experience and provides the rationale for the dis-tinctive collocation of Isaiah's "remnant" concept in Isa 10:22 (quoted in Rom 9:27) and Deuteronomy's "zeal" theme in Deut 32:21 (quoted in Rom 10:19). Here is the path to Paul's solution of Israel's plight.[79]

To the present and desperate plight of Mosaic Israel, Paul then responds in 7:25 in thanksgiving rhetoric on behalf of messianic Israel. Messianic Israel lives in the Rom 3:21 "but now" reality of inaugurated eschatological transfiguration with the coming of Messiah, having re-sponded positively to the word of faith,

χάρις δὲ τῷ θεῷ διὰ Ἰησοῦ Χριστοῦ τοῦ κυρίου ἡμῶν.

But thanks be to God through Jesus Messiah our Lord!

Here, the first person singular of Rom 7:24 transitions immediately into the first person plural possessive of Rom 7:25, a tour de force of Paul's carefully constructed authorial *ethos* in Romans. So, ostensibly, Mosaic Israel serves the law of God. Yet, in real life corporately (τῇ δὲ σαρκι, "but in the flesh," 7:25) and outside Messiah's transforming death and resurrection, Mosaic Israel really serves the law of Sin—an ironic but even more tragic recapitulation of the Elijah crisis.

In a nutshell, Paul's use of "I" is empathetically plural as he works through the dichotomy between Mosaic and messianic Israel upon the occasion of Israel's eschatological denouement inaugurated by the un-recognized arrival of Messiah ("but now," 3:21). In a role similar to Eli-jah, Moses, and the prophets, Paul speaks in Jewish lament mode as a representative of Israel as did those responding to Israel's devastating divine judgment sitting by the rivers of Babylon (Ps 137:1).

[79] Cooper, "The Intertextual Link between *Parazēloō* and *Leimma* in Rom 11:1–15," 171–82, particularly the chart comparing Paul and Elijah, 174.

IMPLICATIONS

We started with often observed notable features of Romans 7 thought to be enigmatic and difficult for exegesis that include topics of grammar, semantics, style, theology, and context. We first summarize how this presentation has made the case that Romans 7 is about Israel, and that understanding brings into focus these areas regularly felt to be confusing about Romans 7, or even inherently contradictory.

Notable Features

Grammar

These features concord well with the thesis that Romans 7 is about Israel, not gentiles in general, or Adam, or even Paul as autobiography. The tense shift is historical, covering the experiences of Mosaic Israel and messianic Israel. The voice shift from first person plural to first person singular fits precisely the authorial rhetoric Paul has developed in the *prescript* as Jewish to the core and as rhetorically fluid and corporate. Like the prophets, the psalmist, and those lamenting the destruction of the nation in the exile, Paul melds his person to his nation's destiny, just as did Moses and other Jewish leaders, which simply could be no more clearly and poignantly voiced than in Rom 9:1–5. This passage above all others in Romans demonstrates how the element of authorial *pathos* is highest when thought of Israel's plight is closest. Therefore, when we encounter the notably high *pathos* of Rom 7:24, we immediately should be clear rhetorically who is speaking and what is the topic.

Semantics

The sematic range of words such as "death," "life," and "law" do not really "drift" as often alleged if the right subject of Israel is in mind. The complexities of describing the present eschatological crisis of Israel under the curse of law but Israel simultaneously offered the new covenant of Messiah would not generate ideas easy to grasp nor a "tweet" theology. Even the apostles took some time to assimilate all that Jesus encompassed, if Acts is any indication (Acts 1:1, 6).

Style

The personification of Sin, Death, and Law in Romans 7 is clear, but the personification of the "I" has raised questions. While several suggestions have been offered, the best one is rather straightforward: authorial empathy for Israel precisely in the vein of traditional Jewish lament rhetoric. The force of this observation, however, requires attention to the *pathetic pattern* of authorial rhetoric throughout the preceding chapters in Romans 1–6.

Theology

The question of theology boils down to the question of the language of "Spirit" so dominant in the very next chapter in Romans 8 thought to be "missing" in Romans 7. Since this category is considered equivalent in Pauline theology to the basic definition of being "Christian" (Rom 8:14), then questions of the supposed "pre-Christian" or "pre-conversion" status of Romans 7 often are raised. Exegetically, these questions are anachronistic. More importantly, such questions are unsympathetic to Paul's Jewish worldview and show lack of rhetorical understanding. We should remember that the term "Christian" is not one Paul actually ever uses. The letter of Romans suggests that the one category most on Paul's mind is Israel, since he spent a minimum of three chapters explicitly working that topic in Romans 9–11. Israel, therefore, is the best frame for discussion of being "in Christ," which in Paul likely better is rendered "in Messiah," and is the better frame for what might be meant by the contemporary term "Christian."

Taking up discussion of the Spirit in Romans 7 would be premature and not really to the point. We should keep in mind that Paul chose to unpack the Spirit in Romans 8, not Romans 7. We should let the author determine what is his rhetorical target in his argument. Law is the target in Romans 7, not the Spirit, and Paul has designed that discussion as an apology for the law under the covenant of Moses, not as an explication of the role of the Spirit in messianic Israel. The point about the absence of the category of "Spirit" in Romans 7 is moot.

Context

Paul is establishing interrelationships among Grace, Sin, and Law in the new eon of Messiah (Rom 3:21). An apology for the law in Romans 7 provides foundation for the premier connection between old covenant in Moses and new covenant in Messiah expressed in Rom 10:4, τέλος γὰρ νόμου Χριστὸς εἰς δικαιοσύνην παντὶ τῷ πιστεύοντι, "For Messiah is the consummation of the law unto righteousness to every-one who believes." Thus, Romans 7 as about Israel fits the overall argument and integrates seamlessly into the entire discourse of Romans 1–11.

SUMMARY

Authorial rhetoric according to the ancient rhetoricians must have a proper and balanced development of the combined elements of ἔθος (ethos) and πάθος (pathos), or character and emotion. The *prescript* (Rom 1:1–7) and *exordium* (Rom 1:8–15) of Romans show careful construction of the authorial voice in terms of *ethos* and *pathos*.

First, in terms of authorial *ethos*, this characterization in Romans is Jewish, fluid, and corporate. Authorial ethos is Jewish to the core, with focus on Israel's prophets, Israel's Scriptures, Israel's Messiah, and Israel's destiny. Authorial ethos in Romans likewise is fluid and corporate. Authorial voice fluidly shifts from first person singular to first person plural without changing *ethos*. The "we" is the author, but specifically with a view to speaking on behalf of corporate Israel from within a messianic-eschatological perspective. This *ethos* also has a corporate dimension maintained consistently throughout Romans 1–7. Paul's "we," that is, can be read consistently as Paul speaking as a (Jewish) apostle on behalf of messianic Israel moving toward her eschatological destiny to bring about the obedience of faith among the nations. Interestingly, the pluralized "we" tracks in parallel with a pluralized "you." This plural "you" is messianic Israel, especially in force in Romans 6, a "you" not framed as individual believers. Correspondingly, any singular "you" form rhetorically is marked as part of the argumentative method.

Second, in terms of authorial *pathos*, this emotion as developed in the *prescript* and *exordium* is thematic and patterned. As thematic, authorial *pathos* is integrated seamlessly into the theme statement of Rom 1:16–17 as a key component. The theme statement, however, has a negative frame, "I am not ashamed," a striking rhetorical feature. This negative frame is totally unexpected, since the authorial ethos has been positive in honorable associations with God and with Messiah.

The theme statement already hints that authorial *pathos* increases when Jewish *ethos* is dominant. Shame will prove to be an authorial *topos* for Paul in Romans. Authorial *pathos* also is patterned. After the theme statement in Rom 1:16–17, we see a heightened pathos in Rom 3:1–8 right when we have higher levels of Jewish *ethos*, similar to the theme statement. In other words, the pattern in Romans is, the closer discussion moves to issues of Jewish identity, the higher the levels of authorial *pathos* registered in the rhetoric. Thus increased *pathos* is related directly to the authorial voice in Romans and gives silent witness to the concerns of the theme statement throughout Romans.

Study of authorial rhetoric in Romans shows that Romans 7 is not *prosōpopoiia*. Rather, the *ethos* of the "I" is authorial, but not as individualizing autobiography. This authorial voice can shift from singular to plural and back without registering a change in *ethos*. First person plural "we" is the author speaking on behalf of corporate Israel, exactly as in the *prescript*. The function of first person rhetoric in Romans 7 is to speak for ("we") or identify with ("I") Israel in her present historical and eschatological crisis due to the unexpected coming of Messiah. Such authorial rhetoric has a scriptural profile in matching corporate contexts related to Israel in Jewish Scripture. This authorial rhetoric in Romans 7 also has a prophetic profile similar to prophets personifying Israel through their own person or a representative figure from Israel's past. Most closely matched of all, though, are Jewish lament contexts. All of the salient features of Romans 7 are in full force in Jewish lament rhetoric spoken on behalf of Israel in exile: authorial *ethos* augmented with high *pathos* using unmarked voice change from first person plural to first person singular in a lament context.

Since Romans 7 in the argument of Romans 1–7 is an apology for the law, the problem in Romans 7 for Paul is that his authorial credibility is at stake. He is supposed to be Jewish to the core but appears grossly to have maligned the law of God. Rhetorically framed, the *putative* problem of law's *ethos* is a *rhetorical* challenge for Paul's own *ethos*. If the author loses credibility in a collapse of his own Jewish *ethos*, as he established clearly in the *prescript* and augmented in the *exordium*, by what he thereafter says about the law of God, the persuasive force of his whole argument is lost even if his logic is flawless. However, Paul does maintain authorial credibility by evoking Jewish lament rhetoric produced at another crucial junction in Israel's history in which her destiny as the people of God was at stake.

Romans 7, then, can be read most easily and naturally—without extraordinary leaps of logic and egregious semantic contortions—as the conundrum Paul faced with Mosaic Israel revealed in the process of attempting to preach in Jewish synagogues throughout the Diaspora. The past tense is Israel facing Moses at Sinai; present tense is Israel facing Messiah at the present time. Similar to the past, Mosaic Israel is in the deadly grip of Sin, revealed by rejection of Messiah, her only hope. The intransigence of this rejection forebodes a tragic plight. This plight creates difficulty for understanding how messianic Israel can come into her fullness in order to achieve Israel's intended destiny to fulfill the promise to Abraham. Paul first gives the answer to the extraordinary lament in Rom 7:24–25 by establishing God's eschatological gift of the Spirit that inbreathes life into messianic Israel in Romans 8. Paul then proceeds in Romans 9–11 to bring to consummation the entire argument of Romans 1–11 by taking up and resolving Israel's plight set up dramatically in Romans 7.[80] Only someone completely consecrated to a Jewish worldview would be so preoccupied with the story of Israel to take eleven chapters to hammer out that story on the anvil of Scripture, as does Paul in Romans 1–11.

---

[80] Even a passage so commonly assumed as about gentiles as Rom 9:21–24 can be argued as about Israel; cf. Campbell, "Divergent Images of Paul and His Mission," 198–200.

4

The Narrative of Israel

Paul's Worldview in Crisis

ROMANS SITS ON A FAULT LINE of worldview crisis for Paul. The initial shock was the Damascus Road. Not only was a crucified Jew to be understood as Messiah, the resurrection had happened without the world coming to an end. A Pharisee could not possibly be more confused. Yet, even considering the extraordinary questions of soteriology and eschatology raised by the Jesus event, the deepest mystery for Paul in the coming of Jesus as Messiah was Israel.[1]

Paul's letters offer a brief glimpse into a brilliant mind with Pharisaic presuppositions and synagogue sympathies. Paul defined Israel and her destiny in these terms. The Jesus event forced re-envisioning this story of Israel. Jews faithful to the law, however, had serious difficulty not only comprehending that story but abiding that retelling. Whether Sadducee, Pharisee, Essene, or Zealot, all Jewish sectarians knew law was the center of Israel. Paul gets thrown out of synagogue after synagogue in Acts. This story concurs with his own testimony.[2] One reason for this reaction one could suspect is how he is retelling Israel's story in the synagogue specifically related to Moses. How did the synagogue picture Moses?

---

[1] Petersen, *Rediscovering Paul*, helpfully explores another perspective on Paul's narrative world, the sociological angle, through a study of Philemon.

[2] Cf. 2 Cor 11:24. In Acts, note Damascus (Acts 9:23–25); early Jerusalem (Acts 9:29); Antioch of Pisidia (Acts 13:40–46); Thessalonica (Acts 15:5); Berea (Acts 17:13); Corinth (Acts 18:6); Ephesus (Acts 19:9); Corinth again (Acts 20:3); Jerusalem again (Acts 21:27–31); Rome (Acts 28:24).

FIGURE 4.1. Masada Synagogue. This Herodian synagogue is one of the best examples of early synagogues before the Jewish war. Jewish Zealots who fled Jerusalem's destruction in the First Jewish War held out here against Flavius Silva's Tenth Legion.

FIGURE 4.2. Capernaum Synagogue. Capernaum's synagogue was a focus of Jesus's ministry (Mark 1:21–28). These 4th cent. remains are built on a 1st cent. foundation.

FIGURE 4.3. Salamis Synagogue Inscription. Ancient Salamis was a port city on the eastern side of the island of Cyprus that was Barnabas and Saul's first stop on the first missionary journey. Salamis had several synagogues, so had a significant Jewish population among its estimated 150,000 residents. The column at left stood in one of those synagogues. The inscription at the bottom of the column, enlarged in the image above, is evidence of a major restoration project: "Joses the elder with his son Synesios restored the whole building of this synagogue." The elder designation indicates Joses was part of this synagogue's leadership (NAM).

FIGURE 4.4. Corinth Synagogue Inscription. Paul visited Corinth on the second missionary journey and preached first in its synagogues (Acts 18:4), which, according to Acts, was his custom in every major city he visited. This pattern makes quite literal Paul's statement in Romans, "to the Jew first" (Rom 1:16). The inscription above identifies the structure as a "synagogue of the Hebrews" (AMAC).

FIGURE 4.5. Corinth Menorah Relief. Moses constructed a seven-branched lampstand made of pure gold for the tabernacle that in later generations was placed in the temple in Jerusalem. Its image became one of the most ancient symbols of Judaism regularly found in synagogue reliefs. This menorah burned constantly to symbolize the continuous presence of the Spirit of God in the temple. Paul in Romans 8 indicated he experienced the presence of that Spirit in a new way in Messiah (AMAC).

FIGURE 4.6. Aphrodisias Synagogue Column. This nine-foot tall column recording over 100 names stood at the entrance to one of the synagogues at Aphrodisias, a city near Ephesus. Image to the right is an enlargement of the bottom section (AMAC).

FIGURE 4.7. Aphrodisias Synagogue Inscription. A synagogue honorific column at Aphrodisias recorded those making synagogue donations. The top section recorded names socially more Jewish. The bottom section, separated by a middle blank space, recorded names socially more Hellenistic. The names in the bottom section are introduced with the adjective "God fearers" (first line, ΘΕΟCΕ BIC, θεοσεβις, *theosebis*). This terminology may illustrate Luke's verbal noun expressions, "one who fears God" (φοβούμενος τὸν θεὸν, *phoboumenos ton theon*) and "worshipper of God" (σεβομένος τὸν θεόν, *sebomenos ton theon*), both used of devout gentiles worshipping in or associated with the synagogue, such as Cornelius, Lydia, Titius Justus, etc. (Acts 10:2, 35; 13:16; 16:14; 17:17; 18:7). Acts 17:17 indicates this group was the target of Paul's synagogue preaching for initially reaching gentiles in any city (AMAC).

FIGURE 4.8. Sardis Synagogue. The Sardis synagogue is the largest Diaspora synagogue ever found, with a standing capacity of 1,000 worshippers (cf. Rev 3:1–6).

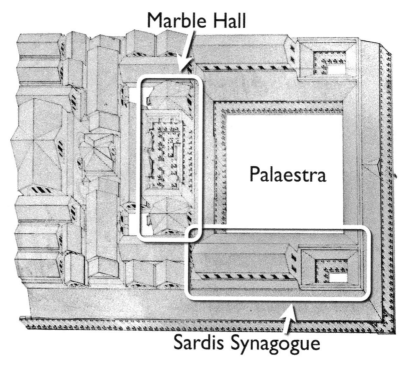

Marble Hall

Palaestra

Sardis Synagogue

FIGURE 4.9. Sardis Bathhouse Complex. The "Marble Hall" is the colloquial name for the huge Roman bathhouse complex in Sardis that was the central social hub of the city. Notice that the Sardis synagogue was located as an essential component of that social setting, fully integrated architecturally as one entire side of the complex.

FIGURE 4.10. Sardis Synagogue Inscription. This long inscription on a support lintel runs along the interior wall of the Sardis synagogue. Names of Jewish patrons who donated to the needs of the city included city counselors, a procurator, and several imperial financial administrators.

FIGURE 4.11. Sardis Synagogue Furniture. A table with eagle reliefs on either side was recycled from an existing Roman monument. The two 6th cent. double-lion pairs are similar to those used in Cybele monuments. The eagle, of course, was a symbol of Rome. Even if reinterpreted for use in the synagogue, these artifacts show strong acculturation to Roman life among Jews in Sardis.

FIGURE 4.12. Ostia Synagogue. Ancient Ostia was the major port city of Rome in the later first century, overtaking the southern port of Puteoli on the Bay of Naples in this role only a few years after Paul and Luke disembarked on Italian soil at Puteoli on Paul's way to Rome (Acts 28:13). The Jewish synagogue at Ostia is one of the oldest in the world, dating to emperor Claudius (41–54), but its use as a synagogue in the first century is argued (cf. Levine, *The Ancient Synagogue*, 274–76).

FIGURE 4.13. Ostia Synagogue Menorah Relief. One of the support columns of the Ostia synagogue seen in the image above is decorated with a relief of the Jewish menorah. As Paul testifies in Rome to the synagogue elders with whom he has requested an audience upon his arrival, he announces, "For the sake of the hope of Israel I am wearing this chain" (Acts 28:20).

THE SYNAGOGUE CONTEXT

Bible readers are surprised to learn Hebrew Scripture never mentions a synagogue even once.[3] This silence seems so strange only because we are so familiar with the New Testament. In the Gospels and Acts, synagogues are everywhere. If you wanted to find Jesus, you regularly

[3] Synagogue origins are unclear, but likely the institution is an exilic or postexilic phenomenon that has some connection to maintaining Jewish life in the exile after loss of the temple in the destruction of Jerusalem in 586 BC, eventually becoming the center of Jewish life. Cf. Ferguson, *Backgrounds of Early Christianity*, 573–74; Safrai, "The Synagogue." This institution propagated Pharisaic influence throughout the Jewish world.

could find him teaching there (Matt 4:23; 9:25), and he was concerned about the hypocrisy to be found there in pious activities (Matt 6:2, 5; 23:6), as well as the judicial floggings administered by that institution (Matt 10:17; 23:34). He taught in his hometown synagogue (Matt 13:54). Mark and Luke make clear that Jesus constantly was in the synagogue.[4] John, while not focused on the synagogue, does not hide that Jesus habitually taught in the synagogue (John 6:59; 18:20). The book of Acts, of course, is replete with synagogue references, a tradition that begins with reference to opposition to the Hellenists in Acts 6:9, but especially related to the activity of Paul in the Diaspora. We should not forget that Saul sought to extend his pursuit of followers of Jesus to the synagogues even outside Judea in Damascus (Acts 9:2), which conforms to his own statement in this regard (1 Cor 15:9). Paul organized his congregations on the pattern of synagogue leadership (Acts 14:23; 20:17), as did James (Acts 15:2, 4, 6, 22; 16:4). James also assumed the synagogue was the place of regular worship for believers (Jas 2:2). John in Revelation still dealt with synagogue opposition later in the first century with his harsh and pejorative "synagogue of Satan" appellation (Rev 2:9; 3:9).

Outside the New Testament, Philo noted the centrality of synagogues in Jewish life, and Josephus spoke casually of synagogues around the world.[5] This institution became essential as the Jewish house of prayer, the schoolhouse for training Jewish children (which inherently meant study of the law in order to be able to do the law), an assembly hall for general community meetings, and even as a hospitality inn for wayfarers. Thus, the first-century synagogue was an institution core to Jewish life and experience around the world.

In short, Jesus centered his teaching on the synagogue, his apostles followed suit, and the early church across the board functionally derived its leadership, worship, and organization from the synagogue paradigm. All the evidence regarding the centrality of the synagogue suffusing the New Testament world and New Testament texts should

---

[4] Mark 1:21, 23, 29, 39; 3:1; 6:2; 12:39; 13:9. Luke 4:15, 16, 20, 28, 33, 38, 44; 6:6; 7:5; 8:41; 11:43; 12:11; 13:10; 20:46; 21:12.

[5] Philo, *Free* 81. Josephus mentioned an incident of sacrilege involving men of the region of Doris, a small mountainous district in ancient Greece bounded by Aetolia and southern Thessaly (*Ant.* 19.6.3); he noted successors to Antiochus IV restoring brass donations to the synagogue in Antioch of Syria (*J.W.* 7.3.3).

make quite unremarkable saying that Paul is all about the synagogue.[6] Our point is, Paul's synagogue context should be our first hermeneutical impulse toward parsing almost any problematic statement in Paul. Such a hermeneutical lens should be particularly true about reading Romans, since Romans is all about Israel. So, we arrive at the pertinent question. What was the "story behind the story" of Israel in Paul's first-century synagogue? This "story behind the story" is the legend of the Great Assembly.

THE SYNAGOGUE NARRATIVE

Legend of the Great Assembly

A legend developed in synagogue traditions later preserved in the Mishnah and the Talmud about the "Great Assembly." The story is told that after the time of the prophets during a period from 410–310 BC (until just after Alexander the Great), a group of 120 Jewish leaders were concerned over the miserable state of the postexilic spiritual condition of Israel. Israel's kingship had imploded. Her prophets nearly had disappeared. The national destiny of Israel was at stake after the exile. Some leaders came forward to save the day. Postexilic leaders came up with their own sanctioned preservation of Israel by self-effort to revive Torah religion.[7] In the venerable legend of the Great Assembly, Ezra with his reforms was claimed as the first leader. The august company of various leaders included the postexilic prophets Haggai, Zechariah, and Malachi, as well as the hero Mordecai (of Esther fame), Nehemiah (rebuilder of Jerusalem's walls), and the high priests Joshua and Simon the Just.[8] These leaders, however, historically are situated after the exile. How, then, can the jump be made across the historical Grand Canyon of postexilic realities of Ezra all the way back to Sinai?

---

[6] Why the synagogue is not ground zero of Pauline study is an enigma, other than a propensity to divorce Paul from his Jewish context. Growing recognition of this "synagogue factor" is seen in the brief comments by Porter, *The Apostle Paul*, 91–92.

[7] That is how Paul told the story in Gal 4:24–25, where he evokes an uncanny parallel between present Israel post exile and patriarchal Abraham post childlessness. Abraham tried to insure his progeny and destiny by assisting God in keeping God's promise of progeny through his own scheme with Sarah's handmaiden, Hagar.

[8] Simon the Just, reputed to be the last of the Great Assembly, is understood variously as Simon I (310–291 BC) or Simon II (219–199 BC). See Josephus, *Ant.* 11.8.4–5; 12.2.5; Babylonian Talmud, *Yoma* 69a.

The mythical "Great Assembly" becomes the trick card in that her-meneutical card deck. The "Great Assembly" story validates the author-ity of postexilic Ezra teachings preserved in Pharisaic oral tradition through inventing a mythical direct line of transmission from the post-exilic Great Assembly all the way back to Moses himself. As stated in the Mishnah,

> Moses received Torah at Sinai and handed it on to Joshua, Josh-ua to elders, and elders to prophets, and prophets handed it on to the men of the great assembly.[9]

In this historical card trick, the authority of Moses is directly behind the Great Assembly, though separated by centuries. That line of trans-mission is imperative since Moses is assumed unparalleled and unsur-passed as a teacher of Torah, because he saw God face-to-face on Sinai. Only Moses saw God face-to-face, which makes Moses the absolute au-thority on God. As stated in the Talmud, "All the prophets gazed through an opaque glass, whereas Moses our teacher gazed through a translu-cent glass."[10]

The Synagogue Legacy

In this worldview, even the prophet Isaiah's comprehension of God comes out as dense as granite ("opaque") compared to Moses. Isaiah is on the worse end of the deal in the story of king Manasseh, probably the wickedest king of Judah, according to the author of the Kings materi-al.[11] The Talmud preserves a story of Isaiah's inglorious death.[12] The story is that Manasseh called for Isaiah's execution for "false prophecy." What that really means is that some of Isaiah's pronouncements were judged as directly contradicting Torah. Multiple versions exist. Either

---

[9] Mishnah *Avot* 1:1.

[10] Babylonian Talmud, *Yeva.* 49b. See p. 102 and 1 Cor 13:12 discussion.

[11] He brought to naught the religious reforms of his father, King Hezekiah. He rein-stituted polytheism, including worship of Baal, Asherah, and the Assyrian astral cult (2 Kings 21). He participated in the worship of Moloch in sacrificing children in a fire ritual (2 Kgs 21:6). God's prophets were put to the sword (Jer 2:30). Strangely, the author of 2 Chr 33:11–15 makes a decided effort to rehabilitate the image of Manasseh, report-ing extraordinary actions in the Assyrian court, including Manasseh's imprisonment, repentance, restoration to the throne, and abandonment of all idolatry, about all of which 2 Kings says nothing.

[12] Babylonian Talmud, *Yeva.* 49b.

a cedar tree engulfed Isaiah for his sin, or he simply went and hid in a cedar tree to avoid Manasseh. In any case, a woodsman later cut down the tree. As the saw came to Isaiah's mouth, Isaiah died. This death was declared divine punishment for saying, "And in the midst of a nation of unclean lips I dwell" (Isa 6:5). A contemporary interpreter remarked, "The prophet was punished for this denunciation, even though he had said many other harsh things about the Jewish people for which he was not punished, including, 'Oh, sinful nation, a people laden with iniquity, a seed of evil-doers, corrupting children' (1:4)."[13]

Thus, the prophets are relegated to secondary status for knowing God. They may be canonized, but they play second fiddle to Moses. Moses in this way of telling the story of Israel has an unrivaled and unchallenged grasp of God (Torah) that not even Isaiah could match, much less anyone else who would have the audacity and hubris to try to interpret Torah. The question is, if Moses saw God most clearly and taught Torah most transparently, then who saw Moses most clearly? No surprise here. Ezra did. That is, those closest to catching a glimpse of the God revealed by Moses are the men of the Great Assembly. That is the point of the legend of the Great Assembly—buttressing their authority alone to speak for God. So, in later generations after the exile, *halachic* oral tradition associated with the teaching of Ezra and his followers becomes just as legal and authoritative as Moses.

With supposed validation for oral tradition maintained by the Great Assembly coming directly from Moses, the Great Assembly might be credited with establishing the trajectory of Judaism after the exile in the movement that eventually would coalesce into Rabbinic Judaism after the First Jewish War. This Great Assembly tradition contributed to synagogue scriptural formation not only by finalizing the form of the Twelve Minor Prophets, Daniel, Ezekiel, and Esther, but also by establishing the Hebrew canon (Tanakh, "Hebrew Scripture"). They contributed to synagogue worship by composing the *Shemonah Esreh*, or *Amidah*, otherwise known as the "Eighteen Benedictions," still in use today. They transformed Jewish education into synagogue study of the Torah, extending this educational enterprise from the domain of the priests prior to the exile to all the people after the exile.

[13] Avraham Fischer, "My Jewish Learning," on Lev 16:1—20:27, accessed April 27, 2021, https://www.myjewishlearning.com/article/constructive-criticism/.

What is the story of Israel? Depends on who is telling the story, of course. The priests had their story centered in Mosaic ritual and a temple. Supporters of the house of David had their story centered in royal dynasty and a throne. The Sadducees had their story centered in Hasmonean politics and aristocracy. The Zealots had their story centered in violence and a war. And so forth.

During postexilic years, everything was changing in Jerusalem. Priests were losing their traditional grip on power as authorities on the temple and its service. New authorities on Moses arose with a new class of scribes after the return from exile. Aligned with these scribes was a new postexilic sect of the Pharisees, a grassroots lay movement. In a further stunning postexilic development, the Romans designated Hasmonean rulers as high priests; no longer were the high priests chosen from the line of Zadok, who had served as David and Solomon's high priest and whose line had provided all the high priests for centuries. The cacophony of postexilic voices offering competing visions had become deafening. Everything was in flux. Israel was up for grabs.

The story of the Pharisees during this tumultuous time is tightly wound up with the story of the Hasmonean king Alexander Jannaeus (103–76). The Pharisees despised Jannaeus. He was cruel, vindictive, and at odds with the Pharisee agenda in Israel. While acting as high priest, he intentionally poured the water libation at his feet to insult the Pharisees. The crowds, many of them Pharisees, pelted him with the lemons in their hands as part of the festivity. Jannaeus reacted in rage and killed six thousand. In a later incident, he forced eight hundred Jews, including Pharisees, to witness the execution of their wives and children as he crucified them while he ate at a banquet.[14] Jannaeus's impending death obviously threatened the stability of his throne. The rising social and political force of his opponents, the Pharisees, was a swelling tide with which his dynasty would have to reckon. Jannaeus advised his wife, Queen Alexandra (76–67), to reconcile with the Pharisees to stabilize her rule. She did. She gave Pharisees power on the ruling council. Pharisees then went to work immediately to actualize their vision of Israel in legislation. They legislated using a lunar calendar for temple ritual calculations. They began to apply regulations in the law

---

[14] Josephus, *Ant.* 13.372–373 (13.13.5); 13.380 (13.14.2).

meant strictly for the priests in their temple service to be obligations for all Jews all the time.

FIGURE 4.14. Qumran Caves. The Dead Sea Scrolls, first discovered in 1947 in an area north of the Dead Sea near the Kirbet Qumran settlement, are a library of canonical and non-canonical religious texts written mostly in Hebrew. Evidence from coins, radiocarbon dating, and paleography date the scrolls in the three centuries before Christ and in the first century to the First Jewish War (66–73). Pictured is Cave 4 oriented to the south of the main plateau of the Qumran settlement. This cave yielded the mother lode, almost ninety percent of all of the Dead Sea Scrolls discovered.

This volatile point in Jerusalem's history is where the community responsible for the Dead Sea Scrolls enters the picture. The recently minted and controversial sect of the Pharisees coming into power and enforcing their vision of Israel was the catalyst for the rise of the figure known from the Qumran scrolls as the Teacher of Righteousness. This charismatic priest deeply steeped in his own understandings of Scripture rejected Pharisee innovations in Jerusalem regarding temple service and ritual. Formerly among the elite of the priestly circle in Jerusalem, this priest was ostracized, disenfranchised, and eventually attacked by Jerusalem powers including the Pharisees after expressing his dissent. He was forced into desert exile along with his followers. Their writings chronicling their on-going protest against Pharisee innovations as well as their copies of religious texts were not discovered until 1947 in jars in caves surrounding Kirbet Qumran. The writings came to be known as the Dead Sea Scrolls, and the nearby settlement was used as short form to refer to this collection. Qumran stands as an early example that neither Jesus nor Paul was the first Jew to find fault with the Pharisee vision of Israel buttressed in authority with its mythic Great Assembly.[15]

The Synagogue Impact

The oral tradition evangelized to the Jewish world in the synagogue is the crux of the issue. Weekly in the Sabbath sermon the preacher demonstrated to the audience union of oral law with the biblical text; in particular, the prophets "became by ingenuous homiletics the bridge that coupled the Written law with the Oral law."[16]

The synagogue claimed only Moses saw God face-to-face, so only he was the ultimate authority to speak for God interpreting the Torah. Jesus dared a bold counterclaim, "Whoever has seen me has seen the Father" (John 14:9; cf. 6:46). Jesus was blunt to those who confronted and contradicted him. He called them liars. He asserted, "Before Abraham was, I am" (John 8:54–58). Such claims were a direct body blow to the Great Assembly pretended patent on Torah interpretation. Presumed entitlement to unquestioned authority to know God's will and speak for God was conceit. More importantly, Jesus rejected the postexilic Great Assembly vision of Israel. He used the Pharisaic halachic "law" of Corban as an example of just how self-serving oral law could be (Mark 7:11). Josephus testifies to this law (*J.W.* 2.175 [2.9.4]).

James of Jerusalem

James also gives witness to the impact of Great Assembly tradition in Israel. According to Acts, leaders from various constituencies of the

---

[15] Also note protest against Hasmoneans in *Psalms of Solomon*. N. T. Wright warned of a "Late Judaism" caricature of postexilic Judaism as "corrupt and degenerate," to which Jesus and Paul gave reaction (*Paul and His Recent Interpreters*, 20). Yet, Wright himself later wrote about the rabbis in the same volume, "but the retreat into Torah-piety was precisely a retreat from the larger story which had led to the cataclysm, the story of God, Israel and the world" (75). Wise (*The First Messiah*) makes clear that the Dead Sea Scroll community was a frontal assault on the Pharisee vision in his fascinating study of the Teacher of Righteousness refracted from the *Thanksgiving Hymns*, intense and personal reflections documenting the career of the Teacher of Righteousness.

[16] Mann, *Bible as Read and Preached in the Old Synagogue*, 24, 27. Cf. Acts 15:21.

early church gathered in Jerusalem to consider the question of the law of Moses, circumcision, and entrance into messianic Israel (Acts 15). Assiduous believers in Jerusalem insisted on circumcision as an entrance requirement for Paul's gentile proselytes. A likely venue would be Jerusalem synagogues. Their claim was the voice of conservative Jerusalem synagogues that did not buy Paul's version of messianic Torah in Jesus. The Great Assembly myth, in other words, was still in play in the Jerusalem church, and that Jewish worldview conflicted the Jerusalem church. Affirming Moses was not the problem, because Jesus affirmed Moses (Matt 5:17–20). The problem was Moses *as interpreted by the synagogue*, so the issue was not circumcision per se but how the synagogue interpreted circumcision as defining Israel. Some Jewish believers interpreted Moses within the Great Assembly vision of Israel, so gentiles must be circumcised to be full members of the Israel of God—Moses said so; end of story. When James of Jerusalem rendered the decision reached by the leaders assembled for this conference, he obliquely gave witness to the on-going impact of the Great Assembly tradition and the synagogue context of Paul's ministry: "For from ancient generations, Moses has those who have preached him every Sabbath, being read in the synagogues in every city" (Acts 15:21).

FIGURE 4.15. Tarsus: St. Paul's Well. In the middle of downtown Tarsus, excavations have revealed a water well dating to the Roman period, which would infer today's market area actually sits on top of the ancient center of the city. Connection of the well to Paul is traditional, not historical, but the remains are ancient. The area in the background covered by Plexiglas allows for viewing remains below of Roman buildings that date second to third century.

Saul of Tarsus

FIGURE 4.16. Tarsus: Roman Road. This ancient Roman road discovered during 1993 construction measures 23 feet wide and points toward St. Paul's Well. For the author's video, see https://drkoine.com/movies/1mj/TarsusRomanRoad.mp4.

Paul also gives witness to the impact of the Great Assembly tradition in Israel. If Romans is all about Israel, then Paul is all about the synagogue. One of the lesser-explored features of Pauline discourse is its likely context in the synagogue. If Acts is to be believed, the synagogue was Paul's first target in every major city he visited. But we do not need Acts for this point. Paul himself indicates he cannot leave the synagogue alone. He himself confides he was willing to endure official synagogue "lashing" on *five* different occasions (2 Cor 11:24). The likely background for that many judicial actions on one individual is consistent synagogue activity (and consistent reaction).[17] When we keep in mind such judicial action by synagogue officials was serious and could do injurious physical harm (so was regulated tightly and closely monitored to prevent death), then Paul's insistence on operating within the synagogue to discharge his ministry in the face of such life-threatening resistance is bewildering to say the least.[18] Even more curious if Paul is "apostle to the

---

[17] Cf. Barclay, *Jews in the Mediterranean Diaspora*, 395. Fine noted that in rabbinic literature, "not a single text reflects any positive attitude toward this religion or its founders" ("Non-Jews in the Synagogues," 233).

[18] See Stevens, *Acts*, 588, n34; 603, n75: "Negative and quick synagogue reaction to Paul's preaching is constant, consistent, and ubiquitous throughout Paul's story in Acts."

gentiles" why he always is in a synagogue in the first place. Paul's "to the Jew first" (Rom 1:16) has to have *some* theological inspiration both for its rationale and its *modus operandi*.

Synagogue tradition may surface in Paul more than is recognized, including halahka.[19] Phrases may be allusive. Note the metaphor about seeing "dimly" (1 Cor 13:12). Paul may evoke Mishnaic description that only Moses saw spiritual matters transparently.

Another example of the continuing influence of the synagogue on Paul, even after the Damascus Road, is the little-noticed "obedience of faith" (ὑπακοὴν πίστεως) phrase Paul coined in Rom 1:5. Delrio has shown that this phrase is only the tip of the iceberg to a running synagogue debate over how to read Isa 11:10 on the inclusion or exclusion of gentiles in Israel. After studying various textual traditions, Delrio concluded, "Paul's rhetorical use of ὑπακοὴν πίστεως is direct polemic to the exegetical tradition as witnessed in *Tg. Isa.* 11:10. The

genesis of Paul's phrase ὑπακοὴν πίστεως was not found in the LXX or MT versions of Isa 11:10, but rather in the intertextual dialogue of Paul's inclusive reading of Isaiah against the particularistic reading of the Isaiah Targum."[20]

Much more explicit, however, is Paul's analogy of the veil of Moses. His veil analogy evokes Paul's on-going conversation with

FIGURE 4.17. Jerusalem's Western Wall. Reading Scripture at the Western Wall, the one surviving part of the Herodian temple complex destroyed by the Romans in AD 70 in the First Jewish War.

the synagogue. Paul wrote to the Corinthians,

> and not just as Moses, who used to put a veil over his face in order that the people of Israel not gaze until the end of the glory that was being set aside. But their minds were hardened.

[19] Cf. Tomson, *Paul and the Jewish Law*, on the *halakhah* traditions in Paul's letters.

[20] Delrio, *Paul and the Synagogue*, 120. Romans 7 could be another synagogue discourse Paul is co-opting. Note that by working directly with the Targums, Delrio significantly advanced beyond Garlington's "The Obedience of Faith" series of articles.

> For until this very day, the same veil remains over a reading of
> the old covenant, since it is not uncovered, because in Christ it
> is put aside. Indeed, to this very day whenever Moses is read, a
> veil lies over their heart; but when one should turn to the Lord,
> the veil is removed (2 Cor 3:13–16).

Here, Paul, like Jesus, directly challenges the tradition of the Great Assembly. Jews in most synagogues he preached simply did not buy his
gospel to Israel that Torah comes to consummation in Messiah Jesus,
not in the "Moses" as interpreted by the Great Assembly tradition preserved in the synagogue (Rom 10:4).

This issue of Paul's relationship to Jerusalem crops up at the end
of Romans. Paul asked the Romans to pray for his safety. As he anticipated going to the nerve center of Judaism with his collection from
his gentile churches (Rom 15:31), he feared trouble. We rarely ask why
if all he is doing is offering a charitable donation should he necessarily
expect resistance? The context of the synagogues in Jerusalem perhaps
is involved, even though Luke is not at pains to indicate the context.[21]

When Paul arrived in Rome, the epicenter of the gentile world, he
did not pull together a planning committee for suggestions on how to
conduct a citywide revival in the marketplace after his release.[22] Rather,
Paul immediately sought audience with synagogue leadership as soon
as he stepped foot in the capital of the empire. His clarion call was,
"For, I am wearing this chain because of the hope of Israel" (Acts 28:20).
If Luke got one matter right, he herein concisely stated the essence of
Romans. We always must keep in mind that Paul being "apostle to the
gentiles" is only in behalf of being apostle to Israel (Rom 1:5). Readers
of Romans often have not thoroughly integrated into one consistent
mission for Israel *both* Paul's activity in the synagogue *and* his work
among gentiles. Paul has become so "gentilized," so to speak, across
two millennia of church history—and its hero worship of Paul—that
Christians have lost touch with the mindset and worldview of the
apostle. We long ago forgot that Paul was not a gentile, and he never
intended to be. Consequently, we inevitably find ourselves in an alien
world trying to parse τὸν Ἰσραὴλ τοῦ θεοῦ, "the Israel of God" (Gal
6:16), or ἡμεῖς γάρ ἐσμεν ἡ περιτομή, "we are the circumcision" (Phil

---

[21] Does not suit Luke's narrative objectives; see Stevens, *Acts*, 451–56.

[22] Romans authorities in Jerusalem already had "wanted to release me" (Acts 28:18).

3:3), or ἀμεταμέλητα γὰρ τὰ χαρίσματα καὶ ἡ κλῆσις τοῦ θεοῦ, "for the gifts and calling of God are irrevocable" (Rom 11:29). Thus, the triumphant climax of Rom 11:26, καὶ οὕτως πᾶς Ἰσραὴλ σωθήσεται, "and thus all Israel will be saved," becomes no climax at all. A quixotic dilemma of unfulfilled promise long endured finally being resolved speaks nothing. Connection to the theme statement is lost. God's glory and the vindication of the apostle not to be ashamed of the gospel he preached to Israel are mute (Rom 1:16).[23] Like Jesus, Paul "came unto his own, and his own people did not receive him" (John 1:11). We still do not. Perhaps, though, history still may reveal in the end that Saul of Tarsus was the greatest rabbi Israel ever had.[24]

THE PAULINE EXPERIENCE

The Pharisees had their patented and proprietary story centered on the Great Assembly myth. We have focused on the Pharisee story because this story is where Paul started as he set out on his way to Damascus. He not only was a Pharisee, he excelled all others in his zeal for preserving the postexilic traditions of the Great Assembly (Phil 3:4–6). That life, of course, changed in a moment, in the twinkling of an eye, blinded by the light.

Transformative Apocalypse

Paul's transformation came through a revelation of Jesus as Son of God (Gal 1:9, 12).[25] Paul grounded his story of Israel in that vision of Jesus. When he speaks this way, he is making a gambit to trump Great Assembly rhetoric on the role of Moses. Paul's revelation introduced him to the transparency of Jesus's knowledge of God and the divine authority through which Jesus spoke, which undercut the synagogue traditions about the singularity of Moses. Luke also subverts the Great Assembly

---

[23] Gentile believers likely read Rom 11:26 apathetically. Those preaching *sola fide* as concerned only with individuals unknowingly have divorced themselves from Paul.

[24] "If the test of sound and seminal thinking is its ability to generate speculation, certainly Paul's thought qualifies as profound and seminal" (Roetzel, *The Letters of Paul*, 156).

[25] Encounters with the risen Christ show an eschatological enthusiasm that appears "unprecedented in Jewish history between the return from exile and the Talmudic period" (Hengel/Schwemer, *Damascus and Antioch*, 28).

rhetoric that singularized Moses as seeing God face-to-face, therefore knowing God's will, in carefully composed words of Ananias to Saul,

> The God of our ancestors has chosen you to know his will, to see the Righteous One and to hear his own voice (Acts 22:12).

Like a blinking neon sign, this way of speaking of Saul challenges the Great Assembly myth of the uniqueness of Moses as a revelatory agent of God.[26] Paul's vision was apocalyptic, since he witnessed resurrection. As Barr observed, the problem for Paul "was not how to understand the Old Testament but how to understand Christ."[27]

We need to be clear: Paul's revelatory experience along the road to Damascus appealed to everything Paul was as a Pharisee zealous for God. For one, the revelation did not force him to give up his Pharisaic zeal. Paul maintained his zeal—only as "enlightened" (Rom 10:2). We should remember that he urged Roman believers not to lag in zeal, which is pure Pauline Pharisaism at its pragmatic heart (Rom 12:11).

For two, this revelatory experience concurred with some of his most cherished and fundamental Pharisaic doctrines, including resurrection, final judgment, angels, spirits, and divine immanence.[28] Thus, Paul no more "converted to a new religion" with his revelatory vision of Jesus on the road to Damascus than did the prophet Isaiah, who also in the temple "saw the Lord high and lifted up," became convinced of his utter sinfulness, went through a cleansing ritual, and was sent off on a new mission with an urgent message from God to Israel focused on repentance in light of God's new revelation (Isa 6:1–13).[29]

For three, this revelatory experience gave Paul deeper understanding of the canonical authority of the prophets vis-à-vis Moses, Isaiah in particular, for example. This new appreciation for *the authority of the prophets to speak to Moses* rather than vice versa is what facilitated Paul's grasp of essential ingredients of the Christian preaching of Jesus as a crucified Messiah to which before he had been oblivious or

---

[26] Revelation seems behind Paul's calling Jesus "Lord" (κύριος, *kyrios*), notably in Scripture about God (e.g., Joel 2:32 in Rom 10:13). For Paul's mysticism and seeing God's throne room (2 Cor 12:2–7), cf. Evans, "Paul and the Prophets," 118, and references in n10; Segal, *Paul the Convert*, 60; Humphrey, "Why Bring the Word Down?" 138.

[27] Barr, *Old and New in Interpretation*, 139.

[28] All rejected by the Sadducees (Acts 23:6–8), for example.

[29] *Contra* Segal, *Paul the Convert*, 117. Paul saw the Lord in the temple (Acts 22:17–21).

considered hands down heretical according to the law, as in "cursed is everyone who hangs on a tree."[30] The preeminent Fourth Servant Song of Isaiah already was core to Christian preaching of Jesus.[31] Paul interpreted the same song as foundational to his gentile ministry.[32] Rereading Isaiah messianically of Jesus fired the thrusters to catapult Paul out of the centripetal force and closed loop of the Great Assembly hermeneutic.

For four, this revelatory experience gave Paul new appreciation for Hillel's focus on gentile proselytism. If Paul sat at the feet of Gamaliel as recorded by Luke (Acts 22:3), then he was of the house of Hillel among the two great Pharisaic teaching traditions in the first century. The Hillelites were less concerned with temple worship than were the Shammaites, and more favorable to the possibility of gentile inclusion into Israel.[33] To be clear, Saul disagreed with this Hillelite perspective, made clear by Luke through Saul's stark contrast to his teacher, who had advised the Sanhedrin to leave the Jesus movement alone (Acts 5:38). That advice Saul rejected, and he made himself a central figure in the attempt to eradicate this heretical Jesus movement. We should note Saul's persecution picks up precisely when the Jesus movement in the story in Acts 8 begins criticizing the premier institution of the Great Assembly, the Jerusalem temple, and its legal sacrificial efficacy (Stephen, Acts 7), and, as well as when this movement began broaching boundaries set by the Great Assembly (Ethiopian eunuch, Samaritans, Acts 8).[34] Saul's revelatory experience, however, as Luke indicated,

---

[30] Deut 21:23; cf. Gal 3:13.

[31] Matt 8:17; Luke 22:35–38; Mark 15:28; Acts 8:26–35; 1 Pet 2:22, 24–25.

[32] Rom 10:16 (Isa 53:1); Rom15:21 (Isa 52:15).

[33] Note Jesus's observation of seeking proselytes around the world (Matt 23:15), as well as the conclusion of this Gospel in the great commission (Matt 28:19). Jesus may have had more Pharisee sympathy than recognized, because we cannot get past his excoriation of the Pharisees in the unrelenting "woes" of Matthew 23. Forgotten here is that one criticizes that about which one cares. Jesus cares to transform the Pharisees.

[34] Eunuchs, deformed in body, could not participate in temple worship in the law of Moses, nor be incorporated fully into Israel (Lev 18:18). Samaritans were considered despicable Jewish half-breeds, remnants of the Northern Kingdom left over from Assyrian captivity, religiously syncretistic, perverting worship of Yahweh (2 Kgs 17:21–41). The Samaritans tell an entirely different story. For a critical reassessment, see Pummer, *The Samaritans: A Profile*. Cf. Barton, *The Samaritan Pentateuch*; Bowman, *The Samaritan Problem*; Macdonald, *The Theology of the Samaritans*; Montgomery, *The Sa-*

included a commission to gentiles (Acts 22:15), which concords with Paul's statement of an agreed division of mission labor between him and Peter (Gal 2:2–8). Thus, the Damascus road experience actually seems to have pushed Saul at the time back more in line with his own Pharisee teacher, Gamaliel, particularly in adopting a Hillelite attitude to the possibility of gentile inclusion into Israel.

In sum, Paul's apocalyptic moment in the sun of a different solar system helped him to envision how he could be the best Pharisee he ever desired to be. At the same time, Paul's apocalypse of resurrection also exposed the myth of the Great Assembly's unique, correct, and exclusive knowledge of Moses and God's will and its accompanying presumed authority alone to speak for God. After his apocalypse, Paul thereafter reconfigured his hermeneutic of Israel through the story of Jesus as Messiah. So, what changed in Paul's narrative of Israel?

Transcending Moses

Paul transcended Great Assembly myth and ceased pivoting on Moses for a definition of Israel. That reorientation is what Jesus as Messiah revealed, and Jesus became canon for Paul. After his revelatory insight, Paul realized that he no longer could say Moses correctly reveals God except only as Moses could be interpreted as in concord with Messiah Jesus (Rom 10:4). No first-century Jew controlled by the synagogue's Great Assembly tradition likely would agree with this quite radical reconfiguration of Moses and his authority. We must be sure to read Paul's declaration in Rom 10:4 in Paul's synagogue context as radical and extremely controversial. This declaration most assuredly is *not* a *kekrimenon* (rhetorical accepted opinion) among even believing Jews. Luke's narrative is clear on this point. A significant contingent of even *believing* Jews in Jerusalem did not agree with Paul's gospel, or at least their understanding of Paul's mission teaching among gentiles. Upon Paul's unexpected arrival in Jerusalem, James cautioned him that "thousands" of Jewish *believers* in Jerusalem who were "zealous for the law" were a serious threat to Paul's leadership and mission (Acts 21:18–21). This faction of the Jerusalem church shows how Great Assembly traditions continued to have impact among even Jewish believers. Paul

maritans: The Earliest Jewish Sect; Purvis, *The Samaritan Pentateuch and the Origin of the Samaritan Sect.*

was "forsaking Moses" by supposedly teaching Jews not to circumcise their children or observe the "customs."[35] James's dilemma in Acts 21 inadvertently reveals that the so-called "decision" in Acts 15 really more just temporarily tamped down vocal dissent. Paul's story of Israel was problematic for the early church, and that legacy continues.[36]

Pivoting on Abraham

If Paul did not pivot on Moses, upon whom or what did he pivot? He pivoted on what Jesus Messiah revealed about Abraham, as insinuated in the Gospels. For example, Matthew takes the genealogy of Jesus back to Abraham (Matt 1:1). When pointing out that God is God of the living to prove resurrection doctrine, Jesus did not speak of God as the God of Moses but as the God of Abraham, Isaac, and Jacob (Matt 22:32; Mark 12:26; Luke 20:37). Jesus inferred that the trajectory of his story and fulfillment of Scripture goes back to Abraham (John 8:56). Jesus told a parable about a rich man and Lazarus. The rich man postmortem in torment in Hades seeks help from Abraham to warn his five still living brothers of their impending fate. Abraham ironically points to Moses and the prophets for a witness to warn the brothers. The rich man on the far side of Hades, however, was acutely aware that even this witness never would be enough for genuine repentance (Luke 16:29).

Abraham Remembered

A key concept to focus discussion for telling the story of Israel is that the "Abraham" remembered in Great Assembly traditions is not the Abraham of Genesis, since the profile of the "remembered Abraham" functional in the minds of first-century Jews was extra-biblical.[37] In these traditions, Abraham was sublimated to Moses (just as were prophets such as Isaiah). In this sublimation, Abraham was redrawn as Mosaic in his relationship to God, already performing the law centuries before Sinai. In this revisionist history, Abraham was declared righteous *because of his sacrifice of Isaac in Genesis 21*. The hermeneutical move

---

[35] Acts 21:21. "Customs" (ἔθεσιν, *ethesin*) is an allusion to the traditions of the Great Assembly, such as the *halakhah* of the oral law. Thus, this interpretive debate is a synagogue confrontation and has synagogue discourse written all over its *ethos*.

[36] Cf. Grenholm and Patte, *Reading Israel in Romans*.

[37] Cf. VanHorn, "Arguing from Abraham." Note Sir 44:20; 1 Macc 2:52; Jub 15:1–2; 16:20–21.

taught that Abraham's *future* action God already took into account as the basis for the earlier divine declaration of his "righteousness" in Genesis 15. In effect, in Great Assembly tradition, "Abraham our father" translates into "Abraham our father in Moses." Abraham remembered this way is transformed into just another son of Moses.

Thus, the "Israel" of the Great Assembly no matter from which direction one looks in history before or after Sinai is "Mosaic Israel," start to finish. Anyone claiming to be messiah but not conforming to the Mosaic oils as put to canvas by the Great Assembly by default would be a false prophet and a heretic cut off from the Israel of God. Paul, however, clearly rejected this Mosaic frame of the Great Assembly for interpreting the Genesis account of Abraham. Paul dared to turn the Great Assembly picture on its head. He reversed the sequence back to the original text order. The Genesis 15 divine declaration of righteousness to Abraham came before the Genesis 21 Isaac episode. Paul made his entire point temporally depend on the Genesis 15 declaration coming *before* the Genesis 21 sacrifice of Isaac. That rereading made Abraham's declaration of righteousness *entirely independent of the Mosaic covenant* four hundred years later (Romans 4). After his revelatory vision of Jesus resurrected, declared righteous by God, Paul no longer read "Abraham our father" as "Abraham our father in Moses." By seeing Abraham as declared righteous *before* law came, Paul saw how Israel's covenant always worked: God's prevenient promise through grace, which in the messianic age was through faith in the resurrected Son of God whom the Sanhedrin had declared by the law of Moses a criminal of the state. *Abraham was the father of many nations, not one.*

To be sure, three world religions today call Abraham father. Jews, Muslims, and Christians all derive their genus from Abraham. A claim to fatherhood normally refers to blood and ethnicity. The Christian claim, then, could appear suspect, since that claim is not based on the grounds of blood relationship. When parental rights are contested in court, one standard state procedure is to do blood tests to establish paternity. The procedure of adoption, however, also legally establishes fatherhood for legal purposes in our courts without the requirement of blood relationship. So, some of the pertinent consequences of being in a family are recognized in our own judicial system on grounds other than blood that are just as legitimate from the point of view of the law. Thus, one legally can be incorporated into a family without being born into a family (Rom 8:15). Paul's adoption analogy in Romans—though unique to Paul in the New Testament and derived from his Roman background, not Jewish—is no innovation on the Jesus tradition. Jesus explicitly taught that being descendants of Abraham does not make children of Abraham (John 8:37–39).

Incorporative Legality

The question would be the legality of the incorporative process. For a proselyte to Judaism, this process would be circumcision and taking on the law of Moses. Since circumcision was commanded in the law (Lev 12:3), this matter was not in dispute for Mosaic Israel. Household slaves and resident aliens could not participate in the Passover meal without being circumcised (Exod 12:44, 48). The original families who had escaped Egypt, however, were not too zealous about the matter, since no Israelites born on the wilderness journey after Sinai had been circumcised, which is why Joshua was commanded to perform the rite on all of those descendants before the conquest (Josh 5:2–5).

However, lack of circumcision compliance was less of a problem after the exile. In seeking to avert their disaster of national judgment again, postexilic Jewish traditions from Ezra on in the development of Great Assembly traditions focused on keeping the law. In such a post-exilic environment, circumcision and diet became supreme identifiers of an Israelite. Jews faithful to the law under the Syrians even suffered martyrdom for circumcising their children and refusing to eat pork.[38] Luke is careful to document that both John the Baptist and Jesus were circumcised on the eighth day as required by law (Luke 1:59; 2:21).

Moses's own teaching made clear, however, that the problem with external rituals such as circumcision always would be matters of the heart, which should have been a crucial warning to Ezra and all those surfing in his postexilic wake (Deut 10:16).[39] For this very reason, Jesus

---

[38] Cf. 1 Macc 1:60; 2 Macc 6:10; 4 Macc 4:25. On not eating pork, note the famous story of a mother and her seven sons, 2 Macc 8.

[39] Cf. Jer 4:4; 9:25. The Teacher of Righteousness at Qumran coined "The Way of God's Heart" for obedience that pleases God in meditations on Isaiah preserved in his *Thanksgiving Hymns*. His later disciples wrote similarly, "So he [God] raised up for them a Teacher of Righteousness to make them walk in the Way of his Heart" (CD 1:11). DSS citations are from Abegg, "Qumran Non-biblical Manuscripts," Ver. 3.3, Accordance, OakTree Software. Cf. Wise, *The First Messiah*, 94.

challenged this postexilic incorporative process, as well as the Jewish claim of having Abraham as father: "And don't presume to say to yourselves, 'We have Abraham as our father.' For I tell you that God is able to raise up children for Abraham from these stones" (Matt 3:9). In spite of centuries of postexilic tradition on the pattern of Ezra reinforcing circumcision as the definitive rite of a child of Abraham and incorporation into Israel, Jesus made clear something else was now operative in this eschatological new age of the Spirit brought about by Messiah for being incorporated into the Israel of God. Regardless, one still finds a circumcision faction criticizing Peter in Jerusalem over the Cornelius affair, including acceptance of table fellowship (Acts 11:2).[40]

The Great Assembly picture of Israel was the only one to survive the war.[41] The only counterpoint to the Great Assembly juggernaut for defining Israel after the war was the sect proclaiming Jesus as Messiah, but after the war this movement became almost exclusively gentile.[42] The effort to interpret the Great Assembly picture of Israel in the new age of Messiah, however, was not easy, not even for the church. Given the obvious ambiguities, even contradictions, of the answer among Jewish believers in Jerusalem before the war, the weight on Paul's shoulders to define Israel as he wrote Romans was immense.

THE PAULINE NARRATIVE

If he were asked directly, "Paul, what is the story of Israel?" we do not know the precise details of how he would respond. We are hobbled by having to guess between the lines. However, positively we do know the title: "The Gospel of God."[43] We might tease out some trajectories of the main plotline of this "Gospel of God."

---

[40] Of course, in every generation someone has to interpret the law of Moses to say how the law applies. Even Moses had to interpret the law of Moses. He became so burdened with the task, his father-in-law, Jethro, had to effect an intervention in his own form of "Behold, I show you a better way." Cf. Exod 18:1–27.

[41] No more Sanhedrin debates over resurrection doctrine (Acts 23:6)!

[42] Luke presents Hellenist believers as carrying the torch of messianic Israel. These Hellenist believers become the heart and soul of the designation "Christian" in Acts (Acts 11:26). See Stevens, *Acts*, 73–111.

[43] Paul begins Romans saying his apostleship is all about telling this story of "the gospel of God" (Rom 1:1). For methodological difficulties in using narrative dynamics for the study of Paul, cf. the essays in Longenecker, *Narrative Dynamics in Paul*.

The Gospel of God

The "of God" phrase in Rom 1:1 subtly reflects two dimensions. One is source. This gospel comes from God. The other rarely considered option is object. Not only humans get "good news" with Jesus. God gets good news too. How is Jesus good news for God? Paul already had said that Jesus is how God fulfills every promise he ever made (2 Cor 1:20). Fulfilling all promises includes the promise to Abraham to be a father of many nations, which is why his name changed from Abram to Abraham (Gen 17:2). This promise Paul called a proclamation of the gospel beforehand (Gal 3:8).[44] How would Paul as a Jew begin to tell the great gospel drama? As any Jew would. He would begin at the beginning. Further, his story would turn on individuals who turned the plot.

FIGURE 4.18. Ivory Table: Adam and Eve. This ivory table had carved reliefs around its circumference depicting biblical scenes, approximately six inches high. This vignette depicts the moment of the fall for Adam and Eve in the Garden of Eden (IAM).

Adam—Israel and Creation

For one, Paul would start with, "In the beginning, God" (Gen 1:1). The first verse of Hebrew Scripture makes clear that monotheism and creation theology are the bedrock of all Jewish storylines. Note how God is assumed, not argued, and God is assumed creator. Without the first theological datum, "God is," faith has no point. Without the theological datum, "God is creator," salvation has no promise. Only the One who created life has the power to sustain life. If any reality threatens life, the only reality that can save life is God. If he is the God of creation, by

---

[44] Cf. Brawley, "Multivocality in Romans 4," 88.

default he is the God of salvation. Further, this fundamental datum about created life is that life is an act of grace. "I did not ask to be born." Correct. Creation means humans are obligated to God for this act of grace. The grace infers divine purpose, a destiny toward which God wills the creation. God wills life, not death. Life is not an accident. Proper response to the act of grace is to fulfill the creative purpose for life. Since God is the only God, he is the only one deserving of human attention and allegiance. Humans need relate to no other to determine proper response to the gift of life.

The next theological datum of creation is evil, unexplained, "Now the serpent" (Gen 3:1). God is creator. Evil is destroyer.[45] Destruction is a fundamental characteristic of evil. By denying, destroying life, evil contradicts God's design, purpose, and goal in creating life. Adam is the story of evil at work, but, more importantly, is prototypical of the story of Israel: life created, land prepared and given, covenant requiring faith response, agent in the land as tempter to idolatry, disobedience, and expulsion from land.[46] Without God's intervention through God's grace, humankind is doomed, the story of Noah.

FIGURE 4.19. Ivory Table: Abraham and Isaac. This ivory table had carved reliefs around its circumference depicting biblical scenes, approximately six inches high. This vignette depicts Abraham's preparations for the sacrifice of Isaac (IAM).

The final theological datum of creation is community. God desires humans to live in community, that two "become one flesh" (Gen 2:24).

---

[45] In Rev 9:11, evil is named "Destroyer" (Hebrew, "Abaddon"; Greek "Apollyon").

[46] Cf. Postell, *Adam as Israel*, 124–25. Postell goes beyond often noted parallels between the garden of Eden story and Israel at Sinai, as well as between primal sin in the garden and the golden calf incident at Sinai. Postell postulates that Genesis 1–3 conveys the creation story molded specifically to be an introduction to Israel, Sinai, and exile.

So the problem of evil, which in part destroys community, has to be solved through community. God's community solution is a people. Noah after the flood failed this goal, but Abraham holds promise.

Abraham—Israel and the Nations

The locus of community after the failure of Noah to fulfill this purpose is Abraham, who is promised as a blessing to all the families of the earth (Gen 12:3). Abraham is the story of call and faith. If humans respond with faith to God's gracious call, then salvation comes, community is preserved, and creation restored. Israel, then, is the on-going saga of Abraham to be a blessing for all humankind through his paradigmatic call and faith (Gen 12:1; 15:6). To seal this covenant of call and faith, God gave Abraham circumcision (Gen 17:10). Abraham received his promised son (Gen 21:3), but the promised land took longer to fulfill (Gen 15:7). In fact, four centuries of slavery intervened (Gen 15:13).

FIGURE 4.20. Abraham's Gate at Tel Dan. Called "Abraham's Gate" on speculation that Abraham would have passed through this gate during the rescue of his nephew Lot, who had been taken captive by an alliance of four Mesopotamian kings (Genesis 14). This mud-brick gate now sits in a nature reserve near Mount Hermon and the Golan Heights. Constructed about 1750 BC, the gate is nearly 4,000 years old.

Moses—Israel and the Law

God redeemed Israel from Egyptian slavery, the exodus story. To seal the covenant of this redemption, God gave Israel law in order to form a nation out of slaves (Exod 19:5). Law is God's will customized for ancient nation building as the foundational document that created a nation among the nations. Like the United States has its constitution, so also Israel had its law. Foundational documents give people their identity. The law is what defined Israel as Israel. The goal for Israel in the end, however, was not an end in itself. Israel's destiny was to reach the nations with the claims of God as the only God and as the creator and thereby fulfill the promise to Abraham. Unfortunately, law was compromised by sin.

Compromised by sin, the law has limits on expressing God's will. The law allowed for divorce, but even the prophets warned divorce was not God's will (Mal 2:16). How could a destroyer of community that weakens the fabric of human society be God's will (Matt 19:7)? Compromised by sin, law cannot effect that which is commanded. The matter of the sincerity of the human heart in obedience to law is left unresolved in Moses. Thus, law inherently anticipates a future for Israel in which God sends forth a prophet greater than Moses who will be able to penetrate the human heart through the Spirit of God.[47] A coming prophet-like-Moses was the key

FIGURE 4.21. Michelangelo's Moses. Renaissance artist, Michelangelo Buonarroti, carved this statue of Moses in the San Pietro in Vincoli Church in Rome for Pope Julius II's tomb. Horns on the head derive from a Latin Vulgate mistranslation of Exodus 34.

to Samaritan eschatology, which figures into Jesus's conversation with the woman at the well (John 4:25–26).[48]

Since law was compromised by sin, the history of Israel is fraught with failure. The people of God more were defined by their disobedience than their obedience. One story of disobedience is paradigmatic—the golden calf. Before Moses even could come down from the top

---

[47] Deut 18:15–19; Jer 31:31–34; Isa 32:15; 44:3; 59:21; Ezek 36:27; 37:14; Joel 2:28–29. Cf. Fee, *God's Empowering Presence*, 811–16; Evans, *Paul and the Prophets*, 128.

[48] "Christ" (Χριστος, *Christos*) as Jerusalem's Davidic equivalent of the Samaritan term, *Taheb* (prophet-like-Moses of Deuteronomy 18). This coming prophet would execute the great day of God's vengeance and retribution. Cf. *Memar Marqah* 4.12.

of the mountain, the people of Israel had made an idol to worship. The golden calf incident shadows the very terminology used in Rom 1:18–32, which ostensibly is supposed to be about gentiles.

David—Israel and Kingship

Another story of disobedience is kingship. God did not desire Israel to have kings like other nations, just like he did not desire divorce. Instead, God called upon Israel to be a kingdom of priests in his service (Exod 19:6). The people predictably rebelled, insisting on a king. So, kingship was the concessional result of the failure of prophetic leadership in Samuel's family. Had Samuel's sons not failed in their spiritual leadership, kingship would not have held as much attraction.[49] Israel's hardness of heart forced God to allow kingship. Unfortunately, the inevitable story of the nation after kingship came on the scene was a tragic vortex spiraling down into destruction. The summary at the end of the Chronicler's narrative is succinct and tragic.

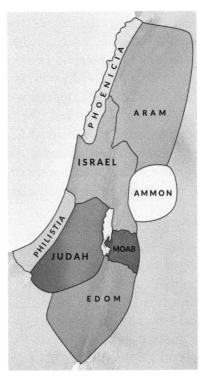

FIGURE 4.22. Divided Kingdom. David and Solomon's kingdom was divided into Northern and Southern Kingdoms.

But Yahweh, the God of their ancestors sent word against them by the hand of His messengers, sending them time and time again, for He had compassion on His people and on His dwelling place. But they kept ridiculing God's messengers, despising His words, and scoffing at His prophets, until the LORD's wrath was so stirred up against His people that there was no remedy (2 Chr 36:15–16, NRSV).

---

[49] Specifically, 1 Sam 8:4–9, 19. The whole narrative, however, is context.

The kings showed abject failure to represent God to the people and the people to God. As a result, God's prophets brought messages of judgment to this corrupt institution in Israel.

Failed kingship is the point of the promises of a Davidic Messiah. Kingship set in motion the sin of a dynasty that could be solved by God only through a king like no other—the promised Messiah.[50] The language of Messiah is the redemption of kingship in Israel. This future Messiah is the only reason that kingship has any future in the storyline of Israel. God will redeem the kingship in the Messiah.

In sum, Israel's kingship was concessional, corrupted, and judged, but, later, to be redeemed. The nature of that redemption, however, as the prophets foresaw, would be counterintuitive. According to Zech 9:1–6, God's Messiah would come humbly, welcome outcasts, bring peace, and rule in true righteousness—no typical pagan profile for king, and no Jewish profile either, after the successful Maccabean revolt.

Isaiah—Israel and Exile

Kingship split Israel as a nation into two kingdoms, north and south. In the end, both were lost. Kingdom destruction resulted in the law's curse of dispossession of the land and exile. Assyria destroyed the Northern Kingdom in 722 BC. The kingdom never was reconstituted as a nation. Loss of the Northern Kingdom set up the historical issues related to the Samaritans. The Southern Kingdom survived another century plus, but eventually succumbed to Babylon in 586 BC with most of the population taken off into exile for seventy years. The city of Jerusalem and its territories were left in utter ruin.

FIGURE 4.23. Assyrian King Relief. King Ashumasirpal II (883–859 BC) is presented as a divinity in this palace relief (PAM).

[50] Isa 7:14; 9:6; Dan 9:25–26.

The prophet Isaiah captured the essence of Israel before the exile in his Servant Songs. Those who would conjure Israel and her destiny after the exile would find their deepest and most transformative truths in Isaiah, not Moses. Most dramatic of all prophecies about the post-exilic future of Israel is Isaiah's vision of the end.

> For I know their works and their thoughts, and I am coming to gather all nations and tongues; and they shall come and shall see my glory, and I will set a sign among them. From them I will send survivors to the nations, to Tarshish, Put, and Lud—which draw the bow—to Tubal and Javan, to the coastlands far away that have not heard of my fame or seen my glory; and they shall declare my glory among the nations. They shall bring all your kindred from all the nations as an offering to the LORD, on horses, and in chariots, and in litters, and on mules, and on dromedaries, to my holy mountain Jerusalem, says the LORD, just as the Israelites bring a grain offering in a clean vessel to the house of the LORD. And I will also take some of them as priests and as Levites, says the LORD (Isa 66:18–21, NRSV).

FIGURE 4.24. Babylon: Ishtar Gate. King Nebuchadnezzar II of Babylon constructed this gate about 575 BC as part of the grand processional road into the city leading to the temple of Marduk in the form of a ziggurat. The ceremonial road was surrounded on either side with 50 feet high walls of blue glazed brick with high gold reliefs depicting mythological animals and deities (PMB).

Ezra—Israel and Return

Exile became the big question mark in the story of Israel. Restoration was promised (Isa 40:1–5). Under Persian kings, several waves of returnees made their way back to a devastated Judea. Reality after return was not nearly as expected (Ezra 4:4; Neh 5:1). Even Ezra confessed they seemed still in slavery (Neh 9:36–37). Time was momentous for changing Israel from the ground up—yet not with Isaiah's profile in view.

FIGURE 4.25. Cyrus Cylinder. This imperial inscription on a clay cylinder in Akkadian cuneiform script dated to 539 BC records the order issued by Cyrus the Great after conquering Babylon releasing all Babylonian deportees, including the Jews (BML). Credit: Renate Hood.

The story of Ezra's impact on postexilic Jerusalem is instructive. Ezra is both celebrated and cautionary. Ezra is celebrated for bringing religious emphasis back into Israel after the exile. However, Ezra also is a figure of caution. Ezra was authorized to reconstitute the temple-cult ritual in Jerusalem by Artaxerxes I, "for the hand of the LORD his God was upon him" (Ezra 7:6). This positive propaganda disguises Ezra's detrimental overemphasis on law observance. Ezra's extreme actions defined Israel after the exile.[51] His law emphasis became the seedbed of a new scribal class preserving the law and the Pharisaic movement zealously living out their interpretation of that law through their oral traditions. They propagated their vision of Mosaic Israel into Jewish culture by a novel postexilic institution in Jewish life, the synagogue, facilitated by the Great Assembly myth. This alternate vision impacted not only Judea and the mission of Jesus, but also the Diaspora around

---

[51] Quite clear in the storyline of Ezra-Nehemiah. We already have discussed elements of this problem in the Great Assembly tradition of the synagogue.

the world and the mission of Paul. Ezra portends troubling elements dramatically affecting Israel's tale and her destiny after the exile.

Messianic expectations also became a vexing conundrum after the exile. Isaiah's promised Davidic ruler was designated quite marvelous titles, but theses images were combined with complexities of a Servant Messiah with both corporate and individual dimensions. In any case, the promised Davidic ruler never appeared. Zerubbabel, who led the first wave of returnees to Judah and laid the foundation for rebuilding the temple, may have had messianic notions associated with his leadership.[52] Outside possibly Zerubbabel, expectations for Messiah after the exile went unfulfilled until the Maccabee brothers initially revived hopes shaped by a martial profile. Mattathias and his sons had more control over the image of Messiah in popular expectations than Isaiah. When Jesus arrived as Isaiah's Servant Messiah, he was not recognized due to martial expectations evolving out of the Maccabean period.

Also unrecognized after exile was the land's changing status. Possession of land was conditional (Deut 30:18–19). Thus, land, hence nationhood, is provisional. Stipulations ignored, then possession of land wrongly could be made imperative for Israel's story. We should note that Paul never speaks of land as what defines Israel. Often noted about the land promises that are given to Abraham, Isaac, and Jacob is that they are not unconditional, nor exclusive, nor exhaustive.[53]

Answering the question whether Israel after exile proved she had learned her lesson is problematic. The two dynasties that eventuated in this postexilic setting were neither Davidic (the Hasmoneans) nor Jewish (the Herodians).[54] Further, by the first century, another foreign empire ruled over the nation in Paul's day whose ruler had his own gospel of good news for the world.[55] Israel after the exile categorically was different in critical ways than Israel before the exile. The story had gotten quite muddled by competing voices inside and outside Israel. Thus, Paul's Jewish worldview was in crisis when he wrote Romans.

---

[52] Ambiguities swirl around whether "signet ring" in Hag 2:23 infers kingship and messianic rule, as well as the title "Branch" in Zech 3:8; 6:12.

[53] Cf. Gen 15:18–21; 26:3; 28:13. Cf. Bruce, *Romans*, 221.

[54] Even though a temporary reprieve from total foreign domination.

[55] Priene Calendar Inscription noting the birth of Augustus as "good news" (εὐαγγέλιον, *euangelion*) for the world; cf. Mark 1:1. Cf. Evans, "Mark's Incipit."

Conclusion

Postexilic challenges were extraordinary: synagogue demands, messianic expectations, national aspirations, and no Davidic dynasty. The story of Israel clearly was unfinished, if God's promises are in view. A viable question would be, had the ruin of exile been resolved?[56] Any satisfactory answer would have to involve the trajectories evolving out of the stories of key individuals who turned the plot, Adam, Abraham, Moses, David, Isaiah, and Ezra, within the overarching metanarrative of creation and monotheism. That is, if the only God is sovereign over his creation, and he called Israel as his solution for the world's ruin by sin, but Israel is in some strange limbo after exile unforeseen by any of her prophets, God surely could not be done. The profile of his answer had to be a son of Abraham to consummate the promise (Gal 3:16; Rom 4:23), an eschatological prophet like Moses to consummate the Torah (Rom 10:4), and a son of David to consummate the kingship (Rom 1:3). Further, all this consummation would have to happen through Israel, whom he elected for this purpose. In this storyline, God through Israel would bring creation to consummation according to all his original designs. Adam would be reborn as eschatological Adam (1 Cor 15:45).

Paul resolved his worldview crisis with his theology of the gospel of God. For Paul, the gospel of God is good news from God and good news for God. The good news from God would be the efficacious work of God's agent to create salvation by consummating the goal of Torah through a prophet who would empower obedience to God's will for all those who believe like Abraham, becoming a true child of Abraham. The good news for God would be a Davidic Messiah who would empower Israel's destiny to consummate creation's goal.

In short, the gospel of God is the good news that God fulfills every promise he ever made, and particularly those to Israel. The only God and creator sovereignly fulfills all his purposes. Paul tries to tell that story in Romans 1–11 and make presumptive application in Romans 12–15. Whether he was successful can be argued, since he is argued.

---

[56] This question becomes a lynchpin of Wright's theory of postexilic Israel's plight. Cf. N. T. Wright, *Climax of the Covenant.* The postexilic conundrum also is picked up in Pate, *et al., The Story of Israel,* but the supersessionism of the Pauline material is disappointing and must be challenged.

5

The Context of Romans

Setting the Document Background

Paul, Rome, and Jerusalem are the three life settings that intersect to establish a crucial part of contextualizing Romans. Establishing these life settings is essential for formulating the purpose of Romans. Strange for a letter so esteemed among the letters of Paul—and indeed, among all the New Testament documents for many—that we struggle so to say why Paul wrote it. The purpose of Romans is one of the most contested contextual issues of this letter.[1] Wisdom would hesitate to go there, but fools rush in . . .

LIFE SETTINGS OF ROMANS

Life Setting of Paul

Without the book of Acts, we would struggle to put anything together on Paul.[2] The date of Romans is pretty clear based upon its sequence comparing notational content in other letters and in Acts. Paul has completed the collection by the time he writes Romans (15:23, 25, 26).

---

[1] From an older generation, see Donfried, *The Romans Debate*. Sparring over the thematic "righteousness of faith," of course, takes pride of place among scholars for theological debate. See chapter 2 of this book.

[2] Though the historical value of Acts is debated, use of Acts for a study of Paul is defensible. The classic arguments against Acts by scholars such as Goodenough, Vielhauer, and Haenchen were rehashed in Smith and Tyson, *Acts and Christian Beginnings*, but has reasonable response for reading usefully as an apologetic historical monograph in Keener, *Acts*, 1:221–57. Cf. Stevens, *Acts*, 23–25.

In 2 Cor 13:1, written from Macedonia after Paul had left Ephesus, Paul announced, "I am coming to you." Yet, the Corinthians still needed to finish up the collection so that when Paul got there, they would not be embarrassed (2 Cor 9:4). This sequence infers that Romans is written after 2 Corinthians toward the end of the third missionary journey, probably from Corinth about AD 57.[3]

Paul is in multiple ministry crises at the time he writes Romans. He lost Ephesus, after he was run out by a riot, so has lost his mission base.[4] In the same time period, he almost lost Corinth, one of his premier churches where he ministered longer than the year at Antioch.[5] Finally, he plans personally to deliver the collection to Jerusalem, a problem in and of itself, and he also is aware this destination threatens his life (Rom 15:31).[6] The Ephesian crisis would suggest he reasonably could be concerned about the viability of conducting future ministry projects because he is absent a sending and supporting church, hence Rome is on the radar. The Corinthian crisis involved the validity of his claim to apostleship, as well as Rome is not a church he started, hence his relationship to the church in Rome is on the radar. Finally, the impending Jerusalem crisis involved his ministry among the gentiles, so the gospel he preaches for Rome to consider is on the radar.

Ephesian Crisis

Paul lost Ephesus. The riot of the silversmiths caused immediate implosion of the ministry (Acts 19:23–40). This loss was a disaster in terms of the Lukan characterization of Ephesus as Paul's crown jewel.

> Ephesus is Pentecost abundance, the apex of gentile mission. Six narratives drive home that Ephesus is the crown jewel of the Pauline missionary enterprise, unsurpassed in success, without

---

[3] Luke states only that Paul was in "Greece" (Acts 20:2), but information in 2 Corinthians indicates the city likely is Corinth.

[4] Cf. Stevens, *Acts*, 416–23. Paul already lost Antioch. Supposed implicit indications of reconciliation with Antioch later in Acts argued by Taylor (*Paul, Antioch and Jerusalem*, 204–05) are not persuasive.

[5] Documented in part in two letters we have and two letters we do not have, that is, 1-2 Corinthians, and a "previous" (1 Cor 5:9) and a "harsh" letter (2 Cor 7:8).

[6] The problem is God's will vis-à-vis Paul's presence in Jerusalem. Cf. Stevens, "The Character Saul-Paul," *Acts*, 113–43.

peer in comparison. Ephesus is where gentile mission was heading until Paul himself got in the way.[7]

After losing Ephesus, and close to losing grip on the wealthy congregation at Corinth, Paul wanders off into Macedonia anxiously looking
for Titus with no mission base and no sponsorship for future mission
immediately in sight (Acts 20:1). Catastrophic collapse of the Ephesian
ministry means Paul needs Rome for Spain (Rom 15:22–24). The question why *Spain* in particular is taken up later in this chapter.

Corinthian Crisis

Paul nearly lost the church at Corinth. One read of 2 Corinthians 10–13
shows significant leadership opposition. Alien leaders Paul sarcastically
dubbed "super-apostles" had moved in and challenged his authority
and questioned his motives (2 Cor 11:5). Add on top of this information
a painful and embarrassing visit to Corinth in which Paul publically was
humiliated by the Corinthians (2 Cor 2:1), as well as the existence of
Paul's harsh letter to the Corinthians prior to 2 Corinthians, but which
we do not have (2 Cor 2:4), then the story gets even more complex. Paul
with the harsh letter apparently drew a veritable line in the sand for the
congregation in Corinth after his painful visit. He put all his chips on
the table in one dramatic poker move. Matters could have gone either
way. Fortunately, Titus rendezvoused with Paul in Macedonia bringing
good news of community remorse and reconciliation after receiving the
harsh letter (2 Cor 7:6).

As Paul writes Romans, Gaius, patron of the church in Corinth,
is hosting him. He also sends greeting from Corinth's city treasurer,
Erastus, and from Quartus (Rom 16:23).[8] The patroness of his writing
project is Phoebe, deaconess at the nearby port city of Cenchreae, who
likely also has donated the services of her scribe, Tertius, for the composition of Romans.[9] Phoebe's lead position recommendation and its
content infer she is the letter bearer. Further, that the Romans should
"welcome her in the Lord in a manner worthy of the saints and assist

---

[7] Stevens, *Acts*, 412. This perspective on Paul requires close reading of Luke's text.
Cf. Stevens, *Acts*, 113–43; 337–49; 412–24.

[8] Taking Romans 16 as original. See later discussion.

[9] Bruce (*Romans*, 12) speculated Paul's current host in Corinth, Gaius, supplied the
scribe; less likely due to Phoebe's primary recommendation position in Rom 16:1–2.

her in whatever matter she should need" consequently infers she is responsible for interpreting the letter of Romans during her time in Rome and that her room and board during that time is their obligation.[10] These personal connections in Corinth and nearby Cenchreae suggest that Paul has resolved the Corinthian crisis. Yet, its challenges to his apostleship and authority in a Diaspora congregation of his own work could raise the specter of acceptance of Paul's authority in Rome, a church he did not even found.[11]

Jerusalem Crisis

While Luke portrays a regular relationship with Jerusalem for Paul that is not as obvious in Paul's letters, he does not whitewash Paul's tension with Jerusalem. Luke does not fail to document the Jerusalem Council questioning Paul's ministry to which all church leadership, Jerusalem and otherwise, was called to decide (Acts 15). Luke also does not gloss over Paul's problem at the end of the third missionary journey. The moment Paul showed up unexpectedly in Jerusalem attempting to deliver the collection from his gentile churches, James immediately was placed in a most difficult predicament. He had a political hot potato he was not sure how to handle (Acts 21:20–22). In fact, at one point, Luke is rather blunt about Paul in Jerusalem. He gives an often-ignored narrative vignette of Paul's temple vision shortly after the Damascus Road, dramatically time-delayed for narrative effect (Acts 22:17–21).[12] In the temple vision, Paul argues with Jesus about the value of his witness in Jerusalem! Jesus, however, is unequivocally blunt, clearly commanding Paul, "get out of Jerusalem quickly, because they will not accept your testimony about me" (Acts 22:18).

Paul too is witness to tension. His most revealing comments are in Galatians. The opening verse that his apostleship is "not from men or by man" (Gal 1:1) is an immediate shot across the bow of Jerusalem authority. His gospel is not taught him, nor from a human source (Gal 1:11). After the revelation of Jesus, Paul "did not immediately consult with anyone" (Gal 1:16), nor did he "go up to Jerusalem to those who

---

[10] Cf. Rom 16:1–2, 22, 23.

[11] Fitzmyer, *Romans*, 71–73, tables Paul's echoes in Romans of themes and phrases in other letters, but 1 Corinthians easily gets the lion's share.

[12] Stevens, *Acts*, 459–61.

had become apostle before me" (Gal 1:17). When first in Jerusalem, he met Cephas and James only, and that only for fifteen days (Gal 1:18–19). Leaders "recognized as important" added nothing to Paul's gospel (Gal 2:6). Jerusalem "pillars"—James, Cephas, and John—agreed to Paul's gentile mission (Gal 2:9). Yet, the relationship was problematic. Cephas equivocated gentile contact after "certain men from James" came to Antioch. Paul upbraided Peter, but likely lost Jerusalem (Gal 2:11–14).[13]

Paul's difficult relationship with both Jerusalem and its church, clear in his own testimony and in the text of Acts, is the subterranean faultline of Romans. The problem, however, is not the church alone. The problem, as already suggested, is Paul's insistence on attempting to function within the synagogue. The gravitational force of the synagogue on Paul suggests that house churches for Paul were a secondary solution at best, only a necessary work-around when local synagogues refused to receive him.[14]

Life Setting of Rome

Age of Augustus

Paul lived in a world of empire. His mission work met imperial Rome from cities to provinces, tribunes to proconsuls, even to the emperor himself. Why would imperial themes not surface in his writings? Certainly "barbarian" (Rom 1:14) is a Greco-Roman social classification, not Jewish. A crucial passage in what could be called the "theological heart of Romans," Rom 3:21–26, has unnoticed imperial undertones.[15] Having "access" (προσαγωγήν, prosagōgēn) to God's grace (Rom 5:2) has undertones of access to the imperial throne room on Rome's Palatine Hill in rare imperial audience by the emperor's "favor." Again, the unusual designation "weak" and "strong" in Romans 14–15 is a deliberate rhetorical move beyond "Jew-gentile" polarities to parlay Roman imperial ideology propagating values of superiority and dominance assumed by Romans as proven by its world conquest and subjugation.

---

[13] Dunn, *Romans 1–8*, xlii, but not Lüdemann's "anti-Paulinism" (*Opposition to Paul*).

[14] Implicit throughout Acts (Acts 13:5, 14, 50; 14:1–2; 17:1–2, 10, 17; 18:4–7; 19:8–9). Jerusalem was *not* the secret address of Romans (Jervell, "The Letter to Jerusalem").

[15] Metropolis of Asia Minor inscription calling Augustus "reconciler" (ἱλαστέριον, *hilasterion*). Cf. Rom 3:25; Wilson, "*Hilasterion* and Imperial Ideology." For the author's video description, see https://drkoine.com/movies/3mj/MetropolisInscriptions.mp4.

General Octavian ended two hundred years of Roman civil wars by defeating Antony and Cleopatra in the naval battle of Actium in 31 BC uniting Rome's interests east and west. He transformed the imploding pieces of the Roman Republic into an empire that lasted for a thousand years. He reorganized the army as a professional force with lifelong military careers loyal to him only. He innovated a brilliantly successful provincial system divided into imperial and senatorial rule that harnessed local elites in a deftly executed patron-client, pyramid relationship. He rebuilt Rome with fountains, temples, gardens, aqueducts, baths, and theaters, and organized Rome's first fire brigades and police protection. He secured crucial grain shipments to feed the unemployed urban masses. He mollified senate aristocrats by disguising totalitarian rule as rule by the "princeps," or first, most eminent man of the state.

FIGURE 5.1. Augustus Statue. Augustus depicted in nude, heroic Greek pose as divine (TAM).

He ushered in an unrivaled era of peace and prosperity—the Peace of Rome, or *Pax Romana*.[16] He harnessed state propaganda to portray his rule as divinely ordained, inevitable, legitimate, authoritative, ruled by law and virtue conceived in Roman terms of aggression, dominance, power, conquest, victory, and subjugation. Images of empire ideology

---

[16] Earl, *Age of Augustus*; Ferraro, *Republic of Augustus*; Hill, *Ancient Rome*; Liberati and Bourbon, *Ancient Rome*. Rejected by Perriman, *Future of the People of God*, 98.

were stamped on coins, carved in marble, framed in friezes, chiseled in inscriptions, and built into architecture and monuments. One could not buy, sell, trade, travel, worship, legislate, socialize, or find leisure without imperial ideology propagated front and center.[17] Even Herod the Great built a temple to Augustus, the first visible artifice greeting mariners who entered his new Roman harbor at Caesarea Maritima.[18] Thus, Octavian's victory at Actium created a new world for which the world's population gave due honor. Citing honors to Augustus in the provinces, rare Senate triple triumph award, building of imperial cult temples in Asia, and numismatics, Wilson concluded, "Octavian's victory is thus portrayed as the restoration of the republic to the people of Rome, which implies reconciliation with his supporters as well as his former enemies. The erection of these altars in Metropolis then was part of an empire-wide expression whereby hundreds of cities around the Mediterranean erected altars and temples to Augustus at this time."[19]

FIGURE 5.2. Priene Calendar Inscription. Second tablet of the Priene Calendar Inscription that uses the Greek word "good news" (εὐαγγέλιον, *euangelion*) for Augustus's birth. Compare Mark 1:1. The inscription records the proclamation in 9 BC to adjust the beginning of the calendar for Asia Minor to the birthday of Augustus in September (FBM).

The Priene Calendar inscription illustrates the extraordinary impact of Augustus on the world.[20] Ancient Priene in Asia Minor was the sister port city to Miletus where Paul addressed the Ephesian elders at the end of the 3MJ (Acts 20:15–36). The proconsul Fabius Maximus

[17] Zanker, *The Power of Images in the Age of Augustus*. Winter (*Divine Honours for the Caesars*) argued the *inevitable* confrontation Christians faced in imperial demands.

[18] Holum, "Building Power: The Politics of Architecture."

[19] Wilson, "*Hilasterion* and Imperial Ideology," 4.

[20] Mommsen and Wilamowitz-Mollendorff, "Die Einführung des asianischen Kalenders." A copy of the inscription has been found in Metropolis; cf. Dreyer and Engelmann, "Augustus und Germanicus im ionishen Metropolis."

proposed Augustus's birthday, September 23, as the birth of a new era, so New Year's of the Julian calendar. His assembly letter follows.

> Decree of the Greek Assembly in the province of Asia, on motion of the High Priest Apolionios, son of Menophilos, of Aizanoi whereas Providence that orders all our lives has in her display of concern and generosity in our behalf adorned our lives with the highest good: Augustus, whom she has filled with *arete* [virtue] for the benefit of humanity, and has in her beneficence granted us and those who will come after us [a *Saviour* (σωτῆρα)] who has made war to cease and who shall put everything [in peaceful] order; and whereas Caesar, [when he was manifest], trans-cended the expectations of [all who had anticipated the good news], not only by surpassing the benefits conferred by his predeces-sors but by leaving no expectation of surpassing him to those who would come after him, with the result that the birthday of our God (τοῦ θεοῦ) signalled (ἦρξεν δὲ τῶι κόσμωι τῶι δι᾽ αὐτὸν εὐαγγελίων ἡ γενέυλιος ἡμέρα τοῦ θεοῦ) the beginning of Good News for the world because of him; . . . (proconsul Paul Fabius Maximus) has discovered a way to honour Augustus that was hith-erto unknown among the Greeks, namely to reckon time from the date of his nativity; therefore, with the blessings of Good Fortune and for their own welfare, the Greeks in Asia Decreed that the New Year begin for all the cities on September 23, which is the birthday of Augustus; and, to ensure that the dates coin-cide in every city, all documents are to carry both the Roman and the Greek date, and the first month shall, in accordance with the decree, be observed as the Month of Caesar, beginning with 23 September, the birthday of Caesar.[21]

The two-tablet inscription found in the Priene market in reply to this ordinance of the Asian assembly, dated 9 BC, is given below.

> On this day [*i.e.*, the birthday of Augustus] *the world has been given a different aspect. It would have been doomed to destruc-tion* if great good fortune common to all men had not appeared *in him who was born on this day.* He judges aright who sees in this birthday the beginning of life and of all living powers for himself. Now at last the times are passed when man must regret that he has been born. From no other day does the individual and all humanity receive so much good as from this day, which has brought happiness to all. It is impossible to find words of thanksgiving sufficient for the great blessings which this day has

---

[21] Danker, *Benefactor*, 217.

brought. *That Providence which presides over the destinies of all living creatures has fitted this man for the salvation of humanity with such gifts that he has been sent to us and to coming generations as a saviour. He will put an end to all strife and will restore all things gloriously.* In his appearance, all the hopes of the ancestors have been fulfilled. He has not only surpassed all former benefactors of mankind, but *it is impossible that a greater than he should ever come. The birthday of this god [i.e., Augustus] has brought out the good news of great joy based upon him. From his birth a new era must begin.*[22]

FIGURE 5.3. Fragments of the *Res Gestae Divi Augusti*. One of the surviving copies of the "Deeds of the Divine Augustus," his own account of his life and accomplishments as Rome's first emperor. The funerary inscription, preserved in several copies across the empire, epitomized the essence of Roman imperial ideology that became standard for generations. Cf. Augustus bragging his honors, *Res Gestae* 6.34 (YMY).

Roman Gospel

Luke's last narrative nugget about Paul in Acts is the verb about Paul proclaiming (Acts 28:31). Proclamation is what the Roman Empire was all about—the imperial propaganda codified across the empire in the *Res Gestae* inscriptions of Augustus's will and pushed on the world's population by all subsequent Julio-Claudian emperors in images on coins, buildings, statuary, inscriptions, literature and every other con-

---

[22] Massey, *Ancient Egypt*, 760. For the Greek text of the inscription, cf. Dittenberger, *Orientis Graecae Inscriptioines Selectae*, 2: 48–60. For the significance of the use of εὐαγγέλιον, *euangelion*, "good news," "gospel" and Mark 1:1, cf. Evans, "Mark's Incipit."

FIGURE 5.4. Ostia: Temple of Augustus. Ostia had a large, commanding temple to Roma and Augustus before Augustus died, served by the flamines of the imperial cult.

FIGURE 5.5. Antioch of Pisidia: Temple of Augustus. At the highest point of the city sat this magnificent temple to Augustus carved into the bedrock. Paul would have seen this imperial temple and its ongoing rituals while he was in the city.

ceivable venue of propagation of a world kingdom with divine rights to rule all of humankind and whose heart was in Rome.[23] Temples to Augustus were already across the empire, including the nearby port city of Ostia, but also in far away provincial cities Paul missionized, such as Antioch of Pisidia on the 1MJ, with its elaborate Augustan

[23]Consult Galinsky, *Augustan Culture*.

temple complex at the very top of the city. The Palatine hill in Rome was becoming the centerpiece of imperial palace luxury overlooking the Forum of Rome below, and Nero, to whom Paul had appealed, would soon launch a palace building project after the fire of Rome that would dwarf anything conceived previously after draining the marsh below the Forum to facilitate this immense monument to his reign.

FIGURE 5.6 Rome: The Palatine Hill. One of the "seven hills of Rome," the Palatine hill was the residence of the emperor of Rome overlooking the Forum below. Here lived the ruler of the world.

Roman emperors asserted divine right to rule the world. Their own narrative, however, disguised a perfidious lie. The "peace" of the Augustan Age was no true peace but only defeat by brute force, violent conquest—a submission at the hands of an overwhelming military might. A perverse ideology of violence and dominance was legitimated as divine right to rule and then reinforced by violent,

FIGURE 5.7. Amazon Warrior Grave Relief. Homer's *Iliad* spoke of a race of Amazon warrior women fierce in battle, becoming an imperial motif epitomized in this grave relief of a Roman soldier to honor his courage in battle (OAM).

brutal, and bloody gladiatorial combat in amphitheaters across the empire. Rome told its beginnings as the legend of two violent brothers, Romulus and Remus, twins conceived by Mars, god of war, abandoned, suckled by a she wolf. Romulus later murdered Remus over where to found Rome. This empire began in violence, breathed violence, bred violence, and baptized violence to the world in her legends and her legions—a kingdom aggrandizing force, dominance, and intimidation.

FIGURE 5.8. Cuirass of Hadrian. The legend of Rome's origins in the she wolf that suckled twin brothers Romulus and Remus is the centerpiece of this military cuirass of emperor Hadrian (117–138) standing in the ancient Agora of Athens. Nike, or Victory, is supported on the back of the she wolf. The she wolf legend tacitly codes the foundational truth that Rome even in its imperial ideology acknowledges its fundamental wild, aggressive, and violent DNA.

The Ara Pacis Augustae monument in Rome celebrates this Roman gospel and its kingdom. The Roman Senate in 13 BC commissioned a new altar in Rome dedicated to the goddess Peace to honor Augustus after his conquests of Gaul and Spain. Short wall reliefs depict scenes of peace and Roman ritual. Long wall reliefs depict the imperial family in sacrificial attire and procession. All the common motifs that would become foundational imperial ideology, including the imperial cult, already manifest in these reliefs. Lower register reliefs depict a harmonious intertwining of vines and nature to symbolize the "harmony and peace" Augustus has forged with its inevitable abundance and prosperity. The Ara Pacis is the greatest surviving monument propagating the grand themes of the Roman Empire, preserving for generations to come the Roman gospel about the Augustan dynasty, its divine right to rule, and the benefits to the world of this glorious empire.

FigUre 5.9. Ara Pacis Augustae. The Altar of Augustan Peace was commissioned by the Roman Senate in 13 BC to honor Augustus after his victories subduing Gaul and Spain. Reliefs promote the imperial cult and family and sacrifice to the goddess Peace.

Paul's proclamation in Rome at the end of Acts is about another kingdom and Messiah, new realities transcending the Jewish nation and Mosaic law, but also the imperial gospel already being proclaimed in Rome. Confessional titles in Acts 28:31 echo Paul's early proclamation in Damascus after the Damascus Road. "Lord" nuances Son of God in the context of Caesar (Acts 9:20), and "Christ" nuances the promised Messiah in the context of Moses (Acts 9:22). Paul's gospel is non-imperial—the multicultural *laos* of Amos's dreams, and the realization of James's message of Jews and gentiles united by faith in Jesus the Messiah to become the eschatological, messianic Israel of the last days (Acts 15:16–18)—for Luke a new vision of the people of God and good news for the world, perfectly imaging Paul's "gospel of God" as "the hope of Israel" (Acts 28:20).

Luke in effect walks his readers around the Ara Pacis to subvert the message of its reliefs. Not lost on Luke is that Paul traveled to Rome on an Alexandrian grain ship; Luke even noted the irony of the ship's figurehead (Acts 28:11). This ship was part of the imperial fleet constantly cutting the seas to supply plebian Rome free bread. God, however, is the essence of Israel's Pentecost celebration. Another Pentecost usurper in Acts besides Herod Agrippa is Rome, who falsely promised conquered peoples nature's abundant harvest, carved into the imagery Ara Pacis reliefs, but who ravaged world wealth and resources in her own insatiable appetite for luxury.

An imperial gospel already was being proclaimed in Rome long before Paul arrived with his own: the good news of Caesar versus the good news of Christ. Rome told its story in the legend of Aeneas, divinely conceived of the goddess Aphrodite, escaping Troy's destruction by the Greeks, his son Lulus on his back, and arriving in Italy to become the progenitors of the imperial families of Julius and Augustus. Augustus is hailed by the

FIGURE 5.10. Roman Aeneas Legend. Aeneas, son of divine Aphrodite, escapes Troy to become progenitor in Italy of the imperial families ruling Rome (AMA).

Roman poet Virgil as Rome's peace, the world's savior, reconciler of enemy forces of a war-torn, dying Republic disintegrating away for two hundred years, herald of a new golden age of human history promising security and nature's profuse abundance.[24] Luke carefully connects Jesus's birth as true son of divinity to the reign of Augustus (Luke 2:1).[25] Paul also critiques Rome: "Insofar as Paul deliberately used language closely associated with the imperial religion, he was presenting his gospel as a direct competitor of the gospel of Caesar."[26]

[24]Virgil *Ecl.* 4. The *Kaisaros hilasteriou* (Καίσαρος ἱλαστηρίου) inscription from Metropolis near Ephesus calls Augustus "reconciler" (dated after Antony's Actium defeat in 31 BC); Augustan imperial rhetoric might shed light on ἱλαστήριον in Rom 3:25. Cf. Wilson, "*Hilasterion* and Imperial Rhetoric."

[25] Jesus's reign as true good news, true salvation, true peace; Luke 2:10, 11, 14; Acts 2:1.

[26] Horsley, "Paul's Counter Imperial Gospel: Introduction," *Paul and Empire*, 140. Note Rock's evocation of multiple connections, *Romans and Roman Imperialism*, 165.

The choice between these two gospels was stark and life changing. Considering Paul's gospel for the first time would face challenges in moving from Caesar to the Christ. Such a decision would involve—as for Paul on the Damascus Road—a total shift into a new worldview, associating with a new community following God's Messiah. New life in God's messianic community would require nothing less than mind transformation through an infilling Spirit power (Rom 12:1–2). Paul's gospel had a dynamic power Rome's did not by reaching depths of the human soul, recognizing the quintessential truth that man does not live by bread alone—not even in Rome.

Aphrodisias Illustrations

Aphrodisias, an ancient city about 19 miles west of Denizli, Turkey (near Laodicea), illustrates Roman imperial propaganda advancing the goals of Rome through local provincial elites.[27] This ancient city's remains are the epitome of the imperial message and Roman support.

FIGURE 5.11. The Aeneas Legend. Three panels in the legend of Aeneas: (1) divine conception by Aphrodite; (2) flight from Troy with son, Lulus; (3) final arrival in Italy (AMA).

Roman Legend. In Roman legend, the Trojan hero, Aeneas, was the son of the goddess Aphrodite, born from divine conception of the goddess with the prince Anchises. Aeneas escaped the destruction of Troy by the Greeks with his son, Lulus. His journey as a brave refugee brought him to Rome, where he and his son would become the forebears of Julian and Augustan families. Aphrodisias was named after Aphrodite, the mother of legendary Aeneas, progenitor of emperors.

---

[27]Another fine resource is deSilva, *UnHoly Allegiances*. Galinsky, *Augustan Culture*, prefers *auctoritas*, "authority" (prestige, influence toward one's will), to "propaganda."

Thus, Roman origin legends meant the city of Aphrodisias always held high status and favored relationship with Rome for its namesake.

FIGURE 5.12. Zoilos Remembrance Monument. Part of a massive monument complex commemorating the famous Aphrodisias patron Gaius Julius Zoilos (AMA).

Patronage. Gaius Julius Zoilos, a former slave in the house of Augustus, was freed and returned home to Aphrodisias, where he became a wealthy, enterprising businessman who maintained close, powerful relations with Rome due to his imperial family connections. He brandished his power and social status through benefactions to his home city. He was patron to the city theater construction (7,000 capacity), the north portico, the north agora, and the temple of Aphrodite, with its elaborate colonnaded court framed by an impressive two-story façade on the east side and extensive porticos on the other three sides.

FIGURE 5.13. Aphrodisias Theater and Temple of Aphrodite. Major benefaction to the city of Aphrodisias by the patron Zoilos, who had strong ties to the imperial family.

FIGURE 5.14. Aphrodisias Stadium and Bouleuterion. The Aphrodisias stadium held up to 30,000 spectators and shows the impact of trade guilds on social life. Statues honoring local patrons of Aphrodisias garnished the entrances to the bouleuterion, often emphasizing connection to Rome, imitation of Roman style, and the status of priest of the imperial cult.

Stadium. The stadium at Aphrodisias was 886 feet long with 30 tiers of seats holding up to 30,000 spectators and is the best preserved in the ancient world. Inscriptions in stadium seats show reserved places for various trade guilds, such as the Association of Tanners and the Association of Goldsmiths, as well as for individual citizen elites not only of Aphrodisias but of surrounding towns. The near end of the stadium later was modified for Roman-style spectator sport, gladiatorial combat.

Bouleuterion. The entrances to the bouleuterion (council chamber) were lined with statues of patron benefactors of the city. One of these patrons was Antonius Claudius Demetrious, who is depicted wearing civic dress and a heavy, priestly crown ornately decorated with a bust of Aphrodite and the Roman

FIGURE 5.15. Grave Stele, Supervisor of the Linen Workers. This workman had achieved significant social status and business clout in Aphrodisias as supervisor of the linen workers guild. He would represent the kind of citizen who would have had a reserved seat at the stadium (AMA).

emperors. Another statue is of Claudia Antonia Tatiana, with hair imitating the empress Julia Domna, and the god Eros at her side. The plinth is signed by the master craftsman, Alexandros, son of Zenon, indicating the expense of these public honorariums.

FIGURE 5.16. Antonius Claudius Demetrious. Honored by the city of Aphrodisias at the entrance to the bouleuterion. Civic dress, heavy priestly crown, decorated with bust of Aphrodite and Roman emperors (AMA).

FIGURE 5.17. Claudia Antonia Tatiana. Statue adorning one of the entrances to the bouleuterion of Aphrodisias. Roman aristocratic hairstyle in deliberate imitation of empress Julia Domna. A small figure of the god Eros was at her side. Work signed by master craftsman, Alexandros, son of Zenon (AMA).

FIGURE 5.18. Leading Citizen. A member of the social elite class and aristocrat of first-century AD Aphrodisias. Portrayed wearing a priestly crown, so in the cult service of a patron god of the city (AMA).

FIGURE 5.19. The Goddess Aphrodite. Best preserved statue of the goddess Aphrodite in Aphrodisias, from the bouleuterion. Head veiled, with heavy symbolic casing in multiple rows of images, including the famous sculpture of the three Graces, the sun and moon gods, Aphrodite on the seat of a goat, and Eros figures making sacrifice (AMA).

FIGURE 5.20. Drawing of the Sebastion Entrance. Architectural schematic depicting the view of the grand entrance into the three-tiered, open courtyard of the Sebastion temple complex (AMA).

Sebastion. The Sebastion was the cult center of the worship of the emperor. Horsley noted, "A reassessment of the emperor cult as a major factor in the world of Paul's mission is in order."[28] The architecture was designed foremost to provide ostentatious, public display of standard Roman imperial propaganda. The "storyline" of the friezes and

---

[28] Horsley, "General Introduction," *Paul and Empire*, 4. Yet, note cautions voiced on imperial cult study in the essays in Brodd and Reed, *Rome and Religion.*

statuary aggrandized the power of Rome and the mighty expanse of her empire. Rome's success was divine favor of the emperors. Her victories were inevitable. Resistance was futile. Besides, Rome did the world a favor subduing barbaric hinterlands and bringing peace, stabilization, civilization, commercialization, and the benefits of world empire to all peoples. "You should be grateful we conquered you" was the message.

FIGURE 5.21. Sebastion of Aphrodisias. One corner of the ruins of the Sebastion sanctuary for emperor worship in Aphrodisias has been reconstructed to suggest the original three-tiered portico flanking the inner courtyard. Nearly 70 reliefs illustrative of Roman imperial propaganda were discovered in this area.

The friezes on the second story of the north Sebastion featured a series of fifty personifications of places and people from East Africa to Western Spain. They were designed to look like statues between the columns of the portico. These friezes represented conquered territories and peoples subjugated by the overwhelming, irresistible power of Rome. Inscriptions on the frieze statue bases identified the conquered: Andizeti, Arabs, Besse, Bosporans, Callaeci, Crete, Cyprus, Dacians, Dardani, Egyptians, Ethiopians, Iapodes, Judeans, Phaeti, Piroristi, Sicily, Trumpilini, and more. In effect, this series was a visual listing of the extraordinary expanse of the Augustan empire. Some of the selections specifically were chosen to emphasize the wilder people on the edges of the world, barbarians, uncivilized. Few of the inhabitants of Aphrodisias even ever had heard of some of them. The grand scale and emotional impact must have been stunning. Message received.

FIGURE 5.22. Sebastion Friezes, North Second Story. A series of 50 personifications of conquered peoples from East Africa to Western Spain. The four represented here are the Pirousti, Dacian, and Besse peoples, and the island of Crete (AMA).

FIGURE 5.23. Sebastion Frieze, ETHNOUS IOUDAIŌN. Inscription of one more conquered nation in the north second-story series, the Jewish people (AMA).

The friezes of the third story of the south Sebastion focus on the Roman emperors and their imperial victories shown in concert with Olympian gods. The symbolic message here is clear: the emperors are today's powerful warring deities and are mixed with the old gods as near-equal partners. The superscription of the entire series is *Theoi Sebastoi Olympiori*, or "Olympian Emperor Gods." The principal emperors depicted are Augustus, Tiberius, Claudius, and Nero, because their most important activities were their victories over barbarians. So, we visualize and vicariously experience emperors in their signature victories: Claudius is conquering Britannia (the furthest west), and Nero is conquering Armenia (the furthest east). The style is imitative, Romans affecting the Greek heroic style.

One frieze depicts the emperor and the Roman people. The emperor is shown in the classic Greek style as naked warrior. He is being crowned by Romans, personified, wearing a toga, the stately civilian dress of Roman citizens. The crown is an oak wreath, which is the civic crown (*corona civica*), which is awarded for saving citizens' lives. The emperor sets up his battlefield trophy as a sign of victory. Beneath him in humiliation pose is the pathetic image of a kneeling, anguished, barbarian woman captive. In this way, the "message" of the imperial political agenda is symbolized figuratively

FIGURE 5.24. Emperor and Roman People. Gratitude to heroic emperor civilizing barbarians, protecting Roman citizens' lives (AMA).

in images that have no need for a prose explanation of the drift of the message. Symbols, figures, and images are a normal way of "talking."

FIGURE 5.25. The Goddess Hemera and the God Oceanus. Hemera left, Oceanus right. Both are framed with billowing cloak behind the head, a symbol of a divine epiphany to mortals. These gods served Roman imperial ideology (AMA).

Another frieze is of the goddess Hemera (Day). The style is "still action," as she steadies a dramatic billowing cloak framing the head. Use of a billowing cloak behind the head was the standard figure for a divine epiphany to mortals. Why would the Romans be interested in the gods Day and Night? They had political interest, not religious. These gods proved useful for advancing imperial propaganda. They became stock images in Roman friezes for signifying the eternity of the Roman imperial rule. "Eternal Rome" is still an expression used even today. One could move from a temporal point to a terrestrial point. In a similar vein, the mutual depiction of the bearded god Oceanus alongside the goddess Earth again was a Roman imperial line for representing the empire as without end over land and sea.

One of the standard Roman goddesses was *Dea* Roma, the city of Rome, with the city of Rome itself a symbolic representation of the entire empire. By picturing *Dea* Roma together with a fecund Earth, one could represent earth's fertility and abundance as in the control of and administered by the wise stewardship of Rome. In this particular frieze, Roma holds a spear and wears a crown in the form of a city wall (symbolic of civilization). Earth reclines, half naked, leaning on fruit and holding a cornucopia of fruit, indicating abundance and fertility. An innocent child climbs the horn wisely provisioned and secure.

FIGURE 5.26. Roma and Earth and Victory of the Emperors. Imperial ideology of Rome as wise manager and protector of earth's abundance, and of the prominent victory theme common in so much Roman imagery (AMA).

Another frieze is titled "Victory of the Emperors" (*Nike Sebastin*). This frieze, another "still action," pictures the goddess Victory as she swoops across the panel bearing a military trophy on her shoulder. This image is meant to convey one of the most prominent themes of Roman imperial ideology—victory. This victory theme was a key *topos* of imperial rhetoric. Rome and her legions were victorious on the field of battle. Conquering by force of military supremacy was the constant story of the Roman empire and her continual expansion to global domination, and Rome never let you forget that story. Her generals were honored with grand victory parades, or triumphs, in the heart of Rome with thousands to witness and laud success on the field of battle. Simon ben Giora, one of the Jewish Zealot leaders, was paraded down Rome's streets before his execution at Titus's triumph after Titus defeated the Jews in the First Jewish War.[29] This victory rhetoric provides background to John's "conquering" language in Revelation's seven letters ("to the one who conquers," Rev 2:7, 11, 17, 26, 28; 3:21).[30]

[29] See Stevens, *Revelation*, p. 20, fig. 1.23.

[30] See the excellent discussion in Horn, "Let the One Who Has Ears," for four important terms telling the story of Revelation: almighty, conquer, throne, and lamb. Each of these terms has imperial ideology in view.

FIGURE 5.27. Tiberius, Captive; Claudius Conquers Britannia. Every generation of emperors continues Rome's victorious conquest theme (AMA).

From generation to generation, the Roman emperors never fail in their military task as successful generals on the field of battle to vanquish their enemies and conquer and civilize barbarian hinterlands of a world empire. In a frieze about the reign of Tiberius (14–37), the emperor is depicted next to one of his captives in the Greek heroic style of the naked warrior. He stands frontally, in a pose of total dominance, holding spear and shield and wearing a cloak and sword strap. Beside him stands a captive barbarian, intentionally rendered at half size as a sign of humiliation and shame. The prisoner wears cloak and trousers, but has his hands tied behind his back, signifying captivity.

In another frieze again symbolizing a victorious conquest theme, Claudius (41–54) is depicted in heroic Greek style as naked warrior, wearing helmet, cloak, and sword-belt. He is captured at the moment he is about to deliver the death blow to this slumped female figure representing all of Britannia. She is styled bare-breasted in imitation of the legendary Greek Amazon myth.

Another of the imperial friezes shows Agrippina (d. 59) crowning her young son Nero (54–68) with a laurel wreath. Nero is styled in high honor, since he wears military armor and the cloak of a Roman commander, and with a helmet at his feet. The early reign of Nero universally was praised as a time of peace and prosperity. He was under the tutelage of the Stoic philosopher, Seneca (d. 65), for political matters and the prefect of the Praetorian Guard in Rome, Burrus (d. 62), for military matters. Nero's early reign widely was associated with the sun

FIGURE 5.28. Nero and Agrippina. Agrippina crowns her young son, Nero, emperor. Rumored to have had her husband, Claudius, poisoned to advance her son, she wisely supervised Nero's early reign through court advisors Seneca and Burrus (AMA).

god Helios. The frieze of Nero and Agrippina is interesting for its timing, because its production had to be before A.D. 59, when Nero had his mother Agrippina murdered and got rid of both of his advisers. Even though the story of the emperors has such mundane matters as intrigue for accession to the imperial throne, Roman imperial ideology ignored these realities and continued to propagandize conquered peoples with their alternate version of the "glory" of the imperial world.

FIGURE 5.29. Claudius, Master of Land and Sea. With the billowing drape framing the upper torso, emperor Claudius is depicted in a divine epiphany. The image is of a divine ruler who is master of land and sea, so Claudius guarantees abundant prosperity for all those under his domain (AMA).

One last example from the imperial friezes is Claudius as master of land and sea. In this frieze, Claudius is depicted as a god striding confidently forward in an intimidating divine epiphany, signified by the drapery that is billowing behind his head just like in the depiction of the gods when they manifest themselves to mortals. A figure is emerging from the ground and gifts Claudius with a cornucopia of fruits of the earth. The symbolism is clear: the emperor god is worthy of worship because he guarantees prosperity of land and sea. The image is remarkable for illustrating how in the outlying provinces of Rome, and most especially in the eastern province of Asia of the seven churches and of Paul's mission work, the Roman worldview not only is accepted but advanced. The emperor's role as universal savior and divine protector is affirmed enthusiastically and vigorously promoted by the local elites such as at Aphrodisias. Considering this city was only a short distance from Laodicea toward the east and Ephesus toward the west, both in the orbit of Paul's mission, the pervasive presence of the Roman imperial world and its ideology is transparent.[31] Philo illustrates how the imperial "point of view" becomes such a natural part of the warp and woof of ancient society as to be integral to the normal rhetorical flourish even for Jew.

> This is Caesar, who calmed the storms which were raging in every direction, who healed the common diseases which were afflicting both Greeks and barbarians, who descended from the south and from the east, and ran on and penetrated as far as the north and the west, in such a way as to fill all the neighboring districts and waters with unexpected miseries. This is he who did not only loosen, but utterly abolish the bonds in which the whole of the habitable world was previously bound and weighed down. This is he who destroyed both the evident and the unseen wars which arose from the attacks of robbers. This is he who rendered the sea free from the vessels of pirates, and filled it with merchantmen. This is he who gave freedom to every city, who brought disorder into order, who civilized and made obedient and harmonious, nations which before his time were un-

---

[31]Galinsky, "The Cult of the Roman Emperor: Uniter or Divider?" 2–6, cautions not to conceive the imperial cult in monolithic, undifferentiated terms, such as suggested in "*the* imperial cult." Rather, local practices varied; the imperial cult was more a civic activity amalgamated into existing local religious, social, and economic structures. Much depended on patronage, social advance, and local elites. Cf. Spaeth, "Imperial Cult in Roman Corinth," 77. Care also must be taken not to conceive that Jews or Jesus followers responded in a monolithic manner to imperial cult interactions. Cf. White, "Capitalizing on the Imperial Cult: Some Jewish Perspectives," 188–89; Carter, "Roman Imperial Power: A New Testament Perspective," 142.

sociable, hostile, and brutal. This is he who increased Greece by many Greeces, and who Greecised the regions of the barbarians in their most important divisions: the guardian of peace, the distributor to every man of what was suited to him, the man who proffered to all the citizens favors with the most ungrudging liberality, who never once in his whole life concealed or reserved for himself any thing that was good or excellent.[32]

Rome's most famous and greatest poet has the last word on the official imperial ideology suffused throughout society. Virgil's *Aeneid*, modeled on Homer's *Iliad* and *Odyssey*, eclipses his famous poems, *Eclogues* and *Georgics*, and became Rome's national epic, a foundational worldview narrative based on Augustus, whose birth Virgil effused,

Now a generation descends from heaven on high . . . smile on the birth of the child . . . and a golden race spring up throughout the world! Thine own Apollo now is king! . . . He shall have the gift of divine life, . . . and shall sway a world to which his father's virtues have brought peace. . . . O thou dear offspring of the gods, seed of Jupiter to be![33]

Luke's "born for you a Savior, who is Messiah the Lord . . . and on earth peace" (Luke 2:11, 14), subverts this Roman gospel, as does Paul.

Jews in Rome

Background to Romans is the history of Jews in Rome. Jews arrived in Rome in numbers with General Pompey's conquest of eastern territories. He seized Judea in 63 BC, and sent Jewish exiles to Rome.[34] The Jews were semi-hostages to insure the cooperation of the Judean province.

---

[32] Philo, *Embassy* 145–47. Again, "Our houses of prayer are manifestly incitements to all the Jews in every part of the habitable world to display their piety and loyalty towards the house of Augustus" (*Flacc.* 23).

[33] Virgil *Ecologue* 4.4–52. On the "gospel of Rome" as a serious and pervasive challenge to Paul's own gospel of God, cf. Rock, *Romans and Roman Imperialism*, 232–35.

[34] With Herodians (Josephus, *Ant.* 14.4.5). For Jews in Rome, see Barclay, *Jews in the Mediterranean Diaspora*, 282–319. Jews already had had contact with Rome. Judas Maccabees sent envoys to make alliances (1 Macc 8:17–22); Simon Maccabees also sent an embassy (1 Macc 14:24). Roman texts indicate early Jewish presence, as in Valerius Maximus *Memorable Sayings and Doings* 1.3.3. Jewish delegations often had contact with Rome (Josephus, *J.W.* 2.6.1). Jewish proselytizing surfaces in Horace, *Satires* 1.4.142–43, and the significant and noticeable synagogue attraction of outsiders paved the way for Jewish Christian mission, but especially for the Pauline message (Hengel/Schwemer, *Damascus and Antioch*, 76).

Later freed, they joined the freedman class.[35] By 59 BC, Jews were a significant enough presence in Rome to figure into Cicero's argument in a court case, even if exaggerated.[36] Julius Caesar confirmed that the Jews of Rome were allowed to assemble and follow their religious customs, and Jewish honor of Caesar at his funeral pyre was notable above all others.[37] More than eight thousand Jews gathered to support the Jewish delegation from Judea sent to register complaint to Augustus about the rule of Herod's son, Archelaus.[38] Jewish funerary inscriptions document at least thirteen synagogues in Rome.[39] Among the political elite of Jewish society, Herod Agrippa I, who ruled as king of Judea from 41–44, was schooled in Rome and personally knew both Caligula and Claudius, later emperors who promoted Agrippa's meteoric rise to power in Judea. Judean Jews likely were regular channels of Jerusalem news to Rome (Acts 28:21). Nero's second wife, Pompaea, looked well upon Judaism, so may have had a positive influence in Nero's court on behalf of the Jews.[40] Philo said Jews in Rome mostly lived across the Tiber River.[41] This part of Rome served as a Tiber river flood plain, so typically, was comprised of a population of lower class and economy.

This history reveals that Jews of Rome became a significant part of Rome's minority demographic in the century before Jesus was born, had their main source directly from Judea, and retained strong Jerusalem connections throughout their time in Rome, especially among the elite, but commercially among the business class as well. Historically close ties with Jerusalem meant that Roman Jews would incline in a conservative direction toward the cultic and social sensibilities of Jerusalem. Thus, as Paul writes Romans, Jews have been in Rome for almost a century, comprising forty to fifty thousand of Rome's one million inhabitants, about four percent of the total population.[42]

[35] Cf. the Synagogue of the Freedmen in Jerusalem that opposed Stephen (Acts 6:9).

[36] Cicero, *Flac.* 66–67.

[37] Josephus, *Ant.* 14.10.8. Suetonius, *Jul.* 84.5.

[38] Josephus, *Ant.* 17.11.1.

[39] Leon, *The Jews of Rome,* 135–66. Here, *synagōgē* means the "congregation" not the building, which more often is referred to as a "house of prayer" (*proseuchē*).

[40] Josephus, *Ant.* 20.8.11.

[41] Philo, *Embassy* 23.155–56.

[42] Leon, *The Jews of Rome,* 15. No European city rivaled Rome in size until London of the industrial revolution.

These combined assemblies were absent any central authority, as had Jerusalem with its high priest, so operated autonomously but co-operatively as needed.[43] Note Acts 28:17: "leaders of the Jews," is τοὺς ὄντας τῶν Ἰουδαίων πρώτους, "those who were first among the Jews," likely inferring the "leader" (*archisynagogos*) of each assembly.[44]

Early Church in Rome

The Roman church probably developed as a result of Pentecost. Luke indicates that Jews from Rome were present at Pentecost (Acts 2:10).[45] Pilgrims likely returned to Rome after the festival with their newfound faith. The earliest church in Rome, then, would have been totally Jewish and totally operational within the context of the synagogue.

FIGURE 5.30. Ancient Ostia Port Facilities. This area near the docks likely served as hotel and other shops for the bustling commercial activity of Rome's port city.

Another social ingredient playing into the origin of the church in Rome is commerce. Rome was the hub of the ancient mercantile world. Roman merchants traveled the world to bring the world's goods to this city. If all roads led to Rome, then all ships, so to speak, sailed to Rome. The second-century Roman, Aelius Aristides, gave this eulogy to the city of Rome as an encomium on behalf of his emperor.

---

[43] For absence of central authority in Rome, see Leon, *The Jews of Rome*, 167–94.

[44] Cf. Jairus (Mark 5:22); Luke 8:49; 13:14; Acts 13:15 (note plural); and Crispus and Sosthenes at Corinth (Acts 18:8, 17).

[45] No need to doubt this report as if anachronistic, as does Jewett, *Romans*, 60.

Around that sea [Mediterranean] lie the great continents [Africa, Asia, Europe] massively sloping down to it, forever offering you in full measure what they possess. Whatever each culture grows and manufactures cannot fail to be here at all times and in great profusion. Here merchant vessels arrive carrying these many commodities from every region in every season and even at every equinox, so that the city takes on the appearance of a sort of common market for the world. One can see cargoes from India and even, if you will, from southern Arabia in such numbers that one must conclude that the trees in those lands have been stripped bare, and if the inhabitants of those lands need anything, they must come here to beg for a share of what they have produced. Your farmlands are Egypt, Sicily, and all of cultivated Africa. Seaborne arrivals and departures are ceaseless, to the point that the wonder is, not so much that the harbor has insufficient space for all these merchant vessels, but that the sea has enough space (if it really does). Just as there is a common channel where all waters of the Ocean have a single source and destination, so that there is a common channel to Rome and all meet here: trade, shipping, agriculture, metallurgy—all the arts and crafts that are or ever were and all things that are produced or spring from the earth. What one does not see here does not exist. So it is not easy to decide which is the greater: the superiority of this city relative to cities that presently exist, or the superiority of this empire relative to all empires that ever existed.[46]

FIGURE 5.31. Ancient Ostia Mill Shop. Imported grain was processed at port millhouses with large stone grinders.

Commodities from "every region in every season" poured into Rome from India, Arabia, Egypt, Sicily, Africa, and points beyond, even silk from China, in the attempt to satiate Rome's lust for luxury. Most important was the supply of grain from the breadbasket of the Nile. A grain ship brought Paul to Rome through Puteoli, but Ostia later was Rome's port. Ostia helps document first-century Roman life in Italy. The city's extensive port facilities,

[46]Aristides, *To Rome* 11–13.

warehouses, market area, temples, luxury and *insula* apartments, and close contact with Rome illustrate life in Paul's Rome.

FIGURE 5.32. Ancient Ostia Market Shops. Shops around the forum advertised their owners and products through the mosaic art in the street at each shop entrance. This art included titles, fish, milling, elephants (an owner from Africa), and ships (grain).

FIGURE 5.33. Ancient Ostia Ship Mosaic. The grain ship mosaic advertises that this shop owner offered milled grain imported from Egypt on one of Rome's grain ships.

The economy of Rome was stratified without much of a middle class. Society had the wealthy, the common laborer operating on day wages, and the mass of unemployed poor. Wealth was limited to aristocrats and businessmen. Landed aristocracy formed the elite families of Rome with inherited wealth. A fast-growing empire sustained new commercial enterprises that created a new business class of wealthy merchants. Commercial activity also employed common day laborers, such as porters and warehousing labor, and supported shop owners with small businesses, such as taverns for food.

FIGURE 5.34. Ancient Ostia Wheat Warehouse. Numerous warehouses lined the streets near the harbor. This large wheat warehouse belonged to a merchant fortunate to be part of the wealthy businessmen's class who could serve as patrons in Roman society. Phoebe of Cenchreae likely served as Paul's patron for Paul's letter to the Romans.

FIGURE 5.35. Ancient Ostia Thermopolium. A thermopolium was a tavern serving ready to eat hot food. The selling counter on the left open to the street had a "menu" display on the right (center column) with an illustrative fresco above that would have been accompanied by food dishes displayed on the shelves below.

This merchant activity likely contributed to the development of the church at Rome. Merchants brought with them more than their goods

FIGURE 5.36. Ancient Ostia In-ground Storage. These large cisterns had been buried into the earth to keep cool the contents stored within them, such as wine and olive oil.

but their spiritual sensibilities as well. Of this number would be Prisca and Aquila (Acts 18:1). From various parts of society, then, the church at Rome conceivably had quite early, unstructured beginnings. While we can be confident of a general Jewish connection between Jerusalem and Rome, what we do not know is the connection of Peter and James to Rome. Direct connection of the church in Rome for its founding to either Peter or James is highly unlikely historically.[47]

Early Christianity in Rome mainly was located in four areas. Two areas were lower class, and two areas were upper class.[48] One lower class area was the Trastevere region, a flood plain west of the Tiber River creating a swampy terrain at the second lower bend in the river. The Trastevere region near the river supported a shipping economy of dock and warehouse workers, importers, tradesmen and their shops, millers

[47] Church origins in Rome are unknown. Apostolic traditions are late (Irenaeus *Adv. Haer.* 3; Gaius of Rome, in Eusebius *H.E.* 2.28). Fitzmyer (*Romans*, 36) asserted that Paul "recognizes that Christianity at Rome has been shaped mainly by that of Jerusalem and Judea, especially by that associated with James and Peter, . . ." Brown, however, is more cautiously judicious: "The paucity of hard evidence in the preceding paragraph indicates why in studying the history of Roman Christianity we do not turn first to the Peter and Paul stories, . . ." (*Antioch and Rome*, 98). Longenecker ignores Brown's caution, arguing Romans 1–4 is Peter's Jerusalem viewpoint (*Romans*, 9). Schweitzer dé·jà vu.

[48] The watershed study of early Christianity in Rome by Lampe, *Die stadtrömischen Christen in den ersten beiden Jahrhunderten* (1987) later was translated as *From Paul to Valentinus* (2003); cf. xiv, 410.

to grind grain, furniture, apparel, and other commodities. This dense population was housed in the *insula* apartments common to this urban demographic. A second lower-class area was situated near the Porta Capena, the gate that gave name to that region at the end of the Via Appia about 220 yards east, southeast of the curved end of the Circus Maximus. Lampe concluded the Romans 16 names reveal dominantly Greek background, so likely immigrant origins; a high proportion of the names was quite common to the slave class.[49] If these factors characterize these individuals, then the majority would have lived and labored in the lower class Trastevere and Porta Capena areas.

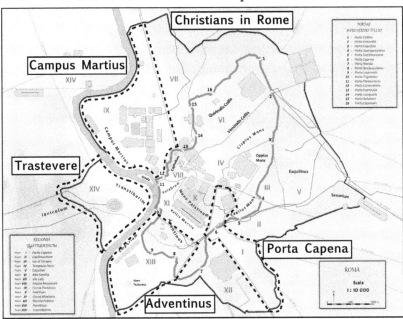

FIGURE 5.37. Christians in Rome. The classic study by Lampe has established the four main areas of habitation by Christians in Rome. The Campus Martius and Adventinus districts were wealthier. The Trastevere (Transtiberium) and Porta Capena districts housed the poorer classes.

The other two areas of Christian presence in Rome represented those of higher economic status. These districts were the Campus Martius (Field of Mars) and the Aventinus districts.[50] The Campus Martius was another flood plain, originally a marshy area at the upper bend of

[49] Lampe, *From Paul to Valentinus*, 182–83.
[50] Ibid., 59–63.

the Tiber River that was drained and used for martial activity but later hosted some of the magnificent building projects of the emperors. The Aventine distinct got its name from the Aventine Hill prominent in the area—a possible location for the residence of Prisca and Aquila, for example, the only actual "house church" mentioned in Romans 16.

In sum, early Christianity in Rome would be a Jewish movement within the synagogues until AD 49. That movement, while likely conservative, distinctively was non-apostolic in origin, so in some ways was independent of Peter, James, and Paul. Early growth seems to have been spontaneous. Later growth, due to historical events, moved decidedly toward a more multicultural, multiethnic profile enhanced by a major port city at the heart of an empire. As a result, the Roman church had unclear leadership structure, undifferentiated demographic profile, and unknown authority for its traditions. Roman Christianity without trying presented an unknown wild card in the early church endowed with its own sense of authority with which all Christian leadership at some point would have to come to terms. Paul made his bid in Romans.

Edict of Claudius

The Edict of Claudius, dated by Orosius to AD 49, changed Jewish life in Rome.[51] This edict responded to disturbances in synagogues.[52] The edict created two major changes. First, synagogue leadership was impacted.[53] Gentile proselytes potentially had to become leaders; so leadership

FIGURE 5.38. Chrestus Inscription. Roman sarcophagus with common name CHRESTVS, "Chrestus" (EMS).

---

[51] The date is challenged, but generally accepted. Cf. Jewett, *Romans*, 18–19.

[52] Suetonius (*Claud.* 25.4) indicts "Chrestus" ("Christos"?), i.e., preaching of Jesus as Messiah in synagogues in Rome? Cf. Riesner, *Paul's Early Period*, 163–66. For dissent, cf. Kim, *God, Israel and the Gentiles*, 50–56; Nanos, *Mystery of Romans*, 375–76.

[53] Elliott (*Rhetoric of Romans*, 48) argued only *Christian* Jews were targeted, a minority view, and implausible: Romans not yet were distinguishing Christians as Christians.

positions changed by necessity.[54] When the Edict of Claudius was rescinded in AD 54 after the ascension of his successor, expelled Jews returned, as apparently did Prisca and Aquila.[55] Return of such individuals might have caused leadership conflict in the synagogues.

Some synagogues may have had to close due to the effect of the decree. An earlier incident of Jewish expulsion from Rome under Tiberius resulted in four thousand punished as indentured soldiers, but an even "greater number" refused this route, so the total affected was around 25–33% of Jews in Rome at the time.[56] If Claudius's edict had a similar impact, Roman house churches could have had their historical impetus. Prisca and Aquila's home served in this capacity by the time Paul wrote Romans.[57] Early on, the numbers assembling in house churches were probably small. Still, these smaller, more informal assemblies in private homes naturally would be more conducive to gentile participation, so inherently were predisposed to have greater penetration into a broader social spectrum of Rome's inhabitants.

Romans may have tolerated Jewish presence in Rome, but edicts under Tiberius and Claudius reveal problems in that toleration, most especially if the attitudes of the Roman satirist Juvenal reveal popular prejudices.[58] The Edict of Claudius likely had significant impact on the social and racial composition of the church as well as its relationship to the synagogue. These relationships would endure inherent tensions. Social identity crisis would come into play. Furthermore, a change in the nature and location of the believing community seems already in progress with the new phenomenon of house churches as Paul writes.

[54] Luke indicates proselytes among Jews from Rome for Pentecost: Ἰουδαῖοί τε καὶ προσήλυτοι, "both Jews and proselytes" (Acts 2:10). "God-fearers" (Acts 10:1–2; 16:14; 18:7) might be another Roman synagogue demographic; cf. evidence from Aphrodisias, p. 99.

[55] Compare Acts 18:1 and Rom 16:3. Most edicts ceased at the emperor's death.

[56] Josephus, *Ant.* 18.3.5; Tacitus, *Ann.* 2.85. Cf. Merrill, "Expulsion of Jews." Oakes (*Reading Romans in Pompeii*, 73–75) unpersuasively rejects the edict's social impact.

[57] Rom 16:5 (cf. 1 Cor 16:19; Col 4:15; Phlm 2). A second assembly includes Asyncritus, Phlegon, Hermes, Patrobas, and Hermas (Rom 16:14). A third includes Philologus, Julia, Nereus, his sister, and Olympas (Rom 16:15). Finally, "household of" might allude to Aristobulus and Narcissus as hosts (Rom 16:10, 11). Whether these are all patron "house churches" is argued. Jewett, *Romans*, 64–69, argued for "tenement churches" with lower economic realities, discussed later. For the distinctly new social matrix of house churches, cf. Meeks, *The First Urban Christians*.

[58] Juvenal, *Satires* 14.96–106. Cf. Nanos, *Mystery of Romans*, 100.

Such changes redefine and relocate the church, offering a likely reason why the letter has so many greetings in Romans 16. Some of those greeted are the new leaders of individual house churches in Rome, loosening the early historical connection with the synagogue. From Paul's point of view, that loss might not be taken as so positive. Connection to the synagogue might have been one of the reasons that "many times" he "planned to come to you" (Rom 1:13).[59] Further, new leadership dynamics might calculate into the issue of the weak and the strong dealt with in Romans 14–15. Thus, the Edict of Claudius may have impacted Roman believers in multiple ways Paul thought undesired.

Emperor Nero

Claudius's successor, Nero, also had significant impact on the Roman context of Paul's letter. His administrative policies were raising issues long before the fire of Rome. Crucial to understand about Nero's reign to contextualize Romans is that Nero's career had two distinct phases: a good early reign (54–59), but a bad later reign (59–68). Paul composed Romans right in the middle of Nero's early reign (AD 57).[60] While taxation policies that agitated the public figure into Paul's advice in Romans 13, only later did Nero transform into the infamous megalomaniac ruler. When not under the guidance and oversight of his advisors, his real personality eventually came out. Nero lost all good advice and all good sense. This later tyrant is the Nero of the fire of Rome, the Nero most Christians "know."

Thus, the Nero infamous in Christian history is not the Nero Paul knew nor the Roman government with which Paul was familiar. Paul's own encounters with Roman governmental officials in the main were positive as far as can be determined from Acts.[61] Paul converts the Ro-

---

[59] The translation, "as I have had among the rest of the gentiles," is misleading. The "gentiles" term, ἔθνος (ethnos), more likely means "nations" here, an allusion to Isaiah's prophecies of the nations bringing offerings to Jerusalem, the essence of the collection for Jerusalem Paul is about to deliver (Rom 15:12, 16, 21). The expression, that is, is eschatological, not ethnic. The point is Israel's destiny with regard to the nations.

[60] Dividing Nero's reign into two parts, with an early five-year good period first was noted by the historian Aurelius Victor, Caes. 5.1–2.

[61] One exception is the negative experience when civic leaders inappropriately jailed Paul as a disturber of the peace in Philippi (Rom 16:19–24). Owners of a slave girl who abused her for commercial purposes manipulated Jewish prejudice and made false charges to imprison Paul after he healed the girl, causing their lost profit. Magistrates

man proconsul Sergius Paulus on Cyprus (Acts 13:12), is exonerated by the proconsul Gallio in Corinth (Acts 18:12–16), declared innocent by the Roman tribune Lysias (Acts 23:29), and declared innocent by the procurator Festus in Caesarea (Acts 26:25). Roman law, applied correctly, had kept Paul out of harm's way in multiple provinces of the empire. In these terms, government was serving its God-ordained purpose of keeping anarchy at bay and preserving general public order. This early Nero is the context of Romans 13.[62]

Life Setting of Jerusalem

By the time Paul wrote Romans, Jerusalem was on its way to war with the empire. Judea had a brief reprieve with the reign of Agrippa I as king (AD 41–44), but his untimely early death threw Judea back into its second procuratorship when his son, Agrippa II, was considered by the Romans too young and inexperienced to rule so problematic a province. Unfortunately, this second period of Roman procuratorship of Judea by the late 50s simply poured gas on the smoldering embers of resentment. Tacitus, even if exaggerating, gives the general profile by describing Felix, before whom Paul appeared multiple times (Acts 24–25), as "practicing every kind of cruelty and lust, he exercised royal power with the instincts of a slave."[63] Jesus in the early 30s anticipated increasing political turmoil in Judea inspired by false messiahs and false prophets agitating against Roman rule (Mark 13:21).

Jesus was prescient. Only thirty years later, Jewish nationalism had become intense. A religious attitude of zeal modeled on the action of Phineas (Num 25:1–11) evolved into a Jewish movement advocating armed rebellion against Rome, perhaps as early as Judas the Galilean in AD 6. Judas revolted against Rome turning Judea into a province with a census for taxation after Archelaus was banished to Gaul by Augustus. Zealotism turned refusal to pay taxes into a litmus test of Jewish fidelity to God (Matt 22:17). Paying taxes is an ancillary issue

immediately rectified the situation when violation of Roman legal procedure was discovered (Acts 16:35–39). Charges at Thessalonica came to naught (Acts 17:5–9).

[62] Paul's advice in Romans 13 is not a blank check for totalitarian regimes. The other side of the coin is the beast in Revelation 13 applied to the same Roman government. That is, government operating in direct opposition to God's purposes does not carry divine approbation. In fact, God will bring that government down (Revelation 18).

[63] Tacitus, *Hist.* 5.9.

Paul also felt compelled to deal with in the context of Neronian Rome. Recorded insurrection revolts by Theudas, Judas the Galilean, and the "Egyptian" infer still others unmentioned.[64] A group Josephus labeled as the Sicarii ("knife men") show the increasingly violent actions of the later 50s. Hiding daggers under their cloaks, they used the stealth of crowds to draw close and kill Jewish leaders in Jerusalem blacklisted in collusion with Rome.[65]

Paul's story intersects with that of the Sicarii. The Roman tribune in Jerusalem seized Paul from a rioting mob. The tribune accused Paul of being the Egyptian leader of the "assassins" (Acts 21:38). Paul knew Jerusalem's political tensions first hand. The tribune allowed Paul to address the riotous mob. "I was zealous for God just as all of you are today," Paul confessed (Acts 21:3). He defined that zeal as willingness to put to death followers of the Way (Acts 22:4). In a twist of irony after the accusation of the tribune, Paul admitted he once reflected the Sicarii goal of execution for religious purposes.

FIGURE 5.39. Tribune Sarcophagus. Mounted tribune in battle (KAM).

The riot just days later showed that James had every right to be concerned about Paul's presence in Jerusalem. James had to contend with thousands of Jewish believers "zealous for the law" suspecting Paul's Jewishness (Acts 21:20). Suspect Jewishness in the face of rising nationalism and intense political agitation was a powder keg James was trying to keep from exploding. So, the Jerusalem church was not immune from the political turmoil of the times and intense pressure toward Jewish nationalism. Who is a true Jew and what does true Jewishness look like? That question had a multitude of answers in the late 50s when Paul wrote his letter to Rome. Life and death for many depended on the answer, as even with those enduring the persecution of one Saul of Tarsus brandishing letters of Sanhedrin authority (Acts 22:5). Paul knew Jewish zeal firsthand (Rom 10:2).

[64] Josephus, *Ant.* 20.5.1; 18.1.1 (*J.W.* 2.8.1); 20.8.6 (*J.W.* 2.13.5).

[65] Josephus, *J.W.* 2.13.3; 4.7.2; *Ant.* 20.8.10.

FIGURE 5.40. Arch of Titus. Built by his brother, Domitian, in Titus's honor after Titus's death in AD 81, the Arch of Titus holds a commanding position at the apex of the "Sacred Way," or main processional street of Rome. The route visually connected the Colosseum valley to the Forum valley. For centuries, public triumphs paraded down this "Sacred Way." The Roman triumph was a military tradition dating to the legendary founding of Rome by Romulus, who celebrated his victory over king Acron of Caenina with a public parade. Generals in the later Roman Republic repeated this military tradition and built memorial columns and arches to commemorate the occasion. The victorious general's face was stained red with cinnabar to evoke the reputed countenance of the god Jupiter. Titus and Vespasian celebrated their victory over the Jews in the First Jewish War (AD 66–70) with such a parade in AD 71, vividly described by Josephus, a likely eyewitness (*J.W.* 7.116–62; 7.5.3–7). After the First Jewish War, the world changed irrevocably for Jerusalem, the temple, and the Jewish nation. Inheritors of the Great Assembly traditions totally had to reimagine Jewish faith and life. For author's video, see https://drkoine.com/movies/4jr/RomeArchTitus.mp4.

FIGURE 5.41. Arch of Titus Menorah Relief. The southern interior passageway of the Arch of Titus shows Jewish temple items paraded down the streets of Rome in AD 71. The relief stands about seven feet high. Temple items displayed include the gold menorah lamp, the gold trumpets, and the table of showbread. Recent work shows that the gold objects were painted a dramatic yellow ochre against a blue background. Mosaic ritual disappeared, but the Law lived on, totally reimagined for a new day.

FIGURE 5.42. Arch of Titus Chariot Relief. The northern interior passageway of the Arch of Titus depicts triumphal Titus being led by lictors (bodyguards to magistrates) carrying *fasces* (bound wooden rods symbolizing jurisdictional power) and *genii* (symbolic representations) of the Senate, the Roman people, and Virtus, the Roman god of bravery and military strength (Greek: Arete). Titus drives the quadriga four-horse chariot. Goddess Victory crowns him from behind with a laurel wreath.

The First Jewish War was a watershed moment in Jewish history. This war broke out only six years after Paul had appealed to leaders of Rome's synagogues about Jesus as God's Messiah (Acts 28:17–28).

FIGURE 5.43. Jerusalem Shekels. Jewish Revolt silver shekels minted in Jerusalem AD 68/69. Obverse: omer cup with pearled rim, date above, "Shekel of Israel." Reverse: sprig of three pomegranates and "Jerusalem the Holy" (PMB).

SLAVERY AND HOUSING

Slavery as Society

Everyone recognizes right away with zero need for explanation that if the Wall Street institution of the New York Stock Exchange vanished overnight, the economy of the United States would collapse catastrophically and irrevocably, and the country would be plunged into chaos and ruin. Slavery, in effect, was the Wall Street of the ancient world. The institution of slavery was the essence of the entire economic and social system. No ancient person even could conceive a world without slaves, most especially since slaves made up an incredible proportion of any population, particularly the urban centers. Slaves comprised from a third to almost one half of the population of Italy alone.[66] Thus, in the ancient world, we should speak not so much slavery *in* society as slavery *as* society. Even the law of Moses presumed slavery without comment over its propriety.[67] The New Testament does as well.[68] At the same time, New Testament writers set new standards for slave-master relationships and new trajectories of thought that eventually would challenge slavery's legitimacy in a just society.[69]

The main source of slavery was war. Lose a war, become a slave. Be a general on the battlefield one day, and a slave on the market the next. Thus, after losing the First Jewish War, thousands of Jewish captives from Judea were deported as slaves to Rome. In a strange twist of fate, Jerusalem temple treasury funds and Jewish captives from the First Jewish War financed and built the Roman Colosseum.

[66] Jeffers, *Greco-Roman World*, 221.

[67] Gen 17:12–13; Exod 12:44; 20:10; 21:2, 20; Lev 19:20; Deut 5:14; 15:7.

[68] Matt 6:24; 8:9; 10:24; 24:45; 26:51; Mark 10:44; Luke 7:2; 12:43; Jesus's parables.

[69] Acts 2:18; 1 Cor 7:21; 9:19; 12:13; 2 Cor 4:5; Gal 3:28; 4:7; Phil 2:7; Eph 6:5; Col 4:1; 1 Tim 1:10; Titus 2:9; Phlm 16; 1 Pet 2:18.

FIGURE 5.44. Roman Colosseum. Financed and built with Jewish temple treasury funds and Judean slaves from the First Jewish War, the Flavian Amphitheater became one of the greatest monuments of the ancient world. Construction took eight years from AD 72–80, begun by Vespasian and finally completed and dedicated by Titus.

One also could sell oneself into slavery for various reasons: financial, agricultural, commercial, or social distress. Any child born to a slave was a slave. Manumission (freedom) was possible over time. Liberty usually was purchased after saving money over time, or granted according to concluding the legally specified service period. Freedom even could be given by a grateful slave owner, or for some other reason in a relationship, a situation Paul seems to anticipate for Onesimus (Phlm 12–21). However, once a slave, even if freedom was purchased, granted, or given beneficently, one socially never escaped slave status. Hence, after manumission, one was frozen in status as only a "freedman," never anything more.

FIGURE 5.45. Slave Bill of Sale. Bill of sale for a female slave: "Titos, son of Lykos, buys from Amphotera a two-month old slave girl. The girl's name is Nike. The price is set at fifteen silver pieces" (TAM).

Yet, even for freedmen, power and wealth still could be

FIGURE 5.46. Slave Manumission. Grave stele commending the freeing of a female slave by her mistress. The slave joined the "freedman" status in society (TAM).

FIGURE 5.47. Comic Actor as Slave. First to second-century AD bronze statue of a comedian, from Egypt. The actor is playing the role of a slave in a comedy. As did all actors on the ancient stage, he wears a mask suited to the role played, with the typical funnel-shaped mouth. Theater masks were worn to project an emotion appropriate to the role played to an audience seated at a distance in the cavea. This actor is wearing a chiton tunic high-girdled at the chest with a belt, along with a close-fitting theater costume. The stereotypical comic plot is that the slave has run away from his strict master and seeks salvation at an altar in a nearby sanctuary where he has been lucky to find asylum. Runaway slaves were a frequent problem in ancient society, usually caught, with severe penalties, even death (PMB).

attainable. Slaves functioned everywhere—home, field, business, education, construction, and civic administration—because these were places they functioned before enslavement. Slaves were chattel to be traded indiscriminately, even separating family members. Laws universally disfavored slaves, who had few rights. Some slave owners treated their slaves decently, but others were quite cruel, inducing runaways.[70] Most slave work was menial, but some could achieve upward mobility and status in society. They could earn money, own property, and have families.

FIGURE 5.48. Herculaneum: House of the Freedman. Also known as the House of the Black Hall, the freedman Lucius Venidius Ennychus owned this mansion. Pictured is the peristyle (open courtyard surrounded by columns) whose covered ambulatories were paved with gray and black mosaic floors in rows of white tesserae and a white double border. The columns were stuccoed brick. The courtyard had a small garden.

One example of upward mobility is the house of the Vettii in Pompeii. This largest domus in all of Pompei was owned by two successful freedmen, Aulus Vettius Conviva and Aulus Vettius Restitutus. Another example of upward mobility for some slaves is the House of the Black Hall in Herculaneum, one of most luxurious mansions of the city, owned by the freedman Lucius Venidius Ennychus. Its monumental front entrance on the street side still retains the carbonized remains of the huge wooden beams of the doorposts and lintel after destruction by Vesuvius in AD 79. A video walk-through is available online.[71]

---

[70] Probably the cruelest, most inhuman of all were slave traders themselves, universally condemned. Of their vice, see Harrill, *Slaves in the New Testament*, 119–44.

[71] Video: https://drkoine.com/movies/4jr/Herculaneum09-HouseBlackHall.mp4.

Calculating sociological dimensions of ancient slavery for under-standing New Testament texts is not easy. How did becoming part of a house church impact slaves, especially those of menial servitude? How would that slave "hear" certain New Testament texts? To answer these type questions, Oakes used space allocation analysis of an insula block in Pompeii to construct a sociological model to show the structure and relationships of a house church of a typical craftworker in Pompeii. He then adjusted the model to compensate for urban differences be-tween Pompeii and Rome and the density of population. What would that house church look like? Oates's model suggests about thirty non-elites exhibiting significant social diversity and hierarchy. Relationships still would endure complications conflicted by patronage and honor-shame codes. In one of many problematic scenarios, if one belonged to a household whose head was an unbeliever, and that person joined a house church sponsored by another head of household with differ-ent social obligations and loyalties, social tensions could result.[72]

Take, for example, Iris, mentioned in tavern graffiti in Pompeii, slave of a woman tavern owner. Food and drink taverns were not the equivalent of a neighborhood Starbucks. Roman jurists exempted fe-male tavern workers from adultery prosecution since prostitution sim-ply was assumed part of business, so charges of adultery did not apply, even as late as Constantine.[73] Ancient writers reveal great prejudice to-ward these slaves.[74] Paul's admonitions against sexual immorality and exhortations to sanctification would be difficult for Iris to hear, since she had no volitional control over her body.[75] She would experience sig-nificant cognitive dissonance.[76] Yet eternal life and bodily redemption as in Romans 8 would resonate for Iris in deeply personal terms.[77]

Paul offers guidance for relationships of slaves and masters, as is common in house codes of the first century. Paul, however, provides a

[72] Peter Oakes, *Reading Romans in Pompeii.*

[73] *Theodosian Code* 9.7.1; English translation, Maas, *Readings in Late Antiquity*, 253. Cf. Osiek and MacDonald, *A Woman's Place*, 276, n4.

[74] Detailed by Meggitt, *Paul, Poverty and Survival*, 109–111.

[75] As in 1 Corinthians 5–6; 1 Thess 4:3–8; Rom 6:12–14; cf. Glancey, *Slavery in Early Christianity*, 49–50, 58, 63–70.

[76] Detailed by Oakes, *Reading Romans in Pompeii*, 143–49.

[77] Ibid., 149. Sex trafficking is as much a problem today around the world, but not much addressed in the church.

FIGURE 5.49. Pompeii Thermopolium. A *thermopolium* was the ancient equivalent of a fast food restaurant exposed to pedestrian traffic on the street, often in an open "L" or "U" shape. Pompeii had over 150 of these establishments, indicating a significant number of the population got their lunch and dinner this way. The customer base was mostly plebeian, who could not afford their own kitchens, so could not prepare hot food at home. Customers sat at the marble countertops to eat food, drink wine, and socialize. The round circles are the openings to large storage jars called *dolia* recessed into the counters that stored hot food. A stove or oven was recessed into the wall for heating and cooking. Fish, cheese, and bread were staples, as well as honey and spiced wine for a sweet taste. Since drunkenness and vagrancy were associated with these establishments by upper class Romans, they would not be found frequenting them. The owner of the establishment usually domiciled in the connected apartment space. Sometimes the owner of the property rented out the street space to a tavern proprietor (man or woman).

FIGURE 5.50. Pompeii Amphorae. Jars with two handles flanking a thin neck, amphorae had pointed bottoms both for tight cargo stacking in ships and for stable pouring. They stored wet and dry goods, but mostly wine, servicing, for example, the many *thermopolia* of Pompeii.

foundation for ennobling those relationships in ways that go beyond the typical mores of his culture. Paul also regularly uses the imagery of slavery as a metaphor for descriptions of how sin works, as well as for the spiritual transition from one lordship to another.[78] Still, the sociological structures of ancient society would make this particular aspect of the world a quite difficult maze to negotiate on any terms. We must not forget that Paul himself seemed resigned to these realities of slavery as society, not slavery in society. The institution was pervasive and impervious to change in one lifetime. He advised Corinthians not to let social status, particularly slavery, be a concern (1 Cor 7:20–24).

Paul used the institution of slavery in multiple ways in his letters. Romans illustrates this usage from several angles. Significantly for a study of Romans, the very first word that Paul invokes after giving his name at the letter's beginning, literally the second word in the Greek text of Romans, is the word "slave" (δοῦλος, *doulos*). "Paul, *slave* of Messiah Jesus" (Rom 1:1). The premier idea Paul wanted the Romans first to associate with his name was not "apostle." Rather, he considered the word "slave" the crucial word to associate with his name for the believers in Rome. That tidbit is a key exegetical nuance to notice, most particularly when you know where he is going when in Romans 6 he extends the slave metaphor for five continuous verses and then hooks the following discussion into that metaphor (Rom 6:16–20; 7:6). The key issue of life is not freedom. For Paul, we are all born slaves (Rom 7:14). The key issue of life is lordship. Human existence is slavery to some lord from start to finish, true since Adam (Rom 5:12). Gaining spiritual life, then, is not so much gaining individual freedom for Paul as a change of lordship. Experience of transferred lordship is Israel's own story from Egypt to Sinai—from Pharaoh to Yahweh. Covenant was a way to live out that new lordship. So, the very first descriptor Paul wants the Romans to know about himself is whose slave he is. That slave reality (lordship issue) becomes foundational to Paul's explanation of the hidden power of the life of messianic Israel (Rom 8:9) as well as Paul's solution to the weak/strong issue troubling at least some house churches in Rome (Rom 14:7–8).

---

[78] Rom 6:16–20; 7:6, 14, 25; 8:15; 1 Cor 7:21; 9:19; 12:13; 2 Cor 4:5; 11:20; Gal 3:28; 4:1, 7, 22, 30; 5:1, 13; Eph 6:5, 8; Phil 2:7; Col 3:11, 22; 4:1; 1 Tim 1:10; 6:1; Titus 2:3, 9; 3:3; Phlm 16.

Another example in Romans of Paul interacting with social constructs related to slavery is the word "barbarian" (βάρβαρος, *babaros*).[79]

Since slaves often came from foreign wars in the far-flung borders of the empire, Romans, following Greek tradition, regarded slaves culturally as uncivilized and not inclined to be civilized. These barbarians were wild, cultureless, and lawless. Gladiator combat was constructed to propagate Roman ideology and cultural values. In these contests, barbaric costumes and weapons stereotyped the outer wild regions of the world to be conquered and subdued for peace and security of all, and the combatants often were foreign slaves. The contests were rigged to insure gladiators representing Rome and her values won the victory. Paul's gospel, he tells Roman believers, is precisely for these "wild,"

FIGURE 5.51. Gladiator Stele. Alkeiaes from Ephesus, who fought as a thraex-class gladiator (Thracian style) armed with crested helmet, greaves, small shield, and curved short blade (*sica*) to injure his opponent's exposed back. Usually staged against a murmillo-class gladiator armed as a Roman legionary. The murmillo gladiator usually won, as with Alkeiaes, epitomizing Roman conquest of barbarians (AAM).

uncultured humans of no worth to civilized people (Rom 1:14). This rare rhetoric in the New Testament prepares for later mention of Spain

---

[79] Rom 1:14. Foreign speech sounded to the Greeks like "nonsensical" repetitions, similar to "bar-bar-bar." They mimicked such sounds by doubling syllables as "bar-bar," thus creating "barbarian" (onomatopoetic formation); cf. Herodotus *Hist.* 2.158; Ps 114:1.

on the empire's western fringes (Rom 15:24).[80] Spain's "barbarian" will be Paul's mission focus, hopefully Rome's as well, pending prejudices.

Tenement Housing

FIGURE 5.52. Ancient Ostia *Insula*. Steps leading up to crowded *insula* apartments at the port city of Ostia about eighteen miles outside of Rome.

FIGURE 5.53. Ancient Ostia Baths of Neptune. Beautiful mosaic bathhouse floor built by emperors Hadrian (117–138) and Antoninus Pius (138–161). Neptune drives a chariot encircled by marine creatures: dolphins, tritons, and Nereids riding sea monsters.

[80] Acts 28:2, 4; Rom 1:14; 1 Cor 14:11; Col 3:11.

FIGURE 5.54. Caesarea Aqueduct. Herod the Great built Caesarea Maritima (22–10 BC) as the capital of the province of Judea at the site of Strato's Tower. He capitalized on Roman underwater construction technique to create the breakwater, as well as building a ten mile long aqueduct for water supply from the springs near Shuni.

First, we must not romanticize or modernize ancient city life. Life in the city was full of threat, darkness, disease, death, squalor, refuse, fire— all of which served as metaphors in Paul's letters.[81] Second, when we speak of "house churches," we easily can assume we mean houses like middle-class, suburban America. An ancient house church is a small assembly of people challenged for space and privacy, unless one had the good fortune of a wealthy patron, perhaps as were Prisca and Aquila.[82] They might have owned a domus in Rome accommodating twenty to thirty people, like the House of the Freedman in Herculaneum.

The vast majority of residents in Rome, however, lived in crowded, multistory, tenement housing.[83] These were apartments, or *insulae*, and

[81] Cf. Williams, *Paul's Metaphors*, 7–31.

[82] Their residence in multiple places such as Corinth (Acts 18:2) and Ephesus (Acts 18:19), as well as permanent residence in Rome (Rom 16:3), indicate a couple with business class status of some means; *contra* Oakes, *Reading Romans in Pompeii*, 45, 76–77.

[83] Jeffers, *Greco-Roman World*, 59. For the meaning of ancient *insula*, cf. Wallace-Hadrill, "*Domus* and *Insulae* in Rome." Oakes (*Reading Romans in Pompeii*, 33) cautioned dichotomizing house churches into only elite houses or non-elite apartments.

can be illustrated at the ancient site of Ostia, port city of Rome at the mouth of the Tiber River.[84] The single-room spaces might be no more than 1000–1200 square feet for one family.[85] Challenges in such spaces included privacy, maintenance, tenure stability, personal hygiene, and general safety due to frequent fires. A manager often fed tenants by delivering food from a common kitchen. If without windows, these spaces could be dark, damp, and without good ventilation. Such living arrangements set the context for the ritual of Roman baths supplied by Roman aqueducts. Here one caught up with daily news, conversation, business, and relaxation. The ubiquitous bathhouses offered rare relief from the stench and squalor of typical city life.

The matter of residence accommodations plays directly into conceptualizing church meetings in Rome. The tenement housing could not accommodate patron-style church meetings of the "house church" paradigm met elsewhere in the New Testament.[86] "Church" of necessity would have to take place in rented and shared space. This type of arrangement may be represented in the four groups in Romans 16. They operate without a patron and without obvious internal hierarchy. Economic support and charity efforts would rely on contributions from all as a collective, egalitarian effort. Meetings and ritual likewise would take community cooperation. A communal shared meal would function on multiple levels as social event, sustenance provision, and shared ritual integrated as a "love feast" that included observance of the Lord's Supper on a pattern insinuated in 1 Cor 11:17–22. Attempting to express authority or offer exhortations in such amorphous social settings might have been a challenge for Paul as he wrote Romans.[87] Oates, however, considers this distinction not nuanced enough, since individuals still would be confronted with a highly stratified economic and social structure even within a tenement setting of typical craftworkers. Oates charges that Jewett's tenement "egalitarian" model ignores these social dynamics still in play.[88]

---

[84] Ruins of Ostia date to the first century. Cf. Packer, *The Insulae of Imperial Ostia*.

[85] Frier, *Landlords and Tenants*, 3–5.

[86] Acts 16:15; 17:7; Rom 16:5, 23; 1 Cor 1:11; 16:15, 19; Col 4:16; 3 John 5–6.

[87] For a fuller presentation, see Jewett, *Romans*, 64–69. He suggests the labeling of "tenement churches" rather than "house churches" to evoke the social difference.

[88] Oakes, *Reading Romans in Pompeii*, 70, 91–92.

PURPOSE OF ROMANS

Literary Exigencies

Letter Frame

Romans has an unusual connecting frame. Matters said ambiguously in the beginning are made explicit at the end. Why did not Paul state matters clearly at the beginning?

As an example, when Paul says at the beginning that he has been hindered from coming to Rome (1:13), why does he not just say at that point what has hindered him, that is, first delivering his collection to Jerusalem, which he does say at the end (15:20–22, 25)? This initial ambiguity is especially puzzl-

Rhetorical Strategy: General to Specific	
Romans 1	*Romans 15*
"hindered" (1:13)	collection (15:22)
"come" (1:11)	"through" (15:28)
"evangelize" (1:14)	Spain (15:28)

FIGURE 5.55. Rhetorical Ambiguity. The letter frame discloses ambiguous rhetorical strategy.

ing since Paul could give the impression, absent such explanation, that he wanted to come to Rome in order to take over. Further, when Paul does get specific in Romans 15, the topic is mostly about Paul himself: his mission strategy, travel, plans. Why does Paul wait fifteen chapters to make his intentions clear? Perhaps the material in the middle (i.e., the letter body) is *necessary* before he can state his *intentions* clearly. The Romans connecting frame reveals two literary elements: (1) intentional rhetorical strategy that delays being specific until the end, and (2) a specificity that makes everything about Paul. The letter of Romans is as much about Paul as about the Romans. The rhetorical feature of general to specific suggests the body of the letter is meant to define Paul, an intention that percolates to the surface sometimes in the pronouns, such as the curious expression "my gospel" (Rom 2:16; cf. Rom 16:25; 2 Tim 2:8). Thus, the letter frame reveals Paul himself is integral to the purpose of the letter. What is crucial to Paul becomes the focus of the letter. However, we need to rethink whether this focus is summed up *exclusively* by the word "gentile." Romans is all about Israel.[89]

---

[89] "Instead, what is needed to understand Paul's Gentile concern is a more Israel-centered framework" (Donaldson, "Israelite , Convert, Apostle to the Gentiles," 77).

Letter Body

The body of the letter is befuddling, because the letter starts off like a personal letter, but the body of the letter is anything but. Descriptive terms for describing the literary character of the body such as treatise, literary dialogue, letter essay, or ambassadorial letter are trying to peg this enigma. Scholars have a tendency to want to turn this enigmatic body of the letter into Paul's stab at systematic theology. Bornkamm's "last will and testament"[90] and similar ideas that Romans is a summary of Pauline theology do not get out of the gate. They offer no exigency for the long exhortation in Romans 14–15, or come off as sleight of hand trying to hide that the word "church," for example, never occurs once in all of Romans 1–15, or that the term "righteousness" crucial in Romans never occurs even once in 1–2 Thessalonians or Colossians, and only once in 1 Corinthians (and that only at the beginning).

The letter body, however characterized, intends to interpret Paul to the Roman believers. The letter body needs to define Paul for what Paul is trying to accomplish with the Romans. First, Paul is trying to offer a gospel solution to perceived divisions in Rome, but he does not want to do this offensively. Second, Paul also is working his mission to Spain. Roman support would ground his mission financially. Roman believers cannot contribute to the collection for Jerusalem. In the first place, the collection is from churches Paul founded. Yet, the Roman church can assimilate into the Pauline mission if they have a mind to do so. If they choose to align with Pauline churches in support of Paul, they can align with the intent of the collection to represent the Pauline mission. Romans therefore could "give" to the collection by giving in support of the Spanish mission of which the collection is symbolic.

Letter Length

Another interesting area is the letter's length. The letter of Romans is very long, even by ancient standards. The long letters of Cicero are not nearly as long as Romans. Ironically, this Paul's longest letter was written to a church not even his own! Thus, a rhetorical enigma surrounds this letter's length. One might wonder if Paul wore out his welcome

---

[90] Bornkamm, "The Letter to the Romans as Paul's Last Will and Testament," 31. Melanchthon's "compendium of all Christian doctrine" comment has been misrepresented; cf. Plummer, "Melanchthon as Interpreter of the New Testament," 1–3.

before Phoebe even started reading the "letter." Roman believers may have had their doubts the moment she first pulled out this obviously lengthy document that feigned being a personal letter.[91]

Length is not the only letter enigma. The letter also is hard to understand. Paul's complex arguments go on for chapters. What is this? An immediate guess is that the length and complexity of the letter is probably because Paul never has met the Roman church face-to-face. Paul carefully walks a fine line with an unknown community. Even so, surely Paul would not have expended such energy, expense, and time without something important on the line.[92]

Letter Audience

Of course, the letter is written to "all who are in Rome" (Rom 1:7).[93] Beyond the formulaic letter opening, though, Romans has a curious addressee enigma. Romans is one of the vaguest of Paul's letters on this score. Rather than say Jews and gentiles, as often assumed in the context of interpeting Romans 14–15, Paul says "the weak and the strong." To whom is Paul talking?

We can ask this question of Paul in many verses of the letter. Commentators differ concerning Paul's particular addressees throughout the letter. Paul will say "gentile" when the material sounds Jewish, and "Jew" when the material sounds gentile. Statements Paul makes in Romans are like a boomerang. He looks like he is shooting for a particular target, but later the statement travels all the way back around to hit the unsuspecting reader in the back of the head. If Paul looks like he is trying to hit the Jew, then chances are that he really is aiming for the gentile. Likewise, if Paul looks like he is trying to hit the gentile, then chances are that he really is aiming for the Jew.

In addition, Romans rhetorically often is not what appears on the surface. One might identify kerygma, diatribe, ambassadorial rhetoric, or midrashic elements on the surface, but Paul uses a variety of rhe-

---

[91] Or, Phoebe and Tertius together; cf. Jewett, *Romans*, 23.

[92] Richards estimated weeks, if not months, were necessary to compose and copy Romans, at a cost of over $2200 (*Paul and First-Century Letter Writing*, 161–70). Adjusted for inflation, the figure today would be more like $3200.

[93] The phrase "in Rome" at Rom 1:7, 15 is missing in one Greek manuscript (G) and inferred missing in a few others. The issue is minor. Cf. Fitzmyer, *Romans*, 47–48.

torical strategies to communicate his point innovatively. The nature of his innovation is not always easy to catch.[94]

Integrative Purpose

Three life settings in Paul, Rome, and Jerusalem combine with strange literary exigencies of letter frame, letter body, letter length, and letter enigma to suggest an occasion matrix to tease out the purpose.[95] This purpose of Romans in general terms is to gain support for three goals.[96]

First, Paul is trying to gain *support for his gospel*, an apologetic aim. If Paul gains support for his gospel, then he will be able to help the Romans with their internal conflicts. He is confident his gospel brings God's power to bear in merciful ways to Jews and Greeks alike. He wants to unleash that power upon the Roman church in ways he perceives they critically need precisely at this time.[97]

Second, Paul is trying to gain *support for his leadership*, a pastoral aim. In other Pauline letters, Paul is assumed writing congregations because he is their pastor. However, Paul is not the pastor of the Roman church; why would he even be concerned? Why does Paul even have a pastoral inclination toward the church? For one, his gentile mission provokes him with a sense of obligation (Rom 1:6, 13–14). Roman congregations for the last seven or eight years since the Edict of Claudius have been evolving away from their historical Jewish roots in Roman synagogues, likely becoming more gentile. Thus, the Roman church almost uniquely has met the profile of both Pauline missions (Israel, gentiles). At first, the church had a profile to meet Paul's Israel mission; hence, he has wanted to come for "many years" (Rom 15:23). Recently, however, the church has become less Jewish, so has evolved to express more Paul's Diaspora mission.

This important *Roman context* to the "gentile" issue seems often unrecognized in commentaries so focused on the "Jew-gentile issue."

---

[94] Such as making elements of Romans 7 look like *prosōpopoiia* (speech in character) when he really more simply is just modeling Jewish lament rhetoric.

[95] A helpful analysis of classic arguments is Wedderburn, *The Reasons for Romans*.

[96] Building on Dunn, *Romans 1–8*, liv–lviii.

[97] Asking whether Paul was aware of problems in Rome seems moot considering the massive literary task at hand. Prisca and Aquila, close partners in Corinth (Acts 18:1–3) and Ephesus (Acts 18:18–19), returned to Rome (Rom 16:3), are one probable source.

Not only is this church becoming less Jewish. More importantly, *the church in Rome is becoming more Roman.*[98] A Roman hubris has manifested itself in the house churches since the edict. Non-Jewish converts bring latent Roman prejudice against Jews. These attitudes have gone unchecked since the silencing of the previously dominant Jewish voice of the church due to Claudius's edit.[99] Upon the return of Jewish church members to Rome, these latent, prejudicial Roman attitudes have flared. Paul writes hoping that he can offer pastoral leadership without being perceived as lording his authority over the Roman church. He has himself been the target of prejudicial attitudes of a different kind in Corinth by what he dubbed as his "super-apostle" opponents, a crisis only recently resolved (2 Cor 11:5).

New, Augustan social mores also figure in. Paul's Greco-Roman world was an honor-shame, patron-client world.[100] The Augustan cultural value of pietas often is translated as "piety," which comes up short. *Pietas* was showing proper respect for tradition that brought honor. Augustus built his world on the foundation of showing proper pietas. This emphasis shows up in statuary. Replacing the old style of representing the emperor in Greek heroic nude evoking divinity, Augustan Roman statuary started portraying the emperor as the epitome of *pietas*. A new imperial "brand" displayed covered head performing religious duties as *pontifex maximus*, that is, as "high priest" of Roman religion (12 BC). The point of showing *pietas* was in order to compete for honor, thereby gaining glory. Yet one wanted to do so subtly enough so that others did your boasting for you. Augustus as the Roman "high priest" instantly was

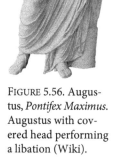

FIGURE 5.56. Augustus, *Pontifex Maximus.* Augustus with covered head performing a libation (Wiki).

[98] Note the sociological analysis applied to Rome and Antioch that reveal differences in Roman profiles in Hood, "A Socio-Anthropological Analysis."

[99] Later turned on Christians themselves; cf. Wilken, *The Christians as the Romans Saw Them*; not adopting here Jewett's anti-imperial hermeneutic of European colonialism (*Romans*, xv), dedicating his commentary to anti-colonialist, John William Colenso.

[100] Malina, *New Testament World*; deSilva, *Honor, Patronage, Kinship and Purity*; Hanson and Oakman, *Palestine in the Time of Jesus*.

ahead of the pack in competing for *pietas*. We already noted how Philo was so impressed with how Augustus handled himself in this way. One need not boast as long as others like Philo were boasting for you.

Note that boasting is a root cause of problems addressed in Romans 9–11. This motif is a key ingredient to Paul's discussion. He is targeting Roman attitudes toward Israel, which ironically only inverts Jewish attitudes to pagans (Rom 11:18; 2:17). Boasting in this context is not a nebulous "gentile thing" happening in some amorphous "gentile way." Boasting in Romans 11 is Roman, heritage of the Augustan Age.

Third, Paul is working to gain support for his *mission*, a missional aim. Admittedly, this goal is not explicit until the end in Romans 15. The question looms. Why would Paul think the Romans *should* be involved in his mission? They most certainly are not a church he has founded. They also are not like Antioch in which he faithfully labored for a year and consequently was commissioned by them on mission (Acts 11:26; 13:2–3). The answer requires understanding the symbolism with which Paul endues the collection, clarified in Romans 15. The collection represents the fruit of Paul's missionary labors on behalf of Israel among the nations. Paul wants the collection to represent Jerusalem's acceptance of the fruit of his Diaspora mission. Indued with this symbolic significance, the collection Paul believes can have Roman "participation" as symbolic support of Paul's work. Paul has lost his base in Ephesus, so is without a sponsoring church. Corinth just has completed their collection contribution; request for more assistance for yet another program from Paul would be unseemly. Thus, Rome could help with the "collection" by helping Paul with Spain.[101]

Yet, pastorally, Paul has two other goals with the collection he wants to accomplish in Rome. Paul endows the collection as a symbol of unity. In Paul's message, no unity means no gospel. Gentiles being accepted by Jerusalem would show the church being unified in Christ. Jews and the nations together praising God would fulfill the prophets related to eschatological Israel (Rom 15:7–12). By participation in the collection, Rome would be showing the concord of the Roman church as a part of messianic Israel as well. Rome's position on this point Paul would not assume, given its Jerusalem origins but obscure traditions in

[101] A point emphasized by Kümmel as a purpose for Romans (*Introduction*, 305–07).

the context of Paul's troubled relationship with Jerusalem. So, Paul also desires Rome's external confirmation of the unity of the church.

However, even more, he needs internal confirmation as well. The external confirmation rings rather hollow if the church internally is divided. Paul needs the Roman church itself to be unified. If the collection symbolizes the unity of the church, including acceptance of the Pauline mission, then Paul also wants to achieve unity in Rome so that the Roman church itself can symbolize what the collection represents.

In sum, Roman Christians are being asked to participate in the Jerusalem collection both tangibly and intangibly. Tangibly, they can give to the "collection," not by sending money to Jerusalem, since that deadline already has passed with Paul already on his way to Jerusalem as he writes. However, they learn through the letter that Paul intends to pass "through Rome" on his way to Spain. Therefore, the Romans can give to the "collection" by helping send Paul on his mission to Spain. Intangibly, the Romans are being asked to cast their lot with Paul and his understanding of the gospel. They can do this by modeling in their congregations what the collection symbolizes, which is the unity of both Jews and gentiles in Christ, a sticking point for Jerusalem, as well as the unity of the weak and the strong, a sticking point for Rome.

Paul, Rome, and Jerusalem—three life settings that explain Romans and the exigencies of the letter itself. Paul wants to introduce himself as a legitimate apostle to a church he did not establish. He wants to introduce his gospel as a legitimate interpretation of Rome's own traditions. He wants to bring that gospel power to bear on the church in Rome and his mission to Spain. He wants Rome herself to symbolize tangibly and intangibly the collection he will deliver to Jerusalem.

Much is at stake for Paul. Winning Rome is crucial because he no longer has a mission base after losing Antioch fighting Barnabas, and Ephesus in the silversmith riot. Roman support for the Pauline gospel would be Paul's golden parachute for his new mission west, regardless what happens with the symbolic collection in Jerusalem. Paul realizes that if he can win Rome, he wins period. Rome is Paul's trump card over Jerusalem.

Historically, Rome was the future. When Paul reached Rome he reached the heart of the empire, and, in effect, reached the entire empire. If all roads lead to Rome, then all roads lead from Rome. The Jerusalem church vanished from history after the Jewish War, so the church destined to become the church universal was the enigma of a non-apostolic Roman Christianity on which Paul left his mark.

SPAIN

The simple question *why* Paul would want to go to Spain in the first place (Rom 15:24, 28) is thoroughly without agreement among scholars. Further, if the big deal is just being "apostle to the gentiles," so hammered as an expression by those without proper focus on Israel as crucial to Paul's narrative worldview, anywhere in

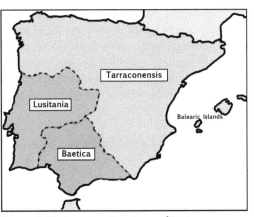

FIGURE 5.57. Augustan Provinces of Spain.

the world would do. We look briefly first at the empire's relationship to Spain and then move to discussion of this Pauline mission goal.

Rome's involvement in the Iberian Peninsula began in war with the famous Hannibal of Carthage in his campaign in Spain during the days of the Roman Republic. Rome eventually won, but local Iberian tribes continued fierce resistance until Augustus permanently subdued the territory. The former Republican province of Hispania Citerior ("Near Spain") Augustus basically simply renamed as the new province of Tarraconensis. The old former province of Hispania Ulterior ("Far Spain") from the days of the Roman Republic Augustus subdivided into the two provinces of Baetica and Lusitania.

Diodorus of Siculus wrote that kingdoms fought over Spain for its abundant natural resources, especially rich silver and gold deposits, of which exploiters were "ever coming upon more splendid veins."[102] These mines powered the Carthaginian Empire and provoked the wars between Carthage and Rome. The Spanish mines were worked by up to forty thousand slaves laboring in utterly cruel conditions. Here is how Diodorus described the mines in Spain.

[102] Diodorus, *Hist.* 5.37.2.

But to continue with the mines, the slaves who are engaged in the working of them produce for their masters revenues in sums defying belief, but they themselves wear out their bodies both by day and by night in the diggings under the earth, dying in large numbers because of the exceptional hardships they endure. For no respite or pause is granted them in their labors, but compelled beneath blows of the overseers to endure the severity of their plight, they throw away their lives in this wretched manner, although certain of them who can endure it, by virtue of their bodily strength and their persevering souls, suffer such hardships over a long period; indeed death in their eyes is more to be desired than life, because of the magnitude of the hardships they must bear.[103]

FIGURE 5.58. Slavery Mining Operation. Rare Greek illustration of the backbreaking labor and rough conditions of mining operations by Greek slaves, perhaps in the Macedonian mines where famous gold deposits enriched the Macedonian kingdoms of Philip and Alexander the Great. The suspended oil-burning lamp indicates poor lighting, with exhaust fumes and smoke generating poor air and lower oxygen levels. General dust and grit hanging in the stale air clogged the mouth, eyes, and lungs (TAM).

[103] Diodorus, *Hist.* 5.38.1.

Numerous famous Romans hailed from Spain, including the three later emperors Galba (68–69), Trajan (98–117), and Hadrian (117–138). Seneca the Elder was from a wealthy equestrian family of Cordoba and lived in the days of Augustus, Tiberius, and Caligula. He wrote on rhetoric and history. Seneca the Younger was a famous Stoic philosopher who served as Nero's tutor. Seneca the Younger's brother, Gallio, was proconsul of Achaia. Paul appeared before Gallio's tribunal in Corinth (Acts 18:12). Lucan, uncle of Seneca the Younger, was a famous Roman poet. Quintilian (35–100), one of the most famous rhetoricians, wrote the classic handbook on rhetoric. Martial (38–102) was a Roman poet and satirist best known for his *Epigrams* (c. 86–102).

Mission Motivation

Numerous theories have floated as to why Paul would want to go to Spain. Three main theories typically crop up in various forms. These theories are: (1) completion of Isaiah's prophetic circle of the gentiles and thereby inaugurating the parousia, (2) counter-proclamation within areas of imperial strength, and (3) attraction of Jewish populations.

Parousia Expectation

Johannes Munck popularized the theory that Paul's mission strategy was inspired by the prophetic idea of Messiah and the circle of the gentiles laid out by Isa 66:19. This reading of Isaiah, however, required Munck to interpret Isaiah's ambiguous designation of "Tarshish" as Spain.[104] Munck connected this prophetic fulfillment scheme with Paul thinking he thereby would provoke the *parousia*. The theory continues to attract attention, at least in terms of prophetic geography and Paul's mission strategy.[105]

Imperial Critique

Wright offered his own theory of deliberate imperial critique. Paul deliberately chose imperial strongholds to stage his gospel counter-proclamation. His goal was to demonstrate that gospel power combined

[104] Munck, *Paul and the Salvation of Mankind*, 39, 55, 299.

[105] Dunn, *Romans 9–16*, 872; Aus, "Paul's Travel Plans," 234; Riesner, *Paul's Early Period*, 245–46.

with the glory of God could conquer the conqueror.[106] Wright argued that Spain had a significant Jewish presence (as have others). Wright, however, argued from literary caricatures by ancient writers about the ubiquity of Jews around the world.[107] This *literary* argument fundamentally is flawed. Hyperbolic rhetoric by ancient writers on gnomic generalities about Jewish demographics is not evidence. Wright simply is not persuasive. Archeological evidence speaks much more strongly to this point, but this evidence Wright did not engage. Thus, the conclusion, "We may therefore take it that Paul at least believed that there were significant Jewish communities in Spain," is not based on evidence of the right kind.[108]

Jewish Populations

The assumption of Jewish populations and synagogues in Spain attracting Paul like a bee to flowers was common among an older generation of classic commentaries on Romans, and even modern scholars such as Wright try to perpetuate that argument.[109] Significant evidence to the contrary exists. Bowers showed conclusively from available evidence that Spain had few Jews and few, if any, synagogues.[110] Thornton in the same year added how sparse was the archeological evidence for Jews in Spain.[111] Absence of synagogues severely would limit Paul's favored tactic for mission entry into a major province, as is implicit in the text of Acts and the rhetoric of "Jew first" (Rom 1:16).

Citing Bowers and Thornton, Jewett argued Spain was not close to the same league of mission feasibility as were Paul's previous fields in Asia Minor, Macedonia, or Greece. Jewett asserted all of Rome's three Spanish provinces presented immense logistical and tactical problems.

---

[106] Wright, *Paul and the Faithfulness of God*, 1502. The idea echoes the sentiment in the apocryphal prediction Paul supposedly made to Nero who, Paul said, thinks himself the conqueror, but will know he has been conquered by Paul's unconquered King when Paul appears in a vision to Nero after Paul's execution; cf. Pseudo-Linus *Martyrdom of the Blessed Apostle Paul* 8 (Eastman, *The Ancient Martyrdom Accounts*, 155).

[107] Such as Strabo, Seneca, Josephus, and Philo; Wright, *Paul and the Faithfulness of God*, 4999, n. 55.

[108] Wright, *Paul and the Faithfulness of God*, 1500.

[109] For a classic example, Käsemann, *Romans*, 383.

[110] Bowers, "Jewish Communities in Spain," 395–402.

[111] Thornton, "St. Paul's Missionary Intention in Spain," 120.

Linguistic barriers alone would be significant, as even Latin was limited to the large urban areas only, and not pervasive in urban indigenous populations. Native peoples regularly favored their own local deities and resisted Romanization in religion. Paul's Lystra experience would be paradigmatic (Acts 14:11). Roman generals repeatedly had to fight in Spain, and Julius Caesar and Pompey engaged their legions against each other on Spanish soil. The Cantabrian War (29–19 BC) illustrates the on-going tendency to revolt even after Augustus came into power.[112]

Mission Exigency

FIGURE 5.59. Roman Provinces. Paul said he had preached from Jerusalem all the way around to Illyricum, a Roman province north of Macedonia and east of Italy.

Regardless the difficulties, Paul indicated his plans to go to Spain. He considered his work in the east completed, from Jerusalem around to Illyricum, a Roman province north of Macedonia on the Adriatic Sea across from Italy (Rom 15:19).[113] Acts gives no clue of any activity of Paul in the province of Illyricum. He possibly could have taken a long detour up into that province on his way from Macedonia to Greece toward the end of the 3MJ, but that is speculation (Acts 20:1–2).[114]

[112] Jewett, *Romans*, 74–79.

[113] Modern nations of Croatia on the coast, Bosnia-Herzegovina, and Yugoslavia.

[114] Farrar (*Life and Work of St. Paul*, 420) is certain Paul missionized Illyricum during the time on the 3MJ in Macedonia he postponed going to Corinth to allow completion of Corinth's collection contribution that had languished due to church conflicts.

With few synagogues and minimal Jewish Diaspora in Spain, Jewett thought Paul's patrons there of necessity would have to be politically connected Roman elite. Political patrons would be a new mission strategy wrinkle. Populations discontent with Rome's presence would require political savvy in choosing patrons. Members of the Roman church might prove invaluable to Paul for Spain. Jewett concluded the Spanish mission complicated by imperial attitudes to "barbarians" was the core purpose of Romans, explaining not only issues and rhetoric in Romans 9–11 and Romans 12–15, but also Phoebe's role as patron, both of Paul and his letter, as well as the Spanish mission, for which she was to lobby personally in Rome. Thus, Paul's vague reference to Spain was in deference to Phoebe's "delicate negotiations" required in person to gain support for Spain.[115]

Jewett's dyadic proposal for the purpose of Romans is a complex interweaving of two missions, Spain and Phoebe, within a challenge to imperial ideology and Roman cultural honor-shame codes that were problematic to Paul's gospel and future plans. The principal strength of this hermeneutic is its appeal to a holistic approach to the entire text of Romans without prejudicing one section over another, as in perennial debates over Romans 1–4 versus 5–8, or the persistent question whether Romans 9–11 is integral to Romans 1–8, or how Romans 12–15 pertinently follows from all of Romans 1–11. Jewett's proposal of the mission to Spain as a heuristic device for all of Romans is helpful and concords well with our previous integrative purpose statement of gaining support for Paul's gospel, leadership, and mission.[116]

TEXT AND INTEGRITY

Letter Text

Critical commentaries on Romans assume the edited text of the *Novum Testamentum graece*, based on the Alexandrian Greek text.[117] Though

---

[115] Jewett, *Romans*, 88–91.

[116] However, less emphasis should be put on Phoebe's role; more than letter bearer and interpreter is a reach. Paul here notably eschews politics of "friendship" terms (φίλη, *philē*) typical of reciprocal relationships involving money; cf. Winter, *Roman Wives*, 196.

[117] Given as NA28; cf. *The Greek New Testament*, United Bible Societies (UBS5). For a history of textual criticism, cf. Metzger, *The Text of the New Testament*. For a contemporary update, see Jewett, *Romans*, 9–18; Longenecker, *Romans*, 29–39.

we have thousands of pieces of early Greek manuscripts on papyrus (paper), not one of them has the entire text of Romans. The most important Greek papyrus is 𝔓46, Chester Beatty Papyrus II in Dublin, Ireland. Some parchment (leather) copies have the entire text, as does Sinaiticus (ℵ, British Museum) and Vaticanus (B, Vatican Library).

Letter Destination

One textual issue is the designation "in Rome" in 1:7, 15. This location is missing in one Greek manuscript, codex G. We have a few other secondary indications (Origen, Ambrosiaster) of its absence in these two verses. While explanations for the absence of "in Rome" play into arguments supporting diverging theories about the composition of Romans, the general consensus is that the missing designation is intentional excision to generalize the text for catholic use.[118]

Letter Doxology

A second textual issue is the doxology's presence and position (Rom 16:25–27). In the Greek manuscripts, the doxology either is missing entirely or positioned differently five ways. The doxology can be found after Rom 14:23 only, after 15:33 only, after 16:23(24) only, or after both 14:23 and 16:23(24), and after both 14:23 and 15:33 (without Romans 16). In other words, the doxology either is missing entirely or no set place, ending chapters 14, 15, and 16. The manuscript evidence raises suspicion about the doxology's integrity.

Letter Benediction

A third textual issue is the final benediction's duplication. The closing grace benediction occurs in three places, with only minor difference in wording: "The grace of our Lord Jesus be with you" (16:20b), and "The grace of Lord Jesus Christ be with you all" (16:24 or 16:28). The second occurrence creates its own separately numbered verse as Rom 16:24. Reduplication, however, is supported only in later and inferior Byzantine manuscripts, which were the only Greek texts available to the King James translators—the reason why the KJV has this additional verse, Rom 16:24, that is missing in all modern translations.

---

[118] Gamble, *Textual History*, 115–16.

The majority of scholars reject the second benediction as original. Gamble proposed Paul concluded, was unexpectedly asked to add more personal greetings from his associates, did so, but then needed to repeat the benediction to conclude the letter. He noted that the benediction at 16:24 is lost or displaced to 16:28 only when the doxology intrudes. His argument for 16:24 as original has not persuaded scholars. Yet, a grace benediction as the invariable conclusion of a Pauline letter has become crucial to arguing the integrity of Romans 16.[119]

Letter Integrity

Questions of the text raise questions of integrity. Theories of minor interpolations of smaller sections, such as Rom 13:1–7, generally have not garnished wide acceptance.[120] Two major areas of discussion, however, concern the ending of Romans and the authenticity of the doxology. Since the manuscripts have evidence for these questions, they need to be addressed. These two issues turn out to be interconnected.

Letter Ending

What is the ending of Romans? All of our Greek texts have Romans 15 and 16, but the issue in the manuscripts has some complexity. The problem is the placement of the doxology (Rom 16:25–27).

Ending Evidence. This doxology by its content clearly is meant to conclude the document. Yet, the doxology is found in various places. The question of the doxology is, Will the real Romans please stand up?

Romans 1–14. Did Romans end with Rom 14:23? Some Greek manuscripts have the doxology here (though also including Romans 15–16). Latin evidence adds to the discussion. Old Latin manuscripts used *capitula*, summary titles, for each section of Romans. Several Latin copies have no *capitula* after Romans 14. Another old Latin piece of evidence is the use of subject headings, which go missing in some Latin copies after Romans 14. Finally, some major patristic fathers, such as Irenaeus, Cyprian, and Tertullian, never quote from either Romans 15 or 16, while quoting extensively from the rest of Romans. Such

[119] Gamble, *The Textual History of Romans*, 130–31. A few manuscripts do not have 16:20b (D, F, G), whereas significant manuscripts are missing 16:24 (𝔓46, 𝔓61, ℵ, A, B, C, 81, 1739, 2464, as well as the Vulgate version).

[120] Kallas, "Romans XIII:1–7; an Interpolation."

Greek and Latin evidence suggests a form of Romans with only fourteen chapters circulated in the early church.

FIGURE 5.60. Codex 𝔓46 Doxology. Our oldest copy of Romans has the doxology at the end of Romans 15, raising the question of an earlier manuscript that concluded here. Image of CBL BP II f.47r, © The Trustees of the Chester Beatty Library, Dublin.

Romans 1–15. Did Romans end with Rom 15:33? The discovery of 𝔓46 in the twentieth century muddied the waters. This papyrus codex is our earliest copy of Romans (c. AD 200). Strangely, the doxology occurs at the end of Romans 15, even though 𝔓46 continues with Romans 16. Does 𝔓46 suggest a form of Romans ending with chapter 15?

Romans 1–16. Did Romans end with Rom 16:23(24)? A number of Greek manuscripts have the doxology here. These witnesses are ancient, geographically widespread, and dispersed across multiple text family streams. Scholars use these factors to conclude Romans 1–16 is likely the original form of the text on text critical terms. Our exegesis assumes Romans 1–16 as the original letter to Rome.

Ending Theories. Multiple placements suggest multiple editions of Romans. The speculation would include how many, who, and when. Some theories assume Paul himself is responsible for different editions. Other theories assume someone else is responsible.

Pauline Editions. A set of symmetrical theories is that Paul either wrote Romans 1–16 to Rome but subsequently created Romans 1–14 for general distribution, or, that Paul first wrote Romans 1–14 generally but subsequently added Romans 15–16 to send to Rome. Both these theories ignore that between Romans 14 and 15 Paul still is continuing his weak/strong exhortation, which runs all the way to Rom 15:13.

Another Pauline theory is the "Ephesian Hypothesis," which goes back at least to 1829. T. W. Manson's 1948 re-popularization of the theory held sway for decades due to the surge of interest created by the discovery of $\mathfrak{P}^{46}$. This manuscript seemed to support the hypothesis that Paul originally wrote Romans 1–15 but later expanded this work with Romans 16 and its greetings in order to send Rome's letter to leaders in Ephesus.[121] The idea had much in its favor. The character of Romans 16 is strikingly different and has an abrupt transition from Romans 15. Notable patristic writers never quoted from Romans 16. The form of giving a name, identity, and request for favor is much like a recommendation letter. Many individuals named have both Ephesian and Pauline connections. The strong warning in Rom 16:17–20 is incongruous in its authoritarian tone with the rest of Romans. Each of these arguments, however, meets strong counterarguments.[122] Gamble definitively ended this theory's relevance by showing that Rom 15:33 is thoroughly at odds with Paul's consistent letter ending form.[123]

Non-Pauline Editions. These fall as either Marcion or the church. Marcion joined the church at Rome but later was excommunicated as a heretic (AD 144). Origen asserted that Marcion was responsible for

---

[121] Manson, "St. Paul's Letter to the Romans—and Others." The "Ephesian Hypothesis," though often associated with Manson, has been championed by others. Fitzmyer (*Romans*, 57) lists Schulz (1829) as original, followed by Bartsch, Bornkamm, Bultmann, Feine/Behm, Feuillet, Fitzmyer (changed positions), Friedrich, Georgi, Goodspeed, Harrison, Heard, Henshaw, Jewett, Käsemann, Kinoshita, Lake, Leenhardt, McDonald, McNeile, Manson, Marxsen, Michaelis, Moffatt, Munch, Refoule, Schenke, Schmithals, Schumacher, Scott, Suggs, Taylor, and Widmann.

[122] Fitzmyer, *Romans*, 59–61, but he abandoned his earlier acceptance (*Romans*, 64).

[123] Gamble, *The Textual History of Romans*, 57–95.

creating the fourteen-chapter form of Romans. Origen accused Marcion of "cutting away" everything after Rom 14:23.[124] Numerous scholars support this "Marcionite Hypothesis." However, Origen's evidence is equivocal. Another problem is implicit evidence of Latin fathers such as Tertullian using a fourteen-chapter version of Romans with no hesitation as if by a heretic.[125] If Origen's assertion is not correct on the origin of Romans 1–14, who is? God alone knows.

Another non-Pauline theory is later ecclesial activity. This theory notes the link of the absence of the last two chapters of Romans in the Greek manuscripts with the absence of the designation "in Rome" in Rom 1:7, 15 at the beginning in the same manuscripts. The intention to generalize the text of Romans for a wider audience is suggested.[126]

Summary Conclusion. A Romans 1–14 edition can be inferred from doxology placement here as well as from Latin evidence, but no actual manuscript without the last two chapters exists. Further, ending at Rom 14:23 in the middle of a discussion of weak/strong would have been logically inept, and without a grace benediction, would have been un-Pauline style. A Romans 1–15 edition is speculated on the singular inference of $\mathfrak{P}^{46}$, but such an ending without a trace of other Greek evidence would be incredulous, and without a grace benediction, un-Pauline style. Thus, (1) all current Greek manuscripts with the ending of Romans have both the last two chapters, (2) text critical and form considerations favor Romans 1–16 as original, and (3) the unusual form and content of Romans 16 can be explained satisfactorily.

Paul originally wrote Romans 1–16 addressed to Rome. Why we have what appear to be different endings suggesting multiple editions of Romans circulating in the early church is unknown. The bottom line for exegesis is, Romans 16 contextually helps determine the social profile

---

[124] Origen, *Rom.* 10.43 (PG 27.43.61–62 [1290]).

[125] Cf. Leenhardt, Sanday/Headlam, Zuntz, Goguel, Manson, Kümmel, Guthrie, Barrett, Donfried, Moo, Jewett. However, Origen continued, *In aliis vero exemplaribus, id est in his quae non sunt a Marcione temerata, hoc ipsum caput diverse positum invenimus,* "Indeed, in other copies, that is, in those which are not contaminated by Marcion, we find this same section differently placed." Note Gamble, *The Textual History of Romans,* 22–23, 100–114, but Gamble supplies inadequate exigency if not Marcion.

[126] Gamble, *The Textual History of Romans,* 115–16. Rejected by Moo, *Romans,* 8, for illogically truncating the conclusion of the weak/strong discussion at the end of Romans 14 that is continued right on into Romans 15.

of the Roman congregation, as well as supports the idea of Paul's awareness of matters in Rome when he writes.[127]

Letter Doxology

The issue of the integrity of the doxology (Rom 16:25–27) is about as complicated as the ending of Romans. Most scholars conclude the doxology is not original to Romans.[128] The minority report has offered arguments for integrity but have not persuaded others.[129]

Weima argued the doxology summarizes the content of Romans, but *notes parallels only in Rom 1:1–7*. Schreiner spun that as an *inclusio*, but ignored that that is no summary. Longenecker noted Paul ended other sections of Romans with doxologies, but ignored that none of these have such signficant textual critical issues. Further, such an ending is atypical of letter genre and Pauline style. For the cumulative effect of arguments related to form, content, length, wording, and textual issues, then, the doxology likely is not original to Romans. Fitzmyer indicated for some purposes the doxology should be studied even if ancillary to the original letter: "Even if not authentically Pauline or originally part of Romans, it forms a fitting conclusion to the letter, for it catches the spirit of the Pauline message of the letter."[130] While we understand the sentiment, our exegesis contradicts this assessment.[131]

---

[127] For other minor and idiosyncratic proposals challenging the unity and integrity of Romans, such as a conflation of multiple letters, or a redactor editing in elements such as Rom 13:1–7, other minor secondary glosses, or a letter originally composed to the Jewish Christian synagogues of Rome, cf. Fitzmyer, *Romans*, 64–65.

[128] Cf. Käsemann, *Romans*, 421–23; Dunn, *Romans 9–16*, 913; Jewett, *Romans*, 8; Fitzmyer, *Romans*, 753; Hultgren, *Romans*, 601.

[129] Hurtado, "Doxology at the End of Romans," 185–99; Marshall, "Romans 16:25–27"; Weima, "Neglected Endings," 135–44, 229–30; Marshall, "Romans 16:25–27"; Moo, *Romans*, 936–37, n2. Schreiner, *Romans*, 816–17; Longenecker, *Romans*, 8, 1083–85. Hultgren noted that the language reflecting a presumed Deutero-Pauline Ephesians or Colossians is not the problem; the unusual word phrase *combinations* are unparalleled in Paul (Hultgren, *Romans*, 601). On a proposed atypical ending, Schreiner said, "A majestic ending is appropriate" (*Romans*, 817), but the issue is not appropriateness.

[130] Fitzmyer, *Romans*, 753. Marshall ("Romans 16:25–27," 183) concluded similarly that the doxology's effect was "to gather together the main themes of the letter."

[131] As our exegesis will show, this "summarizing Romans" idea is wrong. Further, if reflecting Romans, the doxology mostly reflects only the *opening* of Romans. As well, alien elements from other Pauline letters intrude into the doxology. Finally, one of the most important themes of all of Romans is missing entirely in the doxology—Israel.

STRUCTURE OF ROMANS

Romans: Two Parts

Romans naturally falls into two parts, Romans 1–11 and Romans 12–16, easily intuited on first impressions. For example, content in these two parts is different. They also have differing rhetorical strategies. Topics have sustained arguments in the first eleven chapters but jump around much more frequently in the last five. Again, though twice as long, the first eleven chapters have only thirteen imperatives (commands) versus forty-nine in the last five. Clearly, exhortation is much more dominant in the last part. Thus, the two big parts of Romans are clear. Yet, what is the internal organization of each part, and what is their logical relationship to each other? Finally, all observe that in each major part, two subunits easily stand out, Romans 9–11 and Romans 14–15.

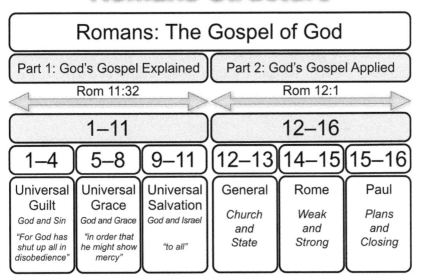

FIGURE 5.61. Romans Structure. The tripartite structure of Rom 1–11 is in Rom 11:32.

Romans: Part One

The disputed outline is in the first part of Romans 1–11. The easily identifiable Romans 9–11 quickly subdivides part one into Romans 1–8 and 9–11, but the question is their relationship. Centuries of church hermeneutic painting Paul as gentile has destroyed any sense of Paul's

Jewishness. Framing Paul only as "apostle to the gentiles" justifies discarding Romans 9–11 as an irrelevant detour on Paul's part away from the theology of gentile mission established in Romans 1–8, so to be ignored safely.[132] Paul, distracted by his Jewish past and his own problems in the synagogue, got off track from his call to be apostle to the gentiles, and pretty much wasted his time as far as church theology was concerned. The exact opposite is true. Romans 9–11 is the focus, point, and climax of the whole argument of Romans 1–11.[133] The argumentative apex is expressed in the summary statement in Rom 11:32, which thereby supplies an outline to Romans 1–11 when Paul summarizes and concludes all he has said and the logical progression of his argument with the words: "For God has shut up all in disobedience in order that he might show mercy to all" (Rom 11:32). Paul here is summarizing everything that he has argued up to this point. This verse's tripartite phrasing reveals a three-part division of Romans 1–11.

The first phrase is "For God has shut up all in disobedience," the argument for universal guilt in Romans 1–4. This part deals with God and sin. Divine righteousness responds to human sin. Romans 1 seems to have gentiles in view, but the rhetoric shadows Israel, Sinai, and the golden calf. Romans 2 with its Jewish interlocutor seems to have Israel in view, but the rhetoric shadows gentiles. All speak with one voice: all humanity is implicated in Adam's primal sin of not trusting

---

[132] As did C. H. Dodd, *Romans*. Eighty years later, Longenecker simply rehearsed well-trodden reformed paths, one of which is to dismiss Romans 9–11 as anything essential to Paul's message. Longenecker chose Romans 5–8 as the essential message of Paul. Reading Romans 5–8, however, as the "essential" Paul with an exclusive focus on his gentile mission facilitates discarding Romans 1–4 and Romans 9–11 and simply turns back the clock a century to Schweitzer's mystical, non-forensic Paul of the inner Spirit communion. In Longenecker's take, "forensic" categories as in Romans 1–4 and "Israel" categories as in Romans 9–11 are forced on Paul only by the weight of Jewish tradition and the disproportionate, unfortunate impact of Jerusalem on the history of Roman Jewry. Without this historical Jerusalem encroachment on the history of early Christianity in Rome, Paul would be freed from Jewish categories and Jewish framing of the essence of Messiah, which, according to Longenecker, Paul had to do to have a successful gentile mission. Thus, Longenecker leaves the abiding impression that if Paul did not have to deal with Jerusalem's impact on Rome, we might never have seen Romans 1–4 or Romans 9–11 in the first place, and Paul's task in writing Romans could have been dispatched with much more alacrity in fewer chapters.

[133] Cranfield, *Romans*, 2:445; Dunn, *Romans 9–16*, 519–20; Stendahl, *Paul Among Jews and Gentiles*, 28.

God. The Adamic destiny shadowing the discussion surfaces explicitly in Romans 5. The solution is a human graced with faith (Romans 4). Here, God's righteousness is efficacious unto salvation.

Even before Romans 5, Paul already is setting up trajectories of grace while discussing the righteousness of God. A change of eschatological epochs is compressed into the "But now" in Rom 3:21. God's great act of redemption is "by his grace" (τῇ αὐτοῦ χάριτι, *tēi autou chariti*, Rom 3:25). Here in the tight unit in Rom 3:21–26 Paul anticipates the eschatological reality driving the Adam/Christ typology in Romans 5, where grace becomes central. Abraham's paradigmatic story of faith in God's promise in Romans 4 reveals the required divine-human relationship demanded by the divine grace and the final act of grace that would arrive in the eschaton (Rom 4:18)—a divinely sent agent of redemption descended from on high in whom to believe, the true reconciler of the world.

The second 11:32 phrase is "in order that he might show mercy," the argument for universal grace in Romans 5–8.[134] This part deals with God and grace. All are guilty, but all are offered grace through faith. Abraham's story reveals that even before Moses, divine grace expresses divine righteousness through faith. The advent of Messiah now signals the eschaton for which Abraham was the prototype, a new epoch in human experience that transcends the Adamic destiny by the arrival of the grace that powers salvation through faith (Romans 5). This grace reigns triumphant, having conquered Sin (Romans 6) and consummated law (Romans 7). The key to the effective power of grace in messianic Israel is the indwelling Spirit (Romans 8).[135] The operation of the Spirit will bring all the cosmos into original creation order.

Commentators often unquestioningly read Romans 5–8 in individualistic, subjective, and experiential terms, epitomized in outline headings such as "the believer's life in Christ." Ignored here is that in critical phrases throughout Romans 5–8 the pronouns and verbs are *plural*. Take, for example, the headline verse kicking the entire unit off

---

[134] Sequencing Romans 5 is problematic. Four major views are: (1) before = Romans 1–5, (2) after = Romans 5–8, (3) split = 5:1–11 *before* and 5:12–21 *after*, and (4) isolated. Fitzmyer gives persuasive reasons for after = Romans 5–8 (*Romans*, 96–98).

[135] "Only by Paul's having himself so experienced the Spirit at the beginning of his life in Christ can one easily explain how the Spirit came to play such a significant role in his theology," Fee, "Paul's Conversion as Key," 181.

(Rom 5:1). All the verbs and pronouns are *plural*. This rhetoric signals that Paul is working within a corporate, eschatological narrative. His narrative is messianic Israel and Mosaic Israel caught in the eschatological drama of the sudden arrival of Messiah in the last days. Paul does make statements to and about individuals, but such rhetoric has its hermeneutical context only within this cosmic drama that does not unfold fully with all its rhetorical force until the climactic Romans 8. So, Adam/Christ typology is not about the experience of individuals but the corporate headship that establishes the corporate experience of all humanity and relegates all to one of only two possible destinies. Again, the baptism language in Rom 6:1–11 is *not* singular. The rhetoric *exclusively* is plural, except once in a participle in Rom 6:7 and in any reference to Christ. The upshot is that baptism has its theological significance only as *incorporation* into messianic Israel. To repeat for emphasis, Romans is all about Israel. Exegesis of Romans 5–8 will reflect corporate ideas.

The third 11:32 phrase is "to all." Israel now is caught between a rock and a hard place after Romans 1–8, because the proposition that Christ is greater than Moses and consummation of the law is hard to fathom within the Great Assembly narrative controlling the Jewish worldview. This use of "all" in Rom 11:32 is another classic example of Paul's boomerang rhetoric. Saving gentiles is not all of God's salvation. The "to all" phrase shows us that God is not finished with Israel. Gentiles might think that God is through with Israel, but Israel gets grace just as do gentiles. In fact, if Israel does not get grace, gentiles have no reason to be confident they do. So, when Paul says "to the Jew first, and then to the Greek" (Rom 1:16), he is indicating a primacy in both direction *and* intention: That is where the gospel first went, and that is where the gospel will last return. Paul is addressing gentile believers: "Do not get too high-minded about being saved, because this grace is for all." The argument of Romans 9–11 is, then, the argument for a universal salvation, a salvation that goes out to those not looking, but then comes back to those looking in the wrong place. God made a promise to Abraham that he would bless *all* the families of the earth, and *Israel itself is one of those families.* God is going to fulfill his word. By fulfilling his promise to Abraham, God saves the world, Jew and gentile—and barbarian for that matter. The whole story is based upon the promise that God has made. In sum, in the three-part division of

Rom 11:32, we see universal guilt, universal grace, and universal salvation.[136] Thus, Rom 11:32 sums up the gospel of God.

Romans: Part Two

The second major unit is shorter, with a clearly defined weak/strong subunit, so the Romans 12–16 outline is simpler (once Romans 16 as integral to the letter is decided). The second part starts with an appeal to the "mercies of God" (Rom 12:1), another way to condense the sense of Romans 1–11. The gospel of God is about the mercies of God. Human relationships are defined by God's relationships, which are defined by mercy. Therefore, all human relationships also should be defined by mercy. The following exhortations, then, are based on the mercy central to the gospel of God. In this way, Rom 12:1 expresses the logical connection between the two major parts of Romans. By topic and content, Rom 12:1—13:14 comprises general exhortations on church and state that would address the church in general but with an eye on the mission to Spain. Romans 14:1—15:13 offers exhortations on the weak and strong addressed specifically to Rome.[137] Finally, Rom 15:14—16:28 concludes the letter with Paul's plans and letter closing.

INTERTEXTUALITY

Intertextuality is a new name for an old discussion of Paul's use of the Old Testament. Quotations or allusions to the Old Testament happen in Romans anywhere from 56–88 times, depending on who is counting. On any count, this frequency is much more than all his other letters combined. Paul overwhelmingly uses the Septuagint version. Paul puts the burden on himself at the beginning of Romans when he claims the gospel is in Scripture (Rom 1:2) and has the audacity to make his theme statement for eleven chapters a quotation of Habakkuk (Rom 1:17). The question of use of the Old Testament is one of the Pauline polarities among scholars. One question is whether Paul is proof-texting or contextual in this process.[138] Another question is whether he is faithful to

[136] Not in terms of the universalism of systematic theology.

[137] The Romans 15 chapter division, as noted, is illogical and misleading.

[138] Cf. Ellis, *Paul's Use of the Old Testament*; Evans and Sanders, *Paul and the Scriptures of Israel*. For how to pursue this question, cf. Stanley, *Arguing with Scripture*, 9–21, 62–71.

Israel's story. That question already has been discussed, but will be pursued again in the process of commenting on the text.[139]

GRECO-ROMAN LETTERS

The form of a standard Greco-Roman letter is our launching pad into exegesis of the letter of Romans. We will discuss the formulaic parts of a typical ancient letter to establish how much the same or how different is Paul's use of the letter genre for his communications to his churches. Attention to these matters can be helpful for yielding clues for exegesis of a Pauline letter.

Letters have formulaic parts even today. For example, even if a person is writing a complaint letter to a company, the address still is "Dear Sirs." That wording is just the expected letter form for the opening address. In reality, the complaining letter writer holds nothing "dear" about the company officials. Likewise the letter conclusion regularly has the word, "sincerely," simply because that is the expected form. Ancient letters also had formulaic parts with similar formulaic expressions, and in a typical format.

Six Parts

The six parts of an ancient letter were author, reader, greetings, thanksgiving, body, and a closing. These parts had stereotypical forms of expression, usually with concision. Brevity saved space, and composing letters with trained scribes to write them was not cheap. The author and reader parts functioned like our envelope. They quickly identified who wrote the letter and who received the letter. The greeting part often was just the word "greetings,"

FIGURE 5.62. *Chaire* in Funerary Epitaphs. Use of *chaire* ("rejoice," "be well") has a fascinating history, since death in the Archaic period was considered tragic and afterlife miserable. See Sourvinou-Inwood, *'Reading' Greek Death*, 180–216 (MANRC).

[139] See the previous chapter, "The Narrative of Israel."

using the verb, χαίρειν, *chairein*. A typical letter opening, then, was simple: "X to Y, greetings." A "most excellent" title might be added for social status, but should not appear to fawn or be obsequious. Then, a thanksgiving was optional. If used, this element said "I give thanks," accompanied by some object of thanks, such as the favor of the gods, good health, prosperous business, or other life status of the recipient used to generate positive rapport. A benediction, "blessed be," could substitute for the verbal "I give thanks." The letter body expressed the reason for writing the letter after opening pleasantries were dispensed. In today's terms, this part would be like the college student writing home, rambling along, and finally saying, "By the way, send money" (almost like Paul in Romans). The letter closing, like the greeting, was concise, often the one word, "Farewell" (Ἔρρωσθε, *errōsthe*).

Letter Examples

One easily can see this ancient letter format in letters embedded into the narrative Luke has composed in Acts, perhaps using some archive source for these documents. Acts offers several examples of embedded letters. Take, for example, the letter of James of Jerusalem to churches of the Antiochene ministry led by Barnabas and Saul embedded into the narrative in Acts 15:23–29. James writes on behalf of leaders assembled to offer these churches a summary of the Jerusalem Council decision. Notice that the author here is not one person. Anyone named in the "from" section of an ancient letter had some contribution to make to the letter. This letter from James is not from James alone. The letter is a corporate production of the apostles and the elders. Thus, when Paul names someone else in the "from" element of one of his letters, which he often does, that person or persons had some contribution to make to the letter.[140] If no one else is named, Paul alone is the author. Paul alone is the author of Romans. This feature means the content of Romans exclusively is tied to what Paul himself wanted to communicate.

> *Author:* "The brothers, both the apostles and the elders"
> *Reader:* "to the believers of Gentile origin in Antioch and Syria and Cilicia"
> *Greetings:* "greetings" (χαίρειν, *chairein*)

[140] Sosthenes (1 Cor); Timothy (2 Cor; Phil; Col; Phlm); members of God's family (Gal); Silvanus, Timothy (1 Thess; 2 Thess).

Thanksgiving: [absent]

Body: "Since we have heard that certain persons who have gone out from us, though with no instructions from us, have said things to disturb you and have unsettled your minds, we have decided unanimously to choose representatives and send them to you, along with our beloved Barnabas and Paul, who have risked their lives for the sake of our Lord Jesus Christ. We have therefore sent Judas and Silas, who themselves will tell you the same things by word of mouth. For it has seemed good to the Holy Spirit and to us to impose on you no further burden than these essentials: that you abstain from what has been sacrificed to idols and from blood and from what is strangled and from fornication. If you keep yourselves from these, you will do well."

Closing: "Farewell" (Ἔρρωσθε, *Errōsthe*)

Another Acts example is the letter of the Jerusalem tribune Lysias to Governor Felix about the prisoner he is remanding to Caesarea in Acts 23:26–30, although Luke has omitted the closing. Notice that neither of these embedded letters in Acts has a thanksgiving section, which is optional. Also notice that both of these letters are only seven and five verses respectively. One papyrus sheet would do. That length is typical. Suddenly we are confronted with how strange are the documents of Paul we want to call "letters." Romans is longer than anything Cicero wrote, and Cicero was long winded. Thus, scholars have debated how to classify the form of Paul's letters. The discussion is inconclusive.

Pauline Distinctives

Even so, still obvious is that Paul used standard Greco-Roman letter format when he wrote to his churches. As these elements are used, Paul shows three distinctives related to this ancient genre form.

Customized Expansions

Paul customized his letter parts by expanding the typical elements to make them his own and not so formulaic. The focus of all expansions was Christ and Christian life—with a keen eye on features to come in the "body" of the letter. Paul would set up trajectories of themes, emphases, and key ideas in all these expansions. His wording was not verbiage. One gets the solid impression after close reading of Paul that his wording was calculated by almost each word. This feature is ever more true of the opening verses of Romans.

Paul's expansions could be quite lengthy. Thus, the identification of the writer in Romans runs on for six verses (1:1–6)! He does not get to the "to" until Rom 1:7. The most obvious expansion is the body of his letters. His "letters" could be so unbelievably long. Expansion of the letter body length is where Paul's "letter" form becomes something else, almost incomparable. The one letter he wrote that pretty much stayed within expected bounds of a stereotypical first-century letter was Philemon. This letter could fit on one sheet of papyrus. Even here, however, we still see the distinctive Pauline traits.

Thematic Thanksgivings

Further, whereas our two sample letters embedded into Acts do not have a thanksgiving section, Paul regularly had a thanksgiving. In fact, the thanksgiving is so distinctive of a Pauline letter that its absence can be counted as exegetically significant. Galatians is our poster child for this feature. Galatians has no thanksgiving. Paul is in the white heat of his anger when he writes, reflected in his harsh rhetoric (Gal 3:1; 5:12). So, ancient letters often do not include a thanksgiving section, but Paul usually did. Why?

Paul regularly seems to have used the thanksgiving to anticipate themes or emphases to come. Scholars are keen to identify the Pauline thanksgiving for this reason. Notice how in the thanksgiving section of 2 Cor 1:3–7, Paul hammers the reader with the noun "comfort" (or, "consolation," παρακλήσεως, *paraklēseōs*) and its cognate verb ten times in only five verses.

> Blessed be the God and Father of our Lord Jesus Christ, the Father of mercies and the God of all **comfort**. He **comforts** us in all our affliction, so that we may be able to **comfort** those who are in any kind of affliction, through the **comfort** we ourselves have been **comforted** from God. For just as the sufferings of Christ overflow to us, so also through Christ our **comfort** overflows. If we are afflicted, it is for your **comfort** and salvation. If we are **comforted**, it is for your **comfort**, which produces in you patient endurance of the same sufferings that we suffer. And our hope for you is firm, because we know that as you share in the sufferings, so you will also share in the **comfort**.

Already in this thanksgiving section of 2 Corinthians, Paul is alluding to the good news Titus brought to Paul somewhere in their rendezvous in Macedonia that Paul's breach with the Corinthian church had been reconciled (2 Cor 7:6–14). Notice that the noun "comfort" and its cognates again occur multiple times in this later biographical unit. This "good news rendezvous" with Titus is the whole storyline behind 2 Corinthians, and the theme of that story clearly is "comfort." Hence, the thanksgiving section of a Pauline letter is not to be ignored by a rushed reading to hurry on to get to the body of the letter. Reading this way, one might miss Paul's main point, even the purpose of the letter.

Romans is an excellent example of Paul using the thanksgiving section with exegetical significance. In Romans, the significance is in stealth mode. Paul hides suggestion of the purpose of the letter in its opening with coyly ambiguous wording, whose significance is not fully disclosed with specificity until the letter end.[141] Thus, the thanksgiving's long shadow is cast all the way to the end of Romans. This connection to the end allows the thanksgiving itself to function literarily as the "envelope" of the body of the letter. This envelope "frames" the letter's significance in terms of what hermeneutical lens to use to focus the meaning of the body of the letter. In short, the thanksgiving section of Romans discloses the meaning of the body of Romans and integrally is tied to the purpose of Romans.

Formulaic Conclusions

A third Pauline distinctive of Pauline letters besides customized expansions and thematic thanksgivings is a formulaic conclusion. Paul always concluded a letter with formulaic elements in a specific order: exhortation, peace wish, greetings, and grace benediction.[142] An element might be missing, but the order of the remaining elements would be maintained. His letters invariably concluded with a grace benediction ("May the grace of our Lord Jesus be with you," Rom 16:20). The formulaic elements of the Pauline conclusion help to establish that neither an ending at Romans 14 nor at Romans 15 likely would have been original, even though we have manuscript evidence of the circulation of Romans in at least two forms (Romans 14, Romans 16), and possibly

---

[141] Rom 1:8–15 with 15:22–28; see figure 5.55, p. 180.

[142] Gamble, *Textual History of the Letter to the Romans.*

three (Romans 15). A fully satisfactory explanation of these apparent multiple editions of Romans circulating in the second-century church does not have scholarly consensus. Yet, wide agreement does exist that the original Romans had sixteen chapters.[143]

In conclusion, understanding the standard Greco-Roman letter form helps in exegesis of Pauline letters. The thematic thanksgiving helps analyze the beginning of Romans, and the formulaic conclusion helps analyze the problem of the ending of Romans. Paul's customized expansions draw attention to key thoughts that will loom large later.

JULIO-CLAUDIAN FAMILY

The graphic on the following page lays out the complex family history that produced the first emperors of The Roman Empire. This chart is hoped to be of some use not just for reading a book on Romans but for negotiating any discussion related to parsing the history that gives the New Testament its context. The imperial line always is the monster in the room for New Testament study.

Renaming individuals with the same names of previous generations just was not a problem, rather habitual, and even what seems to modern sensibilities, illogical. Of course, such a practice produces a fairly extreme headache on occasion just trying to decipher exactly to whom an ancient author might be referring. As a result, a certain degree of ambiguity attends any and all reconstructions attempted from the primary sources available for historical research. Anyone who tries to dig into this material will encounter this difficulty within only a paragraph or two of reading. Bon voyage!

One of the most pertinent points to recognize about the line of Roman emperors illustrated in this table and to keep in mind while investigating the Julio-Claudian family is that the imperial line under review thoroughly was built on the process of adoption, not inheritance. Even the very first official emperor, Octavian (Augustus), who established the foundation for what would become an empire, was adopted by the general-turned-dictator, Julius Caesar. This reality that adoption was crucial to maintaining the imperial line, as will be seen, becomes core to the exegesis of Romans 8.

---

[143] See previous discussion in this chapter.

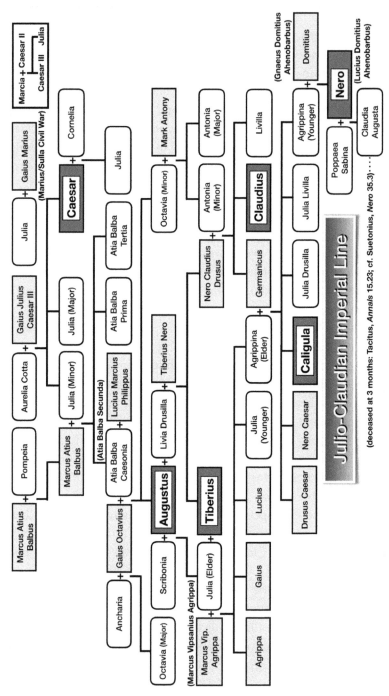

FIGURE 5.63. Julio-Claudian Imperial Line. © 2021 Gerald L. Stevens.

PART 2

Exegetical Analysis

Paul's Letter to the Romans

6

Introduction

A Good Beginning

Pᴀᴜʟ ᴡʀɪᴛᴇꜱ ᴛʜᴇ Rᴏᴍᴀɴꜱ ᴀ ʟᴇᴛᴛᴇʀ ᴛʜᴀᴛ for millennia has captured the attention of readers to whom the letter never was addressed. Yet, most readers feign the letter was written exclusively to them. Further, why the letter was written has no consensus. The purpose is illusive and has to be teased out from multiple angles.

So, the letter is difficult, no doubt. Intimidating is the knowledge that major theological systems harvest their theological axioms from this document. For all this, from the top, our guiding principle is this: Romans is all about Israel. That means Romans is not all about you. Only if your story properly folds into Israel's story is Romans about you. This principle is clear even in the letter's introduction.

In terms of the introduction to Romans, like every good book has a good beginning, every good letter also has a good beginning—and what a good beginning Romans has! The beginning of Romans reveals that Paul meticulously has thought out every part of this letter.

KEY WORD: GOSPEL

The key word in the introduction is "gospel," which occurs in all three sections of the opening, thanksgiving, and theme statement:

- 1:1   opening section: "set apart for the gospel of God"

- 1:9   thanksgiving section: "announcing the gospel of his Son"

- 1:16 theme section: "For I am not ashamed of the gospel"

The word "gospel," then, is thematic, the controlling thought of the introduction. This gospel is the "gospel of God." Fundamentally, the story is divine.

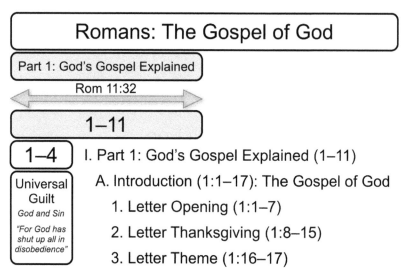

FIGURE 6.1. Outline: Introduction (1:1–17).

The gospel story involves God. God is creator. God is sovereign over creation. God intends a cosmos teeming with life, so God has purpose. Creation, however, was damaged by sin. Sin brought death. The story of God's sovereignty involves overcoming sin and death. He overcomes sin and death by calling a people, the story of Israel. God made promises to Israel. He has promises to keep. Israel will bring forth Messiah, and Messiah as Isaiah's Servant of Yahweh will consummate all things in God's purposes through messianic Israel.

The gospel story involves Paul. God was pleased to reveal his Son to Paul. God's Son is Messiah who establishes messianic Israel. Paul's understanding of Jesus the Messiah fulfills Paul's every aspiration as a Pharisee and has become Paul's life work, his mission. To accomplish this mission, Paul still has miles to go, and he intends to go.

The gospel story involves the Romans. The whole world lives under a dominion soaring high into heaven claiming divine authority to rule over all creation. A gospel already was being preached in Rome before Paul ever got there. This gospel was the gospel of Augustus. This Roman gospel promoted an imperial ideology of a ruling dynasty, a universal kingdom, a world peace, and an abundance of life's goodness—their own story of an Eden of their own making. The dynasty, however, was human, not divine, the kingdom was imposed not chosen, the peace was subjugation not reconciliation, and the abundance was rapacity not stewardship. In the process of building an empire, Romans have cultivated cultural and social prejudices that run counter to the gospel of God and render their picture of Eden thoroughly corrupt.

The gospel story, then, involves God, Paul, and the Romans. The gospel is still more. That more is the letter of Romans. The letter of Romans will explain the gospel of God and then apply this gospel to Roman believers. The introduction to the letter has the letter opening (1:1–7), letter thanksgiving (1:8–15), and letter theme (1:16–17).

Introduction: Letter Format

Greco-Roman Letters	Pauline Expansions	Exegetical Significance
Writer (1:1–6)	intriguing omission: no co-senders	letter content exclusively Paul's
	use of Roman creedal tradition	attempt to establish shared faith
Recipient (1:7a)	use of Jewish covenant language	redefining "Israel," anticipating 9–11
Greeting (1:7b)	combining Greek and Hebrew ideas	alluding to gospel universality
Thanksgiving (1:8–15)	personal emphasis, Paul's work, plans	alludes to the purpose of Romans

FIGURE 6.2. Expansion of the Writer Identification.

LETTER OPENING (1:1–7)

Identification of the Writer (1:1–6)

The writer element in the letter opening has two notable features. One is the intriguing omission of any co-senders, even though he often has co-senders in his letters, and is in the company of numerous cohorts when he writes Romans, including Timothy, Lucius, Jason, Sosipater, Gaius, Erastus, and Quartus, all of whom send greetings, along with the scribe of the letter, Tertius (Rom 16:21–23). The letter content is exclusively Paul's. That observation makes the letter all the more important, because Romans winds up being the longest letter Paul wrote that we have. Paul has a lot to say, and he is writing on his own. These are not the fleeting, haphazard thoughts of a casual daily diary.

The second notable feature of the writer element is how the identification of the writer is expanded like in no other letter of Paul. First, such extraordinary expansion means the obvious—the recipients do not know the author personally. Exegetically, however, one must realize that that lack of connection constrains the rhetoric Paul can use to be persuasive. He will have to be subtle and nuanced. The bully pulpit of Galatians will not do. The expansion of the writer element mainly is accomplished by the use of Roman creedal tradition (Rom 1:3–4). As he identifies himself, Paul establishes shared faith with a church he did not found. He skillfully turns the expressions to show how the Roman tradition substantively agrees with his gospel. He works to build rapport on the basis of gospel themes.

Romans 1:1

The writer is styled simply "Paul, a slave" (**1:1**). The name Paul conjures his life setting at the time he writes, and this life setting, as already discussed, involves the matrix of the three life settings of Paul, Rome, and Jerusalem. Paul's life setting is multiple crises. The Ephesian crisis is a loss of mission sponsorship that puts in stress Paul's future mission plans. The Corinthian crisis is a challenge to leadership and authority that casts a shadow over a relationship with Rome. The life setting of Rome is the age of Augustus and the Roman gospel. Rome also involves the story of Jews in Rome, their influence, and Roman synagogues that already have had history with the preaching of Jesus as Messiah. Further, Rome involves Roman cultural prejudice to Jews that has become endemic among the populations of Rome. Rome also involves the story of a non-apostolic church, with unclear leadership structure, undifferentiated demographic profile, unknown sources for its Jesus traditions, and its own, independent sense of authority. The life setting of Jerusalem is a tensioned relationship with other groups in the Jesus movement that question the Jewish integrity of his gospel. Jerusalem also was a nation standing at the political precipice of war with Rome, a powder keg of nationalism and patriotism ready to go off at any time. The soul of Jewish identity was in dispute. Everyone in their own way was saying, "And, thus, all Israel will be saved."

The first thing Paul absolutely wants the Romans to know is not that he considers himself an apostle. The premier mark of his identity is as a "slave."[1] In the Old Testament, the term is a title of honor, but in Greek culture, dishonor. Whereas Paul is fully conversant with the Old Testament usage, he is not oblivious to the institution of slavery in his world. He particularly will use this term to capitalize later in Romans on the issue of lordship, who is master (Romans 6). The issue for humans is not the illusion of freedom, but the reality of to whom you are indentured. Paul thinks only two choices are available. Those who imagine themselves to be free are really the walking dead of the devil, or in Pauline terms, Satan.[2]

The writer is a slave "of Messiah Jesus." The translation "Christ" should be avoided. Thousands of years of saying "Jesus Christ" with the second term almost as the equivalent of a last name, as well as the all too common slang use of the phrase for exasperation have rendered "Christ" totally meaningless in today's vernacular. An entire Jewish worldview is lost. Paul means "Messiah," and not any messiah. He means the *Jewish* Messiah—the coming Jewish prince that many false messiahs pretended to be.[3] This term for a Pharisee, in other words, is *confessional*. A confession of Messiah for a Pharisee is declaring the end of days has come and every expectation of Israel is being fulfilled.[4] Paul evokes the confession of Jesus as "Messiah" five times in the first eight verses of Romans. That authorial *ethos* is thoroughly Jewish.

Ascription of "Messiah" by Paul to Jesus brings into play the Edict of Claudius. With "Messiah" (Χριστός, *Christos*, in Greek), Paul has navigated his wording close to the shores of imperial history in

---

[1] The term δοῦλος, *doulos*, often is translated "servant." This rendering is *much* too mild, minus the rhetorical edge here. Paul has a different term for "servant" (διάκονος, *diakonos*), and he uses this term as appropriate (Rom 13:4; 15:8; 1 Cor 3:5; 2 Cor 3:6; 6:4; 11:15, 23; Gal 2:17; 3:7; Phil 1:1; Col 1:7, 23, 25; 4:7; 1 Tim 3:8, 12; 4:6).

[2] Rom 16:20; 1 Cor 5:5; 7:5; 2 Cor 2:11; 11:14; 12:7; 1 Thess 2:18; 2 Thess 2:9; 1 Tim 1:20; 5:15.

[3] Of whom Jesus forewarned (Mark 13:21) and Josephus informs (*Ant.* 18.1.1; 20.5.1; *J.W.* 2.8.1; 2.13.5; 20.8.6).

[4] As did the most famous rabbi of his day, Akiba, who fatefully declared Simon bar Kokhba to be messiah in the Second Jewish War of 132–35.

Rome. Only eight years before Paul's letter, Rome already had had trouble with "Chrestus" preaching in Jewish synagogues. Fortunately for the moment, Paul's "Chrestus" message was flying "under the radar" due to the new, socially obscure house church venue for the assembly of believers as a result of the edict. In the highly structured, patron-client network of the first-century world, however, that cloaking device could not last forever. Further complicating matters were the growing problems in the province of Judea with increasing grumbling about the Roman yoke in Zealot circles and whispers about war.

The writer also is characterized as "called apostle." That call is God's initiative in Paul's life, the Damascus Road. Here is the fundamental issue of the essence of what Paul experienced—call or conversion? Paul never uses the term "conversion" to describe the Damascus Road, though he does use that term to describe the experience of gentiles in his ministry.[5] More likely the call of Isaiah (Isa 6:1) is the paradigm. The call deepened Paul's understanding of grace. He fully is aware of the mercies of God (12:1). The call also clarified his Pharisaic aspirations, purified his zeal, and transformed his sense of Israel as the called of God. The call became the foundation of his apostleship, since his call was a sending out on mission to the nations for Messiah in gathering eschatological, messianic Israel (15:14–21). He became an ambassador for Messiah.[6]

Paul's adamant claim to apostleship, however, was in dispute in the early church. Paul did not even meet Luke's own definition for an apostle set in the replacement of Judas among the Twelve (Acts 1:21–22).[7] This issue of Paul's claim to apostleship made the problem of the "super-apostles" at Corinth brandishing their Jerusalem letters of recommendation such a sting and threat for Paul (2 Cor 11:5). Paul had reason to wonder what was the Roman church attitude to his sense of call. Since they were non-apostolic in origins, perhaps they would be more receptive to Paul's broader sense of call as "apostle" than was Jerusalem, particularly since the Roman gentile base was his bailiwick. Paul

---

[5] The term for conversion is ἐπιστρέφω, epistrephō, "I turn, return" (1 Thess 1:9).

[6] 2 Cor 5:20; Eph 6:1.

[7] Paul is called an apostle—only once—in Acts 14:14. Luke here likely is using Antiochene tradition for this information, tradition that could have used the term only as applied to the Antioch church as the mission sending body related specifically to the two leaders delegated for that mission, Barnabas and Saul.

is God's authorized agent on gentile mission. If Jerusalem would not accept him, he still could work as Rome's apostle, particularly if they "helped" him on his way to Spain (15:24).

The writer is "set apart." To be set apart is the idea of the concept of a "Pharisee" as one "set apart" to God.[8] Paul, like Jeremiah (Jer 1:5), was set apart for exactly what he was doing right at that moment, to preach Messiah as resurrected Lord to the nations. The separation is to the "gospel of God." Gospel is the key word in all three units of the introduction. The next five verses build on this gospel, joined by a series of connectors: "which" (1:2), "concerning" (1:3), and "through whom" (1:5). This grammatical series supplements the meaning of gospel.

Romans 1:2

The first supplement to the gospel is "which he promised beforehand" (**1:2**). This statement codes the whole narrative of Israel. Paul insists the gospel of God is in concord with the Hebrew Scripture. This claim here in the second verse explains why the argument in Romans by far has more Scripture quotations than any other letter of Paul. In effect, Paul has the veritable eight hundred pound scriptural gorilla sitting on his back. "Promised beforehand" is nothing less than a hermeneutical burden. His argument is with the synagogue and its Great Assembly myth about the significance of Moses for defining the Israel of God.[9] Postexilic changes had created extraordinary challenges for Israel in synagogue demands, messianic expectations, national aspirations, and no Davidic dynasty. Almost universally agreed was that the story of Israel post exile was unfinished. Neither Hasmoneans nor Herodians cut the mustard. The Teacher of Righteousness already had attempted his alternate vision in the desert, and his followers still were active in the time of Jesus and Paul. Israel, God's solution to sin, was in an odd limbo. Competing definitions of Israel provoked a cacophony of solu-

---

[8] The verb is ἀφορίζω, *aphorizō*. One nuance of the verb is separation to avoid contact. Cephas "separated" himself from the gentiles at Antioch (Gal 2:12), and God called Israel to "separate" from idolatry, Paul reminded the Corinthians (2 Cor 6:17). The other nuance is to be selected out from a group for a purpose, to be "appointed." Paul sees God as separating him out from the womb (Gal 1:15), and the Antioch mission team was so appointed from among the leadership at Antioch (Acts 13:2).

[9] As Luke faithfully presents in Acts 28:23. For details of the Great Assembly and its postexilic impact on defining Israel, see chapter 4, "The Narrative of Israel."

tions to unfulfilled promises. The "gospel of God" is Paul's answer of how God fulfilled every promise he ever made in Jesus the Messiah. Through Jesus's resurrection, God will transform this world damaged by sin back into his creative design and purpose. This story of Jesus is good news for the world and good news for God. Gentile members of messianic Israel need to get their heads screwed on straight about whose story they are living.

The second supplement is "concerning his Son." Jesus is the son of Abraham who consummates the promise (Gal 3:16; Rom 4:23). Jesus is the eschatological prophet-like-Moses who consummates the Torah (Rom 10:4). Jesus is the son of David who consummates the kingship (Rom 1:3; 15:12). If Isaiah's vision is in view, this kingdom will have a striking impact on the gentile world (Isa 66:18–21). In effect, Isaiah's vision is Paul's argument with the church. All are witnessing that the power of God is poured out on gentiles through Abraham's faith, not the synagogue's tradition.[10] Abraham's faith in God's promise of a son is the heart of believing in God's promise of a Savior.

Romans 1:3

Paul smoothly incorporates a traditional Roman creed into the story of Israel (1:3). "Seed of David" is not a typical Pauline emphasis. He uses this expression only one other time (2 Tim 2:8). The only two other times he mentions David are here in Romans, and each time Paul subordinates David's testimony to his presentation of the gospel of God. The first instance is to show David's affirmation of righteousness without works in Paul's use of the story of Abraham (4:6). The second instance is to show David's affirmation of Israel's righteousness failure (11:9). Davidic descent is a characteristic Jewish emphasis on Messiah. Davidic language in the Roman creed seems to suggest the synagogue origins of the early church in Rome. Paul does not have a problem with Davidic theology. He himself quotes the "root of Jesse" theme in the prophecy of Isa 11:10 in Rom 15:12. Even here, though, Paul uses this quotation to support the idea "gentiles will hope in him," a phenomenon of the gospel of God he carefully has presented in Romans. In general, then, while Paul can incorporate Davidic tradition, Paul does not naturally focus on David, nor other Davidic motifs, such as land.

---

[10] The thought captured well by Luke in Acts 15:12.

"According to the flesh" is added to the seed of David. This use is the first for the term "flesh" in Romans, which can be crucial to Paul's argument. Whether use here carries a *double entendre* with a negative or pejorative sense of its use in Romans 8 is unclear, as in "weakened by the flesh" (8:3), "likeness of sinful flesh" (8:3), and "live according to the flesh" (8:5). Perhaps the idea would be dependence upon efforts in the flesh, human, rather than God's power, as in Abraham's fleshly efforts to produce progeny through his handmaiden, Hagar.[11] The problem would be exclusive focus on Messiah as Davidic. Such focus would overemphasize the human side of the equation. False Davidic aspirations swirled around Zerubbabel after the exile for this very reason.[12] If joined with the expectation of military prowess due to the impact of the Maccabees, as with false messiahs such as Athronges, Theudas, and Simon bar Kokhba in the first and second centuries of the church, such emphases could downplay or miss Isaiah's crucial Suffering Servant vision (Isaiah 53), as well as Zechariah's own distinctive vision of the humility of this future ruler (Zech 9:1–6).[13]

Romans 1:4

God's Son has been "designated Son of God" (**1:4**). The verb has the root behind "set apart for the gospel" in 1:1. The question is raised whether this idea is a remnant of adoptionist Christology in the early church. Likely not. The similar thought in 3:25 makes more likely divine public demonstration. God has made a public demonstration of what he is up to through the resurrection of Jesus. God's public demonstration of Jesus's sonship by resurrection validates the self-testimony of Jesus.[14]

The modifying phrase "with power" could go with the verb, "designated powerfully," or the associated noun, "Son in power." Either way, "power" emphasizes that God is at work, which coordinates with

---

[11] Imagery Paul uses in Gal 4:24–25. Note the Spirit and "flesh" contrast in Gal 3:3.

[12] Hag 2:23; Zech 3:8; 6:12.

[13] Cf. Josephus, *Ant.* 17.278–84; 20.97–98; Jerusalem Talmud, *Ta'anit* 4:6 (68d–69a); Gruber, *Rabbi Akiba's Messiah*.

[14] Matt 7:21; 10:32; 11:25; 12:50; 15:13; 16:17, 27; 18:10, 19, 35; 20:23; 24:36; 25:34; 26:29, 42, 53; 28:19; Mark 8:38; 13:32; 14:36; Luke 1:32; 2:49; 10:21–22; 22:29, 42; 23:34, 46; 24:49; John 1:14, 18; 2:16; 3:35; 5:17, 19–23, 26, 36, 43; 6:32, 40, 44, 57; 8:16, 18–19, 27, 38, 42, 49, 50; 10:15, 17, 25, 29, 36; 11:41; 12:27; 13:1, 3; 14:2, 6, 9–31; 15:1–15, 23, 26; 16:10, 15, 23, 25, 32; 17:1–25; 18:11; 20:17, 21.

"according to the spirit of holiness," an expression that sounds odd but is likely a Semitism for "Holy Spirit," another indicator of the early Jewish flavor of this creed.

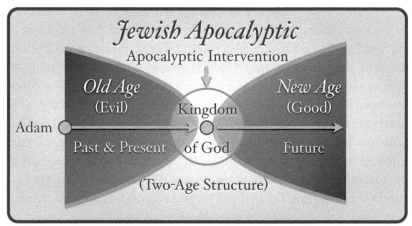

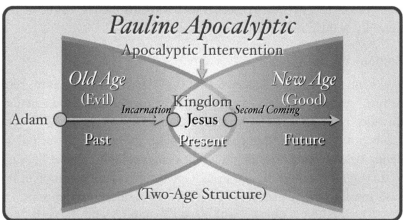

FIGURE 6.3. Jewish Apocalyptic and Pauline Adaptation.

The Son's status is designated "by the resurrection of the dead." Resurrection is core belief for Paul (10:9). Of the many elements of the Jewish story Paul capitulated in order to preach to the purely pagan audience at Athens, resurrection he did not—and he lost his audience precisely at that moment. Greek dualism of body and soul would have made resurrection repugnant or inconceivable, certainly undesirable.[15]

---

[15] Acts 17:16–31; see Stevens, *Acts*, 372–78.

The early disciples, however, like Paul, gave their own clear witness to resurrection as the essence of the gospel.[16]

Resurrection doctrine invokes a whole system called eschatology. The eschatological framework of Pauline theology is another of the Pauline polarities among scholars.[17] Arguments over the nature of the eschatological thought of Paul tend from Paul already accommodating to Hellenistic philosophical thought moving away from ancient ideas based upon mythology to Paul being totally sold out to an "apocalyptic eschatology" (however defined). Most agree the Jewish foundation of Pauline eschatology builds on a "two age" structure. The old age of evil dominated by sin and death resulted from the epic event of the fall of Adam. This old age incorporates the past and present. The new age of good dominated by righteousness and life is triggered by the epic event of the divine coming. This new age anticipates the future. The sudden appearance of God or God's appointed agent would break into human history, banish sin and death, and thus realize the kingdom of God on earth. Typically, the idea of "breaking into history," thereby interrupting its normal processes, is the essence of apocalyptic mentality.[18]

Discussion of New Testament eschatology further is complicated by evidence of multiple frames of reference for the kingdom timing in the Gospels. The kingdom can be a future reality (Matt 10:23; 25:31, etc.), but the kingdom also can be a present reality (Matt 3:2; 5:3, etc.). If one thought Jesus put all emphasis on the future element, awaiting a kingdom to come in the future, that would be "futurist eschatology."[19] If one thought that Jesus sublimated all eschatological ideas to the present reality of his person and ministry and the movement that would follow after him, that would be "realized eschatology."[20] In this view, no end of the world was in sight for Jesus. All end time language was only metaphor for present time reality. Oscar Cullmann split the difference. He conjured up an "inaugurated eschatology" explained in

---

[16] Acts 1:22; 4:2, 33; 17:18, 32; 23:6; 24:15, 21; 26:23 1 Cor 15:1–4, 12, 21, 42; Phil 3:10; 2 Tim 2:18; Heb 6:2; 1 Pet 1:3; 3:21.

[17] See chapter 1, "Polarities," pp. 6–7.

[18] The matter is disputed on whether the two ages are completely discontinuous (Martyn, Campbell) or have some interconnection (Wright).

[19] Schweitzer's "thorough-going eschatology"; sometimes "consistent eschatology."

[20] J. A. T. Robinson (1919–1983), Joachim Jeremias (1900–1979), Ethelbert Stauffer (1902–1979), C. H. Dodd (1884–1973).

popular terms as a "now-not yet" duality. Some of the kingdom is now (Holy Spirit, resurrection of Jesus, messianic Israel), while some of the kingdom is not yet (second coming, final judgment, rewards). So, the kingdom is *both* present *and* future—inaugurated, but not consummated.[21] In this inaugurated eschatology view, the two-age structure of Jewish eschatology is modified by an overlap of the two ages. With the coming of Jesus, the old age is passing away but is not completely finished, while the new age is coming around, but is not yet consummated. The coming of God's agent (Messiah) instead of being one point in time (Jewish eschatology) is stretched out across two points in time as incarnation and second coming (Pauline eschatology).

Inaugurated eschatology dominates the New Testament landscape. The view successfully synthesizes and holds together two extremes of a spectrum. The problem for understanding Paul is the imminence elephant in the room. The view does not address the clear impression Paul leaves that he thought not in terms of millennia of church history for the period of overlapping ages but of his lifetime.[22] Hard to calculate is whether Paul's ethics and admonitions might carry specific eschatological presuppositions regarding imminence that if changed would impact how he would choose to express himself and to negotiate issues of church and life. On this point, one could engage Munck regarding his thesis of Pauline mission strategy as motivated by completing Isaiah's circle of the gentiles to inaugurate the parousia, a theory which itself presupposes the power of imminence thinking.[23]

Our basic approach is to assume this inaugurated eschatology as a framework for understanding Paul's thought. Thus, for example, the "But now" in 3:21 is not just a grammatical clause. This brief "but now" codifies a huge leap across the eschatological boundary of the ages. The "now" is epic, a new aeon, a new reality in human experience. The Messiah has come. The end of days has arrived. Nothing is the same.

[21] Cullmann, *Christ and Time*; cf. John 3:16, 36; 5:24; 1 John 2:8; 3:2, 14; 5:11–12. Ladd (*Theology of the New Testament*) brought Cullmann's inaugurated eschatology to evangelicals.

[22] For example, 1 Thess 4:17; Rom 13:11–12. Advice on marriage, "in view of the present crisis" (1 Cor 7:26), is difficult to decide as to whether eschatological; for a balanced discussion, see Ciampa/Rosner, *The First Letter to the Corinthians*, 335–38. Some try to scrub imminence from Paul; cf. Campbell, *Paul and the Hope of Glory*.

[23] See Chapter 5, "Context," p. 186.

Paul finishes the Roman creed with double appositional phrases. The first phrase identifies the subject of the creed as a historical reality ("Jesus") and a confessional faith ("Messiah"). The second phrase climaxes the identification of Jesus Messiah with high Christology, "our Lord." Paul ascribes to Jesus the same terminology used of God in Hebrew Scripture, "Lord" (κύριος, *kurios*). In Romans and elsewhere, Paul will quote Scripture originally referring to God but be referring to Jesus.[24] "Our Lord," then, theologically anticipates the church's later trinity doctrine. One should note that Paul regularly adds "our Lord" to "Jesus Messiah" throughout Romans.[25] So, this connection between messiahship and lordship is fundamental in Paul's thinking, actually explicit in Rom 16:18 ("our Lord Messiah").[26] Paul's consistent use of "Lord" with "Jesus" in Romans seems to reflect the Damascus Road dialogue as presented by Luke.[27] This habit of thought to join "Lord" with "Jesus" seems to have been present from the beginning of Paul's experience of the risen Jesus. Paul seems regularly to be setting up in these opening verses of Romans rhetoric that will carry exegetical significance throughout the letter. In short, one could say that in these two appositional phrases Paul uses to conclude the Roman creed is the mother lode of New Testament Christology: Jesus—Messiah—Lord.

Finally, in "our Lord" we have the first occurrence of Paul's first person plural in Romans. This "we" is fraught with exegetical significance. This "we" is the beginning of the development of the authorial *ethos* in Romans that will become critical for interpretation of the "I" in Romans 7. In chapter 3, we observed that the thematic development of authorial *ethos* in the prescript of Romans is unique among the letters of Paul. We also observed this authorial *ethos* is:

- *Jewish*—Paul thoroughly identifies himself as a Jew who will be reflecting Jewish issues as he writes

- *fluid*—Paul smoothly without interruption or marked rhetoric transitions between singular "I" and plural "we"

---

[24] As in Rom 10:13 (Joel 2:32).

[25] Rom 1:4, 7; 5:1, 11, 21; 6:23; 7:25; 8:39; 13:4 ("the Lord"); 15:6, 30; 16:8 ("our Lord Messiah"); 16:20 ("our Lord Jesus").

[26] Which soon is followed up for balance in Rom 16:20 with "our Lord Jesus."

[27] "'Who are you, Lord?' Saul said. 'I am Jesus, the one you are persecuting,' he replied" (Acts 9:5).

- *corporate*—Paul subsumes the corporate reality of messianic Israel into "we"

Paul integrally ties this authorial *ethos* development to authorial *pathos* development. The degree of rhetorical *pathos* is thematic. That is, the closer discussion moves to issues of Jewish identity, the higher the levels of authorial *pathos* in the rhetoric. Increased *pathos* is related directly to the authorial voice. Simply put, Paul emotes more when Jewish issues are at stake. Anytime one sees a high level of emotion in Romans, *the issue is Jewish by default*. That observation includes Romans 7.

Rhetorically, Paul uses the Roman creed to build rapport with his audience. He is attempting to establish a shared faith with this unknown church. "We are of the same theological stock" is his message. "Our core confessions resonate." His job is to try to make the proposal stick through the rest of Romans.

Romans 1:5

The third supplement through which Paul explains the gospel of God that continues to expand this lengthy writer identification is "through whom" (**1:5**). Paul here transitions out of the Roman creed to his own thoughts. The "whom" refers back to Jesus-Messiah-Lord. "We have received" again infers the divine initiative, similar to rhetoric of being "called." If God did not take initiative, no human would be saved. One divine gift Paul has received is "grace" (χάρις, *charis*). This occurrence is the first in Romans. The word is so fundamental to life in messianic Israel that Paul will end every letter formulaically with a "grace benediction." Grace is fundamental to ethics and behavior. Paul begins the second part of the letter with exhortation "by the mercies of God."[28] The term grace appears five times in Romans 1–4, but then six times just in Romans 5, revealing a shift in Romans 5–8. Grace almost disappears from Romans 9–11 (four times, two verses, 11:5–6), then four more times in Romans 12–16. A second divine gift Paul has received is "apostleship." This apostleship configures in his mind his relationship to the Romans, so relates to the purpose of Romans.

The purpose[29] of the apostleship is the "obedience of faith." The "of faith" prepositional phrase could be either obedience that consists

---

[28] Rom 12:1. A synonymous term is used (οἰκτιρμός, *oiktirmos*, "compassion").

[29] The significance of the preposition "unto" (εἰς, *eis*).

in faith (faith itself) or faithful obedience (i.e., faith's faithful living). Faith's faithful living seems more likely in context due to the mention of "for the sake of his Name." If this second option holds, this thought would enhance the idea of the "gospel" as good news for God too.

This verse is crucial, generally taken as a programmatic declaration of Paul's ministry among gentiles. The problem is, little noticed is that Rom 1:5 and 16:26 are the only two occurrences of this phrase "obedience of faith" in all of ancient literature.[30] Totally unrecognized by commentators is that this phrase is the tip of the iceberg to crucial synagogue arguments. Paul uses this phrase in the context of gentiles, and first-century synagogues were debating the status of gentiles particularly related to whether the prophet Isaiah was inclusive or exclusive on the matter.[31] The Isaiah Targum reveals this debate. Paul's phrasing engages this debate in a polemic against Jewish particularism that assumed forced submission of gentiles in the coming kingdom.[32] If gentiles are obedient to God, what more could the synagogue demand of them? If faith is the path to obedience or their paradigmatic act of obedience according to the pattern of Abraham when he himself was a gentile, either way, God receives glory from the gentiles that Israel was supposed to facilitate according to Isaiah's vision.[33] That vision means, "Circumcision does not matter, and uncircumcision does not matter. Keeping God's commands is what matters" (1 Cor 7:18).

The obedience of faith is "among all the *ethnē*." A translation choice may disguise a subtle redirection of the thought in a way missing Paul's meaning. The word ἔθνος, *ethnos* (plural: *ethnē*), can be translated either "gentile" or "nation" (also, "people"). However, rather oddly, most English translations at Rom 1:5 exclusively opt for "gentiles," never "nations." A look at Rom 15:12 reveals a problem here at Rom 1:5. Paul in Rom 15:12 is quoting Isa 11:10 with two occurrences of *ethnos*. Almost without fail, all English translations opt for "gentiles" for both these occurrences in Rom 15:12. This choice is odd. Almost all English translations *take the opposite gloss in translating the source text of Isa 11:10*, that is, exclusively as "peoples" and "nations." Why do we never

---

[30] Provoking the question whether Paul coined the term (Jewett, *Romans*, 110).

[31] Kebede, *Universalism and Nationalism in the Book of Isaiah*.

[32] DelRio, *Paul and the Synagogue*.

[33] Isa 11:10; cf. Rom 15:12.

FIGURE 6.4. *ETHNOUS* in Imperial Inscriptions. Romans used *ethnē* as "peoples" or "nations"—not "gentiles." The Sebastion friezes in ancient Aphrodisias formulaically list over fifty conquered nations. Above is *Ethnous Piroustōn*, "Nation of the Pirousti," a Balkan warrior tribe Tiberius defeated in AD 6–8. The figure wears classical dress, cloak, and helmet, and carries a small shield in the left arm; the right hand probably held a spear. See pp. 144–46 for more description of these friezes (AMA).

see Isaiah's original "peoples" and "nations" in translations of Paul's quotation of Isa 11:10 in Rom 15:12? Instead, *consistently* we have *only* the "gentiles" option? Inconsistent handling of Rom 15:12 in terms of the original source text in Isaiah may reveal a problematic habit of thought that has resulted from constantly calling Paul "apostle to the *gentiles*." We never can think of nations. Paul does. So do the Romans.

Yes, this point makes an exegetical difference. The proposal here is that a better translation in Rom 1:5 is "nations," as in "among all the nations." This translation better supports Rom 1:5 as a programmatic statement of Paul's mission. Paul understands himself to be fulfilling the eschatological vision of Israel given in the prophets, particularly Isaiah.[34] Isaiah's vision is for the nations, as all translations of Isa 11:10 recognize. Paul is not focused so much on gentiles as on *Israel's eschatological destiny for the nations*. The real issue for Spain is not reaching gentiles ("uncircumcised"). If Spain had any Jews, Paul would want to reach them too. Spain for Paul is working out Isaiah's program for the nations. Gentiles are everywhere. Nations are not. Nations have a specific geography like gentiles do not. Thus, translating "among all the gentiles" is not "wrong" (that is an option for a gloss), but that option totally misses the prophetic frame of the Pauline worldview. Paul winds up being misconstrued, and the whole point of Romans is turned into Galatians. In this exegetical tradition, Romans conveniently just becomes "Galatians, Part 2." Yet, contextually, Romans most assuredly is not Galatians. Note how the issue at Rom 15:12 dominoes into 15:16.

To be sure, Paul does use *ethnos* to mean "gentile," but this use will have the typical Jewish sense of "uncircumcised." These cases usually are clear, however, because circumcision is either explicit or implicit in the immediate context.[35] Since Paul has said nothing about circumcision yet in this letter, this "gentile" gloss at Rom 1:5 should be rethought. The gloss prejudices Paul's meaning and misdirects Paul's point so that his concluding quote of Isaiah 11:10 in 15:12 is obscured and English translations of 15:12 fail. The next verse is a case in point.

---

[34] For Paul's prophetic emphasis, see Evans, "Paul and the Prophets."

[35] An excellent example is Gal 2:1–9. The issue here is Titus's circumcision status (Gal 2:3). Paul's statements of missions of Peter and Paul are framed in the context of the circumcision status of Titus. If Jerusalem had not proselyted circumcision (Gal 2:12), Paul would not have crossed swords with Peter's behavior at Antioch (Gal 2:11), nor would the Galatians have been "bewitched" (Gal 3:1). Circumcision is Jerusalem.

Romans 1:6

Paul then includes the Roman believers into the orbit of his mission, "among whom you also are called of Jesus Messiah" (**1:6**). Notice that he is not describing Roman believers as "gentiles," so that we have here the social location of the audience, as assumed ubiquitously in commentaries. The translation issue at Rom 1:5 ("among all the ?") comes home to roost. Notice here in 1:6 Paul defines this group, *not* as the uncircumcised ("gentiles"), but as the "called of Jesus Messiah." Thus, "you" is *not* socially identified. "You" is messianically identified. *This group is messianic Israel,* the Israel Messiah is calling unto himself, the eschatological Israel as a nation transformed by inclusion of the nations. The obedience of faith in 1:5 is "among all the nations." This program is Isaiah's vision of eschatological Israel among the nations being a light to the nations to turn them to God, as God always had intended Israel to do. "You" in 1:6, then, is neither Jew nor gentile, circumcised or uncircumcised. "You" is the Israel of Messiah. This message strikes home of all places in Rome. Rome touted itself as the divinely appointed empire for all the nations. The friezes of the Sebastion of Aphrodisias are graphic portrayals of this ideology. The imposing figure of Tiberius dwarfs a captive barbarian representing a nation. Claudius strides land and sea and conquers Britannia. Nero is crowned as military victor. An almost endless sequence of conquered peoples and nations are carved into fifty frames, including the Jews. More could have been added were space available.[36] The "called of Jesus Messiah" challenge Rome's claim of divine destiny to rule the world. "The earth is the Lord's and the fullness thereof," claimed the psalmist (Ps 24:1). Isaiah thought so too (Isa 66:18–21). Israel's eschatological destiny was to make this so. Paul extends his apostleship role (1:1) to Rome for this purpose and to speed his way to Spain. The concept of "call," both Paul's and the Roman believers', creates an effective literary *inclusio* bracketing off the beginning and end of this identification of the writer unit that opens Romans.

---

[36] Aphrodisias illustrates Roman ideology; see chapter 5, pp. 125–48. Kim, *God, Israel, and the Gentiles*, 76, argued for "among all the gentiles" at 1:5 but both ignored the evidence of Rom 15:12 and wrongly asserted Rome did not think of itself as a nation. Kim followed Nanos's gentile audience (*The Mystery of Romans*, 41–84), but the rhetoric is more complex (cf. 7:1, "speaking to those who know the law" versus 11:13, "speaking to you gentiles"), and Kim later capitulated to "nations" anyway at 15:19 (pp. 87–88).

Identification of the Recipient (1:7a)

Following the traditional Greco-Roman letter format, Paul next identifies the recipient (**1:7a**). This section is expanded by use of standard Jewish covenant language. This use is unusual, since Jewish tradition would be loathe to apply this language to anything but Mosaic Israel. Already early in Romans Paul is anticipating Romans 9–11, which climaxes this first part of the letter in Romans 1–11. Paul even now this early in the letter begins redefining the meaning of "Israel." Now that the New Aeon has broken into human experience through the arrival of God's Messiah from heaven, the Israel of God is brought forth out of an infertile womb solely by the promise and power of God.

Introduction: Letter Format

Greco-Roman Letters	Pauline Expansions	Exegetical Significance
Writer (1:1–6)	intriguing omission: no co-senders	letter content exclusively Paul's
	use of Roman creedal tradition	attempt to establish shared faith
Recipient (1:7a)	use of Jewish covenant language	redefining "Israel," anticipating 9–11
Greeting (1:7b)	combining Greek and Hebrew ideas	alluding to gospel universality
Thanksgiving (1:8–15)	personal emphasis, Paul's work, plans	alludes to the purpose of Romans

FIGURE 6.5. Expansion of the Recipient Identification.

Paul addresses his letter "to all God's beloved." This "beloved" is Jewish covenant language. God loves Israel, and this love is the essence of God keeping the covenant. A distinctive Hebrew word, *chesed*, often translated "steadfast love," is used to describe this covenant love, both for the patriarchs and for Israel.[37] This *chesed* defines the essence of being merciful and gracious.[38] Keeping the covenant with Israel is found-

---

[37] Cf. Abraham and Joseph (Gen 24:12; 39:2), the redemption of slaves from Egypt (Exod 15:13; 20:6; Hos 11:1), and Job (Job 10:12).

[38] Exod 34:6; Ps 86:15; Joel 2:13.

ed on this *chesed*.[39] Worship in the temple is inspired by this steadfast love and is the object of faith.[40] Synonymous terms for love should be reflected in those who claim to be God's people and often describe God's behavior to Israel and Israel's expected behavior to God.[41] Yet, the story is tragic. God's steadfast love was spurned. Israel's love for God was adulterated by chasing after other gods. Hosea's marriage experience becomes a metaphor for all Israel. Hosea is told to "love a woman who is an adulteress, just as the Lord loves the people of Israel."[42] Responding to this tragedy, God promises a solution out of his own spurned steadfast love, so great are his mercies and faithfulness to Israel. Isaiah declared of a coming ruler, "then a throne shall be established in steadfast love in the tent of David, and on it shall sit in faithfulness a ruler who seeks justice and is swift to do what is right."[43] The ruler would be acclaimed as Wonderful Counselor, Mighty God, Prince of Peace (Isa 9:6). Paul has seen in Jesus Isaiah's ruler expressing the "steadfast love" of God for his covenant and his people. For Paul, Jesus is God's steadfast love, even to the point of death on a cross (Phil 2:5–11). Israel's covenant relationship is redefined in the eschaton. God's greatest covenant with Israel is not Moses. His greatest covenant is the new covenant in Jesus's blood.[44] Indeed, because of Jesus, Paul can write "to all God's beloved." Because he violently persecuted those faithfully following Messiah, he considered himself least deserving (1 Cor 15:9).

Specifically, all those beloved are "in Rome."[45] This city rules the world and sets the pattern of life for four to five million people among the nations.[46] This city should be the focus, therefore, for those wanting to reach the nations. Paul will reveal, "many times I purposed to come to you" (1:13). Rome has been part of Paul's mission strategy for a while. Reaching the nations is likely one good reason.

[39] 1 Kgs 8:23; 2 Chr 6:14; Neh 1:5; Dan 9:4.

[40] Ps 5:7; Ps 13:5.

[41] Lev 19:18; Deut 7:8; 11:1; Josh 23:11.

[42] Hos 3:1. Paul will apply Hosea to those who are "not my people" (Rom 9:25).

[43] Isa 16:5, NRSV.

[44] Matt 26:28; Mark 14:24; Luke 22:20; John 6:53–56.

[45] For the minor textual issue, see pp. 189–90.

[46] Census figures documented by Augustus himself (*Res Gestae* 8).

"Called" is the second occurrence of Jewish covenant language in this unit. The called are the elect.[47] God has elected Israel to be his people and to reach the nations. To be called is to be chosen. To be chosen is to have status. Even a slave who had no familiarity with Israel's Scripture would resonate with this designation. God's call is the ground of the inherent worth of humans. In 15:16 the call involves the offering of the nations: "to be a minister of Messiah Jesus to the *ethnē* in the priestly service of the gospel of God, so that the offering of the *ethnē* may be acceptable, sanctified by the Holy Spirit."[48] All Rome's subjugated nations forever memorialized in the friezes of Aphrodisias are intended to be included in this offering.

They are "called saints." Saints is ἁγίοις, *hagiois*, which is the root of "holy." Modifying "Spirit" (πνεῦμα, *pneuma*) the phrase is *pneuma hagion*, or "Holy Spirit." The gift of the Holy Spirit clearly defines a member of messianic Israel (Rom 5:5). Paul flatly declares, "Anyone who does not have the Spirit of Messiah does not belong to him" (Rom 8:7). The outpouring of the Spirit would be the clear mark of the last days (Joel 2:28–29). Peter pointed to Pentecost as fulfillment of Joel's prophecy (Acts 2:16–21). Thus, the presence of the Holy Spirit in early church prophecy and worship is written large across the pages of the New Testament, but especially in the letters of Paul. Paul struggled to control Corinthian enthusiasm on the matter (1 Corinthians 12–14). Use of the term "saints" for followers of Messiah is not because of their perfection, the popular misconception of the designation. Paul's use is the obvious reality he could not dispute: pagans had *pneuma*, God's Spirit. The heritage of this dynamic element of the Spirit in the early church is the continuing use of this term, "saints," for Jesus followers.

Greeting (1:7b)

This "grace and peace" greeting is characteristically Paul and characteristically innovative. From the Greek background, Paul creates a play on words. The standard Greco-Roman letter term for "greetings" is the simple infinitive form of a verb, χαίρειν, *chairein*. This verb appears

[47] Deut 28:9; Isa 62:12; Hos 11:1.

[48] Given the context of the recent quotation of Isa 11:10 in 15:12, surely these two occurrences of *ethnē* in 15:16 properly should be translated as "nations," as already discussed.

in the letter of James in Acts 15:23.[49] Paul turns this formulaic *chairein* in an alliterative twist using the foundational term of new life in Christ, χάρις, *charis*, which is "grace." Paul thus turns *chairein* into *charis*, that is, he turns "greetings" into "grace" (**1:7b**).

Introduction: Letter Format

Greco-Roman Letters	Pauline Expansions	Exegetical Significance
Writer (1:1–6)	intriguing omission: no co-senders	letter content exclusively Paul's
	use of Roman creedal tradition	attempt to establish shared faith
Recipient (1:7a)	use of Jewish covenant language	redefining "Israel," anticipating 9–11
Greeting (1:7b)	combining Greek and Hebrew ideas	alluding to gospel universality
Thanksgiving (1:8–15)	personal emphasis, Paul's work, plans	alludes to the purpose of Romans

FIGURE 6.6. Expansion of the Greeting.

From his Jewish background, Paul uniquely pairs "grace" with the Hebrew concept of *shalom*, or "peace."[50] *Shalom* is a beautiful concept difficult to describe because the idea is applied broadly to many areas of life. The basic concept is completeness, soundness, and welfare, as in "safe and sound" in body (Ps 38:3), or an unattended tent found safe and secure (Job 5:24). Personally, *shalom* is used to ask, "Is it well with you?" (Gen 29:6; 37:14; Exod 18:7), or, corporately, one could speak of the "peace of Jerusalem" (Ps 122:6; Ezek 13:16). In another range of meanings the term could refer to quiet, tranquility, and contentment, as in sleeping in peace (Ps 4:9), or going back to your home in peace (Exod 18:23), or dying in peace (Gen 15:15). As Isaiah promised, "My people will abide in a peaceful habitation, in secure dwellings, and in quiet resting places" (Isa 32:18, NRSV). In these terms, one could have peace from war (Josh 9:15). *Shalom* has its greatest impact on the idea

---

[49] See p. 202.

[50] The Hebrew term is שָׁלוֹם.

of relationships. In terms of human relations, a peaceful relationship infers the soundness and security of relationship or friendship (2 Sam 15:27; Zech 6:13). In terms of relationship with God, his covenant can be described as a covenant of peace (Num 25:12; Isa 54:10; Mal 2:5), and this idea can be used as a blessing formula, as in "the Lord lift up his countenance upon you, and give you peace" (Num 6:26). Notice how steadfast love, faithfulness, righteousness, and peace all merge together in the psalmist's meditations (Ps 85:10).

The context in Rome is added to the mix of "grace and peace." Grace puts the Jewish law in place, and peace puts the Roman empire in place. Augustus's *Pax Romana*, "peace of Rome," claim to fame has to be in view, especially since the magnificent Ara Pacis Augustae, the Altar of Augustan Peace, had been standing in Rome for six decades, commissioned by the Roman senate in 13 BC to honor Augustus after his victories subduing Gaul and—yes indeed—Spain. The Roman poet Virgil waxes eloquent celebrating Augustus for the peace he brought to the world. Augustus himself brags about this altar and the empire-wide peace he brought in his own last will and testament, and inscriptions on sacrificial altars in Asia Minor celebrated Augustus as the "reconciler" of former enemies in that province after winning the battle of Actium against Antony and Cleopatra, making peace for the whole Roman world for the first time after centuries of civil war.[51] The greeting of grace and *peace* evokes imperial resonance in Rome, an implicit challenge in the heart of empire to the imperial gospel.

Paul concludes the word of greeting by identifying the source of grace and peace. These realities come from "God our Father." The Hebrew Scripture preserves the notion of God as father of the Jewish nation (Deut 32:6), and the psalmist meditates on God as father (Ps 89:26; 103:13). The prophets Isaiah and Jeremiah use the image of God as father (Isa 9:6; 63:16; 64:8; Jer 3:19; 31:9). However, one of the most characteristic elements of the Jesus tradition is how frequently Jesus called God "Father," including the double combination with the Aramaic *Abba* (Mark 14:36), echoed by Paul (Rom 8:15; Gal 4:6). Even the model prayer given to his disciples begins with "Our Father" (Matt 6:9).

[51] Virgil *Ecl.* 4; Augustus *Res Gestae* 12, 13; Wilson, "*Hilasterion* and Imperial Rhetoric." On imperial overtones of "peace," see Rock, *Romans and Roman Imperialism*, 176–82; all such imperial overtones are rejected by Perriman, *Future of the People of God*, 98.

Thus, the language of the relationship of Jesus and God translated into the devotion and worship of the early church.

FIGURE 6.7. Arch of Titus: *Apotheosis* of Titus.

FIGURE 6.8. Arch of Titus: Inscription.

At the same time, an audience in Rome probably also would hear imperial resonance. On Feb. 5, 2 BC, Augustus was honored with the title *pater patriae*, "father of the country," which was an act of political patronage.[52] The idea was that the entire population was in debt to Augustus as clients to a patron for all he accomplished for the empire. The Caesars also were divinized at their death, called the *apotheosis* of the emperor. A current ruler would recognize a predecessor as divine, an act formalized by a decree from the Senate. After this decree, a new

[52] A title conferred by the Roman Senate for notable accomplishments on behalf of the Romans, for example, general Camillus in 386 BC after fending off the Gallic siege, Cicero in 63 BC for suppressing the Catilinarian conspiracy, and Julius Caesar after becoming dictator, temporarily ending civil wars.

title was added to the former emperor's name in imperial inscriptions to recognize this status. He was called *divus*, referring to a mortal who had become divine (in contrast to *deus*, one by birth a god). The *apotheosis* of Titus, the general who destroyed Jerusalem and later became emperor, is symbolized in a relief in the top interior of the Arch of Titus. He is portrayed symbolically as an eagle taking wings of flight to heaven.[53] This divine status is memorialized in the exterior inscription at the top of the arch, originally inlaid with gilded bronze letters. The inscription reads, "The Senate and People of Rome, to Divus Titus, son of Divus Vespasian, Vespasian Augustus."

Paul concludes the greeting, "and the Lord Jesus Messiah." God and his agent of the New Aeon, Jesus Messiah, work in concert. The divine grace and peace are channeled into human experience through Jesus. This concluding phrase here echoes the conclusion of the Roman creed with its own appositional, "Jesus Messiah, our Lord" (1:4). Jesus Messiah is God's divinely appointed agent consummating all the purposes of God in creation. Paul has innovated the opening of his letter to infer that Augustus is neither the prince of peace, nor divine agent of heaven graciously doling out gifts of civilization and culture to nations, nor true father, nor truly divine. These accolades and honors are fictions of imperial propaganda. Eternal grace and peace come from God, and God only, and this reality is in his Son, so declared by his resurrection from the dead. Messiah is about the nations and God's rule.

In conclusion, by combining the ideas of grace and peace, Paul has customized the typical Greco-Roman greeting to transform this formulaic element into a sermon and a benediction in two words with an assertive affirmation from whom these realities derive. In doing so, Paul already declares the gospel's universality for all the world, Jew and Greek, against any other gospel, building to a climax in Romans 9–11.

LETTER THANKSGIVING (1:8–15)

Thematic Thanksgivings

As discussed earlier, the thanksgiving section of a Pauline letter is loaded with exegetical freight.[54] Whereas having a thanksgiving section is

---

[53] For more on this monumental arch, see figure 5.3, p. 161.

[54] See pp. 203–05.

optional in a standard Greco-Roman letter, Paul almost always has one. He purposefully converts this formulaic element into a preview of attractions to come. In the thanksgiving, he rehearses important terms, concepts, or themes in the letter.

Introduction: Letter Format

Greco-Roman Letters	Pauline Expansions	Exegetical Significance
Writer (1:1–6)	intriguing omission: no co-senders	letter content exclusively Paul's
	use of Roman creedal tradition	attempt to establish shared faith
Recipient (1:7a)	use of Jewish covenant language	redefining "Israel," anticipating 9–11
Greeting (1:7b)	combining Greek and Hebrew ideas	alluding to gospel universality
Thanksgiving (1:8–15)	personal emphasis, Paul's work, plans	alludes to the purpose of Romans

FIGURE 6.9. Expansion of the Thanksgiving.

The thanksgiving of Romans is no disappointment here. The significance of the Romans thanksgiving, we discover only later, is that Paul has hidden the purpose and theme of Romans in these words. Yet, like an

(Beginning)	Literary Echoes	(Ending)
Paul's Plans 1:8–15		Paul's Plans 15:14–33
Text	Terminology	Text
1:1, 9	"serve"	15:16
1:1, 9	"gospel"	15:16
1:5, 8	"obedience of faith"	15:18
1:10, 13	"desire to come"	15:22–23
1:14	"indebted"	15:27

FIGURE 6.10. Literary Echoes: Rom 1:8–15 and 15:14–33.

Easter egg hunt, one has to do a little digging around to find the egg. The reason for this subtlety is an intentional ambiguity in the thanksgiving that does not become clear until the end of the letter. Romans is thereby imbued with an unusual connecting frame. The beginning is connected to the end.

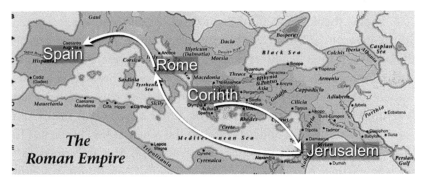

FIGURE 6.11. The Pauline Itinerary in Romans.

The letter frame, once inspected carefully, reveals that Paul himself is integral to the purpose of the letter.[55] The entire emphasis in both the beginning and ending units is Paul himself, his work, his plans. Terminology echoes between 1:8–15 and 15:14–33 show a deliberate reflecting back to pick back up the thanksgiving. We discover that "hindered" (1:13) really means the collection (15:22, 25), the Jerusalem itinerary; again, "come" (1:11) only means "come through" (15:24, 28), the Rome itinerary; and "evangelize" (1:14) coyly means not only edifying Rome, but missionizing Spain (15:24, 28), the Spain itinerary. Only at the end do we perceive the Pauline itinerary after Corinth of Jerusalem, Rome, and Spain as integrally tied to the purpose of Romans.

Thanksgiving Expansion

Romans 1:8

Two statements in the thanksgiving are quizzical. The first is the declaration in **1:8** that "your faith is proclaimed." If so, why does Paul need to go? Suddenly the reason for Paul spending the next *five* verses on his intent to visit stands in bold relief. The tension is not resolved until Paul has worked all the way through the text, like a slow reveal until he has supplied specificity at the end in Rom 15:14–33.

The second is the curious expression, "reap some harvest among you," in 1:13. What harvest? They already are strong believers, an emphatic point in 1:8, because their "faith is proclaimed throughout the world." The "harvest" wording may hide a rhetorical *double entendre* about help with Spain that Paul not yet is ready to put on the table.

---

[55] This featured already has been discussed briefly; see p. 163.

Paul is thankful for all of them because their faith is proclaimed "throughout the world." Here his concern for the nations percolates to the surface in what he observes about Roman believers. Paul's thought about Rome as central to impacting the very edges of the empire already is manifest. He is not wishing this statement were true, and he is not feigning a false compliment. He knows. Rome already sent Prisca and Aquila to Corinth and Ephesus right in the midst of his campaigns in those cities. So Paul has personal experience with Roman believers already impacting gospel mission in the province of Asia Minor. Since his purpose is reaching the nations of the world inspired by Isaiah, he can extrapolate that association with Roman believers would offer an effective tool for enhancing his future mission work just about anywhere.

Romans 1:9–10

Paul calls God as his witness. He is quite serious. He serves God by "announcing the gospel of his Son" (**1:9**) Here is the second of three uses of gospel as the word tying together all three opening units of Romans.[56] The testimony to which God will assent is that "without ceasing I remember you always in my prayers." One can believe the full force of this prayer as a perpetual offering to God on Paul's part, since prayer was a leading aspiration in Pharisee piety. This statement, however, is not to persuade Rome of Paul's piety, but rather reveals forethought about Rome, as the next phrase makes clear, "asking that by God's will I may somehow at last succeed in coming to you." Paul's itinerary is emphasized three times in four verses.[57] This plan could cause concern in Rome. What is Paul up to? Does he want to move into the pastor's office and pretend Rome is his church to lead? Only later does Paul make clear that he wants only to pass "through" Rome, not park in Rome.

Prayer forms a literary *inclusio* over Romans. Paul prays for Rome here at the opening in **1:10**. He then asks Rome to

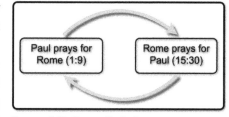

FIGURE 6.12. Prayer *Inclusio*.

---

[56] The introduction (1:1), thanksgiving (1:9), and theme (1:16).

[57] Cf. "succeed in coming to you" (1:10), "longing to see you" (1:11), and "often intended to come" (1:13).

pray for him at the end in 15:30. Paul wants to go to Rome. The ominous shadow of Jerusalem, however, looms over his plans. The Romans need to join with him in prayer if he is to get to Rome.

Romans 1:11–13

Paul expands the prayer topic by giving the details of his prayer's content, which is to see, share, and strengthen through a spiritual gift (**1:11–12**). He backtracks to avoid any impression of offensive condescension on his part about their spiritual maturity. Here, his experience at Corinth is informing the rhetoric. He clarifies he intends a mutual encouragement, which, once they learn of Spain later and agree to help, would be precisely true. This effort is reiterated four times in five verses.[58] Paul apparently already senses some mutuality with Roman believers.[59]

Paul says he often had planned to come, which was news to this church, to have "some fruit" (**1:13**). To be pastor? This rhetoric could be very unclear. He waits fifteen chapters to make clear his actual plans, which means those chapters are essential to expressing his plans more clearly. The church just will have to wait for "the rest of the story."

Almost all English translations gloss *ethnē* as "gentiles," a clear misdirection of Paul's thought.[60] Paul reflects Isaiah's vision of Israel as a nation leading the nations to God, so, "among the rest of the *nations*." "Nations" flows smoothly into the following categories that identify the object of Paul's preaching indebtedness, *not* in *Jewish* categories (Jew-gentile) but in *Roman* categories (civilized-uncivilized)—imperial ideology about the *nations* of the world. If we read Paul carefully, gentiles are not the point. Paul is writing this letter to Rome, not to Jerusalem.

Romans 1:14–15

Paul says, precisely, "I am indebted both to Greeks and to barbarians, both to the wise and the foolish" (**1:14**). These categories are Greco-Roman, how Greece, and later Rome, divided the world. Either one was Greek, wise, and therefore civilized, or one was barbarian, foolish, and therefore uncivilized. Paul expresses his indebtedness for preaching

---

[58] Cf. "share some spiritual gift" (1:11), "be mutually encouraged" (1:12), "reap some harvest" (1:13), and "proclaim the gospel" (1:15).

[59] Perhaps on the basis of those in Rome he already knows indicated in Romans 16.

[60] In discussion of Rom 1:5; see pp. 223–4.

the gospel *in terms of Roman imperial ideology of civilized and uncivilized nations of the world*. Paul boldly is making a direct claim for Israel's destiny on behalf of Isaiah. Israel has the divine obligation of leading the nations to God. That is her covenant. Rome has claimed divine prerogatives to rule the world and usurped Israel's covenant with Yahweh about the nations of the world. Brutal conquest celebrated by bloody gladiator contests to laud victories over nations is not God's will. Rome is just another empire of violence, subjugation, intimidation, and dominance, and that is not Israel's divine destiny. Israel's profile is as the Servant of Yahweh speaking love, joy, peace, and grace—everything Messiah revealed in his life and death. That message will be good news to anyone brutalized by Rome. Yes, Augustus had conquered the "barbarians" in Spain, but Paul also had sights on that nation as a part of his "indebtedness" to all the nations. If Rome proclaimed a gospel, Paul proclaimed a better gospel. He spoke eternal grace and peace. His mission to the nations under the shadow of Rome on behalf of that gospel would be the culmination of his call as apostle. As Paul makes clear, "hence my eagerness to proclaim the gospel to you also who are in Rome" (**1:15**)—that is, at the heartbeat of an empire, in the middle of the world's melting pot of peoples, making a clarion call in the capital of the empire ruling the nations. The gospel of God is for the nations.

LETTER THEME (1:16–17)

The movement from thanksgiving to theme pivots on literary ties and literary context. The literary ties include a grammatical tie in the connecting "for" conjunction, which indicates the thanksgiving and theme continue the same thought, and a key

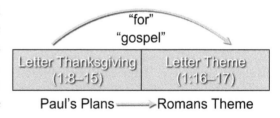

FIGURE 6.13. Thanksgiving and Theme Connections.

word tie, "gospel," which is the word common to all three units of the opening of Romans in the introduction, thanksgiving, and theme. In fact, Paul has strung together an entire series of clauses joined by "for" (γάρ, *gar*) in 1:9, 11, 16, 17, and 18. The grammatical ties mean not only that the thanksgiving flows logically immediately into the theme statement, but also that the theme statement flows logically immediately into the first rhetorical proof substantiating the theme proposal. All of Romans 1, then, is a continuous movement in Paul's rhetorical strategy. One practical implication of this logical flow of a string of "for" conjunctions is understanding that the key opening idea of the obedience of faith, is the controlling idea over all of Romans 1.

So the unit pivots on literary ties, and the unit pivots on literary context, which is the Pauline thanksgiving section. Considering the grammatical and linguistic connections above, then the theme can be interpreted as the logical extension of the thanksgiving. In addition, the thanksgiving is the logical foundation of the theme statement. In other words, Paul's *plans* (thanksgiving section) are *integral* to the exegesis of the Romans theme. Paul's plans involve his mission to the nations.

God's Gospel (1:16)

Paul introduces the theme in a strange and unexpected manner. First, he makes the theme about himself, "For I" (**1:16**). He might have just moved directly to a statement of God's power in the gospel. He could have said, "For in the gospel the power of God." He does not. As the thanksgiving was all about Paul, so is the theme.

Second, not only is the theme about Paul himself ("I"), another strange and unexpected element suddenly appears for which we have had no preparation whatsoever in either introduction or thanksgiving sections of the letter—the motif of shame. We note that Paul introduces this alien motif with an asseveration framed in the negative, "I am *not* ashamed." Well, OK then. Thanks, but what is the problem? To this point, Paul has not been on the defensive in anything he has said, so this new attitude rhetorically catches the audience off guard and gains their full attention. Catching the full rhetorical impact of this negative asseveration requires an understanding of first-century honor/shame codes. Throughout the introduction, the *ethos* of the author has been associated with God, Jesus, Messiah, and Lord. These associations all are honorable. Why does the author introduce shame into the theme?

The motif of shame in the theme statement of Romans is because Romans is all about Israel. Shame is tied directly to the prophetic word about Israel. The motif of shame is picked up again in Rom 5:5, where "hope does not put to shame." Contextually, this hope is "of sharing the glory of God" (5:2). The glory the nations presumed to themselves God will reclaim, even as with Pharaoh of Egypt (Exod 14:4, 17) and Nebuchadnezzar of Babylon (Isa 13:19).[61] Israel will be vindicated by God's glory (Isa 62:2), and to this glory all the nations shall be gathered (Isa 66:18–19). Paul's hope for God's glory in Israel he is confident will not be put to shame.[62]

Hope for the glory of God expressed briefly in 5:5 is Paul's thought in Romans 9–11, throughout which he takes his cues from Isaiah. Note that in Romans 9–11, the motif of shame suddenly reappears. During the Assyrian crisis, Isaiah warned Israel about its national policy of foreign alliances that evidenced lack of faith in Yahweh. Isaiah used the figure of Yahweh's trustworthy stone in Zion (Isa 28:16). This text likely resonates with Isa 8:14, in which both houses of Israel become a stone one stumbles over, "a trap and a snare for the inhabitants of Israel." The stumbling stones of the houses of Israel are set in contrast to the sanctuary of Yahweh himself, a stone against which one strikes. In Isa 28:16, some not having faith in the stone of Yahweh's provision would put their trust in foreign alliances and stumble over the stone meant to save. They subsequently would be put to shame by Assyria. Others having faith in the stone of Yahweh's provision would believe on him. In that belief, they would not be put to shame by Assyria. Paul in Romans 9–11 applies Isaiah's Zion stone imagery to Messiah (9:33). Notice that Isaiah's wording is the negated form of the verb ("not be put to shame," which Paul imitates in his own wording in the theme of Romans. The shame motif is related to Israel's rejection of the stone placed in Zion, Messiah, over which Mosaic Israel now is stumbling. Paul, on the other hand, has trusted in the messianic stone Yahweh has placed in Zion. Paul knows he will not be put to shame, as will other Jews trusting in the wrong object of faith. This passage in Isaiah Paul quotes twice in only a few verses (9:33; 10:11), revealing its crucial significance to Paul and why the shame motif appears in the theme statement of Romans. Paul is reflecting on Israel's eschatologi-

---

[61] This glory led Israel in the wilderness (Exod 16:10), filled the tabernacle (Exod 40:34), left Israel because of the ark (1 Sam 4:21), was over all the earth (Ps 57:5, 11), and to be declared among the nations (1 Chr 16:24, 28; Ps 96:3; Ps 102:15–16; Isa 24:15–16; 42:12; Ezek 39:21; Hab 2:14; 3:3).

[62] Mark 8:38 (Luke 9:26) may be background, but the main idea is from Isaiah.

cal crisis of stumbling over the stone meant to save. This crisis, indeed, may be paralleling the Assyrian crisis in an uncanny and foreboding way. One only needs to consider that the destiny of a nation is at stake.

One also might venture to say that the shame motif is personal, although Paul does not say so explicitly. Paul's take on the gospel is not everyone's cup of tea in the early church. Thousands in Jerusalem were not happy with him, according to James.[63] The synagogue must not have been happy with him either, as he endured formal punishment of the synagogue lash on five separate occasions, probably the record for one person at the time.[64] According to Acts, he is rejected in every synagogue in which he attempts to be an ambassador for Messiah.[65] Many Jews treat him as having betrayed Moses, the law, and Israel. He is sensitive to the charges made against him, because the false accusations surface on occasion in the argument in Romans (3:8).

Paul's thought transitions logically and consistently with what he just has said about being indebted to all the nations. Regardless his rejection in synagogue after synagogue (or coming riot in Jerusalem over his presence), he is not ashamed. He is called as an apostle and set apart for the gospel of God, and he is confident that hope in God's glory in Israel will not shame him in the end. God's glory will be declared and manifested to the nations as the prophets promised. That glory is Israel's destiny. Paul is faithful to God and to Israel and sets his mission compass for the nations of the world in total commitment to the vision of Isaiah: "For I am not ashamed of the gospel."

The gospel "is the power of God." Power language invokes the lordship frame over created life. God lays claim to creation. Paul dives in head first to the beginning of the narrative of Israel: God is. God is creator.[66] The evidence to this power is the resurrection (1:4). The issue is God's sovereignty over the nations. That issue would involve Rome. The term in Roman imperial inscriptions that is translated "emperor" is ΑΥΤΟΚΡΑΤΩΡ (AUTOCRATŌR), from which we get the word "au-

---

[63] Acts 21:20–22. The debacle of Paul's insistence on going to Jerusalem ended up in riot and turmoil. James had warned Paul his presence was a problem. He was right.

[64] 2 Cor 11:24. Any one occasion could have threatened Paul's life.

[65] Damascus (Acts 9:23–25); early Jerusalem (Acts 9:29); Antioch of Pisidia (Acts 13:40–46); Thessalonica (Acts 15:5); Berea (Acts 17:13); Corinth (Acts 18:6); Ephesus (Acts 19:9); Corinth again (Acts 20:3); Jerusalem again (Acts 21:27–31); Rome (Acts 28:24).

[66] See pp. 113–14.

tocrat," which means a ruler who has absolute power. The emperor
claimed absolute power over the nations.

FIGURE 6.14. Roman Imperial Inscription. The beginning of this inscription reads
ΑΥΤΟΚΡΑΤΟΡΙ ΚΑΙΣΑΡΙ, *AUTOKRATORI KAISARI*, "To Emperor Caesar." The
inscription probably was part of a dedicatory monument to the emperor cult (AAM).

A similar term in the Hebrew Scripture is *El Shaddai*, associated
with the name of Yahweh, which the Septuagint Greek version translates as Παντοκράτωρ, *Pantokratōr*, "Almighty." This designation is one
of the most common titles for God in Hebrew Scripture.[67] (Sometimes
LXX translators rendered the term as "God of hosts.") Thus, the claim
of the emperor is in direct conflict with God's own prerogatives. The
emperor might claim to be *autokratōr*, but God is *pantokratōr*.[68] As a
feature of the eschaton, God would show his power by regathering his
sons and daughters from among the nations of their dispersion, as in
Isa 49:22, "Thus says the Lord God: I will soon lift up my hand to the
nations, and raise up my signal to the peoples; and they shall bring your
sons in their bosom and your daughter shall be carried on their shoulders."[69] Developments in Judea since the exile have left much to be desired in terms of these promises. In fact, the story of the Jewish nation
still in Paul's day is one of foreign domination and exploitation. Surely
that state of affairs is not what Isaiah had in mind. The gospel of God
is the narrative that concludes that story with God's power on display.

The power of God is "unto salvation." Pop quiz. Yours, mine, or
ours? All of the above, of course—but what is the emphasis in this context? Likely corporate, for multiple reasons. One is the emphasis upon

---

[67] Cf. 2 Sam 5:10; 1 Kgs 19:10; 1 Chr 11:9; Job 5:17; Hos 12:5; Amos 4:13; Mic 4:4;
Nah 2:13; Hab 2:13; Zeph 2:10; Hag 1:2; Zech 1:3; Mal 1:4; Jer 3:19.

[68] See Stevens, *Revelation*, 229, 458, 488.

[69] Cf. Isa 43:6; 60:4; also, Hos 1:10. Note that in 2 Cor 6:16–18, Paul alludes to an
amalgam of texts with the common imagery that God is a Father to Israel, whose members are his sons and daughters.

getting translation of *ethnē* properly focused.[70] Paul's general thought throughout both the introduction and thanksgiving sections has been corporate. Further, Paul's pluralizing rhetoric in Romans 6–8, for example, regularly is ignored by commentators, so the matter is disguised from the general reader.[71] The second reason salvation in the theme rhetoric likely has corporate emphasis is because the entire movement of Romans 1–8 is headed toward a first person plural corporate climax.

> For the creation with eager expectation is awaiting the revelation of the children of God. For the creation was subjected unto futility, not willingly, but because of the one who subjected in hope, because even creation itself will be set free from the slavery of decay unto the freedom of the children of God. For we know that all creation is groaning together in pain together until now. And not only that, but we also ourselves groan in ourselves awaiting adoption, the redemption of our bodies (Rom 8:19–23).

Salvation is cosmic in Romans, so the theme unit likely includes these eschatological dimensions.[72] A third reason salvation likely is corporate in the theme statement is how Paul addresses ethics from a corporate perspective. All the verbs and pronouns are plural in Rom 12:1–2. Further, the premier imagery Paul uses in Romans 12 as foundation to his exhortation is of believers as a corporate body (12:4). The fourth reason salvation is corporately conceived in Rom 1:16 is that such a perspective provides the necessary theology for addressing the weak and the strong in Romans 14–15.

Salvation is "to the one who believes." Belief does not make salvation—God does—but belief is the channel salvation flows in a dyadic relationship between believer and God. Belief language gives voice to the mutuality of the divine-human relationship.

Availability for the one who believes is "to the Jew first, and to the Greek." The "Jew and Greek" rhetorical combination is a common pattern in Paul.[73] What is its meaning here? The statement could be observation of simple historical circumstance. Naturally, Jews such as Mary,

---

[70] See discussion of "among all the *ethnē*" (Rom 1:5), pp. 227–29.

[71] On the pluralizing rhetoric of Romans, see pp. 50, 198. The tradition of interpreting Romans as about the individual believer is the default hermeneutic, especially since the Reformation, but needs to be challenged.

[72] Deliverance from destruction; cf. 1 Cor 3:15; 5:5; Phil 2:12; 1 Thess 5:8–9.

[73] Rom 2:9; 3:9; 10:12; 1 Cor 1:24; 10:21; 12:13; Gal 3:28; Col 3:11.

Zechariah, the shepherds, Simeon, and Anna were the first to hear the gospel and rejoice in a Savior sent from God.[74] Yet, here in Romans, the "first" wording emphasizes covenant priority. But how does Jewish covenant priority play into the reality of faith?

Faith is fundamental, and fundamentally faith is obedience (1:5). The "obedience of faith" in the context of the introduction to Romans is obedience of the nations to the worship of God and ascribing glory to God, as in Isaiah's vision (Isa 66:18–21). At this point, we have to pay careful attention to how Paul expresses himself to see how Isaiah's vision is, in fact, the underlying narrative in this theme statement with its focus on covenant priority. Notice the categories of humankind Paul chooses when he speaks to Jewish priority. He does *not* say, "to the Jew first, and to the gentile." Rather, he chooses "and to the Greek." The common denominator in the use of "Greek" is Jewish focus on polytheism—the fundamental evidence of not being obedient to God.[75] The issue is not so much circumcision as polytheism. Note that polytheism will be the main problem identified in the next section in Rom 1:21–23. For that matter, even the circumcised can be polytheistic.[76] Note how Paul establishes obedience of faith as a move away from polytheism in the story of uncircumcised Abraham, who was called by God to leave his polytheistic context, Ur of the Chaldees.[77] In this he is the father of many nations for those who follow Abraham's footsteps (Romans 4). God intends the nations to show obedience of faith by hearing his call in the gospel and forsaking their polytheism. This call to forsake polytheism is precisely how Paul describes the response of the Thessalonians (1 Thess 1:9). For God to accomplish this goal, as with the Thessalonians, Israel will have to embrace God's mission des-

---

[74] Luke 1:46, 67; 2:8, 25, 36.

[75] Reflected in Acts and in Paul, especially in terms of polytheists attracted to the worship of one God in the synagogue. Cf. Acts 14:1; 18:4; 19:10, 17; 20:21; Rom 2:9; 3:9; 10:12; 1 Cor 1:24; 10:21; 12:13; Gal 3:28; Col 3:11. Greeks were not attracted to Jewish circumcision. They were attracted to Jewish monotheism, and that belief comes with a built-in story, no extra charge. See p. 113. Inherently, a Greek would not be circumcised (Acts 16:3), of course, but the issue here is broader than just circumcision.

[76] The golden calf is paradigmatic (Exodus 32). Moses warned of the problem (Exod 20:4; Deut 4:19; 5:8; 27:3), and the prophets had to continue to warn (Amos 5:25–27; Zeph 1:5; Jer 7:18; 8:2). Stephen reminds Jewish rulers that even in the wilderness, the Israelites were idolatrous (Acts 7:42–43).

[77] Gen 11:28, 31; 15:7; Neh 9:7; Acts 7:4.

tiny on behalf of bringing the nations to worship God alone, as did Paul after a risen Messiah reformulated his Pharisaic traditions.

Unfortunately, not all Jewish narratives had Isaiah's vision in mind in configuring the place of gentiles in the future kingdom of God. This failure of vision is evidenced by the synagogue debate over gentile inclusion or exclusion. Paul's vote is for inclusion. He was trying to redirect the Great Assembly narrative with its emphasis on Moses and circumcision to a messianic emphasis on Isaiah and faithful obedience. In short, Paul is trying to move Jewish discussion from "gentile" and circumcision to "nation" and covenant destiny. To be sure, he was encountering formidable inertia from centuries of postexilic Great Assembly tradition. As a zealous Pharisee, he knew fully what he was up against, but he believed the Scriptures, and he believed Messiah.[78]

God's Righteousness (1:17)

Paul introduces two revelations inaugurated by the coming of Messiah. One is the revelation of God's righteousness (**1:17**). The other is the revelation of God's wrath (1:18).[79] Revelation is God's activity whereby he discloses truth that humans otherwise would not have known. The full truth about God's righteousness and wrath was not known until Jesus came. With all the information about God's righteousness and wrath in the Scripture, what possibly could be unknown? That, Paul now knows, is the mystery of the cross. Not even Paul with all of his Pharisaic training had a clue about what the cross revealed about God. After his encounter with the risen Jesus, which was a revelation, Paul's theological quest was to reflect on the meaning of Jesus Messiah, and him crucified (1 Cor 2:2). Paul now introduces the Romans to what he understands as the revelation of God's righteousness in Jesus, crucial to his understanding of the gospel story.

> For in it the righteousness of God is being revealed from faith unto faith just as it has been written: "But the one righteous out of faith will live" (Rom 1:17).

[78] "Gentile" will be an appropriate topic when circumcision directly is in view. As argued above, circumcision is not directly in view in Rom 1:16.

[79] Both revelations of righteousness and wrath are expressed in present tense (ἀποκαλύπτεται, *apokalyptetai*, "is being revealed"). These revelations are concurrent with the preaching of the gospel to which they are associated (1:16).

The conjunction "for" ties this verse to the previous verse. Thus, the neuter pronoun in the phrase "in it" in 1:17 refers back to the neuter noun, "gospel," in 1:16. So, only in the gospel is this truth about the righteousness of God revealed. "For" also continues tying this unit back to the thanksgiving. Therefore, the revelation of righteousness in the gospel also is interconnected with Paul's plans, that is, his mission to Spain. Paul later will indicate the gospel reveals that God's righteousness is a public affair (3:25). From the introduction to Romans, we can surmise that that public affair involves the nations and the obedience of faith. The target of the nations for God is the story of Abraham inheriting the world. Israel never was about Israel only. God is not God of Jews only (3:29). That the whole world belongs to God is the whole point of monotheism (Ps 24:1–3).

Commentators regularly have agreed that "the righteousness of God" is the crucial phrase that makes this statement the crucial verse of Romans. Yet, amazingly, this particular phrase occurs nowhere else in Paul outside of Romans except in 2 Cor 5:21, written just months before Romans. The phrase occurs only eight times even in Romans, but five are clustered in one series in chapter 3.[80] We already discussed in depth three recent scholars' widely differing hermeneutical frames for parsing this phrase.[81] That presentation was given to show just how complex are the issues. In brief, the major theories on how righteousness functions in Romans revolve around attributes or activity:

- *attribute of God*, either his retributive justice (negatively), or his own faithfulness to the covenant (Watson, Wright)

- *attribute of humans*, divinely conveyed, either as forensic (alien) status (Luther) or as genuine (moral) quality (Augustine)

- *activity of God*, his power to establish what is right, typically salvation for his people (Psalms, Isaiah, Käsemann).

We really do not have to choose. First, each of these has good support in Scripture, and that is why so many famous names can be attached to each option. Second, commentators often will opt for some combination of at least two in various relationships. Some even combine all

[80] Cf. Rom 1:17; 3:5, 21, 22, 25, 26; 10:3 (2x).
[81] See chapter 2, "The Righteousness of God."

three.[82] At the same time, we do need to decide what Paul's emphasis would be here given what he knows he will be saying later.

Imperative is to realize this verse begins a discussion that will go for eleven chapters. We have to be careful to understand this passage such that we have the appropriate foundation for the concluding declaration of these eleven chapters, "And, thus, all Israel will be saved" (11:26). Romans 9–11, in other words, casts a long shadow onto the meaning of Rom 1:17.

Righteousness as the activity of God on behalf of his people to save is the predominant use in the Scripture (option 3). According to the prophets, God's saving activity especially would be manifest in the eschaton. Yet, that expectation alone creates a problem that turns the question of this righteousness of God into the story of Israel's odyssey through theodicy, justifying the ways of a covenant God, who, in the harsh reality of history, has destroyed Israel by exile, not saved Israel. In the crucible of the exile, the cry of lament still reverberates. Modern readers of Romans should hear this lament.[83]

> How lonely sits the city
> > that once was full of people!
> How like a widow she has become,
> > she that was great among the nations!
> She that was a princess among the provinces
> > has become a vassal.
> She weeps bitterly in the night,
> > with tears on her cheeks;
> among all her lovers
> > she has no one to comfort her;
> all her friends have dealt treacherously with her,
> > they have become her enemies.
> Judah has gone into exile with suffering
> > and hard servitude;
> she lives now among the nations,
> > and finds no resting place;
> her pursuers have all overtaken her
> > in the midst of her distress (Lam 1:1–3, NRSV)

The author of Lamentations lived no illusion about what had happened: "Jerusalem sinned grievously" (Lam 1:8). The result was, "The Lord has

---

[82] Cf. Wedderburn, *Reasons*, 108–203.

[83] See discussion, pp. 69–74.

destroyed without mercy all the dwellings of Jacob; in his wrath he has broken down the strongholds of daughter Judah" (Lam 2:2). Notice that the author immediately connects exile as an expression of the wrath of God. God could not be righteous if he did not condemn sin. God's wrath is his zeal to preserve his holiness. He is righteous to do so. But, what of Israel? Thus begins Israel's long odyssey through theodicy after the crucible of the exile.

Israel's present theological maze after the exile, in other words, is theodicy, justifying the ways of God. The problem is that God's wrath destroys Israel, so jeopardizes God's unfulfilled promises. In the destruction of exile the promise to Abraham appears lost. Other promises to Israel after the exile seem unfulfilled. Isaiah had promised, "For the mountains may depart and the hills be removed, but my steadfast love shall not depart from you, and my covenant of peace shall not be removed, says the Lord, who has compassion on you" (Isa 54:10). And again, Isaiah promised, "The Lord has bared his holy arm before the eyes of all the nations; and all the ends of the earth shall see the salvation of our God" (Isa 52:10). God's pledge of steadfast love to Israel seems lost in events since the exile. Israel has defaulted on two royal dynasties already and now is ruled by another foreign nation, Rome. Is Israel almost back to square one, hardly better off than the author of Lamentations?[84]

Thus, Israel's story has dual perspectives on God's righteousness. In Abraham, righteousness is a status God gives (option 2), but in judgment, righteousness is a quality God lives (options 1, 3).[85] Note: *Israel is in the center of both these stories.* Jesus Messiah both gives and lives this righteousness of God like no other king in Israel. In truth, Jesus is the only true king Israel ever had. Jesus both realizes Abraham's inheritance among the nations and consummates God's steadfast love to Israel.

Although Paul has various ways to use the verb "reveal" (ἀποκαλύπτω, *apokalyptō*), the nuance here is God's eschatological disclosure

---

[84] The prophets give evidence for the feeling that after the exile something still was amiss, that the wrath of God still was on Israel; cf. Hag 1:5–11; Zech 1:3, 19; Isa 64:9. Similarly, Ps 74:1–8; 85:4–6. This climate of thought was fertile ground for theodicy in late wisdom material; cf. Hengel, *Judaism and Hellenism*, 250.

[85] Moo, *Romans*, 70–75, has one of the best discussions of how best to balance the options on interpreting the righteousness of God in Rom 1:17 (but note the emphasis on Lutheran forensic status rather than Augustinian infused character).

of his plan for salvation.[86] That the revelation now is happening in the gospel translates into "gospel knowledge," an understanding that comes into view only inasmuch as the gospel comes into view, so requires gospel proclamation (10:14–15). What about Scripture? Does Scripture testify to this revelation? Paul writes Romans 4 to say yes. Only inasmuch as Scripture has touched on the gospel "promised beforehand" (1:2) would one have a notion of this truth about God's righteousness in the old covenant. The Scripture touches on this gospel truth in the revelation of God's dealings with Abraham. Abraham is the story of a gentile who trusted God to justify the ungodly—a faith God reckoned to Abraham as righteousness. That righteousness from God was the foundation of God's promise that Abraham would inherit the world (4:5, 13).

Two prepositional phrases, "ἐκ (*ek*) faith εἰς (*eis*) faith," are juxtaposed together immediately after the verb "revealed." They could modify the verb or the phrase righteousness of God, but how? These binary prepositions have exhausted reams of paper in the search for translation and exegesis. First, translators do not agree how to construe the doublet series of prepositions, even at times capitulating to paraphrase:

• from . . . unto (ASV)

• from . . . for (ESV)

• from . . . to (CSB, HCSB, KJB, NASB, NET, WEB)

• through . . . for (NRSV)

• by . . . unto (ERV)

• by faith from first to last (NIV)

• shows up in the acts of faith (Message)

Second, as one could expect with such an array of translational options, each with its own slightly different nuance, establishing a consensus on the precise meaning of this series is out of reach. Proposals of degree (from lesser faith to greater faith), direction (from God's faithfulness to human faithful obedience), or emphasis (faith all the way) all have

---

[86] Cf. Rom 2:5; 8:18, 19; 1 Cor 1:7; Gal 1:16; 3:23; 2 Thess 1:7; 2:3, 6, 8.

their proponents. Notice that all three tip the hat to the human side of the equation. This inclination makes sense in the context of "to everyone who believes" (1:16), as well as some of the implications of the Habakkuk quotation to follow. From the Jew first, then to the gentile also could figure in, Israel to the nations, Abraham to his heritage.

"Just as it is written" is the first of Paul's many scriptural quotations in Romans. Paul begins parsing his "promised beforehand" claim made in 1:2. His first text is Hab 2:4: "the one righteous out of [?] faith will live." The original context of Hab 2:4 is a Chaldean invasion crisis confronting the nation. These enemies "continually slaughter nations without mercy" (Hab 1:17). Israel will not be able to resist because injustice and the wrongdoing of oppression and violence are right in front of the prophet, all rendering the law ineffective (Hab 1:3–4).[87] The problem is that every inhabitant of the land is swallowed up indiscriminately in this divine judgment, even those who have kept faith with Yahweh, who have lived righteously with regard to the law: "Why do you look on the treacherous, and are silent when the wicked swallow those more righteous than they" (Hab 1:13, NRSV)? The original import is that God responds to vindicate the faithful Israelite (Hab 2:4). In the end, the faithful Israelite "will live."

The question mark is a missing pronoun in Paul's quotation. The intertextual issue is complicated. The Hebrew original has "the one righteous out of *his* faith," that is, out of the individual Israelite's faith. Against the complaint of the prophet that the righteous Israelite will be judged indiscriminately with the lawless in the land, God responds not so. God sees the righteous. God will vindicate that righteousness.

The LXX translators, on the other hand, significantly altered the meaning. Since Paul most often quoted the LXX translation when he quoted Scripture, then he likely was familiar with this version of Hab 2:4. The problem is that the LXX translators reversed the point and negated the original historical context by changing the pronoun. They translated, "the one righteous out of *my* faith(fulness)," that is, Israel is righteous; therefore, God's covenant faithfulness obligates him to save righteous Israel, which takes the original sinful nation out of the picture. The LXX completely obscures that the lawless in Israel were why God was using the Chaldeans to judge Israel in the first place!

---

[87] Paul was not the first to note the impotency of the law.

Paul chose door number 3: no pronoun. So, whose righteousness are we talking about? Perhaps both. Paul intertwines two stories, that of Abraham, and that of postexilic Israel. Both facets of faith are necessary to understand how the cross works to save, how God will reach the nations, and how Israel will fulfill her destiny.

The quotation concludes, "shall live." Life and destiny are at stake. Life and destiny were at stake for the nation of Israel in the days of Habakkuk, and life and destiny are at stake for all who need to hear the gospel of God. We are back to creation. Life is creation's purpose. Creation, meant for life, has been transmuted into a death chamber. The creator, however, who has the power of life, thereby has the power to save, and he does. Creation's goal ultimately will be achieved. Faith is the key to how the gospel of God works, whether divine or human.

7

Universal Guilt

God and Sin

B EFORE JUMPING INTO THE FIRST UNIT on divine wrath in Rom 1:18–32, let us remind ourselves of how all this fits together in the bigger picture of Romans 1–8. Paul's presentation in Romans 1–8 centers on his eschatology. In these eight chapters, Paul overviews the human experience in terms of two epochs that constitute two eternal destinies, the age of Adam and the age of Messiah. What is implicit behind all of Rom 1:18—3:20 is the assumption of the fall of Adam and the inability of anything in human experience to overcome the results of the fall. The Adamic tragedy has one solution only. This solution is Messiah, as confessed in the creed of the Roman church with which Paul begins Romans (1:3–4). In that creed, resurrection doctrine points to eschatology as the crucial frame for understanding the Christ event. In Romans 1–8, Paul in his discussion is encompassing the beginning and end of human history. In another letter, he spoke of Christ as the "last Adam" as the consummation of human history, and here in Romans is his fuller treatment of that Adam theology.[1] His shorthand for this eschatology surfaces in the "but now" of 3:21–26 and the Adam typology in 5:12–21. The age of Adam is the assumption behind Romans 1–4, and the age of Messiah the assumption behind Romans 5–8. The age of

---

[1] 1 Cor 15:45. Note carefully that Paul does *not* describe Christ as a "second Adam." "Second" implies an on-going series, as in a third or a fourth. Christ is not the "second Adam." He is the "last," a crucial distinction. "Last" is eschatology like "second" is not. "Last Adam" means no other and describes the consummation of human history.

Adam is the Old Aeon of sin and death. The age of Messiah is the New Aeon of grace and life. Life controlled by the consequences of Adam's disobedience is a story of incorrigible sin and the reign of unrighteousness and death—no matter how God reveals himself, whether in the creator-creature bond with humanity as a whole or in the covenant-election bond with Israel in particular. Life controlled by the consequences of Messiah's obedience is a story of overwhelming grace and the reign of righteousness and life. Paul begins the story of the human predicament with the Age of Adam, the Old Aeon characterized by sin and death, the story of God's wrath. Eden is a short story of divine wrath that became the long story of human history.

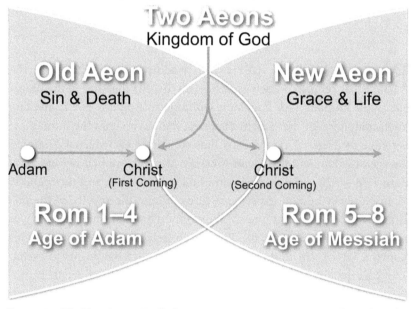

FIGURE 7.1. The Two Aeons. Paul's discussion in Romans 1–8 assumes the reality of two aeons that tell the human story and summarize the beginning and end.

Outlines of the smaller units comprising Rom 2:1—4:25 have considerable variances. The problem is threefold. First, the rhetoric of diatribe confuses the issue of speaker, topic, and background from Rom 2:1 onwards. Scholars disagree, sometimes diametrically opposed.[2]

---

[2] What is the context, and which statements are Paul's and which are his imaginary opponent (polemical context) or student (pedagogical context)? Whether Paul or his dialogue partner can turn the whole point on its head. Contrast Achtemeier (*Romans*), Campbell (*The Deliverance of God*), Dunn (*Romans*), Longenecker (*Romans*), Stowers (*A Rereading of Romans*), and Wright (*Paul and the Faithfulness of God*).

Second, the argument is dense in logic and theology, with some of the phrasing so complex or condensed as almost to defy translation, much less comprehension. An outline is hard to generate when one is confused even about what the author is saying.

Third, Paul detours at Rom 3:21 as any Pharisee would to defend the integrity of the righteousness of God to save humans even in the face of abject human failure (3:10–18). If all humanity stands condemned, nothing need be decided at the judgment. Yet, God saves. That action should render God unrighteous. Thus, Paul takes a spin around the theodicy block on God's righteousness (Rom 3:21—4:25). To do so, Paul has to jump prematurely to the New Aeon reality in Messiah to argue this theodicy before he *formally* introduces the New Aeon reality in the Adam typology of Rom 5:12–21. An outline cannot easily accommodate this logical jump that is grounded in subsequent presentation (similar to Rom 3:1–8 already anticipating the later issues of Romans 9–11). Here is our outline of the first part of Rom 1:18—4:25 on the universal guilt of humankind. The first subdivision in Rom 1:18—3:20 establishes fundamental human unrighteousness in disobedience.

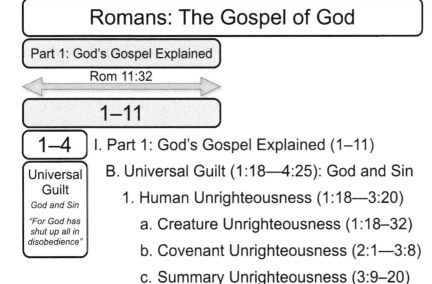

Romans Structure

Romans: The Gospel of God

Part 1: God's Gospel Explained

Rom 11:32

1–11

1–4 | I. Part 1: God's Gospel Explained (1–11)

Universal Guilt
God and Sin

"For God has shut up all in disobedience"

B. Universal Guilt (1:18—4:25): God and Sin

  1. Human Unrighteousness (1:18—3:20)

    a. Creature Unrighteousness (1:18–32)

    b. Covenant Unrighteousness (2:1—3:8)

    c. Summary Unrighteousness (3:9–20)

FIGURE 7.2. Outline: Romans 1–4. Establishing universal guilt (1:18—3:20) leads to a theodicy (3:21—4:25): How is a just and holy God righteous to save anyone?

HUMAN UNRIGHTEOUSNESS

Creature Unrighteousness (1:18–32)

Human Unrighteousness (1:18—3:20)

Romans 1	Romans 2	Romans 3
Creature Unrighteousness	Covenant Unrighteousness	Summary Unrighteousness

FIGURE 7.3. Outline: Romans 1 (Creature Unrighteousness). Universal guilt in three parts in Rom 1:18—3:20 begins with creature unrighteousness.

Divine Wrath in God's Story

God intended life, but Sin created death. Sin provoked human distrust in God, the core cause of unrighteousness and disobedience, which has been pandemic since Eden. So, faith in God has been the issue since the beginning. Eden is the story of God's wrath, because Adam, though initially blessed, was cursed due to his disobedience. Curse is a basic function of divine wrath. God is holy and righteous, so he cannot ignore sin.

Thus, the story of Eden teaches that neither divine righteousness nor divine holiness has any gravitas without wrath. Yet, even though an integral and indispensable part of the story of Eden at the beginning of the biblical narrative, divine wrath is the last topic on God anyone wants to talk about. Indeed, Marcion had his falling out with the church of Rome over his idea that the God of the Old Testament was an angry demiurge not to be trusted. Marcion was prescient of much theological angst over the ages. Yet, even from the very beginning, the story of God as creator cannot be told without the story of his wrath. So, Paul, like the Bible, starts his story of the gospel with the story of divine wrath. What cultural paints already were on the canvas when he wrote that would have predicated how his audience viewed his picture of wrath?

Divine Wrath in Ancient Culture

The language of divine wrath Paul inherited from his world has features that illustrate the ancient mindset upon which Paul had to build his theology of wrath.[3] In doing so, he had to negotiate around some

---

[3] In the following several paragraphs, we are condensing some material presented in detail and at greater length and documentation in Stevens, *Divine Wrath in Paul*.

presuppositions, counteract others, and capitalize on some core ideas. A quick summary of Pauline distinctives in his ancient context will be useful before diving into Rom 1:18.[4]

The term basic to Paul, ὀργή (*orgē*),[5] was basic to Greek usage, as was the synonymous term, θυμός (*thumos*);[6] hence, "wrath" and "anger" could be swapped out in translation when the terms occurred together in series.[7] The problem in Greek myth was characterizing divine anger of the gods of Olympus as comparable to human anger. Human anger, of course, could be capricious and irrational. Capriciousness or irrationality when applied to the gods meant one always was in jeopardy of unknowingly offending some god in some obscure way. Petitions to the gods for help and cultic propitiation to ward off harm were features of daily life laboring under the demands of Olympus.

The irrationality of human anger became a focus and a problem to be solved for the philosophers. They produced various solutions, particularly among Epicureans and Stoics. Anger was to be controlled or eliminated. Since elimination of anger became a philosophical virtue to which to aspire, the philosophers taught that the gods as more than mortals could not possibly express anger. The gods were immutable, but the Yahweh revealed in Scripture clearly was not immutable. How does one convey to such Greek thought that Yahweh has wrath but not irrationality? That was part of Paul's goal in Romans 1.

Greek thought to capitalize on was divine wrath used by Olympus as an instrument to guide human destiny. Divine wrath sets limits on human hubris and cannot be resisted with impunity. Greek thought also understood the divine wrath as preserving the state and defending justice. Thus, expression of *orgē* as a function of the state for "punishment" was the proper and expected emotion of a good ruler serious about avenging injustice in the public arena, on the pattern of King David's reaction to hearing Nathan's parable, even though David himself was the offender (2 Sam 12:1–6). This concept plays into wrath as used in Rom 13:1–6.

---

[4] For detailed development and discussion, see Stevens, *Divine Wrath in Paul*.

[5] Rom 1:18; 2:5 (2x), 8; 3:5; 4:15; 5:9; 9:22 (2x); 12:19; 13:4 (2x); Eph 2:3; 4:31; 5:6; Col 3:6, 8; 1 Thes 1:10; 1 Thess 2:16; 5:9; 1 Tim 2:8.

[6] Rom 2:8; 2 Cor 12:20; Gal 5:20; Eph 4:31; Col 3:8.

[7] Cf. Eph 4:31; Col 3:8.

Another thought to capitalize on was that the Roman historians had a distinctive use of divine wrath as the ground of the welfare of state and government. For the Romans, religion and divine wrath were linked inseparably to state and destiny. Thus, the wrath of God was a literary device for historical interpretation. This aspect Paul capitalized on in Romans 9–11 in explaining Israel and her destiny.

Hebraic understanding of the wrath of Yahweh is distinguished from Homeric thought on the basis of Yahweh's revealed covenant with Israel. The covenant both personalized the divine-human relationship unlike anything that could be conceived by the Greeks and eliminated capriciousness. Wrath was judgment for violation of known covenant stipulations. Another twist in Hebraic thought was the subordination of any expression of divine wrath to the proclamation of the divine Name. Preservation of Israel was not for Israel. Israel did not deserve preservation, as the nation was idolatrous from beginning to end and never held up its side of covenant obligations. Preservation of Israel was for the glory of Yahweh's Name among the nations. The expression of God's wrath as a result, no matter how catastrophic, never was the end of the story, not in God's playbook. Here is the core of Pauline thought about divine wrath.

Other Jewish literature such as the Septuagint, Josephus, and Philo shows a decided trend to deemphasize Homeric terms for wrath, using *orgē* and *thumos* exclusively, with a decided preference for *orgē* for the divine wrath. The linguistic trend seems to reveal an implicit attempt to suppress Greek associations of irrationality with divine anger. Even the rabbis in figures such as the Angel of Destruction seem to show this trend to dissociate God's wrath from human anger. Paul's usage with its decided preference for *orgē* in contexts of the divine wrath is right in line with this Jewish trend.

The Dead Sea scrolls and the Samaritan doctrine of the future Taheb redeemer figure show how divine wrath became integrally associated with eschatology. Full reckoning for sin required a final judgment. Paul's eschatology, while not deterministic, was just as emphatic on final judgment (Rom 2:5–11).

Paul's first problem as he begins in earnest to develop his argument in Romans 1 is that God could not be righteous without wrath. Paul's second problem is that God in his wrath must be righteous. The problem for readers is that Paul's good news starts with God's wrath.

Like the theme statement starting with an unexpected motif of shame, the gospel statement starts with an unexpected motif of divine wrath.

A Revealed Creator (1:18–23)

Paul wrote, "For the wrath [ὀργή, *orgē*] of God is being revealed against all human unrighteousness and ungodliness" (**1:18**). In Paul's ancient world, a god who did not express wrath against ungodliness was neither a true deity nor of any concern. God, however, is holy like Olympus is not, so the expression of his wrath is for other purposes than simply getting miffed or getting revenge. Fundamentally, a fallen world cannot comprehend holiness, so the operation of God's wrath is both alien and unfathomable. Paul will turn Olympus on its head. As Rom 1:18–32 will show, God reveals his wrath in order to save humans. Wrath is the dark side of the moon of grace. Thus, Paul's "wrath" language requires contextualization. Romans 1 most certainly is not Homer's Olympus. God's wrath intends to save. Zeus never did.

Second, notice both that the verb "is being revealed" is present tense, and that the revelation comes "from heaven." Combined, these realities mean that whatever Paul is referencing about what humans can know about God's wrath is happening *now* and available to *all*. The "from heaven" addition emphasizes that this revelation is before all and inescapable to any. We also should note that while the righteousness of God is revealed in the gospel (1:17), so requires the preaching of the gospel of Jesus as Messiah to understand, the wrath of God is revealed in the creator-creature bond ever since the creation of the world, so is understood inherently by any human by virtue of being a creature created by God. So Rom 1:18–32 focuses on unrighteousness of creatures.

Third, the apocalypse of wrath is against "unrighteousness and ungodliness." Probably synonymous, the terms are doubled for emphasis. Every culture has its definition of what constitutes this behavior. Paul's is biblical, the revelation of Yahweh in Scripture as interpreted by the prophets of Israel and the coming of Messiah, but not, as he formerly thought, as interpreted by oral tradition under the aegis of the Great Synagogue. Paul is most careful with his rhetoric. He speaks of the unrighteousness and ungodliness of *human beings* ("man," ἄνθρωπος, *anthrōpos*, here used as synecdoche for "mankind," "humans," "human beings"). Note carefully that nowhere in this passage does Paul use the word "gentile," even though this assumption commonly is made in commentaries. If one qualifies to be on the cover of National Geographic, Paul's analysis applies, so Jews are included in this indictment. This observation will become more telling in a few verses.

Fourth, similar in vein of thought to the above observation, this wrath is against *all* (πᾶσαν, *pasan*) ungodliness and unrighteousness. This "all" first of all globalizes the target of divine wrath as every nation and culture. Paul had said that the obedience of all the nations was his mission target (1:5), and the global apocalypse of divine wrath is the theological basis for global accountability in this global mission. Paul's mission audience already knows something crucial about the God of heaven before Paul even gets there, that judgment is coming, with a judge already appointed to the bench to adjudicate the case.[8] At the same time, this "all" also is a boomerang that will come back to hit the unsuspecting. Even the elect fall into this category of the unrighteous and ungodly. This adjective "all," then, is a rhetorical hook that supplies exegetical efficacy to the intentional choice of a global "humankind" (*anthrōpos*) target of this apocalypse of divine wrath—that is, not particularly "gentiles." Nothing in what Paul says in Rom 1:18–32 is exclusive to gentiles. As the argument develops into chapter 2, we shall see that someone falsely assumes gentiles were the target of this wrath.

Paul wrote that God's wrath is expressed because these humans "by unrighteousness are suppressing the truth."[9] The problem is not that something about God is unknown. The problem is that *what is known about God deliberately is suppressed by unrighteous behavior that denies this truth.* What is known about God? At a minimum, his power and deity as creator, Paul says in Rom **1:19–20**. Paul insists on some fundamental creator-creature bond inherent within the creative act of God, a baseline relationship by virtue of being born a human creature through God's power within God's cosmos. Paul does not explain the *mechanism* of this knowledge. He simply asserts that God "manifested it to them" (1:19). We certainly could speculate, but without gaining much traction, because Paul simply does not say.[10] More important

---

[8] Cf. Paul to the Athenians in Acts 17:30–31.

[9] "By unrighteousness" is taken as instrumental. For adverbial, cf. Godet, *Romans*, 100–101.

[10] As I wrote previously (*Divine Wrath*, 141n5), Paul does not explain how humans have this knowledge, other than through the revelatory activity of God, so not the result of human apprehension alone. We are unconvinced, therefore, this passage is a case

exegetically is the result: "without excuse" (ἀναπολογήτους, *anapologē-tous*) in Rom 1:20. "Without excuse" is the forensic heart of the matter. Otherwise, God has no case to prosecute, and Paul has no reason to worry about Spain. First impulse for any human being is to look for excuses, regardless the offense. Immediately offering excuses seized Adam and Eve in Eden (as well as anyone pulled over by a state trooper). But how lame is the excuse of idolatry? To say God who made the heavens and the earth is a stick or a stone, or much less something a *human made*, is pure foolishness and a deliberate lie when the truth is known. (You sat there and carved the stick yourself.) Idolatry is the rankest unrighteousness and ungodliness, equivalent to self worship.

"Though knowing God" Paul continued in Rom **1:21** (again, not saying how) "they did not glorify God as God." Reducing God to a stick or a stone does not glorify God, but exchanges the truth about God for a human-invented lie. A natural response to God from one of his creatures should have been gratitude for the life freely given ("nor give him thanks"), but the creator God did not even receive thanks for the breath of life.

This fundamental failure and disobedience is the first step down the long and winding road that eventually ends in death (Gen 2:17). This deceitful thinking pattern on the part of humans to lie deliberately about God is destructive and begins a journey into darkness. Darkness begets further darkness. "Reasonings" (διαλογισμοῖς, *dialogismois*) become futile (Rom 1:21), meaning logical thought is skewed toward serving the lie. Hence, deceit piles up on top of deceit. "Hearts" (καρδία, *kardia*) become senseless, which means thoughts about God no longer can have any sensibility to them, because the true God is being denied in these vain imaginings.[11] Further lying ("professing to be wise," **1:22**) only reveals the basic foolishness of the whole enterprise of idolatry.

for "natural" theology, particularly if that phrase intends a rudimentary systematic theology. The knowledge of God contextually is the reality of God himself provided by divine revelation (1:19b), i.e., not the subject of rational effort. Cf. Cranfield, *Romans*, 1:116, n3. For an opposite view, cf. O'Rourke, "Romans 1:20 and Natural Revelation," 301–06. Longenecker, *Romans*, 209, implied a revelation "implanted" into creation and appealing to Psalm 19's "general" revelation for all and "special" revelation in Torah. Jer 14:22 and Acts 14:17 seem similar; note also Bar 6:53.

[11] Emotions were related to the belly, and thoughts to the heart. Bad news distresses digestion, and shocking news can provoke throwing up. The Greek word for "bowels" (σπλάγχνον, *splanchnon*, Acts 1:17) is the same word for "compassion" (Phil 1:8).

An essential exchange takes place: "exchanged the glory of the immortal God" (**1:23**). Rather than worship the creator God in his glory, humans opt for idolatry of creation. A false god is invented. This "god" is seen in images "resembling mortal man, birds, four-footed animals, and reptiles." The gods and goddesses of Olympus certainly qualify here, such as Asklepios, son of Apollo, god of healing, with his entwined snake on a staff. A focus on "birds" and "reptiles" may reflect the prominence these creatures had in Egypt, land of Israel's enslavement to another lord. Horus, the falcon god of kingship and the sky, was one of the most ancient and significant gods in Egyptian religion. In art depicted as a human with a falcon head, he was taken as incarnate in Egypt's pharaoh. Snake gods in Egypt included Nehebkau, god of afterlife, Apophis, serpent foe of the sun god, Ra, and Wadjet, cobra goddess and protector of Lower Egypt. Nekhbet was a vulture goddess and protector of Upper Egypt. The united kingdom merged the symbolic imagery of Nekhbet and Wadjet as protectors of both Upper Egypt and Lower Egypt at the apex of the pharaoh's crown, famously memorialized in King Tutankhamun's funeral mask.

FIGURE 7.4. Asklepios. Numerous healing centers were dedicated to Asklepios, the god of healing, whose iconography featured a snake entwined on his staff (AAM).

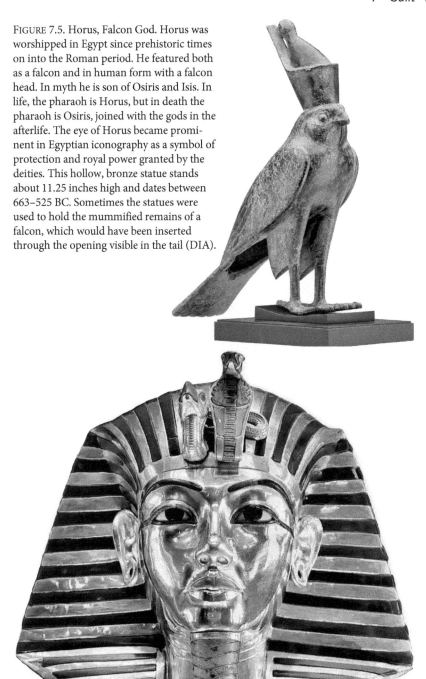

FIGURE 7.5. Horus, Falcon God. Horus was worshipped in Egypt since prehistoric times on into the Roman period. He featured both as a falcon and in human form with a falcon head. In myth he is son of Osiris and Isis. In life, the pharaoh is Horus, but in death the pharaoh is Osiris, joined with the gods in the afterlife. The eye of Horus became prominent in Egyptian iconography as a symbol of protection and royal power granted by the deities. This hollow, bronze statue stands about 11.25 inches high and dates between 663–525 BC. Sometimes the statues were used to hold the mummified remains of a falcon, which would have been inserted through the opening visible in the tail (DIA).

FIGURE 7.6. Tutankhamun's Funeral Mask. Gold, lapis lazuli, carnelian, obsidian, turquoise, and glass paste; top center features Nekhbet (left) and Wadjet (right). Credit: Roland Unger, Wikimedia (CEM).

The emphasis on "reptiles" brings to mind Moses's confrontation with the pharaoh's court magicians and their snake charming prowess (Exod 7:10–11). Egyptian kingdoms had millennia of history with reptiles and their worship, particularly serpentine.

But what about the imagery of "four-footed beasts" in Rom 1:23? That notation is Paul tucking away the story of Israel subtly into the meaning of wrath against "humans." If "since creation" alludes in any way to the story of Adam in this analysis, Adam simply functions as a parable and paradigm of Israel: receiving a gift of life, knowing God, receiving God's word, disobeying, being delivered over to lust, experiencing the wrath of curse, and banishment from the land.[12] This story is Israel at Sinai and afterwards on into Babylonian exile. At the very beginning of Israel's story, even as the elect of God, before Moses can come down the mountain, the people have begged from Aaron a golden calf to worship, a four-footed beast, which, in his disapproved mind, Aaron foolishly provides. The Israelites, although knowing God in all his glory who through his power and deity crushed pharaoh's will and drowned his mighty army before their very eyes, did not honor God as God nor give him thanks. Instead, they made an image of a four-footed beast. That is, Israel continued to live out the Adamic tragedy. The golden calf incident is paradigmatic of Israel's whole story. One clear element in the story of the exodus is God's wrath.

> "Now let me alone, so that my wrath may burn hot against them and I may consume them; and of you I will make a great nation." But Moses implored the Lord his God, and said, "O Lord, why does your wrath burn hot against your people, whom you brought out of the land of Egypt with great power and with a mighty hand? Why should the Egyptians say, 'It was with evil intent that he brought them out to kill them in the mountains, and to consume them from the face of the earth'? Turn from your fierce wrath; change your mind and do not bring disaster on your people" (Exod 32:10–12, NRSV).

To this exodus reality one could add the tragic summary that led to exile in 2 Chr 36:15–16.

> The Lord, the God of their ancestors, sent presently to them by his messengers, because he had compassion on his people and

---

[12] Postell, *Adam as Israel*.

on his dwelling place; but they kept mocking the messengers of God, despising his words, and scoffing at his prophets, until the wrath of the Lord against his people became so great that there was no remedy (2 Chr 36:15–16, NRSV).

Rom 1:23 clearly echoes Sinai. "Exchanging glory" deliberately echoes Ps 106:20, which speaks of Israel at Sinai: "They exchanged their glory for the image of an ox that eats grass." The prophets excoriated Israel for continuing to exchange God's glory even in their day (Jer 2:11). The Sinai problem really never went away. Instead, the golden calf was paradigmatic. The generalizing rhetoric of Rom 1:18–32 ("humans," ἀνθρώπων, anthrōpōn) is intentional so as to include Jewish humanity. The problem of Israel shadows everything Paul says in Romans. Even words like 1:23 that easily could be applied to non-Jews are even more true of Israel. If the nations hold up a faintly flickering candle about God, Israel has the blinding light of holy theophanies experienced at Sinai (Exod 24:15–18). Israel is the most culpable of all the nations.

So, wrath is the exodus story, and wrath is the exile story. Divine wrath is Israel's story. In speaking of wrath being revealed in present tense, Paul is speaking to Israel of the on-going consequences of the exile and its aftermath. Israel may have returned from exile, but Israel never recovered from exile. The only solution is for Messiah to come and establish the kingdom of God. But, to do so, first order of business will be to "banish ungodliness from Jacob" (Rom 11:26). Jesus signaled the beginning of this business by cleansing the temple of the moneychangers, an event all four gospel writers recount.[13] The ungodliness in view in Rom 1:18 *includes* the ungodliness of Jacob.

The potent question for a modern audience is, What functions as an idol? Some idolatry has nothing to do with sticks and stones or ancient mythology.

A Revealed Wrath (1:24–28)

The human "exchange" mentioned in Rom 1:23 actually inaugurates a dramatic triad of paired rhetorical devices pitting three exchange actions of humans against three "delivered over" responses of God. In this triad is the essence of exactly what Paul means when he says that the

[13] Matt 21:12–17; Mark 11:15–19; Luke 19:45–48; John 2:13–16.

wrath of God "is revealed" in Rom 1:18. Three human exchanges (1:23, 25, 28) are counteracted by three divine responses (1:24, 26, 28).

"God delivered them over" Triad (Rom 1:24–28)

Human Exchange	Divine Response
Glory (1:23)	Uncleanness (1:24)
Truth (1:25)	Passions (1:26)
Knowledge (1:28)	Disapproved Mind (1:28)

FIGURE 7.7. "God Delivered Them Over" Triad.

Three present tense verbs are tied to three past tense verbs.[14] The net result is perfective, inferring on-going consequences. What is manifest (1:19), God manifested (1:21); knowing God, they glorified not (1:22); professing to be wise, they became fools (1:22); forsaking natural use, they burned in desires (1:27). The cumulative perfective force means these exchanges are not for a moment but for a lifetime. The perfective idea perfectly captures the human tragedy in all its terrible force and concisely summarizes a lifestyle living out the consequences of enslavement to another lord. The perfective sense is supported by the perfect participle, "being filled," that introduces the vice list beginning in Rom 1:29. Further, the tense sequence is the grammatical marker of God's *personal* involvement in this process of divine wrath.

To exchange God's glory is to lose access to God's wisdom about how humans properly fit into the purposes of the cosmos, to lose sight of the compass showing true north on how to treat the world with proper stewardship (Rom 8:19–21) and how to treat others with proper relationships (Rom 12:10–11). In these terms, exchanging God's glory has the consequence of becoming "unclean" (1:24), unfit for service (as for priests to assume temple duties), and one's uncleanness renders others unclean, like a contagious virus. Becoming "unclean" as a result of the

---

[14] The aorist verbs are indicative, so interpreted as having past time component.

operation of God's wrath basically is being delivered over into a self-chosen subhuman condition unable to function as a real human being created in the image of God, unfit for any service toward anything or anyone.

To exchange the truth of God as creator and only God (1:25) is enslavement to the abuse and perversion of everything God created. Passion is a proper force in human experience ordained in creation for invigorating life so as to be lived to the fullest, abundantly. Lust is perverted passion (1:26). Lust destroys life by destroying its object. Lust is one of the rawest forms of selfishness. Lest lust be misinterpreted as exclusively the domain of sexual behavior, we might need reminding that greed is lust. Status seeking is lust. Envy is lust.

To exchange the knowledge of God is not like missing questions on a pop quiz of God's attributes. To exchange the knowledge of God is to lose relationship with God, because knowing in biblical terms is equivalent to relationship. Since the image of God includes ability to relate to God in ways no other creature in the cosmos can, marring the image of God through sin damages human fulfillment, condemning a human being to a sense of perpetual lostness, like a child who no longer can find the hand of the parent in the store. God delivering over to a "disapproved mind" means guaranteeing a person has to live out the consequences of thinking patterns destined to produce bad decisions, such as deciding to cross the road without looking both ways (1:27).

We need to push back on the translation "reprobate mind." The root verb in Paul's expression, "disapproved mind," (ἀδόκιμον νοῦν, *adokimon noun*) in 1:28, *dokimazein*, means "to test," as in to gain approval for meeting requirements.[15] The converse is testing that fails. The idea is like quality assurance controls on a factory assembly line. If the finished product is "not up to specs," does not meet all of the specifications of the intended design, that item is pulled off the line as "not working as designed." The product works, but not as designed. A failed test results in disapproval. Thus, we would urge that "reprobate mind" is not a good translation, because reprobate in everyday parlance is taken to mean *not working at all*. That sense would destroy the force of Paul's full culpability argument as the *opposite* of Paul's intent (i.e., "without excuse," 1:20).

---

[15] Trench, *Synonyms*, 278–80; Grundmann, *TDNT*, s.v. "δόκιμος," 2:255–60.

A Revealed Consequence (1:29–31)

The vice list is common in the ancient world, especially among Stoics. By them philosophers were making recommendations for how to live a better life to achieve some valued virtue. Paul is not making recommendations for how to live a better life. Paul is profiling lifestyles that prove the effective operation of divine wrath. Divine wrath operates to guarantee the full maturation of abject uncleanness that "disapproved minds" produce in unrighteousness and ungodliness. One need only read about the emperors in Suetonius or Tacitus, listen to the cat-talk in Juvenal's satires, or walk down the streets of first-century Pompeii to catch a glimpse of this lifestyle.[16] Paul speaks of God's wrath as a means of communicating the perilous state of the human condition in rebellion against God. God's wrath is an act of grace that walks every human to the edge of the destiny cliff to experience some judgment vertigo, hoping to sober up a disapproved mind. This revelatory journey is engaged by way of living the life of the vices given as examples.

The vice list is introduced in **1:29** with a perfect tense verb, "being full of" (πεπληρωμένους, peplērōmenous). This grammar encapsulates what might be called the "greenhouse of God's wrath" (**1:30–31**).[17] Sin's consequences are made unavoidable. One can get bogged down in trying to parse out the exact significance of every term and phrase in this list, even more how to nuance specific elements in modern society, particularly, for example, the issue of homosexuality. Exegetically, in all these discussions one sometimes can lose a sense of the forest for focusing too much on individual trees. Paul's point is this. When life is built on idolatry, fundamental rejection of God turns human behavior into subhuman degradation. This behavior corrupts society as a whole and destroys God's purposes in creation. God obviously intended abundant life—just look through a microscope at a drop of pond water or a telescope at a distant galaxy. Sadly, no human is exempt from basic unrighteousness, regardless sexual orientation. Normalizing specific behaviors does nothing to solve the fundamental problem Paul addresses. This problem is summarized in the concluding verse of the passage.

[16] Although from a different social frame, cf. Oakes, *Reading Romans in Pompeii*. Of course, we cannot give credence to every slander recorded in these tendentious sources, but the general impression even toned down is a debased society.

[17] Stevens, *Divine Wrath*, 155.

A Revealed Destiny (1:32)

Paul concluded, "Which ones although knowing God's just sentence—that those who habitually practice such things are worthy of death—not only do these things, but also approve those who practice them" (**1:32**). The death destiny is what divine wrath reveals. Persons know the way they live will kill them. Choosing sin is choosing death. Wrath takes the wraps off that destiny. This destiny is the story of all humans, Adam, his progeny, and Israel. Death here probably has dual significance as both physical and spiritual. Physical death should function as a sign of eternal death. Rejection of God's lordship is rejection of life. The lord of evil, god of this world, takes charge and takes life (2 Cor 4:4).

The tag lines to two legacy television commercials help illustrate Paul's point about how divine wrath works in Rom 1:18–32. The first is from Burger King. The effort was to persuade the American public of the many choices available for constructing a customized burger of choice. The tag line was, "Burger King, have it your way!" You could build your burger any old way you liked. To the sinful human desire to live an idolatrous life, God's wrath responds, "Burger King!" The second is from Toyota. The effort was to persuade the American public that Toyota heard the feedback and customized the new model car to whatever were the current trends in options and packages. The tag line was, "You asked for it, you got it. Toyota!" You got precisely what you said you wanted. To the creature insisting on living life without God, God's wrath responds, "Toyota!"

Finally, often noted is the connection of this material in 1:18–32 with Wis 13:1—14:31, a Jewish sapiential composition written about fifty years before Jesus was born. Some wording even is pretty close. However, gentiles in this document are only foil for takedown as idol worshippers for the purpose of glorifying Jews as pleasing to God by knowing and doing the law.[18] Paul's reflection, in stark contrast, is entirely different in motivation, attitude, and development. Further, Paul's eschatology is radically transformed by the new age of Messiah that has redefined the place of the nations in the kingdom of God, principally invigorated by the eschatological vision of Isaiah for the destiny of Israel in regard to the nations.

---

[18] The best overall discussion is Longenecker, *Romans*, 193–95.

Covenant Unrighteousness (2:1—3:8)

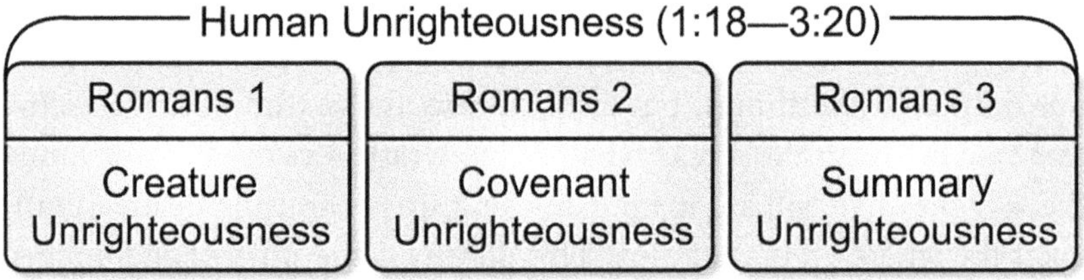

FIGURE 7.8. Outline: Romans 2 (Covenant Unrighteousness). Universal human unrighteousness in three parts in Rom 1:18—3:20 now moves to covenant unrighteousness.

Paul first has demonstrated universal creature unrighteousness, to which God responds in wrath still working to try to save, like a lifeguard slapping a drowning swimmer wildly flailing about, impeding the attempt to save. Romans is about Israel. Paul's real target all along has been Israel. He has nuanced his rhetoric smartly enough in Romans 1 that just when the reader thinks his target is the pagan, the boomerang comes back around in a striking applicability. He starts off Rom 2:1 still referring to the "human being" (*anthrōpos*) that he categorized in Rom 1:18, but the content of his argument following that address shows he already is shifting gears towards the Jew. The force of the rhetoric does not become explicit until Rom 2:17, when the Jew specifically is addressed. In this way, Paul methodically moves from general creature unrighteousness towards a revealed creator in Romans 1, which covers all of humanity, to specific covenant unrighteousness towards an electing God in Romans 2, which covers Israel in particular.

Another prefacing note to offer is the analogical imagery lurking in the rhetoric of both Romans 1 and 2. If Adam is lurking behind the imagery in Romans 1, not to become explicit until Romans 5, Abraham is lurking behind the imagery in Romans 2, not to become explicit until Romans 4. When, therefore, Paul says "gentile" in Romans 2, he subtly is pointing to the example of uncircumcised Abraham.[19] Pointing to Abraham as a pedagogical lesson about the nature of gentile experience is not a typically rabbinic move, for whom Abraham always kept the Mosaic law both before and after circumcision, even though the law was not given until four centuries after Abraham. At least, that was the story of the Great Synagogue. After Paul envisioned Messiah as none

---

[19] As we already have argued, "gentile" is Pauline rhetoric related to circumcision.

other than Jesus of Nazareth, he was forced to reformat his theological hard drive with a new messianic operating system. The new operating system provoked reconfiguring his understanding of the essence of the story of Abraham for Jewish faith, quite contrary to traditions he had learned in the synagogue. The old files just did not work any more.

Lastly, Dunn's approach to this material in Romans 2 always has had probative weight. Paul is using diatribe rhetoric potently to punch a hole in Jewish presumption over election and law. Election has created an illusion of immunity to divine wrath (2:1–11), and law has provoked a presumption of advantage over other human beings (2:12–16). Paul disabuses reliance on these ideas. When the matter is God's judgment, Jews have no exclusion privileges.[20] Strange how the reality of exile did not teach the lesson that rebellion is endemic to the human condition, and having the law before the exile most certainly did not advantage anyone. Nothing fundamentally changed after the exile. The result was the same: the weight of divine wrath was building to judgment.

Election Illusion (2:1–11)

Paul turns to diatribe style, a form of speaking in which the speaker invokes an imaginary opponent who raises questions and points of contention, effectively meeting objections and scoring persuasive points with the audience by disarming their unvoiced doubts and concerns. The grammatical signal is change from third person ("they") to second person ("you"). "He starts with a "Therefore" (Διό, *Dio*), an inferential conjunction that signals that the previous discussion is the basis for the present remarks. The previous discussion was the present revelation of divine wrath in 1:18–32. That divine wrath revelation integrally is connected to the significance of the wrath language soon to appear in 2:5, 8. On the basis of that 1:18 revelation comes another one.

Translations that ignore the vocative of address, "O Man," in **2:1** in order to try to degenderize the translation pay too heavy an exegetical price—the *author-intended* connection directly back to Rom 1:18 is lost.[21] The reader loses immediate access in translation to the insight the grammatical connection infers that the same *anthrōpos* that is object

---

[20] Dunn, *Romans 1–8*, 77.

[21] E.g., CSB: "every one of you"; HCSB: "any one of you"; NIV: "You"; NRSV: "whoever you are," and so forth.

of God's wrath in 1:18 is still the *anthrōpos* directly addressed in 2:1. Whoever is addressed in 2:1, *they presently are under God's wrath*. That connection is crucial to follow the threat of judgment to come. Further, since Paul intentionally repeats almost the exact same phrase in 2:3 ("O Man, the one who judges"), he clearly is using repetition to build the rhetorical force of his argument to a climax. All of this carefully worked out rhetorical precision is lost in modern translations.[22]

This person's problem immediately is condensed into the terse, descriptive phrase that follows the vocative of address, "the one who judges." This descriptor is repeated in 2:3, indicating the thought is crucial to Paul's analysis. Someone is condescending, thereby exposing an inaccurate evaluation of themselves and a gross misunderstanding of God, both problems jeopardizing future prospects in the judgment.

Paul says that such persons who "are judging" problematically are themselves "without excuse" (αναπολόγητος, *anapologētos*). "Without excuse" is the key declaration made in 1:20 that is the entire burden of 1:18–32, and the key declaration of this unit as well. "Without excuse" makes a striking statement in one word in Greek, since the word itself appears nowhere else in the New Testament other than here in Rom 1:20 and 2:1. Further, the word occurs not even once in all of the LXX and Philo, and only once in all of Josephus (*Apion* 2.137). The point of this extremely rare word is to establish the weight of the conclusion of the entire section in 3:19, "that the whole world may be held accountable to God."

The problem is twofold. Disapproved minds are making erroneous conclusions based on false assumptions of both innocence and ability to judge rightly. First, the same condemnation returns upon those who pronounce condemnation. They themselves are not innocent of the fundamental idolatry, if not the exact same vices. Second, such persons have presumed the prerogative to judge rightly when they do not have a clue about true righteousness blinded by their own idolatry. Further, they presume the role that only a holy and righteous God can perform. They are "without excuse" because they know better and behave worse.

They are without excuse because they do the "same things." Does "same things" refer to individual elements of the vice list in 1:29–31 or

---

[22] A pity that we simultaneously cannot be as rhetorically sensitive as we are gender sensitive.

to the three fundamental exchanges of glory, truth, and knowledge (1:23, 25, 28)? The question is moot, since the vice list theologically is connected essentially to the three exchanges. Thus, any vice is simply symptomatic of a prior exchange. The fundamental error is not the vice. The vice is only a symptom. Worse here in the case of these humans is claiming to serve God more truly than someone worshipping Zeus when the hidden heart is full of hypocrisy. The charge here falls in line with Scripture. "Circumcise then, the foreskin of your heart, and do not be stubborn any longer. For the Lord your God is God of gods and Lord of lords, the great God, mighty and awesome, who is not partial and takes no bribe" (Deut 10:16–17, NRSV). Jeremiah clearly echoed this critique, "Circumcise yourselves to the Lord, remove the foreskin of your hearts, O people of Judah and inhabitants of Jerusalem, or else my wrath will go forth like fire, and burn with no one to quench it, because of the evil of your doings" (Jer 4:4).[23] Jesus pointed out that the revered oral law of the Great Assembly was not so revered in God's eyes, not when the intention of the Great Assembly's pronouncements was to profane the very law that ostensibly was being upheld. He gave as example the oral law of Corban (Mark 7:9–13, 22).

They acknowledge such behavior cannot escape the judgment and will not escape the impartiality of God, who upholds the truth (**2:2**). This opinion makes them appear to take God's side in the matter of the condemnation expressed in 1:18–32. In this context, this truth is the truth that wickedness works to suppress (1:18), which is whatever God chooses to reveal about himself (1:19). That revelation might be expressed in creation (1:20) or in covenant (2:17), but the point is, no matter what God reveals, humans rebel. Therefore, the ones judging will not escape, since they too are culpable, and God is impartial (**2:3**).

In 2:4–5, the rhetorical flourish drives deeper into motives and attitudes. In truth, being liable to the same condemnation but ignoring that truth by judging others is equivalent to despising "the riches of his kindness and forbearance and patience" (**2:4**). God's kindness in not executing judgment immediately on sins is because God works in everything to try to save. Repentance, however, is the required response to this kindness, because repentance indicates a willingness to do what is necessary to restore the relationship. The refusal to repent is blatant

---

[23] In other Jewish literature, cf. Ps Sol 15:8; Wis 15:1–6.

refusal to restore the relationship. Another way to describe this refusal to repent is a "hard and impenitent heart." This hardness speaks to a decided resolve not to repent after plenty of opportunity. This condition is dangerous. Continued refusal to repent is "storing up wrath [ὀργήν, orgēn] for yourself on the day of wrath [ἐν ἡμέρᾳ ὀργῆς, en hēmerai orgēs] and the revelation [ἀποκαλύψεως, apokalypseōs] of the righteous judgment of God" (**2:5**). In this future "day of wrath" we meet Pauline eschatology. Paul anticipated a final assize by God as part of the final judgment that would bring human history to a close and settle all outstanding accounts on the books. We now have before us two revelations of the wrath of God in Pauline thought. The first is the revelation of wrath in history in 1:18, which is temporal. The second is the revelation of wrath at the end of history, which is eschatological. After the day of wrath at the end of history, destiny is fixed with no recourse. So, Pauline understanding of divine wrath includes both a revelation in history (1:18), in which God is trying to save, and a revelation at the end of history (2:5), in which God announces the final outcome of his efforts to save.

Who is this imaginary, self-deceived debater? Certainly "a Jew," as becomes explicit in 2:17. But not really so imaginary. Probably Paul is pointing a finger at Saul of Tarsus. Galatians 1:13–14 is a confession: Saul, advancing in Judaism more than most by his account, zealous for ancestral traditions, meaning the Great Synagogue oral traditions after the exile. Yet, confronted by the risen Messiah in personal revelation, he stood condemned in his own malice, murder, strife, foolishness, and haughtiness toward the nascent messianic movement. After the divine encounter, the world turned upside down and values reversed (Phil 3:6–8). Paul most certainly could personalize the divine fiat in 1:28, "God delivered them over to a disapproved mind." Saul on the way to Damascus with Sanhedrin letters was bound for the inescapable judgment of God (2:3). He knew the "hard and impenitent heart" first hand, both in himself and in the synagogue. We do not need Acts to have evidence of this reality, though Acts is thoroughly consistent in its own testimony on this matter.[24] Paul himself said he received the

---

[24] Cf. Damascus (Acts 9:23–25); early Jerusalem (Acts 9:29); Antioch of Pisidia (Acts 13:40–46); Thessalonica (Acts 15:5); Berea (Acts 17:13); Corinth (Acts 18:6); Ephesus (Acts 19:9); Corinth again (Acts 20:3); Jerusalem again (Acts 21:27–31); Rome (Acts 28:24).

life-threatening, formal punishment of the synagogue lash five times.[25] When one such experience was plenty for a lifetime, Paul's testimony was extraordinary. So, in part, one might say that Paul is shadow boxing Saul in Romans 2. The contention was real for the original audience. Storing up wrath for a day of wrath, as well as judgment on the basis of deeds, both were common themes in synagogue traditions on final judgment, so this diatribe has a clear synagogue tone.[26] Paul is arguing with the Great Assembly. But he also is arguing with Rome. This argument applies to the Romans, because their own synagogues already have had a distinctive track record of rejecting the preaching of Jesus as Messiah, if the Edict of Claudius is any indication.

Here is Paul's prophetic call to Israel, particularly its mythic Great Assembly beginning to dominate first-century Israel's story, based on his own personal experience. Reprising the prophets of old, he was trying to warn recalcitrant compatriots before a new tsunami of judgment destroyed the nation again (9:1–5). Paul evokes Joel's plea to the nation before the judgment of exile.

> "Yet even now, says the Lord, return to me with all your heart, with fasting, with weeping, and with mourning; rend your hearts and not your clothing." Return to the Lord, your God, for he is gracious and merciful, slow to anger, and abounding in steadfast love, and relents from punishing. Who knows whether he will not turn and relent, and leave a blessing behind him, a grain offering and a drink offering for the Lord, your God? (Joel 2:12–14, NRSV)

He sets out to warn the delusional, as did Amos. Amos tried to warn those falsely presuming the coming of God in judgment on the day of the Lord would be vindication for Israel and condemnation for Israel's enemies. Amos 5:18 is blunt: "Alas for you who desire the day of the Lord! Why do you want the day of the Lord? It is darkness not light!"

In 2:6–11, Paul drives home the point of God's impartiality. God will repay according to deeds (**2:6**), but "deeds" here have to have the contextual parameters of Romans, whose whole point is the gospel of God (1:1). "Doing good," then, is circumscribed within Romans as the

---

[25] 2 Cor 11:24.

[26] Preserved in Targum readings; cf. Stevens, *Divine Wrath in Paul*, 163. Perriman, however, argued second temple literature does *not* evidence a "final judgment," only judgments in history (*Future of the People of God*, 44–45, 49, 54, 92, 119, 121, 122).

work of advancing the gospel (10:14–15). That background context reveals the import of the Edict of Claudius for defining "doing good" or "doing evil" (2:7–9). Eternal life is at stake (**2:7**). Self-seeking means seeking one's own interests, not God's, so not obeying the truth (1:25). Doing so only promotes unrighteousness—back to 1:18. Present wrath intends to be salvific, but, facing recalcitrant obstinacy, becomes "furious wrath" (the sense of the doubling effect of combined synonyms for wrath, ὀργὴ καὶ θυμός, *orgē kai thymos*) in the judgment (**2:8**). These words are a warning shot across the bow of Roman synagogues. That warning shot now brings up the boomerang effect of rehearsing a previous phrase (1:16), "the Jew first, and the Greek" (**2:9**). If first in the offer of the gospel, then first in the inescapable judgment to come. The salvific counterpart is "glory and honor and peace to everyone who works the good, Jew first, and Greek" (**2:10**). "The good" is the gospel.

Paul concluded, "For God shows no partiality" (**2:11**). Election is no inoculation from divine wrath. Election knowledge can produce a dangerous false overconfidence, and any professed wisdom based on that overconfidence is foolishness. The condemnation "through the lusts of their hearts" on general humanity in 1:24 has its corollary in the "hardness and impenitent heart" of Jewish humanity in 2:5. Thus, the profile of 1:18–32 is made clear as the problem of postexilic Israel in 2:1–11. In a sense, Paul as he writes Romans has a premonition of the impending disaster of the First Jewish War.

Law Presumption (2:12–16)

Sin is sin, and sin against God is known, has accountability, and invokes judgment (1:32). One does not need the law for accountability toward the creator God for idolatry ("perish apart from the law," **2:12**). On the other hand, one has engaged incredible accountability if one is in a direct covenant relationship with God based on his revealed law. In that case, one who has "sinned under the law will be judged by the law." Righteousness is doing right, not simply agreeing with platitudes on good behavior (**2:13**). This verse has Paul's fundamental definition of righteousness: combined hearing and doing. Anyone who hears what God says do and then does what God says to do is righteous before God. The question is parsing what God says to do. Law is static, but life is dynamic, constantly rearranging the game board pieces to create new conundrums to solve. Parsing what God says to do today on the basis of a new arrangement of pieces or a new set of factors tomorrow requires knowing God, his character, his designs, his will, his heart. If one cannot sense the beat of God's heart, one cannot envision how the law expresses God's will and sense proper ways to apply that vision in daily life such that God in all things would be honored and glorified. That was the conundrum of the oral law, parsing an old law in a new day. Somewhere along the way, letter became more authoritative than Spirit. A sense of God's heart grew faint. Someone who could say "Abba, father" (8:15) in the context of a genuine relationship with God was needed to guide others how to re-envision doing the law after the devastating judgment of exile. Promoters of the oral law of the Great Assembly missed this mark. They missed the heart of the matter. "Then Jesus came from Galilee to the Jordan to John to be baptized by him" (Matt 3:13). The heart of the matter arrived in the flesh (Rom 1:3–4).

Romans **2:14** has caused quite the discussion. Raising the specter of gentiles doing "what the law demands," so becoming "a law to themselves even though they do not have the law" seems instantly to render the Mosaic law useless, even insensible. Proposals on who is in view focus on following descriptions in **2:15**, such as "written on their hearts," "consciences confirming," and "competing thoughts" that either "accuse" or "excuse," as well as on the conclusion in **2:16** based on eschatological judgment, "when God judges what people have kept secret, according to my gospel through Messiah Jesus." Who are these gentiles? Proposals have included: (1) a basic moral sensitivity among pagans, (2) some rudimentary ethical conscience, (3) an inward moral conflict within every human being, and even (4) gentile believers after being saved, which, since Paul is arguing pre-gospel realities for the logic to hold, makes little sense. Dunn pointed to Stoic thought of the natural bond between humans and the cosmos implicitly teaching what is fitting in conduct.[27] Moo has the best summary of the options. He takes the innate moral sensitivity route, like Dunn, but insists such gentiles are not thereby saved—which begs the question.[28] These speculations are problematic, lacking support in the rest of the Pauline canon. Paul never employs the suggested gentile scenarios anywhere else as key to

---

[27] *Romans 1–8*, 105.

[28] *Romans*, 149–51.

an argument about the gospel. More importantly, Paul never does so in the rest of this letter, Romans 7 absolutely not excepted.[29]

We cut to the chase with two strategic observations. First, ἔθνη (*ethnē*) here rightly is translated as "gentiles," not "nations," *precisely because circumcision is in view*, as we have argued already in dealing with the crucial phrase "obedience of the *nations*" in 1:5. The issue of circumcision becomes explicit and is pursued relentlessly in 2:25–29. Thus, our first observation about this passage is that the crux of the matter is circumcision, which is a Jewish issue. Second, we point out again that like Adam shadowed 1:18–32 on behalf of moving to 5:12–21,[30] Abraham shadows 2:12–29 on behalf of moving to Romans 4. Therefore, when Paul introduces "gentiles" into the discussion in 2:14 (for the first time in Romans), by "gentile" he implicitly means Abraham. Thus, what we really are discussing in Rom 2:12–29 is the story of Abraham, who was, in fact, a Chaldean gentile when we first encounter him in the Chaldean city of Ur (Gen 11:31). As a Chaldean gentile, Abraham was uncircumcised. He was ἄνθρωπος (*anthrōpos*). Yet, God spoke to Abraham (law), and Abraham did what God said (faith). That response of faith is the *anthrōpos* with whom God can work to overcome the Adamic tragedy. Abraham then becomes an exemplar of how saving relationship to God works, and how law as a particular expression of that relationship should work. Whatsoever is not of faith is sin (Rom 14:23). Law without faith is sin, indeed, even exceedingly sinful (7:13). Faith does not save. God saves. God, however, has chosen faith as the venue through which he chooses to release the power of salvation (Rom 1:16–17). Abraham's faith and his story is the missional goal of the entire Pauline enterprise around the world (1:5), the incarnation of the Romans theme (1:16–17), the exegesis of the "work [singular] of the law" (2:15), and the "gentile" of Romans 2. The issue pre or post gospel is responding in faith to whatever God reveals. That response consummates the gospel of God, who now has revealed himself in Messiah Jesus (2:16). Therefore, categorizing *anthrōpos* as either having or not having the law, being circumcised or not circumcised, sets up a false dichotomy for deciding who is righteous in the judgment. Israel was elected, but election is not favoritism, and

---

[29] See chapter 3.

[30] Which itself lays the theological groundwork for Romans 7.

law is not a vaccine against sin. God is impartial. Israel had no inherent or superior quality to be the people of God among other human beings. Israel would not be the elect if Abraham had not had faith. Israel will be judged on the same basis as everyone else.

That word of faith is the gospel of God that will be the basis of the judgment, and that gospel is "my gospel," Paul insisted (2:16). The long view of eschatological judgment is Paul's ground of confidence in his ultimate vindication as a Jew and a true child of Abraham by reason of his faith in Messiah Jesus. That ultimate vindication is why he is "not ashamed" of the gospel (1:16), even in the context of continual synagogue rejection of his gospel in his mission throughout the diaspora, as well as the questioning of his ultimate loyalty to the faith of the fathers.[31]

Jewish Identity (2:17–29)

The illusion about election (2:1–11) and the presumption about the law (2:12–16) now are concentrated into the question of Jewish identity. In Rom 2:17–20, the specific identity in question is a Jew. The specific issue in question is the law. The specific problem in question is boasting.

"But if you call yourself a Jew" (**2:17**) immediately makes explicit what has been implicit all along and drives to the very heart of the matter in Romans 2: Who is a Jew? The answer is Abraham. You can have Judaism without the law (because you did for four hundred years), but you cannot have Judaism without Abraham. Yet, the definition began to change after the exile. Instead of taking Abraham's faith as a paradigm of Jewishness, observing Mosaic law was taken as definitive of being a Jew to the point of strict performance even without faith. Paul enumerates these postexilic characteristics in 2:17–20:

- rely on the law (2:17; 1:21)
- boast in God (2:17; 1:21)
- know his will (**2:18**; 1:19)
- approve superior values (2:18; 1:28)
- receive guidance from the law (2:18; 1:21)

---

[31] Which Luke captured accurately as the "hope of Israel" (Acts 28:20).

- provide guidance for the blind (**2:19**; 1:29)

- bring light to darkness (2:19; 1:21)

- instruct the ignorant (**2:20**; 1:22)

- teach the immature (2:20; 1:32)

- possess embodiment of knowledge and truth in the law (2:20; 1:18)

That list is pretty audacious, even intimidating, but that list also is the Great Assembly myth Paul encountered every Sabbath in the synagogue in action. That list rhetorically is correlated carefully with specific elements in Rom 1:18–32 (suggested by the parenthetical references). Paul transforms the vice list in 1:29–30 into specific violations of the Mosaic code in **2:21–22**, which would illustrate more pertinently the covenant unrighteousness of those who have the specific revelation of God in the law (stealing, adultery, idolatry).[32]

Boasting in the law encumbered with these egregious violations of covenant righteousness dishonors God. In fact, God's name is blasphemed, because God has associated himself and his reputation with Israel in particular among the nations of the world (**2:23**). Paul is not out on a limb here. He has Isaiah's blunt accusation against Israel as support, which he quotes, "The name of God is blasphemed among the nations because of you" (**2:24**; Isa 52:5). Blaspheming God's name revisits the letter opening in 1:5 in which Paul concisely states his missional goal as seeking the obedience of faith among the nations. After God revealed himself in Messiah, his Son (1:3–4), then this blasphemy will have concrete definition as what happens in synagogues when Jesus is preached as Messiah.[33]

---

[32] The idea of robbing temples is difficult to provide background and exegesis. Each option has shortcomings. A good word study and discussion is Moo, *Romans*, 163–64. We can note temple robbery was insinuated against Paul in Ephesus (Acts 19:37).

[33] As in Acts 18:6. Ironic, since Jesus himself was charged with blasphemy during his ministry (Mark 2:7; John 10:33) and then condemned to die as a blasphemer (Matt 26:65). This charge also was conspired against Stephen (Acts 6:11), and Saul of Tarsus punished believers to try to provoke their blasphemy (Acts 26:11). Cf. 1 Tim 1:13. While John's characterization of synagogues in Smyrna is harsh (Rev 2:9), the problem of blasphemy is critical to his plot (Rev 13:1, 5; 16:9, 11, 21; 17:3). James, however, reminded believers they are not immune from this danger (Jas 2:7).

Paul moves directly to the question of circumcision, which, along with diet and Sabbath observance, had coalesced into the preeminent definition of a Jew in postexilic Israel through emphases in the Ezra movement and the struggles with Syria in the Maccabean era. First-century Romans got the point, as the satires of Juvenal illustrate.[34] Breaking the law as a form of not trusting God invalidates the point of circumcision as a sign of the covenant (**2:25**). Paul now directly alludes to the story of Abraham in **2:26–27**:

> So, if an uncircumcised man keeps the law's requirements, will not his uncircumcision be counted as circumcision? A man who physically is uncircumcised, but keeps the law, will judge you who are a lawbreaker in spite of having the letter of the law and circumcision.

These verses precisely describe the difference between Abraham and the Great Assembly Jew. Abraham did not have the letter of the law, as did the circumcised Pharisee observing Sabbath every week in the synagogue, such as a Saul of Tarsus. Abraham, however, kept the law's requirements because fundamentally the law requires faith in God, and he had faith in God. That faith is what made him righteous before God, even as an uncircumcised gentile (Gen 15:6). So, Abraham will sit in judgment on the one calling himself a Jew because he is circumcised and has the law, but does not show the law's core requirement of faith in God, which is the true definition of a Jew for Paul, which, in nuce, is the profile of Abraham at the point in time he is declared righteous before God as a gentile. Paul then summarizes the entire argument of Romans 2 in the final two climactic verses in which he spills the beans on the difference between Saul of Tarsus and Paul the apostle.

> For not the one who in outward appearance is a Jew, nor is circumcision manifest in the flesh. Rather, the one who in secret is a Jew, even that circumcision of the heart by the Spirit not the letter, whose praise is not from humans but from God (Rom 2:28–29).

Here is Abraham, for those who have eyes to see. His faith in God's promise while an uncircumcised gentile was neither seen nor praised by any human, but assuredly seen and praised by God, and he transformed Israel's entire story on that legacy of faith.

---

[34] Juvenal, *Satires* 14.96–106. Cf. Nanos, *Mystery of Romans*, 100.

What can be an idolatry carved in stone (1:23) can be an idolatry carved in flesh (**2:28**). Paul is asking Jews enamored with the Great Assembly picture of Israel to contemplate Moses's meaning in Deut 10:16, "Circumcise, then, the foreskin of your heart, and do not be stubborn any longer." That is the heart of the matter, and reveals that the Jew Mosaic law really intended as defining Israel was the gentile Abraham, who was circumcised in the heart long before he was circumcised in the flesh (**2:29**). "Praise from God" alludes to Gen 15:6 (4:3).

Jewish Advantage (3:1–8)

So, if Abraham's story rightly understood means that you can be a Jew without having the law, what is the law for in the first place? Pretty obvious and pertinent question for postexilic Israel. Just jumps right out there immediately on the basis of Paul's stunning presentation in Romans 2 in which he rhetorically by stealth has introduced the story of Abraham to reject the Great Assembly postexilic definition of Israel. The question cannot be ignored, but Paul is not ready to take up the matter in full. He has yet to bring to conclusion his argument that humanity is in a sin spiral to destruction. Therefore, he will broach an initial response in 3:1–8, not to answer fully, but only to stave off insistence by those whose inquiring minds just have to know right now. After this cursory response in 3:1–8, he will table the matter until he is ready to offer preview development in Romans 4 and 7, and then finally consummate his response in its fullest form in Romans 9–11.

In Rom **3:1**, Paul gives voice to the obvious question of the advantage of the Jew, or, its twin question in postexilic Israel, the benefit of circumcision. Does the story of Abraham nullify the point of the law? Paul immediately responds in **3:2** with an adamant, "Much according to every consideration" (πολὺ κατὰ πάντα τρόπον, *poly kata panta tropon*). Of foremost importance are the life-transforming promises of God that eventually become Scripture ("the oracles of God"). With the idea of "oracles," Paul will be pivoting on two defining events for these oracles: Abraham and Moses. Paul is getting ready to spell out exactly what he means in this case by the oracles of God as he moves to tell the story of Abraham and the promises God gave Abraham in Romans 4. In this coming chapter, Paul makes clear that Abraham's story is the locus of these "oracles." Abraham's covenant promises are key to defining Israel. At the same time, Paul also pivots to Moses and Sinai, similar to Stephen in Stephen's reprise of Jewish history to the San-hedrin (Acts 7:2–50). Sinai and the story of Moses is one of the most momentous events in human history. Stephen summarized this truth in the words, "he received living oracles to give to us" (Acts 7:38). No other nation on the face of the earth ever could make this astounding claim: living words from the God of the cosmos. Talk about a reality that instantly would put a nation at the head of the line in God's world! God never communicated to any other nation in this way.

Yet, with great privilege comes great responsibility. The law en-coded a covenant that had both blessing and cursing. Unfaithfulness, fundamentally the unrighteousness of idolatry, brought the curse, and curse brought death and exile. Does Jewish unfaithfulness and the con-sequence of curse forever overwhelm God's intention to bless (**3:3**)? The quandary of human unfaithfulness raises the question, How does God "prevail" in judging? That is, knowing God's goals in creation, if God intends life, but to be just he has to condemn all to die, has he not lost everything? God's faithfulness to the covenant in this series of unfor-tunate events is rendered meaningless in the long run. To this blunt question Paul delivers one of his most characteristic turns of phrase so definitive and recognizable of Pauline style: μὴ γένοιτο, *mē genoito*, "Absolutely not!" (**3:4**).[35] Truth is, God always and forever will be both true to his word, including those that promise blessing, and true to his character, including being holy and just. Paul quoted Ps 51:4 to this effect: "That you might be justified in your oracles and that you prevail when you judge."

Of course, God's ways are a mystery, because fulfilling oracles and being entirely just appear mutually exclusive. Naturally, in this case, if one thinks with the limited logic one can muster struggling to process matters with a faulty "disapproved mind," one could make specious arguments, which is what Paul means by the tacked-on disclaimer, "I speak according to a human way" (**3:5**). One such specious argument would be that human unrighteousness sustains the righteousness of God, provoking the question, "Is God unrighteous to inflict the wrath

---

[35] Almost exclusively Paul's in the New Testament, 13 of 14 times, with the lone ex-ception of Luke 20:16, which might indicate Pauline influence on Lukan style. Cf. Rom 3:4, 6, 31; 6:2, 15; 7:7, 13; 11:1, 11; 1 Cor 6:15; Gal 2:17; 3:21; 6:14. In colloquial speech, this remonstrance is similar to, "Say it ain't so!" Paul is being as forceful in his rejection of an idea as he can.

[ὀργήν, *orgēn*]" (3:5)?[36] First, is this wrath the present revelation in history (1:18) or the eschatological wrath at the end of history (2:5)? Scholars are divided.[37] We suggest Paul is referring to wrath in history, but not the general revelation of 1:18. Rather, Paul here refers to Israel's experience of the wrath of God in exile, because this entire excursus is all about Israel. This wrath is the catastrophic Babylonian destruction of Jerusalem and its temple in 586 BC and the ensuing exile, God's revealed wrath of the law, the covenant wrath that could have wiped the nation off the face of the earth had God not been merciful for the sake of his Name and allowed a return from exile. God is righteous and just to inflict wrath at any point in time, and Israel is called first on the witness stand to testify to this absolute truth.

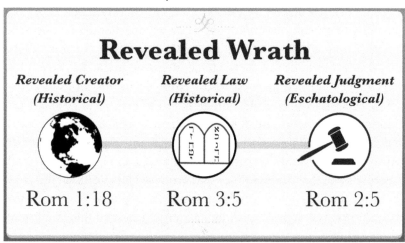

Revealed Wrath

| *Revealed Creator* | *Revealed Law* | *Revealed Judgment* |
| *(Historical)* | *(Historical)* | *(Eschatological)* |

Rom 1:18   Rom 3:5   Rom 2:5

FIGURE 7.9. Pauline Perspectives on Revealed Wrath.

[36] The verb "afflicts" (ἐπιφέρων, *epipherōn*) is a participle. In context, the verbal could be read as temporal ("while inflicting") or causal ("because he inflicts"), but attributive seems best in the diatribe rhetoric, which can be rendered as an infinitive.

[37] For eschatological, cf. Sanday and Headlam, *Romans*, 73; Käsemann, *Romans*, 83; Bultmann, *Theology*, 1:288–89. For present wrath, cf. Dodd, *Romans*, 45; Hanson, *Wrath*, 88; Smith, "ὀργὴ θεοῦ" 91–92. Jewett (*Romans*, 247–48) and Dunn (*Romans 1–8*, 135) opt for both. Neither Fitzmyer (*Romans*, 329) nor Longenecker (*Romans*, 349–50) even raise the question. Dunn accused Paul of getting off track and becoming self-contradictory: "The trouble is that Paul's argument now seems to be going in two contradictory directions. The powerful exposition of God's wrath in chaps. 1–2 has been thrown completely off course by the gratuitous assertion that God nevertheless remains faithful to faithless Israel" (*Romans 1–8*, 141). Dunn missed Paul's actual point about revelatory wrath in history and its connections with the end of history.

Second, Paul now has completed the triad of ideas unpacking his thought on God's revealed wrath. The first divinely revealed wrath is in 1:18, from the revealed creator, manifested in history on creature unrighteousness. The second divinely revealed wrath is in 3:8, from the revealed law, manifested in history on covenant unrighteousness. The third revealed wrath is in 2:5, from a revealed judgment, manifested eschatologically at the final judgment on all unrighteousness, absent propitiation (3:21–26).

Third, the assertion, though phrased as a question, really is an accusation that impugns the character of God and functions as just another attempt to find "excuse" from God's judgment. Israel knows God's wrath evidenced in history is absolutely just, so any wrath reserved for eschatological judgment will be just. This divine justice is ground zero for any theology of wrath in Paul. God is absolutely and always just anytime, anywhere, and in any way he inflicts the wrath. Paul responds to the charge briefly with his characteristic, "Absolutely not!" (**3:6**). Otherwise, how could God judge the world? Good question. If God cannot be righteous in history, he most certainly cannot be expected to be righteous at the end of history. But Israel knows God is righteous in his judgments in history.

Paul briefly pursues the point in **3:7**. With "my lie" Paul's first person assumes the role of recalcitrant Israel, anticipating his style of argumentation in Romans 7.[38] "My lie" read this way is Israel's claim to be covenant keepers when history already has proven them to be covenant breakers. Supposing that my lie results in God's truth abounding to his glory is claiming that God righteously responding with the wrath of exile to defend holiness brought him glory, so God gets the glory anyway. So, bluntly, "Why am I still being judged as a sinner?" Rationalizing that more human unrighteousness advances more divine truthfulness is downright perverted, proof positive of a "disapproved mind." We are back to the issue of God's glory and truthfulness (1:23, 25).

Romans **3:8** unfolds the curtain just briefly on Paul's mission experience: "And why not say, just as some people slanderously claim we say, 'Let us do evil so that good may come'?" In the present context in 3:1–8 with its topic of the advantage of the Jew, this slander derives

---

[38] Again, see chapter 3.

from the synagogue. Paul apparently has been slandered in this way. All he says at this point to this slander is, "Their condemnation is deserved." "Condemnation" in this context presumes another tsunami wave of historical wrath on the nation as in the days of Joel and Amos. That is all Paul says at this point in the letter. He first has to lay the groundwork in several more chapters for a thorough response. Paul here suspends exoneration of God's character until Romans 9–11.

Summary Unrighteousness (3:9–20)

Human Unrighteousness (1:18—3:20)

Romans 1	Romans 2	Romans 3
Creature Unrighteousness	Covenant Unrighteousness	Summary Unrighteousness

FIGURE 7.10. Outline: Romans 3 (Summary Unrighteousness). Universal guilt in three parts in Rom 1:18—3:20 ends with summary unrighteousness.

So, we have an irony that an advantage actually translates into a disadvantage. The Jew has an advantage in greater revelation (3:1–8), but that truth invokes greater culpability, with the result of greater condemnation because of what really happened in Israel in history. The Jewish advantage is insufficient for solving the problem. Instead, in the race to righteousness, a stumbling has occurred, and Jewish humanity is not ahead of anyone.

Sin as Power (3:9)

After an aside, Paul transitions to his closing summary using a question based on the previous unit, "What then? Are we any better off? Not at all! For we already have charged that both Jews and Greeks are all under sin" (**3:9**). This statement is the equivalent of the first part of the closing summary of all of Romans 1–11 in 11:32, "For God has shut up all in disobedience." Note that "Jews and Greeks" strategically ties each unit with repeated rhetoric, moving from the theme statement (1:16) into creature unrighteousness in 1:18–32, then to covenant unrighteousness (2:9–10), then to summary unrighteousness (3:9). Notice in these categories Paul distinctly eschews use of the term "gentile" for his rhetorical purposes in categorizing humanity. Use of "gentile" ter-

minology makes too many Great Assembly assumptions about the nature of humanity and Jewishness for Paul's messianic understanding
of Israel. Only something as momentous as meeting the Messiah could
facilitate that new perspective. That new understanding subsequently
invigorates fresh insight into Isaiah's eschatological vision for Israel.

Sin is introduced as a power in 3:9 in the phrase "under sin." This
idea is crucial to Romans and what now has contributed to Paul's movement away from the Great Assembly's take on Israel's postexilic problem (insufficient zeal) and its solution (sufficient zeal = oral law).[39] Sin
is not a smudged shirt that needs washing. Sin is a panther lunging for
the jugular. Stark reality is ignored by all self-effort schemes, so New
Years resolutions simply are not going to work, as they do not take sin
seriously enough. Sin as a power also exposes self righteousness as the
most devious and potent form of sin's manifestation in human experience. One even could crucify the Lord of glory and still regard oneself
undefiled for observing a religious feast (John 18:28). The theology of
sin as power is crucial to the Pauline enterprise, because the solution
to sin is not redoubled human effort but the need for a higher power.
This sin problem applies to all humanity, Jewish or Greek, Jerusalem,
Rome, or Spain. Sin as power levels all Greco-Roman social categories
from the educated, civilized, and cultured (Greeks) to the foreigners,
uneducated, and uncivilized (barbarians). Sin as power levels all Jewish
social categories, from those chosen, under God's favor, with Torah
blessings (Jews) to those not chosen, not favored, supposedly ignorant
of God, and sinners (gentiles). All social categories disguise arbitrary
superiority constructs and distract from understanding the problem of
sin and rebellion as universal to humankind of any stripe or color, whether conceived as the dyad of Jerusalem and Rome (Jew and gentile),
or the dyad of Rome and Spain (Greek and barbarian).

Scriptural Catena (3:10–18)

In **3:10–18** Paul launches into a catena salvo (series of scriptural
quotations). He shows Scripture testifying to the problem of universal
depravity. This depravity covers a depraved mind (Ps 14:1–3), depraved
speech (Ps 5:9; 140:3; 10:7), and depraved behavior (Isa 59:7–8). Basically, "no one" means no one. Jews are not excepted. They deny their

---

[39] As expressed clearly in the "former way of life" outlined in Gal 1:13–14.

own Scripture to say they are. The catena concludes with Ps 36:1, "No fear of God is before their eyes" (3:18). Absence of fear inspires willful rebellion. The Adamic tragedy permeates all humanity.

Conclusion (3:19–20)

In 3:19–20, Paul concludes his entire development of creature unrighteousness, covenant unrighteousness, and summary unrighteousness. He starts with a "we know." He identifies as a Jew under the law. He speaks as a synagogue Jew. What "we know" is not, however, what "we" are saying in the synagogue. Paul is countermanding the Great Assembly narrative propped up in synagogue worship every Sabbath. The Jews cannot have their cake and eat it too. One cannot claim God's offer of election and blessing without acknowledging the law's threat of condemnation. What the law says is spoken to those under the law, and the law says no one is righteous, not even one (**3:19**). The law's blanket condemnation *should* shut every self-justifying mouth, but not so much so in the synagogue. Paul here is just amplifying the criticism with which Jesus already had confronted his opponents in the parable of the publican and the Pharisee praying in the temple.[40] The deliberate "whole world" here is another way of pushing the point, "and I mean our Jewish world too!" Future judgment is coming. Future wrath in the face of incorrigible corruption is inevitable.

Romans **3:20** preserves the essence of the matter of God and sin related specifically to Israel, which seems to be an intertextual echo of Ps 143:2: "Therefore, out of the law no flesh will be justified before him, for through the law is knowledge of sin." As Dunn wrote,

> This verse delivers the *coup de grâce*, the final and fundamental reason which actually serves as the basic theological underpinning of the whole argument. All this must be so (the *whole* world answerable to God for its unrighteousness) because "by works of the law shall no flesh be justified before him." Its importance for Paul is confirmed by his use of the very same as-

---

[40] Luke 18:9–14. Luke notably introduced Jesus's parable with, "He also told this parable to some who trusted in themselves that they were righteous and held in contempt all the rest." Only Luke has this parable, and his inclusion and framing shows him tracking closely to distinctively Pauline patterns. In many subtle ways as this, Luke's first volume is setting the stage for his second volume with its exclusive emphasis in its second half on the apostle Paul. See Stevens, *Acts*, 22–23.

sertion in Gal 2:16, where it clearly fills the same role of expressing a fundamental axiom of Christian thought (agreed by Christians from both Palestine and beyond).[41]

Protestant "Works" System

Our problem is parsing "works of the law." Paul has introduced a new idea into the argument, its first occurrence in Romans.[42] The phrase is crucial to Pauline theology, since its use and placement are in critical points of the argument in the defining texts of both Romans (3:20, 28) and Galatians (2:16; 3:2, 5, 10). This phrase, therefore, is crucial to the traditional Protestant exegesis of Paul. Yet, that exegesis is not as free of problems as Protestants are wont to assume. We surveyed Watson's canonical tensions hermeneutic, Campbell's false gospel hermeneutic, and Wright's covenant God hermeneutic to show just how complicated can be integrating the expression "works of the law" into the question of the meaning of the righteousness of God.[43]

Traditional Protestant exegesis proposes a "works" system. This interpretive theory presupposes (and that is the problem) that all religions are works based. Acceptability to the gods is based on accumulating a sufficient reservoir of good works to come out in the good in the heavenly accounting office. In the first case, this presumption is patently false as in Homeric mythology. Greeks simply were trying to avoid stepping on the toes of the pantheon of personalities. If inadvertently (or even advertently) one made a misstep, one made appropriate supplication and sacrifice to propitiate the offended god or goddess. Pro-

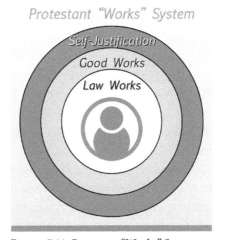

FIGURE 7.11. Protestant "Works" System.

---

[41] Dunn, *Romans 1–8*, 158.

[42] Paul spoke without reservation of a judgment "according to works" (2:6), which suggests we need to be careful here not to undermine what he clearly said there.

[43] See chapter 2, "The Righteousness of God." We concluded, "The meaning of the phrase [works of the law] always is hostage to the hermeneutic applied" (p. 43).

pitiate the gods, and one pretty much was left alone and could resume going about one's business doing whatever one pleased. That type of system really has nothing to do at all with a "works religion," much less earning a final and permanent "OK" from Olympus with a sufficient pile of good deeds. Besides, Greeks were not known for eschatology. They even argued whether an afterlife existed (Plato versus Epicurus). Consequentially, they had no scheme of "final judgment," which itself requires a linear philosophy of history synthesized into an elaborate eschatological system (some type of "the end" process). Such a view of history did not fit their concept of time as cyclical. They thought of an indefinite cycle of ages ("aeons"), one rolling over into another, with each age having its own defining characteristics. Everyone striving to accumulate sufficient good works to get a stamped passport to the afterlife simply was not in the cards in Greek religion. Elysian Fields for the heroic and virtuous was about as far as a few were able to envision, but only for those who even thought an afterlife existed.

Further, any quick investigation into Roman religion as religion (non-enlightenment presuppositions) would discover little connection between moral behavior and religious activity, which is a modern construct. Instead, religion involved a concept of *pietas* (piety), defined as showing proper respect for ancestors of the family and observing care for the welfare of the state. Once again, Romans, like the Greeks, had no thought of eschatology. Further, moral behavior was the quest of philosophy, not religion. As a result, Stoics and Epicurean philosophers took on the challenges of morality.[44]

Thus, to level all world religions, ancient and modern, as "works religions," all seeking to warehouse sufficient good works to pass the test of divine judgment through behavior defined as righteous in some self-justifying system is simply a false presupposition. From this false premise arises the accusation, "Well, Judaism is nothing but a works religion," inferring this is the problem with all religions of all time, and insinuating the Jews as a race are the poster child of them all.

The effort here is not to disavow the Protestant gemstone of *sola fide*. The effort is to advise rethinking the "works religion" construct better so as not to wind up effectively denying Rom 2:5–11 on the way

---

[44] For source documentation on Greek and Roman religion, see Stevens, *Divine Wrath*, 46–49. Cf. Parker, *Miasma: Pollution and Purification in Early Greek Religion*.

to affirming Rom 3:20.[45] Moo has an excursus to address the issues of Paul, works of the law, and first-century Judaism that has lucid critical discussion from which much can be learned from an expert in Pauline literature. Yet, in the end, he winds up proposing an understanding of Judaism that strikingly has not advanced in its critical fulcrum past the 1500s, evoking classic stereotypes and presuppositions, evidenced in his concluding summation, quoted here in full.

> We conclude, then, that Paul criticizes Jews for thinking that the Mosaic covenant is adequate without that perfection in "works" without which any system of law must fail to bring one into relationship with God. The Jews become, as it were, representative of human beings generally. If the Jews, with the best law that one could have, could not find salvation through it, then *any* system of works is revealed as unable to conquer the power of sin. The "bottom line" in Paul's argument, then, is his conviction that sin creates for every person a situation of utterly helpless bondage. "Works of the law" are inadequate not because they are "works of *the law*" but, ultimately, because they are "works." This clearly removes the matter from the purely salvation-historical realm to the broader realm of anthropology. No person can gain a standing with God through works because no one is able to perform works to the degree needed to secure such a standing. This human inability to meet the demands of God is what lies at the heart of Rom. 3. On this point, at least, the Reformers understood Paul correctly.[46]

The above representation of Judaism does not square with the ideas of Rom 2:5–11. Here are Paul's words in these verses in full again.

> But according to your hardened and impenitent heart you are storing up unto yourself wrath in the day of wrath and the revelation of the righteous judgment of God who will repay to each according to his works. On the one hand, to those who according to persistence of good work seek glory and honor and immortality—eternal life. But, on the other hand, to those who out of strife both disobey the truth and obey unrighteousness—

---

[45] Such as arbitrarily putting Rom 2:6 into the mouth of the interlocutor in the diatribe rather than accepting the statement as affirmed by Paul. No need to sacrifice exegesis to preconceived notions of what Paul could or could not have said just to support the predefined system for interpreting Paul brought into the text when no substantive rhetorical devices are present in the text to justify such a radical move.

[46] Moo, *Romans*, 217.

furious wrath. Tribulation and distress upon every human flesh that works evil, both to the Jew and the Greek, for no partiality exists with God (Rom 2:5–11).

Besides not seeming to represent forthrightly and logically these clear words of Paul, the synthesis Moo has condensed in his concluding paragraph subtly introduces issues Paul never once has raised in all of Romans 1–3, which at the least confuses the logic of the thought. Never once has Paul spoken of *perfectionism*, yet Moo *does* ("without that perfection in 'works' without which any system of law must fail to bring one into relationship with God").[47] Not once has Paul said or implied the problem in works of law is lack of perfection in keeping the law. In this case that what is required is perfectionism, provision of sacrifice is a strange waste of lambs without point. Further, Scripture characterizing any person in first-century Israel as "righteous" with obvious covenant inferences becomes nonsensical, or even misleading. Passing Hebrew Scripture straight into the New Testament, we have Joseph "being a righteous man" (Matt 1:19), or God sending his rain on the "righteous" (Matt 5:45), or many prophets and "righteous people" longing to see the realities of the days of Messiah (Matt 13:17), or Herod fearing John because he was "a righteous and holy man" (Mark 6:20), or Luke's claim that Zechariah and Elizabeth "both were righteous before God, both walking in all the commandments and ordinances of the Lord" (Luke 1:6), etc. The logic of "righteous" becomes impossibly opaque in the face of such statements, most particularly when they are the purest expressions of covenant righteousness as possible: "walking in all the commandments and ordinances of the Lord." Such a description in no way qualifies for this "tribulation and distress upon every human flesh that works evil" (Rom 2:9). Obeying the law is not automatically de facto working evil nor requires perfection to accomplish. The very problem that Habakkuk had with the impending disaster of God's wrath was not that God would judge Israel for working gross evil in the land but that the righteous in Israel would be swept up in this cataclysm (Hab 1:13).

This Protestant "works" system is a theoretical construct built up to service *sola fide* doctrine, but the system has numerous problems.

---

[47] Gal 3:10 is *not* insistence on perfection. Paul is addressing circumcision adoption *as if that one act fulfills the law*. He points to the obvious: circumcision is taking on the whole covenant burden, not an isolated act standing alone, independent of Moses.

First, "good works" is not the prototypical problem of humankind, and most emphatically God never has required perfectionism for a human to be in relationship to himself.[48] The concentric circles of this traditional "works" system make a neat and simple diagram (law works = a special form of good works = *all* human self-righteousness systems = the fundamental human problem), but the syllogism is based on a skewed anthropology. Humans left to themselves are not trying to be righteous. They are trying their best to be unrighteous (Rom 1:18–32), and, in fact, pretty proud of their efforts (Rom 1:32). Second, the "Jew" is not the prototypical sinner,[49] which is slanderous. No race nor ethnic group is more prone to sinning than any other. Paul himself presents Adam as the prototypical sinner (Rom 5:12) which has nothing to do with being a Jew, possession of the law no exception. Law simply makes a person forensically more culpable. Third, and most importantly, *sola fide* does *not* require the proposed "works" system construct for viability. In truth, at this point we are back to the problems raised by the issue of worldview polarities briefly discussed in chapter 1.[50]

Israel's Messianic Conundrum

What is our way out of this problematic Protestant presupposition that winds up obfuscating Paul's logic and actual statements?[51] The problem Paul is addressing by using the phrase "works of the law" is *when obedience to the law is not an expression of faith in God.* The premier evidence of "works of the law" for Paul is *propagandizing the precepts of the law while simultaneously performing gross evil that is either rationalized or ignored.* That behavior was Israel before the exile,

---

[48] Ironically, the pernicious error 1 John struggles to circumvent (1 John 1:7—2:2).

[49] "Thus are people (and especially Jews) led by the law into sinning" (Moo, *Romans*, 210). Moo in the accompanying note references Bultmann, Käsemann, and Schmithals, paradigmatic sources of this skewed anthropology. Again, "The Jews become, as it were, representative of human beings generally." (Moo, *Romans*, 217). The extraordinary danger here is playing into the racial stereotyping and bigotry of anti-Semitism.

[50] See pp. 6–8 on "Worldview Polarities." Even the term "religion" itself is claimed a post-Enlightenment invention foreign to the first-century mind. We still have to grapple with the "new perspective" on Paul, and the more radical perspectives spawned later. Nuancing "works of the law" in Romans first needs reframing Paul within Judaism.

[51] Without a Pelagian "works of the law" as reference to the temple rituals and ceremonies (refuted by Calvin, *Institutes*, 3.11.19) or the reductionist effort to make the expression no more than the "legalistic" aspect of law. What aspect of law is not legal?

and, we might add, Paul before the Damascus Road. In the days before the exile, Habakkuk fully was aware that injustice, oppression, and violence were rife in a land in which law was performed daily in the temple ritual (Hab 1:3–4). So, *works* of the law are performed punctiliously, but the *work* of the law is not accomplished (Rom 2:21–24). This evil of propagandizing precepts but performing evil was a virus that infected the leadership of Israel and then expanded out to Israel itself. This situation was the result of kingship in Israel that begged for the wrath of exile. Paul insinuates using Habakkuk's context just prior to the wrath of exile as our exegesis of "works of the law" by including a quotation of Hab 2:4 in his theme statement of Romans in 1:17. "Works of the law" is Paul's rhetoric of the condition of Israel's religious leaders, the high priests, the Sanhedrin, the Sadducees, and the Pharisees, expressing impenitent and hardhearted response to the preaching of Jesus as Messiah, all the while claiming to do the law as required by God—"works" Paul encountered in synagogues as he tried to preach Jesus as Messiah in the Diaspora. Israel's present religious leaders, as before, were storing up wrath for the nation. Tragically, also as in the days of Habakkuk, all the righteous also would be swept up in that terrible national cataclysm.[52] The coming of Messiah was a revelation that nothing had changed in postexilic Israel, even with Ezra, the Great Assembly, and the religious traditions of oral law. The solution to avoid postexilic Israel's juggernaut into national destruction was genuine faith in God, truly as a child of Abraham, as in Zechariah and Elizabeth, or Joseph and Mary. Faith in Jesus as Messiah revealed true faith in God and a true child of Abraham, for whom performance of the law was an opportunity to express a vital relationship with God until Messiah came (Luke 2:22–24), for all those looking for the consolation of Israel, as righteous Simeon, the prophet in Jerusalem (Luke 2:25). Romans is all about Israel.

No one is justified by works of the law when the heart is evil. One can be declared righteous performing the precepts of the law when the heart is good, meaning faith is genuine, and the one God is worshipped, and the works are an expression of that faith relationship. Otherwise, we have a most difficult time explaining how Luke and other gospel

---

[52] Invoking Jesus's words to the faithful of the need at that time to flee to the mountains to avoid the siege of Jerusalem (Matt 24:16–20; Luke 21:21–22). As Luke explained, "For these are the days of vengeance" (Luke 21:22).

writers are not making outright duplicitous declarations of righteousness. Further, we have to understand that that one God now at the end of the ages has revealed himself in his Son, Jesus Messiah. With the coming of Messiah, one cannot reject God's Son and have a good heart toward God; in that case, works of the law only reveal and amplify that rejection, since Jesus is now the ἱλαστήριον (*hilastērion*, "mercy seat; place of reconciliation," Rom 3:25) toward which performance of the law was our guide all along to foster understanding of the significance of the Son of God hanging on a cross (Gal 3:24), which consummates the law (Rom 10:4). Either Jesus was a blasphemer as charged by the high priest (Matt 26:25), or he was speaking truth to power as the future prophet Moses promised like himself to whom if any Israelite did not listen, God would judge that disobedience (Deut 18:18).

So, the conundrum for Israel and her leaders is that Messiah, the prophet like Moses, the one that had to be listened to, finally has come, and Israel's leaders are not listening. His coming has exposed evil hearts among those most responsible for leading the covenant people. In this case of messianic disobedience, law performance of any kind on the part of these leaders is shown not to be the work of faith but vain "works," inconsequential actions, useless exercises, with no connection to the obedience of faith God desires for transforming human lives.

Law brings knowledge of sin (3:20). Law by its very existence exposes the conceit of the evil heart and refuses to let that heart operate without conscience, similar to the work (singular) of the law among gentiles (2:14–15). With greater knowledge comes greater culpability. "Without excuse" comes home to roost (1:20; 2:1). Now, however, for a "disapproved mind" that claims "works" but works evil, the problem is worse than being without excuse. Sin has revealed its true nature as more than simply bad behavior; rather, sin is a devious power. Sin is the Terminator with only one purpose: termination. The deeper problem for an evil heart is not a judicial "without excuse" but being under the lordship of sin. Sin's unbroken power in an evil heart gains free reign to wreck the worst havoc and destruction. Life becomes death. Creation is destroyed. Bottom line: this problem has no solution. No solution, that is, unless God takes radical action by his creative power, unprecedented in human history, action to which the only stunned response a human could utter would be amazing grace. However, he still must remain holy and just in doing so. A deep mystery is in the making.

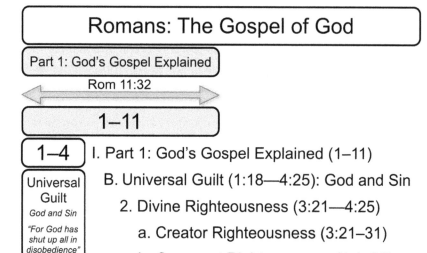

FIGURE 7.12. Outline: Romans 1–4. Establishing universal guilt (1:18—3:20) leads to a theodicy (3:21—4:25): How is a just and holy God righteous to save anyone?

DIVINE RIGHTEOUSNESS

Creator Righteousness (3:21–31)

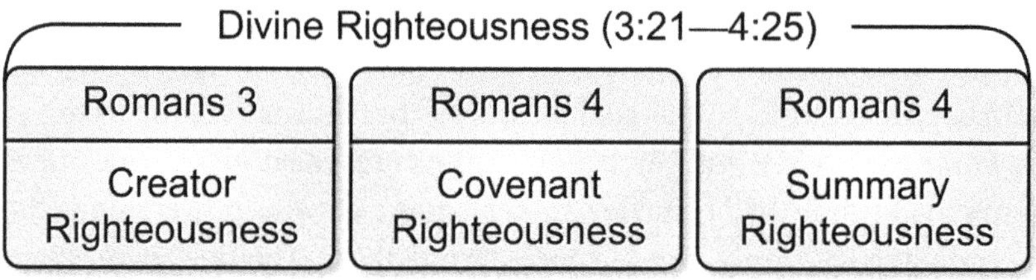

Divine Righteousness (3:21—4:25)

Romans 3	Romans 4	Romans 4
Creator Righteousness	Covenant Righteousness	Summary Righteousness

FIGURE 7.13. Outline: Romans 3 (Creator Righteousness). Three part human unrighteousness is paralleled on the divine side by righteousness in Rom 3:21—4:25.

Justification by Faith (Rom 3:21–26)

This unit often is identified as the heartbeat of Romans, and rightly so. Paul uses terms here that are rare and yet loaded theologically. Since the terminology includes rare words, exegesis is hampered by lack of ability to use word studies to build comparisons and contrasts, or even to use the author himself as his own exegesis in other letters. So, we have to acknowledge right away that this difficulty naturally will create lack of consensus on various questions that can be raised. Still, the passage has served Christendom for thousands of years, so benefit still accrues from diving right on in.

To the devastating analysis of the human predicament in 1:18—3:20 Paul suddenly passes through a worm-hole in the theological time-rhetorical space continuum to travel at light speed to another world. He does this dramatically with just two little words, "But now" (3:21). That little adverb "now" is the worm-hole into the New Aeon of Messiah.

God has done something stunning and spectacular in the story of God and sin. He has ushered humans back to the future. He has bent the power of creation's glorious consummation into the present by sending his Son into the world to forgive sins to those asking in faith and by the resurrection power released in Jesus to vivify mortal bodies for those who die in Messiah. God himself becomes the answer to the problem that had no solution. God thereby remains righteous in his character and in his conduct and manages to save the ungodly in the final judgment. God wins. Satan is confounded. Humans are amazed.

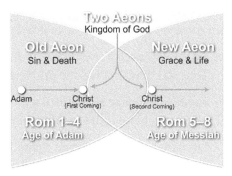

FIGURE 7.14. The Two Aeons.

The Righteousness of God. This divine action now is "apart from the law" (**3:21**) because law is an abstraction, a command, a principle, a precept—that is, letters chiseled in stone, a still-life portrait, inanimate, lifeless, fundamentally powerless to break the power of sin when sin is going for the jugular. The answer to sin is the "righteousness of God" (δικαιοσύνη θεοῦ, *dikaiosynē theou*), which, Paul declared in 3:21, "has been revealed" (πεφανέρωται, *pephanerōtai*). Paul returns to the theme statement that in the gospel, "the righteousness of God is being revealed from faith unto faith" (1:17). The two verbs for "reveal" in 1:17 and 3:21 are different (*apokalyptō* versus *phaneroō*), but often are used synonymously. The two tenses are different. The verb in 1:16

is present, which makes sense in the context of revelation taking place in the gospel as the good news is preached. To point out a problem that has no solution is not news, but to announce that God himself suddenly has done something decisive on his own to solve an unsolvable problem is big news, but news not revealed until heard. In contrast, the verb in 3:21 is perfect, which makes perfect sense with its emphasis as on-going consequences. The cross and resurrection are an ensemble event, epic in human history, dividing the ages for eternity.

We have summarized already three major proposals for understanding the righteousness of God in Paul in Watson, Campbell, and Wright.[53] That chapter should at least indicate the issues are complex. Across the centuries, three major views have dominated discussion.[54] All three propose some type of *attribute transference*:

- *legal view* (declare righteous), a *forensic* attribute transfer of righteous standing, but has the problem of a legal fiction

- *moral view* (make righteous), a *moral* attribute transfer of righteous character, but has the problem of a moral fiction

- *covenant view* (incorporate righteous), a *corporate* attribute transfer of righteous community, but the problem of an individual fiction

In terms of Romans, Hultgren landed on the covenant view as seeming strongest for integrating well with nuances in various statements in Romans, but the view requires sensitivity to overcoming the deficit of a tendency for obscuring the individual sense. In this approach the bad news is that God is the aggrieved party in a covenant arrangement. The covenant could disintegrate. The good news is that God beneficently chooses to sustain the covenant. Paul expresses the issue as a matter of lordship, the power one serves. Law righteousness tacitly is still being under sin's lordship. Messianic righteousness is a transfer to Messiah's lordship. The crux of the matter is Jesus Messiah. Jesus is the apocalypse of God's righteousness, and the locus of God's salvific activity. Paul labeled incorporation into this new covenant of righteousness secured by divine action as being "in Messiah." "Justification" comes by accepting God's salvation in faith. Thus, the eschatological turning of the age

---

[53] See chapter 2, "The Righteousness of God."

[54] See Hultgren, "The 'Righteousness of God' in Paul," *Romans*, 605–15.

in 3:21 is a crucial turn in Paul's argument because *this reality is outside the law covenant*, news to the Jews. Yet, they should reread Scripture ("law and the prophets") one more time, as the coming of Messiah has resurfaced truths buried under layers of Great Assembly traditions.

Faith or Faithfulness? The agency is "through" (διά, *dia*) "faith [of/in] Jesus Messiah" (**3:22**). The preposition is unexpressed, which creates grammatical ambiguity with the case of the inflected genitive noun, "Jesus." Genitive infers two options for the preposition, "in" or "of," but is this "faith in Jesus" or "the faithfulness of Jesus"? Both are viable grammatically, but each puts different spin on the thought. One spin focuses on the object of the believer's faith ("faith in Jesus"). The other spin focuses on the subject of Jesus's own faithfulness. We can summarize Hultgren's excellent overview.[55]

While the expression occurs seven times in Paul, the problem of translation is that either view ("faith in, faithfulness of") is defensible, but involves major discussions of syntax, key texts, and theology.[56] The traditional option is for "faith in," represented in many translations, but discussions on "faithfulness of" have gained renewed interest. In terms of syntax, the expression does not have the Greek article in any of its six occurrences in Paul, a shame, since the article could have made "faithfulness of" much more clear. So "in" or "of" options have to be decided on the more ambiguous case syntactically of the noun without the article. When Paul means "of" in the genitive, he typically will have the article, but not always. Examples can be adduced in which Paul means "in" by the genitive noun. So, both meanings are observed in Paul when the article is absent, and nothing decisive is gained. In Greek the preposition is not required, but examples of prepositions preceding the genitive noun also support both "in" and "of" meanings in Paul as well. Another syntax is to have both the noun faith and the verb believe in the same context, as here, but this construction happens in Paul only in Gal 2:16, so, again, offers too little to be decisive.

In terms of key texts to consider, one is Rom 4:16, involving a similar expression, but related to Abraham. Here the faithfulness of Abraham is the clear sense. The analogy with 3:22, however, breaks down, since the matter in 4:16 is not the personal faith of Abraham

---

[55] Hultgren, "Pistis Christou: Faith in or of Christ?", *Romans*, 623–61.

[56] Rom 3:22, 26; Gal 2:16 (2x), 20; 3:22; Phil 3:9.

itself, but those following in the pattern of Abraham's faith. However, the topic of Abraham in the very next chapter does make clear that the faith in view in the following example is the faith of the one believing, and the analogy is believing in God's promises.

What about the issue of redundancy of "faith in" in the context of the explanatory "to the one who believes"? This issue is involved in the three occurrences in Gal 2:16; 3:22; and Phil 3:9. In these contexts and observing the following verses makes clear that "faith in" is the sense. The emphasis is on the universality of faith.

In terms of theological observations, one would have to involve the idea of narrative, or story, as part of how Paul's theology "works." If one considers the broad sweep of Israel's story, the idea of God's faithfulness to the covenant has great support. Still, the immediate context in 3:22 does not emphatically support that the issue is Christ's faithfulness, and Paul elsewhere does not put a clear emphasis on this aspect. One could worry that the "faith in" option turns faith into a good work, but this inference is not made in the scholars arguing for this option. The reverse could be worried about the "faithfulness of" option as a good work. If, hypothetically, one takes the "faithfulness of" option, then some type of participation construct for the believer is requisite. Yet, exactly how the believer would appropriate or execute on this participation is unclear. Therefore, the actual details of a participation idea are vague. A further question would be, What role does Christ play after he has performed his "faithfulness," presumably by dying on a cross? Another problem would be that some type of sequence seems inferred, as in a gift-participation-salvation scheme, but that seems rather alien to Paul's thought. In the argued verses, why if so crucial to theology is the actual discussion of this participation in Christ's faithfulness absent? Whenever Paul speaks of justification elsewhere, the faith of the believer is clear in context. As well, outside of Paul, the faith of the believer is a regular feature.[57] Finally, in terms of the history of interpretation, the Greek church fathers regularly took the "faith in" option, so this option is not a Reformation invention or unobvious to others. Hultgren decided for "faith in."

While Paul was not habited to including a preposition in these type constructions, he may have intended both meanings. The issue in

---

[57] As in Eph 2:8–9 (depending on authorship issues) and Jas 2:17.

salvation is as much God's as human in terms of vested interest. The issue of God's Name haunts the discussion. God's saving action is not exclusively for human beings. God, after all, does seem interested in the reputation of his Name among the nations. The case may be in the faithfulness of Jesus as in the faith of the believer. Since Jesus was the only one who *could* get the job done, Jesus *had* to get the job done. He had to be faithful to his mission of being sent into the world. As we have suggested before, the gospel of God is as much good news for God as good news for humans. We would suggest the exegesis of *dia pisteōs Iēsou Christou* does not have to be either, or. We would opt for both, and. Both are grammatically defensible and theologically coherent. Paul has in view both the believer's faith and Christ's faithfulness. That theological dyad is the gospel of God, which works two ways.

Paul continued, "For all sin and are coming up short of the glory of God" (**3:23**). The verb "sin" is a gnomic aorist, a generally observable truism. What is true is across time, cultures, and societies. All sin. If any truth ubiquitous in human experience illustrates the power of sin, "all sin" covers the case. Two words, and Paul is done. This verse is a virtual restatement of the entire unit on human unrighteousness in 1:18—3:20, and functions as Paul's own "Paradise Lost."[58] The glory of God that is humanity's glorious destiny features in Paul's own "Paradise Regained" in Rom 8:18–22. This issue of God's glory reinforces the idea that something in the gospel of God is good news for God as much as for humans. The faithfulness of Jesus and believers showing faith in Jesus both are essential to the future glory of God.

"And they are justified as a gift by his grace through the redemption that is in Messiah Jesus" (**3:24**). "Justified" is the first of a series of three, powerful metaphors Paul fires off for probing the mystery of the death of Christ. The other two are "redemption" (3:24) and "propitiation" (3:25).[59]

---

[58] Cf. Rom 1:23; 2:7, 10; 3:7.

[59] We must remind ourselves that metaphors are analogies. Analogies can be pushed too far, overextended, and the meaning more confused than clarified. We transgress the invisible boundary between metaphor and some aspect of reality to which the metaphor is intended to point by making too much of the metaphor, such as trying to establish a one-to-one correspondence with every element in the metaphor, similar to treating each minor detail in a parable as if hiding some deep theological truth.

Justification is the metaphor of the law court. The point is a verdict. Theologically, however, justification is eschatology. The verdict of the final judgment bends back in time. Jesus has brought the reality at the end of time to now (3:21), almost like a back to the future. Paul's justification language is the root source of forensic righteousness theology and those systems of thought. One question is whether God intends for human righteousness to be a fiction for eternity, since being only *declared* righteous is not ever *being* righteous in reality. Of course, one could invent a two-stage salvation sequence (justification + sanctification), and that would solve the problem—assuming, that is, that everyone moves down the continuum from sinner ("justified") to righteous ("sanctified") at a sufficient and steady enough pace to arrive at the end when at the end.

The offer is "as a gift," which, essentially, means beyond human ability. The offer also is "by his grace," which, essentially, means God's initiative. So human effort cannot achieve this result, even assuming humans were so inclined (unlikely in the face of "all sin"). The result is quite the predicament without God taking the initiative. The gospel is the announcement that God took the initiative. In an honor-shame society as in the first century, grace would be interpreted as a benefit offered by a patron to a client. The client would be obligated to show loyalty to the patron as a result of this benefaction.

"Redemption" is the second analogy and is taken from the slave market. In the ancient world, the most common source of slaves was war. People who were conquered were enslaved. They were sold for a price in the slave market. Yet, someone could intervene and free the slave by paying a redemption price, that is, the price of the slave in the open market. The point in this metaphor is the freedom gained, not the price paid.[60] Within the narrative of Israel, freedom from Egyptian slavery to become a nation provides a strong correlation to the power

---

[60] This "redemption" metaphor is the root source of expressions such as, "Jesus paid the price." We have to remember, however, that metaphors make only analogies with real world elements for the sake of a point. Here, the point is freedom secured, not price paid. We need not confuse extending an analogy about freedom gained by making a further analogy about paying a price. The problem is, theological statements using such extensions can get dogmatic.

of this metaphor.[61] This redemption is in Messiah Jesus. Jesus is the righteousness of God in providing redemption without price.

The verb here in the expression, "whom God put forward" (3:25), infers "publicly" or "in view of all." God's action is public, so available to know and understand. While this emphasis could counter the mystery religions with their secretive rites, the more likely sense is just the public nature of the crucifixion event itself. Nothing about this action was "done in a corner."[62] Further, this highly public event is the initiative of God. God did not have to save sinners, but he took initiative to do so. When he did so, he was quite public.

Jesus was put forward "as a propitiation" or "expiation" (ἱλαστή-ριον, *hilastērion*, **3:25**). Propitiation is the third metaphor utilized by Paul on the death of Christ. Paul has moved from the law court, to the slave market, and now to temple sacrifice. We have two thoughts to consider hermeneutically, one well traveled, the other quite less so. The well-travelled idea is from the Hebrew sacrificial system. The word *hilastērion* in Hebrew Scripture in the LXX was used for the golden covering of the ark of the covenant.[63] This covering was the place where once a year the high priest sprinkled the blood of two sin offerings.[64] This event was the holiest of person, time, and place in all of Jewish ritual. No Jew, however, ever saw the high priest take this action from within the inner sanctum of the temple. Yet, the Day of Atonement that God effected though Christ notably, Paul said, was public. Further, the place of atonement had moved from temple to Messiah.

The less traveled road on the way to exegesis of this term *hilastē-rion* takes in mind the Roman audience.[65] The story involves emperor Augustus when he was Octavian the general. Octavian defeated Mark Antony and Cleopatra in the famous naval battle of Actium in 31 BC. He thereby gained control of all Roman territories east and west and permanently ended the long history of Roman civil wars as the Roman Republic was disintegrating.

---

[61] Note that God did not pay Pharaoh anything for these slaves in this redemption story. Jewish slaves simply were freed against Pharaoh's will.

[62] The idea evokes Paul's statement to King Agrippa II in Acts 26:26.

[63] Exod 25:17–22.

[64] Lev 16:12–19.

[65] Cf. previous discussion, pp. 128–29, 136n4, 235; Stevens, *Acts*, 561–66; Wilson, "*Hilasterion* and Imperial Ideology."

Most of Asia Minor had pledged loyalty to Antony's forces.[66] The cities could have faced devastating war reparations. Octavian, however, acted magnanimously, showing leniency to Asia Minor and favoring supplications for clemency. His unexpected behavior inspired gratitude for such grace.[67] Octavian was hailed for bringing both peace to the world and reconciliation to all as the *hilastērion*, the "reconciler."

FIGURE 7.15. Theater at Metropolis. The theater at Metropolis, excavated in the 1990s, revealed an important find related to Roman imperial inscriptions.

FIGURE 7.16. Metropolis Dedicatory Altars. The three dedicatory altars with imperial inscriptions to Octavian and Germanicus were discovered in the Metropolis theater.

[66] Plutarch, *Ant.* 56.1.

[67] Cassius Dio, *Hist.* 51.4.1.

Excavations in the early 1990s at Metropolis,[68] an ancient city only twenty-one miles north of Ephesus, found three early Roman imperial inscriptions on dedicatory altars honoring Octavian (Augustus) and Germanicus. The inscription to Octavian calls him the *hilatēriou*, the "reconciler" of the world.[69] A Roman audience likely would have heard an echo of imperial rhetoric in Paul's use of this term so rare in the New Testament.[70] Further, we could have intratextual resonance in Romans with this imperial propaganda between Rom 3:25 and 5:10, "For if, while we were enemies, we were reconciled to God by the death of his Son, much more, being reconciled, we shall be saved by his life."

FIGURE 7.17. Metropolis Dedicatory Inscription. The inscription is KAISAROS EILASTĒRIOU, Καισαρος Ειλαστηριου, "Caesar, the Reconciler."

The propitiation is "in his blood," which clearly makes the context sacrificial and points to the ark of the covenant mercy seat imagery. In this analogy, Christ's death is a sin offering. As God himself provided

[68] The city of Metropolis is on the main road from Ephesus to Smyrna. Luke indicated Paul impacted the whole province of Asia; the word of the Lord spread widely from Ephesus (Acts 19:10, 20). Likely Metropolis, so close by, was impacted by Paul's preaching. Paul even may have been aware of this city and its inscriptions. In the background material, we noted that Romans was written soon after Paul left Ephesus.

[69] See the author's video at https://drkoine.com/paul/rome/italy/index.html in the section, "JR Italy—Imperial Monuments," and then down to "*Hilastērion* in Rom 3:25."

[70] Note that its only other occurrence in the New Testament is in the letter of Hebrews (Heb 9:5), a document also associated with a provenance in Rome in church tradition.

propitiation in the law of Moses, he now does so in the death of Christ.[71] "In his blood" is as clear as Paul can be that the law of Moses is fulfilled in Messiah's self-sacrifice (10:4). Self-sacrifice as efficacious for propitiation was the one offering never considered in the law of Moses.[72] In Roman thought, however, self-sacrifice as propitiation of the gods was a feature of the Roman military.

> The most potent expiation of divine wrath was the cultic-military rite of "devotion" to death, a drastic action to vitiate impending divine wrath. In 340 BC, the consul Decius so devoted himself to divert divine wrath from his legions to his own person and to the enemy troops whom he had dedicated along with himself. Legionnaires, witnessing their comrade expiating the divine wrath, renewed the attack with fresh vigor, their spirits relieved of religious fears.[73]

We are not framing Jesus's death theologically as a military cultic rite of devotion to death like the consul Decius. However, we do suggest a Roman audience could hear as reasonable the thought expressed in Rom 3:25 in terms of both sacrificial language from the Jewish cult (mercy seat) as well as expiatory self-sacrifice on behalf of others. Yet, even though expiatory self-sacrifice is found on rare occasion, as in later Maccabean-era Jewish martyrdom contexts, atoning human self-sacrifice nowhere was anticipated in the law of Moses. Human sacrifice, in fact, was anathema.[74]

Even so, one rare and allusive prophetic tradition that tends in the direction of human self-sacrifice but without explicit connection to the law of Moses is the curious figure of the Servant of Yahweh, abused by the nations, in the Servant Songs of Isaiah.[75] In Jewish tradition, the Servant figure, though sometimes singular in the text, has been taken as the suffering Jewish people across the centuries. Isaiah's Servant motif became core scriptural testimony for interpreting the death of Jesus in the early church due to Jesus's own claim to fulfill the role of Isaiah's

---

[71] Dunn, *Romans 1–8*, 180–81.

[72] Human atoning self-sacrifice, of course, is evidenced in later Jewish thought in 4 Macc 17:21–22. This context, however, is martyrdom language, which Paul's is not.

[73] Stevens, *Divine Wrath*, 48. Cf. Livy, *Ab urbe cond.* 8.9.

[74] As in sacrificial offering of children to the god Molech (Lev 18:21; 20:2–5; 1 Kgs 11:7; 2 Kgs 23:10; Isa 57:9; Jer 32:35).

[75] Particularly the final and climactic Isa 52:13—53:12; cf. Isa 42:1–4; 49:1–6; 50:4–7.

Servant of Yahweh.[76] Paul interestingly utilizes the fourth Servant Song in Romans both for contextualizing disobedience to gospel preaching and Israel's mission to the nations (10:16; 15:21).

When we note that the surrounding context of Romans 1–3 is suffused with the language of the wrath of God, and given the context of Hebrew Scripture that sacrifice is spoken of as staying the wrath of God, then the conclusion is almost inevitable that this propitiation here in 3:25 is meant to be understood as turning away God's wrath. That conclusion can be acknowledged without inferring another idea that is altogether different: that on the cross Jesus endured the wrath of God in his person. We need to be clear that neither Paul nor any other New Testament writer makes such a statement explicitly. We need to be clear theologically that *turning away God's wrath is not enduring God's wrath.* When a devastatingly destructive hurricane is turned away from doing damage to the eastern coastline of the United States by the upper steering winds of an approaching warm front, nothing endures the storm's wrath, whether coastline or warm front. The storm simply turns and dissipates harmlessly over the open waters of the Atlantic. So, we can affirm that in Rom 3:35 Paul meant by using the analogy of sacrificial propitiation that Jesus turns away God's wrath. That affirmation, however, does not have to mean God spent his wrath on Jesus like the designated royal whipping boy. If God would be unrighteous for not judging the guilty, he certainly could not be righteous for judging the innocent. Righteousness has to work both ways to be right.

Jesus's self-sacrifice *by definition* was a once in a lifetime event. One sacrifice now has fulfilled perpetual sacrifice regulated in the law. Once fulfilled, however, covenant obligations no longer adhere to the perpetual sacrifices, which become vain. After the coming of Messiah, the efficacy of the temple cultus transfers to Messiah by default. This transcendence and transfer of covenants is the new revelation of how God has manifested his righteousness in the New Aeon brought about by Messiah to justify the ungodly. He has done so mysteriously, unexpectedly, and miraculously so as to transcend all deficiencies of the law of Moses.

---

[76] Luke 22:37; cf. Matt 8:17; Mark 15:28; John 12:38; Acts 8:32–33; Rom 10:16; 15:21; 1 Pet 2:22.

The mediation of this efficacious self-sacrifice is "through faith." The element of faith in Jesus takes the law of Moses out of the picture. Belief must be placed in the only sacrifice that is efficacious to break the power of sin.[77] That power is in the gospel (1:16). Messianic faith consummates the covenant God made with Abraham to declare faith in God's promise as righteousness. God promised Jesus. Thus, faith in Jesus consummates the covenant with Abraham.

Paul now gives two reasons for the death of Christ. Both take up the issue of the righteousness of God. The first reason is "as evidence of his righteousness" (3:25, 26).[78] The noun "evidence" (ἔνδειξιν, *endeixin*) is a sign that functions to point to a reality, like a tremor points to an earthquake. God intends the death of Jesus to be evidence that points to his righteousness when other evidence might suggest the contrary. The other evidence is "passing over sins previously committed." What are these sins to which Paul referred? Moo performed a word link between "forbearance" in 3:26 and its use in Rom 2:4.[79] He decided from his previous interpretation of the forbearance in 2:4 having to do with sins in general that the "sins previously committed" would be all sins in "the period of time before the cross."[80] This approach surely heads in the wrong direction exegetically. The hermeneutic neither properly has contextualized Rom 2:4 as about Israel (*not* forbearing the general sin of all humans), nor Rom 3:25, for the same reason.

Israel is the key to "sins previously committed," not a vague category of humans in general. The reason is straightforward and obvious: the context is propitiation imagery of the Mosaic covenant (*hilastērion*), the mercy seat furniture of the temple and the Day of Atonement ritual of the high priest for the nation of Israel. God had no such propitiatory covenant with gentiles. The covenant that backgrounds the imagery is the Mosaic covenant that offered a place of expiation that now has a new place of expiation. So the subject of "passing over sins committed beforehand" has to be about Israel. The problem is justly enforcing the

---

[77] Cf. Rom 8:3; 2 Cor 5:21, 14; by also sharing fully in resurrection (Rom 6:3–11).

[78] Moo discussed the two major interpretations of the meaning of righteousness here, *Romans*, 237–38.

[79] Because "forbearance" (ἀνοχή, *anochē*) occurs only twice in the NT in these two verses in Romans. The linkage is correct, but Moo's interpretation misses the mark.

[80] Moo, *Romans*, 239–40.

terms of the covenant. A rejected Mosaic covenant according to the terms of the agreement should have resulted in a rejected people. As Jeremiah warned Israelites who fled from the Babylonian destruction of Jerusalem to establish a colony in Egypt but continued their idolatrous ways,

> And now thus says the Lord God of hosts, the God Israel: Why are you doing such great harm to yourselves, to cut off man and woman, child and infant, from the midst of Judah, leaving yourselves without a remnant? Why do you provoke me to anger with the works of your hands, making offerings to other gods in the land of Egypt where you have come to settle? Will you be cut off and become an object of cursing and ridicule among all the nations of the earth (Jer 44:7–8, NRSV)?

So what about the problem of allowing Israel to survive exile, return to their land of disinheritance, and become a nation among the nations again, when covenant stipulations were clear that they should lose the land and the nation and no longer be the people of God? The "forbearance" in **3:26**, as in 2:4, is about forbearing Israel, restraining the divine wrath from being exhausted to its fullest extent, granting a reprieve by granting a remnant and a return. As Ezra confessed, "you, our God, have punished us less than our iniquities deserved and have given us such a remnant as this" (Ezra 9:8, NRSV). Ezekiel fell down and cried out fearful of the divine wrath if expressed to the fullest, "Ah Lord God! will you make a full end of the remnant of Israel" (Ezek 11:13, NRSV)? Micah most directly hit the nail on the head, "Who is God like you, removing iniquities and passing over ungodliness for the remnant of his possession" (Mic 7:18, LXX)? The problem for theodicy is both defending allowing a remnant, then explaining passing over the remnant's continued penchant for sinning. Of course, God did promise a remnant,[81] and God can have mercy on whomever he decides to have mercy,[82] yet, such statements call into question how to understand the righteousness of God when the claim made in the absolute is that God shows no partiality (Rom 2:11).

After the exile, God passed over the remnant's continued sin. He deferred judgment again, because the next time would have eschato-

---

[81] Isa 10:20–22; 11:11, 16; 28:5; 37:31; 46:3; Jer 6:9; 23:3; 31:7; Mic 5:7–8.
[82] Exod 33:19; cf. Rom 9:15.

logical consequences for the nation, the final, exhaustive wrath of God because the last days had arrived in the arrival of Messiah. At the turn of the ages, judgment will turn to the Messiah, who has been set forth publically by God as the propitiation of Israel, the Day of Atonement. Rejection of the Messiah thus means no atonement for Israel and sins passed over since the exile no longer will be passed over. The nation will be called to account as the day of the Lord arrives and the Lord suddenly appears at his temple.

> . . . and the Lord whom you seek will suddenly come to his temple. The messenger of the covenant in whom you delight—indeed, he is coming says the Lord of hosts. But who can endure the day of his coming, and who can stand when he appears? (Mal 3:1b–3, NRSV)

God thus demonstrated forbearance (ἀνοχή, *anochē*) by passing over sins.[83] Messiah, however, radically had changed the entire situation.

So, the first reason for Christ's death is to solve Israel's postexilic predicament. After the exile, Israel despised the divine grace that had granted a reprieve of the divine wrath of exile. That reprieve meant that exilic wrath was not executed exhaustively to the fullest according to the terms of the Mosaic covenant. This despising of God's reprieve is manifested in on-going idolatry and sin. Some, such as those with whom Jeremiah dealt down in Egypt, still were carving idols of sticks and stones. Others had improvised a new species of idolatry by promulgating the law's precepts while performing gross evil. The power of sin had increased to its most insidious form of evil, hypocrisy of the impenitent. God broke into this death-spiral of sin in Israel to reveal a new covenant with a new Day of Atonement through the self-sacrifice of the Messiah. This sacrifice is efficacious because this death comes with the power of life. The power of the destroyer is overcome by the power of the creator. Incorporation into the death of Messiah is incorporation into his life through resurrection. The death which sin has effected God has nullified. The Adamic curse is broken. Jesus's action is efficacious for turning away the wrath of God on Israel and

---

[83] The inexplicable new verse insertion (3:26) into the middle of the continuing Greek clause from 3:25 obtusely has broken the connection between the propositional phrase, "in the forbearance of God," at the beginning of 3:26 and the previous phrase of the passing over of sins in 3:25, as most English translations recognize.

on all the nations. This death that transforms into life consummates all of the purposes of creation. Easter came, and the evening and the morning were the first day, and a new creation had dawned.

Paul now gives the second reason for Jesus's death in 3:26. God had a second demonstration to accomplish with the death of Messiah. This, again, is expressed as "in order to demonstrate his righteousness in the present time." God's righteousness in the past is clear, and now God's righteousness in the present is clear. Here again we interface with Pauline eschatology of the two ages. God was righteous in the Old Aeon because he always determined to consummate all his purposes in Messiah in the New Aeon. He is just to delay consummation until he can consummate creation according to all his purposes. He does this through Jesus, whose coming at one point in time changed all time. God, therefore, is just in all his expressions of wrath, but also all his expressions of mercy. He is consistent, because he always had declared righteous the one who believed in his promises. Further, justifying the one who has faith in Jesus is justifying the ungodly in a godly way, because Jesus died to sanctify that faith.

Three Dialogical Questions (Rom 3:27–31)

Paul's "dialogical" rhetoric (imaginary opponent) takes up a question and answer style of argumentation that is frequent in Romans.[84] The background came from philosophy. The method was used regularly by Socrates, popularized by Plato, and later developed in two venues. One venue was street preaching, with a polemical function. If Paul is operating in this mode, the assumption in terms of context would be a style he developed in his disputation in the synagogues. The other venue was school teaching, with a pedagogical function. If Paul is operating in this mode, the assumption in terms of context would be a style he developed in his exhortation in house churches. Since a synagogue setting (Rom 1:5) and a house church setting (Rom 16:5) both are a part of the rhetorical context of Romans, the answer for which direction Paul is taking with his dialogical style in Romans (polemical, pedagogical) would have to be nuanced contextually. The Jewish focus and temple ritual of sacrificial language in Rom 3:21–26 puts forward as the more probable context in the present verses the longstanding

---

[84] Romans 2; 3:1–8; 3:27—4:1; 8:31–39; 9–11.

debate in Roman synagogues over the role and function of Jesus as the Messiah. The Edict of Claudius indicates this debate had engaged Roman synagogues long before Paul ever arrived, and, beginning in Rom 3:21, Paul was just diving right on into the debate. So, his rhetoric here is polemical. His point, however, eventually will target the evolving new situation of Roman house churches, which also was pushing the issues involved in another wrong direction related to the significance and place of gentiles in messianic Israel (Romans 9–11). So, the rhetoric here also is pedagogical, for those who had ears to hear.

Paul asks three dialogical questions to anticipate typical objections by Mosaic Israel to Jesus as the place of sacrifice and the reconciler of the world to God. The first is, "Where then is boasting" (**3:27–28**)? This question reveals ignorance about how God works in salvation. Paul responds that boasting is excluded, clarifying what "apart from the law" means in 3:21. Paul's nuance is not law per se, but "works of the law," law as performed in postexilic Israel under the aegis of the Great Assembly hermeneutic. Mosaic Israel has nothing in which to boast. Ezra's postexilic religious reforms devolved into a Pharisaic movement that so opposed Jesus and his understanding of the law they crucified him. Again, Nehemiah's postexilic political efforts devolved into Hasmonean and Herodian dynasties that either attempted to kill Jesus or to throttle his disciples by killing their leaders (Matt 2:16; Acts 12:1–4). All this time, Israel boasted of performing the works of the law—as did Saul of Tarsus himself.

> For we are the circumcision, the ones who are serving by the Spirit of God, and we boast in Messiah Jesus, not having trusted in the flesh, though I was confident even in the flesh. If anyone thinks to have confidence in the flesh, I all the more: circumcised on the eighth day, of the family of Israel, the tribe of Benjamin, a Hebrew of the Hebrews, according to the law, a Pharisee, according to zeal, persecuting the church, according to the righteousness which is in the law, I was blameless (Phil 3:3–6).

Being blameless according to the righteousness which is in the law is a point of view. Mosaic Israel's postexilic works of the law is the wrong point of view on being blameless, not when that point of view crucifies the Lord of glory (1 Cor 2:8). Thus, Paul rhetorically has set up tension between "law of faith" and "law of works." The *same law*, however, is involved. These phrases are just two different points of view on this law, encapsulated poignantly in Paul's own story before and after his "moment in the sun" of the epiphany of Jesus (Gal 1:16).

The second question is, "Is God of Jews alone" (**3:29–30**)? This question exposes ignorance about who God is related to election. The doctrines of monotheism and election inherently are in tension. Claiming a God of all is hard to explain when proclaiming a God of the few. For postexilic Israel, election stops at Sinai for defining who God is. Yet, Paul takes the question all the way back to creation. Eden trumps Sinai on this question. No understanding of election is adequate that does not square fully with the doctrine of monotheism. Paul works out this doctrinal tension with the story of Abraham and how that patriarchal story defines Israel (Romans 4, detailed more fully in Romans 9–11). In short, if God is both one God and God of all, election of the few is only to insure that the many can be included.

The third question is, "Do we destroy the law" (**3:31**)? This question exposes ignorance about what Paul preaches. Paul's understanding of Israel has been integrated into his understanding of the God of all. His gentile mission is on behalf of his apostleship to Israel.[85] Paul insists he establishes the law (which readers of Romans need to cogitate seriously). The assertion in 3:31 is simply another facet of the claim that the gospel of God is that "which he promised beforehand through his prophets in the holy Scriptures" (1:2). Faith always has been the law's true basis. We are back to Paul's theme: "the one righteous by faith shall live" (1:17). What Paul says here clarifies the exegesis of both the quixotic Romans 7 and the quintessential Rom 10:4.

Covenant Righteousness (4:1–22)

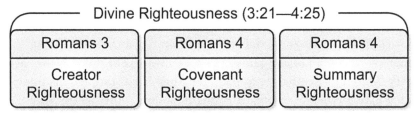

FIGURE 7.18. Outline: Romans 4 (Covenant Righteousness). Three part human unrighteousness is paralleled on the divine side by righteousness in Rom 3:21—4:25.

---

[85] More about nations than gentiles as gentiles; cf. "obedience of faith" in Rom 1:5.

Setting up the Proof Case (Rom 4:1–3)

Paul now enhances his three dialogical assertions against synagogue objections to his preaching of Jesus as Messiah with his proof from the life of Abraham, ground of all that is Jewish and definitive of Israel, even more than Moses (**4:1**). Since God's covenant is foundational to the story of Abraham, this development of the divine covenant *righteousness* functions as Paul's rhetorical counterpoint to Jewish covenant *unrighteousness* presented in Rom 2:1–29. The probing question is whether one is justified by works of the law (**4:2**). This issue involves confusion within Mosaic Israel about Abraham's story and its implications for a definition of Israel. What is Abraham's story?

The Genesis narrative has traced the story of abject human evil (Genesis 6), the consequent judgment of flood (Genesis 7–10), and the tower of Babel as prelude to the story of Abraham through genealogy (Genesis 11).[86] Terah leaves Ur of the Chaldeans for Canaan, but we are not told why. He is accompanied by Abram, Sarai, and Lot. Terah arrives in Haran but never leaves. Abram, however, receives a direct word from God to leave his father's house "to a land I will show you," and is promised progeny as a great nation and that "all the peoples on earth will be blessed through you" (Gen 12:1–3). The Scripture then states succinctly, "So Abram went" (Gen 12:4), and thus began Abram's life of faith. Abram gets to Shechem in the land of Canaan, the land for which Terah started out but never arrived, and Abram is promised this land for his offspring (Gen 12:7). The story moves through famine and sojourn in Egypt and back to Bethel where a land dispute with nephew Lot causes separation. God, however, reiterates his promise of offspring and land (Gen 13:14–17). Warfare among kings of the valley entangle Lot and his family as prisoners because they had settled in Sodom (Gen 14:12). Abram bravely defeated king Chedorlaomer and his confederate kings, pursuing them beyond Damascus to the north, thereby rescuing Lot and family (Gen 14:13–16). For this decisive victory, Abram made offering to "God the Most High" through the priest-king Melchizedek of Salem. The king of Sodom, duly noting Abram's success against the kings of the valley, offered an alliance with Abram, but Abram refused (Gen 14:17–24). Abram's refusal of human alliance was commitment to the protection of the Most High.

---

[86] Noah, Shem, Arpachshad, Shelah, Eber, Peleg, Reu, Serug, Nahor, Terah, Abram.

The larger literary backdrop to the story of Genesis 15, then, is the story of absolute human failure and perpetual corruption (evil, flood, Babel). The immediate backdrop is the contrast offered by the story of Abram's life of faith and trust in God, not human alliance. That backdrop is the very reason why the Scripture notates, "After these events, the word of the Lord came to Abram in a vision" (Gen 15:1). In other words, the Genesis storyline is the narrative equivalent of Rom 1:18—3:31, including the essence of what makes Moses and the law work or not work in Israel before ever arriving at Sinai. By Romans 4, Paul has arrived at Genesis 15. In this way, one could say that the story of Genesis is the story of Israel,[87] that the gospel was promised beforehand in the prophets (Rom 1:2), and that Romans is all about Israel.

We see the narrative logic, then, why in Rom **4:3**, Gen 15:6 is used to answer the question whether one is justified by works (specifically as defined by Great Assembly traditions perpetuated and propagated in the synagogue). In the immediate prelude in Genesis 14, Abram has sacrificed to God the Most High through the priest-king Melchizedek for Abram's victory over the kings of the valley in saving his nephew Lot and simultaneously has refused human alliance with the king of Sodom for securing his family and future life. These actions are the essence of faith as both properly worshipping the only God for his gracious provision and righteously living life trusting in this only God.

Paul explains two key phrases: "he believed," which is the nature of Abraham's faith, and "was reckoned," which is the nature of Abraham's justification. Paul discusses the phrases in reverse order to the text ("was reckoned" first in 4:4–8, then "he believed" in 4:9–21).[88]

Explaining the Proof Case (Rom 4:4–22)

Paul first discussed "was reckoned" (4:4–8). He started with a business analogy (**4:4–5**). Wages are pay for work performed. Oddly, Abraham did no work, but got "paid." Paul then made a scriptural analogy (**4:6–8**). David has a similar take on one's relationship to God as not based on work performed in Ps 32:1. Since humans are sinners, "pay" would be judgment for sin. A human could be blessed in this case only if God does *not* reckon sin! Thus, if God's "reckoning" results in a declara-

---

[87] See remarks on Postell, p. 114, n46.

[88] Following Dunn's analysis (*Romans 1–8*, 194–241), still one of the best.

tion of righteousness, such a declaration represents a unique operation of divine grace at God's own initiative beyond wage earned. The mediated divine righteousness is the security of the relationship.

Phrase two explained is "he believed" (4:9–21). Paul here focused on the later chronology of Abraham's circumcision (**4:9–12**). When was the kind of "blessedness" of which David spoke pronounced over Abraham? The "blessedness" spoken in Genesis 15 is pronounced *before* God enjoins Abraham's circumcision in Genesis 17. Thus, this chronology is crucial for establishing that circumcision was given as a seal of Abraham's *uncircumcised faith*. Abraham was a *gentile* when God declared him righteous in Genesis 15. Now surfaces the identity of the gentile to whom Paul was referring when he wrote in Rom 2:26, "Therefore if an uncircumcised man keeps the requirements of the law, will not his uncircumcision be counted as circumcision?" Paul was alluding to the uncircumcised Abraham being declared righteous by God in Gen 15:6.

This chronology of Abraham's circumcision uniquely makes him simultaneously father of the uncircumcised, to whom righteousness is "reckoned" by faith, and father of the circumcised, to whom righteousness *likewise* is "reckoned" by faith *before* works. Such reckoning shows law only a *seal* of faith without presuming a works performance component. The logic here is the logic of the inward circumcision of the heart in Rom 2:29 as what expresses true relationship and trust in God, not "works of the law." That inward reality is the life of Abraham.

So God gives Abraham a promise, and faith is the channel of that promise, not law (**4:13–16**). In fact, making works performance the channel of God's promise will guarantee to void the promise, because law brings wrath (1:18). For this reason, promise never automatically is transferred from generation to generation by genetics. *Every* generation must receive the promise by faith. Faith is the only security in any generation for the future, because faith is how the just will live (Rom 1:17). Thus, "Abraham our father" must be infused with a faith component, or no genuine representation of Abraham is conveyed. In this sense, Abraham is "father of us all," that is, gentile and Jew (4:16).

Abraham's faith also is imbued with a "resurrection" character that gives that faith ever much a gospel-reflecting core (**4:17–21**). Abraham was getting much older and Sarah had been barren her entire life. They had nothing to contribute to God's promise of a son to them, but God miraculously brought forth a son out of that hopeless death. Paul has claimed that Abraham's faith is paradigmatic for messianic Israel not only because this faith encapsulates the path to God a gentile can walk without the law, as did Abraham from Ur to Canaan, but because this faith foreshadows the resurrection character of the God believed: a child brought forth out of death. So, Paul concludes, "Therefore, (his faith) was reckoned to him as righteousness" (**4:22**). In this statement, "righteousness" is interpreted by the later chronology of circumcision. "Was reckoned" presupposes faith as the channel for the efficacy of God's promise. "His faith"[89] is framed in terms of its resurrection character: believing God and his seemingly impossible promise.

When Genesis 15 is integrated into Genesis 22 and Exodus 20, the issue of trusting faith is thrust forward dramatically as the issue of the law in Israel. In Genesis 15, Abraham responds to God's gracious promise of a son with trusting faith. In Genesis 22, Abraham responds to God's mysterious demand for the sacrifice of that promised son with trusting faith. In Exodus 20, the question is whether Israel will respond to God's gracious gift of the law with trusting faith. History already has shown that Israel did not emulate "our father, Abraham" on this score. Abraham was asked to sacrifice his son for God, and he obeyed in faith. Israel was asked to sacrifice her Great Assembly take on the law of Moses for Messiah, and Israel rebelled in unbelief. Israel's reliance on her own take on the law over that of the Messiah thereby was proven as idolatry, not faith, and just as culpable as the idolatry at Sinai with the golden calf, or the idolatry that led to the judgment of exile, or any pagan idolatry that begs for the wrath of God (1:23).

Summary Righteousness (4:23–25)

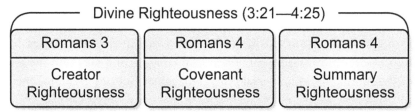

FIGURE 7.19. Outline: Romans 4 (Summary Righteousness). Three part human unrighteousness is paralleled on the divine side by righteousness in Rom 3:21—4:25.

---

[89] Presuming the reference of the third person "it" in the verb.

Paul finally drew the wider corollary by extending Abraham's story into the present. The Scripture recording Abraham's story was written not just for ancient generations, but "for us" (**4:23–24**). "Us" is messianic Israel of the New Aeon that burst upon human experience in the coming of the Messiah, which creates an entirely new "now" ("but now," 3:21). We too will have righteousness reckoned in the same way, that is, to those who, like Abraham, "believe in him," but now with the reality of resurrection anticipating God's new promise of eternal life, "who raised Jesus our Lord from the dead" (4:24). Through Messiah, God calls Israel *now* just as Abraham *then*. The foundational story of faith still is foundational to what makes Israel "the Israel of God." Paul now is back to his theme statement in 1:16–17,

> For I am not ashamed of the gospel, because it is the power of God unto salvation to everyone who believes, to the Jew first, then to the Greek. For in it the righteousness of God is revealed from faith to faith, just as it is written, "The righteous shall live by faith."

This theme statement now has been reframed in Abraham: *the gospel story is Abraham's on-going story.* The very character of Abraham's faith in God's promise (life out of death) now has been woven tightly into the very creed already existing among the Roman house churches with which Paul opened his letter to them in 1:2–4,

> which he promised beforehand through his prophets in the Holy Scriptures—concerning his Son, Jesus Messiah our Lord, who was a descendant of David according to the flesh and was appointed to be the powerful Son of God according to the Spirit of holiness by the resurrection of the dead.

Inasmuch as Israel-in-the-flesh (Abraham our forefather) stubbornly refuses to incorporate into Israel-in-the-faith (Abraham our father) through God's promised Messiah, then Israel-in-the-flesh ceases to fulfill God's purposes in election and in creation and falls into the lot of that humanity in universal rebellion against God the creator. Thus, Messiah was "delivered up for our trespasses and raised for our justification" (**4:25**). Those trespasses include disbelieving Messiah.

Thus, Abraham is integral to the story of Messiah, and Abraham becomes the paradigm of faith in Messiah. Abraham's faith is prior to and the basis of the law, which opens the door to gentiles to respond to God's promise in the gospel like the gentile Abraham to God's promise in progeny. Further, Abraham's oracles from God become key to understanding where God is going with messianic Israel in fulfilling creation's purpose ("bless all the families of the earth"). Finally, Abraham's salvation illustrates how God justifies the ungodly.

So what does the story of Abraham suggest about the law? This story infers that the law properly understood signals the need for faith (4:11) and always is subordinate to promise (4:14). Abraham trumps Moses for defining Israel. Law misunderstood in non-Abrahamic terms voids faith, aborts the promise, and provokes God's wrath.

What does the story of Abraham suggest about creation? This story infers that Scripture presents *two* gentile paradigms, not one as claimed by the Great Assembly. The first paradigm is the Adamic gentile, the tragedy of rebellion overviewed in Genesis 1–11. This gentile suppresses God's revelation (Rom 1:18), exchanges God's lordship in God's glory, truth, and knowledge (Rom 1:23, 25, 28), and confirms the reality and power of the Old Aeon leading to death (Rom 1:32). The second paradigm is the Abrahamic gentile, the triumph of faith recorded in Genesis 15–22. This gentile affirms God's revelation, embraces God's lordship, and anticipates the reality and power of the New Aeon leading to life. The question for first-century Jewish identity is not how gentiles can become more like Mosaic Israel but how Mosaic Israel can become more like Abraham. The problem is Adam. The solution is Messiah. The key is Abraham. Hence, Rom 5:12–21.

To conclude this discussion of Paul's use of Abraham, not Moses, to parse the meaning of being declared righteous, we can observe that, theologically, we are beginning to see how Paul consistently has focused on God's promises as the appropriate hermeneutic in the New Aeon of messianic Israel for parsing the meaning of God's law. Mosaic Israel reversed the hermeneutical process: Moses was everything.[90] Even the promises were subordinated to the primacy of law.

Finally, by this time through the argument of Romans 1–4 we have seen Paul affirming three major Jewish traditions that summarize God's promises to Israel through his covenants with Israel. As the discussion has progressed, Paul also has insisted that Jesus fulfills all these covenant traditions as God's Messiah and is the "yes" to every promise of God (2 Cor 1:20). Paul has affirmed Jesus as fulfillment to the promised

---

[90] Hence the term, "Mosaic Israel." See previous discussion, pp. 95–105.

Davidic covenant (1:3–4), the promised Mosaic covenant (3:24–26) and the promised Abrahamic covenant (4:23–24).

8

Universal Grace

God and Grace

ROMANS 1–4 HAS DEVELOPED THE first part of the summary state-ment in Rom 11:32, "for God has shut up all in disobedience." Paul now develops the second part of that statement, "in order that he might show mercy." Romans 5–8 is about God's grace as the basis of God's response to human sin and Israel's predicament in God's wrath.

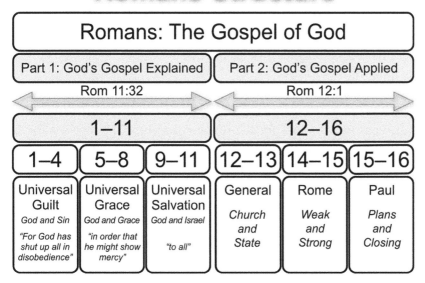

Romans Structure

Romans: The Gospel of God		
Part 1: God's Gospel Explained	Part 2: God's Gospel Applied	
Rom 11:32	Rom 12:1	
1–11	12–16	

1–4	5–8	9–11	12–13	14–15	15–16
Universal Guilt	Universal Grace	Universal Salvation	General	Rome	Paul
God and Sin	*God and Grace*	*God and Israel*	*Church and State*	*Weak and Strong*	*Plans and Closing*
"For God has shut up all in disobedience"	*"in order that he might show mercy"*	*"to all"*			

FIGURE 8.1. The Structure of Romans. Paul moves from establishing universal guilt to developing universal grace as God's response to human sin in Romans 5–8.

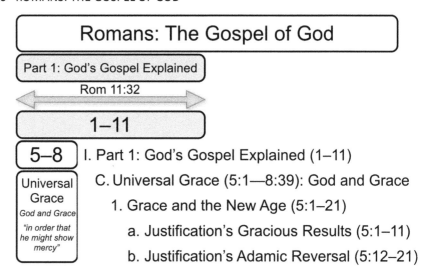

FIGURE 8.2. Outline: Romans 5 (Grace and the New Age). Romans 5 is results now for those who have accessed justification by grace in Messiah, and the reversal of Adam.

GRACE AND THE NEW AGE

Justification's Gracious Results (5:1–11)

Paul has presented God's divine righteousness working in Jesus as Messiah to provide justification of the ungodly through faith. God thereby fulfills all of his covenant promises to Israel. Paul now reflects on the realities of the New Age brought about by the coming of Messiah already in play for those who have accessed this justification by grace. In part, he is describing his own experience.

Peace with God (5:1)

The first result of justification is "peace with God" (**5:1**). This word of peace has two contexts for the Roman churches. The first context is Roman via the state ideology inspired by Augustus himself of the *Pax Romana*, the peace of Rome. This background is the same as presented in 3:25. The backdrop is the general Octavian's defeat of Antony, consolidation of all Roman territories east and west, and a conclusive end to centuries of internal civil wars in the dying Roman Republic.[1] After Augustus further subdued Gaul, the Roman Senate honored him with a sacrificial monument to peace, the Ara Pacis, and Roman poets

---

[1] See pp. 307–09.

celebrated the new age Augustus's birth inaugurated for Rome. Augustus himself bragged in his last will and testament about the peace he brought to the world. Roman imperial propaganda continued state funded support for this Roman gospel through imperial inscriptions, coins, statues, friezes, monuments, and imperial cult temples.[2] Thus, at Jesus's birth was not the first time anyone heard a poetic proclamation of peace on earth. A word of peace is analogous to the military struggles of Octavian and Antony and Octavian's subsequent reconciliation to cities of Asia Minor. In a similar vein, rebellion against God is a seditious compliance with the losing forces of Satan in his designs to destroy God's creation. In sin, we are aligning with the wrong forces and thereby treating God as if an enemy. God, however, magnanimously has offered unexpected reconciliation, whose consequence is peace.

The process of reconciliation with Octavian involved a transfer of allegiance by cities of Asia Minor from Antony to Octavian. This transfer inherently also was a change of lordship. Similarly, peace with God is evidence of a lordship exchange. The lordship of Satan is exchanged for the lordship of God. Lordship exchange connected to the concept of peace is precisely why Paul at the end of Romans—after giving a sudden stern warning to avoid contentious heretics (16:17–19)—concludes with, "And the God of peace soon will crush Satan under your feet" (16:20). Martial terminology at the end of Romans in 16:20 alluding to Satan's warfare with God supports the likely context of Roman imperial conquest in 5:1 behind another use of the motif of peace in Romans.[3]

The second context for Paul's word of peace is Jewish in the eschatology that anticipated life in the kingdom of God. The concept rich in meaning that carries this complex of ideas is "shalom." Shalom is the background also to Paul's opening benediction of "grace and peace" (1:7).[4] Notice that this opening peace benediction also presumes a lordship exchange ("from God our Father and the Lord Jesus Messiah"). From this Jewish background of future life in the kingdom of God to come, an eschatological component to "peace" in messianic Israel is

---

[2] See the "Age of Augustus" discussion, pp. 127–54.

[3] The verb translated "will crush" is συντρίψει (suntripsei), meaning to break, break in pieces, break down, crush, bruise, or break the power of, evokes the imagery of city siege, breaking down city walls, and other images of military conquest (cf. Rev 2:27).

[4] For the Hebrew term and its rich background, see discussion, pp. 127–31.

derived and used by Paul. Thus, dual Roman and Jewish background to the concept of peace in 5:1 powerfully presents the incredible value to be gained by justification, both now and in the future. Peace is the messianic community's present experience (Rom 5–8), Israel's future hope (Rom 9–11), and creation's ultimate goal (8:21).

Entrance into Grace (5:2)

The second result of justification is "entrance into this grace" (**5:2**). The word translated "entrance" once again, draws on imperial imagery.[5] Imagine the imperial palace at the top of the Palatine Hill, one of the famous seven hills of Rome, overlooking the Roman forum, the heart of Rome and Roman rule. Being allowed entrance into this palace was an extraordinary privilege and rare experience. Direct access usually was granted to the immediate family members only. A plebian Roman passing through the forum on his way to gathering his daily ration of corn or wheat and glancing up to the top of the hill never in a lifetime could imagine entrance into that palace, even less to have the "favor" of the emperor to gain a personal audience with the ruler of the whole world who dwelled within.

Paul wrote this access is through "our Lord Jesus Messiah."[6] This expression encapsulates the exchange of lordship that is crucial to the theological realities of the hidden problem in human unrighteousness. The issue is not a matter of New Year's resolutions. The issue is lordship, to which higher power one is enslaved and does the bidding ("Paul, *slave* of Messiah Jesus," 1:1). Paul emphasized the permanence of this access through marking the tense of we have.[7] Likewise, being inside the royal palace is permanently to stand in the rarified atmosphere of this sphere of grace.[8] The avenue is faith, not works, blood, ethnicity, or religious heritage (Romans 4).

---

[5] The word is προσαγωγή, *prosagōgē* (approach, access, admission, entrance).

[6] Carried over from verse 1 into verse 2 as the antecedent of the relative pronoun phrase, "through whom" (δι'οὗ, *di ou*).

[7] The tense of "we have" (ἐσχήκαμεν, *eschēkamen*) is perfect, with emphasis on the on-going consequences of God's act of justification.

[8] Again, the tense of "we stand" (ἡστήκαμεν, *estēkamen*) is perfect, with emphasis on the on-going consequences of God's act of justification. One of the notable realities of ancient urban life was the constant stench on city streets, for many obvious reasons. Thus, elite urban property tended to take to the hills for cooler breezes and fresher air.

Cause for Boasting (5:2–11)

The third result of justification is ironic: "we boast" (5:2). Since boasting has been challenged throughout Romans 1–4, one would have to suspect Paul rhetorically catches his audience off-guard with this word.[9] Now becomes clear, however, that Paul does not denigrate boasting per se but false boasting. False boasting has the wrong object. Paul's objects of boasting are "hope" (5:2), "tribulation" (5:3), and "God" (5:11). All three relate directly to God himself and his designs in salvation.

The first object of boasting is "in hope of the glory of God" (5:2). Here, we are back to the issues of the ungodly exchange of the glory of God in 1:18–32. Divine glory is the goal of creation. Since obtaining that glory is yet to be consummated (Romans 8), then the reality for believers with boots on the ground is that this glory can be affirmed only in hope during the present "now-not yet" eschatological tension of messianic Israel. At the same time, the resurrection of Jesus already is the harbinger of the harvest to come. Hope goes well beyond wish.

The second object of boasting is "in tribulations," another eschatological reality (5:3). These tribulations likely are the "birth pangs" of the approaching end, analogous to a woman's labor pains significantly intensifying just prior to birth (Rev 12:2); this image then becomes an eschatological *topos* (Matt 24:21). Another analogy could be the devastating time of warfare with its city siege that intensifies into hunger, famine, disease, and terrible distress just before the walls crumble and the end comes.[10] Paul developed a sequence based on eschatological realities that suffering produces endurance, that produces character, that produces hope (5:4). So, God strengthens every step of the way to glory. This type of hope "does not make ashamed" (5:5). With this assertion, we are back to the theme statement of Romans, "For I am not ashamed" (1:16). Paul's gospel of the justification of the ungodly, both Jew and gentile, has gotten him thrown out of synagogue after synagogue. He has another justification for which to look forward—his reputation as a faithful Jew and teacher of Israel.[11] His day will come.

Believers are persuaded even in tribulation that they are in God's care and will make the journey to glory successfully because God's love

[9] Romans 2:17, 23; 3:27; 4:2.

[10] Cf. Josephus's gruesome description of the fall of Jerusalem, *J.W.* 6.1.1; 6.8.1, etc.

[11] Like his Pharisee brother, Nicodemus (John 3:10).

"has been poured out in our hearts through the Holy Spirit which has been given to us" (5:5). The verb tense communicates the permanent nature of this pouring out action.[12] Pouring out of the Spirit was a sign of the last days for Joel (Joel 2:28–32), and Peter interpreted the pouring out of the Spirit at Pentecost precisely in this way (Acts 2:16–21). Paul resonates with this prophetic tradition and Peter's interpretation. Messiah has inaugurated the prophetic last days.

We boast in tribulations because our confidence in its outcome is (1) persuaded by God's poured out love, (2) channeled by possession of God's eschatological Spirit, and, finally, (3) proved in Messiah's death on the cross (5:6–10). This death comes at just the right time in human history to accomplish God's redemptive purposes for the entire cosmos (**5:6**). The timing was the point of greatest weakness. What marked that desperado situation? Israel. Israel has failed miserably after the exile properly to reflect the law of Moses as a revelation of the heart of God, so the chance offered in preserving a remnant for Israel to fulfill her mission to the nations has been squandered with no plan in sight post remnant. The word of a remnant is where the prophetic voice in Israel came to an end. If the remnant fails, what then? Then came Jesus from Galilee to John at the Jordan to be baptized by him (Matt 3:13). Just in the nick of time, the remnant is preserved for her mission to the world through the propitious coming of Messiah to reformulate messianic Israel to reveal the heart of God and call to the obedience of faith the nations of the world (Rom 1:5). In human terms, for a good person one might die, but Messiah died for the no good, the ungodly (**5:7**).

The language of Romans 5 reflects the thought Paul has been developing all along. For example, "weak" in 5:6 reflects the enslavement that is the universal predicament of humanity in Rom 1:24, 26, and 28. These verses repeat the "God gave them up" signature of how God's wrath works through allowing a lordship exchange because humans asked for that exchange. Human nature thereby corrupted into a distorted, perverted, debased subhuman nature through enslavement to the bidding of evil. Again, "ungodly" reflects the objects of God's wrath met recurrently in Rom 1:18; 2:5; and 3:5, encompassing both Jews and gentiles. Clearly, this unit is summarizing the argument made.

---

[12] Again, the tense of "has been poured out" (ἐκκέχυται, *ekkechytai*) is perfect, with emphasis on the on-going realities of God's love.

Paul then provides a carefully crafted, two-verse statement summarizing soteriology in a nutshell in **5:8–9**. In this summary, Paul reiterates that God proves his love by saving sinners.

Statement, 5:8–9	Reiteration, 5:10
1. while sinners	1. while sinners
2. Messiah died for us	2. reconciled, son's death
3. much more then	3. much more
4. having been justified	4. having been reconciled
5. we shall be saved	5. we shall be saved
6. through him	6. in his life
7. from the wrath	7. [blank = 5:12–21]

FIGURE 8.3. Soteriology in Rom 5:8–9. The concise overview of soteriology in Rom 5:8–9 is repeated for emphasis in 5:10, but with an important missing element.

Paul repeats the two-verse summary more concisely in one verse in **5:10**. Each phrase in 5:10 sequentially mirrors its corresponding element in 5:8–9 in thought, if not verbally. Repetition, of course, is a way of emphasizing importance. Paul again builds on the Roman context of what act inaugurated the entire epoch of the Augustan age. The victor in the conflict unexpectedly and magnanimously offered peace and reconciliation to former enemies who wrongly aligned with the losing forces, even as Paul explicitly frames the circumstance, "while we were enemies." Paul then translates into political terms for Roman believers God's act of justification in Messiah as the relational idea of reconciliation (element 4), echoing Augustus's treatment of his own enemies in Asia Minor allied with Antony. This salvation is "in his life" (5:10). Life (ζωή, zoē) and wrath (ὀργή, orgē) are eschatological polarities in Paul's semantic universe.

However, one crucial element is missing in 5:10 from the previous statement in 5:8–9: "from the wrath." This wrath is God's future coming judgment. Paul goes back to the future to the judgment that consummates the wrath of God that even now is being revealed but then will be finished. Paul obviously has pulled a page from the dog-eared folder of his mission preaching (1 Thess 1:9–10). This missing element, however, insinuates something even more. The story of Eden is not concluded. The story prematurely is interrupted by the wrath of banishment, just like Israel's story prematurely is interrupted by the wrath of exile. The metanarrative of Israel in sin, then, is Adam, and Moses can do nothing about the Adamic curse. Humanity needs more than the law to resolve the problem of sin. Posting another speed limit sign simply does not stop speeding. Adam chose another lordship and thereby invited into human experience the evil that continually incites the wrath of God against all ungodliness and unrighteousness of humans who suppress the truth by their unrighteousness (1:18). Humans, including Israel, have been enslaved to evil's lordship ever since. A power that can overcome Adam's fall is needed to reverse the course of human history, and Moses and the law are not that power. Messiah is that power (1:16)—and even more. This Adamic curse and the transcending accomplishment of Messiah over against this curse soon will be summarized in 5:12–21.

The third object of boasting is "in God," which is on the basis of his initiative in Jesus Messiah (**5:11**). This divine initiative, completely undeserved, suddenly opens up the possibilities of a new relationship, the essence of "reconciliation" (καταλλαγή, *katallagē*). The source of confidence for this boasting is that the process already has begun (5:1–5, 9, 11). Since the reconciliation already is taking place ("now," νῦν, *nyn*), the future of this boast is founded historically (5:6–11).

In summary, justification's gracious results include numerous realities experienced by messianic Israel even now, with some realities to be anticipated in the future. These descriptions evoke the "now-not yet" tension of eschatological living that is the hallmark of the present time. Paul primarily has been focused on what already is true in the present time, because these can be taken as harbingers of the future. These present realities include peace, entrance, hope, tribulation, Spirit, love, and reconciliation. Still to be anticipated in the future are salvation and glory, the "not yet" portion of eschatological destiny.

Justification's Adamic Reversal (5:12–21)

Paul has been reflecting on the realities of the New Age brought about by the coming of Messiah, particularly those already in play for believers. He has insinuated the problem goes well beyond Moses and the law, due to contemplation of what Messiah has accomplished already in messianic Israel.

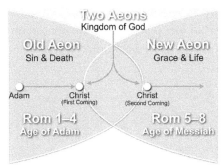

The problem goes all the way back to creation. The narrative is of two epic events that have defined human existence and destiny. Paul first presents the epoch event in Adam (5:12–17). He then presents the epoch event in Messiah (5:18–21). The epoch events set up the realities of the two aeons under which human life forever is set. Paul

FIGURE 8.4. The Two Aeons. Prior Adamic allusion in Romans now becomes explicit.

launches a comparison that is burdened with more contrast than comparison. He still sallies forth, because he wants to establish the point that Adam is a "type of the Coming One."[13] His typological comparison has only one element: the action of one person in each case establishing an entire aeon of human experience.

Epoch Event 1: Adam (5:12–17)

Paul begins with a "therefore" that is a conjunction of logical inference (**5:12**). What he says here is meant to enhance the magnitude of Messiah's offer of reconciliation mentioned in 5:11. The best way to show the stunning accomplishment of reconciliation is to go back to the stunning consequences of the original estrangement.

Sin is personified as an actor on the stage of life. Adam through one act of disobedience facilitated Sin's entrance onto the stage (5:12). The syllogism is simple. Adam brought Sin. Sin brought death. All sin.[14] All die. The idea, however, is complex. Did all sin "in Adam," making

---

[13] The Greek is, Ἀδὰμ ὅς ἐστιν τύπος τοῦ μέλλοντος, *Adam, hos estin typos tou mellontos* (5:14). The use of typology as a hermeneutic by New Testament authors raises a number of issues that cannot be resolved here.

[14] The Greek expression (ἐφ᾽ ᾧ, *eph hōi*) before the verb is ambiguous, because the relative pronoun gender is not clear in the form. If neuter, the idea could be "because," or "in view of the fact," "wherefore, it follows," "that is the reason," or "inasmuch as." If the relative pronoun is masculine, then one could translate "in whom all sinned" (as did Augustine when developing his influential federal headship of Adam theory).

Adam's sin the sin of all? Did Adam's sin corrupt human nature genetically such that a tendency to sin is congenital? Did Adam simply set an example inevitably followed by all (for no given reason)? Morris pointed to the emphasis of the word "one" throughout this entire unit inferring that the logic is built on what one person did, not what many do. He then listed the following expressions as demanding the sense of all sinned in Adam:

- "many died by the trespass of one" (5:15)

- "the judgment followed one sin" (5:16)

- "by the trespass of one man, death reigned" (5:17)

- "the result of one trespass was condemnation for all men" (5:18)

- "through the disobedience of one man the many were made sinners" (5:19)

Morris then pointed to the similar expression in 2 Cor 5:14, "one died for all, and therefore all died."[15] Yet, the rhetoric of "one" in this context does not have the one reading as suggested by Morris. What Paul simply said was that by Adam's disobedience, Sin "entered." This action of "entering" reads more like letting an animal out of its cage. Once loose, the animal prowled about seeking its prey (1 Pet 5:8). To be sure, one person acted, but not all humans yet unborn themselves acted in that singular act. Further, rhetoric such as "Death reigned," as if speaking of a ruler such as Nero in Rome, makes little sense without understanding personification. The weakness of Morris's take that all sinned in Adam is insufficient integration of the role of personified Sin into his reading of Paul in this context. Highly likely is that the personification Paul is using here is because he is speaking of Satan.[16] Further, Morris has a faulty understanding of verbal aspect when reading the aorist tense in "all sinned" as a singular event.[17] Satan loosed means all sin.

---

[15] Morris, *Romans*, 232. Paul's meaning in 2 Cor 5:14 surely is not universalism, which is the inevitable consequence of Morris's typological twist here. So many other statements in Paul, particularly in Romans itself, make clear that "therefore all died" in Christ would presume "for those who believed."

[16] Rom 16:20; cf. 1 Cor 5:5; 7:5; 2 Cor 2:11; 11:14; 12:7; 1 Thess 2:18; 2 Thess 2:9; 1 Tim 1:20; 5:15.

[17] "The aorist points to one act" (*Romans*, 231)—a classic misunderstanding of the aorist. Compare the same expression in Rom 3:23, where Morris contradicts himself:

Paul does not finish his sentence in 5:12. He breaks his grammar to chase some caveats in 5:13–17. He finally gets back to his original thought in 5:18.[18] His main idea can be grasped, but his actual thought in these caveats is compressed, so, difficult and illusive. Dunn noted, "What comes to expression is rather what we also see in the same broad stream of Jewish reflection on the Genesis account of Adam's fall— viz., the tension between the inescapableness of human sin operating as a compelling power from within or without."[19]

The first caveat in Rom **5:13–14** makes a point about the law.[20] Commentators struggle with the meaning of 5:13.[21] One possibility is that Paul is undermining Jewish presumption of the necessity of law before condemnation can be charged (i.e., transgression). If so, death should not have reigned from Adam to Moses. The weakness is that this thought looks back to verse 12 when the grammar of the strong adversative (ἀλλά, *alla*, "but," "rather") looks forward to verse 14. In this way, is Paul pointing to the contradiction that sin not reckoned (no law transgression) means death should not have happened, but death *did* happen, so law never was the point? Or, is this universal law (though quite unrevealed by God in any way) that all transgressed, but without knowledge? Or, could verse 14 be another way of showing by death's reign that all sinned in Adam, though not volitionally?

Perhaps what Paul is arguing, admittedly compressed and almost convoluted, is critiquing Israel's attitude to the law as able to give life. In the face of evil's overwhelming lordship over human experience, even those who do not sin like Adam by transgressing an explicit command—Israel's own paradigm—still sin against God so as to deserve death, such as Noah and the flood. Imagining that the law actually could

---

"The aorist pictures this as past, but also as a completion, It certainly does not mean that sin belongs wholly in the past, for Paul goes on to a present tense when he says *fall short of the glory of God*" (Romans, 176–77). The aorist at 5:12, similar to 3:23, can be read as gnomic (or timeless, the categories are sliced deli thin at this point), that is, a generally true principle. Another example is Peter's "the grass withers," which also is aorist (ἐξηράνθη ὁ χόρτος, *ezēranthē ho chortos*, 1 Pet 1:24).

[18] So, for example, the KJV puts 5:13–17 in parentheses.

[19] Dunn, *Romans 1–8*, 274. He noted Philo, *Moses* 2.147, 1QS 3:18—4:1, 4 Ezra's "evil heart" but human responsibility (4 Ezra 8:35); Apoc Bar 54,15, 19.

[20] The "jump" to making a point about the law immediately upon engaging the Adam typology often is read as abrupt, even illogical—but not if Romans is all about Israel.

[21] Bultmann famously labeled 5:13 "completely unintelligible" (*Theology*, 1:252).

bring life in the face of such overwhelming evidence of the human propensity to perversion of everything God created so as ultimately to be cursed with judgment and death (which, by default, would have to include the law itself) is a hubris absolutely devoid of historical reality. That Sin "reigned" from Adam to Moses should have been the starting point for predicating what law would do to Israel: only make Sin more powerful in its most insidious and sinister form—self-righteousness.

The next caveat in Rom **5:15–17** is a little easier. Our exegetical north star is the repetitious "much more" grammar (πολλῷ μᾶλλον, *polloi mallon*). Whatever is the contrast or comparison, the New Aeon in Messiah is so much more transcendent a reality as inherently to defy the contrast or comparison. Paul's struggle to work his typological analogy between Adam and Messiah is that what God accomplished in Jesus is beyond words both quantitatively and qualitatively. In quantity, Adam's act of disobedience required his attempting to overcome only one trespass. Messiah, on the other hand, had to overcome a tsunami of trespasses to accomplish his one act of obedience. So, Adam's disobedience is quantitatively inferior to Messiah's obedience. Again, Adam's one act destroyed creation's purpose, no small feat, to be sure. Messiah, on the other hand, not only fulfills creation's purpose, he transcends creation by transforming the cosmos into the eschatological destiny that was God's ultimate goal in creation all along. So, Adam's temporary reign of death is qualitatively inferior to Messiah's eternal reign of life. The work of salvation is grounded in a flood of grace overcoming the flood of sin, and righteousness as a gift to access undeserved life, not a gratuity to acknowledge service performed.

Paul's two caveats in 5:13–17 have exposed Israel's hubris about the law as harmless in the light of Sin's devastating reign and his own admission of the deficiencies of his typology. He now moves to finish his typology, so he picks back up in 5:18 where he broke off in 5:12. In **5:18–19** Paul reengages the comparison between Adam and Messiah, which, the second caveat already has admitted, has more contrast than comparison. Adam's epoch event inaugurates the fateful series of transgression, condemnation, and death. Human disobedience has resulted in sinners and unrighteousness. Messiah's epoch event inaugurates the fateful series of righteous deed, justification, and life. Messianic obedience has resulted in saints and righteousness, a holy people consecrated to God.

In **5:20–21**, Paul concludes the Adam typology of the two aeons in human experience by picking up the topic of law raised in the first caveat. In the light of the overwhelming power of Sin that "reigns" over human behavior throughout the Old Aeon, law only multiplies trespasses, and culpability and consequences for disobedience become even more grave. The only contravention of Sin's power is intervention of God's power. That power is divine grace released in the gospel of God.

So, we have two epochs, two dominions, and two reigns. We have Sin's reign in death versus grace's reign in life. Eternal life is the consequence of justification in the New Aeon of Messiah. Justification is the final and complete Adamic reversal in the economy of salvation. Messiah inaugurates the eschatological blessings of which Adam only could dream even in the abundance of Eden. The Adam-Messiah typology of 5:12–21 is the Pauline soteriological fulcrum of the turn of the ages, but so much more. The Adam-Messiah typology is the fullness of the gentiles and the salvation of all Israel.

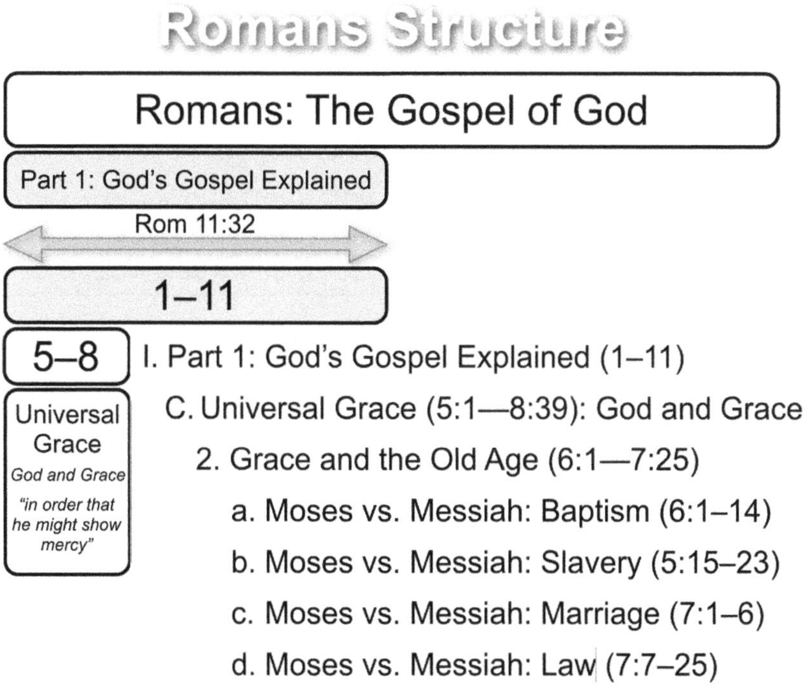

Romans Structure

Romans: The Gospel of God

Part 1: God's Gospel Explained

Rom 11:32

1–11

5–8

Universal Grace

God and Grace

"in order that he might show mercy"

I. Part 1: God's Gospel Explained (1–11)

C. Universal Grace (5:1—8:39): God and Grace

   2. Grace and the Old Age (6:1—7:25)

      a. Moses vs. Messiah: Baptism (6:1–14)

      b. Moses vs. Messiah: Slavery (5:15–23)

      c. Moses vs. Messiah: Marriage (7:1–6)

      d. Moses vs. Messiah: Law (7:7–25)

FIGURE 8.5. Outline: Romans 6–7 (Grace and the Old Age). Israel's old redemption story in Moses in the Old Aeon and Israel's new redemption story in Messiah in the New Aeon. The initiative of divine grace is both parallel and essential to both sagas.

GRACE AND THE OLD AGE

The Adam-Messiah typology has raised the issue of the purpose of law in Israel during the Old Age of the Adamic curse, since law's coming brought extraordinary culpability for sin with deadly consequences for the nation. This conundrum of the divine purpose of law in Israel is the issue of Romans 7. Paul will set the stage for Romans 7 by using motifs from Israel's story of deliverance—baptism in Moses, slavery in Egypt, and covenant at Sinai—as images of justification in Messiah. Paul parallels Israel's old redemption story in Moses during the Old Aeon with Israel's new redemption story in Messiah in the New Aeon. The initiative of divine grace is essential to both sagas. First up is Israel's exodus from Egypt as God's gracious response to slavery. Second up is Israel's covenant at Sinai on the relational pattern of a marriage covenant as divine expectation for God's initiative and deliverance. These images of baptism, slavery, and marriage in Romans 6–7 thus set the stage for the discussion of Israel and the law in Rom 7:7–26, famously misread as Pauline autobiography, or Christian conscience, or the existential angst of gentile Everyman.

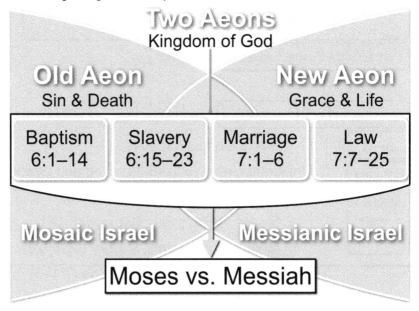

FIGURE 8.6. Moses versus Messiah. Israel's election and calling are circumscribed by the Adamic curse. Law creates the dilemma of Mosaic Israel increasingly bound in a spiritual slavery greater than Egyptian servitude. Unless Israel follows the path of the faith of Abraham, law will bring only wrath and destruction. Messiah alone saves.

Moses vs. Messiah: Baptism (6:1–14)

Paul has presented God's divine righteousness working in Jesus as Messiah to provide justification of the ungodly through faith. God thereby fulfills all of his covenant promises to Israel. Paul now reflects on the realities of the New Age brought about by the coming of Messiah already in play for those who have accessed this justification by grace.

Romans 6–8 almost universally is assumed to be Paul describing the individual believer's experience.[22] To say otherwise simply sounds wrong. In this case, one hardly can see the forest for all the trees. What is the forest? *The rhetorical context is corporate, not individualizing.* The pronominal grammar overwhelmingly is plural throughout this entire series of chapters in Romans 6–8. Reading this material as about the individual believer's experience blinds the exegetical eye to this dominantly plural rhetoric.[23] The author throughout Romans 1–7 discloses his addressees in consistently corporate terms. This corporate reality is messianic Israel. In Romans 6, therefore, Paul continues his quest to provide exegesis of the meaning of Israel now that Messiah has turned the page of the age.

The election and calling of Israel fatefully are circumscribed by the Adamic curse (Romans 5). In this creation context of a power that reigns over God's creation, law creates a dilemma for Mosaic Israel.

---

[22] Illustrations can be compounded easily. "He who believes in Christ has, through Him, entered into the new age and now lives his life 'in Christ'" (Nygren, *Romans*, 230). According to Cranfield, "In more than one sense the Christian has already died and been raised with Christ" (*Romans* 1:296). Käsemann is similar, "Verse 11, however, solemnly sums up a first train of thought . . . according to which Christians are set free from sin with a definitiveness which death alone can achieve" (*Romans*, 163). We can note that Dunn's title for Rom 6:1–11 is, "The Believer Has Died to Sin" (*Romans 1–8*, 303). Fitzmyer's unit title, similar to Dunn's, is "Freedom from Self through Union with Christ," and he started his discussion with the comment, "Paul's description of the Christian experience proceeds a step further" (*Romans*, 429). In referring to 6:2, Jewett applied the passage to the individual believer (also invoking the wrong inference from verbal aspect) with the comment, "The aorist verb ἀπεθάνομεν ("we died") harks back to the singular, punctiliar moment in the life of believers when they appropriated the death of Christ for themselves" (*Romans*, 395). In framing the "now–not yet" eschatological tension of the passage, Hultgren compared references to Christ in this unit by noting, "Other references are to the baptized person and to that person's destiny with Christ" (*Romans*, 243). Longenecker revealed his assumption as he observed, "factors that still exist in every Christian's experience" (*Romans*, 609).

[23] For the rhetorical significance of this point, see previous chapter, "The Rhetoric of Romans 7"; note pp. 48–50. Cf. Son, *Corporate Elements in Pauline Anthropology*.

Like Chinese handcuffs, the more Israel struggles to free herself from the power of the old age, the more she is bound to a spiritual slavery even greater than the original Egyptian servitude. Unless Israel follows the path of the faith of Abraham, law is destined to bring wrath and destruction for the nation. History dramatically already has proven this lesson. The faith of Abraham is crucial, as this way of relating to God by trusting his promises anticipates the coming of Messiah as the ground of being declared righteous in the gospel (Romans 4). So, the question boils down to Moses or Messiah. Paul demonstrates the transcending power of grace over Sin for Israel in the New Aeon through Messiah by analogy with Israel's previous redemption story, her own baptism, slavery, and marriage contract with Yahweh from the exodus story. In this process he provides clarification of the nature of God's grace.

Grace Is Not Indulgence (6:1–2)

Paul raises rhetorical objections to the gospel of God's grace. Paul just had said that "where sin multiplied, grace multiplied even more" (5:20). One could infer God desires sin to multiply, as that only would magnify his grace, so we should assist in the effort (**6:1**).[24] This logic that grace is no more than divine indulgence hides false assumptions. First, arguing sin can multiply without consequence assumes sin is no more serious than a misstep. In truth, sin has only one consequence—death (1:32). God's grace, if only indulging sin, would destroy his own creation, which is absurd. Second, the assertion ignores that new life in Messiah crosses the eschatological boundary between the two ages. Such an objection is specious and ignorant. So, asserting that Paul's understanding of grace infers that more sin is more glory for God calls forth Paul's characteristic rejection out of hand in **6:2**, "Let it not be!" (μὴ γένοιτο, *mē genoito*).[25]

Corporate Baptism Illustrates (6:3–11)

Paul illustrates the transition between two ages with Israel's own story of Mosaic baptism in the Old Aeon that anticipates messianic baptism

---

[24] Arguing the source of the objection (inherent in the logic of the argument or encountered in synagogue missionizing) is unnecessary to establishing the point.

[25] Almost exclusively in Romans and Galatians (Rom 3:4, 6, 31; 6:2, 15; 7:7, 13; 9:14; 11:1, 11; 1 Cor 6:15; Gal 2:17; 3:21; 6:14). Otherwise in the New Testament, only Luke 20:16. The "Say it ain't so!" slang expression captures the emotional punch.

in the New Aeon. In Israel's baptism into Moses, Israel crossed a lordship boundary from Pharaoh to Yahweh. Paul already had written of Israel's exodus deliverance as baptism into Moses in 1 Cor 10:2, "And all were baptized into Moses in the cloud and in the sea." That is, Israel had a corporate baptism in its escape from slavery in Egypt to serving a new lord at Sinai, effected through Moses. Paul's thought moves in similar patterns here in Romans 6. The new baptism is into Messiah. In this baptism, Israel similarly is offered opportunity to cross another boundary of lordship from Sin to God.[26] Paul thus speaks of baptism into Moses as analogous to baptism into Messiah because both represent the crossing of a lordship boundary. The earlier Mosaic baptism defined a nation (and, after the exile, Mosaic Israel), but was crippled by the Adamic disobedience of the Old Aeon. The new messianic baptism redefines the Israel of God as the Israel of the prophetic last days, even now enabled with realities of the New Aeon (5:1–11).

Faith initiates this life-transforming transition from the Old Aeon into the New Aeon. This New Aeon provides new power that is the basis of new life. "We" are buried with him by baptism into death that like as Messiah was raised up from the dead by the glory of the Father, even so "we" ought to walk in newness of life (**6:3–4**). "We" is messianic Israel. The Messiah has brought the power of resurrection from the New Aeon into the Old Aeon (**6:5**), and "our old humanity," that is, Mosaic Israel, is crucified in the move from Moses to Messiah (**6:6**).[27] The rule of Sin over the corporate experience of Israel is nullified in the New Aeon.[28] Israel once again is redeemed from slavery: "that we no

---

[26] Applied to gentile idolatry in 1 Thess 1:9, but unrighteousness reigns over all humanity, including Jewish (Rom 1:18—3:20). Imaging redemption through the sea as a baptism is unique to Paul; cf. Thiselton, *1 Corinthians*, 722; Hayes, *1 Corinthians*, 160.

[27] Notice how Paul's grammar joins a *pluralized* "our" pronoun with a *singularized* "humanity" noun (ὁ παλαιὸς ἡμῶν ἄνθρωπος, *ho palaios hēmōn anthrōpos*).

[28] The clause is ἵνα καταργηθῇ τὸ σῶμα τῆς ἁμαρτίας, *hina karargēthēi to soma tēs hamartias*. This expression in Rom 6:6 of τὸ σῶμα τῆς ἁμαρτίας, (*to soma tēs hamartias*) resonates with the exclamation "this body of death" in Rom 7:24. Paul employs this verb "nullify" (καταργέω, *katargeō*) multiple times in Romans when asking important rhetorical questions or making crucial points. In 3:3 he asks whether Israel's unfaithfulness will nullify God's faithfulness. In 3:31 he asks if messianic faith nullifies law. In 4:14 he asserts if law makes heirs, the promise is nullified. Most importantly, its use here in 6:6 anticipates the point he will make in the forthcoming marriage analogy about making Sin's rule "powerless" or null (7:2) and then how death "nullifies" the obligations of a marriage contract (7:6).

longer be enslaved to sin" (6:7). Incorporation into Messiah's death involves a lordship transaction, since Death (so personified) no longer "lords over" Messiah (6:9, κυριεύει, *kyrieuei*). Breaking Sin's lordship in Death through resurrection is permanent, as Messiah forever is raised, and Israel is incorporated (6:8–10). This reality is how messianic Israel should think of her corporate life: dead to sin, now alive to God (6:11).[29]

Behavioral Implications (6:12–14)

Understanding God's grace as a transition into a New Aeon breaking the power of Death and the lordship of Sin has behavioral implications (6:12–14). We should caution here that the English translation, "Do not let Sin reign in your mortal body" (6:12), disguises that the "your" is plural in Greek. Note a *pluralized* pronoun has a *singular* "body." This grammar reflects the corporate nature of the logic. This move is exactly what Paul does later in Romans 12 in referring to the church as one body that has "many members" (12:5). Thus, the thought in 12:5 of one body that has many members applied to the corporate realities of messianic Israel precisely parallels the dynamic of the thought of 6:12 in exactly the same way and is the basis of the plural grammar. The logic of the grammar when interpreted as the individual believer actually misses the whole point of these corporate analogies between Israel as defined in Moses and in Messiah, that is, Israel as refracted from the perspective of the defining characteristics of the two aeons. The issue is lordship. The case is corporate.[30] In the case of Moses, after being freed from Pharaoh's power, Israel no longer was to let Pharaoh rule (6:12, βασιλεύω, *basileuō*). Similarly, after being freed from Sin's power, the community of messianic Israel no longer is to let Sin rule.

The essence of these verses is that believers in their corporate life should affirm the lordship of grace, not sin. Each individual believer, of course, contributes to the effort (6:13), so the point is not that the individual believer does not count. However, *the effort is defined in terms*

---

[29] Corporate, since both pronouns in this summation verse are plural ("you" and "yourselves").

[30] Others are recognizing the importance of the corporate nature of the rhetoric of Romans. This perspective becomes more apparent the more the Jewish background to Paul and his Old Testament covenant themes are recognized. Cf. Holland, *Romans: The Divine Marriage.*

of the goals of the community, not the personal life goals of any given believer. "Weapons of righteousness" as *corporate*, then, would reflect *community* goals to present a *covenanted* group to the world that is:

- transforming itself and its society through a transformed mind controlled by the values of the gospel of God, not the gospel of Caesar (Romans 12–13)

- modeling the unity proclaimed in the gospel by the manner of its handling of internal differences (Romans 14–15)

- supporting the point of the spear of gospel proclamation Paul plans to carry westward on into Spain to achieve the unity of faith among the nations according to Isaiah (Rom 1:5 and 15:9–12, 22–24)

- recognizing the strength of messianic Israel to accomplish this goal to the nations is in its social and ethnic diversity as reflected in its house churches, not only in Rome, but the world (Romans 16)

Quite simply, Paul's corporate emphasis here in Romans 6 already is laying the theological foundation for the exhortations to come in the second part of Romans. Note that in the **6:14** summary verse, "For Sin will not lord over you, for you are not under law but under grace," the "you" in every case is plural. "You," messianic Israel, no longer live in the Old Aeon under its power. "You" live in the New Aeon. Behave so.

Moses vs. Messiah: Slavery (6:15–23)

Paul continues to work his historical theme of the exodus redemption under the aegis of Moses by God's grace to show its parallel in Messiah for messianic Israel. He introduces another perspective on the operation of God's grace in the New Aeon by using the linking word of law from the previous summary verse "not under law."

Grace Is Not Lawlessness (6:15)

Once again, in **6:15** he uses a rhetorical question, and, again, the point is preposterous for not cognizing the change of these aeons: "What then? 'Let us sin because we are not under law but under grace?' Let it not be!" The issue again is lordship, as in the unit on baptism, but now taken up from the perspective of the slave, not the lord. "Not under law" interpreted as freedom to sin is equivalent to permission to speed through the subdivision if the sign is knocked down. The issue is deeper than no sign posted. The issue is creation and the will of the Creator who is lord of creation. The issue is not a speed limit sign. The issue is a known will that already has expressed itself in creation and obedience to that will (Rom 1:20). The act of life itself establishes relationship with the Creator, and all slaves must be obedient to their masters.

Corporate Slavery Illustrates (6:16–23)

Now the rhetorical force of the identification of the sender in the letter opening in 1:1 comes into full force: "Paul, slave of Messiah Jesus." Paul in this introduction already has hinted that the basic issue of human existence is not law keeping but lordship living, here expressed in the common image of slavery. Here in **6:16** Paul harnesses the power of his own self designation: "Do you not know that if you present yourselves to anyone as obedient slaves, you are slaves of the one whom you obey." A slave to Sin exhibits disobedience and death, but a slave to God exhibits obedience and righteousness (**6:17–18**).

The argument in **6:19–21** is straightforward and rehearses 1:18–32. The conclusion is the same: Sin evokes only more sin and results in eternal death (1:32). Paul calls upon a "fruit" analogy (cf. 6:21–22). He points out that lordship produces a crop: unrighteousness that leads to death or sanctification that leads to life. The slave, then, should show the characteristics of the household under which the slave lives (6:19–20). Incorporation into Messiah is becoming a slave of Messiah (1:1), a new lordship that is characterized by righteousness and sanctification. Righteousness evokes sanctification and results in eternal life (**6:22**).

Paul then summarizes living in the two aeons: "For the wages of sin is death, but the free gift of God is eternal life in Messiah Jesus our Lord" (**6:23**). The idea of wages brings up the question: So, what do you really want God "reckoning" to pay you (cf. 4:4)? "Gift" is χάρισμα, *charisma*, which is the same root as grace. Transference between aeons is an act of God's grace, not human endeavor. That grace is the power of the gospel that empowers a new life (1:16). Thus, the idea of continuing in sin as suggested in these objections to Paul's understanding of God's grace for Paul are absurd, representing a fundamental category confusion, a contradiction of aeons. *Mē genoito!*

By analogy, while living in Egypt, Israel was ruled by the power of Pharaoh. Freedom from Pharaoh, however, did not mean freedom from any lordship. Freedom from Pharaoh's power was gained only by the gracious action of a new and higher power. Living outside of Egypt did not mean living with no lord. Moving from Egypt to Sinai constituted a transfer of lordship. Life changed to reflect that new lordship. However, whoever stayed in Egypt remained under the old power and lordship. Those lives did not change.

We need to recognize in Romans 6 that slavery is the premier language of Israel's story. When Israel was in slavery in Egypt, Israelites presented themselves as slaves obedient to Pharaoh. God redeemed Israel from slavery to Pharaoh, and Israel then presented themselves as slaves obedient to God. That is to say, the issue in Israel's story always has been that of lordship. Later in Israel's story, when Israel rebelled against God, she was "delivered over" to another lord, Nebuchadnezzar, and Israel became slaves again.

We also need to recognize in Romans 6 that slavery is a dominant experience of believers in Rome. The majority of names in Romans 16 are typical slave names. They would have lived in the lower class Trastavere and Porta Capena areas supporting the shipping economy.[31] Slaves were as much as half the population of Italy, so the issue is not so much slavery *in* society as slavery *as* society. Even the term "barbarian" (Rom 1:14) would evoke slavery images, since many of Rome's slaves derived from conquered foreign peoples. Once a slave, one's social status never changed, even if manumitted. One then only went to being a freedman, always socially marked as a former slave. While slaves could have upward mobility economically, most slaves had little to no control over their lives, or even their own bodies, as with prostitute slaves. New Testament writers such as Paul did ennoble slave-master relationships in their own household codes, but the matter of lordship never changed. Since lordship was the very fabric of first-century life both through the institution of slavery as well as imperial rule, Paul presented the gospel in those terms.[32] The language worked both as Israel's story and as the experience of believers in Rome. Paul scored twice with the same image.

---

[31] See discussion, pp. 160–62.

[32] See discussion, pp. 169–77.

Moses vs. Messiah: Marriage (7:1–6)

Marriage is the third image Paul harnesses from the exodus redemption to explicate God's grace in the New Aeon. In this imagery, Paul follows an Old Testament prophetic motif. "For your Maker is your husband, the Lord of hosts is his name" (Isa 54:5, NRSV); "And I will take you for my wife forever; I will take you for my wife in righteousness and in justice, in steadfast love, and in mercy" (Hos 2:16, NRSV).[33] The Sinaitic covenant prophetically interpreted as a marriage is common:

- Sinai as a marriage covenant: Ezek 16:8–14

- God as Israel's husband: Isa 54:4

- Israel's marriage devotion to God: Jer 2:2

- Israel's covenant adultery: Jer 3:20

- Israel's divorce from God: Hos 2:2

- God's call to his bride to return: Hos 3:1–3

- Israel's marriage covenant restored: Isa 62:4–5

This marriage motif of God's relationship with his people is continued into the New Testament.[34]

Strategically in Romans 7, this imagery does double duty as both an analogy about grace in the marriage metaphor in 7:1–6 but also as transition to taking up the issue of the law in the next unit in Rom 7:7–25 that has been dogging the discussion almost since Paul began. Even the very first verse that initiates the marriage analogy clearly tips the hat to the Sinaitic covenantal foundation behind all of Paul's thought throughout Romans 6–7 on into the climactic discussion of Israel and the law that concludes Romans 7.

Death Annuls Covenant Obligations (7:1)

Paul begins in **7:1** with the rhetoric of feigned ignorance as a device to affirm what assuredly is well known: "Or, are you unaware, brothers and sisters." They are aware, well aware, in fact, because the rhetorical

---

[33] Cf. Isa 54:5–8; 61:10; 62:4–5; Hos 2:19.

[34] Jesus as the bridegroom in John 3:29 and the church as the bride of Messiah in 2 Cor 11:2 and Rev 19:7–9.

dissimulation is disclosed immediately: "for I am speaking to those who know the law." Once again, as throughout the sequential imagery in Romans 6–7, Moses, exodus, and the covenant at Sinai during the Old Aeon is the point. Paul could not be more clear that he is addressing the metanarrative of Israel that contextualizes the coming of Messiah. Paul directly is addressing Mosaic Israel through the transformative perspective of messianic Israel—Moses versus Messiah.

What does Mosaic Israel "know"? The obvious time limitation to the authority of the law to rule over a person's contractual obligations: "that the law rules over [κυριεύει, *kyrieuei*] a person in as much time as that person is alive." One key reality even recognized in the law itself is that the application of law is limited by death. Once again, the issue is lordship. The question is when the authority of that lordship ends. Death ends the lordship of law. This conclusion is not radical in any way, as Paul's following example of a marriage covenant's contractual obligations makes clear. No one would argue the point.

Corporate Marriage Illustrates (7:2–6)

Death annuls the law's jurisdiction (**7:2–3**). Marriage law expects relationship fidelity, because marriage without fidelity is only legal fiction. The charge of infidelity in intimacy with another person, however, immediately disappears upon the death of a spouse. Covenant obligations are nullified (καταργέω, *katargeō*), the same verb Paul has used several times already in similar contexts.[35] In the case of death, a surviving spouse is "free" then to marry another without censure from the law. In this case of covenant obligations, death changes law's censure as an adulteress to law's approbation as a duly covenanted wife. All would agree with these principles, as they are embedded in the law itself.

However, no one applied the point to God's covenant with Israel. That application indeed was radical. Yet, as Paul already has described, believers are incorporated into the covenant altering death of Jesus (3:21–26). Thus, a changed jurisdiction of the law because of death is precisely the situation of those believing in Messiah (**7:4–6**). Faith is a death experience to the law and a dominion exchange that changes the very character of the law from its enfeeblement by the Adamic curse of enslavement to evil in the Old Aeon ("letter") to its vivification by the

[35] Rom 3:3, 31; 4:14; 6:6.

messianic blessing of enslavement to God in the power of the New Aeon ("Spirit"). Since this transfer between the ages is an act of God's grace (5:21), then Israel's redemption story remains the same whether in Moses or in Messiah: God's prevenient grace and initiative to save those otherwise enslaved, helpless, without purpose, destiny, or future. While law was the covenant meant to bless a people in possession of a land for obedience to God, law never was intended as the mechanism to facilitate eschatological salvation. Rather, law had the more limited role of a guide for those looking for the heart of God until the coming of Messiah revealed God's heart transparently (Gal 3:24–26).

The limited role of the law is where Paul lost the synagogue. As a question of God's will, Paul insisted law never was absolute. This insistence directly contradicted some rabbinic traditions, which commonly asserted the eternal character of the law. Yet, from the beginning, law had constraints, including inherent limitations.[36] Other rabbinic traditions recognized the law itself awaited its own consummation when God would restore Israel. Some traditions maintained that elements of temple ritual would be hidden until Messiah would come to integrate them into the consummation of the messianic age.[37] In another vein, Israel expected Messiah to function as the great arbitrator of the law, or even transcend the law with his own messianic precepts.[38] None of these traditions, however, actually anticipated the law's authority to be annulled entirely.

So, what say ye, Paul, of Israel and the law? Does your gospel of God's grace render law in Israel a historical exercise in futility? Have you disparaged irreparably the character of law as an expression of God's will in the life of Israel? Paul's series of Sinaitic covenant metaphors of baptism, slavery, and marriage in Romans 6–7 have dressed the stage for the denouement of the question that has been implicit all along that now surfaces potently—law in Israel, Moses versus Messiah.

---

[36] The law of divorce is one famous example from the teaching of Jesus; cf. Matt 5:32 (with its exception clause); Mark 10:11; Luke 16:18.

[37] As one example, for sealing up in an unknown cave by Jeremiah, cf. 2 Macc 2:4–8. Another related to the secret activity of an angel is 2 Bar 6:7–9. Cf. Kalimi, "The Hiding of the Temple Vessels in Jewish and Samaritan Literature."

[38] Assuming second-century rabbinic traditions have interpretive trajectories back into the first century, as in the Tannaitic Rabbi Ishmael, "At the end, the Torah will be forgotten," *Mekilta, Masechet Piska* 2 (Lauterbach).

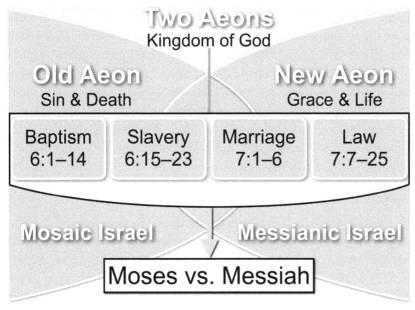

FIGURE 8.7. Conclusion: Law in Israel (7:7–25). Paul's Sinaitic covenant imagery of baptism, slavery, and marriage under the aegis of Moses has prepared the way to discuss the dilemma of Mosaic Israel still enslaved to Sin in the Old Aeon. Messiah's power is Israel's only redemption through the Abrahamic righteousness by faith.

Moses vs. Messiah: Law (7:7–25)

As Paul presents the dilemma of Mosaic Israel he has presented at the same time the dilemma of one of the most hermeneutically problematic passages in the entire Pauline corpus. The fault is not Paul's. Two thousand years of Hellenization and gentilization of Paul has silenced his Jewish voice. We numb our exegetical conscience in nullification of his Jewish voice by incessantly assigning to Paul the invented cognomen "apostle to the gentiles," which quietly eliminates the category of Israel from his thought. In this way, even our nomenclature predetermines who Paul must be before we even read Romans.[39]

In fact, Paul is apostle to Israel, guided on his journey to worship Messiah by the north star of Isaiah's eschatological vision of Israel as light to the nations, resonating with Isaiah's declaration how beautiful are the feet of those who proclaimed the gospel to Israel (Rom 10:14).[40]

---

[39] On contextualizing the division of mission effort between Peter and Paul in Galatians 2, see p. 229, note 35.

[40] Quoting Isa 52:5.

Isaiah's proclamation of good news for Israel forms a thematic *inclusio* over the beginning and ending of Romans in 1:15 and 15:20. Isaiah's thought of Israel's eschatological destiny consummating her purpose for the nations likewise forms a thematic *inclusio* over the beginning and ending of Romans in 1:5 and 15:12 (Isa 11:10).[41] One could say that Isaiah's thought "frames" Romans literarily and theologically. Paul goes to the gentiles to facilitate Israel's destiny.[42] That goal is what made the Damascus Road commission naturally congruent with the life of a zealously committed Pharisee.

Exegetical Decisions

One question of 7:7–25 is who is the speaker? The first-person "I" of the passage is variously understood as autobiography of Paul's supposed pre-conversion despair, or the individual believer's moral vacillation in daily living, or Adam's paradigm in a post-conversion retrospective on all human experience, or Mosaic Israel's dilemma after the coming of Messiah. The last option is best, with Rom 7:7–25 read as prophetic lament on behalf of Israel.[43]

Another question is what experience is described? This question is complicated by the passage divided clearly between past tense (7:7–13) and present tense (7:14–25). The answer varies between individual or corporate. The individual option subdivides into either the believer or the non-believer, or even a combination (non-believer for the past tense unit, believer for the present tense unit). The corporate option is Israel by way of anticipating fuller development in Romans 9–11.

Argumentative Clue

Our argumentative clue is to observe closely the wording earlier in the marriage analogy in 7:5. First, the expression "Sin *through* the law" makes clear personified Sin is the villain, not the law itself. Second, the plural pronoun in the expression "in *our* members" already insinuates

---

[41] On *ethnē* in 1:5 being "nations," not "gentiles," see discussion, pp. 226–29.

[42] Luke captures the essence of this guiding thought in Paul's affirmation to synagogue leaders in Rome: "For the sake of the hope of Israel I am wearing this chain" (Acts 28:20). Paul may have intended a double entendre; cf. "hope of Israel" as a title for the Lord in Jer 14:8; 17:13. Paul, however, interpreted God's redemptive activity as focused in God's Messiah and his resurrection (Acts 23:6; 24:15, 21; 26:6–8).

[43] For extensive rhetorical arguments for this case, see chapter 3.

the corporate nature of the thought, verified by the expression, "you [plural] also were put to death in relation to the law through the body of Messiah" (7:4). Further, this corporate activity as accomplice to Sin is still an unwitting situation, an idea paralleling 10:2–3, which clearly is about Israel, in which Paul testified:

> I can testify about them that they have a zeal for God, but not according to knowledge. Since they are ignorant of the right-eousness of God and attempted to establish their own righteous-ness, they have not submitted to God's righteousness.

The marriage analogy already has made clear that the real problem is not law. Sin commits the crime by using unwitting law. Indeed, Israel is complicit by submitting to Sin's lordship. All this argumentation prepares the way for the following 7:7–25 as a defense of the law, even though law does bring curse on Israel.

Israel Is the Point

If law is the topic (7:1), Israel is the point. Notice how the pluralizing about those who know the law continues without change in the move-ment from the end of the marriage analogy in 7:6 to the beginning of the law defense in 7:7, which simultaneously is a theodicy for God:

- 7:1: "Do you [plural] not know, brothers and sisters—for I am speak-ing to those who know the law"

- 7:4: "in the same way, my friends, . . ."

- 7:5: "While we were living in the flesh . . . our members"

- 7:6: "But now we are discharged from the law . . . not under oldness of the letter"

- 7:7: "What then should we say?"

Other alternatives for understanding what Paul is addressing in 7:7–25 ignore the immediately preceding marriage analogy in the first place as being about the law, which Paul made explicit. These alternatives also ignore the powerful *corporate* point for Israel under the Sinaitic code. *They are oblivious to the quite straightforward historical argu-ment Paul is making here*: Israel, enslaved to Sin, died as a nation under the curse of the law. The consequence of ignoring this corporate perspective means other alternatives that these verses are about Paul's supposed misery as a Pharisee, or any person's angst over a conflicted conscience striving for moral mastery, or the non-believer's existential crisis over unrequited union with the universe immediately have to start contorting the logic and distorting the words trying to hammer these square interpretive pegs into an exegetically round hole.

Paul's effortless shift from first-person plural to first-person singular easily is documented in Jewish literature *when the nation Israel is the subject*, especially among the prophets, but never more true than in Jewish lament rhetoric. Jewish lament rhetoric shifts fluidly back and forth between "we" and "I" as the speaker takes on the voice of corporate Israel in both the first-person singular and the first-person plural.[44] Jewish lament overwhelmingly is about the woe and humiliation of exile, and this exilic crisis continued into the first century with another foreign empire dominating and ruling over the nation. That empire happened to have as its capital and heart of its reign the very city of Paul's addressees. You just cannot invent a more pertinent and direct problem for Israel and the addressees of this letter. Seeing that tensions between Judea and Rome already were on the rise by the time Paul wrote Romans, and that all out war eventually did break out less than ten years later, one would be justified in saying the matter was pressing for Mosaic Israel to comprehend the Pauline analysis of their predicament with the law and spiritual blindness to Messiah to stave off yet another impending national calamity.[45]

The three definitive moments in Israel's history orbit around the narratives of three persons whom Paul has engaged in his discussion in this part of Romans: Abraham (4:1), Moses (2:17), and David (1:3). Abraham is the story of the birth of a faith-based people. Moses is the story of the birth of a law-based nation. David is the story of the birth of a messianic-based kingdom. Paul is integrating these storylines into the story of the coming of Messiah. The Messiah brings the New Aeon and its age of the Spirit ("newness of Spirit," 7:6). Messiah touches the heart like the law cannot (5:5; 2:27) and quickens messianic Israel out of Mosaic Israel. History has proven the law impotent from any other result than invoking the covenant curse of death. Israel's future and

---

[44] Examples are Ps 44:4, 14–15; 129:1–3; Isa 38:20; 63:15–16; 64:1–12; Jer 10:19–20; 31:15; Lam 1:9; 2:11; 3:47–48; Ezek 37:11; Dan 9:1–19; Mic 7:8–10. See chapter 3.

[45] See the earlier discussion, "Life Setting of Jerusalem," pp. 165–69.

destiny thereby are threatened. Romans 7:7–25 is Paul's adoption of the prophetic mantle on behalf of Israel to offer a corporate lament of national grief for Mosaic Israel that concludes with messianic Israel's triumphant word of corporate repentance. This Romans 7 profile of eschatological Israel revealed by Messiah's coming fluidly transitions into anticipation of the coming eschatological revelation of the "children of God" consummating all God's purposes in creation in Romans 8.

Romans 7:7–13 (Israel and Sinai)

Paul defends the law with a highly compressed, triadic retrospective of Israel's past, reflected in the past tense grammar in this unit. This story of Abraham told from the perspective of the coming of the law divides on Sinai—before Sinai, Sinai, after Sinai. Thus, the story is corporate—about a nation and its destiny—not individuals. The pre-Sinai story is compressed into "alive apart from the law" (**7:7–9**), which means at this point, Israel's national destiny is not threatened by law. The Sinai story is compressed into "the commandment came" (7:9), a covenant which was to commemorate God's exodus redemption. The post-Sinai story first is compressed into "Sin came alive" (7:9), which is the foreboding note in the story. Israel's national destiny now was threatened because Sin intended to manipulate law's intent for life into an instrument of death for the nation. The second stage of the post-Sinai story is compressed into "I died . . . killed me" (**7:10–11**), which is the national disaster of judgment and exile. God's purposes in Abraham's covenant to bless all the families of the earth through Israel are on the line.

Paul summarized this compressed story of Sinai in **7:12–13**. The real problem for Israel is that Sin came alive, not that law was evil. God's law is holy and good, but abused by Sin. The law intended life, but Sin perverted that intent into its own death design. So, in the light of this story of Israel and Sinai, the question can be asked, What was the law's purpose? The answer in 7:13 is so that through the commandment Sin could be revealed as "exceedingly sinful" (ὑπερβολὴν ἁμαρτωλός, *hyperbolēn hamartōlos*)—that is, deadly (1:32; 6:23). Sin is deadly serious.

Romans 7:14–23 (Israel and Messiah)

But now is a new day for Israel (3:21). Paul shifts to present tense to reflect the experience of messianic Israel now that Messiah has come. The law came, but then Messiah came. Messianic Israel affirms that law is spiritual (**7:14**). But messianic Israel is encumbered in its task to fulfill Israel's destiny: Mosaic Israel persists in rebellion against God.

Paul turns to Jewish lament rhetoric in a pattern characteristic of postexilic Jewish writers. First person ("I," "we") rhetoric is used to speak on behalf of a community: "I am flesh, sold into slavery" (**7:15–21**). This slavery characterizes Mosaic Israel's dilemma in the age of grace inaugurated by Messiah. Instead of moving forward into Israel's destiny in Messiah, Mosaic Israel is choosing to move backward into its slavery as if never redeemed from Egypt. Mosaic Israel is no better off than Joseph sold into Egyptian slavery by his jealous brothers (Genesis 37). The problem is, this enslaved condition of Mosaic Israel holds back messianic Israel from her destiny. Historically, a vicious cycle is engaged: law's good intent, but Sin's evil result. This tragic condition for Mosaic Israel leaves Sin without remedy: "nothing good dwells within me . . . in my flesh," where "flesh" speaks to corporate Israel's conundrum, not that of an individual (7:18). The old law has a new reality: "I find a law . . . want to do good, but evil lies close at hand" (7:21).[46]

Paul then provides a summary of the conflicted state of Mosaic Israel in **7:22–23**. On the one hand, messianic Israel and Mosaic Israel agree: "delight in the law of God in my inmost self" (7:22). This reality is messianic Israel as defined by the New Aeon of grace in Messiah in which this law is fulfilled that Paul soon will describe further in 8:1–4. Yet, Mosaic Israel itself is conflicted: "another law at war with the law of my mind." Again, Paul is anticipating the coming discussion in 8:1–2. Here, two conflicting law experiences are at work: "Therefore, there is now no condemnation for those in Messiah Jesus, because the law of the Spirit of life in Messiah Jesus has set you free from the law of sin and death." The "law of my mind" would be the law one is taught and trained to understand, an allusion to the "Great Assembly" traditions maintained in synagogues across the Diaspora, particularly including the oral law.[47] The sphere of activity for this law of the mind is "in my members," that is, the corporate representatives of Mosaic Israel, seen

---

[46] "Law" here is not "principle," as so many commentators assert. Paul consistently in Romans means Torah with νόμος (*nomos*); cf. Dunn, *Romans 1–8*, 392–93; Jewett *Romans*, 469. The translation as "principle" actually obfuscates the whole point of this expose of Mosaic Israel confronted by Messiah.

[47] "Mind" here has just as much corporate sensibility as does "mind" in 12:2. Commentators often seem oblivious to the connection; cf. Hultgren, *Romans*, pp. 290, 441.

in the Gospel accounts in those individuals and groups acting on behalf of Mosaic Israel such as Caiaphas, the Sadducees, and the Pharisees crucifying Messiah and persecuting the church, as did Saul of Tarsus himself.

This unit concludes with a dramatic exclamation (7:24–25). First, a Jewish lament over Mosaic Israel is offered in **7:24**. Here, Paul takes on the mantle of Jewish lament on behalf of Mosaic Israel. The current dilemma for Mosaic Israel is its rejection of Messiah. That rejection portends a wretched nation with a cursed destiny, because the wrath of God is being revealed against all unrighteousness and ungodliness of humankind (1:18). Hence comes the exclamation of 7:24: "Wretched humanity that I am! Who will deliver me from this deadly body?" The nation's curse destiny is expressed, again in quite personal terms, in 9:3: "For I could wish that I myself were cursed and cut off from Christ for the benefit of my brothers and sisters, my own flesh and blood."

Then, Paul immediately offers the Jewish praise of messianic Israel in **7:25a**. Once again, Paul takes on a prophetic mantle on behalf of messianic Israel. Praise is offered to the Lord Messiah for the blessed destiny to come: "Thanks be to God through Jesus Messiah our Lord!" This destiny is rehearsed in the following chapter in 8:18–19: "For I consider that the sufferings of this present time are not worth comparing with the glory that is going to be revealed to us. For the creation eagerly awaits with anticipation for the children of God to be revealed."

Paul concludes with a summary recapitulation of Israel's dilemma in the face of Messiah in **7:25b**: "So then, therefore, on the one hand, I myself with my mind am serving the law of God, but on the other hand, with my flesh, the law of Sin." These are the two laws of the next two verses in 8:1–2. We have slavery either way, since the issue is the lordship of God or Satan. The law of God stands without perversion only as Messiah breaks Sin's power. Then, law's ultimate result is the life law intends, which, by definition is the New Aeon (5:1–11). One should not miss that "with my flesh" rhetorically functions with double entendre as both corporate and spiritual realities in the Pauline semantic universe. In this light, Mosaic Israel thinks to serve the law of God but actually serves the law of Sin, which brings only the death result Sin designs. Absent a change of heart about Messiah, Mosaic Israel will set itself on a collision course with God's wrath for remaining in catastrophic exile.

Romans Structure

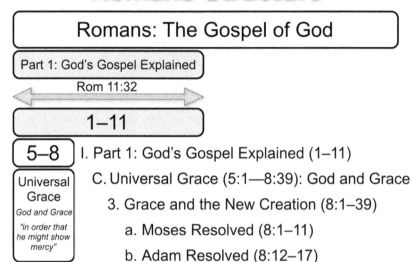

Romans: The Gospel of God

Part 1: God's Gospel Explained

⟵ Rom 11:32 ⟶

1–11

5–8

Universal
Grace
God and Grace

*"in order that
he might show
mercy"*

I. Part 1: God's Gospel Explained (1–11)

C. Universal Grace (5:1—8:39): God and Grace

   3. Grace and the New Creation (8:1–39)

      a. Moses Resolved (8:1–11)

      b. Adam Resolved (8:12–17)

      c. Creation Resolved (8:18–30)

      d. Concluding Praise (8:31–39)

FIGURE 8.8. Outline: Romans 8 (Moses, Adam, Creation). Paul concludes Romans 5–8 by resolving Moses and Adam, moving toward the eschatological climax of divine purposes in creation. The theological continuity of the entire saga is divine grace.

Paul is ready to summarize the saga of divine grace in the creative purposes of God. This saga is focused on the story of Israel. Key figures for analyzing Israel's story have been Adam and Moses. These figures illuminate from the perspective of law and Sin the plight of Israel related to the coming of Messiah.

Before diving in, we need to emphasize rhetoric, topic, and language that continues into chapter 8. First, the rhetoric is *still* plural, so we continue Paul's corporate focus, which concords with the analysis being that of the plight of Israel, not the individual believer. Second, the topic is *still* the law, so we continue Paul's focus on the saga of how the story of redemptive grace in the New Aeon concords with the story of redemptive grace in the Old Aeon. Law is Jewish Torah throughout this discussion, and continues the grand development of Romans 1–8 as setting the stage for Romans 9–11, which is all about Israel and thus demonstrates how Romans is all about Israel. Third, parsing the language of "flesh" (σάρξ, *sarx*) and Spirit (πνεῦμα, *pneuma*) is crucial to the entire reading of Romans 8. An analysis of the complex usage of "flesh" in Paul is not necessary here in light of the corporate context.[48] Flesh is the weakened state of Mosaic Israel corporately caught in the Old Aeon of Adamic tragedy, absent the dynamism of the outpoured, eschatological Spirit of the New Aeon. "Spirit" is the transcendent sign of God's presence and signature of the New Aeon. The imagery likely builds on Ezekiel's "new spirit/my Spirit" language.

> A new heart I will give you, and a new spirit I will put within you; and I will remove from your body the heart of stone and give you a heart of flesh. I will put my spirit within you, and make you follow my statutes and be careful to observe my ordinances (Ezek 36:26–27, NRSV).

In Pauline terms, this "new spirit" would facilitate human obedience, the "obedience of faith" program for the nations with which Paul introduced his letter (1:5). The "my spirit" would be God's Spirit in the New Aeon as the indwelling and transformative power that reshapes corporate attitude and worldview (Rom 12:1–2). This "flesh"/"Spirit" polarity allows Paul to nuance Israel's present situation to show how the issues for Israel are resolved in Messiah.

Thus, Israel's present conundrum is defined by two legal realities. One is the sphere of weakened "flesh" in which the law of Sin operates to create death, the problem of Mosaic Israel. The other is the sphere of empowered "Spirit" in which the law of the Spirit operates to create life, the promise of messianic Israel, a future which the prophet Ezekiel anticipated. These two legal realities have behind them two aeon realities. In the flesh, unredeemed Israel subverts Moses, illustrated by the disingenuous law of Corban whose clear intent was to skirt the law of Moses, as exposed in the teaching of Jesus (Mark 7:11). Even more, Moses could be so subverted as to crucify Messiah with the very claim that doing so would save the nation.[49] In the Spirit, redeemed Israel fulfills Moses, which is precisely what Ezekiel anticipated: "I will put my Spirit within you, and make you follow my statutes and be careful to observe my ordinances" (Ezek 36:37).

---

[48] Dunn has a fine summary of eight major nuances of "flesh" that operate along a continuum with the general sense of human weakness easily abused by Sin, but not as a cosmic power, as in older German constructs (*Theology*, 62–70).

[49] The justification by Caiaphas that John used with great irony (John 11:50; 18:14).

Moses Resolved (8:1–11)

Paul first shows the resolution of the problem of Moses. Since the premier historical result of the law was condemnation, this resolution is in the declaration of "no condemnation." The law's curse is overcome in Messiah. The New Aeon that Messiah inaugurates offers freedom from enslavement to Sin for messianic Israel (**8:1–2**). "Set [you/me] free" is singular,[50] but the corporate rhetoric of the entire section infers that Paul is speaking on behalf of messianic Israel. The statement recapitulates the bondage/release exclamation of 7:24–25 ("O wretched humanity"). The dominance of plural pronouns throughout this unit indicates that while the individual is involved, as here, the context is community.

Romans **8:3–8** actually recapitulates the analysis given in 7:14–23. The polarity described for Israel in 7:14–23 is law's impotence through the flesh, which is the controlling dynamic of Mosaic Israel, and Messiah's power through the Spirit, which is the controlling dynamic of messianic Israel. This conclusion in Rom 8:4 should give context to the exegesis of Rom 10:4, in which Messiah is described as the τέλος (*telos*) of the law. The classic question is whether Messiah is the "end" or the "fulfillment" of the law. Translations notably differ. Yet, in the context of Romans, most particularly with the assertion here in Rom 8:4, the trajectory clearly favors the sense that in 10:4 Paul meant Messiah is fulfillment of the law.[51]

Romans **8:9–11** then personalizes the analysis given in 7:14–23. The Roman addressees are brought into the equation, with Paul signaling he considers the house churches of Rome a part of messianic Israel. The grammar continues a plural emphasis, so English readers should take note that the "you" is plural throughout these verses. "You, however, are not in the flesh, but in the Spirit, if indeed the Spirit of God lives in you. If anyone does not have the Spirit of Messiah, he does not belong to him" (Rom **8:9**). This statement is about as close as Paul ever comes to defining the bottom line of messianic faith.

Notice in the following "If Messiah is in you" in **8:10**, the "you" is plural. Thus, this singular "body" that immediately follows has corporate nuance. This "body," therefore, that is "dead because of sin" is

---

[50] Greek manuscripts vary on the pronoun; cf. Metzger, *Textual Commentary*, 456.

[51] The claim to "uphold the law" in 3:31, or the axiom that the law is "holy, and the commandment is holy and just and good" in 7:12.

Mosaic Israel. The Spirit, however, gives "life" (ζωή, zōē). Messianic Israel, then, fulfills all God's creative purposes for life. "Life" resonates with the theme statement that the gospel of God is the power of God unto salvation (1:16).

Romans **8:11** indicates this messianic life's premier sign is bodily resurrection, even as Messiah was raised from the dead. This resurrection conceptual frame is the reason Paul wove into his introduction a creed of the Roman church in Rom 1:4: "declared to be the Son of God with power, according to the Spirit of holiness, by the resurrection from the dead, Jesus Messiah, our Lord" (1:4). One might infer that "your mortal bodies" clearly shows emphasis on the individual. That false inference, however, fails to focus Pauline thought precisely as Jewish thought. Bodily resurrection in Jewish tradition was not focused exclusively on individuals as individuals, as is the predilection of Western thought. Almost always Jewish resurrection was about the possibility of Israel's future as a corporate, national entity. The clearest expression of this corporate focus was set early on by Ezekiel's vision of the valley of dry bones returning to life in Ezek 37:1–14. This vision anticipated the nation of Israel's return from exile to reclaim its dignity and status as a nation among the nations.[52]

Adam Resolved (8:12–17)

Adam invited into human experience the deadly power of Sin. He thus becomes the prototypical paradigm of "flesh" in as much as this word encompasses all the senses and the physicality of creation. Through the senses and basic physical nature of creation, evil entices humans into destructive behaviors that themselves progressively weaken the will into an enslavement to even more destructive behavior. The eventual result is death, which denies God's purposes for life. Banishment from Eden signals separation from the creative design and ultimate purposes of God and a fundamental breach of the life-giving relationship.

Note that even though Adam is an individual, scripturally he is a corporate representative of all humanity. Thus, the solution to Adam is corporately expressed, and that is why all the grammar in this unit

---

[52] Even in questionable eschatological systems such as dispensationalism, Ezekiel's valley of dry bones is interpreted as a *corporate* affair about the *nation* of Israel. For a critique of this system, see Stevens, *Revelation*, 84–96.

continues to remain plural. Paul is addressing the corporate realities of messianic Israel as resolution of the problem of "flesh" in human experience for which the name Adam functions as metonymy (5:12–21). We must not forget, though, that the story of Adam is preserved in Scripture because the parameters of this story encapsulate the story of Israel.[53] Israel's primal problem always has been Adamic "flesh," not God's law.

Paul's announcement is that of "no obligation" to the flesh (**8:12**). Messiah has broken Sin's power to work death. If the weakened state of Adamic existence ("flesh"), however, is not overcome, death is the inevitable result (**8:13**). "Deeds of the body," in which body is singular, could be read of the individual, yet the "you" of the verb "put to death" is plural, so the expression allows for a double valence. A corporate sense would not be excluded. One could understand the issue having application for an individual, but Paul likely intends the expression to include corporate Israel, which is the major focus of the immediately following three chapters.

In these terms, then, the "deeds of the body" in 8:13 is theological cousin to "works of the law" in 3:20, so 8:13 is a recapitulation of 3:20. Note that 3:20 also uses the crucial term "flesh" in a masterful double entendre of mortal existence but also weakened Adamic nature. This subtle rhetoric Paul now cashes in after his extensive development in Romans 5–7 that has featured Adam, Moses, Messiah, and Sin.

In addition, this corporate understanding of "deeds of the body" likewise flows perfectly into the following verses in **8:14–17**, which runs so continuously in thought as hardly to be subdivided. Here, issues of slavery, sonship, and heirs come immediately into view—all of which have corporate focus, and all of which are part of Israel's exodus, Sinai, and nationhood story. Once again, note how all the pronouns in this entire, seamless unit (e.g., "as many as," "these," "you," "we," "our") are plural. Abraham's trusting belief in God's promise, which God reckoned as righteousness, anticipates messianic faith in Messiah, who, at this critical, eschatological juncture at the fulcrum of the ages now is Mosaic Israel's only escape from the primeval Adamic tragedy of

---

[53] The creation story in Genesis 1–3 purposefully is molded to serve as introduction to the story of Israel, Sinai, and exile (see Postell, *Adam and Israel*, 124–25). See earlier discussion, p. 114.

"flesh" and its sure destiny of death for God's people as a corporate reality. The nation cannot survive rejection of Messiah. Paul, however, is confident that God will accomplish all his purposes in the messianic Israel now being called out in worldwide gospel proclamation.

> For as many as are led by the Spirit of God these are children of God. For you did not receive a spirit of slavery again unto fear. Instead, you received the Spirit of adoption, by whom we cry out, "Abba, Father!" The Spirit himself testifies together with our spirit that we are children of God, and if children, also heirs—on the one hand, heirs of God, and, on the other, coheirs with Messiah—since we suffer together so that we also may be glorified together (Rom 8:14–17).

"These are children of God" is the *core issue* of Mosaic Israel! Israel as the "children of God" thoroughly is grounded in scriptural divine sonship imagery.[54] In these verses, Paul is defining the messianic Israel of God of the eschaton, the last days of God's prophetic, definitive, and conclusive salvation for Israel. The core truth of this anticipated prophetic eschaton always was Spirit empowerment, so Spirit empowerment would be the core truth of eschatological Israel. So, Paul is just "connecting the dots" of what undeniably has happened to him and to Israel through Jesus Messiah, or, as Luke the evangelist would frame the matter—Pentecost.

Also to be noted in these verses is the strange "Spirit of adoption" expression in **8:15**. Adoption (υἱοθεσία, *huiothesia*) is not a part of ancient Jewish culture. The term never appears anywhere in the LXX, Philo, or Josephus. Jewish thought did include sonship in royal ideology and enthronement ceremony, with the Jewish king incorporated into Yahweh's rule as his "son," as in Psalm 2, but that relationship is fictive royal ideology. Jewish society at large had no legal or formal adoption procedure as part of its social structure.

Greeks did have legal adoption procedures, but across the multitude of independent Greek city states, nothing was uniform, and the conventions varied widely. Further, documented regulations are pre-Hellenistic before the New Testament period. Most of what we know are the conventions in classical Athens and in the ancient cultural

---

[54] Exod 4:22; Deut 14:1; Isa 43:6; Jer 3:19; Hos 11:1. Note also Paul's use of Hos 1:10 similarly in Rom 9:26.

center of Gortyn, because of the famous archeological discovery of the Gortyn law code on the curved wall structure behind the bouleuterion (city council assembly). The inscription is about thirty feet long and five feet high written in the ancient Dorian dialect prominent in central Crete. Adoption was one of its topics, prescribing that adopted children had all inheritance rights as legitimate heirs.[55]

FIGURE 8.9. Gortyn Law Code. The Greek city-state of Gortyn in southern Crete was a major cultural center other than Athens. The Gortyn Law code inscription discovered in the 1850s is a treasure trove of pre-Hellenistic Greek culture and the Dorian dialect.

FIGURE 8.10. Dorian Dialect. Inscription is written right to left like ancient Hebrew.

[55] For more on this inscription, see Stevens, *Stevens Greek Workbook*, 32.

Because Romans developed a strong legal code, adoption was a considerable feature of Roman life, particularly among wealthy, aristocratic, and political families that had so much at stake with inheritance issues and so few biological heirs.[56] The Roman father had to initiate the procedure, which formed a legal contract through proper execution of legal procedures.[57] We should remember as Paul writes to inhabitants of Rome that the Roman imperial line was founded on adoption. The most famous Roman adoption of all was that of Augustus, founder of the empire: Octavian was adopted by his great uncle, Julius Caesar. Numerous later emperors came to power by adoption, including the very next emperor after Augustus, Tiberius. Later, emperor Claudius adopted his stepson. That stepson then changed his name to become the infamous emperor Nero.[58] This prominent feature of imperial rule clearly is the background to Paul's noticeable use of the imagery.[59]

In the New Testament, the uncommon term adoption (υἱοθεσία, *huiothesia*) is exclusive to Paul.[60] Paul's use of the term likely reflects imperial Rome. His contexts are incorporation with the thought of inheritance. Rhetorically, adoption is Paul's unique metonymy of the formulation of legal heirs of Israel as the eschatological people of God in the New Aeon. Adoption imagery in 8:15 translates to a Roman audience God's transformation of Mosaic Israel into messianic Israel. A transfer of dynastic authority is taking place, from Moses to Messiah.

Thus, "children of God" and "heirs" in **8:16–17** strikes Jewish and Roman chords. "Children of God" is Jewish covenant language, and

[56] High infant mortality rates, dominantly male-only rights restricting the progeny pool, vicissitudes of life (death in war, disease, political intrigue, etc.) and other factors regularly made generational transfer of family status, power, and wealth ambiguous. See Lindsay, *Adoption in the Roman World*. For an overview of the Roman imperial line, see the chart of the Julio-Claudian family on p. 210.

[57] Roman adoption was a dramatic scene in Metro-Goldwyn-Mayer's 1959 movie, "Ben Hur," starring Charlton Heston, based on the 1880 novel by Lew Wallace, *Ben Hur: A Tale of the Christ*. The Roman consul and general, Quintus Arrius, adopted his famous and eminently successful Hebrew charioteer, Judah Ben Hur.

[58] In the second century, the entire Nerva-Antonine dynasty is adopted up through Marcus Aurelius, the five good emperors of the Golden Age.

[59] As referring to Roman law, cf. Lyall, "Roman Law in the Writings of Paul—Adoption." For the Roman imperial context, cf. Lewis, *Paul's 'Spirit of Adoption.'*

[60] Rom 8:15, 23; 9:4; Gal 4:5; Eph 1:5.

"heirs" is the issue of Abraham's true descendants (Romans 4).[61] Messiah is the messianic origin of the family of God.

In addition, adoption language is quite revelatory of the Pauline semantic universe as code for resurrection doctrine. This theological construct connecting adoption and resurrection is clear in the later appositive grammatical construction in 8:23: "while we eagerly await adoption, the redemption of our body." The appositional grammar defines adoption as "the redemption of our body," which is another way of speaking of resurrection. Thus, becoming children of God in Paul theologically cannot be separated from belief in resurrection. We should note that that resurrection clearly is conceived in this verse as *corporate*.[62] The significance of 8:23 is this: *Whatever messianic Israel is presently in the "now-not yet" eschatological tension of present experience (5:1–11) is not messianic Israel consummated.* Messianic Israel is in a continual state of development. Her storyline is not static, not in suspended animation, not frozen in time. "The rest of the story" is yet to be told, and corporate resurrection is a chapter still to be written of future changes for messianic Israel. That "mystery" of the actual look and feel of a consummated messianic Israel has yet to be revealed in Romans and in time.

Paul also continues in **8:17** the essential connection he established in the opening unit of 5:1–11 between suffering and glory ("if we suffer with him . . . also glorified"). Suffering is conceived in an overarching corporate frame as community labor.

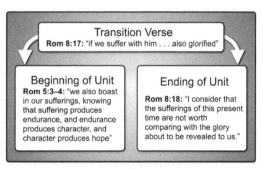

FIGURE 8.11. Romans 5–8 Thematic *Inclusio*.

The eschatological tension of the present time between Mosaic Israel and messianic Israel is a necessary part of the end time labor ushering in the kingdom of God. This corporate suffering theme of the

---

[61] Old Testament inheritance language progresses in Jewish thought from issues of the land of Canaan (Gen 15:7; Num 34:2; Deut 1:7–8; Josh 23:4; Ps 78:5) to issues of Yahweh and Israel (Isa 19:25; Jer 10:16; 16:18; 51:19; Ezek 44:28) to issues of future kingdom blessings (Ps Sol 14:10; 1 Enoch 40:9; 4 Macc 18:3).

[62] Even though the adjectival pronoun "our" is plural in 8:23, "body" is singular.

present time is likely how Paul frames his struggle with the synagogue. Any persecution he endured is a far bigger issue in the messianic scheme of things than personal injury. Rhetorically, 8:17 also functions as a transition verse tying this unit into the next unit of 8:18–30. Using a thematic *inclusio*, Paul thus ties together the beginning and ending of Romans 5–8.

Glorification with Messiah is the final reversal of the Adamic tragedy (5:12) and final reversal of the continual and incorrigible human exchange of lordship persistently provoking the wrath of God (1:23). In short, all God's creative purposes throughout the cosmos will be consummated in messianic Israel.

Creation Resolved (8:18–30)

Some introductory literary observations on this unit's function are in order. First, Rom 8:18–30 actually offers a *triple* literary climax. This unit climaxes not only its own chapter (Romans 8) and the larger unit in which this chapter is embedded (Romans 5–8), but also climaxes the entire corpus of Romans 1–8 from the wrath of God opening in 1:18–32 on. Intent to conclude the entire corpus is easily seen in its skillful employment of thematic vocabulary, theology, and imagery. For example, vocabulary from 1:18–32—glory, creation, creature, futility, body, image—is deftly incorporated. The theology is thematic and notably corporate, which unifies the entire theological movement. The imagery is thematic in its portrayal of the reversal of Adamic rebellion. Second, this thematic construction facilitates emphasis on the cosmic outworking of salvation. Third, this thematic construction is a slingshot orbit to catapult the craft to its literary destination in Romans 9–11. The work to parse the messianic Israel of the New Aeon through an analysis of God and sin and God and grace in Romans 1–8 establishes all the necessary theological foundations for presenting Romans 9–11. Thus, the climactic declaration concluding Romans 9–11 that all Israel will be saved is where our astronaut Paul has been piloting this literary module ever since escaping the synagogue's gravity in Romans 1.[63] Paul now ties his literary bow with Romans 5 on the suffering theme as he moves to the eschatological climax of the story.

---

[63] Given the cosmic focus of the unit, astronautical imagery was irresistible.

Eschatological Suffering (8:18–25)

Speaking of "present sufferings" in **8:18** smoothly transitions to the final resolution taken up by Paul, that of all creation, because right now creation is suffering too. This unit should caution against obsessive individual focus as if personal redemption exhausts the meaning of God's kingdom enterprise. Paul begins this climax by returning to the theme that began the unit in Romans 5, insisting the present sufferings are eschatological and cosmic realities (8:18). He has grounded his logic in the story of Jesus's passion and glorification as he builds on the 8:17 transition and echoes vocabulary from 1:18–32 ("glory," "revealed"). Quizzing Paul for so-called "signs of the times" to prove the final denouement of history is at hand would not return language of earthquakes, wars, or rumors of wars.[64] Paul instead pointed to the suffering of messianic Israel, because these sufferings by their very nature anticipate the eschatological and cosmic realities of salvation that are future: a future consummation (which infers that salvation is unfinished), a future glory to be revealed (presently missing, so part of human "lostness"), and a future new creation that transcends Eden.

All creation has "eager expectation" (ἀποκαραδοκία, *apokaradokia*) for the revelation of the "children of God" (**8:19**). Paul here infers that messianic Israel has something to do with the resolution of all of creation. That connection suggests more complexities are involved in "thus all Israel will be saved" (11:26) than simply a secular nation-state called Israel possessing a small chunk of real estate. This connection also brings into focus how creation's groaning is tied to the groaning of messianic Israel in 8:23, which itself connects back to the shared eschatological sufferings in the bridging verse of 8:17. Present suffering speaks to creation's dilemma, an issue insinuated in 1:8–32 but not resolved. A connection back to 1:18–32 is seen by echoing earlier vocabulary, such as "creation," "revelation," "futility'" "glory," and "body." Paul thus has added a cosmic layer to the consequences of Eden. Creation's "futility" in **8:20** (ματαιότητι, *mataiotēti*) in part is

---

[64] And neither did Jesus, for that matter. The most curious exegetical fallacy is that certain eschatological schemes use wars and rumors of wars as a supposed "sign of the times" from Matt 24:6 when Jesus adamantly said the *opposite*, that these were *not* any so-called "sign of the times," that, in fact, "the end is not yet." See Stevens, *Revelation*, 130–31.

seen in its deification ("Mother Earth"), which directs thinking away from its Creator, and in its brutalization by commercial and industrial conglomerates, which leaves devastation and inability to support life.[65] In these ways and others, creation also is enslaved to corruption.

A lot is at stake for God in the enterprise of salvation. The vastness of the universe boggles the imagination. Even if only one percent of the dimensions and realities astronomers contemplate were true, that would be one-hundred percent more than the human mind could grasp.[66] Contemplate for a moment the huge enterprise of the cosmos, then contemplate for a lifetime the only God who created everything beyond what you can imagine. That is why Messiah is as much good news for God as good news for humans.

Creation will be set free from its bondage to decay (**8:21**). Strikingly, creation is characterized as "enslaved" (δουλείας, *douleias*), which recalls the general condition of humanity (1:24, 26, 28) and the condition of Mosaic Israel (6:15–23). Like a woman giving birth, creation is in its own eschatological labor pains (**8:22**). Having the Spirit now is the "first fruits" of the later harvest, so the matter is Spirit driven start to finish, even as was creation itself (Gen 1:2). We should note that Paul emphasizes that *all* creation (πᾶσα ἡ κτίσις, *pasa hē ktisis*) is in labor. Such a global descriptor infers a cosmic scope to redemption. As part of creation, humans groan too (**8:23**). One of the consequences of sin is physical bodies are not in the state originally intended by God.[67] Part of the redemption story is recovering the lost creative purpose of the divine design of human corporeality.[68] "Adoption" language here

---

[65] Cf. Cate, "How Green Was John's World"; Johnson, "Confronting the Beast," 142–44.

[66] Physicists estimate the (observable) universe is about 93 billion light-years in diameter. Light travels 186,282 miles *per second*, that is, can circle the earth 7.5 times in one second. Our sun around which our planet rotates is only one among 100 thousand million stars in our Milky Way galaxy, and our galaxy is only one of two trillion or more in the universe. We have underestimated God.

[67] More than the simple problem of aging and mortality, as suggested in biblical accounts of angelic manifestations. Resurrection is more than the walking dead.

[68] No details are worked out, but Paul already asserted to the Corinthians that flesh and blood cannot inherit the kingdom of God, that this mortality has to put on immortality that has an essential connection to the Spirit (1 Cor 15:42–50). "Paul's point seems to be that one can assume full *pneumatikos* esistence only as Christ did, by resurrection, which includes a *pneumatikos* body" (Fee, *First Corinthians*, 789).

is connected to resurrection doctrine. Hence, even if adoption is read with present meaning, its fullness in the Pauline sense is temporal and future. The adopted child awaits full inheritance to come. The redemption awaited is of "our" (plural) "body" (singular). Thus, the essence of the future of which Paul speaks is corporate, which is messianic Israel, not a conglomerate of individual entities milling about uselessly doing "their own thing" without point, purpose, or plan and no integration into a synergistic divine design for the cosmos.

Because these realities are future, present faith is founded on future hope. "In *this hope* we were saved" (**8:24**). "This" means a specific hope, not a vague wish. If we do not know what God is doing, he does, and anyone who went to the trouble to create the universe has dibs on the design. "This hope" means creation fulfilled. The Davidic promise has a future yet unseen (1:3), which includes the long-expected gathering of the nations.[69] "This hope," then, comes directly from God, who also consummates its reality. God as source and conclusion of eschatological hope inspires the designation "God of hope" in Paul's benediction in Rom 15:12 and is the reason why eager expectation can be tempered with patience (**8:25**). We suffer, indeed, but in hope.

Assisted Suffering (8:26–30)

While we pray for consummation, the Spirit helps in weakness (**8:26–27**). The confessional tone here, acknowledging dependence, reverses the spirit of Adamic rebellion (1:18–32). The question might be, what is the object of prayer? In this *specific* context, the object would be creation's consummation. Note the connecting idea and the word "groan," which seems tied to creation's own longing (8:22). In context, "mind of the Spirit" would be divine designs to consummate creation. A thematic parallel is found in the early confession, "Come, Lord Jesus!"[70] Thus, messianic Israel shows its lineage in Messiah by working together to pray for Messiah's consummation of creation and to do its part toward achieving that end among the nations. "God works in all things toward the good" or "all things work together for good" is not a crucial trans-

---

[69] Rom 15:12, where the key eschatological theme of "hope" appears again.

[70] Preserved in Aramaic as *marana-tha*; 1 Cor 16:22. Cf. Rev 22:20.

lation decision,[71] particularly when "good" is read in its context (8:28). "Good" here resonates with the thematic creation pronouncement of "good" in the creation story.[72] Understood this way, use of "good" as about creation and its future in 8:28 prepares for the language of future destiny immediately coming up in the famous sequence in 8:29.

Paul now pulls themes together in a compressed and theologically loaded statement. The question of Israel's inheritance, the problem of Adamic failure, and the promise of messianic fulfillment with an eschatological transfer of authority from Moses to Messiah through divine adoption, that is, the entire discussion of Romans 5–8, explodes forth in a rush of phrases in 8:29–30.

> For those he foreknew he also predestined to be conformed to the image of his Son, so that he would be the firstborn among many brothers and sisters. And those he predestined, he also called; and those he called, he also justified; and those he justified; he also glorified (Rom 8:29–30).

"Those he foreknew" would be the Israel of God and her chosen status among the nations. "Predestined" is a sovereign will at work that brings covenanted people to a desired divine destiny. Being "conformed to the image of his Son" is that destiny, because this process reverses out Adam's failure (Romans 5). "Firstborn" is the language of the issue of the right of inheritance. Paul later will argue that the true firstborn in terms of the right of inheritance in the divine economy never has been the biological firstborn. That argument was not novel. The firstborn "among many brothers and sisters," reflects Jewish arguments over the question of how the sons of Isaac and the children of Israel are to be figured. In the eyes of returning Jews of the Southern Kingdom after the exile, Northern Israel had sold off their biological right for a bowl of Assyrian porridge. Thus, in the New Testament, Samaritans were considered not even half-Jews, *regardless* issues of firstborn. The pertinent question now that Messiah suddenly has come to the temple to bring the will of God to Israel would be whether the southern kingdom even would qualify in all fairness for some similar judgment. That Messiah has needed to adopt a family when none seems forthcoming,

---

[71] Compare NRSV and NIV and notes, as long as we do not misinterpret as "all things are good," which is wrong on so many levels.

[72] Gen 1:10, 12, 18, 21, 25, 31.

as God provided Isaac in order for Abraham even to have a family, seems to suggest an answer. Instead of the destiny of Israel being in Moses, her destiny is in Messiah. Those in messianic Israel are the predestined in Pauline terms. These are called by God, which is a Jewish way of saying God adopted them, so an authority transfer has taken place from Moses to Messiah (Romans 6–7). This process of inclusion into messianic Israel provides the benefits of Messiah, whose main benefit for the undeserving ungodly yet adopted is to be "justified" by faith on the pattern of Abraham's covenant. These are covenant children of Abraham and therefore heirs of his promises (Romans 4). Those who are justified are at the beginning of a divine work that God will conclude within his purposes for creation and for humanity, that is, to be "glorified," which is creation consummated and a profound reversal of human rebellion, in which, "although knowing God, they did not glorify him as God" (1:21). Paul, sounding almost confessional, is saying that understanding how God has worked in the past and will work in the future, concisely condensed here in 8:29–30, provides all succor for suffering and the consequent ability to persevere. The Spirit works this assistance on behalf of the community of faith during the difficult, in-between-time crossing from one age to another in moving toward God's ultimate consummation.

God Praised (8:31–39)

God is praised for gracing messianic Israel all things. The praise moves from summary reflection on the divine advocacy for sinners in 8:31–36 to personal response to this advocacy in 8:37–39, Paul's own rabbinic "amen" to God's cosmic salvation.

The summary reflection on divine advocacy for sinners starts with the assurance of final victory in God's gospel of grace (**8:31–32**). The rhetorical question, "What shall we say" (8:31), signals summarization. Logically, "these things" could be Romans 8, or Romans 5–8, or even all of Romans 1–8, but, literarily and thematically, Paul likely intends to merge all thought together like a spacecraft targeting an elliptical orbit around a planet to use as a gravity accelerator along a trajectory that will facilitate the final destination, which, in this case, is Romans 9–11. Romans 8:31–39 is the gravity accelerator toward the resolution of Israel's place in the plan of God.

Paul deliberately develops an intratextual echo of the "delivered over" action of God used in the distinctive analysis of the operation of the wrath of God in Rom 1:24, 26, 28, as well as the statement in 4:25 that Jesus was "delivered over for our trespasses." Paul now recapitulates the idea in the expression "delivered him over for us all" (8:32), using the same verb.[73] Theologically, the delivering over of Jesus counters the effect of the delivering over of humans. As we have argued, however, the wrath of God is obviated, not endured.[74] Paul here used the historical fact of Jesus as the basis of a future hope of glory, in perfect parallel to his encouragement to Thessalonian believers in 1 Thess 5:1–11. The past is ground of the future. A vision of the cross provides assurance that the God who already has sent his Son "will grace us all things" (8:32). Romans 5:1–2 is back in view.

The summary reflection on divine advocacy for sinners continues with the assurance of final vindication in the last judgment (**8:33–34**). The rapid-fire questions, "who brings a charge?", "who condemns?", evoke a forensic setting allusive of Isaiah's third Servant Song (Isa 50:8). The questions function to emphasize the twofold basis of final judgment security by the inferred answers. The first basis is the security of God's justification. The second basis is the security of Messiah's intercession. For one, this intercession is secure because the one interceding is "at the right hand of God," which alludes to Ps 110:1. God as Lord invites Israel's king as master of his subjects to sit in the place of honor in God's heavenly court, so has the direct hearing and audience of God.[75] The experience of this intercession is mediated through the Spirit (8:26–27). In essence, these answers offer up the gospel of God in a nutshell: Messiah's death, resurrection, and intercession. In offering this assurance, Paul anticipates his own personal and ultimate vindication that has bubbled up at crucial turning points in his argument, as in the theme statement of Romans in 1:16, "For I am not ashamed of the gospel" and in 5:5, "hope does not make ashamed."

---

[73] Which theologically functions similarly to the kenosis passage of Phil 2:7.

[74] Stevens, *Divine Wrath*, 153. Also, see earlier discussion on 3:26, p. 311.

[75] The passage used by Jesus to circumvent the attempt of the scribes and Pharisees to discredit him by offending public opinion on John the Baptist (Matt 26:64). Note also Acts 2:34–36.

The summary reflection on divine advocacy for sinners concludes with illustrations coming in part from Paul's own mission experiences (**8:35–36**). The illustrations are introduced through a third rhetorical question, "What can separate us from Messiah's love?" Interesting is how suffering for Paul is a sign of union, not separation. Such an idea is grounded in, and theologically generated out of, the passion of Jesus. The Messiah, after all, even made clear that the life of anyone wanting to follow him would take on its own cruciform shape, just as did his, a teaching, however, his disciples always failed to comprehend.[76] Paul then proposes various difficult life contingencies that could qualify for potentially causing breakdown in trust in Messiah's love:

- "affliction" (or, "tribulation," θλῖψις, *thlipsis*)

- "distress" (στενοχωρία, *stenochōria*)

- "persecution" (διωγμός, *diōgmos*)

- "famine" (λιμός, *limos*)

- "nakedness" (γυμνότης, *gymnotēs*)

- "peril" (κίνδυνος, *kindynos*)

- "sword" (μάχαιρα, *machaira*)

One could illustrate most of these difficulties from the text of Acts. However, Paul's own firsthand catalog of his suffering in his mission work is an even more compelling case that this list in Romans is not arbitrary nor considered in the abstract or impersonally.

> In whatever anyone might dare [to boast]—I speak foolishly—I also dare. Are they Hebrews? I also. Are they Israelites? I also. Are they seed of Abraham? I also. Are they ministers of Messiah? I am speaking as a lunatic—even more (am) I: even more labors, even more imprisonments, so severe floggings as often near death. From the Jews five times I received forty lashes minus one. Three times I was beaten with rods. Once I was stoned. Three times I was shipwrecked. A day and night I have drifted in the deep sea. Frequent journeys: in perils from rivers, in perils from bandits, in perils from kindred, in perils from gentiles, in perils in the city, in perils in the wilderness, in perils in the sea,

---

[76] Mark 8:31—9:1; 9:30–50; 10:33–45. Cf. Matt 16:21–28; 17:22; 20:18–28; Luke 9:22–27; 17:25; 18:31–34.

in perils among false brothers, in toil and trouble, oftentimes in sleeplessness, in hunger and thirst, many times fasting, in cold and nakedness (2 Cor 11:21b–27).

Paul should be dead already. Anyone else would be talking about enduring the wrath of God. Somehow, that conclusion just does not come to Paul's mind. What is his problem? His problem is, during none of these contingencies did he once feel separated from the love of Messiah. In fact, he drew the opposite conclusion: his mission peril was so close to the pattern of the passion of Messiah he had the conviction he was in the center of God's will, as was Messiah as he hung dying on a cross. Paul had presented his body a living sacrifice, holy and acceptable to God and had proven in his absolute commitment and trust in God what was the good, acceptable, and complete will of God in his life (Rom 12:1–2). The perspective for all of Romans 8, and particularly for this concluding praise, is eschatological entirely, taking the long view of the coming final judgment that can facilitate an attitude adjustment that present circumstances are not the end of the story.

Paul then quotes Ps 44:22, "For your sake we are being killed all day long; we are being reckoned as slaughtered sheep." Commentators point out this verse has a trail in Jewish martyrdom literature, but the evidence cited is late.[77] More important is to observe that Psalm 44 is a *lament psalm*, so this use here is resonating with the rhetoric of Rom 7:7–25 and the immediately following Rom 9:1–5. This lament context infers the focus is messianic Israel. Thus, the opening "for your sake" (ἕνεκεν σοῦ, *heneken sou*) of the quotations is applied to Messiah.

Paul offers his own personal response to bring to a climax this concluding praise of God (**8:37–39**). After the previous and grievous catalog of perils and persecution, the literary turn around is signaled with a strong, contrastive conjunction, translated as "but" or "rather" (ἀλλά, *alla*) in 8:37 to change the tone from negative to positive. The storm clouds immediately lift and reveal a brilliant light of triumph. The reference in "all these things" at a minimum is to the immediately listed perils and dangers of 8:35–36, but likely is to the whole chapter. Moses has been resolved (8:1–11). Adam has been resolved (8:12–17). Creation has been resolved (8:18–30). Suffering on behalf of messianic Israel for the sake of Messiah has meaning (8:31–36). Paul employs a

[77] As in Dunn, *Romans 1–8*, 505–506; cf. Jewett, *Romans*, 548. Cf. Rev 12:11.

FIGURE 8.12. Victorious Hadrian (117–138). Marble statue from Hierapytna, Crete of emperor Hadrian in traditional ceremonial military cuirass with conquest, subjugation pose of a humiliated, shamed barbarian in disproportionate size underfoot. A conqueror with vanquished enemy underfoot is a common motif in the Ancient Near East also used in biblical messianic images; cf. Ps 110:1; Acts 2:35; 1 Cor 15:25 (IAM).

rare verb, "more than conquerors" (ὑπερνικῶμεν, *hypernikōmen*), but the context in imperial ideology of empire, war, conquest, domination through divine right to rule lurks in the background. Paul offers a provocative spin on imperial propaganda of conquest and subjugation by turning upside down and inside out all Roman values presumed in that imperial ideology, which is the Roman gospel of the age of Augustus that so dominated the city of Rome's world throughout the age of the early church.[78] The initial audience of this letter to Rome would have high political and cultural resonance with how Paul expresses himself. One of the more striking evidences of this "conqueror," "victorious" imperial ideology is a colossal, marble statue standing nine feet tall of emperor Hadrian (117–138) found in ancient Hierapytna on the southern coastline of Crete. Hadrian is presented in traditional ceremonial military cuirass. He strikes a conquest pose. His vanquished barbarian enemy is depicted in disproportionate small size and underfoot as a sign of humiliation and subjugation. A vanquished enemy underfoot is a common motif in the Ancient Near East that is incorporated into biblical royal and messianic images.[79] Paul had used this image of the royal victory of Messiah already with the Corinthians: "For he must reign until he has put all his enemies under his feet" (1 Cor 15:25). For Paul, however, the victory is not gained by force and subjugation, as in imperial ideology, but by faith and sacrifice. For Paul, this "more than conquerors" motif consummates the "for I am not ashamed" opening declaration (1:16).

The concluding confessional is grouped in pairs (**8:38–39**). The organizational principle for the pairing sequences seems to express eschatological realities. Some of the terms have figured directly into the developing discussion as integral to the complex present and future dimensions of the New Aeon in Messiah. For example, "life" in the first pair seems at first blush a strange category to consider as a threat to one's sense of God's love. However, the immediate context of 8:35–36 taken as allusive to the perils of Paul's mission work, as itemized in 2 Cor 11:21b–27, brings into better focus how "life" can be just such a threat when nuanced as inevitable adverse circumstances surrounding the preaching of the gospel. Other pairs are less clear in reference. One

---

[78] See previous discussion, "Life Setting of Rome," 127–50.

[79] Cf. Ps 110:1; Acts 2:35.

may have to fill out the meaning through similar words or ideas in the entire Pauline universe of thought.[80]

- *death nor life*: cf. 1:32; 5:10, 12, 14, 17, 21; 6:3, 4, 5, 9, 16, 21, 23; 7:5, 10, 13, 24; 8:2, 6; cf. 2 Cor 11:21b–27

- *angels nor rulers*: cf. 1 Cor 4:9; 6:3; 11:10; 13:1; 11:14; 2 Cor 12:7; Gal 1:8; 3:19; Col 1:16; 2:18; 2 Thess 1:7; 1 Tim 3:16; 5:21; 1 Cor 15:24

- *things present nor things to come*: e.g., divine wrath as both historical (1:18; 3:5) and future (2:5; 5:9; 1 Thess 1:9–10)

- *powers*: 1 Cor 15:24; Eph 1:21; 1Cor 12:28; Gal 3:5; 2 Thess 2:9

- *height nor depth*: 2 Cor 10:5

- *nor any other created thing*: Rom 16:20; cf. 1 Thess 2:18; also, 1 Cor 5:5; 7:5; 2 Cor 2:11; 11:14; 12:7; 2 Thess 2:9; 1 Tim 1:20; 5:15

For example, an "angel" as a threat might have meaning against the rhetoric of Satan described as disguising himself as an "angel of light" (2 Cor 11:14). The idea of all things as created in Jesus in Col 1:16 includes all "thrones" (θρόνοι, *thronoi*), "lordships" (κυριότητες, *kyriotētes*), "rulers" (ἀρχαί, *archai*), and "authorities" (ἐξουσίαι, *exousiai*). These broadly cast descriptions are universal in scope, that is, anything the listener can conceive in the general category. Paul uses "angels" to make clear what "rulers" by itself does not, that is, that he intends to encompass the entire universe whether visible or invisible, spiritual or earthly. Things present or to come likely has eschatological focus in light of Romans 1–8 on final judgment, particularly the wrath of God in both its historical and eschatological dimensions.

Easily noted is that the element of "powers" (δυνάμεις, *dynameis*) sitting by itself breaks the paired sequencing and balance of the whole. Some are wont to incorporate the solo "powers" backwards into the "angels"/"rulers" dyad.[81] The inclusion of "power" in a similar expression in 1 Cor 15:24 (cf. Eph 1:21), also in an eschatological context, might favor this suggestion. Such a move, however, destroys the obvious symmetry in that earlier pair. Jewett tried to advance a rhetorical

---

[80] For the purposes of establishing the general point of how the rhetoric works, disputed Pauline authorship is not crucial to the argument here.

[81] Cf. Dunn, *Romans 1–8*, 513.

argument as a tie-in to the following "will be able [to separate]," both built on the same cognate root, but such a rhetorical ploy would be neither obvious nor meaningful, begging on a rather trite effect.[82] Moo regarded the reason for its solitary presence was impossible to know.[83] He might be right.[84]

At the same time, the semantic domain of this word "power" as including working "miracles" (1 Cor 12:28; Gal 3:5; 2 Thess 2:9) might be suggestive, especially for the eschatological context of 2 Thess 2:9 about Satan who uses all "power" to deceive in that end time scenario. This satanic force at work would be poised over against the power of God and the Spirit, which features in Romans regularly.[85] In this sense, "powers" as a solitary item may suggest the cosmic spiritual conflict of heavenly powers conceived in the totality of all forces engaged, along the lines of the metanarrative John develops in Revelation 12 with the great, red Dragon and its sea and earth beasts persecuting followers of the Lamb.[86]

If this cosmic conflict is in view with "powers," then the singular element "powers" here forms an *inclusio* with the concluding singular element of "any other created thing," since, in a monotheistic world, Satan is a created thing, so without any hesitation could be included in this "any other created thing" category and give that category its final and climactic punch. The gospel of God goes all the way to taking down the Devil. Nothing in the universe more wants to separate believers from assurance of God's love than the Devil. Paul leaves the category open in case the reader by any stretch of the imagination can conjure anything in the universe worse than the Devil. This exegesis also then lays theological foundation for the grave and strong warning against a group causing dissention and offenses at the end of Romans that ends

---

[82] Jewett, *Romans*, 553.

[83] *Romans*, 546.

[84] The casual suggestion with a shrug of the shoulders of some momentary lapse of concentration or distracted dictation in which Paul forgot himself and did not return to correct this rhetorical gadfly simply does not fit the rhetorical exigency of a crucial *tour de force* climax to all of Romans 1–8.

[85] Rom 1:4, 16, 20; 9:17; 15:13, 19; cf. 1 Cor 1:18, 24; 2:4; 4:19; 5:4; 6:14; 15:56; 2 Cor 4:7; 6:7; 13:4; Eph 1:19; 3:7, 20; Phil 3:10; Col 1:11, 29; 2 Thess 1:11; 2 Tim 1:8.

[86] See Stevens, *Revelation*, 422–40.

with the assurance, "The God of peace shortly will crush Satan under your feet" (16:20). This statement is nothing more than 8:38–39 again.

The "height nor depth" dyad is hardest to interpret.[87] First, the terms are rare. "Height" (ὕψωμα, *hypsōma*) is quite rare, only twice in the New Testament, both Paul.[88] "Height" in its only other occurrence in 2 Cor 10:5 is an obstacle raised up against the knowledge of God, the hubris and vanity of human reasoning. This concept corresponds to suppressing revealed truth about God, which provokes the wrath of God in Rom 1:18–23. Second, "depth" (βάθος, *bathos*) has a few more hits in the New Testament, but often just literal, as deep soil or water, or simple metaphor, such as deep poverty, or deep riches, wisdom and knowledge.[89] Use in Eph 3:18 actually inverts the dyad of height and depth into a positive appropriation of the love of Christ. The context in Romans is negative, threatening separation. One possibility is domicile, that is, the domains of heaven and earth (or under the earth) and unknown forces or entities residing therein potentially threatening God's relationship to his people, like a snake in a garden. Nothing hidden in any dark crook, cranny, or cave anywhere in the universe is a candidate for being able to separate believers from the love of God.

The bottom line for this whole sequence is "anything you possibly can think of in your wildest imagination," like your worst, B-grade science fiction nightmare. Taken seriously, however, and we have the richest, most powerful, most personal celebration of the gospel of God as anywhere in the New Testament.[90] Paul confesses the new lordship of the New Aeon in "Messiah Jesus, our Lord" (8:39)—the perfect conclusion to Romans 1–8. "No separation" means the basic consequence of sin is destroyed. Analysis of the problem through the topic of God and sin in Romans 1–4 leads to analysis of the solution through the topic of God and grace in Romans 5–8. Paul now is ready to bring on the heat in his climax of the topic of God and Israel in Romans 9–11.

---

[87] Highly unlikely are speculations about astrological powers or astronomical extremities used to subsume the whole universe (apogee, perigee). Such topics simply have no resonance in Romans, nor does Paul show any interest in them elsewhere.

[88] The alternate noun form, ὕψος (*hypsos*), occurs in Luke 1:78; 24:49; Eph 3:18; 4:8; Jas 1:9; Rev 21:16, used consistently literally as simply "height" or "on high."

[89] Matt 13:5; Mark 4:5; Luke 5:4; Rom 11:33; 1 Cor 2:10; 2 Cor 8:2; Eph 3:18.

[90] In a tongue-in-cheek tease on the "once saved, always saved" Baptist mantra, this passage comes to mind most often when daring to think Paul might have been Baptist.

9

Universal Salvation

God and Israel

ROMANS 5–8 HAS DEVELOPED THE second part of the summary statement in Rom 11:32, "in order that he might show mercy." Paul now
develops the third and last part of that statement, "to all." Romans 1–8
has made clear Israel's predicament in God's wrath now that Messiah
has come inaugurating the New Aeon to consummate creation. Is Israel
finished? Depends on definitions and destiny. Who is your father?

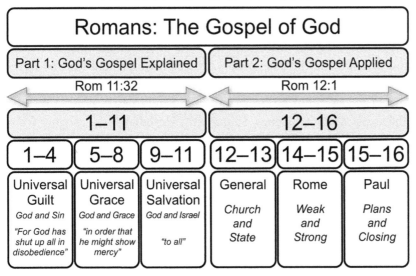

FIGURE 9.1. The Structure of Romans. Romans 9–11 is about God and Israel.

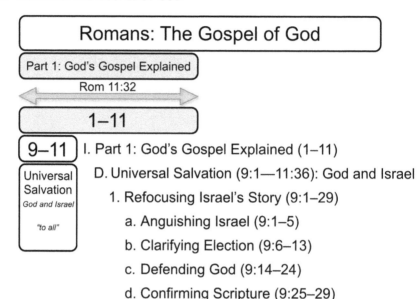

FIGURE 9.2. Outline: Romans 9 (Refocusing Israel's Story). On God and Israel, Paul first refocuses Israel's story by way of clarifying election among the patriarchs.

REFOCUSING ISRAEL'S STORY

Preliminary Reflections

Reflections on Crisis Settings

First, Jewish identity was in crisis in the first century. The two centuries before and the first century after Christ saw an extraordinary surge in spirited competition for the very soul of Jewish identity. Everyone and their brother in their own ways were saying, "and thus all Israel will be saved." Paul most certainly was not the first. A veritable cacophony of voices could be heard—priests, Sadducees, Davidic royalists, Pharisees, Zealots, Essenes, Samaritans, Herodians—all ranging from passive quietism to outright war.[1] This crisis should be sobering when recognizing that only eight, or possibly nine, years after Romans was written, Judea *was* in outright war with Rome.

Second, messianic identity also was in crisis in the first century. This crisis surfaces in Jesus's question to his disciples at Caesarea Phil-

---

[1] See earlier discussion, pp. 95–105.

ippi, "Who do people say that I am?"[2] The variety of answers shows people generally are clueless. Worse, careful reading of Mark indicates Peter's messianic answer was inadequate, because his thought could not abide an image of suffering and persecution (Mark 16:31–33). As a result, Jesus had to warn of the problem of false messiahs (Mark 13:21), of which the historian Josephus corroborates several.[3] We should keep in mind that using the term "messiah" for a Pharisee was *confessional* and included a world of expectation. A premier example would be in Rabbi Akiba's declaration about the insurrectionist Simon bar Kokhba in the Second Jewish War of 133–35.[4] Keep in mind that Paul evokes the confession of Jesus as Messiah five times in the first eight verses of Romans. Messianic identity already was problematic in Rome. The Edict of Claudius a few years before Romans implicates preaching of Jesus as Messiah in Jewish synagogues in Rome, creating such conflict that the Roman emperor himself had to become involved.

Reflections on Israel Language

The term "Israel" central to Romans 9–11 occurs sixty-eight times in the New Testament, mostly in Matthew, Luke-Acts, and Paul.[5] Of the seventeen times in Paul, eleven are in Romans, and all of these are in Romans 9–11 exclusively.[6] Grasping Israel is essential to Romans 9–11.

Semantic Domains. "Israel" has two semantic domains, biological for descendants of Jacob, and political for the nation of those descendants. The family name is tied to the patriarchal history of Jacob, the grandson of Abraham. Jacob's name was changed to "Israel" by the angelic opponent Jacob successfully wrestled (Gen 32:28). Josephus speculated the etymology as "one who struggled with a divine angel."[7] The descendant domain logically subsumes related ideas of "family" (*genos*), as in Phil 3:5, as well as "house" (*oikos*). This domain probably is the sense of "Israel according to the flesh" in 1 Cor 10:18.

---

[2] Mark 8:27–30; Matt 16:13–20; Luke 9:18–20.

[3] *Ant.* 18.1.1; 20.5.1; *J.W.* 2.8.1; 20.8.6; 2.13.5.

[4] Jerusalem Talmud, *Ta'anit* 4:6 (68d–69a). Cf. Gruber, *Rabbi Akiba's Messiah.*

[5] Matt 12x, Mark 2x, Luke 12x, Acts 15x, John 4x, Paul 17x, Heb 3x, Rev 3x.

[6] Rom 9:6, 27, 31; 10:19, 21; 11:2, 7, 25, 26. Cf. 1 Cor 10:18; 2 Cor 3:7, 13; Gal 6:16; Eph 2:12; Phil 3:5.

[7] *Ant.* 1:333 [1.20.2].

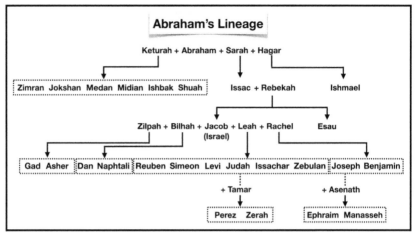

FIGURE 9.3. Abraham's Lineage. Proving lineage was crucial to Jewish culture for purposes of inheritance and priestly service, so genealogies were important.

A cognate term uncommon in the New Testament is "Israelite" (Ἰσραηλίτης, *Israēlitēs*).[8] This term is used as a biological marker that distinguishes patriarchal lineage between Jacob (Israel) and his older brother Esau, as well as from descendants of Abraham's other sons.[9] The biological import of "Israelite" evidences lineage always has been integral to Jewish culture for priesthood and inheritance of land given by God.[10] Maintaining genealogies was essential for these purposes, as indicated in the biblical text.[11] Further, newly discovered inscriptions reveal that Samaritans referred to themselves as "Israelites."[12]

[8] Mostly in Acts, but two of the three times in Paul in Romans 9–11. Cf. John 1:47; Acts 2:22; 3:12; 5:35; 13:16; 21:28; Rom 9:4; 11:1; 2 Cor11:22. The term "Judea" or "Judeans" may have similar semantic connotation in certain contexts; cf. Jdt 6:2; 1 Esd 1:30; Matt 2:6. "Hebrew" (Ἑβραῖος, *Hebraios*), quite rare in the New Testament (only four times: Acts 6:1; 1 Cor 11:22; Phil 3:5) and an alternate for "Israelite," is always ethnic, but with focus on capability in the Hebrew language.

[9] Ishmael from Sarah's handmaiden Hagar (Gen 16:3), and Zimran, Jokshan, Medan, Midian, Ishbak, and Shuah from Abraham's second wife, Keturah, whom he married after the death of Sarah (Gen 25:2; 1 Chr 1:32).

[10] Provable lineage was crucial in the work of Ezra reconstituting temple service after the exile; unproven lineage prevented service (Ezra 2:59–63). Family lines of returnees tediously are detailed in Ezra 2. Ezra's own priestly genealogy is given in Ezra 7:1–5.

[11] Seen throughout the biblical text. Cf. Cain (Genesis 4), Seth (Genesis 5, 11), Noah (Genesis 10), Book of Ruth (Naomi to David), 1–2 Kings (kings of Judah and Israel), exile returnees (Ezra 2, 7), Jesus (Matt 1:1–16; Luke 3:23–38).

[12] In second-century BC dedicatory inscriptions from Samaritan synagogues on the Greek island of Delos. For images, transcriptions, see Pummer, *Samaritans*, 92–94.

The political domain crosses over with the biological, seen in the use of similar related terms, such as "people" (*laos*), "family" (*genos*), and "house" (*oikos*). Political use occurs in dominantly genitive constructions ("of"), such as "cities of Israel" (Matt 10:23) or "twelve tribes of Israel" (Matt 19:28; Luke 22:30; Rev 21:12).[13] Other cases are used as well, of course.[14] This political domain has an interesting history after the divided kingdom. Originally, the Northern Kingdom established by Jeroboam was the "house of Israel," and the Southern Kingdom under Rehoboam was the "house of Judah." Thus, politically, "Israel" meant the Northern Kingdom of Israelites. After the exile, however, southern Jews centered on the cult in Jerusalem dropped the "house of Judah" and arrogated the political designation "Israel" exclusively to themselves as though the Northern Kingdom never existed.

This quick survey suffices to show that biological and political uses of "Israel" easily overlap, so semantic ambiguity leaves the sense mostly driven by immediate context. However, the good news here is, "Israelite" is exclusively biological. From this semantic clarity we draw two inferences. First, the general tenor of Paul's reflection in Romans 9–11 is biological (cf. Rom 9:4; 11:1). Exegesis must deal with this reality rather than ignoring the elephant in the room. Thus, Campbell's conclusion that "all Israel" in Rom 11:26 equals *only remnant* Israel is less than satisfying.[15] First, this exegesis struggles with the obvious ethnic sensibility of Rom 11:30–32, as even Campbell admits.[16] Second, this exegesis inadvertently plays into the hands of supersessionism.[17] Third,

---

[13] Cf. "commonwealth of Israel" (Eph 2:12); "consolation of Israel" (Luke 2:25); "elders of Israel" (Acts 4:8); "God of Israel" (Matt 15:31; Luke 1:68; Acts 13:17; "hope of Israel" (Acts 28:20); "house of Israel" (Matt 10:6; Acts 2:36; Heb 8:10; "king of Israel" (Matt 27:42; Mark 15:32; John 1:49; 12:13); "kingdom of Israel" (Acts 1:6); "land of Israel" (Matt 2:20); "people of Israel" (Luke 2:32; Acts 4:10; Phil 3:5); "salvation of Israel" (Acts 5:3); "sons of Israel" (Luke 1:16; Acts 5:21; 7:23, 37; 9:15; 10:36; 2 Cor 3:7; Heb 11:22; Rev 2:14; 7:4; 21:12); "teacher of Israel" (John 3:10).

[14] Nominative, accusative, dative, or even vocative. Cf. "redeem Israel" (Luke 24:21); "manifested to Israel" (John 1:31); "repentance to Israel" (Acts 5:31); "the Israel of God" (Gal 6:16); "in Israel" (Matt 8:10); "to Israel" (Luke 1:80); "O Israel" (Mark 12:29 [Deut 6:4]).

[15] Campbell, *Paul and the Hope of Glory*, 250.

[16] Ibid., 251.

[17] This view holds that the church replaces the Jews and their nation of Israel as the covenanted people of God entirely with no remainder forever. The view is ancient. Its trajectory is anticipated in the apocryphal *Epistle of Barnabas*, a late first or early second

this exegesis historically leaves hardly any other impression than that God, even though gaining gentiles, thoroughly lost his gambit on Israelites—which, lest we forget, is where the discussion started (Rom 9:4). Neither Romans 9:6–13 nor 11:26 should be interpreted in such a way as to ignore the whole burden of the discussion. Paul never expressed a wish to be anathema for the sake of gentiles. If Paul launches Romans 9–11 with the rhetoric of biology (Israelite), *the question of who is your father is not eliminated in the ensuing discussion.*

Jesus Tradition. The teaching of Jesus on what comprises "Israel" is rather complex, so, somewhat difficult to negotiate. First, we have both biological and political domains in his use of "Israel," which complicates the picture. Second, we may have intimations of teaching on election that transcend either of these elements, which adds even more complexity.

Both biological and political domains are present in the teaching and ministry of Jesus. He sent out disciples on mission exclusively to "the lost sheep of the house of Israel," specifically eliminating gentiles and Samaritans (Matt 10:5–6). He made similar distinction to his disciples when the Canaanite woman begged for healing for her daughter (Matt 15:24). When he spoke to a Samaritan woman, he told her she did not know what she worshipped and countered, "salvation is from the Jews" (John 4:22). Jesus himself was challenged with the issue of lineage in attempts to cast aspersion on the nature of his heritage. The status of his birth was questioned, which would disqualify him in the minds of his opponents from pretense to speak to Israel (John 8:41).[18] Jesus wryly agreed the question of fatherhood was without doubt important, but noted the devil is in the details (John 8:44).

Another element to be considered related to Israelite lineage is the prophetic motif of a coming Davidic ruler presented in the image

century Christian writing. At the close of the second century, Clement of Alexandria quoted the work as having scriptural authority, as did Origen a little later (d. 254). The work also is included at the end of Codex Sinaiticus, a Greek copy of the Bible dating about 330–350. Thus, even though not eventually canonized, the book was read and received with high regard in various Christian communities of the early church. The author argued that Jewish sin with the golden calf incident at the foot of Mount Sinai aborted God's covenant before even getting ratified. Thus, the Jews never understood the law rightly from the very beginning and never were, nor could be, the covenanted people of God. Covenant promises belong exclusively to the church (Epis. Bar. 4:6–8).

[18] The original "birther" controversy.

of a shepherd. This imagery has a clearly political nuance as a metaphor for a ruler of the nation. Further, prophets promised that God would send a shepherd to gather the lost and scattered sheep of his people.[19] A shepherding role figures into descriptions of Jesus's ministry (Mark 6:34), which likely traces directly back to Jesus's teaching he was the good shepherd (John 10:11–16). He also inferred he fulfilled messianic prophecy of the shepherd being struck and the sheep scattered (Mark 14:27). This theme of Jesus as the shepherd continued to be preserved by his disciples and in later generations of his followers.[20]

Yet, to complicate matters, at the same time as speaking of "Jews," the "house of Israel," and a Davidic shepherding role, Jesus also spoke in terms of "other sheep" that did not belong to the fold that he must gather (John 10:16). The narrator later explained that what facilitated this gathering activity was the death of Jesus, which not only was for "the nation" but to gather "together into one the scattered children of God" (John 11:52). Interpreters regularly jump to explain reference to "other sheep" as meaning gentiles. Gentiles, of course, would not be excluded in the messianic mission eventually, but that issue is another discussion altogether in terms of election.

Before we go so quickly to gentiles as the "other sheep," we have to consider the issue of unfulfilled prophecy about the reunification of the original united kingdom of David and Solomon, such as found in Micah and Hosea, and implicitly in Jeremiah. Micah prophesied: "then the rest of his kindred shall return to the people of Israel" (Mic 5:3, NRSV). The reference to "kindred" returning in context would be Israelites of the Northern Kingdom, not gentiles. Also referring to the Northern Kingdom, Hosea spoke of the "not my people" from the perspective of the covenant once again becoming "my people" (Hos 1:9–10). Hosea then declared: "The people of Judah and the people of Israel shall be gathered together, and they shall appoint for themselves one head; and they shall take possession of the land, for great shall be the day of Jezreel" (Hos 1:11, NRSV). Actions of appointing one ruler and possessing the land are both political and national language. This expectation is compatible with Jeremiah's claim that both houses of Judah and Israel would come together again in the future under one

---

[19] Jer 50:4–6; Mic 5:3–5; Ezek 34:23–24; 39:7.

[20] Heb 13:20; 1 Pet 5:4; Rev 7:17.

covenant (cf. Jer 31:31–34; LXX, Jeremiah 38). Zechariah had a similar vision (Zech 10:6). Such prophecies envision reunification of the nation after David's kingdom fractured in the days of Rehoboam and Jeroboam. Longing for a reunified kingdom continued through the centuries. A vestige of the idea of two political entities becoming one still lingers into the New Testament in the dual designation, "house of Israel" and "house of Judah," found in the quotation of Jeremiah in Heb 8:8.

In the context of both this unfulfilled prophetic expectation of a unified nation, as well as the intentional mission exclusivity of Jesus, a more likely candidate for "other sheep" would be other Israelites disenfranchised from the covenant. The interest of the Gospel of John in the Samaritans is obvious by the prominence given to the dialogue of Jesus with the Samaritan woman in John 4. Thus, "other sheep" even in John may not be a reference to gentiles. As well, when Jesus gave a parabolic example of fulfilling the law, he himself used a Samaritan as his example (Luke 10:25–37).

The Samaritan Enigma. We have an enigma in New Testament research. New Testament scholars consumed by the "new perspective on Paul" hardly have paid attention to the insistent blip on the radar of another "new perspective" coming up on the horizon. This trend is the new perspective on the Samaritans. We may have been just as obtuse to the historical Samaritans being Israelites as we have been to the historical Paul being a Jew. Major presuppositions need to be challenged.

How could Jesus even think to use a Samaritan as an example of fulfilling the law of Moses? Samaritans were considered so un-Jewish by southern Jews of the Jerusalem temple cult, they could insult Jesus with the "slander" that Jesus was a Samaritan, which obviously meant the polar opposite of truly Jewish and true worship of Yahweh. Being a Samaritan in this sense would insinuate that Jesus's religious door was wide open to paganism and its associated demonic forces (John 8:48). Was this Jewish picture of the Samaritans true? Probably not. If untrue, how did this image develop? The way all ethnic stereotypes do: deliberate reframing of historical reality to achieve tendentious religious and political agendas. Three myths about the Samaritans play into such agendas: paganization, Samaritan Pentateuch, ethnic purity.

That northern Jews completely paganized, and that their texts of Moses were untrustworthy sectarian perversions, and that Jews of the southern cultic center in Jerusalem were the *only* "Israelites" left to history after Assyrian destruction of the Northern Kingdom of Israel are all myths meticulously exposed by Pummer.[21] Each myth's sole purpose is to disenfranchise Samaritans as a legitimate Jewish group and to discredit their story as a legitimate expression of Jewish faith. In truth, the actual history of the Samaritans exposes the myth of their paganization. Again, actual study of the Samaritan Pentateuch reveals the myth of sectarian readings. Finally, carefully preserved Samaritan genealogies expose the myth of southern Israelites as the *only* ethnic Israelites.

The crucial myth is Samaritan paganization. Pummer argued that the famous passage in 2 Kings 17 has a more favorable reading than the one traditionally given that responsible exegesis must recognize. Interpretation as a statement of the paganization of northern Israel is a tendentious reading propagated by Jews of the Jerusalem cultus. In fact, the Hebrew text of 2 Kgs 17:24–41 admits of an alternative reading that undercuts pagan defamation.[22] Jerusalem temple Jews suppressed this alternate reading for purposes of rewriting "Jewish" history after Jerusalem Jews returned from exile. Such a "paganization" reading of the passage naturally facilitates the historical rewrite by the southern Jews of Judah after the exile as if endowed with canonical authority. The intent of the rewrite was to delegitimize the surviving Israelite population in the north and its competing sacred mountain, Gerizim. Pummer notes the irony that, historically, Gerizim has an even longer Jewish history behind its centrality as a Jewish worship center than does the cultic site in Jerusalem invented by David (Jacob vs. David).

Thus, seizing upon this tendentious reading of 2 Kings 17, southern Israelites literally wrote northern Israelites out of existence. They propagated the defamatory claim that the northern Jewish population was paganized so completely by the Assyrians that any semblance of Israelite identity in the north was lost irretrievably.

Historically, however, that "story" just is not true. Southern Jews compounded the effect of the historical rewrite by a subtle but powerful linguistic maneuver. They abrogated the northern term "Israel," formerly used exclusively of the Northern Kingdom, to apply exclu-

---

[21] Pummer, *The Samaritans: A Profile.*

[22] The issue is translation of the Hebrew term, הַשֹּׁמְרֹנִים, with specific ethnic value as "Samaritans" (RSV), or less specifically as simply "people of Samaria" (NRSV), which would not have to implicate northern Israelites. On the issue of "Samaritans" in the Hebrew Bible, see Pummer, *Samaritans*, 27–35.

sively to the Southern Kingdom of Judah returning from exile. Thus, the preexilic term, "kingdom of Judah," disappeared after the exile, which meant the "kingdom of Israel" was not your father's kingdom. Thus, "Israel" as referring to the reality of the Northern Kingdom of Israel simply ceased to exist in both public discourse and in literature. As Jews associated with the cultic center in the south eventually gained overwhelming political dominance after the exile, the usurpation of the Northern Kingdom name "Israel" was secured. "Israel" as reference to a northern Israelite kingdom magically "disappeared" from history.

This kingdom language sleight of hand coordinated perfectly as confirmation of the Southern Kingdom myth of Northern Kingdom paganization. This mythic historical rewrite by Jerusalem temple Jews of the fate of their northern brothers was compounded, for example, by historians such as Josephus, who perpetuated the defamation in his writings. Recent archeology has proven Josephus to be demonstrably wrong on numerous accounts about Samaritan history.[23] Christians uncritically dependent on Josephus sealed the deal by perpetuating the myth. In this way, Christians "canonized" the southern Jewish rewrite of northern Jewish history.[24]

To counter this historical myth, Pummer carefully documented a different social-religious history for the remnant Jews of northern Israel. The reality is, the surviving Samaritan enclave today still worshipping on Mount Gerizim does, in fact, legitimately represent the historical remnant of the Northern Kingdom of "Israel." Pummer pointed out that in many ways, ironically, Samaritans are even more strict in their interpretation of the law of Moses than Yahwist Jews of Jerusalem.[25]

---

[23] Josephus was wrong on multiple counts related to Samaritans, Gerizim, Shechem, and Samaria: (1) the Gerizim temple was constructed in the fifth century BC, *not* the fourth; (2) Shechem was *not* the capital of the Samaritans in the time of Alexander the Great (*Ant.* 11.304); (3) the Gerizim temple was *not* destroyed in 130 or 129 BC, but twenty years later in 110 BC (*J.W.* 1.62; *Ant.* 13.254).

[24] As in asserting northern tribes "had largely disappeared" and "dissolved among the various peoples" in Pitre, Barber, and Kincaid, *Paul, A New Covenant Jew*, 68, 69.

[25] Another irony is that the Jerusalem church, composed predominantly of southern Jews, never once initiated a gospel mission to reach Samaria. This passivity stands in stark contrast to the direct command of the risen Jesus explicitly designating just such a mission (Acts 1:8). Only *after* persecuted *Hellenist* believers made their own move to evangelize Samaria independently of Jerusalem was Jerusalem suddenly forced to take notice of Samaria only a few miles to the north. Even then, Jerusalem only begrud-

So what does "other sheep" mean in the Jesus tradition in the Gospels? We simply cannot exclude Samaritans. But, would Samaritan eschatology have prepared them to receive Jesus favorably as an eschatological figure? Likely, through their "prophet like Moses" tradition. A prophet like Moses was fundamental to Samaritan eschatology. This figure was called the Taheb, which means "the returning one." This figure is based on a promised prophet like Moses in Deut 18:18, who would explain fully all questions about the law and cult and worship so as to bring to an end the Age of Disfavor that engulfed Israel with Eli's cultic defection, in Samaritan view, from Shechem to Shiloh by arrogating to himself illegitimately the high priesthood of Uzzi. The prophet like Moses would straighten all this out and thereby bring the Age of Favor. The Samaritan eschatological figure, then, while not directly equated with Davidic messianic expectation, could be compatible with the preaching and teaching of Jesus, since he was received by some as a prophet (Mark 8:28).[26] The possibility of interpreting Jesus as the coming prophet of Samaritan eschatology is illustrated in the Samaritan woman's response, "Sir, I see that you are a prophet" (John 4:19). Jesus interpreted as the prophet like Moses had the potential to draw Samaritans into his circle. The Samaritan woman likely represents the "other sheep" of whom Jesus spoke, that is, *other* Israelites of the "lost sheep of the house of Israel" (Matt 10:6).

Likewise, the story in Acts 8 of the movement of Hellenist missionaries into Samaria is another indication of the place of Samaria in the advance of the gospel, which accords with the command of Jesus (Acts 1:8). As an integral part of this Hellenist movement, at least in Luke's portrayal, one could suppose Paul would not be unaware of Samaritan developments in the story of the advance of the gospel and their potential significance for the prophetic future of Israel. One might presume that Paul as a good southern Jew never would consider Samaritans qualified as "Israelites." Perhaps. Yet, given his openness to missionizing gentiles so much so that he was charged with not being Jewish enough by a Jerusalem mob who themselves appealed to fellow

gingly sent a delegation to "verify" the legitimacy of the Spirit already obviously at work in Samaria—as if the Spirit needed Jerusalem's validation before Samaritans could be considered "real" believers. See Stevens, *Acts*, 231–38.

[26] John translates the woman's titles from the Samaritan "Taheb" language into its messianic equivalents ("Messiah," "Christ," John 4:25). Why is not apparent.

Israelites (Acts 21:28), then the issue of the Samaritans may have had more favorable reception in Paul's thinking after his epiphany of messianic revelation than his heritage alone would suggest. Paul never directly addressed the matter of the Jewish status of Samaritans, so we are speculating, of course. Still, the matter should be considered as one of on-going historical and theological discussion.

Thus, drawing from the new perspective on Samaritans that is beginning to express itself in New Testament study, the question of the Samaritans—hardly mentioned at this point in the study of Romans— might should figure into the calculus of the meaning of "Israel." This issue at least should be entertained more seriously by Pauline scholars, especially in light of unfulfilled Hebrew prophecy that labored over reunification of two cultic camps of Israelites as integral to what the Messiah would accomplish. We could point out that Jesus did directly address the issue of the place of cultic worship in his response to the Samaritan woman when she brought up this core issue dividing Judean Israelites and Samaritan Israelites (John 4:19).

The Election Enigma. Jesus may have added one more layer to the complexity of the meaning of "Israel" in his teaching. He made a comment that is hard to figure as to whether meant as ironic for the sake of making a point almost humorously, or as a serious reflection on the nature of election and the character and power of God. He may have insinuated the character of election goes beyond biology in his remark about raising up children to Abraham from the stones lying around on the ground (Matt 3:9). If one recalls that not only was Abraham aged but his wife was both aged and barren, then, in fact, Isaac was created from stones to begin with, since Abraham and Sarah actually offered nothing physically, that is, on the "flesh" side of things. So, the possibility that Jesus may not have been speaking hyperbolically for rhetorical effect has to be considered. He may, instead, have been trying to provoke self-reflection on the meaning of a promise of God and how promise actually works. If so, Paul's comments on the matter of Abraham having a child of promise may have more Jesus tradition informing the thought than appears on first blush.

Election has to be ethnic or election cannot be shown working out in history. Anyone can claim to be elect, because everyone does. Ethnicity functions as a historical delimiter to the claim to be elect. If God calls a particular people as a nation among the nations to declare his

Name to the nations, this people as a group have to evidence and maintain a recognized, corporate existence or the purpose is aborted.[27] How
would one know Jesus was the Jewish Messiah if he was not Jewish?
Further, how could one say that Jesus is the fulfillment of 2 Sam 7:12–13
if he were not demonstrably of David's *seed*?[28] How could a promise of
God *based on progeny* be seen as fulfilled without any identifiable ethnic
markers in the subsequent generation claiming fulfillment?[29]

So election of a particular people as distinct from other peoples
by default is ethnic. When that group is governed by rules and regulations that establish cultural and religious behavior, then the basic ge-
netic base evolves with cultural and religious shape. Since ethnic clans
associate together, *ethnos* involves a geographical component that is
important in personal formation; person and land form a symbiotic
relationship crucial to developing personal identity.[30] Others by nature
not of that *ethnos* genetically, culturally, religiously, or regionally still
can incorporate into the group. Incorporation has to take place in ways
that maintain the ethnic integrity of the cultural and religious profile,
which often involves initiation rituals for this purpose. Here we have
the story of Ruth, the Moabite widow absorbed into an Israelite clan.[31]

Israel Language Summary. Thus, when we speak of "Israel," we
first have to balance a mix of both biological and national connota-
tions. We then have to contend with the enigma of the Samaritans, that
is, we simultaneously also have to adjudicate the complicated historical
question of who qualifies as Israelite. We finally have to contend with
the enigma of election. How do we balance existing election obligation
made by sovereign choice with the possibility of any future sovereign
choice? That is, what is the exegesis of "God is able from these stones
to raise up children to Abraham" when the God of whom we speak is
described as steadfast in love and faithfulness (Exod 34:6)?

---

[27] Exod 9:16; 19:3–6; Ezek 23:49; 39:7.

[28] Hence, the importance of the genealogies of Jesus in Matt 1:1–16 and Luke 3:23–
38. Their differences are more than exegetical curiosities. For discussion, cf. Fitzmyer,
The Birth of the Messiah, 89–99.

[29] Gen 15:5; 18:9–15; 22:17–18. Garroway's argument (*Paul's Gentile-Jews*, 60, 85)
that Paul makes believing gentiles ethnic Jews (Bhabha's "hybridity") is a non-starter.

[30] Leach, *Creative Land*, 31.

[31] Transformation details are embedded; Ruth 1:16–17; 2:1–2, 10–14; and 4:13.

Reflections on Jew Language

Another term also used with some multivalence like "Israel" is "Jew" ('Ιουδαῖος, *Ioudaios*), which also has patriarchal roots as a derivative of "Judah" ('Ιούδας, *Ioudas*), fourth son of Jacob (Israel) from his first wife, Leah.[32] Judah's lineage became the tribe of Judah,[33] and territory allotted to this tribe after the conquest of Canaan became the "land of Judah."[34] The twelve tribes coalesced into the kingdom of David, who innovated a move of the central worship center to his capital city of Jerusalem in his territory of Judah. Thus, the kingdom period saw the centralization of all Israelite cult and culture into the tribe of Judah, its worship center, and its territory. Inhabitants in this kingdom became "Judeans" politically and culturally. The Davidic kingdom split after Solomon into the Southern Kingdom of Judah and the Northern Kingdom of Israel. Assyria then destroyed Israel, which never afterwards regained political identity, but survived as a distinct group with Israelite identity and culture as the Samaritans. Babylon destroyed Judah. In contrast to the northern Israelites, southern Israelites regained political identity. At that point, the term "Jew" began to be used exclusively for these southern Israelites. Thus, the term "Jew," depending on context, could be ethnic for the Jewish people, geographical for the inhabitants of Jerusalem and surrounding territories, political for the authorities ruling in Jerusalem, religious for cultic and religious observance centralized in Jerusalem, or social for rejection of northern Israelites as Israelites by southern Israelites after the return from exile.

New Testament usage varies as well. The Synoptic Gospels have only seventeen occurrences, all by foreigners, often in the designation, "king of the Jews."[35] John is notable for use of the term, seventy times, usually for inhabitants of Judea and their distinctive politics, customs, and culture. In contrast, "Israel" is quite rare in John, only four times, all political and national in focus.[36] "Jew" in Acts is similar to John's use as a globalizing category, but applied to Diaspora Judaism.

[32] Gen 29:35; Matt 1:2.

[33] Judg 1:2; Mic 5:2; Heb 7:14; Rev 5:5.

[34] Josh 11:21; Matt 2:6.

[35] Matt 2:2; 27:11, 29, 37; 28:15 (narrator); Mark 1:5 (countryside); 7:3 (narrator); 15:2, 9, 12, 18; Luke 7:3 (elders of); 23:3, 37–38, 51.

[36] John 1:31, 49; 3:10; 12:13.

Paul's use is similar to John and Acts as a globalizing category, but Paul has a distinct rhetorical trait of synecdoche, that is, using singular number categorically for the entire group.[37] Paul's usage of "Jew" also has another distinction. His use of "Jew" often has narrow focus on law observance as a way of relating to God. While "Jew" for Paul can have an ethnic component in some contexts (Gal 2:15), other contexts do not require ethnicity as key to the essential element of law observance (Rom 2:17; 1 Cor 9:20). In these contexts, Paul could be talking about proselytes to Judaism, or even more generally to those simply attracted to the synagogue or, culturally, a Jewish lifestyle. Such contexts are not centered so directly on the issue of Israel and her destiny as a nation among the nations. "Israel," however, almost always circumscribes national destiny for Paul. Thus, "Jew" and "Israel" are not exact equivalents nor automatically synonymous in Paul.

Anguishing Israel (9:1–5)

Asseveration of Anguish (9:1–2)

Paul begins Romans 9–11 with an asseveration of anguish (**9:1–2**). We probably should take him at his word. That is, the language is not superficial rhetorical flourish to feign a point, since he makes such a fuss about the matter: (1) speaking the truth, (2) speaking the truth in the Messiah, (3) not lying, (4) conscience bearing witness, (5) conscience bearing witness in the Holy Spirit. Paul never swears something more forcefully in any other letter. The emotional load is peaking the meter. The point is important, because observing authorial rhetoric is crucial for interpreting Romans. We already have established that authorial *pathos* in Romans is *thematic*, that is, authorial *pathos* tracks directly parallel to questions of *Jewish identity*, and carries the full rhetorical burden of the theme statement, "for I am not ashamed" (1:16).[38] The depth of authorial *pathos* reaches its height here, which means we have reached the very heart of Paul's *ethos* development as author in the letter. By this feature alone we know that a matter crucial to Paul's

---

[37] A general rhetorical habit across the board for Paul ("to the Jew first, and also to the Greek," Rom 1:16). Compare Rom 10:12, "For whether Jew or Greek is no distinction," and 1 Cor 1:22, "For Jews demand signs and Greeks desire wisdom").

[38] See earlier discussion, pp. 51–56, and summary on p. 56.

purpose for Romans now comes on stage. Rhetorically considered, we have reached the final, climactic act of the first part of the letter.

Anguish over Kinfolk (9:3–5)

Over what in the world is Paul so anguished? Paul's topic is clear: "my own people . . . according to the flesh" (τῶν συγγενῶν μου κατὰ σάρκα, *tōn syngenōn mou kata sarka*, **9:3**). Paul condenses the target into one word, "which ones are Israelites" (Ἰσραηλῖται, *Israēlitai*, 9:4). Paul emphasizes his Hebrew lineage in 2 Cor 11:22: "Are they Hebrews? So am I! Are they Israelites? So am I! Are they the seed of Abraham? So am I!" Again, he states in Phil 3:5: "of the family of Israel, the tribe of Benjamin, a Hebrew of the Hebrews." Biology clearly is the point of reference in all these remarks, and biology is where the argument of Romans 9–11 starts. Romans is all about Israel, and Israel is all about ethnicity and nation, or no definition has any historical sense. Further, "Israelite" has as its semantic reason for existence specifically answering the question who is your father. Even more pertinently, paternity is all directed toward claiming God's covenant, which is the only reason for preserving the patriarchal story in the first place.[39] "Israelites" makes explicit a biological domain. This domain serves the rhetorical exigency. Paul with "Israelites" thrusts the larger issues of election and covenant instantly on the table. Thus, "Israel" as a covenanted nation among the nations is the topic inescapably.

What is the problem? Paul here does not say immediately but later acknowledges that the issue for him is that his fellow Israelites have stumbled over the gospel.[40] By this one should not think Paul is as much exercised over individual Israelites as he is about the Israelite nation as a whole missing the boat.[41] This stumbling seems to have become ever more problematic for Paul as his mission work expanded from province to province, and as he anticipated trying to push even further westward into Spain. By Paul's own self-admission here in Rom 9:1–5, Jewish rejection of the gospel is becoming a growing mission crisis for

---

[39] "Who are Israelites" renews the problem of the Samaritans previously discussed. Reunification of the tribes of Israel is a wild card in Hebrew prophecy. Pitre, Barber, and Kincade (*Paul, A New Covenant Jew*, 69) assert the prophecy is fulfilled, but only by making Samaritans gentiles—ignoring actual progeny, perpetuating Judean slander.

[40] Rom 9:32; 11:11.

[41] The grammar for "Israelites" is plural, which likely infers a more corporate focus.

Paul as an apostle that is entangled in existing Jewish messianic and identity crises to explode in war with Rome in less than a decade.

Paul is confronted with broad Jewish rejection of the gospel not only at the national level among leaders in Judea itself, but in almost every synagogue he attempts to reach across the Diaspora.[42] He probably finds hard contemplating that state continuing indefinitely. Not that he could not empathize with this spirit of rejection, since his own life was a premier example of the problem.[43] He may have contemplated, even hoped for, a revelatory event for his Jewish brethren as was made available personally to him, since he probably realized that that grace event was the only reason salvation broke through for him. His trigger was an epiphany on a journey; perhaps theirs would be an epiphany over jealousy.

Why not just shake the dust off his sandals and forget the Jews? They are being recalcitrant and obstinate, so they just need to lie in the bed they made. Paul has bigger fish to fry than that as a result of the Damascus Road. The Great Assembly traditions he had absorbed from his extensive Pharisaic training indicated in Phil 2:5 were exploded out of existence by the revelation of Messiah to him. This point is crucial hermeneutically. Under the spell of the Great Assembly myth about the authority of their traditions and their authority alone to speak for Moses, Paul's ability to contemplate the significance of the prophets for providing a profile of the Messiah and Israel's destiny in the world was diminished significantly. Paul likened the effect to having a veil over the face when trying to read Scripture that is unveiled by Messiah to contemplate the Lord's glory (2 Cor 3:12–18). The matter of Paul's revised hermeneutic of the Scripture is clear in Gal 1:12–14. Paul is clear his understanding of the gospel is a "revealed" knowledge, not a taught knowledge, as he had been taught Pharisee traditions formerly. His knowledge of the gospel is a revealed knowledge that transformed, even revolutionized from his point of view, the way he read Scripture.[44] Since these Great Assembly traditions of his former training demoted the authority of the prophets, then one severe deficiency Paul had was

---

[42] Receiving the synagogue lash five times is silent testimony to the struggle (2 Cor 11:24). Luke, unfortunately, does not document any cases.

[43] Acts 8:3; 9:1–2; 22:3–4; 26:9–11; 1 Cor 15:9; Phil 3:5–6.

[44] One can compare a similar thought pattern in Eph 3:9.

in understanding the role of the prophets to speak to Moses. The Great Assembly made the prophets subservient to their take on Moses when the prophets clearly critiqued the nation's inability to be faithful to the law.[45] This demotion of the authority of the prophets meant that Paul missed some important insights from the prophet Isaiah, particularly about Israel's destiny to bring about the confession of God as a nation among the nations. Allowing the authority of the prophets to speak to Moses allowed more focus on Isaiah's eschatological vision for Israel.[46]

Paul cannot forget the Jews because through Isaiah he has come to a worldview understanding of Israel *as a nation* to be central to the destiny of the other nations of the world by God's design. So, he has intent on moving that plan forward not by indiscriminately going to gentiles haphazardly, any gentile anywhere will do, but by going to the *nations*, and particularly those barbarian regions on the outer fringes of the empire.[47] He also understands, however, that this divine design can be effected *only* through the Messiah, but also as working *in* Israel and *through* Israel, not in spite of Israel. Given Israel's present state of unbelief and rejection of Messiah that haunts Paul's mission, he wrote in a moment of extreme vulnerability and transparency, "I have great sorrow and unrelenting anguish in my heart" (9:2). Something is not working, and Paul's spirit truly is vexed over the conundrum.[48]

[45] See discussion, pp. 96–97.

[46] "Jesus fired the thrusters to catapult Paul out of the centripetal force and closed loop of the Great Assembly hermeneutic," p. 107. We should note that Paul was not the only charismatic figure in Judea inspired by Isaiah. The Teacher of Righteousness at Qumran wrote his beautiful *Thanksgiving Hymns*, a series of personal devotions, while mediating on Isaiah. In doing so, he coined the phrase, "the way of God's heart," that became a dominant mode of expression for his community, which emphasizes the difference between performing Moses and living Moses. Paul likely has similar thought in the way he discusses law performance in Romans 2. Of course, the theme is hinted in Moses (Deut 30:6, 10; 32:46) and in the prophets (Jer 31:33; 32:39–40). See similar points, p. 111 and note 39.

[47] Why he expresses his indebtedness explicitly as "Greeks and *barbarians*" (1:14). Other missions perhaps are not aggressively targeting this mission strategy toward the nations, in spite of Matt 28:19. This strategy targeting nations might be the gist of how Paul conceives he fulfills not preaching on another's foundation (Rom 15:20).

[48] The extraordinary nature of Romans 9–11 almost leaves the impression that the process of writing the letter functioned in part as catharsis through this mission crisis that inspired this theological and eschatological synthesis regarding God and Israel. We see nothing else even close in emotional intensity and conceptual complexity in

"I myself could long to be anathema from Messiah on behalf of my kinfolk" (**9:3**).[49] Paul is doubly emphatic in Greek, combining both the personal and emphatic pronoun, "I *myself*" (αὐτὸς ἐγὼ, *autos egō*). His serious and intense rhetoric continues unabated. The core sense of "anathema" (ἀνάθεμα, *anathema*) is "that which is devoted to God," which could be positive or negative. The positive sense is used in the description of the beautiful stones and gifts that adorned the temple (Luke 21:5). The negative sense is devoted to God "for destruction," so had the derivative idea of "accursed" (Deut 7:26). This statement is extraordinary in two ways. First, Paul invokes the deepest spirit of self-sacrifice. Often mentioned is Jewish martyrdom ideology, and a case from Roman military history is interesting for its direct connection to expiation of divine wrath.[50] Paul, however, is not thinking expiation. Paul fully is aware that Jesus is the atonement (3:21–26), so this anathema expression is not expiatory in tone.[51] While Paul does say "*from* Messiah," which carries a note of separation, we cannot presume final judgment. Further, whatever is contemplated abstractly here simply cannot be proposing a more efficacious substitute for the atoning death of Messiah—not in the face of all of Romans 1–8.

A more likely Pauline thought here with "anathema from Messiah" is not expiatory but conciliatory (11:28). Paul so desires Israel's salvation he would sacrifice heart, body, and soul to conciliate fellow Israelites to God, even if he himself were destroyed in the process. (In fact, he was destroyed in the process.) Following the Messiah for Paul involves adopting the mind of Messiah (Phil 2:5; 1 Cor 2:16). Having this mind means in ministry suffering "brand marks" that conjure Jesus's own passion (Gal 6:17). Being "in Messiah" for Paul is significantly more than quiet time devotionals. Jesus in facing the cross had to anticipate and endure the deepest suffering on behalf of God's people (Luke 22:44), and Paul seriously tries to contemplate and absorb that type of devotion and self-sacrifice on behalf of the gospel of God, per-

---

any other letter of Paul, hard to parse. Exegesis of Romans 9–11 is more of a mystery than the mystery Paul thought he revealed (hardening as partial and temporary).

[49] The verb "I could long" (ηὐχόμην, *ēuchomēn*), rendered here like a contingency mood, is notoriously hard to translate into English. Its imperfect indicative grammar has to be morphed to express the contextual sense of prayer-like wish.

[50] See discussion, p. 310.

[51] In terms of relationship of 3:21–26 to divine wrath, see pp. 309–11.

haps even to the point one would cry out, "My God, my God, why have you forsaken me?"[52]

Second, the anathema expression is extraordinary for its context, that is, this separation from Messiah comes right on the heels of the overwhelming conviction and testimony that nothing can separate from God's love in Messiah (8:38–39). The thought is staggering. We could reject the sincerity and claim lack of integrity, or we could say we have here the very core of Pauline mission. Paul is not so much apostle to the gentiles as the exclusive point of his call, even though he can self-describe his ministry as directed to gentiles (11:13). Paul is apostle to Israel. He is set apart to the gospel of God (1:1), which, we must not forget, he immediately characterizes as "promised beforehand through his prophets in the Holy Scriptures—concerning his Son, Jesus Messiah our Lord, who was a descendant of David" (1:2–3). All this language is clear: *That gospel has Israel at its heart.* Paul frames his gentile mission as working for the salvation of Israel. We cannot rush by this verse as if a trivia question of no import in a board game. Romans 9:3 makes clear the generative theological center of Pauline mission. That center is Israel, from Jerusalem arching through Illyricum past Italy on to Spain (15:19). All those footsteps are on behalf of Israel.

First Set	Second Set
1. **adoption** (Sinai: nation building; cf. 8:15–17)	1. **Torah** (Sinai: national covenant obligations)
2. **glory** (Shekinah, divine presence: fire, cloud)	2. **temple** (divine presence, purified worship)
3. **covenants** (Abraham, Moses, David)	3. **promises** (especially Abrahamic)
4. **ancestors** (patriarchs = national destiny)	4. **Messiah** (national destiny realized)

FIGURE 9.4. Jewish Privileges in Parallel Sets. In Rom 9:4–5 Paul outlines Jewish privileges in two parallel sets that figure into the saga of God and Israel.

Paul hammers home the focus on Israel as a lineage and a legacy in **9:4–5**. He uses catchwords in parallel sets to summarize the saga. Paul starts with lineage by using the term "Israelites." These are the descendants of Jacob. Their legacy was to become a nation. But exactly how did they become a nation among the nations? This epic is the story of Moses, pharaoh, Passover, exodus, and Sinai. Paul innovates on this epic with a word unique to him in the New Testament.

---

[52] Matt 27:46; Mark 15:34.

Paul innovates with his unique term "adoption" applied to the standard Jewish term "Israelites"—not typical Jewish terminology for election. Paul likely surprises the Jewish reader by insisting that adoption into the people of God is not exclusive to gentiles (8:15). Paul has spoken this way before about those under the law (Gal 4:5).[53] To be sure, the exodus is God's election of a nation.[54] Yet, for Paul, the exodus also is God's adoption agency at work. As Paul soon will make clear, divine election is the essence of mercy, the evidence of prevenient grace. To be an "Israelite" is to be adopted by God by grace, and grace will be required all the way to the end of the story. The flip side of the human element of "from faith to faith" (1:17) is the divine element from grace to grace, as Paul forms the story here in Romans 9.

To Israel is the adoption also because Israel carries the promise of resurrection, accomplished through the Messiah. Resurrection is an eschatological event related to the final judgment. Important here to remember, though, is that resurrection in Paul's thought is another phase of God's adoption process (8:23). Through the promise of resurrection effected though Israel, God is moving all humanity towards his goal of consummating all creative purposes from the beginning.

Thus, "adoption" is Paul's own unique way of speaking of how God worked with both Abraham and Moses toward the grand plan of the ages to consummate creation. Through election, God adopted a family in Abraham and then adopted a nation in Moses. God always has worked by adoption in the saga of Israel.

"Glory" is the Shekinah divine presence. In the exodus story, the divine presence is the night and day guidance in fire and cloud. "Covenants" are the three critical stages of Jewish history keyed on the figures of Abraham, Moses, and David. Abraham sets up Israel. Moses sets up Mosaic Israel. David sets up messianic Israel. "Ancestors" trace that story through history. These ancestors begin with the patriarchs, whose progeny define Israel and constitute national destiny.

The next set is parallel. "Torah" is a restatement of adoption, the covenant obligations of nation building from the family of Abraham. "Temple" is the localized divine presence of Shekinah glory in Israel

---

[53] Indeed, Paul is unique in the New Testament in his use of this term: Rom 8:15, 23; 9:4; Gal 4:5; Eph 1:5; so, the point is pure Pauline orange juice, fresh squeezed.

[54] Exod 19:6; Deut 7:6; 14:1.

through purified worship after wilderness wanderings. "Promises," with premier focus on Abraham, is restatement of the covenants motif, but with sharper focus on a prevenient grace as the ground of all of God's dealings with Israel. "Messiah" is the national destiny of the ancestors realized. Messiah fulfills Israel's purpose as a nation among the nations.

In this way by using these parallel sets of terms, Paul makes clear he is talking about the Israel everyone knows and recognizes. By using adoption language, however, he also has signaled he has a different way of framing the saga of Israel. Fundamental to that saga is the doctrine of election. Paul must clarify how election works in the story of Israel from his perspective. This clarification will confront and challenge the traditions of the Great Assembly propagated by synagogues around the world, for whom Israel was by birth inherited and by law retained. A vision of Messiah reformulated for Paul how God's election is another way of speaking of God's adoption and grace in every generation.

Clarifying Election (9:6–13)

Paul uses the first two generations after Abraham in the patriarchal story to define how election works in every generation of Israel. He first defines Israel in Isaac (9:6–9). He then defines Israel in Jacob (9:10–13).

Paul invokes a simple statement of observation in **9:6**: Not all out of "Israel" (Jacob) are "Israel" (heirs). This statement sets up the general principle of how Israel always has worked. Three crucial factors must be kept in mind. First, Paul presumes lineage is integral to the meaning of Israel. He is talking about progeny, so inescapably he is dealing with seed. Second, though speaking of Jacob ("Israel"), the principle he invokes applies retroactively to the first generation. Third, the principle applies to every subsequent generation after Jacob as well. What is the principle?

Legal heirship is not how "Israel" ever has worked. In the first generation of Abraham, the firstborn was Ishmael, who should have been heir. God chose otherwise (**9:6–9**). In the second generation of Jacob, the firstborn was Esau, who should have been heir. God chose otherwise (**9:10–13**). Even within the arena of progeny, then, *God's choice is what makes heirship in Israel.* If God says so, what the law says simply does not count. Election never has been a legality or a generational right of passage by birth alone. Election always has been by God's choice—in every generation from the first forward. In this way, from the beginning, "Israel" always has been a remnant of the seed. Thus, "Israel" has two constituent conditions to its definition. Israel is God's prevenient promise (Abraham) subsequently shaped by God's gracious choice in each generation (Isaac and Jacob). Thus, even assuming the arena of progeny, "Israel" is defined as promise plus grace. Birth means nothing without a prior promise that involves understanding the design and purposes of God in making that promise, and law fundamentally is impotent to supersede grace. Thus, election may involve progeny, but that progeny is circumscribed by the dynamic of promise plus grace in every generation.

But what constitutes progeny? Traditionally, progeny would be defined biologically. However, progeny as biology cannot be applied exclusively. How would Abraham have been included into the family in the first place if biology were the exclusive condition? The entire line started by God's adoption, thereafter perpetuated by God himself by another act of grace through his promise of a son in Isaac. Without the promise of a son, Abraham had no family through Sarah. In these terms, God created Abraham's family by a miracle of grace in Sarah's womb; Abraham did not. So, as at the beginning, God can adopt into the existing lineage whomever he so chooses, and he perpetuates that lineage as an act of grace to fulfill a promise, even as he did originally with Abraham "our forefather" (4:1). Israel is indeed progeny, but that progeny is perpetuated only by prevenient promise and grace. Further, the shape of that family always is God's to define in his sovereignty by an act of his grace in any generation. Thus, Israel in any given generation never is by birth alone inherited nor by law retained.

Defending God (9:14–24)

Appealing to Moses (9:14–18)

Paul anticipates the "not fair" gambit. The charge is that his definition of "Israel" as "promise plus grace" acting within the arena of progeny impugns the character of God as "not fair," which instantly places God in the docket for being unrighteous, which, in covenant terms, means not keeping his side of the bargain. This charge is because the electing choice of Jacob over Esau before birth by default could have nothing to do with performance. The patriarchal story flies in the face of Jewish tradition that framed election as deserved by inherent excellence of character (which should infer Jacob was going to be such a good boy; ironic, since the actual story is of a swindler and a cheat). Alternatively, Jewish tradition could point to anticipated punctilious performance of obligations as the reason for election, which was the standard interpretation of Abraham's declaration of righteousness in Gen 15:6.[55]

Paul exposes the objection directly in **9:14**, "Is there unrighteousness with God?" Paul responds with his characteristic μὴ γένοιτο, *mē genoito*, "Absolutely not!"[56] He counters with the testimony of Moses himself, which is his only option in the context of a Jewish objection in a Jewish discussion (**9:14–18**). Paul basically is appealing to Mosaic Israel to "hear" Moses once again, but with non-synagogue ears. Paul invokes one of the most famous passages in the exodus narrative offering insight into the divine character: "I will have mercy on whom I will have mercy" (Exod 33:19). God said this to Moses as Moses appealed to God to show himself to Moses. Instead of showing himself directly to Moses, which Moses could not have endured, God agreed to reveal himself only partially, and instead emphasized who he was in his character, not what he looked like in his countenance. God emphasized his character, because that is what Israel most needed at that moment in her history. Moses already had destroyed the tablets of the law when he encountered the golden calf idolatry of the people after coming down from the mountain (Exod 32:19). God could have walked away from this rebellious, bull-headed people, but he chose to stay, and Moses learned thereby that the most important reality about God in terms of his relationship to humans is not his countenance but his character. He is merciful. Otherwise, Israel had no hope and no future. God chose to redo the tablets. He chose to be merciful, even upon an ungodly and unrighteous people suppressing the truth of God in their unrighteous and ungrateful behavior toward the God who only shortly before had redeemed them from slavery and slaughter.

---

[55] Abraham being declared righteous in Gen 15:6 because his willingness to sacrifice Isaac later in his life in Genesis 22 already was known and calculated into that earlier declaration by God. Abraham's law-keeping, thus, was credited in advance to him before he ever did the work. Abraham "pre-earned" his declaration of righteousness. He already had his own layaway payment plan going in his righteousness bank account.

[56] See p. 287, note 35.

In regard to this exodus saga, Paul pointed out that Scripture informed Pharaoh, "For this reason I raised you up so that I might show by you my power and so that I might proclaim my Name in all the earth" (**9:17**).[57] God uses even his own enemies to further his own designs. God's power was on full display in the exodus saga, whether this Pharaoh was sitting majestically on his throne or riding menacingly in his chariot. So even hardening has divine purpose, and God hardens whomever he chooses (9:18).

Accountability Objection (9:19–24)

By acknowledging God's hardening of Pharaoh, Paul appears to have dug his hole only deeper in attempting to defend God, but he knows exactly what he is doing. He is heading for the denouement of the argument in the hardening of Israel as the ultimate expression of divine mercy for the world, a mirror-reverse image of Pharaoh and Israel. The appearance of raw injustice in the argument, however, cannot be avoided. If God hardens by his own sovereign choice, capriciousness reigns, and human accountability is out the window.

Paul in his response in 9:19–24 pretty much has the attitude of the narrator of the book of Job. We can point to the "Who has become his counselor?" rhetorical question in the concluding praise in 11:34 often taken as probable allusion to Job 41:11. This part of Job is Yahweh's speech declaring his sovereignty over all creation. Brute reality is, humans never have gotten anywhere trying to put God on trial. You can ask God questions demanding answers all day long and gain nothing for your trouble. God just does not work that way. Paul acquiesces to that reality. At the same time, Paul can spot a ruse too, so he does.

"You will say to me, therefore: 'Why does he still find fault? For who has resisted his will?'" (**9:19**)—another way of saying, "Don't blame me; God made me do it!" Paul's diatribe response in **9:20**, "O Man" (ὦ ἄνθρωπε, ō anthrōpe), rhetorically signals we are back to Rom 2:1 in a parallel rhetoric of "O Man."[58] That unit, "Covenant Unrighteousness (2:1—3:8)," was subdivided into "Election Illusion (2:1–11)." In other

[57] Quoting Exod 9:16, but not following any known textual tradition. As Dunn suggested, Paul worked the ambiguous Hebrew to his advantage (*Romans 9–16*, 563).

[58] In fact, four of the five uses of ō anthrōpe in the New Testament are Pauline, three of these in Romans alone (Rom 2:1, 3; 9:20; 1 Tim 6:11; Jas 2:20).

words, the discussion in Rom 2:1 had turned decidedly to Jewish critique. In Romans, Paul uses the rhetoric "O Man" to address the Jew. He employs this rhetorical move intentionally to level the Jew onto the same playing field as the original *anthrōpos* in Rom 1:18 who is suppressing the truth of God in unrighteousness.[59] Thus, "O Man" in Romans is the Jew as *anthrōpos* still living in the forces of the Old Aeon of Adam seeking any excuse for sin in the vain attempt to evade God's wrath. The only person who would make such an objection is one in the grip of evil, knowing guilt, desperate for any wiggle room at the judgment. That person has no real objection. They are only excuse baiting. Someone who had experienced the grace of God in Messiah would not be looking for excuses.

Paul exposes this ruse of Mosaic Israel confronted by the gospel of God. The person who "talks back" (ὁ ἀνταποκρινόμενος, *ho antapokrinomenos*) to God in this way with such a specious objection lives in election illusion. That is, presuming election is by birth inherited and by law retained includes the presumption God has no right to harden anyone he has elected. Conceived this way, election doctrine is perverted into a false guarantee of herd immunity, inoculation from judgment. This thought of election as inoculation deluded Israel before the judgment of exile. How this attitude could have revived in postexilic Israel in the light of the reality of the exile is a mystery. Election never has eliminated accountability in judgment.

Not only Israel's own history, but contemplating Pharaoh also explodes this myth of divine hardening as exclusion from responsibility and accountability. If God has hardened Pharaoh, he has done so not violating Pharaoh's own accountability for his actions. That is, Pharaoh *already* had rejected the word of God through Moses to let God's people go. You cannot violate a direct command from a sovereign God with impunity. God's hardening Pharaoh is simply simmering Pharaoh in his own stew. That is how God's wrath works (1:18–32). God "delivers over" to the reality of the consequences of rejection of God, whose end is death (1:32). The consequences for Pharaoh were that dramatic, not only the death of all Egyptian firstborn, but even his own death and that of all his elite soldiers drowned in the sea.

---

[59] On the importance of maintaining gender in the translation, "O Man" to perceive the logical connection between Rom 2:1 and Rom 1:18, see discussion, pp. 275–76.

FIGURE 9.5. Roman Potter's Wheel. Replica as in multiple artisan production shops. Rotary motion allows symmetrical curving of objects. A vertical axle connects a smaller top disk to a larger bottom disk. An amorphous lump of wet clay on the top surface is shaped with the hands and wooden mold forms (hanging on nails at the top). The potter sat on the angled bench seat and rotated the larger disk at the bottom with his feet. The larger disk was naturally heavier, sometimes having added weight, to utilize a flywheel principle to conserve rotational energy to counterbalance the weight of the clay the potter was manipulating on the top wheel. Animal fat applied on the axle helped reduce the high friction coefficient for smoother spinning (HMM).

FIGURE 9.6. Roman Pottery Storage Vessel. A typical example of a storage jar for various purposes that did not require an enclosed top or lid for the contents. This vessel was turned on a potter's wheel to create the grooved edges in the side and has fairly consistent shape. The decoration on the side, however, lacks the requisite symmetry and is rather simple and rudimentary (BMB).

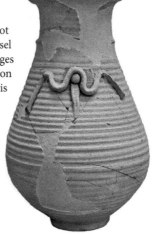

FIGURE 9.7. Roman Pottery Drinking Cup. An exquisite example of first-century Roman pottery found in ancient Corinth with ingenious applique of grape vine and grape clusters in high relief and accurate detail surrounding the body of this wine drinking vessel with curved handle evoking a branch. A beautiful piece of consummate artistic skill on the part of this Corinthian craftsman (AMAC).

Paul then gives an example building on the natural roles of former and formed, of potter and clay (**9:20–21**). Even though they both derive from the same lump of clay, one potter's piece has mundane use (dishonorable) and another exquisite use (honorable). The use is decided solely by the potter forming the clay for whatever intended purpose. The craftsmen of Corinth were renowned for their bronze and pottery manufacturing, a likely source of firsthand knowledge by Paul that he could be reflecting as he wrote the letter of Romans from Corinth.

Paul assigns God the role of the potter, but he immediately adds, however, a new and unexpected twist—divine wrath (**9:22–24**). Who was talking about divine wrath? Paul was. All along. This addition reveals that Paul has been thinking of the wrath of God throughout the entire discussion of Israel, indeed, throughout all of Romans, because Israel is enduring the wrath of God. Paul is back to the dramatic beginning of Romans, the wrath of God presently revealed. This wrath is divine response to both creature unrighteousness (Romans 1) and covenant unrighteousness (Romans 2) that concludes with a statement on summary unrighteousness (Romans 3). Paul is consummating the entire thrust of Romans to this point: confrontation of Mosaic Israel in its dire predicament in persistently rejecting Messiah. He is restating Mosaic Israel's present gospel conundrum. Can God handle that, or was he caught by surprise? Does God have a plan?

Paul insists God has a plan. Here is where Paul leaves the analogy of the potter, whose work is, in fact, arbitrary, and why many, misunderstanding the point, balk at the analogy. Analogies pressed too hard break down, this one particularly. In the real pottery world, an object once made forever has that design and purpose. Dishonorable objects by definition naturally do not transform into honorable objects. Who would use a chamber pot for a drinking vessel at a feast? Right. Paul's application, however, is *transformational*. Objects of wrath made for destruction *can transform* into objects of mercy. Paul's potter analogy of its own contemplates no such transformation. Yet, the possibility of transformation sustains Paul's hope for Mosaic Israel. He believes his own story of incorporation into messianic Israel can be Mosaic Israel's story corporately ("even us, whom he called," **9:24**).

Possibility of transformation that in itself transforms the potter analogy means Paul has the essence of the analysis of Rom 7:7–24 back in view. Vessels of wrath made for destruction would be Mosaic Israel rebelling against the gospel of God. Vessels of mercy made for glory also would be messianic Israel receiving by faith the gospel of God. So, in the definition of Israel as promise plus grace, what the potter now is doing is executing on another prevenient promise of a Son (Messiah) subsequently shaped by God's gracious choice in this new generation to continue adopting children by grace (justification) into his eschatological family of the New Aeon, who otherwise could not be counted as progeny. Jews who have the right lineage but lost their inheritance by rebellion also have to be reincorporated as anyone else by adoption. Without faith in Jesus Messiah, they are vessels of wrath. Fortunately, God is defined by his mercy, so he chooses mercifully to adopt those of Israel (Jacob) who are not Israel (heirs). This family has biological continuity, but that biology in itself is not what constitutes belonging. Belonging to the people of God requires divine adoption. Adoption, unique to Paul in the New Testament, is essential Pauline soteriology. Messiah's eschatological Israel includes adopted Jews, such as Paul, and adopted gentiles, such as believers in Rome (**9:24**).[60]

Confirming Scripture (9:25–29)

Hosea: Israel as Expanded (9:25–26)

The prophets confirm this definition of Israel, which includes the two fundamental ideas of expansion (Hosea) and remnant (Isaiah). Once again, Paul fulfills his promise to show how the gospel was promised beforehand through the prophets in the Scripture (1:2).

Hosea had declared that the "not my people" would become "my people" and the "unloved," "loved" (Hos 1:10; 2:23). Love language in this context, of course, is God's special and sustaining covenant love for his people. This language is exclusive to God's people, so not used of others. Paul using the language of divine love for gentile believers at the beginning of Romans has this nuance (1:7), which, of course, would have been quite controversial within the synagogue.

Hosea's original application was to the ten tribes of the Northern Kingdom of Israel. Those rejected can be reinstated. The historical trail

---

[60] We suddenly thrust into the discussion a word that has been *entirely* absent since its last occurrence in the unit on Abraham in Rom 4:17: "gentiles" (ἔθνη, *ethnē*). Paul drops the term in 9:24 in preparation to shift gears into a new unit beginning in 9:30.

of these ten tribes resides in the Samaritans, and in the first century, Samaritans were despised among many southern Jews even more than gentiles. If a prophet could anticipate a northern Israelite (in current contemplation, now a Samaritan) being reincorporated into the covenanted community, surely gentiles just should not be that much of a stretch for a southern Jew to contemplate. Thus, Paul's application to messianic Israel's gentiles is a legitimate extension in the first-century context of the prophet's word of restoration. After all, God made Adam before he made Israel. Surely he has some intention there. Thus, the "my people" of Sinai covenant fame always have had a prophetic anticipation of expansion.[61] The point is, those rejected can be reinstated, whether rebellious Northern Kingdom inhabitants in the days of Hosea, or rebellious gentiles in the days of Messiah, or even rebellious Mosaic Israel. God anticipated Jewish rebellion against his Messiah, no less than the initial rebellion against even Moses.[62] God peremptorily made a way around current rebellion, Jew or gentile, through faith and the justifying of the ungodly.

Isaiah: Israel as Remnant (9:27–29)

The second fundamental idea included in a definition of Israel derived from the prophets is Isaiah's remnant theology. In the face of the devastating destruction of God's judgment, is Israel history? Once again, a prophetic word to the Northern Kingdom eerily now seems to prefigure Mosaic Israel in Paul's day.

Isaiah's prophecy in Isa 10:22 quoted in **9:27**, like Hosea's word, also was addressed to the Northern Kingdom in the same context of imminent destruction by the Assyrians. Isaiah announced that even if the number of the "sons of Israel" (τῶν υἱῶν Ἰσραὴλ, *tōn huiōn Israēl*) were as the sand of the sea, "the remnant will be saved" (τὸ ὑπόλειμμα σωθήσεται, *to hypoleimma sōthēsetai*). Reference to the sand of the sea seems to point to fulfillment of God's promise to Abraham about his progeny.[63] The crucial point is, God already has been faithful to fulfill his promise to Abraham. So, doing anything else at this point is grace

---

[61] Exod 3:7, 10; 6:7.

[62] Acts 7:35; cf. Exod 2:14.

[63] Gen 22:17; cf. Gen 32:12; Hos 1:10.

going unexpectedly beyond the promise. Providing a remnant is a new word of promise that goes beyond the patriarchal promise.

The quoted next verse of Isa 10:23 in **9:28** is difficult to translate and, thus, difficult to understand: "For the Lord will execute [finishing] and [shortening] (his) word on the land." That God would execute his sentence of judgment ("word," λόγον, *logon*) throughout the land of Israel (Northern Kingdom) is clear enough. That idea makes clear the devastating effect Assyria will have. The entire Northern Kingdom will be destroyed, no territory or village spared.[64] The meaning of the participles (given in brackets), however, is not clear.[65] Perhaps the idea is that God in this judgment will act "quickly and decisively."[66] However, the implication of that thought of swift and decisive judgment when applied to the present status of the Jewish nation in general rebellion against the gospel is not a happy one. While we cannot be sure due to the admitted ambiguity of specific translation and meaning, if that dilemma of impending judgment but shortening of time is what Paul contemplated, then the statement of anguish that opens this unit on Israel in 9:1–5 tells an even more acutely and urgently felt crisis than typically considered.

Paul's last in this series of quotations is Isa 1:9 in **9:29**. He turns to the prophet again for reflection on the remnant. Without the remnant, Isaiah ironically observed, the result for Israel would be no better than the dramatic Sodom and Gomorrah saga in Genesis 18–19. The allusion is appropriate. This story of total and permanent destruction of these paired pagan cities out of historical existence also has a remnant preserved by God in Lot and his family. The irony is the judgment is what these pagans received for sins so grave as to attract God's direct attention in heaven (Gen 18:20). Abraham pled with God, and God finally relented if only ten righteous could be found not to destroy the

---

[64] Often invading armies focused on siege of the large, armed citadels of a country, and left small villages alone as of no account, unless the intent was for revenge.

[65] If anarthrous adjectives, they both would modify the noun, "word." If adverbial, they would modify the verb, "execute." Neither option provides entirely clear thought. They also conceptually could connect to the patriarchal promise itself, so, the idea of "finishing" would be allusion to God's fulfilling his promise to Abraham, and "shortening" would be allusion to the reality of only a remnant left out of that promise. That option, however, is a logical stretch for the given grammar.

[66] The typical option seen in most modern English translations; cf. NIV, NRSV, etc.

city, since Abraham's nephew, Lot, and his family lived there. That the city was destroyed meant not even ten were found. Notably, Isaiah now characterizes Israel as in no better condition than godless Sodom and Gomorrah. Paul by deduction sees Isaiah's warning in Isaiah's day as even more pertinent to Mosaic Israel in Paul's day. Sin could not pile up to heaven any higher than crucifying the Lord of glory (1 Cor 2:8).

Paul's presentation has worked to refocus Israel's story from the perspective of Messiah. What he has said also can be summarized in the inverse from the perspective of Mosaic Israel.

- Rom 9:1–5:   Mosaic Israel causes Paul extreme anguish
- Rom 9:6–13:   Mosaic Israel has misunderstood God's Israel
- Rom 9:14–18: Mosaic Israel has misunderstood God's purposes
- Rom 9:19–24: Mosaic Israel is still accountable to God's Messiah
- Rom 9:25–29: Mosaic Israel has a future hope in God's grace

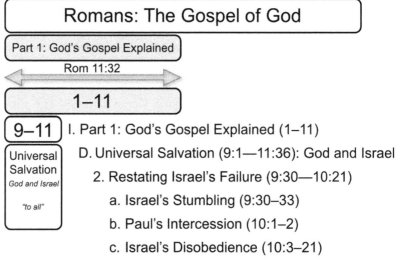

FIGURE 9.8. Outline: Romans 10 (Israel's Failure). After refocusing Israel's story, Paul next moves to restate Israel's failure to respond properly to the coming of Messiah.

RESTATING ISRAEL'S FAILURE (9:30—10:21)

Paul has refocused Israel's story by revisiting the patriarchal saga to establish Israel's identity as revealed in God's actions in each generation. The story is traced within a seed, but God's adoption is crucial, secured by prevenient promise and maintained by grace—in each generation. Without God's sovereign adoption, promise, and grace, Israel never existed and does not exist. More importantly, by definition, God is free to adopt whomever he chooses to be his children in any given generation. In doing so, however, he will not fail to keep his promises. While he will be just and righteous in all his actions, he also will give mercy a preeminent role in how he chooses to behave toward all humans, in the family or not in the family. As a result, he inherently always is seeking to transform the "not my people" into "my people," and "my people" do best whenever they comprehend that divine penchant. Otherwise, "my people" will stumble. Paul now restates Israel's failure.

Israel's Stumbling (9:30–33)

A faulty chapter division unhelpfully obscures that the argument turns at **9:30** to a new progression in the thought. Not only do we have the rhetorical question that signals a transition, we also have a new term strategically dropped recently in 9:24 to prepare for this transition that now becomes the center of attention: "gentiles" (ἔθνη, *ethnē*). Logically and rhetorically, Rom 9:30 should be the beginning of Romans 10.

The new thought is Israel's failure through stumbling. The irony of what is going on after arrival of Messiah should strike anyone: Those not seeking obtain; those seeking fail to obtain. Paul first takes up the case of gentiles. They did not pursue righteousness—pretty obvious, for example, in the story of Noah and the flood, Sodom and Gomorrah, or worship of Molech with its child sacrifice in fire.[67] Yet, they obtained the righteousness which is by faith when they put their faith in Messiah as God now requires in the New Aeon (9:30).

In contrast, Israel pursued righteousness through the law ("the law of righteousness"). Yet, Israel did not reach law's goal of righteousness (i.e., "unto law not obtaining," εἰς νόμον οὐκ ἔφθασεν, *eis nomon ouk ephthasen*, **9:31**). One particularly can see this failure illustrated in the kingdom period in kings such as Ahaz and Manasseh.[68] After the exile, the Hasmonean dynasty blazed no trail of righteousness, in spite of the initial Pharisaic enthusiasm for the rule as represented in the attitudes prevalent in 1 Maccabees. Herod the Great, of course, the following

---

[67] Genesis 6–9; Genesis 18–19; Lev 18:21; 2 Kgs 16:3; 21:6; 23:10.

[68] 2 Kgs 16:3; 21:6.

dynasty in Judea, was notoriously cruel even to his own family, and figures infamously into a nativity story on the birth of Jesus.[69] Scribes, Pharisees, and Sadducees themselves plotted how to murder Jesus and found their opportunity one Passover.

Paul asks, "For what reason?" in **9:32**. He responds because faith was eliminated out of the equation. They pursued ritual performance ("out of works") without concern for right heart. We have circled back to Rom 2:17–29. Paul's contemporary, Josephus, claimed Jews worldwide performed the law uniformly and completely, a view Saul of Tarsus also espoused for himself.[70] Pursuing this way, however, Mosaic Israel "stumbled over the stone of stumbling," fulfilling Scripture.

Isaiah had seen in the Assyrian crisis both houses of Israel would face God's judgment, but God by his grace would provide a remnant. The remnant would survive by its unwavering faith in God. That faith metaphorically would function like a foundation stone in a city's great wall of defense protecting from enemy assault. Those without appropriate faith in God in the crisis would stumble over that very issue. In contrast, the literal defensive walls upon which Samaria or Jerusalem depended would fall, to the shame of all their inhabitants. Thus, Isaiah declared God's defense available for the remnant, "Behold I am laying in Zion a stone of stumbling and a rock of offense, and the one who believes on him will not be put to shame" (**9:33**).[71] Works of the law are not proof of righteousness because they are not faith grounded. Instead, they cause stumbling. They look to the wrong defensive wall. The only "wall" able to withstand the siege of God's coming judgment is the wall God builds through the obedience of faith. Such faith that is grounded in the messianic cornerstone is available not only to Israel, but to all nations, because faith in Messiah offers a universal language for relationship to God (1:5).

---

[69] Massacre of the Bethlehem infants (Matt 2:16–18), though unconfirmed in any other first-century sources.

[70] Josephus, *Ant.* 3.223; Phil 3:6.

[71] Combining Isa 28:16 and Isa 8:14. Paul adapted the quotation noticeably, but within the constraints of acceptable methods of his day, such as word linking to join two different texts into a synthesis for application (e.g., merging the stone of faith in Isa 28:16 with the stone of stumbling in Isa 8:14). The Hebrew text indicates a foundation stone, so one among others. The LXX makes a foundation clear as well (θεμέλια, *themelia*). Paul overlooks this nuance in the original MT and the LXX translation. He narrows focus to a single stone, which suits application exclusively on the Messiah.

Notice that the theme of shame resurfaces once again in a discussion of Jewish issues over Messiah. Introduction of the theme of shame into the theme statement of Romans in 1:16 is because Romans has underneath its surface structure Paul's on-going struggle with Mosaic Israel, the consistent rejection of his gospel in synagogues around the world. He now has brought that struggle directly into the argument in Romans 9–11. His reputation and honor as a Hebrew of the Hebrews is open to dispute and is disputed. Paul has reason to be ashamed. He has received the synagogue lash, which would put him close to death, five times already. But he is not ashamed. He has reread Isaiah's prophetic word with messianic insight. He has not stumbled over the stone God laid in Zion, the stone which has become Mosaic Israel's rock of offense. Messiah eventually will be his ultimate vindication in the day of final judgment. Paul will be declared a Hebrew of the Hebrews.

Paul's Intercession (10:1–2)

Paul prays on behalf of Israel. The strong emotion here reiterates the emotional opening of 9:1–5 and indicates that Israel is the metanarrative of Romans.[72] Further, "brothers" (Ἀδελφοί, *Adelphoi*) continues to reveal Paul's corporate perspective throughout Romans, and "salvation" (σωτηρίαν, *sōtērian*) shows that the salvation of Israel guides the whole argument Romans 9–11, and moreover, is stalking the rhetoric of all of Romans 1–11. The discussion certainly is not academic for Paul.

So he prays. The good pleasure of his heart and his prayer to God is for "their" (αὐτῶν, *autōn*) salvation (**10:1**). In context, "their" refers back to the recently mentioned "vessels of wrath" on the way to destruction minus messianic intervention, in other words, Mosaic Israel (9:22). *Paul cannot dissociate the topic of salvation from the category of Israel.* This synthesis should be retained in any overview of Pauline theology. We also should remember that the "them" in "for them" used to include Paul (9:24). He speaks to a zeal without knowledge because he knows exactly what he is talking about (**10:2**). Besides giving him a new frame on eschatology, the revelation of the Son of God to him (Gal 1:16) has revealed that while zeal can be a religious person's best asset, ironically, zeal can be God's worst problem. Paul is the poster child.[73]

---

[72] Similar to Pate, *et al.*, *The Story of Israel*, but minus the supersessionism.

[73] Paul self-confesses the zeal he sees in his murderous Jerusalem mob (Acts 22:3).

Zeal is a key component of Pharisaism, as even Jesus himself noted (Matt 23:15), and such a mindset Paul used to cultivate as a "virtue" of his religious devotion to God. Paul testifies to Mosaic Israel's zeal here in 10:2, but that coin has two sides. Paul is dealing with the side that blinds to the truth and self-justifies behavior that otherwise never would be approved, such as Paul's own persecution of disciples of Jesus.[74]

Israel's Disobedience (10:3–21)

Zeal misdirected can turn obedience into obstinacy, which culminates in persistent disobedience, as for one Saul of Tarsus. Saul's "virus" now is pandemic in Mosaic Israel in synagogues throughout the Diaspora, but particularly Rome, whose synagogues already have had "Chrestus" preaching disturbances so serious as to provoke a decree from Emperor Claudius expelling Jews from Rome. Paul had firsthand knowledge of this decree, particularly its synagogue context in Rome, through the eyewitness testimony he received from Prisca and Aquila.[75]

Two Ways of Righteousness (10:3–4)

Paul presents two ways of righteousness: God's way and Israel's alternate way (**10:3–4**). Paul already has encoded these as the singular "work of the law" (2:15) versus the plural "works of the law" (3:20; 9:32). The righteousness of God is the righteousness of faith (9:30), which issues in life through the Spirit (8:10) from a new lordship (6:19) of Messiah (5:21). Messiah as the object of faith is new, but this "faith-way," or righteousness by faith, as the proper way of relating to God is not new, as Abraham's life illustrates (Romans 4). Unhappily, faith righteousness did not survive the transition into the Mosaic law needed for nationhood in practice, though the truth was inscribed.[76] Sin seized opportunity to make sin exceedingly sinful through the law, and most certainly did (7:13). One of these methods was to innovate a way of self-righteousness defined as the absence of a true heart for God. Not submitting to God's righteousness from the heart as if performance alone were sufficient to self-justify is stubborn enough, but a blindness

---

[74] Gal 1:14; 1 Cor 15:9; Phil 3:5–6.

[75] Acts 18:2, 18, 26; 1 Cor 16:19; Rom 16:3; cf. 2 Tim 4:19.

[76] The "heart" language of Deut 4:6, 9; 10:12–22; also, the prophets, Jer 4:1–4.

that looks the other way when canonizing an oral tradition that itself encourages unrighteousness, such as the law of Corban, is obstinacy.[77]

What does righteousness from the heart whose generative core is a true heart for God look like? Jesus. Thus, Paul says: "For Messiah is the *telos* of the law unto righteousness to everyone who believes," τέλος γὰρ νόμου Χριστὸς εἰς δικαιοσύνην παντὶ τῷ πιστεύοντι, *telos gar nomou Christos eis dikaiosynēn panti tōi pisteuonti* (**10:4**).

This verse famously divides commentators into two camps, as the inferences drawn from two choices are consequential for a theology of Paul. The word *telos* (Messiah is *telos* of the law) has two main translation options: (1) *end*—Messiah is the end of the law, (2) *completion*—Messiah is the consummation, fulfillment, goal of the law. The internal rhetoric of Romans in the end seems most persuasive. That is, "fulfillment" seems fully amenable to and harmonious with explicit statements about the law upon which Paul has insisted throughout both prior supporting units of Romans 1–4 and Romans 5–8:

- 2:26: "[Gentiles who] keep the requirements of the law, will not their circumcision be regarded as circumcision?"

- 3:27: "[boasting] is excluded, By what law? By that of works? No, by the law of faith."

- 3:31: "Do we overthrow the law by this faith? By no means! On the contrary, we uphold the law."

- 7:12: "So the law is holy, and the commandment is holy and just and good."

- 8:4: "So that the just requirement of the law might be fulfilled in us."

Romans 8:4 is decisive. Law as a genuine expression of the will of God does not slink away in disgrace as if having no grace and sharing none of the glory of God.[78] Law, read messianically, is grace. The life of Jesus

---

[77] Mark 7:11; cf. Josephus, *J.W.* 2.175 (2.9.4); see "Synagogue Impact," p. 100.

[78] 2 Cor 3:7–8. Messiah's glory outshines all glory of heaven, of course, so outshines the glory of anything by comparison, including the law (2 Cor 3:10). That idea is *relative comparison*, not a verdict sending law off to some God's will garbage dump. Law as "letter that kills" (2 Cor 3:6–7) is not axiomatically true of law inherently. The meaning of 2 Cor 3:6–7 should not ignore the entire argument of Rom 7:7–25 that law was not the culprit. Sin was. Neutralize Sin as a power, and law can guide toward God's will (Gal 3:24–26). For interpretive options on *telos*, cf. Badenas, *Christ the End of the Law*, 7–37.

is the proper hermeneutic of the law of Moses, and read straightway enough, Jesus's own teaching displays an unmistakable attitude about the permanence of the law in God's economy (Matt 5:18). Paul enhances that attitude by showing how through the Spirit by faith in Messiah, the goal of the law is achieved. The Spirit of God infused into the believer by Messiah (5:5) penetrates ever more deeply into the lives of believers daily than the Mosaic law ever could in the absence of that empowering Spirit. This Spirit available indiscriminately to all in the New Aeon neutralizes for believers the premier tool of the law used by Sin in its continuing war on flesh (8:1–13). So, law *can* be fulfilled, and Messiah is the fulfillment of the law to all who believe.

Moses's Own Testimony (10:5–8a)

Moses speaks his own testimony on *righteousness by law* (**10:5**). Of the righteousness from the law, Paul quotes Lev 18:5 and its clear promise, "The one who does these things will live by them." Obedience means life. This straightforward statement is distorted and misinterpreted by those trying to build a case for a universal system of "works religion" ubiquitous throughout human history in all religions, the Jews and their law of Moses offering the worst example. To make this system work, a doctrine of perfectionism unilaterally has to be shoehorned in to guarantee failure of all these hypothetical religious systems automatically and instantly against the human impossibility.[79] On the contrary, Moses here does not infer a word about any doctrine of *perfectionism*. Otherwise, why would sacrifice be provided for sin, which inherently assumes no one can live perfectly obedient? So, to what does Moses speak?

Moses speaks corporately to *national Israel* about how to maintain her covenant blessings of land and life. Moses most certainly is not insisting every single Israelite perform every single dictate of the law every twenty-four hours of the day perfectly, or Israel is finished. National covenant faithfulness was possible, even in the face of sin, if true repentance accompanied sin's sacrifice. Israel's great conundrum historically, however, was lack of genuine covenant faithfulness. Israel failed to repent of even egregious sin. Sacrifices performed for Yahweh took place while simultaneously showing idolatry toward other gods. Israel's sin was that she performed prescribed works but had no true,

---

[79] Convenient self-fulfilling prophecy by presupposition. See discussion, pp. 293–97.

unadulterated faithfulness to God. For this rampant and heartless sin, Israel was judged. The exile was God's judgment on this *national failure* of covenant faithfulness, not that some Israelite in some village failed to sacrifice a pigeon along the way. Chronicles summarizes succinctly.

> The Lord, the God of their ancestors, sent persistently to them by his messengers, because he had compassion on his people and on his dwelling place; but they kept mocking the messengers of God, despising his words, and scoffing at his prophets, until the wrath of the Lord against his people became so great that there was no remedy (2 Chr 35:15–16).

National death in exile proved performance righteousness failed. That is what "shall live by them" means in Lev 18:5. Corporately, that was a doable deal, but historically, that became a miserable failure due to the illusion of performance righteousness absent true repentance.

Moses also speaks on *righteousness by faith* (**10:6–8**), or else the gospel was not promised beforehand in the Scriptures (1:2). Paul uses Deut 30:12–14. The idea is basic (up, down), but the meaning argued. Is the reference metaphorical to Moses going up Sinai to bring down the law or to Messiah's incarnation and resurrection? The focus on Messiah, however, is explicit. Clearly, Paul has turned the text messianically to focus on the life of Jesus. The "Who will go up to heaven?" Paul explains as "That is, to bring Messiah down." Then, "Who will go down into the abyss?" Paul explains as "That is, to bring Messiah up from the dead." In its original context, Moses's point was that God's commandment was both doable (not too hard) and reachable (not too far). In this way, the message of law as revelation of God's will is near in the "mouth," metonymy for teaching and transmission from generation to generation, and near in the "heart," metonymy for requisite obedience from any given generation. Moses's point would concord with the intent of Lev 18:5 (obedience is life). Obviously, what originally was reference to the *commandment* for Moses is now reference to the *Messiah* for Paul. Paul's Mosaic hermeneutic is in line with Messiah as fulfillment of the law, and exactly what Paul said in 3:31. Once again, the foundation of law obedience is a faith relationship, trusting God.

Paul's Conformity to Moses (10:8b–10)

Paul shows his message is faithful to Moses. This famous verse shows up in many pamphlets of gospel presentations, and rightly so: "That if

you confess with your mouth the Lord Jesus and believe in your heart
that God raised him from the dead, you will be saved" (**10:9**).[80] First,
confessing Jesus as "Lord" is the essence of incarnation doctrine and
testifies to the truth that Jesus reveals the heart of God, which is the
point of the law. If you know God's heart, you know God's will. Jesus
teaches God's heart, and that is foundational to the "work of the law"
to which every believer happily is obedient through the Spirit. Second,
believing that Jesus is raised from the dead is the essence of eschatological doctrine and testifies that Jesus reveals the heart of the future,
which is the point of the Spirit. We must not miss in this confession
that with the symbiotic key terms "Lord" and "resurrection" in this
two-fold formula, Paul quite beautifully and with exquisitely planned
exegetical strategy has circled back to the opening Roman creed with
which he opened the letter of Romans with keen purpose to buttress
this confessional (Rom 1:3–4). He thereby has integrated the Roman
creed now into the story of Israel and the crux of his mission strategy.
This literary flower is opening into full bloom. The follow-up verse in
10:10 reemphasizes the reality that the righteousness God has sought
all along, as Jeremiah had said, was in the flesh of the heart, not flesh
of the foreskin (Jer 4:4). Righteousness and salvation are dyadic operations, not two stages of some linear process. Inability to recognize such
righteousness in the life of Jesus reveals dangerous obduracy. Mosaic
Israel seems poised to reprise the role of Pharaoh.

Paul's Unashamed Gospel (10:11–13)

Paul comes back to the shame theme—again—as he quotes Isa 28:16
(**10:11**). This "not be put to shame" is about Paul's faith gospel in the
face of synagogue rejection built into the letter's theme statement in
1:16 as a key component.[81] He adds second allusion to the letter theme

---

[80] The title "lord," κύριος (*kyrios*), was applied to Roman emperors from the time of
Augustus; Rock (*Romans and Roman Imperialism*, 156–57) emphasized the imperial,
political overtones of the title. In terms of punctuation, Paul's reference to "word" in
"the word of faith" at the end of 10:8 could be a *backward-looking* hook to "the word"
that is near in the prior quotation of Deut 30:14, which requires a period at the end of
verse 8; so the editors of both the UBS5 and NA28. On the other hand, the expression
could be a *forward-looking* introduction to the content of the word preached that is
expanded in verse 9, thus requiring a colon at the end of verse 8; so some English
translations, such as CSB, NIV. ERV punts the ball by innovating *two* colons.

[81] Cf. also 5:5 and 9:33.

by restating the "no distinction" motif (**10:12**).[82] This motif justifies his multicultural mission. He grounds the motif in the Jewish doctrine of monotheism—again—in "The same Lord of all richly blesses all who call upon him" (10:12).[83] The link word of "call" calls up the quotation of Joel 2:32 in **10:13**: "For whoever will call on the name of the Lord will be saved." The context for this salvation promise in Joel, of course, is the decisive action of Yahweh coming to Zion's aid after judgment.

> You shall eat in plenty and be satisfied, and praise the name of the Lord your God, who has dealt wondrously with you. And my people shall never again be put to shame. You shall know that I am in the midst of Israel, and that I, the Lord, am your God and there is no other. And my people shall never again be put to shame (Joel 2:26–27, NRSV).

Notice the doubly emphasized "never again be put to shame" motif. The prophet holds out the hope that even devastating judgment does not have to be the end of the story nor Israel's shame be forever. Paul resonates with these thoughts in his own context and finds hope in them for the present condition of Israel. But repentance is key.

Paul knows Joel's "never be put to shame again" is not unconditional. Joel dealt with a historically unidentified locust plague that brought the Judean countryside to its knees. He interpreted the ecological disaster as God's judgment for sin. The solution was national repentance that God would honor with crops flourishing again so much as to make up abundantly for the lost harvests. Joel does not flip the coin to discuss refusal to repent. Still, he was clear that sin always brings judgment. From that realistic prophetic perspective, Paul saw Mosaic Israel's hoped for national repentance ambiguous, so its fate unclear.

The fate of Israel after the exile was undecided. The road back to nationhood had been encumbered with foreign domination through the centuries that had followed the exile. The nation had endured two local dynasties that had nothing to do with David, the present family being Idumean, not even Jewish, and sold out to Rome and its patron-client political arrangements. Disparate groups vied with one another to promote and propagate their competing, even conflicting, visions of

---

[82] Cf. also 3:9, 22–23.

[83] The doctrine of monotheism is used similarly in 3:29 as Paul follows up on the justification of the ungodly through the death of Messiah in 3:21–26.

Israel. Worse, Messiah had come to his temple at the most inopportune time, since Israel seemed not at all ready, and destiny was on the line. Israel was in a tight spot. Politically and religiously the nation was embroiled in an identity crisis exacerbated by messianic confusion. The stakes could not be higher, and Paul could not be working harder. He desperately was trying to break through the veil of Moses obscuring Scripture interpretation in the synagogue with the gospel of God to avert a reprise of national disaster as Joel had experienced. In the meantime, those that called upon the Lord Messiah assuredly would be saved.

Paul noticeably assigns to Messiah the role of Yahweh in this Joel passage, given the confession in 10:9. Whatever is meant is complex, since the confession (like a baptismal liturgy) is "Jesus is Lord," yet that word immediately is followed by the belief affirmation that *God* raised him up from the dead. How this relationship works Paul leaves for others to say in finely nuanced Trinitarian formulas that took the church fathers several centuries to nail in words, but still are mused.

Israel's Clear Accountability (10:14–21)

The requirement to call on the Lord invites Paul's accountability series, "call . . . believe . . . hear . . . sent," offered to stave off another effort at excuse baiting (**10:14–15**). Paul appeals to Isaiah's prophetic mandate in Isa 52:7, "how beautiful" (**10:15**), already taken as a messianic text in Paul's day, which Paul naturally applies to the preaching of the gospel through Isaiah's use of "good news" (LXX: εὐαγγελίζω, *euangelizō*). Isaiah meant God's kingdom realized, characterized by peace and salvation. Jesus sent out his disciples expressly to Israel with this word of the fulfillment of good news (Matt 10:5–7). Paul's application is perfectly in line with this announcement of Jesus. Thus, Paul and all those on mission to and for Israel propagate this prophetic word Jesus said was fulfilled in his own ministry (15:20).

Further, Isaiah's prophetic mandate of preaching the good news applied to Jesus as Messiah is what Paul means appropriating the title "apostle" (1:1). He was not disingenuously pretending to be part of the original band of brothers. *By "apostle" Paul always meant Isaiah's apostleship to Israel.* Paul saw his apostleship as fulfillment of Isaiah's word to Israel. This Pauline perspective informs using Isaiah at this point in a discussion of the salvation of Israel. Two-thousand years of the mantra "apostle to the gentiles" must be redirected. *Mission to the gentiles is sublimated to the larger mission to Israel in Paul.* The gentile mission *does not stand independently on its own in Paul's mission playbook.* To this point, we do well to remember that Paul pulls no punches as he upbraids rogue gentile attitude on this very issue in the next chapter.

A sent preacher means a culpable Israel. "No excuse" ominously shadows the wrath of God discussion as revelation does not obviate human accountability (1:20). Paul deftly transitions "no excuse" to Jewish responsibility in Rom 2:1. The homing pigeon now returns home.

Paul points out that Isaiah anticipated a response of unbelief to the mandated message (**10:16**). So, "Who has believed our message?" Isaiah asked in Isa 53:1, which introduces a Servant Song into Pauline thinking about Israel. The word of Messiah is Isaiah's Servant message because of the crucifixion. The passion of Jesus is perfect fulfillment (3:21–26). As Isaiah had seen, the Servant served Israel, but Israel balked at the offer. Paul gives a triadic witness of Scripture (Law, Prophets, Writings) in the following verses to undercut no accountability arguments. In his series of linked chains of accountability, Paul drives home that "not hearing" in Israel's case is, in fact, *refusal* to hear.

Perhaps unbelief can find excuse due to a faulty link in the chain necessary to establishing accountability—not hearing the word. Paul acknowledges that faith comes by hearing and hearing by the message of that Messiah has fulfilled Isaiah's Servant role of suffering (**10:17**). So, Paul puts a direct question in **10:18** with the strong adversative "but" (ἀλλά, *alla*): "But I ask, 'Did they not hear?' Indeed! (μενοῦνγε, *menounge*)." He uses the negative particle *mē* (μή) with indicative mood, so anticipates agreement: "But of course they heard!" His response is to quote Ps 19:4: "Their voice went out to all the land, and their words to the limits of the inhabited world" (LXX). The psalmist spoke of the heavens giving clear testimony to the creator's glory. As effective in the psalmist's eyes is God's revelation of his glory through that which he has created for reaching everyone everywhere, Paul so understands the gospel mission to Israel. Compare Rom 1:20: God's ability to reveal his eternal power and divinity, even though invisible, through the creation itself, thereby making all earth's inhabitants accountable to him. If God can do that generally and effectively, he certainly can reveal himself in Messiah to Israel—and he has. The global thrust of gospel preaching almost can be summarized in Paul's preaching alone (amazingly), but Paul most certainly is not alone (15:24).

Another faulty link in the chain necessarily for accountability is hearing but not understanding. Fair enough, if true. Paul again uses a strong adversative with the negative particle *mē*: "But I ask, 'Did Israel not understand?'" (**10:19**). "Israel" is corporate, not individual. Paul answers with the jealousy and anger theme of Deut 32:21: making jealous by "not a nation" and making angry by "a nation that lacks understanding." To this text Paul conjoins Isa 65:1 of being found by those not looking and of self-revelation to those not asking (**10:20**). The thought echoes 9:30 about gentiles not pursuing but still obtaining righteousness, but Paul now applies that same process to Israel as well. Why should Paul link Israel coming to Messiah to a gentile-imitating path? These quotations from the law and the prophets have corporate contexts, as does Paul's application, but Paul's own story seems to summarize this plot paradigmatically. Saul of Tarsus fits the category of one "jealous" of messianic claims of Jesus's disciples, because such claims best are the prerogative of Pharisees to discern. He could be angered by those with the audacity to speak for Israel and Torah when they so obviously had absolutely no credentials for such serious tasks. Further, he was found by Jesus when he was not looking for Jesus, and he was granted a self-revelation of the Messiah when he was not asking for one. Again, as we have suggested, perhaps Paul saw in his own experience a microcosm of possible trajectory for the whole nation in macrocosm. Of course, if the similarity were to be maintained, Jesus would have to reveal himself corporately to a nation not asking for self-revelation of the Messiah to shock them into their senses, as for one Saul of Tarsus.

Reality rain on this parade immediately comes in the very next verse of Isa 65:2 that Paul himself must acknowledge in **10:21**: "But to Israel he says, 'All day long I stretched out my hands to a disobedient and denying people.'" The bad news anticipated in Isaiah's moment of reality therapy is intransigent rebellion on the part of God's people. The aura is of a permanent condition. The good news while trying to wrap the mind around such a fatalistic impression is that God never gives up ("all day long"). In spite of recalcitrant unfaithfulness on the part of God's people, God is faithful, as Paul already had stressed in 3:3 of that preliminary unit of Rom 3:1–8 that proleptically anticipates all of Romans 9–11. In this case, God being faithful might anticipate some dramatic, revelatory event. Question, however, still would remain: Even if revelation were possible in the divine plotline, could repentance happen in time before God's "seeking repentance" gig was up? To be or not to be, that, indeed, is the question. So, was Israel (Jacob) going to be Israel (heirs) in time? The problem is, while all depends on God, all depends on Israel too.

Paul's presentation has worked to refocus Israel's story from the perspective of the gospel. What he has said also can be summarized in the inverse from the perspective of Mosaic Israel.

- Rom 9:30–33:   Mosaic Israel mistook divine righteousness

- Rom 10:1–2:   Mosaic Israel still has Paul's prayers

- Rom 10:3–13:   Mosaic Israel is unfaithful to the gospel

- Rom 10:14–21: Mosaic Israel is culpable for gospel disobedience

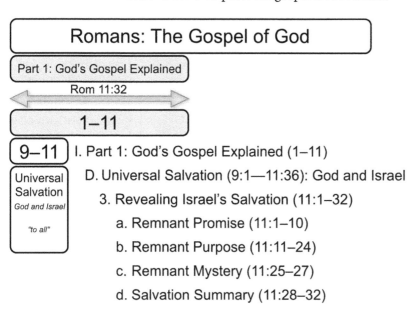

FIGURE 9.9. Outline: Romans 11 (Israel's Salvation). After restating Israel's failure, Paul finally moves to reveal Israel's salvation through remnant theology and mystery.

REVEALING ISRAEL'S SALVATION (11:1–32)

A pretty bleak picture has emerged in Romans 10. Israel is rebellious, almost fatalistically so. Achieving national destiny such as envisioned by the prophets seems a stretch. Yet, Paul hears God say, "I got this." Paul harnesses remnant promise, purpose, and mystery to show how.

Remnant Promise (11:1–10)

Paul is ready to deal with the present crisis of Mosaic Israel caught in the Old Aeon confronted by the coming of Messiah to inaugurate the New Aeon. How is Israel's own salvation ultimately impacted by this decisive collision of the ages? To negotiate an answer, Paul develops two thoughts. First, he comes back to his earlier idea from Romans 9 of a remnant by grace (11:1–6). That discussion introduced the concept of divine hardening, which he now applies to Mosaic Israel as he adds his own new wrinkle to Israel's story in his innovative analysis that Israel's present condition is a hardening by judgment (11:7–10). From a literary perspective, Paul is building on his analysis of Israel in Moses contrasted to Israel in Messiah in Romans 6–7, which he resolved in the Spirit in Romans 8, but now applies to his present mission context.

FIGURE 9.10. Mosaic Israel's Pauline Mission Context. Paul earlier had contrasted Mosaic Israel and messianic Israel as one Israel conflicted by the realities of two aeons using historical analogies derived from the exodus story of baptism, slavery, marriage, and law. Paul now applies this analysis to his present mission.

Remnant by Grace (11:1–6)

Paul asks the obvious question confronted by the reality of synagogue rejection of gospel preaching of Jesus as Messiah prophesied by Isaiah: "Has God rejected his people?" (**11:1**). First, make no mistake. Paul by "his people" is clear he is talking about ethnic profile: "For I too am an Israelite, a descendant of Abraham, from the tribe of Benjamin." With "Israelite" in 11:1, we circle right back to "Israelite" beginning in 9:4. Paul remains laser-focused on his topic. The whole discussion continues to pursue the question of Jacob and his progeny.

Second, Paul still is banking on election: "God has not rejected his people whom he foreknew" (**11:2**). "His people" is ethnic in context, and "foreknew" is election. The whole point is misunderstanding the gentile influx into messianic Israel as God finally and righteously abandoning ethnic Israel over its failed covenant by rejecting Messiah. "Not so fast," Paul admonishes. "God can choose to do what he wants to do, and if he still wants to save those in a state of rebellion, just review your own salvation history, and then we'll talk."

To show God has not rejected ethnic Israel, Paul harnesses remnant theology. "Israel already has been here before," basically is what Paul will say. He will point to Elijah's experience in the Jezebel crisis, which itself anticipates Isaiah's experience in the Babylonian crisis, and which, Paul will infer, anticipates gospel rejection in the messianic crisis currently. If the past is any clue, God is not done with Jacob.

Paul appeals to Elijah's complaint to God (**11:3**). Elijah as a prophet of Yahweh had a crisis with Jezebel, Phoenician princess daughter of the king of Tyre. She married King Ahab of the Northern Kingdom of Israel and brought her Baal worship with her into his royal house. Yahweh altars systematically were demolished and his prophets killed. Elijah's successful showdown on Mount Carmel and slaying of the Baal prophets enraged Jezebel, and she sought his life. Elijah fled to a cave to hide. He pled with God against Israel, thinking he was the only one left zealous and faithful to Yahweh (1 Kgs 19:10, 14).[84] God responded in 1 Kgs 19:18 that Elijah was not in a position to count, that God still had seven thousand to himself who were faithful and had not committed Baal idolatry (**11:4**).

Paul made application to the present crisis: "Thus therefore also in the present time is a remnant according to gracious choice" (**11:5**). He then emphasizes if by gracious choice, the matter does not come down to works (**11:6**). Paul here and in the next several verses will be cutting against the grain of typical synagogue beliefs about the nature of any remnant of Israel. Typical Jewish belief was that a remnant by default would exist due to inherent worth. A remnant had earned by

---

[84] Paul may have empathized with Elijah because Elijah describes his faithfulness to Yahweh as being "zealous" (ἐζήλωκα, *ezēlōka*, 1 Kgs 19:10, LXX). Cooper demonstrated that Paul came to his distinctive collocation of Isaiah's "remnant" concept in Isa 10:22 (quoted in Rom 9:27) and Deuteronomy's "zeal" theme in Deut 32:21 (quoted in Rom 10:19) through his understanding of the Elijah narrative, and this linkage is the path to Paul's solution of Israel's plight. Cooper, "The Intertextual Link between *Parazēloō* and *Leimma* in Rom 11:1–15," 171–82. Note particularly Cooper's chart comparing Paul and Elijah, 174. See previous discussion, p. 81.

works God's attention and protection. If so, their existence was proof of superiority over others.

Remnant Beliefs: Synagogue vs. Paul

Romans 11	Synagogue	Paul	New Aeon
Rom 11:1–6	grounded in inherent worth	grounded in God's grace	Paul as Jewish paradigm
Rom 11:7–10	a proof of superiority	a cause for hardening	hardening as God's plan

FIGURE 9.11. Remnant Beliefs: Synagogue vs. Paul. Understanding grace changes how anything is understood.

Paul, in contrast, had been overwhelmed by God's grace in Messiah even at the moment he thought he was being his most zealous for God, but his zeal was without true knowledge of God. Paul now realizes that *any remnant is grounded in God's grace*, including a remnant in Elijah's day, or in Isaiah's day, or in Paul's day. Isaiah spoke to this characteristic way of God dealing with a disobedient Israel.

> On that day the remnant of Israel and the survivors of the house of Jacob will no more lean on the one who struck them, but will lean on the LORD, the Holy One of Israel, in truth. A remnant will return, the remnant of Jacob, to the mighty God. For though your people Israel were like the sand of the sea, only a remnant of them will return. Destruction is decreed, overflowing with righteousness (Isa 10:20–22, NRSV).

Paul already had quoted Isa 10:22 in 9:27, so he sees this remnant also as a function of God's gracious choice. The point is, Paul sees his own story as the present Jewish paradigm of a remnant by gracious choice (9:24). He will go on to say that superiority attitudes based on works is the cause of hardening, because grace is rejected. Yet, the hardening process itself is not beyond God's redemptive power to save and God's plans for Israel.

Hardening by Judgment (11:7–10)

God's grace puts Israel in a hard spot, because righteousness of the law is impossible to achieve without God's grace. Israel (Jacob) did not find the righteousness sought, but the elect of Israel (heirs) called upon the name of the Lord Jesus and believed that God had raised him from the dead and received grace (**11:7**). This repentance and faith marks the transition from the Old Aeon to the New Aeon, from Mosaic Israel to messianic Israel. The thought in 11:7 resonates with 9:31.

The new twist Paul adds at the end of 11:7 is, "but the rest were hardened." This divine action, Paul implies, is what few properly have calculated trying to interpret the status of present Jewish rejection of the gospel. Mosaic Israel now plays the role of Pharaoh. Having heard a direct proclamation from God in the gospel of God from synagogue to synagogue (10:18), Mosaic Israel has insisted on resisting. Mosaic Israel now has thrown itself into a judgment storm of the wrath of God. God judges this unrighteousness and ungodliness by guaranteeing that insistent resistance inevitably matures into hardened insensitivity ("God delivered them over," 1:24, 26, 28). For scriptural confirmation of this process of divine wrath, in **11:8** Paul merges Deut 29:4 (Moses's point about God not giving a mind to understand, or eyes to see, or ears to hear) into Isa 29:10 (God pouring out a spirit of deep sleep, closing the eyes and covering the heads of the prophets and seers).[85] Like a bird in a covered cage slipping into unconscious silence fooled into thinking night has arrived, the prophetic voice in Israel falls silent with Messiah's arrival to Israel among those most responsible for rightly knowing the time. Unremedied, the national destiny in this judgment of divine wrath eventually is death (1:32). However, divine wrath also is an act of mercy, because divine wrath operates such that God does not judge immediately, even though immediate judgment fully is justified. Divine wrath is divine mercy forestalling immediate judgment in God's persistent quest to save. God in his fundamental character is merciful. Paul likely intends the reader to hear the "to this day" in the Deut 29:4 passage with an eschatological nuance intimating Israel's present messianic conundrum.

In his regular triadic pattern, Paul adds testimony to the Law and Prophets from the Writings by using Ps 69:22–23 in **11:9–10**.[86] David's words of snare, trap, pitfall, darkened eyes, and bent backs were meant for his enemies. The synagogue had appropriated this psalm in times of their own distress from their enemies. Along these lines of natural

---

[85] Interestingly, Isaiah's "spirit of stupor (deep sleep)" is one of only two times the Greek word for "stupor" (κατάνυξις, *katanuxis*) is used in the LXX (cf. Ps 59:5). Further, both contexts relate to God's people corporately in a stupefied state because God has rejected and destroyed and expressed anger.

[86] And possibly conflating Ps 35:8, whether intentionally or unintentionally.

development, Jews long had taken this psalm messianically by the time of Jesus. Paul simply applies that messianic hermeneutic to Jesus. Jesus already had quoted Ps 69:4 in reference to his rejection (John 15:25), and the disciples recalled Ps 69:9 when Jesus drove out the money changers in the temple (John 2:17). Further, Paul uses the last part of Ps 69:9 to speak of the example of Jesus in not pleasing himself (15:3).

What Paul has said to this point is that Israel has a grace remnant (messianic Israel) and a judgment hardening (Mosaic Israel). This simultaneous duality means Israel's eschatological status altogether is in God's hands still. From these verses we can conclude our first of two major remnant deductions: Paul is saying, *Israel's rejection is not total.* This conclusion is crucial to understanding Paul's optimism. In contrast to the judgment of Babylonian exile, in which temple, city, and nation totally were destroyed, Paul is insisting the glass is half full, "At least we are not there yet." Further, the existence of a remnant already called shows God working in mercy through grace. The present remnant must mean that God has a plan and greater purpose in his hardening judgment than meets the eye. Messiah still can be expected to continue to reestablish and renew the Israel of God. The remnant is a promise of God already fulfilled by grace on which an Israelite such as Paul can put his future hope for Jacob.

Remnant Purpose (11:11–24)

How does this eschatological remnant work in the present time for God's purposes with Israel? "Glad you asked," Paul says. "That was my next point." Paul clarifies status among Israelites and gentiles in the Israel of God. But why would he need to?

We must be consciously vigilant to let Galatians and Romans stand on their own, not presuming the Galatians and Romans contexts to be the same or even similar. For one, Paul is in the white heat of his anger when he writes Galatians. Nowhere is his rhetoric more insulting (Gal 3:1) and crude (Gal 5:12). He clearly is functioning in a nonnegotiable either/or logic and rhetoric that leaves absolutely no room for nuance (Gal 4:20). He cannot afford to. The situation is so dire he would lose his point. He clearly is going for shock value, like slapping a drowning person with no other way to get their attention in a life or death situation (Gal 1:9). We could point out no other Pauline letter is absent a thanksgiving section. (Let that thought sink in a minute.) Paul is in consternation how his teaching on grace, promise, law, faith, and Spirit so easily and so soon could have been so corrupted (Gal 1:6). Paul's own teaching on this matter should have been pretty obvious even in casual conversation. In a more dispassionate frame of mind, as in Romans, issues of faith and law can be nuanced more generously and less rigidly.

For two, the situations are entirely different. The problems are opposite. The problem behind Galatians is gentiles evaluating Israel too highly, but the problem behind Romans is gentiles evaluating Israel too lowly. In Galatians, Paul makes no attempt to speak to the situation of Israelites (the term never surfaces even once), but gentiles exclusively. In Romans, Paul makes every attempt to speak to the situation of Israelites, but *also including gentiles* derivatively to address a specific local situation (a much more complex rhetorical target).

One element behind the context of Romans is decidedly missing in the context of Galatians. One of Paul's great deficits in writing Romans is addressing with authority a congregation he did not found.[87] He would not have been integral to development of foundational traditions from the beginning (as in Galatia) nor would the Roman church necessarily inherently reflect Pauline nuances on the gospel of God.[88] Yet, one historical event Paul does know well. He is aware of synagogue disturbances leading up to the Edict of Claudius expelling Jews from Rome. That situation not only would have impacted the demographic profile and worship setting of followers of Jesus in Rome, but likely would have eroded further gentile attitudes to Jews as well. Romans already were predisposed to broad prejudice against the Jewish people and their culture. An incident as traumatic as the "Chrestus" crisis of AD 49 only seven or eight years before Paul wrote Romans likely exacerbated this inbred prejudice, even within the church.[89] Gentiles in the church might have succumbed to increasing racial tension, unchecked in the absence of dominant Jewish church leaders, but now

[87] Even the church in Colossae was in the orbit of the three-year Ephesian mission through Paul's associate, Epaphras, likely founder of all three Lycus valley churches of Colossae, Laodicea, and Hierapolis (Col 1:7; 2:1; 4:12–13). Cf. Bruce's erudite summary (*Colossians, Philemon, Ephesians*, 13–17).

[88] As illustrated, for example, in the crisis with Peter at Antioch (Gal 2:11–14).

[89] See previous discussion, pp. 162–64.

exposed as Jews including Jewish believers returned to Rome as the Claudius edict was rescinded after the emperor's death in October of AD 54. Gentile believers might have found their attitudes changing, inducing a growing tendency to write off Jews and Jewishness as a decided deficit to the church coming into its fullness. They have "done church" without trying to interface nearly as intimately with Jews or Jewish culture for several years, much more so than when a new movement in Rome worshipping in the synagogue. The "fullness" of the church might not need Jews at all anyway. Paul turns all that gentile thinking on its head. While gentiles indeed might have their own "fullness" within God's plans, the church is nothing without the fullness of Israel by definition. Galatia has not a clue about all this.

Reframing Israelite Status (11:11–12)

Israel stumbled. Was Israel then utterly cast down (11:11)? Paul takes the bull by the horns to face head on a developing faulty hermeneutic in Roman churches fed by Roman prejudice that Israel lost its chance in covenant grace. Here we have the seedbed of the supersessionism of the second-century Roman church. This view presumes that the church replaced the Jews and the nation of Israel as the covenanted people of God entirely with no remainder forever. Its full fruit later is seen in the apocryphal *Epistle of Barnabas*, written between AD 70–132.[90] The author argued that Jewish sin with the golden calf incident at the foot of Mount Sinai aborted God's covenant before the covenant even was ratified. Jews were charged with never understanding the law from the beginning. They never were, nor could they be, the covenanted people of God. Covenant promises belonged exclusively to the church.[91] One sees a similar attitude in Justin Martyr (d. 165), a leader in Rome, who wrote an apology for Christianity against Judaism. In this work, Justin interpreted God's promise to Abraham, and to his Jewish literary foil, Trypho, Justin asserted, "Accordingly, He promises to him a nation of

---

[90] Though not eventually canonized, the book was read and received with high regard in Christian communities of the early church. Clement of Alexandria quoted the work as having scriptural authority, as did Origen a little later (d. 254). Barnabas is included at the end of Codex Sinaiticus, a Greek copy of the Bible dating about 330–350.

[91] *Epis. Bar.* 4:6–8.

similar faith, God-fearing, righteous, and delighting the Father; but it is not you, in whom is no faith."[92]

On the assertion Israel utterly has been cast down, Paul responds with another of his characteristic exclamations, "Absolutely not!" (μὴ γένοιτο, *mē genoito*). Apparently, someone in Rome inspired by something is drawing this conclusion, because Paul by his strong response clearly does not. We may have here another impact of the trauma in Roman synagogues that provoked the Edict of Claudius. The challenge to Jewish status in Rome may have emboldened a similar challenge to Jewish status among those confessing Jesus as Lord who no longer were meeting in synagogues but in house churches with gentile patrons who would set the tone and influence and control all social dynamics.[93]

"On the contrary" translates the strong adversative "but" (ἀλλά, *alla*). Paul dramatically draws the *opposite* conclusion: God still is at work. "By their trespass (παραπτώματι, *paraptōmati*)" is a key characterization. "Trespass" is the crucial word describing Adam's failure in 5:12–20. Mosaic Israel patterns itself after Adam's sin, not Moses's law. More importantly here, *Messiah specifically was handed over for such trespasses* (4:25). Messiah already died for this sin too. This theological reality is being ignored by those in Rome who may not realize the gravity of their bad attitude and premature deductions about Israel's disobedience. They are insinuating final judgment already has transpired for Israel like that judgment has not for gentiles.

Instead, Paul announces to the chagrin and surprise of those in Rome with a chip on their shoulders about synagogue Jewry, God, in fact, has worked this trespass into the divine economy of salvation. So, he continues, "By their trespass, salvation has come to the gentiles to make Israel jealous." We perhaps should allow for the possibility that the better translation of *ethnē* here is "nations," not "gentiles." Nations actually would make more sense in terms of the Isaian motif of Israel's destiny as a nation among the nations shadowing the discussion ever since Rom 1:5, which will figure prominently in the quotation of Isaiah at the end of Romans in 15:12 and 15:16.[94] That is, Paul may not be talking about the jealousy of individual Israelites, but rather of Israel

[92] Justin Martyr, *Dial.* 119.
[93] See previous discussion, pp. 161–64; 177–79.
[94] See previous discussion on Rom 1:5, pp. 225–27.

envisioning its national destiny as a light of revelation to the nations. This idea that *ethnē* is more likely "nations" is made more probable by the nature of the jealousy motif to come, in which the context in the original text that speaks to jealousy explicitly is about Israel as a nation and God provoking Israel with "not a nation" (ἐπ᾽ οὐκ ἔθνει, *ep ouk ethnei*), that is, a nation without a covenant with Yahweh like Israel has.

The jealousy motif merges with the zeal motif in a theologically potent way for Pauline remnant theology.[95] The "jealousy motif" is a unique Pauline exegesis of Deut 32:21, already introduced in 9:19. The context of Deuteronomy 32 is national covenant failure through rank idolatry. "Jacob" has abandoned the God who made him, and made God jealous with strange gods (Deut 32:15–16). The summary in Deut 32:21 rhetorically has classic symmetry inversion built on top of typical Hebrew parallelism.

> They made me jealous with what is no god,
>   provoked me with their idols.
> So I will make them jealous with what is no people,
>   provoke them with a foolish nation (NRSV).[96]

Israel made God jealous with a "no god," so God took action. God turns the tables and so makes Israel jealous with a "no nation." The point is, *God's intention is to stir Israel to response,* not to offer a petty tit for tat in a spat. The whole idea is that *God wants Israel back,* not that God is going to ditch Israel in the covenant dumpster.

The second point is, Paul uniquely turns Moses's covenant text of national disobedience characterizing the inevitable outcome of Israel's kingdom period into an eschatological (i.e., messianic) text to reframe for Rome's understanding the present synagogue rejection of Messiah. Then Paul puts in the ringer (**11:12**). *God did this for Rome's gentiles:* "Now if their trespass brings riches for the world [Rome], and their failure riches for the gentiles [nations], how much more will their fullness bring!"[97] This thought is a window into Paul's mission motivation and

---

[95] Cf discussion of Cooper, 81, n79; 425, n83.

[96] The verb translated "provoke" (lines two and four) in the LXX is a compounded form of the verb for being greatly angry or beset with wrath, παροργίζω (*parorgizō*), which suggests more forceful translation as "enraged" here, not just "provoked."

[97] Note here equivalency of "world" (κόσμος, *kosmos*) and *ethnē*, which, again, suggests more the idea of "nations" than "gentiles" for *ethnē*.

provides balance to overemphasis on Paul as "apostle to the gentiles," translated as "Israel has been left in the dust of Pauline mission objectives." Israel's trespass facilitates "riches for the world," which is Isaiah's light to the nations, meaning salvation. *This process is precisely the Pauline missionary narrative throughout Rome's provinces: to the Jew first, but then, strategically also to gentiles among all nations of the world* (1:16; 2:9). Synagogues are scattered throughout the civilized empire. The gospel of God for Israel by having the spectacular advantage of a vibrant, worldwide Diaspora—like no other nation ever had produced before—has automatic entre to all the nations. *Paul is reminding Rome the gospel came to Rome's gentiles through the synagogue—so, to the Jew first, then to the gentile.*[98] The Edict of Claudius gives silent witness to that reality. If Israel's failure can be so productive in Rome in God's hands, just imagine Israel's fullness! Paul produced a wordplay for the thought: from Israel's failure (ἥττημα, *hēttēma*) to Israel's fullness (πλήρωμα, *plērōma*). So, before ever mentioning a "fullness of the gentiles" (11:25), Paul already has spoken of a "fullness of Israel."

Reframing Gentile Status (11:13–24)

Clarifying Gentile Apostleship (11:13–15). Paul's gentile apostleship now comes into sharper focus as he speaks directly to gentiles (**11:13**). First person rhetoric brings in authorial *ethos*, and Paul's *ethos* in Romans is thoroughly Jewish. He works in these verses to reorient gentile status *within* Israel, not in spite of Israel. Paul is sent by God to gentiles, so he is obligated to assist Roman gentile bad attitude. He "magnifies" his ministry by gaining further reach than he has to this point by helping Rome, but also by impacting the premier city center of world empire.

All this effort, however, is to "make jealous" (Deut 32:21) his own "flesh" (σάρκα, *sarka*, **11:14**). Biological use of "flesh" in this context makes clear that he still pursues his opening topic of "Israelites." The concluding clause, "and might save (σώσω, *sōsō*) some (τινάς, *tinas*) of them," suggests two ideas that seem in tension with Paul's concluding summary in 11:26. First, the (aorist) optative verb has an unexpected

---

[98] Not through the synagogue exclusively, of course, but dominantly as a traceable movement originating among Jews in Judea. Merchant trade was a significant factor in Roman economy and social structure and another source of religious activity. Still, Jewish merchants also would be synagogue Jews. See discussion, pp. 156–60.

element of contingency ("might"). Paul does not here express rigid or dogmatic thought about guaranteed future salvation. Second, the indefinite pronoun, "some," suggests he is unsure the relative size of the group in question, but certainly not "all." These two factors appear at odds with the typical reading of 11:26. This grammar also sounds less than a resounding affirmation of the sense of "fullness" in 11:12. The grammar of contingency and indefiniteness in 11:14 puts a governor on the meaning of "fullness" in 11:12 or "all" in 11:26. Among others, several possibilities immediately could be suggested as explanation.

- *Unknown result.* Perhaps the grammatical ambiguity in 11:14 suggests Paul was not working with a concrete picture of what this "fullness" in 11:12 or "all" in 11:26 actually looked like.

- *Unrealized miracle.* Perhaps the ambiguity suggests Paul, in faith, is willing to leave room for another astonishing and unexpected movement of the Spirit, like Pentecost. This category also would include unexpressed thinking related to the expected parousia, or appearing of Messiah.

- *Unfulfilled prophecy.* Perhaps the ambiguity suggests Paul is thinking more traditionally Jewish than allowed. His thought has turned subliminally toward unfulfilled Jewish prophecy of the restoration of Israel and reintegration of the northern tribes into the Israel of God, and he cannot be sure what that reintegration actually would look like (i.e., resolution of the Samaritan question). The chronicle in Acts 8 could preview a harvest to come.

In any case, what is clear in Rome is that, for the moment, Israel's rejection brings "reconciliation" (καταλλαγή, *katallagē*) to the world, or, Rome (**11:15**). Reconciliation from a scriptural angle is summarized in the story of Messiah's propitiation (3:21–26). At the same time, "reconciliation" in Rome counters imperial propaganda related to Octavian (Augustus).[99] The condition of rejection is parallel to those described in 3:3, "What if some were unfaithful?" Further, God brings life out of death. What was true for Abraham's barren wife (4:19) Paul expects to be true for Abraham's barren nation (11:15).

---

[99] See "Age of Augustus," pp. 127–54, and comments on peace and reconciliation at Rom 5:11, pp. 326–27.

This difficult circumstance of rejection has not baffled God. This situation is that of "vessels of wrath" bound for "destruction" that God yet presently is "enduring" for his purposes (9:22), which means God is choosing not to exercise that deserved judgment immediately. Instead, God, as in all judgment situations, directs his sovereignty toward expressing grace. "Their acceptance" would be a transformation into "vessels of mercy" prepared for "glory" (9:23). "Glory" is a key eschatological term, tip of the iceberg for the reality of the future world in Paul, which believers anticipate in this time of overlapping ages as the "hope of glory" (Col 1:27).[100] Entrance into that glory is impossible without resurrection (8:18–25). Or, as Paul expresses the thought here in 11:15, "what will their acceptance be but life from the dead?" He connects what he is anticipating for Israel with the resurrection. Resurrection is a major motif in Romans from the opening bell (1:3–4) and a fundamental proof of the power of the gospel.[101] Connecting the future of Israel with resurrection is linear logic. Resurrection functions for Paul as the messianic paradigm of messianic Israel following in the path already blazed by Messiah. If Messiah is raised, Israel will be. While walking in newness of life now anticipates that future life in resurrection glory (6:4), and that future life of the Spirit already has partial realization now in messianic Israel (8:4), present life is not to be equated with the full manifestation of glory that is to come through resurrection. Resurrection is not simply a metaphor in Paul. Therefore, the "life from the dead" language in 11:15 would tend to suggest that the ambiguity of 11:14 involves at least option 2 above: unrealized miracle.

In short, we gain clarity in these verses on Paul's mission work. He ultimately targets the Israel of God (Gal 6:16). His gentile apostleship transcends exclusive focus on gentiles. Thus, Paul reveals he has two mutually operating goals for Israel in his gentile mission work.

• mission goal 1: to make Israel jealous, provoking return to God

• mission goal 2: to save "some of them" out of Mosaic Israel

Illustrating Gentile Status (11:16). Paul concludes reframing the status of Israel and of the nations through two metaphors of harvest and horticulture whose intent is to remind gentiles how holiness works.

---

[100] For a study of eschatology in Paul, see Campbell, *Paul and the Hope of Glory.*

[101] Cf. Rom 1:4; 4:17, 24; 6:5, 9, 13; 7:4; 8:11; 10:7, 9; 11:15; 14:9.

The reason for this turn to holiness is related directly to God's purpose for transforming Israel into a nation among the nations through the redemption from Egypt. Gentiles are sublimated to that purpose.

> Then Moses went up to God; the LORD called to him from the mountain, saying, "Thus you shall say to the house of Jacob, and tell the Israelites: You have seen what I did to the Egyptians, and how I bore you on eagles' wings and brought you to myself. Now therefore, if you obey my voice and keep my covenant, you shall be my treasured possession out of all the peoples. Indeed, the whole earth is mine, but you shall be for me a priestly kingdom and a holy nation. These are the words that you shall speak to the Israelites" (Exod 19:3–6, NRSV).

Being a treasured possession of God out of all peoples is strictly for the purposes of holiness. Paul wants to explore how God intends his holiness to permeate all creation through his people. Holiness spreads out from part to whole, the basic idea in both metaphors.[102]

The first metaphor is harvest, firstfruits, given in **11:16a**. The first sheaf or early part of a later harvest indicates the promise of the quality and fullness to come. Eschatologically, firstfruits is indicated in the resurrection of Messiah (1 Cor 15:20) and the messianic Israel he has created (9:24).[103] Paul is promise of more Israelites to come. Thus, from Messiah, holiness permeates into Paul and messianic Israel, and out from messianic Israel to the whole of creation (8:21).

The second metaphor is horticulture, roots, given in **11:16b**. The health of the root determines the health of the branches. Nutrients from the root flow upward and outward to the branches. Once again, holiness spreads out from a central part to the whole plant.

The holiness Messiah brings consummates God's purpose in the exodus to create a treasured possession unto himself whose holiness as a people would permeate outward to all the nations and all creation. Messiah's fulfillment is for Mosaic Israel. Messiah's fulfillment is for the Samaritans. Messiah's fulfillment is for the nations.[104] Messiah's fulfillment is for all. Somewhere in all this is "all Israel."

---

[102] Pauline emphasis on holiness is regular in Romans and elsewhere; cf. Rom 1:7; 6:19, 22; 12:1; 1 Cor 6:11; 1 Thess 4:3–4, 7.

[103] Compare the similar thought in 2 Thess 2:13.

[104] Gentiles, if you must.

FIGURE 9.12. Ancient Olive Tree. The Mount of Olives across the Kidron Valley from Jerusalem used to have large olive groves. Olive oil was a major part of the Judean economy. On the slopes today is this olive tree several centuries old.

Challenging Gentile Attitude (11:17–24). Paul harnesses these illustrations of holiness to confront gentile attitude in Rome. He now extends his olive tree metaphor.[105] Farmers tend their plants by selective pruning. Careful pruning of old and unproductive branches provokes new, more vigorous growth using root system resources. The new growth has better yield quality and volume. Cultivated clips can be grafted into wild stock too.

"Some of the branches are broken off," Paul states (**11:17**). This allusion is to hardening of Mosaic Israel, which now manifests as a state of unbelief in Messiah (9:18). The earlier metaphor was of a potter who creates "dishonorable vessels," or, theologically, "vessels of wrath" (9:21–22). Other wild branches subsequently are grafted in to access the rich resources of the olive tree root. A holy root means holy branches. The root is Israel or Messiah (Rev 5:5). Wild shoots and cultivated plants, however, do not mix effectively in the real world, so the metaphor has lost verisimilitude. That would take a miracle. Ah, but of course. Miracle might just be Paul's point when the transformation of the ungodly and unrighteous into Israel is in view, and not that he is that ignorant of horticultural practices. He overextended his metaphor, but perhaps intentionally. He intended to

---

[105] Metaphor extension is dangerous, violating verisimilitude or making false inferences. False inference is Esler's error, who distorts Paul as if urging the *superiority* of Jews, destroying the whole argument ("Ancient Oleiculture and Ethnic Differentiation").

point to impossibility to arrest attention rhetorically of his listener and turn the overextension into a subtle but effective comment on the stunning achievement of Messiah. Touché.

The bad attitude surfaces in **11:18–19**. This problem is particular to the Roman house assemblies. Boasting to be better is no better than the *anthrōpos* condemned in Romans 2. This attitude reveals a proud and haughty mind, a judgmental spirit that is inviting the wrath of God to activate to secure the destiny that that mind has determined to own by darkening even further that senselessness (1:21). Boasting is the key signature of belonging to Mosaic Israel (2:29) and reveals a hardened heart not truly belonging to messianic Israel in the first place. Boasting forgets that one stands by faith and not deservedness in the first place (**11:20**). Such arrogance against Jewish unbelief is dangerous, because *this type of arrogance reveals lack of true belief in the first place.* If God did not spare the natural branches for unbelief (now the overextended metaphor scores its mark), neither will he spare unnatural branches for the same unbelief.

Therefore, arrogant gentiles are on the edge of a disaster just as much as anyone in Mosaic Israel, because they also stand in disbelief. This gentile ought to contemplate with grave seriousness that God's character is balanced on both sides of kindness and severity. God has been severe with his own nation among those who have fallen in unbelief and kind to those who have been part of "not a nation" for the reason of their belief and confession, which testifies to total humility and dependency on the Lord Jesus Messiah (10:12–13). Only the righteous by faith will live (1:17). The fate of a gentile boaster, then, is the fate of an unbeliever, that is, as cut off from the covenant, just as with Mosaic Israel (**11:21–22**). Indeed, consider the "kindness and severity (ἀποτομίαν, *apotomian*)" of God, an idea encountered already at 2:4 directed to Mosaic Israel.[106] Jewish wisdom featured this parallel kindness and severity motif, so Paul here likely follows this wisdom theme.[107] Paul seems to align the idea of severity with the operation of divine wrath.[108]

---

[106] "Severity" (ἀποτομίαν, *apotomian*) occurs only here in biblical Greek. Cognate nouns add only six, all in Wisdom of Solomon: ἀπότομος, *apotomos*, Wis 5:20; 6:5; 11:10; 12:9; 18:15; ἀποτόμως, *apotomōs*, Wis 5:22.

[107] Note Wis 5:20; 6:5. cf. Koester, *TDNT*, s. v. "τέμνω," 8:108.

[108] So Barrett, *Romans*, 218.

If so, God's wrath is implicit in context. Further, while the grafting in of a wild branch was a miracle of horticulture only God could perform (so contemplate that for a moment) surely the gardener by the same reasoning, can graft back in a cultivated branch to its native root. The idea powerfully undercuts the arrogant gentile's brag of belonging that yet admits how they got into the root in the first place (**11:23–24**).

The boasting issue raised here Paul will return to in later exhortations in the second part of Romans. This issue sets up the need for a statement about being "transformed" through a process that functionally is by "renewing your minds" (12:2). This exhortation strategically is placed right at the beginning of all exhortations, indicating this type of "transformation" is a core need of the Roman house church assemblies across the board.

Remnant Deductions: Rom 11:1–24

Text	Deduction	Implication
Rom 11:1–10	#1: Israel's rejection not total	Optimism
Rom 11:11–24	#2: Israel's rejection not final	Future

FIGURE 9.13. Remnant Deductions. Paul draws two deductions about the remnant from the Scripture in his discussion in Rom 11:1–24.

Paul has correlated his understanding of the gospel of God and Israel's eschatological status. He has pointed out that stumbling serves the purpose of gentile mission. At the same time, stumbling also serves the purpose of Israel's future fullness. Paul, as could be expected, is committed to affirming that God fully is in control, even though he himself has had to struggle with understanding his own mission crisis in Jewish synagogues across the Diaspora. By now, he has drawn a second deduction about the remnant: Israel's rejection is not final.

Paul has emphasized two major deductions about the remnant so far in this chapter of Romans. First, Israel's rejection is not total. This deduction allows Paul to be optimistic still about Israel's prospects. Second, Israel's rejection is not final. This deduction allows Paul to anticipate a future for Israel. Paul is obligated now to address that future.

Paul's presentation has worked to refocus Israel's story from the perspective of stumbling. What he has said also can be summarized in the inverse from the perspective of Mosaic Israel.

- Rom 11:1–6:   Remnant Israel is by God's grace only

- Rom 11:7–12: Hardening of Mosaic Israel is neither total nor final

- Rom 11:13–16: Gentile apostleship is sublimated to Israel

- Rom 11:17–24: God's power can fulfill all promises to Israel

Remnant Mystery (11:25–27)

Paul's statement of remnant mystery is one of the greatest mysteries of Romans. Given comments of the last two thousand years, we entertain little hope of relieving the exegetical angst. Still, we dare forge ahead.

Mystery Revelation (11:25–26)

First, we need to point out the literary purpose of this revelation is *to mitigate gentile conceit* (**11:25a**). Gentile conceit, explicitly exposed in 11:20, discloses spiritual ignorance at best, as conceded in the opening clause ("I do not wish you to be ignorant"). At worst, the conceit more dangerously may expose a religious cloaking device for rank Roman prejudice that disguises its own hardheartedness and unbelief and has no place whatsoever in messianic Israel. Paul will give further attention to the problem of conceit afflicting the body of believers in general in later exhortations (12:16).

Second, the literary content of this revelation is the knowledge of the divine hardening of Israel: "a hardening in part has come upon Israel" (**11:25b**). This idea of hardening is not actually what is unknown. Paul already had introduced the hardening topic in his discussion of Pharaoh in 9:18, and then applied that topic to Israel in 11:7. Also not really new in 11:25b is that the hardening of Israel is "in part."[109] Again, this very emphasis already was addressed in 11:7–10.

What is new is "until" (ἄχρι, *achri*) in **11:25c**. This adverbial preposition introduces the element of time. Time could suggest a specific idea, something measurable by a clear, identifiable marker on the way. Such thought of time specificity is dashed immediately by a thoroughly ambiguous phrase that Paul uses nowhere else: "the fullness of the *eth-*

---

[109] The adjectival phrase, ἀπὸ μέρους (*apo merous*), can be hardening "in part," like slices of a pie (ASV, KJV, NIV, NRSV), or "partial" hardening, like dilution of a liquid (CSB, ESV, NASB). Dilution just does not make as much logical sense in the context of discrete entities in which this hardening is registered (from Israelite to Israelite).

nōn.[110] "Fullness" is πλήρωμα (*plērōma*), used by Paul twelve times, enough to suggest his general meaning. He typically does not mean a mathematical quantity. Typical use is ideas such as maturity, intended goal, fulfilled objective, completeness.[111] If we use the general sense of "fullness" as completeness or fulfilled objective as in other passages, and combine that idea with the translation of "nations" for *ethnē* rather than "gentiles," some fog dissipates from the expression. We have "until the fulfilled objective for the nations." This fullness is not a discrete, arbitrary number of uncircumcised males. The expression becomes a thoroughly prophetic, messianic, eschatological thought. Paul's remnant mystery integrates Isaiah's vision of national Israel fulfilling its destiny as a light of revelation and salvation for the nations of the earth. God has left to himself a remnant Israel, composed not only of Israelites, progeny of Jacob, responding in faith, but expanded by gentiles also responding in faith as anticipated by the prophets.

Paul is working through a biblical déjà vu. His synagogue context reprises Elijah's complaint. Elijah complained so of being the only one faithful to God in an Israel overwhelmed by Baal idolatry. The premise was false. God had many faithful Israelites Elijah was not in a position to count. God now in Paul's context likewise has a sufficient remnant of Israelites still faithful to him who can get the job done. But Paul has an eschatological wildcard Elijah did not. Paul has those who formerly were "not a nation" now integrated into messianic Israel as God's own. These gentiles have a capacity to supercharge the effort of completing Israel's destiny to the nations right at the very moment Mosaic Israel has abandoned the task. Hardened in unbelief, Mosaic Israel is unresponsive to the call to tell the good news envisioned by Isaiah (10:15).

The fullness of the nations "enters in" (εἰσέλθῃ, *eiselthēi*). Such language would be appropriate for entering into a covenant. This goal

---

[110] The issue again is whether Paul thinks of an aggregate of uncircumcised males, "gentiles," or in broader terms as "nations," the far more dominant perspective of the *ethnē* in the prophets of Israel so notable in the LXX translation.

[111] As in love is the fulfillment of the law (Rom 13:10), the fullness of the blessing of Messiah (Rom 15:29), the earth and its fullness being the Lord's (1 Cor 10:26), the fullness of time for sending the Son (Gal 4:4), the fullness of time eschatologically (Eph 1:10), the fullness of him who fills all in all (Eph 1:23), filled with all the fullness of God (Eph 3:19), the full stature of Messiah (Eph 4:13), all the fullness of God dwelling in Messiah (Col 1:19; 2:9).

is the incorporation of all nations into the worship of God through the Messiah. In Pauline terms, this goal is Paul's "obedience of faith" that spreads God's glory and Name throughout the earth, a motif with which Paul both opens and closes Romans.[112]

"And thus all Israel will be saved" (**11:26a**). The meaning of every word is contested, even the adverb. The adverb, "thus" (οὕτως, *houtōs*) is an adverb of manner, so generally is "in this way," but one has to ask, in what way? In what way is Israel saved? By the previously mentioned divine action of judgment hardening? Or, by the previously mentioned Pauline mission goal of causing jealousy in Israel through achieving the "fullness of the *ethnē*"?[113] If we take *ethnē* as "nations," as argued, then the scope of Isaiah's vision comes into play, which would be entirely reasonable as a means of causing jealousy. Jerusalem is swelled with worshippers, so to speak, but they are not Israelites.

The meaning of "all" (πᾶς, *pas*) in "all Israel" is argued. "All" has been equated with the "church" as the so-called "spiritual Israel."[114] The problem here is no attempt to integrate Paul's use of "church" into his use of "Israel." In short, Paul uses both, not necessarily inter-changeably. This sophisticated domain range makes the facile equation of "church = Israel" exegetically unlikely. Another option is to equate "all" exclusively with the "Israelite" and "patriarchal" ethnic markers in the context (9:4; 11:1, 28) to think this category must be the sum of all converted Jews through the ages. The problem here is no reality check on the absolutely meager historical results of that sum total. Such contemplation is not nearly compatible with an exultant, triumphant hymn that concludes the whole discussion. Further, logically, if this meager historical result is what Paul meant, then the expression "all Israel" be-comes practically meaningless. A similar criticism would be true of the

---

[112] Rom 1:5; 15:9. Note the centrality of the Name in God's encounter with Pharaoh picked up by Paul in 9:17 and the antithetical blaspheming of the Name in Rom 2:24.

[113] Particularly if *ethnē* is read without contextual nuance as just the generic "gentile," in which case, avoiding the idea of reaching some arbitrary mathematical quantity of uncircumcised males is almost impossible.

[114] Like the equally infelicitous "true Israel," "spiritual Israel" is distinctly *not* a Pauline category. "True Israel" begs the question by not addressing that others exist. Even Paul's own expression, "not all who are descended from Israel are Israel" (9:6), inherently recognizes multiple linguistic categories for "Israel" exist simultaneously. For positions on "all Israel," cf. Moo, *Romans*, 720–23. Fitzmyer (*Romans*, 623) noted the underlying Hebraism, *kol-Yisrae'el*, is used 148 times in Scripture for historic, ethnic Israel.

cousin idea of a "Jewish revival" at the end of history that is popular in evangelical circles. Once again, we have the problem of meager results of the sum total not really compatible with the exultant heights of the concluding hymn of triumph, and a practically meaningless expression from a historical perspective. More importantly, Paul offers no hint anywhere that he anticipates a two-thousand year interval separating the only two aeons of which he ever speaks. Those who suggest such an interval as integral to Pauline eschatology do not cognize they actually have invented a whole new aeon in its own right never mentioned by Paul. How could Paul possibly exult triumphantly in any logic that Messiah wins only one generation of Jews while he loses all others? Further, that Paul is prophesying in 11:26 is an unlikely presumption. His rhetoric suggests he is *analyzing his current mission situation to try to calculate the possible outcomes*. A mathematician knows full well that to change either the variables or their values in an equation changes the solutions. Paul calculated the best solution with the variables he had.

The meaning of "Israel," obviously, is argued. In most proposals, the meaning of Israel is simply presumed to fit the inherent logic in the proposal. Thus, if one presumes Israel equals the church, then that fits the logic of supersessionism. If one presumes Israel is exclusively ethnic, then that fits the logic of Jews having their own salvation track, as in classic dispensationalism, or opting for a Jewish revival at the end of history, as in evangelicalism. One even could presume "all Israel" is just whatever Paul meant by "remnant Israel," but that is fundamental category confusion. That Paul would not have relieved two thousand years of debate and just said "And thus remnant Israel will be saved" is beyond reasonable expectation of the rhetorical context for begging the question Paul actually is asking: Is remnant Israel all God has for the divine economy of consummating his call of Israel?

Finally, the meaning of "saved" is argued. This salvation could be conceived as simply physical, the Jews fight their way out of a climactic, literal battle with some so-called, legendary figure of Antichrist. Or, this salvation could be completely "spiritual," as in some interior, existential, individual passage into faith. Or, this salvation could be somewhere in between physical and spiritual—or something else altogether.

This brief discussion is not to give an exhaustive history of interpretation of this passage, which already is provided in the critical commentaries. This summary is only meant to alert the reader that we fully are aware that whatever we say about Rom 11:26 will be argued. Yet, we do hope to offer comments to help the reader keep their exegetical balance in this difficult passage. Balance goes back to the beginning.

We go back to the beginning, the anathema wish "for the sake of my brothers, my kinfolk" (9:3). Eliminate the abstract. Substitute the real. Who is he talking about? Perhaps his father or mother. Perhaps his sister or her son (Acts 23:16–22). We know that they existed, but we never hear one word of their involvement in the Jesus movement as followers of the way. They inspired absolutely zero church traditions with episodic anecdotes to illustrate values and priorities of this family of so famous an apostle.[115] Whether Paul was married or had children is unknown from his letters, but if so, they too would be a part of this story. Whatever the actual contours of his actual family, they certainly qualify for "my kinfolk." We do know Paul had high connections in Jerusalem within the Sanhedrin, because he obtained letters from the council to the synagogues in Damascus authorizing extension of his pursuits there, and he was a personal acquaintance of the high priest, Caiaphas, because he was able to go directly to him (Acts 9:1–2). He also was well connected to the Pharisees, by his own testimony advancing beyond most of them (Gal 1:14), and by Luke's testimony a personal disciple of one of the most famous Pharisee leaders of the day, Gamaliel (Acts 5:24; 22:3). These individuals and so many others would qualify as "my brothers." Work through the names in Acts, and one could keep expanding this list, especially in the many synagogues he had visited. After the letter of Romans, on Luke's testimony, one also could add synagogue leaders in Rome as well (Acts 28:17).

The point is this. The anathema burden is quite personal to Paul. When he wrote those words, he likely had images of specific people in his head, family members, religious colleagues, casual but beloved ac-

---

[115] The little we have has nothing to do with Paul's family. The apocryphal *Acts of Paul* (c. AD 160) includes the *Acts of Paul and Thecla*, which chronicles episodically a virgin Thecla's fascination upon encountering Paul's teaching on chastity at Iconium on his first missionary journey and following him faithfully thereafter, trailing miracle after miracle of her protection from persecution and death. This work is first known from Tertullian (*De baptismo* 17.5, c. AD 190), in which he traced its authorship to an Asian presbyter who was deposed upon confession of the fabrication. The original was Greek, but numerous translations indicate wide dissemination and popularity (Latin, Coptic, Ethiopic, Greek, Syriac, and Armenian versions).

quaintances.[116] Thus, "Israel" is kinsmen, kinfolk, acquaintances. They are people bonded to Paul "according to the flesh" (κατὰ σάρκα, *kata sarka*), terminology that surfaces three times in the first eight verses of Romans 9 (9:3, 5, 8), then again in 11:14. In all such ideas, Paul clearly is focused on God's covenant with Abraham as defined by progeny.

Paul does not reject the covenant of progeny when he redefines the meaning of becoming children of God in 9:8. Rather, Paul nuances the concept of a covenant-making God to accommodate a sovereign God. God in his own sovereignty can adopt whomever he choses, and God's sovereign choice is the essence of the God of promise and the children of promise. Whenever God establishes a child of promise to become part of the family (Isaac), that action is an expression of his mercy and his miraculous power. Thus, "Israel" is promise plus grace. The people of God do not get to say who are their brothers and sisters. Thus, if God chooses to establish through the Messiah by adoption children of promise through faith from among the nations outside the nation of Israel, that is his sovereign choice in the divine economy of salvation. Children of the flesh do not get to say who are their brothers and sisters. God does. Any sovereign actions of the God of promise, however, do not mean the God of Abraham is not faithful and will not honor his unconditional covenants, as effected by his gifts (Isaac) and calling (Abram), because they are irrevocable (11:29). God is faithful, so none of this means the word of God has failed (9:6). One just has to nuance carefully the complexities of progeny and promise. We tend to fall off on one side or the other of this Pauline tightrope upon which Paul was balancing his thoughts of "Israel" throughout Romans 9–11.

So what is salvation in 11:26? In these terms, salvation in the context of this complex discussion of progeny and promise is becoming the children of God, which offers the hope of a glorious future (8:18–19). God adopts Abraham by his calling of Abram in Ur of Chaldea. God chooses in his sovereignty to provide Abraham family, though his wife is barren, by his promise that requires performing a miracle. God then chooses in his sovereignty to follow that heritage of flesh, but by

---

[116] The NRSV employs the expression "beloved" in his letters a total of thirty-seven times. Poring through Paul's letters, he clearly leaves the impression of one quite open and affectionate. He even associates himself to the Thessalonians both as a nursing mother (1 Thess 2:7) and as a tender father (1 Thess 2:11) in the space of four verses.

that same sovereignty only by his choice among those of faith in any generation of that progeny, just as with Abraham. From that progeny God in his sovereignty chooses to expand that family by the promise of a Messiah, another miraculous child, born within that progeny, as promised, who will reach the nations by the obedience of faith (1:5). By his death and resurrection, Messiah inaugurates a New Aeon of the Spirit, and confession of Messiah as Lord and belief in his resurrection from the dead is effectual for becoming a member of this family of faith with hope of a glorious future shared with all creation. God in this way honors both his covenant in Abraham and his covenant in Messiah. In a nutshell, Israel is not an arbitrary, aggregate sum of individuals. Israel is the divine economy of completed covenants through Abraham and Messiah among all the nations.[117] "All Israel" in Rom 11:26 is messianic Israel's destiny fulfilled. This destiny consummates progeny, promise, and future. This Israel is the Israel of God.

In terms of covenant, the problem with gentiles is not their state of uncircumcision. Historically, circumcision did nothing for Israel if one considers the judgment of exile. Even after the exile, circumcision did nothing for Caiaphas if one considers the execution of Messiah. In Pauline terms, then, the problem with gentiles, and Israel, is Adamic flesh, not uncircumcised flesh, and only Messiah solves that problem if humanity in Adam is to have any future (5:12–21). Hence, that problem is why circumcision nor uncircumcision is anything (Gal 5:6). In these terms, circumcision is only a mirage of covenant keeping. The pathetically perverted actions of Hasmonean rulers forcibly to circumcize conquered populations, as if that action had anything at all to do with keeping the law, is clear testimony to gross confusion on Moses, even if politically expedient, almost imitating branding slaves.[118]

---

[117] No reason exists from Romans 9–11 why this completed covenant for Paul could not comprehend from the perspective of progeny reunification of the tribes of Israel and Judah, that is, historically resolve the issue of the Samaritans. Faith is the key.

[118] Mattathias (d. 166 BC), priestly clan patriarch who revolted against Syrian rule, forcibly circumcised sons of non-observant Jewish parents (1 Macc 2:45–46). John Hyrcanus (134–104 BC) later circumcised the conquered inhabitants of Edom, or Idumea (Josephus, *Ant.* 13.9.1). Aristobulus I (104–103 BC), after conquering Galilee, forcibly circumcised that population as well (Josephus, *Ant.* 13.11.3). Circumcision as a form of branding to mark Jewish power over gentile bodies is argued by Weitzman, "Forced Circumcision and the Shifting Role of Gentiles in Hasmonean Ideology." In the Levant,

With this revelation of the mystery of the remnant working toward fulfilling *both* Abrahamic *and* messianic covenants—not one over the other whether by exclusion or by abrogation—Paul thereby mitigates gentile conceit in house churches in Rome. This problem, we should recall, preludes the introduction of Paul's famous "all Israel" assertion to the grand scheme of salvation in 11:26a. Some so-called solutions to "all Israel" ironically do not mitigate gentile conceit. Rather, they wind up only exacerbating that conceit. Paul rolls over in his grave.

We should point out that in Rom 11:26 Paul is not prophesying. Instead, he is analyzing his current mission context of this continuing synagogue rejection ("for I am not ashamed," 1:16) to establish why he yet reasonably can be hopeful to pursue his quest on into Spain. Without this hermeneutic for hardening, Paul has no way to explain his mission to Israel through the gentiles as either logical or reasonable. He is confident his hermeneutic of the mystery of the remnant is on track, because he finds confirmation in the prophetic words of Isaiah.

Remnant Confirmation (11:26b–27)

Isaiah prophesied Zion's deliverance by turning away ungodliness from Jacob through a new covenant that takes away sin.

> And he will come to Zion as Redeemer, to those in Jacob who turn from transgression, says the LORD. And as for me, this is my covenant with them, says the LORD: my spirit that is upon you, and my words that I have put in your mouth, shall not depart out of your mouth, or out of the mouths of your children, or out of the mouths of your children's children, says the LORD, from now on and forever (Isa 59:20–21, NRSV).

To this deliverance one can add the thought, "Therefore by this the guilt of Jacob will be expiated" (Is 27:9, NRSV). In the original context of Jewish enemies threatening the nation, the assumption is that Israel repents and confesses sins because enemies are at her gate from God's judgment. Yahweh responds to repentance by coming as redeemer to save. Paul builds on this idea in his quotation in **11:26b–27**.

Paul adapts the quotation in two noticeable ways. First, Jesus takes on Yahweh's redeemer role, but this hermeneutic is common in New

---

since other peoples also practiced circumcision, the rite alone never would suffice of itself to constitute Jewishness.

Testament scriptural quotations that reference Yahweh's actions, as Paul did already in 10:13. Second, this redeemer in Paul's quotation comes *from* Zion, not *to* Zion, as in Isaiah.[119] Since "Jerusalem" has two domains in Paul, earthly and heavenly, opinions divide over the sense of the pronoun change related to Zion.[120] Would Paul intend Zion as literal and earthly? Then perhaps the inference is subtle, as an allusion to Jerusalem as the origin of the resurrection? This prospect is unlikely. Jerusalem as the location of the resurrection never has such an emphasis anywhere else in the New Testament.[121] However, earthly Jerusalem having a heavenly counterpart surfaces in several New Testament contexts.[122] The possibility is that theologically, the thought is working off the idea of heavenly Zion as the origin of incarnation, an idea not far from the kenosis hymn of Phil 2:5–11. Thus, through incarnation, the redeemer has come from (heavenly) Zion to redeem. If so, however, such a theological point would be a thinly-sliced subtlety without pertinent rhetorical traction in context, like serving up a ham sandwich with hardly any ham.

If we keep in mind the rhetorical exigency of a covenant-making, covenant-keeping God whose sovereignty and grace is driving toward begetting "all Israel" (progeny, promise, future), and that the whole point is that the word of God has not failed (9:6), then the redeemer coming "from Zion" means *the redeemer comes from Jews for Jews*. From Jews for Jews is head on the point of a Davidic Messiah (1:3–4), the emphasis of the teaching of Jesus (Matt 15:24), and a key Pauline mission strategy expressed in Romans ("to the Jew first," 1:16). This interpretation is stronger precisely because Paul still is hammering gentile

---

[119] Redemption of Zion has its twin expression, "redemption of Jerusalem," in Luke 2:38.

[120] Literal, earthly, as in Gal 1:17, or metaphorical, heavenly, as in Gal 4:26.

[121] Jerusalem as "where the Lord was crucified" is alluded in Rev 11:18, which shadows the meaning of the exodus (departure) allusion that Jesus would accomplish in Jerusalem in the transfiguration narrative (Luke 9:31), followed by Jesus's lament over Jerusalem as the city that kills the prophets (Luke 9:34). Thus, whereas the crucifixion of Jesus as historically grounded in the city of Jerusalem is a common idea in the New Testament, the New Testament never evidences the same language with resurrection.

[122] For earthly Jerusalem's heavenly correlate, cf. Heb 12:22. Similarly, compare the "new Jerusalem" that comes "down from heaven" in Rev. 3:12; 21:3, 10. A typical reading is that Paul's "Zion" reference is to the second coming of Jesus (cf. Kim, *God, Israel, and the Gentiles*, 139). Such an *ambiguous* allusion is unlikely (contrast 1 Thess 1:10).

conceit in Roman assemblies, and "from Zion" is pretty much right in the face of that conceit.

Rom 1:18	Rom 11:26
"for the wrath of God is being revealed against *all ungodliness*"	"turn *ungodliness* away from Jacob"

FIGURE 9.14. Ungodliness Boomerang. The boomerang launched in Rom 1:18 now lands in Rom 11:26.

Romans 1	Romans 11
"For the wrath of God is being revealed from heaven against all ungodliness and unrighteousness . . . therefore, God gave them up . . ." (1:18, 24, 26, 28)	"But the rest were hardened . . . the Deliverer will come from Zion; he will take away ungodliness from Jacob . . ." (11:7, 26, 32)

FIGURE 9.15. Wrath in Romans. Paul now hits his strategic target in all of Romans 1–11.

More important is what the redeemer does. The redeemer banishes "ungodliness away from Jacob." Say that three times real fast to Caiaphas. Ungodliness circles all the way back to the wrath of 1:18–32, and the rhetorical boomerang Paul threw out in Romans 1 now hits in the back of the heads those watching the weapon twirl through the verses of Romans unsuspecting its eventual target: "For the wrath of God is being revealed against *all* ungodliness and unrighteousness of humankind" (1:18). "All unrighteousness," we now know, includes Mosaic Israel.[123] In this way, "ungodliness" in Rom 1:18 *includes* Israel's unbelief in Messiah. This inclusion of Israel's unbelief by being tucked away into the "all" of the potent phrase, "all ungodliness," means that Paul in 1:18–32 never was focused exclusively on gentiles in that famous passage on the wrath of God, as is so commonly assumed in so many commentaries on Romans. "Being revealed," we now know, includes Israel's hardening. Thus, we have here in Romans 9–11, and most particularly in the climactic "thus all Israel will be saved" of 11:26 and its

---

[123] Consistently pursued throughout; cf. Rom 2:5, 8; 3:5; 4:15; 5:9; 9:22; 11:26, 28.

following quotation of Isaiah 59:20–21, full demonstration of the thesis guiding all our discussion that Romans is all about Israel.

Messiah's premier role for Israel is to be the redeemer who comes from Zion for Zion. He is a deliverer from God's wrath and coming judgment. Rejection of Messiah is not judged immediately. The delay is a further operation of wrath into divine hardening appropriate for the hardhearted. God's basic character, however, is merciful. His mercy is not just for gentiles at the present time. God never does anything such that he is not trying to save, including a judgment by hardening. He always works together in all things for the good of his purposes in Messiah Jesus. Thus, he has a plan for Israel's hardening as well. He has provided a remnant surviving this hardening process by grace. Paul trusts God to use this surviving remnant to consummate the salvation of all Israel, Jew and gentile. Paul's confidence in God's redeeming love means that, in spite of present circumstances across the Diaspora of synagogue rejection of the gospel of God, Paul still is not ashamed of the gospel message he preaches. He will serve to the utmost and trust all results to God.

Salvation Summary (11:28–32)

Israel Summary (11:28–31). We let Paul speak for himself in **11:28–31**. He summarizes the parallel universes of Jews and gentiles in salvation.

> On the one hand, according to the gospel, they are enemies because of you, but, on the other hand, according to the election, beloved because of the fathers; for the gifts and the calling of God are irrevocable. For just as formerly you were disobedient to God, but now you have been shown mercy by the disobedience of these, in this manner also they themselves have been disobedient for your mercy, in order that also they themselves might be shown mercy (Rom 11:28–31).

The symmetrically succinct phrases summarize Romans 9–11. These verses compress the whole story of progeny, promise, and future, from Abraham to Messiah to the Israel of God. "Gifts" would include Isaac. "Calling" would include Abraham. "Irrevocable" would include the provocative court scene question in Rom 8:33: "Who can bring a charge against God's elect? God is the justifier!" The "elect" of 8:33, as *explicitly* identified here in 11:28, *includes* the covenant of progeny: "according to election, beloved because of the fathers." Supersessionism simply should not be allowed to drown out this clarion call by the Jew Paul to wake up to the reality of God's commitment to Israel. God can do whatever he wants in his sovereignty, such as save gentiles, but *for the very same reason*, gentiles need to get off their high horse and recognize that *that very same sovereighty also can decide to hang with Israel*.

Gospel of God Summary (11:32). Paul faithfully has run his eleven-chapter race to explain the gospel of God all the way to the finish line. He summarizes in one verse (**11:32**) the three parts of his outline: "For God has shut up all in disobedience" (Romans 1–4); "in order that he might show mercy" (Romans 5–8); "to all" (Romans 9–11).

Paul has explored God's mystery of Israel's salvation in 11:25–32 in order to warn Roman congregations that gentile spiritual conceit is dangerous. The attitude is ignorant of the workings of God's wrath that intends salvation. The attitude is unaware that the hardening of Israel first is only in part, allowing for a remnant to push forward toward its destiny with the nations, and second is not final, allowing for all Israel to be saved as God fulfills all his covenant purposes with Israel even as the prophet Isaiah prophesied. Thus, even though Israel is conflicted eschatologically as a result of the coming of Messiah and arrival of the New Aeon, gentiles in Roman congregations need to transform their minds about their relationships with the synagogue and Jewish *ethnos* in order to align with the divine program—or God will judge them too.

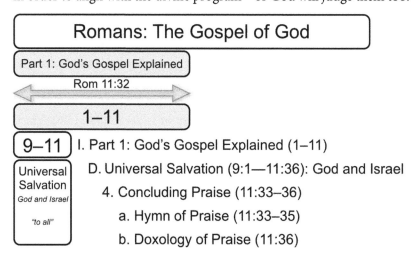

FIGURE 9.16. Outline: Romans 11 (Concluding Praise): Rom 11:33–36. Paul concludes all of Romans 1–11 with a beautiful hymn and doxology perhaps from church worship.

CONCLUDING PRAISE (11:33–36)

Hymn of Praise (11:33–35)

Paul concludes his explanation of the gospel of God with a twofold offering of praise that reflects on the extraordinary wisdom of this gospel. The first offering is a hymn of praise, and the second is a doxology of praise. Hymn and doxology work together to provide a sublime celebration and offering of worship to conclude Part 1 of Romans.

A pair of triads makes a supremely structured and quite beautiful concluding hymn of praise. The lines might reflect an early Christian hymn. Literarily, the function is like the concluding unit of 8:31–39, because the ideas sum up multiple sections at once, so the conclusion is cumulative. These lines conclude Romans 11, Romans 9–11, and all of Romans 1–11. This literary versatility naturally reflects the internal structure of Romans and its overall unit and subunits. The hymn of praise is a sophisticated celebration of God's glory and greatness.

Noun Triad (11:33)

The hymn is quite poetic. Two parts are each subdivided by threes. These subdivisions smoothly follow the grammar of three nouns and three questions.

The first series is a three-noun exclamation that augments the motif of the "depth" (βάθος, *bathos*) of God introduced in **11:33**. First explored is the depth of the "riches" (πλούτου, *ploutou*) of God's grace and mercy in salvation. Resonating here are passages such as Rom 2:4; 9:23; 10:12; and 11:12. Second explored is the depth of the "wisdom" of God, which would have to include the stunning, unexpected atoning sacrifice of Messiah that justifies the ungodly (3:21–26), which needs to be integrated into the stunning mystery of Israel itself (11:26). Third explored is the depth of the "knowledge" (γνώσεως, *gnōseōs*) of God. While the idea of omniscience immediately comes to mind, more specific to Romans would be the foreknowledge and call of God, resonating in passages such as Rom 8:29 and 11:2, and the "unsearchable judgments," such as the potter and clay (9:20–23), and the "inscrutable paths," such as walking in newness of life (6:4). Even the basic idea of God as creator assumes an unfathomable depth of knowledge (1:20–23; 8:19–22).

Question Triad (11:34–35)

The second series is a three-question probing that continues to augment the motif of the "depth" (βάθος, *bathos*) of God in the first series and its own three-noun expansion. This paired structure creates a beautiful chiasm that flows into the thought and then smoothly back out.[124]

    A1: Riches (noun)
        B1: Wisdom (noun)
            C1: Knowledge (noun)
            C2: Knowledge (question)
        B2: Wisdom (question)
    A2: Riches (question)

So, to enhance the thought of knowledge, the question is asked, "Who has known the mind of the Lord?" in **11:34**. While direct quotation is not indicated explicitly, the question is suspect as a probable allusion to Isa 40:13, which appropriately was yet another time when deliverance seemed impossible for Israel. God's ways simply are not in the same universe as human ways. Really, who *has* known the mind of the Lord, other than Messiah?

To enhance the thought of wisdom, the question is asked, "Who has become his counselor?" Once again, though not a direct quotation, the wording seems a probable allusion to Job 41:11. In Job, this verse is part of Yahweh's climactic speech declaring his absolute sovereignty over all creation. He created the mighty beast Leviathan (Job 41:1) that no one even dares to confront and be safe (Job 41:11). How much less could they confront God himself and be safe? Who could counsel God in how to create a beast like Leviathan, much less the universe itself?

Enhancing riches, the question is asked, "Who ever has given to God, that he should be repaid?" in **11:35**. The idea of a creator God owning everything but strangely in need of borrowing from meager human resources and having to repay is preposterous. Salvation never

---

[124] Based on the look of the Greek letter, "chi," which is like an "X" having four interrelated endpoints, so suggesting an a1 b1, a2 b2 interlocking symmetry of thought. The technique of such built-in literary structure is used to aid following the thought flow in oral cultures where one did not read silently, one listened verbally. Note the Ethiopian eunuch described reading "aloud" even though alone (Acts 8:28) and Paul's admonition to Thessalonian leaders to "have this letter read" to those not present (1 Thess 5:27).

would be a matter of putting God in debt in any way, including works of the law.[125] Fundamentally, God owes his mercy to no one, ever.

Doxology of Praise (11:36)

What is evident immediately in these words of a concluding doxology is the Jewish wisdom that proper theology always inspires doxology. Rhetorically, the genre developed as the standard Jewish punctuation mark after making a point.[126] Usually the doxology would be brief, as here, but could be more substantial. We should note that Paul here is being thoroughly consistent with the Jewish authorial *ethos* that he has developed consistently throughout Romans.[127]

Structure and Function

The doxology also has a three-part structure that mirrors the structure of the hymn of praise. This construction seems intentional as a literary way to expand the hymn of praise with a final triad that works in perfect concert to express the genuine wonderment over God's awesome reality. If the hymn of praise came from within the worship of the church, the doxology is pure Paul putting his own personalized amen to the hymn and his finishing touch to this part of the letter in **11:36**.

Triadic Prepositions (11:36)

The third series is a three-proposition celebration of God as the be all, end all of all things. The purpose of the doxology is to put Paul's own Jewish punctuation mark to emphasize the gospel as the gospel *of God* (1:1), an idea that echoes all the way back to the very first verse of the letter in a fitting literary *inclusio* that ties together all of part one.[128]

The inferred sense of each preposition is not difficult, but they do not stand in solitary isolation from one another. All three prepositions

---

[125] Or by insulting his intelligence as if the duplicitous subterfuge of works without heart possibly could hide our motives from God's awareness or view.

[126] Note the similar function in Rom 1:25 and 9:5, for example.

[127] On the significance and literary function of Paul's Jewish authorial *ethos* in Romans, see discussion, pp. 46–48.

[128] An *inclusio* is a literary marker by similarity (word, phrase, idea) at the beginning and ending of a unit to signal macrostructure to the hearer.

build together to make one unified, singular point: God is everything, and God alone.

- "from": God is the singular source

- "through": God is the singular instrument

- "to": God is the singular goal

God, and God only, is to be praised for all the riches of salvation. Paul fulfills the function for which humans were created, to bring all praise to the all powerful God in all loving gratitude. In so doing, he reverses out the Adamic rebellion that doomed the human race (1:21).

10

General Exhortations

Principles of Service and Submission

R OMANS 12–13 INTRODUCES THE SECOND half of the letter, which is
focused on exhortations in a typical theory and practice pattern of
Paul's letters. The unit is briefer, sentences less structured, and the concepts more easily grasped. All, however, thoroughly reflects and depends on the theology and emphases of Romans 1–11. In part two, after
explaining the gospel of God, Paul makes application in Rome.

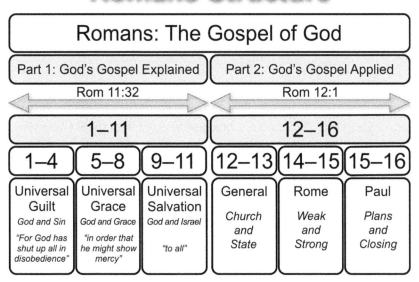

FIGURE 10.1. The Structure of Romans. Romans 12–13 is about church and state.

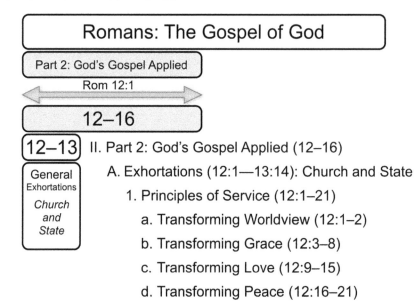

FIGURE 10.2. Outline: Romans 12 (Principles of Service).

PRINCIPLES OF SERVICE (12:1–21)

Paul moves to practicalities. Commentators sometimes wonder if the general nature of Paul's admonitions suggests he does not know much about the Roman congregations because he obviously did not found the church in Rome. Unlikely. First, Rome always has been in his sights (1:13), and he knows much more about the Roman situation than he is given credit. Most particularly ignored is his long mission relationship with Prisca and Aquila, members of a Roman congregation themselves refugee victims of the Claudius Edict banishing Jews from Rome. Paul met the couple when he arrived in Corinth on the second missionary journey and established a joint business venture with them (Acts 18:1–3). The couple continued with Paul when he left Corinth for Ephesus (Acts 18:18–19). We should note that Prisca and Aquila continued to attend synagogue services in Ephesus, because that is where they encountered the gifted Apollos and had to take him aside and explain "the way of God more accurately to him" (Acts 18:24–26).[1] Paul also

---

[1] In Luke's surrounding context of Pauline mission, probably meaning they explained the Pauline gospel to Apollos they had learned in Corinth. See Stevens, *Acts*, 407–08.

specifically sends greetings to this couple at the end of this letter (16:3–4). Paul likely knew much more about the church in Rome and the contours of complex profile through his long association with this couple. They could offer eyewitness testimony to Paul to the synagogue setting, religious development, and social consequence of the momentous Edict of Claudius. Paul potentially could have been in touch with them after they arrived back in Rome sometime after their stay at Ephesus.

Paul first moves to principles of service. Realities of the New Aeon transform all of life and become the universal basis of all conduct. Once worldview is transformed, then grace, love, and peace become defining and transforming principles of service in messianic Israel.

Hopefully. Paul does have concern. Dangerous gentile conceit is lurking at the door, fed by Roman prejudice against Jews (11:20). This unrecognized and imminent danger internally threatens the fellowship and externally threatens God's mission enterprise to all the nations, as Paul just has made clear in Romans 11. Not a trifling matter for Paul.

Transforming Worldview (12:1–2)

Paul changes gears but builds on a key idea of the first part of Romans, the grace of God: "I beg you by the mercies (οἰκτιρμῶν, *oiktirmōn*) of God" (**12:1**). A synonymous term for grace is used (*oiktirmōn*).[2] Grace is fundamental to the reality of messianic Israel. God's grace is the foundation of the New Aeon and the exclusive basis of salvation. God's grace is the entire argument of Romans 1–11. Thus, this word of grace in the opening exhortation is intended to hover over the entire second part of Romans. Paul, as before, uses the affectionate "brothers," which translations degenderize as "brothers and sisters." The tone is familial, a defining characteristic of Pauline expression that later became "canonized church speak" so to speak, in the later centuries of the church. For Paul, the expression was sincere, even if socially the rhetoric was of fictive family. The literary point is the corporate nature of the ethical appeal, showing Romans is a community document start to finish. This corporate dimension is crucial for proper perspective in Romans 5–8.

---

[2] Only four times in Paul. The three others are "Father of mercies" (2 Cor 1:3), "if any affection and mercy" (Phil 2:1), and "put on compassion, mercy, humility" (Col 3:12). The nuanced difference is between receiving a gift (*charis*) versus receiving a kindness (*oiktirmos*), but either understood as an act of mercy.

FIGURE 10.3. Imperial Cult Priest, Ephesus. Note the prominently displayed imperial cult ring of a proud, high status, aristocratic family of Ephesus (IAMI).

Paul beseeches the Romans "to present your bodies a living sacrifice." "Living sacrifice," we need to be reminded, is a basic contradiction in terms. You cannot kill an animal in sacrifice and the animal thereafter be alive. All through the streets of Rome sacrificial rituals were conducted daily in numerous temples. The smell of incense and sounds of ritual were part of the daily lives of Romans. To this ritual should be added activities of imperial cult priests in the provinces, but especially in Asia Minor, where Paul had ministered extensively, such as Ephesus, where Paul just had concluded a three-year ministry before writing Romans.[3] In distinction from what would be pleasing to the emperor, Paul calls for sacrifice that would be pleasing to God. Life in Messiah has been rearranged and reoriented. Idolatrous sacrifices that bring the wrath of God (1:23–25) have been rendered foolish by the propitiation in Messiah's own death (3:21–26). The sacrifice of a contrite heart to God is to be the new norm (Ps 51:17). This goal of holy and pleasing to God fulfills the Mosaic law. Paul still is working Rom 8:1–4. This

[3] For background on the imperial cult, see pp. 144–48. On the city of Ephesus in particular, see Stevens, *Revelation*, 287–98.

pattern of sacrificial living, of course, is the pattern of Messiah and the new covenant relationship with God through Messiah. Paul will use this point in later exhortations to the weak and the strong (15:3).

This "living" sacrifice, a life lived wholly to God, is "your reasonable service," or "true worship," or "spiritual worship." The expression τὴν λογικὴν λατρείαν, (*tēn logikēn latreian*) is ambiguous, though each word by itself is simple enough.[4] The meaning seems to encompass the *non-cultic pattern of messianic worship*, counter to almost anything in the ancient world. Service in the temple in Jerusalem was full of ritual and liturgy. These regulations in Scripture terribly bore modern readers but so absorbed the ancients. In contradistinction, worship in messianic Israel essentially is in living life itself, not in any specific cultic rite—a revolutionary idea. Messianic worship did not even involve a common libation ritual. The believer's life poured out is the libation (Phil 2:17).

FIGURE 10.4. Apollo Kylix. Apollo, crowned with a myrtle-leaf wreath, dressed in white peplos, red himation. Left hand plays lyre as right hand offers wine libation from a navel-phiale (AMAC). Credit: Jean M. Stevens.

[4] This λογικός, *logikos*, is logical, rational thought, which philosophers equated with "spiritual." This λατρεία, *latreia*, is cultic ritual, service, or ministry, that is, worship.

"Do not be conformed to this age" Paul exhorts further (**12:2**). In the context of sacrifice and ritual, the conformity profile is given in Rom 1:18–32. The age is the Old Aeon of Adamic weakness (5:12–21). We are back to the Pauline eschatological framework upon which the analysis given in Romans 1–4 and Romans 5–8 hangs.

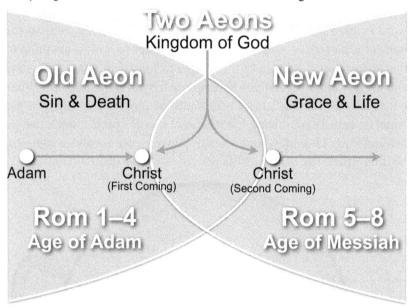

FIGURE 10.5. The Two Aeons. Paul's discussion in Romans 1–8 assumes the reality of two aeons that tell the human story and summarize the beginning and end.

Instead, Paul advises, "be transformed by the renewing of the mind in order that you might approve what is the good, acceptable and complete will of God." Transformation of a mind is the essential work of the Spirit in the New Aeon (8:5–8). This transformation is not working quite as needed in the Roman house churches. The problem of the weak and strong is silent testimony to the need to be more intentional on finding the mind of Messiah. Paul already is laying groundwork for that discussion. Being able to "approve" (δοκιμάζω, *dokimazō*, "test," "discern") the good, acceptable, and complete will of God is nothing less than Messiah bringing about fulfillment (*telos*) of the law in believers (10:4; cf. 3:31). A transformed mind is one of the key signatures of the Spirit in the New Aeon. All other qualities of a life of faith—such as grace, love, peace—flow from those headwaters.

One might note that what Paul describes in these first two verses actually shows how the realities of the New Aeon already are reversing the realities of the Old Aeon. Language echoes in Rom 12:1–2 back to the discussion in Romans 1–2 seem intentional to make this point.

New Aeon Reversal of Old Aeon Problems

Romans 1–2 (Old Aeon)	Rom 12:1–2 (New Aeon)
"to dishonor their own **bodies**" (1:24)	"present your **bodies** a living sacrifice" (12:1)
"**worshipped and served** the creature" (1:25)	"to God, which is your **reasonable service**" (12:1)
"gave them up to a **disapproved mind**" (1:28)	"be transformed by the **renewing of your mind**" (12:2)
"know **his will**, approve excellent things" (2:18)	"that you might approve the **will of God**" (12:2)

FIGURE 10.6. New Aeon Reversal. Romans 12:1–2 reflects the language of Romans 1–2.

Transforming Grace (12:3–8)

The first principle of service derives from transforming grace. Receiving a gift (*charis*) is an act of God's mercy. In this unit is where Paul confronts again the issue of Roman arrogance and conceit (**12:3**). While conceit is a general problem anywhere, the particular version in Rome was insidious because the conceit lived on prejudice. That kind of conceit is hard to exorcise. Gentile believers lording over Jewish believers in Rome had the potential to destroy Paul's vision of all Israel saved (11:18–20). Paul's attempt to persuade Roman believers on the seriousness of the problem pointed out that God measures out faith to the community. The very existence of faith is at the divine initiative in the first place. Properly understanding how faith comes by divine initiative should be the *coup de gras* to conceit. Without that understanding, the community will shortchange God's intended work. Ironically, the attitude of Mosaic Israel would lurk in the shadows (2:17–24).

From the perspective of history, Paul's pastoral concern could not have been more on the mark. Paul was driving for the reconciliation in Rome that God was driving for with Israel (11:15). History seems to suggest he lost his gambit. Dealing with prejudice is a sobering thought to contemplate in any setting of the church for the potential damage to the goal of global outreach of the gospel, whether in the first century or the twenty-first century.[5]

Gifts gifted by God upon which the church depends for doing its work should humble the community gratefully to acknowledge that all credit goes to God for the church. Paul turned to the body metaphor to make this point, a favorite Pauline metaphor for the church (**12:4–5**).[6] This metaphor and its use for illustrating a corporate issue here in Romans 12 is another indication how Paul uses the rhetoric of plural grammar but intends corporate application, as in Rom 8:10.[7] New Aeon corporate priorities are inclusivism, diversity, and community, which also serves as a reminder that belief always is a corporate matter for Paul, not simply private. Any Pauline church will be charismatic in these terms of grace gifts that mean a believer's life is not self driven.

Grace gifts function to equip the church (**12:6–8**). Their individual roles are easy to grasp. Some overlap to some degree, showing that mathematical precision is not the point.

- *prophecy* (προφητεία, *prophēteia*): prophecy interprets and communicates the divine will. Paul functioned this way in the Roman setting notably with the revelation of the mystery of Israel's hardening in part (11:25), which was a crucial word from God for them.

- *service* (διακονία, *diakonia*): acts that are performed specifically on behalf of others; in government, the idea would be civil service, in cult, priestly service, in church, ministerial service. This function probably became more significant as gentile house churches were

---

[5] If we take the measure of second-century patristic attittudes, Paul was not able to stem the tide of gentile conceit. Inherent Roman prejudice against Jews became fertile soil for inculcating gentile conceit in the church about inherent worth over the Jews. The social pathway was the recently evolving gentile house church, a new feature of Roman congregations after the Claudius Edict that had disturbed the social structure of synagogues in Rome. An arrogant superiority complex that already existed at the time Paul wrote Romans (11:20) eventually did have devastating impact on his optimistic forecast of Israel's future. Arrogance never makes anyone jealous, just angry (11:11). In any case, accomplishing reconciliation in Rome did not have the luxury of time. The Judean powder keg was primed to blow soon, and did. Judea went to war with Rome only nine years after Paul wrote Romans. All bets were off the table at that point, and, as they say, the rest is history.

[6] 1 Cor 10:16–17; 12:12–27; Eph 3:6; 4:4, 12, 16; Col 1:24; 2:19; 3:15.

[7] Notable for understanding the intent of plural grammar throughout Romans 5–8.

developing their own gatherings independently of the synagogue and its fully organized system of community service.

- *teaching* (διδασκαλία, *didaskalia*): instruction to bring knowledge, but including the idea of wisdom in applying knowledge to life. This gift epitomizes the letter of Romans itself, which apparently was meant temporarily to substitute for Paul's own presence until he personally could arrive in Rome, as he long had planned to do (1:10–11). Rome was the wild card in early Christianity with its own mysterious track of development. This church had unclear leadership, undifferentiated demographic profile, and unknown authority for its traditions. Paul deftly quoted from the Roman creed at the beginning of the letter (1:3–4) only later to use that very creed as the ground of confession of Messiah unto salvation (10:9). Thus, we can spy over his shoulder to watch Paul intentionally and purposefully trying to build a fundamental rapport with this church in a way congruent with his own gospel. The letter of Romans viewed from this angle was Paul's bid to become an integral part of Rome's story.[8]

- *exhortation* (παράκλησις, *paraklēsis*): encouragement that persuades behavior modification including lifting up the spirits by comfort and consolation. Again, we see this need in issues within the congregations of incipient disunity, increasing problems with acceptance of civil authority, and serious factionalizing over weak and strong parties, not to speak of theological points of the Pauline gospel.

- *giving* (μεταδιδούς, *metadidous*): actually built on the verb meaning to give, impart, share, but with the added stipulation of "sincerity" (ἁπλότης, *haplotēs*), which addresses personal integrity in being upright, sincere, frank, not dissimulating, that is, not manipulative by the act of giving for ulterior motives such as to gain return; another semantic domain for *haplotēs* is "generosity," which would address attitudes of stinginess, giving only the absolute minimum required. This gift potentially could aim for the patron-client relationships upon which the local house churches in Rome were built, but which themselves had decided disadvantages socially and for communion of the saints. A patron could be offering financial support or accommodations for meetings but at the same time expecting certain

---

[8] See discussion, p. 162.

behaviors of compliance and support in return from his or her house church clients.

- *leading* (προϊστάμενος, *proistamenos*): actually is built on the verb meaning exercising a position of leadership, or one with responsibility to direct or be at the head. A derivative meaning is having an interest in a group's success, or showing care for a group's needs, or giving aid. Again, this idea has the added stipulation of "diligence" (σπουδή, *spoudē*), implying swift action or haste to perform, or the ancillary thought of an "eagerness" or "earnestness," or even "zeal." While one might think of those with gifts of prophecy and teaching who are targeted, as those areas do overlap, other "leaders" emerge in the first-century setting not as obvious today, such as the patrons of the house churches.[9] Paul also soon will be exhorting the need for taking the lead in showing familial love, another place this gift needed to be brought to bear more diligently (12:10).

- *having mercy* (ἐλεῶν, *eleōn*): actually built on the verb meaning to show or have mercy, but with the added stipulation of "cheerfulness" (ἱλαρότης, *hilarotēs*); otherwise the act of mercy becomes counterproductive for lifting up the spirits of someone under duress. The problem of arrogant gentiles actually is one of denying mercy to the group most needing the benefit of mercy. The gift of mercy is a sore need in the Roman church on this score, and Paul is trying to boost the stock of those willing to show mercy, but particularly with cheerfulness on behalf of the recipient.

The list is notable in several ways that are important for practical application in a contemporary setting. First, the list is incomplete and not exhaustive. This incompleteness would be true of any list of spiritual gifts in the Pauline letters. Incomplete status suggests the gifts mentioned in any given Pauline letter are those most important to that congregation addressed at that time. Thus, the variety of gifts in various lists in Paul implies God continuously is gifting churches according to particular needs in each setting. We have suggested above how a "targeted" gift list might work specifically, for example, applied to the

---

[9] One only need think of rural churches today that often are owned and controlled by one patriarchal family populating the pews with aunts, uncles, cousins, and in-laws, who block vote at business meetings, meaning only one opinion actually matters.

Roman congregation. The natural inference would be that no gift list of any particular church necessarily should exactly match that of any other church.

Second, the list is notable in that items are unranked. Ranking gifts is antithetical to the whole point: all gifts contribute to the whole, and the whole is less than complete for its task in the world if any one gift is not applied.

Third, the list is notable in that we see Paul presuming automatically that every believer is gifted. Since the Spirit is the absolutely essential ingredient in the life of the New Aeon (8:1–4, 9), then gifts would be a natural function of the indwelling Spirit. That the Spirit would indwell and not make its presence known through Spirit-sourced giftedness was not even a thought that crossed Paul's mind.

Fourth, the list is notable for suggesting that unity is a hallmark of proper attitude toward the presence of gifts. Disunity betrays wrong attitudes about grace gifts, how they are given, why they are given, and how they are distributed by God. Disunity over grace gifts was the story of the Corinthian church. This church then added to Paul's woes by rejecting his authority. Such trouble with Corinth was prelude to writing Romans, which Paul most certainly could hope not repeated in Rome.[10]

If one pays close attention to this list of gifts in Romans, one can perceive that these gifts taken together as a unit show characteristic features overall that probably are true of any list of gifts by Paul. The list reveals how gifts all work ultimately for the goal of empowering God's global outreach. In fact, corporately gifts help incarnate God's global outreach. Thus, gifts, rightly understood and applied, basically should take their cue by modeling the pattern of Jesus as Messiah.

At the same time, gifts can create disturbance in the church. The church at Corinth is defined by this very issue, as the letter of 1 Corinthians illustrates so well. One of the greatest dangers with gifts is their overemphasis. That overemphasis on charism itself is a subtle form of idolatry, worshipping and serving the created thing rather than the Creator (1:22–23). In fact, the problem of Mosaic Israel is mirrored as God's righteousness is perverted into an Adamic-inspired "charism" righteousness similar to Mosaic Israel's "works" righteousness (10:3).

---

[10] The near loss of his authority in the church at Corinth was profiled earlier. See discussion, pp. 125–26.

Transforming Love (12:9–15)

The second principle of service derives from transforming love. Here is another place where a literary *inclusio*, this time on an evil/good polarity, marks the entire unit. Note how the unit opens with "hate evil . . . hold fast the good" (12:9) and ends with "overcome evil with good" (12:21). The *inclusio* shows how Paul regards both virtues of love and peace as a mutually acting pair, even though for purposes of discussion we take them separately.

The sentences become short and choppy, but they are not ad hoc, scatterbrained ramblings. Exegesis is benefited greatly simply by observing that these short clips are short precisely to make them effective rhetorical embellishments reemphasizing the pertinence of the gift list, especially within the context of Rome and these congregations.

Take, for example, the short clip in **12:9**, "Abhor evil and cling to the good." The participle translated "cling" (κολλώμενοι, *kollōmenoi*) is "to glue." Paul in English would have said, "Be glued to good." Pretty graphic. Being glued to good, however, was imperative to resist the rampant immorality of the ancient world. Roman mores of social behavior, especially after the impact of perversions of emperors such as Caligula—the key conceptual target of the word "evil" (πονηρόν, *poneron*) in this context—were thoroughly incompatible with life to be lived in the New Aeon. Abhorring evil in Rome would require the equivalent of moral superglue.

Again, another short clip is that love be without hypocrisy (12:9). Genuine love is the core experience of the New Aeon (5:5), and Paul cannot conceive separation from God's love in Messiah (8:35). "Without hypocrisy" is one word in Greek, ἀνυπόκριτος (*anypocritos*). This word hypocrisy originates in Greek drama for the skill of play acting to imitate emotions, often signaled to large crowds at a distance from the stage by wearing an oversized mask appropriate to the emotion or overall role (tragic, comic) of the actor in the drama.[11] Paul knows that love can be play acted, and, if so, is the death knell of love. He already here anticipates discussion of the problem of the weak and the strong, strategically implying even before he gets to that discussion that the deeper problem is not really the strength of faith but the absence of genuine love, which alone would solve the problem forthwith. Paul

---

[11] See p. 171, and Stevens, *Divine Wrath*, 30–36.

practically says as much when he quickly follows up with, "Be devoted to familial love unto one another," a most unusual way to express showing familial love (**12:10**).[12] In the ancient world, brotherly love inherently assumed strong devotion by default. Exhorting being devoted to being devoted seems redundant, but that is actually Paul's point. The claim to familial love in Rome needs intentional effort at recapturing its reality. The issue of the weak and the strong needs a strong look in the mirror.

The gift of leading comes to bear right at this point of being devoted to familial love. Paul admonishes, "Take the lead in honoring one another." Those gifted with leadership need to show the way on the path toward solving the problem of the weak and the strong. The deeper the division is allowed to grow, the more each faction will begin dishonoring the other in all the ways possible socially as a form of passive aggressive rebuke.

"Do not be slothful in zeal" is the next short clip (**12:11**).[13] This appeal to zeal takes up the stipulation in the gift list of zeal added to the gift of leading. The connection in the immediate context is back to taking the lead in honoring one another. To be effective at solving the weak and strong debate, lackadaisical leadership only will make matters worse, not better, being useless. Energy and determination (the sense of "zeal" in this context of leadership) will be imperative. The next clip parallels the thought, but from the perspective of how this type of zealous leadership is empowered: "be fervent in Spirit." The Spirit is the key to the proper functioning of all gifts, but critically to the gift of leadership. Bearing one another's burdens fulfills the law of Messiah (Gal 6:2), but ministry truly is a load difficult to bear (2 Cor 11:28). Spirit-empowered ministry is essential in this task of leadership. Then, "serving the Lord" uses the verb for being owned by another, being subjected to another, that is, being a slave (δουλεύω, *douleuō*). Paul is back to the first verse of Romans: "Paul, slave of Messiah Jesus." More and more as we go through this incredible letter we see how Paul's opening word throws down the gauntlet to envisioning committed discipleship and true church leadership.

---

[12] The Greek is τῇ φιλαδελφίᾳ εἰς ἀλλήλους φιλόστοργοι (*tēi philadelphiai eis allēlous philostorgoi*).

[13] The Greek is τῇ σπουδῇ μὴ ὀκνηροί, (*tēi spoudēi mē oknēroi*).

In **12:12** Paul pivots to those particular eschatological realities brought about by the New Aeon that Messiah has inaugurated that attend to the burden of being a leader enslaved to the Messiah. The first is an ability to "rejoice in hope." This "hope" always in Romans is the promise of life in the future kingdom of God (5:2; 8:20–25). Rejoicing in hope is a tonic to the sense of burden, since the effort is promised a result on the basis of the faithfulness of God. The second is its eschatological cousin in the present time of the overlap of the ages: "be patient in affliction." Hope becomes the foundation of patience. This sequence of hope and affliction here in 12:12 simply reworks 5:2–4 and its series of affliction, endurance, character, and hope, which is the progression of eschatological life from this age to the next. Equipped in this way with hope and patience, the leader can find the will to "be persistent in prayer," which also is assisted by the Spirit (8:26–27).

These short, seemingly disjointed clips really are not, if the immediate context of the charismata list is foregrounded as the rhetorical exigency for these exhortations. This exegesis makes more sense than that Paul without real purpose is throwing around general maxims to see what will stick on the wall, as if he just tacks these on to fill vague expectations for some type of exhortations to end a letter, mainly because he is clueless of the actual situation in Rome and does not have a better idea what to do at this point.

The next word of exhortation seems to move directly to encourage patrons of the Roman house churches (including some of those at the end of the letter in the greetings in Romans 16). Paul exhorts, "Share with the saints in their needs" (**12:13**). All members of the Roman house churches are saints, and the letter is addressed to all these saints ("to all who are in Rome, loved by God, called as saints," 1:7). Thus, the admonition in effect encompasses the support of the entire church in Rome. In the house church structure, that responsibility basically falls to the patron(ess) for churches with that organizational structure. In this setting, "pursue hospitality" would have been a direct instruction that patrons and patronesses take on the role of seeing after the room and board needs of visitors who had business with the church as did traveling prophets and ministers (such as Paul himself). Hospitality was one of the premier expectations of a church leader in the early church, because ancient inns and way stations were unsafe by reason of robbers and unpleasant by reason of poor living conditions, such as rats and lice.[14] Hospitality was a highly valued virtue, and hosting travelers and visitors was a common need throughout the biblical period.[15] Recommendations for this reason served a vital function of verifying the authenticity of a visitor to a church, and the function of the effusive recommendation of Phoebe (16:1–2), revealed as a leader of the church at Cenchreae and personal patroness to Paul. She would be needing hospitality for her stay in Rome as the likely bearer of the letter of Romans. Thus, Paul already is setting the stage for the Phoebe recommendation and expectation of leaders in Rome with his "pursue hospitality" in 12:13. If the house church is less loosely organized, as Jewett noted for a tenement house setting, then the admonition would be more difficult,[16] particularly true in the Trastevere region across the Tiber river, as well as the Porta Capena region proximate to that gate ending the Via Appia.[17] In any such tenement assembly, sharing with the saints in their needs would have required community effort on the part of most of those participating. Pursuing hospitality in the typical terms of providing lodging and food also would have been a tenuous proposition in these crowded *insula* apartments.

The next clip is "Bless those who persecute you; bless and do not curse" (**12:14**).[18] Suspicion that Paul here begins using a series of Jesus sayings learned from the tradition is voiced often.[19] While the possible influence of dominical sayings seems a fair proposal, exegesis simply left there is not enough. What is the rhetorical exigency of placement just here in Romans? Jesus tradition background is interesting, but the rhetorical exigency is found in integrating the necessary hermeneutic in the Roman context for the specific gifts identified in the list enumerated in 12:6–8. These short clips enhance the pertinence of each gift.

[14] Cf. Earle, "Inn; Lodge; Lodging Place," ISBE Revised, 2:826–27.

[15] Koenig, "Hospitality," AYBD, 3:299–301.

[16] See discussion, pp. 177–79.

[17] See discussion, pp. 160–62.

[18] New unit proposals include here at 12:14, or at 12:15, or 12:16. Commentators disagree on internal organization, whether grammatical (participle constructions, infinitives, etc.), or conceptual (internal relationships with believers, external with non-believers). So-called patterns, however, inevitably have inconsistencies.

[19] See a detailed proposal of four dominical sayings in Longenecker (*Romans*, 938–41). He suggested 12:14–16 (Matt 5:44); 12:17–18 (Matt 5:39–42); 12:19–20 (independent *logion*); and 12:21 (Matt 5:38–48).

The verb for persecute is "pursue" (διώκω, *diōkō*), as in chasing after fleeing prey. After Mattathias began the Maccabean Revolt, the general population fled Syrian forces, who pursued them into the hillside caves. Jews refused to fight on the Sabbath, so Syrian troops easily killed them all, about a thousand, by smoke inhalation from fires at the cave entrances.[20] Jews were well aware of religious persecution, and even though Roman law from the time of Caesar forward set out to protect Jewish rights, local populations took occasion to desecrate synagogues with other offenses. One famous example is the serious disturbance in the Jewish quarter in Alexandria, Egypt that led to Philo's embassy to Rome to plead on behalf of Alexandrian Jews to Caligula; another is the desecration in Caesarea that triggered the Jewish War.[21] The track record of both Jesus and his early followers in Jerusalem is anticipated in the beatitude to bless those who persecute (Matt 5:10). To this add Paul's own track record, and the deduction is obvious that religious persecution always trailed the story of the Jews, which was reprised in the story of those following Jesus as Messiah. Paul as Saul of Tarsus had been on the other side of the story himself, pursuing believers in Damascus. He acknowledged that the Thessalonians were suffering at the hands of their own countrymen (1 Thess 2:14). In Rome, Paul is thinking about the Edict of Claudius. He is anticipating matters could deteriorate even for house churches also associated with "Chrestus" preaching evocative of synagogue disturbances only a few years earlier. The intense irony in this verse, of course, is Paul's martyrdom in Rome, according to church tradition, by the same emperor who was ruling earlier at the time he wrote Romans.[22]

In **12:15** we have the balanced "Rejoice with those who rejoice; weep with those who weep." One instantly thinks of 1 Cor 12:26, which is quite similar in thought, so seems to be a Pauline pattern for general exhortation on the basis of the thought that even when life is good, underneath always is the realization that persecution is unpredictable,

---

[20] Mattathias convinced Jews to fight on the Sabbath (Josephus, *Ant.* 271–77 [12.6.2]).

[21] Cf. Philo, *Embassy to Gaius*. According to Josephus, *J.W.* 2.14.5, Greek merchants in Caesarea offensively sacrificed birds in front of a synagogue, which inspired Eleazar ben Hanania to cease prayers for the emperor at the temple in Jerusalem, starting war.

[22] Interestingly, Paul may have died in Rome, but not as a result of martyrdom after the fire of Rome. See "Epilogue: Intimations of Mortality: On Conjuring Paul's Death and Burial," in Stevens, *Acts*, 577–606.

as Philo discovered in Alexandria. Joy can turn to sadness and struggle rather quickly, and, as new converts in Thessalonica discovered, confession of Jesus as Messiah not always is well received in a community that follows other values, such as those of the Roman emperor.

Transforming Peace (12:16–21)

The third principle of service derives from transforming peace. The exhortation to "live in harmony with one another" in **12:16** does seem to suggest an intended motif for the following series of exhortations.[23] Paul again is driving toward the needed discussion about the weak and the strong in Romans 14–15. Love and peace work mutually to build harmony in the community, which renders the paired exhortations that follow quite pertinent for pointing to the precise problem in attitude that is haunting Roman congregations and fostering the conflict of the weak and strong: "Do not be proud; instead associate with the humble. Do not be wise in your own estimation." Associating with the humble made little to no sense to first-century, Greco-Roman minds. Humility was not a virtue. Humility was sourced in low social status, undistinguished background, having no inherent power or reputation. Such a person by default would be forced to be subservient to others just to meet basic life needs. They would be unpretentious in any relationship. Such a profile was dishonorable and demeaning, so nothing for which to aspire to get ahead in a power-grubbing, position-envying, honor-shame society. Belonging to messianic Israel required value inversions such as this call to associate with the humble that were costly to a first-century sense of self-esteem. Paul continues hacking away at the root of arrogance already manifest in Roman assemblies (11:20).

Another arena for New Aeon peace to manifest itself is in relationships with outsiders, which seems to be the new focus in the turn at **12:17** that continues to the end of the chapter. Not repaying evil for evil reflects Jesus tradition of turning the other cheek to interrupt the path of escalating conflict (Matt 5:38–40). Seeking what is honorable in the eyes of all is persuasion toward cultivating community harmony so as not to impede the progress of gospel penetration into a society.

---

[23] The translation "live in harmony" is a paraphrase. The Greek is "think the same thing unto one another" (τὸ αὐτὸ εἰς ἀλλήλους φρονοῦντες, *to auto eis allēlous phronountes*).

Seeking what is honorable "in the sight of all," however, also is meant to discourage personal vendetta. Any particular case should submit to the common consensus of what is "right." The goal is stated clearly in the follow up expression: to live at peace with "everyone," even to the point of "as far as possible" (**12:18**).

Just how far, though, is "possible"? This quest for peace even includes not seeking unilaterally to avenge a wrong (**12:19**). Yes, that far, Paul exhorts. Again, such an exhortation made little to no sense to the mindset within that ancient context. Gaining vengeance actually was considered required in an honor-shame society in order to retain the balance of the limited quantity of honor to go around.

For countering the vicious cycle of violence provoked by human sensibilities as to appropriate vengeance, the path of wisdom is leaving matters to God. So, restraining personal vendetta meant recognizing some matters inherently belong to God alone. To this end, Paul advises to "give place to the wrath" (δότε τόπον τῇ ὀργῇ, *dote topon tēi orgēi*). Wrath is not specified explicitly as God's wrath, simply given with the article as "the wrath," but the following quotation makes absolutely certain divine wrath is meant.

Paul quotes Deut 32:35 that vengeance belongs to God, who will repay.[24] That the wrath is that of eschatological judgment, as suggested by Käsemann, is unlikely.[25] Wrath in Romans can include its historical manifestation (1:18–32), which is much more likely here in terms of Paul dealing with potential problems in Rome. Divine wrath in Greek thought often was seen as preserving the proper order of government and religion.[26] Further, the immediately following application of wrath language in 13:1–4 explicitly is within the divinely appointed arena of local government.

This poetic line is from a hymn celebrating Yahweh as a warrior who avenges the blood of his children despoiled by conquering pagan adversaries in a judgment on these aggressors in like and kind.

---

[24] Interestingly, the quotation follows neither the Hebrew nor Septuagint, but more closely readings in the Targums; cf. *Onkelos* (Etheridge, 2:550), *Jonathan* (Etheridge, 2:668; *Jerusalem* (Etheridge, 2:668). Similarities might derive from a possible proverb at the time (Myer, *Romans*, 480–81). Similar thought is in Sir 28:1 (LXX): "The one who avenges will discover vengeance from the Lord." See Stevens, *Divine Wrath*, 182.

[25] Käsemann, *Romans*, 349.

[26] See Stevens, *Divine Wrath*, 37–39.

When I whet my flashing sword.
    and my hand takes hold on judgment;
I will take vengeance on my adversaries,
    and will repay those who hate me.
I will make my arrows drunk with blood,
    and my sword shall devour flesh—
with the blood of the slain and with captives,
    from the long-haired enemy (Deut 32:41–42, NRSV).

The imagery is martial and brutal so naturally offends modern sensibilities, but the thought of the eventual vindication of God's people by God himself is a well-trod path in the prophets. What we learn from Paul in Romans that takes reflection deeper than rudimentary and simplistic balancing of an injury scale is that God has mysterious ways of working his wrath toward mercy, which is revolutionary in thinking about God, particularly within the ancient Greco-Roman mindset. Leaving vengeance to God would make room for mercy like humans simply would not, if Romans 9–11 is any measure. Even Greeks were wise enough on occasion, even when grievances with others had been long-standing, to seek the advice of the gods, as did the Spartan king, Archidamus II, before going to war with Plataea in 429 BC.[27]

Instead of vengeance, Paul urges feeding the hungry enemy and giving the thirsty a drink (12:20). Paul quotes Prov 25:21–22, and the thought reflects the teaching of Jesus (Matt 5:44; Luke 6:27). Such action most certainly would be one form of how to bless those who persecute (12:14). While some in the ancient world might understand the action as generosity and magnanimity, others perhaps would be confused, not recognizing any typical honor-shame ritual. The action also would be a most innovative way to "give place to the wrath," not only by showing absolute trust and reliance upon God to choose how to be the ultimate vindicator, but also simultaneously working toward the mercy toward which God always is known to be working, because he reveals his fundamental character in his sovereignty as one who will have mercy upon whom he will have mercy (Exod 33:19; Rom 9:15).

The idea of heaping coals of fire has no sure exegesis, whether in Proverbs or Paul.[28] Best to leave that hound dog sleeping on the porch.

---

[27] Thucydides, *War* 2.74.

[28] Moo, *Romans*, 788–89 has a good summary of options; also, Fitzmyer, *Romans*, 657–58. None are any too persuasive. All require somewhat convoluted logic to get to

Prudent exegesis at least can observe that the context is positive, not punitive, due to the immediately following positive summary that admonishes overcoming evil with good.[29] Thus, the intent of coals of fire likely is redemptive, but any contemporary application lost. That is, since we cannot know precisely the meaning, we are challenged to find a principle to apply.

In **12:21** we have the closing of the literary *inclusio* tying back to the good/evil polarity established in 12:9. The structure is a doublet that reflects a typical Semitic parallelism common in Jewish wisdom and poetry literature: "Do not be conquered by evil, but conquer evil with good."[30] Paul perhaps echoes thought in Matt 5:38–48. In that context, going beyond gentile norms means particularly those that restrict care exclusively to the group to which one belongs (Matt 5:47). Jews did similarly by restricting "neighbor" in the love your neighbor command by the technicality that the alien in the land was not in strictest of terms a neighbor. One thus circumscribed the command to love a neighbor by eliminating obligation to outsiders. This sleight of hand hermeneutical card trick Jesus rejected smartly in the parable of the good Samaritan (Luke 10:25–37). One can make a general observation that the intent here is gaining victory over evil both by not allowing evil to corrupt moral integrity and by giving an example of the character of Christ.[31]

Paul's thought probably runs deeper, with structural mooring in Israel developed in Romans 9–11. Overcoming evil with good is exactly how the wrath of God works. Wrath allows sin to be exceedingly sinful in order to guarantee complete and permanent quarantine in the death of Messiah, which by divine mercy is declared full justification of the ungodly by delivering entirely from all guilt of sin. Wrath hardens Israel after choosing disobedience but by divine mercy preserves a remnant so that in the end, all Israel can be saved. In these terms, overcoming evil with good is by definition the mystery of the cross and the mystery of a future for Israel.

---

application in 12:20. Appealing to an Egyptian repentance ritual from the third century BC compounded by speculation this ritual became widely proverbial for repentance is a stretch; yet, cf. Käsemann, *Romans*, 349; Cranfield, *Romans*, 650; Wright, *Romans*, 10:715; Jewett, *Romans*, 777; Hultgren, *Romans*, 460; Longenecker, *Romans*, 941.

[29] So, for example, Fitzmyer, *Romans*, 658.

[30] Cf. Geller, *Parallelism in Early Hebrew Poetry*.

[31] Moo, *Romans*, 790.

On the motif of peace, the countercultural value of messianic Israel directly challenges the imperial definition of peace foundational to Rome's own ideology and gospel for the world.[32] The difference with the gospel of God hardly could be more radical. The experience of conversion for a Roman gentile and incorporation into this new community of faith inevitably would have involved a serious case of cultural whiplash, requiring a truly transformed mind.

One also should notice the chosen verb in both elements of the concluding parallelism that ends this unit is "conquer" (νικάω, *nikaō*). A deliberate echo back to the conclusion of Romans 1–8 in Rom 8:37 seems to suggest itself. Paul had concluded that "in all these things we are more than conquerors (ὑπερνικῶμεν, *hypernikōmen*) through the one who loved us." These New Aeon principles of service inspired by a transformed mind and empowered by transforming grace, love, and peace facilitated becoming more than conquerors and thereby lay the foundation for the future Israel of God.

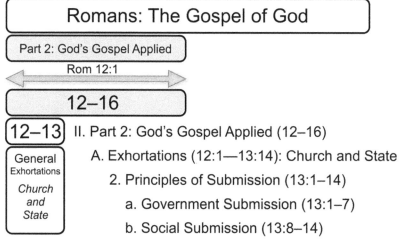

FIGURE 10.7. Outline: Romans 13 (Principles of Submission).

The first order of business for proper exegesis of this material is to become acquainted with first-century history of the Roman Empire. The main task is learning the Julio-Claudian line of imperial succession. Adoption was crucial, but devious schemes in transitions of power also complicate the story (consult fig. 5.63, p. 210).

---

[32] See discussion, pp. 127–37.

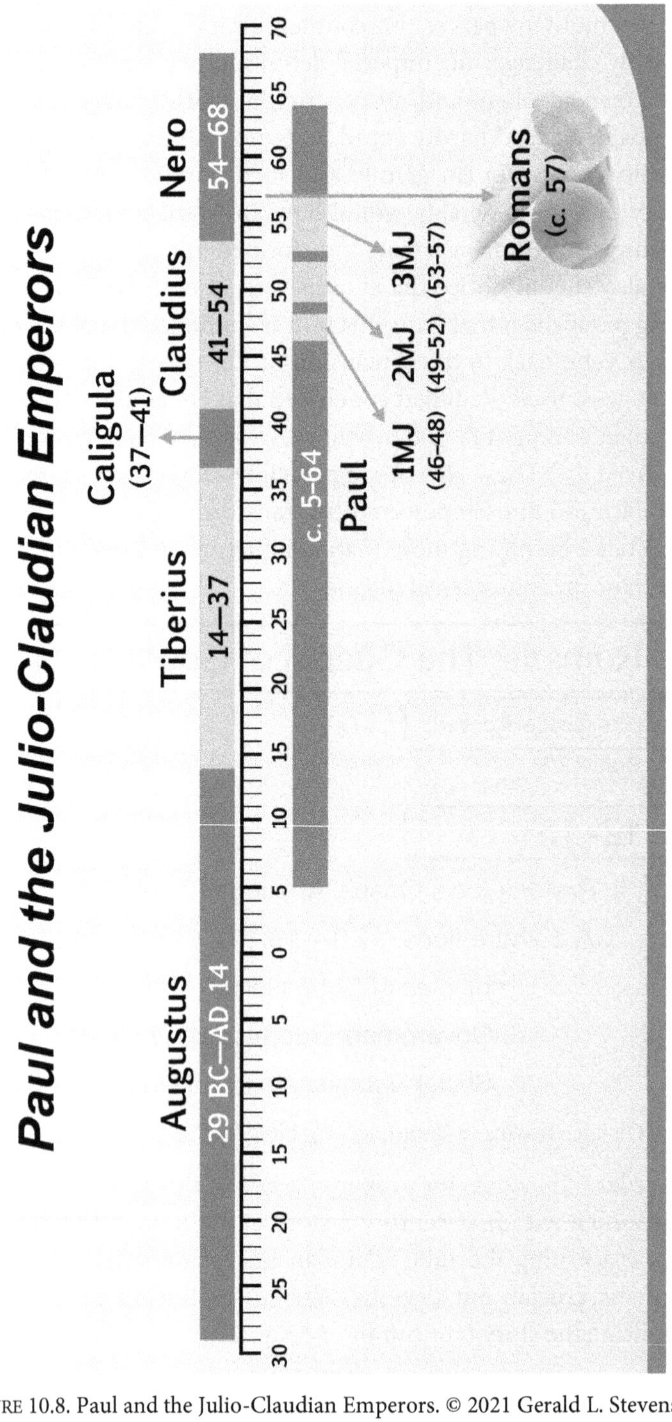

FIGURE 10.8. Paul and the Julio-Claudian Emperors. © 2021 Gerald L. Stevens.

FIGURE 10.9. Emperor Claudius (41–54). Ruler during most of Paul's ministry (NAM).

The material in Romans 13 takes on clearer focus with this historical review, and hermenutical abuse is reduced. Key here is that the main emperor of Paul's missionary work to this point was Claudius.

PRINCIPLES OF SUBMISSION (13:1–14)

Paul turns to issues of government. His message is submission. Why needs to be understood. The first verse becomes dangerous when not carefully contextualized by the two emperors with whom Paul had most experience. Most of Paul's ministry was performed under the rule of Claudius. He was demeaned for some unidentified physical disability, and scorned even by his own family.[33] Yet, contrary to all expectations, Claudius administered a wise, benevolent reign. He improved Rome's grain supply with a new port, repaired roads and aqueducts, worked for greater humanity in treatment of slaves, and guaranteed Jews practice of their religion.[34] Note the Aphrodisias frieze celebrating Claudius as master of land and sea.[35] The Claudius Edict was required to keep peace.

The other emperor under whom Paul ministered and traveled through imperial provinces doing mission work was Nero, and therein is a serious problem of bad press. Most opinions of Nero derive from the infamous fire of Rome and his despicable blaming of Christians for the conflagration and subsequent persecution of them in Rome. Much less known in the general public is that Nero's reign had two distinct stages (54–59, 60–68).[36] The early reign was under the tutelage of court advisors, Seneca the philosopher in political matters, and Burrus, prefect of the Praetorian Guard, in military matters. Nero's later reign was the megalomaniac stage of the infamous fire of Rome. *Paul wrote Romans during the early stage of Nero's reign* when civic matters were handled wisely, administration was stable, and businessmen were expanding their economies.

Government Submission (13:1–7)

Ordained Authority (13:1–5)

Paul makes two points about the institution of government. First, he says government is *God's provision against anarchy* (13:1–3). He opens with a call for submission: "Let every person be in submission to the

---

[33] Suetonius reported that his grandmother Livia "always treated him with the utmost contempt" (Suetonius, *Claud.* 3.2).

[34] Cf. Cassius Dio, *Hist.* 60.11.1–5; Josephus, *Ant.* 19.290.

[35] See discussion, p. 152, and fig. 5.29.

[36] Aurelius Victor, *Caes.* 5.1–2; but cf. Thorton and Thorton, *Julio-Claudian*, 100.

ruling authorities" (**13:1**). Note right away that Paul is using rhetorical generalities, which means his remarks encapsulate general principles. For example, who actually is addressed? Every "soul" (ψυχή, *psychē*). Even emperor Nero is held accountable to submit to God's designs. What is the principal principle? Submission (ὑποτασσέσθω, *hypotassesthō*). The verb τάσσω (*tassō*) means to bring into order by arranging or putting into proper place. God intends citizens to be in proper order in the civil sphere, to "be in proper place." Government is meant to control the tendency to chaos and anarchy in human society.

FIGURE 10.10. Claudius Coin (41–54). Note the *fasces* bundle in the lower left quadrant, the standarad symbol of Roman authority to judge and bear the sword (PMB).

The reason is, "no authority exists except by God." Paul did not say no government exists except by God. The principle is *authority in general*, not any government in particular. God in general ordains a delegated authority for the purpose of establishing civic order in order to stabilize human society from the inevitable chaos of sin. Delegated authority, then, represents God's intention for protecting humans from each other. One place authority is expressed is in government. From the divine perspective, government has a job to do and at a minimum must meet this requirement. "Those that exist have been put in place by God," Paul continues. "Have been put in place" is the same cognate verb as that already expressed by "be in submission." Thus, citizens are to "put themselves in order" just as government has been "put in order" by God, or established. Human government is constrained by divine design. Violation of divine design always has consequences (1:18–32).

Thus, the one who resists authority in general (by breaking the laws meant to order society) resists the divine purpose for delegated authority, so is opposing God's command for an ordered society. Any such opposition brings judgment (**13:2**). Rulers, that is, as defined in the rhetorical generalities of those fulfilling the divine design, do not present a terror to good conduct, only bad (**13:3**). Paul then asks a rhetorical question that seems rather lame, "Do you want to be unafraid of the one in authority?" However, underneath the surface, the question may give silent testimony to on-going problems due to the recent social developments of gentile house assemblies and their increasing need to establish normalized, not hostile, interaction protocols with the former synagogue assemblies of which they used to be a part, particularly if a Jewish minority continues as part of the demographic profile within these house churces.[37] The profile of the weak and strong problem dealt with in Romans 14–15 seems to suggest so. Paul advises to stay within the borders of the expected ("Do what is good.")

FIGURE 10.11. Roman Gladius Sword. The main weapon of a Roman legionnaire was the short sword, or *gladius* (HMM).

After pointing to the need for controlling anarchy in society, Paul second says government is *God's provision for law and order* (13:4–5). This civil authority is "God's servant for you for the good" (**13:4**). The

---

[37] See the Ostia Synagogue, which dates to the reign of Claudius, p. 93, fig. 4.12.

word "servant" (διάκονος, *diakonos*) is a cognate of the church gift of "service" in 12:7, and Paul does see the two functions as similar in their respective roles. Civil service is in behalf of the needs of others. Yet, the person who does wrong, which in context is a terrible wrong that demands the death penalty, needs to be afraid. The civil servant "does not carry the sword in vain." "Sword" (μάχαιραν, *machairan*) is metonymy for the death penalty for a Roman citizen.[38] The fate was to be beheaded.[39] The authority of a Roman magistrate to prosecute and execute was represented in a *fasces* symbol made up of a simple bound bundle (*fascis*) of wooden rods that could include an axe head in the middle. The symbol continues in use today on Mercury dimes of the United States mint and behind the podium of the United States House of Representatives.

The positive role of this civil "servant" shifts radically for the law breaker. The *diakonos* turns into an *ekdikos*, an "avenger," a sharp word play by Paul to show two sides of the same coin. This *ekdikos* is an "avenger unto wrath (ὀργήν, *orgēn*)." Now we see the connection back to wrath in 12:19 that is God's vengeance to which the believer is to give way. That is, 13:4 is a manifestation of the divine wrath of God's vengeance in 12:19 working out in history through the general principle of divinely ordained civil authority.

Paul concludes, "Therefore, fundamental necessity (ἀνάγκη, *anagkē*) requires you to be in submission, not only because of the wrath but also because of conscience (συνείδησιν, *suneidēsin*)" (**13:5**). Appeal to conscience shows that Paul is working on the basis of what reasonable people in society would think, so his idea here is not so much a christological argument (turn of the ages, messianic realities, atonement), as simply theological—the way God has ordered society in general for all the nations. The idea was common in Greek thought.

> In the background study on Greek tragedy, divine wrath was shown to function to maintain the established order. This function had a parallel in Greek government. The Greek ruler was

[38] Tacitus, *Hist.* 3.68; Cassius Dio, *Hist.* 42.27. Cf. Let Aris 254. Menander wryly observed, "A law observed is nothing more than merely Law; when broken it is law and executioner" (*Min. Frag.* 770K [Allison].

[39] Ironically enough, church legend promoted the idea Paul was beheaded, not on the testimony of eyewitnesses, but more by simple deduction from Paul's claim in Acts to Roman citizenship (Acts 22:25). See primary data in Stevens, *Acts*, 590–95.

to preserve order, to avenge injustice. The term *orgē* in this context came to mean "punishment," and the expression of wrath could be righteous. Paul's use in 13:4–5 seems to be thoroughly in line with this Greek background.[40]

Paul here assumes a government properly performing its divinely ordained task of holding back total anarchy in human civilization, not contributing to anarchy. Thus, Rom 13:1 is not a blank check for every brutal and murderous totalitarian regime in human history, as if God had ordained cruelty and murder. The rule of a Hitler, Stalin, or Mao, the Cambodian killing fields, or the Columbian drug cartels propping up puppet governments is not Paul's point of reference for parsing the meaning of God's ordinance of human government to hold in check the chaos inevitably worked by the presence of sin in human society.

In other words, context makes a decided difference on the same topic. One can contrast Romans 13 with Revelation 13. The same government is envisioned, but in two entirely different historical contexts. In Romans 13, government acts as a divinely ordained servant maintaining social stability by putting to the sword law breakers. One could illustrate in Paul's dealings with Roman authorities throughout Acts. Paul converted the proconsul, Sergius Paulus, on the island of Cyprus, who thereby reveals no sense that belief in Jesus is an anarchist threat to Rome (Acts 13:12). Paul is protected against Jewish calumny in court at Corinth by the proconsul Gallio (Acts 18:15–16). He leverages Roman citizenship and the legal system of Rome protecting citizens from illegal judicial procedings when threatened with flogging by a tribune in Jerusalem (Acts 22:25–29). He is declared innocent of all charges by the procurator in Caesarea (Acts 25:25).[41] *That government* is the civil authority with which Paul has had personal experience and of which Paul speaks in Rom 13:1 of having divinely delegated authority to provide a modicum of order and stability in society. In stark contrast, in Revelation 13 we have the complete opposite in the same government. In this context, the emperor and his empire is imaged as a fearsome, malevolent beast itself breaking the law by putting to the sword innocent people of God for their confession of faith. So, on the one hand

---

[40] Stevens, *Divine Wrath*, 188.

[41] For discussion of the passages in Acts, see Stevens, *Acts*, 306–07 (Sergius Paulus); 392–93 (Gallio); 461–62 (Jerusalem tribune); 488–89 (Festus).

you have a Roman proconsul as governor accepting the message of the gospel without incident, but on the other, the anticipation of Roman provincial officials adjudicating confessed believers for execution.[42] One hardly could have more contrasting New Testament images and historical contexts on the same subject.

Paul had the luxury of assuming a government that properly was performing its task because his government was the Roman empire of the extraordinary administration of Claudius and of the early stage of Nero's reign under the wise tutelage of Seneca and Burrus. Paul knew fully that matters could go south. He himself had experienced the crisis under Caligula, who brought Jews in Judea to the edge of rebellion with his order that a statue of his effigy be erected in the Jerusalem temple.[43] But Caligula was only a four-year blip on the imperial scene in Rome, an aberration of the norm. The early stage of Nero's reign showed every sign of the steady administration of Claudius. Thus, bringing the later megalomanic Nero of the infamous fire of Rome catastrophe into an exegesis of Romans 13 is hermeneutical malpractice that sets up potentially dangerous conclusions about existing governments of any kind.[44]

Ordained Submission (13:6–7)

Government is ordained, and submission to government is ordained. The background may be Nero's unpopular taxation policies in Rome that ignored Seneca's advice trying to dissuade Nero of such action.[45] Paul states that paying taxes simply is the necessary support of divinely ordered government that cannot exist without its own budget of oper-

[42] Which actually did start happening only twenty years later after Revelation was written, documented in governor Pliny's letter to his emperor Trajan; Pliny, *Letters* 10.96; cf. Ferguson, *Backgrounds*, 594–95; Stevens, *Revelation*, 314–16.

[43] Josephus, *Ant.* 18.261; Tacitus, *Hist.* 5.9; *Ann.* 12.343.

[44] Note how "Nero" as a notorious villain name was employed blatantly by science fiction writers in the 2009 Hollywood blockbuster, *Star Trek* (Paramount Pictures).

[45] Eduardo Barrón González in 1904 created an outstanding sculpture, *Nero and Seneca*, portraying Seneca advising the young Nero. The art is housed in the Museo del Prado, Madrid, Spain. For the museum image, https://www.museodelprado.es/en/the-collection/art-work/nero-and-seneca/caeace6f-f0f7-4b20-aef5-c770672bf2ef, accessed April 27, 2021. Evaluation of Nero's tax policies is difficult in the primary historical sources such as Tacitus, Suetonius, and Cassius Dio due to tendentious presentations. For an astute analysis of the history of Roman taxation policies from an economic perspective, cf. Bartlett, "How Excessive Government Killed Ancient Rome."

ations. Such administrative officials are "civil servants" (λειτουργοί, *leitourgoi*) serving the need of society by closely attending to this very business of government (**13:6**). While the noun *leitourgos* in a religious domain would apply to the service of priests, in this civil domain the word refers to civil service.

Paul then subordinates paying taxes to the broader responsibility of paying *any* obligation (debt), whether financial or social. (**13:7**). Pay all financial debts, such as tax (φόρος, *phoros*) to the tax collector and toll (τέλος, *telos*) to the toll collector, but also pay all social debts, such as respect (φόβος, *phobos*) to those deserving respect and honor (τιμή, *timē*) to those deserving honor. This social emphasis of paying respect and honor riding immediately on the heels of paying financial obligations may imply a worry that the jeopardy of tax unrest could escalate into more consequential actions of disrespect and dishonor of those in power in administrative positions regarding collecting these finances, which almost inevitably would escalate into use of force whether by the authorities themselves or by bringing in Roman troops to restore order. Any such escalation in those terms automatically was a lose, lose proposition however the cake was cut.[46] The problem is not an academic exercise for Paul. Jewish communities both in Judea and across the Diaspora characteristically evidenced problems with foreign taxation. This issue particularly could be transformed into the core litmus test of Jewish patriotism, as seen in the attempt to corner and discredit Jesus on this matter, or even could inspire Jewish nationalist revolts.[47]

Paul pulls no punches against this type of nationalist agitation. His speaking here makes clear he intends to communicate that nothing in the gospel of God he preaches should be construed as an inherent threat to the authority of the Roman government when that government is accomplishing its divinely appointed task of providing law and order. Government is presented as a shared responsibility of all citizens. Paul drives for peace and harmony in Rome, whether with internal stresses within the house churches or with external stresses with synagogues or even the Roman government. The advice is pragmatic in a context of

---

[46] Note the excellent, forthcoming study on Roman governmental response to social unrest by Browning, *Facing the Mob: Rome, the Crowd, and the New Testament.*

[47] Cf, Matt 22:18; Luke 20:22. Josephus recounts the revolts of Judas, Theudas, and Eleazar in *Ant.* 18.1.1; 20.5.1; *J.W.* 7.8.6.

explosive political and social issues. As far as possible, be at peace (12:18). Paul feels that a path of peace is the wisest for believers in Rome in their own context, but in particular in regard to paying taxes, whatever was the issue then that now is lost to exacting exegesis.

Social Submission (13:8–14)

The Debt of Love (13:8–10)

The theme of submission is extended from governmental to personal relationships in a bridge from civic to social responsibility. The unit is marked by another *inclusio* through the idea, "fulfills the law," in 13:10 and 13:18. Paul continues to work the 8:4 theme of fulfilling the law through the indwelling ministry of the Spirit.

Showing intentional calculation, Paul bridges to the related topic of social submission by the rhetorical hook of obligation from the previous unit: "Owe no one anything except to love one another" (**13:8**). That debt of love is the only one left on the billable account because that debt never can be repaid in full in a lifetime. Paul next shows he never has left Moses, because he comes right back to Moses insisting that love is the core divine command fulfilling all others: "for the one who loves the other has fulfilled the law." Strange if the gospel annuls the law Paul never can get away from the law. Paul then gives Torah examples in adultery, murder, theft, and covetousness, but adds "and any other commandment" (**13:9**), which shows he simply allows no exceptions. This "and any other commandment" insertion into 13:9 provides further confirmation of exegesis of Messiah as the *telos* of the law as meaning fulfillment of the law (10:4).[48]

All these commandments are summed up laconically as, "Love your neighbor as yourself."[49] The reason this one command facilitates fulfilling them all is not because all other commands are performed by observing this one command, but because this one command encapsulates the core principles that fulfill all God's intentions in human relationships. Thus, rightly understood by the principles guiding this

---

[48] The given examples are in Exod 20:13–17; Deut 5:17–21 and almost parallel the response of Jesus when himself asked about the commands of Moses to fulfill in Matt 19:18–19.

[49] Lev 19:18; cf. Jesus in Matt 19:19. Note Matt 22:39; Mark 12:31; Luke 10:27.

one command, this one command generates through apprehension of its principles a mind totally transformed into a new way of life. The principles are: (1) concern to accomplish the total good of God's perfect will,[50] and (2) acting not for self but on behalf of another human being, regardless of merit.[51] Love, rightly understood and applied this way, "works no evil to a neighbor" (**13:10**).[52] The conclusion is, "Love, therefore, is fulfillment of the law." Rote performance completely obscures apprehending God's love. Knowing God's love reveals God's will, and knowing God's will turns law into the obedience of faith. Paul clearly here is working fundamental Jesus tradition, which recapitulates the Romans motif of fulfilling the law.[53] This commandment is law obedience without works performance. For a Pharisee zealous for Moses, the thought was transformational.

Imminence Ethics (13:11–14)

Theologically, ethics and eschatology often are connected in the New Testament.[54] This aspect of New Testament teaching could be called its "imminence ethics."[55] This rhetoric works best in an "either/or" logic in order to persuade behavioral compliance without having to deal with distracting ambiguities that can lose sight of the point. Thus, metaphors common to this type of language include light and darkness and weapons and war. Such metaphors set up clearly understood polarities

---

[50] As suggested by Rom 12:1–2.

[51] As suggested by Rom 5:7.

[52] Often compared to similar statements by luminaries of other world religions (and echoed in the Hippocratic oath of the modern medical profession). Yet, none have their parameters of meaning constrained by the God revealed in Jesus the Son.

[53] Rom 2:15, 27; 3:31; 7:12; 8:4; 10:4.

[54] Note, for example, Matthew 25; 1 Thess 5:2–3; Heb 9:28; Jas 5:7–8.

[55] Campbell's recent study of Pauline eschatology, *Paul and the Hope of Glory*, has much of value, but his attempt to purge any element of imminence expectation from that eschatology is entirely unpersuasive. Imminennce expectation is writ large across the pages of the New Testament. Otherwise, why even preserve the promise given to the awestruck disciples witnessing the ascension of Jesus (Acts 1:11)? Why work so hard to find some way to get around the clear assumption of Paul when he wrote to the Thessalonians early in his ministry (1 Thess 4:15)? This counsel to Roman believers now most simply is read as imminence expectation continuing to be functional in Paul's thinking, as in the beginning, only now, even more close (Rom 13:11).

and, hence, clear choices. The point will be to behave consistent with the future destiny in Messiah's kingdom.

Fulfilling the love command is crucial now, given awareness of eschatological time (**13:11**). "Time" is καιρόν, (*kairon*), which is more season than chronology. A New Aeon had dawned. The season is not the reality that had been true in the previous season of the Old Aeon. Seasons have changed, and seasonal characteristics have changed likewise. A new reality is in place. Know what season you are living in. The hour to wake up already is upon the eschatological community. A call to "wake up" metaphorically is a call to that watchfulness that is inseparable from imminence expectation. Truth is, Paul says confidently, "our salvation is nearer than when we came to faith." In this context, "salvation" is eschatological, that which is anticipated in 5:10 and 8:23–25, and in 1 Thess 1:10. This salvation in 13:11, in other words, is the future salvation from the future wrath of the final judgment brought on by the appearing of Jesus from heaven. The context is eschatological judgment, of which Paul already had warned.

> But according to your hard and impenitent heart you are storing up wrath for yourself on the day of wrath and revelation of the righteous judgment of God, who will repay to each according to his deeds: to those who by patiently doing good deeds seek glory and honor and immortality, he will give eternal life; but to those who are self-seeking and who do not obey the truth but wickedness, even wrath and fury. Tribulation and distress upon every human soul who works evil, to the Jew first and also the Greek, but glory and honor and peace to everyone who does good, to the Jew first and also the Greek. For no partiality exists with God (Rom 2:5–11).

The mention of salvation with its eschatologically loaded theme of final judgment perfectly sets up the following exposé of Roman lifestyles. This type of flagrant sinful behavior while seemingly unknown or ignored, is not.[56] Given this context of near judgment, Paul engages in the typical polarity rhetoric of imminence thinking: "The night has advanced and the day has drawn near. Let us discard therefore the deeds of darkness and let us put on the weapons of light. Let us walk properly as in the daytime" (**13:12–13a**).

---

[56] On the scriptural pattern of Sodom and Gomorrah's sins reaching "up to heaven" to capture God's wrathful attention (Gen 18:20–21).

The counterpart to proper conduct in the day is the improper conduct of the night that Paul now enumerates in pairs **13:13b**. While each term could yield its own profitable word study, Paul likely was aiming for overall impact taken as a whole. The life of darkness in the Old Aeon is obvious in its contrast to a life of light in the New Aeon.

- *reveling and drunkenness:* these are the heavy drinking orgies typical of elite Roman feasts

- *debauchery and licentiousness:* these are the sensual pleasures and sexual sins along with the accompanying immoral lives

- *quarreling and jealousy:* these are the social evils that destroy families and all relationships

In other words, one should note that this list is paradigmatic of the evils of elite Roman society,

FIGURE 10.12. Emperor Caligula (HAMC).

particularly imperial. Caligula's degradations are ready illustration.[57] The sins are paired for rhetorical impact by showing their interconnectivity. The behavior outlined is more of a network of behaviors, like a web of many strands spun by evil such that entanglement on just one never remains just one. All strands pull together, and the more the captured victim struggles for freedom, the more the result of death is guaranteed by ever deeper entanglement. Degrading behavior simply degenerates into subhuman behavior less than even animals. Thus, in this short list in 13:13b, we are looking at illustrations in Roman lifestyles in which the wrath of God is at work (1:24–31). Such Roman

---

[57] Allegations of Suetonius who wrote decades later, such as incest with all three sisters, are hard to judge. They come into question since writers of that day, such as Seneca and Philo, are silent on such charges. Still, that he had an incestuous relationship with his sister Drusilla is not really doubted due to his obvious and constant obsession with her, as well as his behavior at her death. However, that Caligula had numerous affairs with men and women and was despicably cruel and despotic indiscriminately is not in dispute.

lifestyles fulfill the picture of the "disapproved mind" that is "delivered over" to ever more degrading behavior and will be determinative in the final judgment, since "those who practice such things are worthy of death" (1:32). Worse, "they not only do them, but even applaud others who practice them" (1:32). Paul has had his eye on Roman perversion from the beginning of the letter, because such a lifestyle puts the lie to the imperial gospel of Rome hiding the truth about this Roman world.

The contrast in the final verse is, "Instead, put on the Lord Jesus Messiah, and make no provision for the flesh, to gratify its desires" (**13:14**). "Putting on" is a clothing metaphor that is what is meant by a transformed mind (12:2). Paul already had addressed making "no provision for the flesh" in Rom 8:5–14, only there he made clear that the power for such living is not on the basis of any "self-help" program of human origin but only on the basis of the Spirit-enabled life available in the New Aeon inaugurated by Messiah. The Roman congregations have to live in Rome, but they do not have to look like Rome.

11

Rome's Factionalism

The Prospect of Fracture

Romans 14–15 turns to a specific problem in the Roman assemblies of an incipient factionalism, reminiscent of Corinth, of serious enough consequence Paul could not ignore. Factionalism is simply a reemergence of the same problem of arrogance turned inward (11:20). In Corinth, the problem grew to become a challenge to the apostolic authority that had founded the church. Rome should beware.

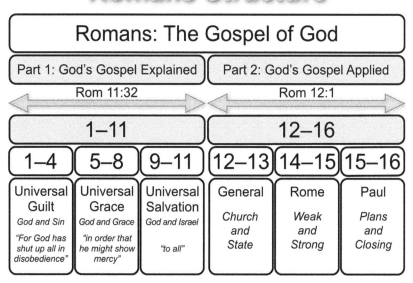

FIGURE 11.1. The Structure of Romans. Romans 14–15 is about the weak and strong.

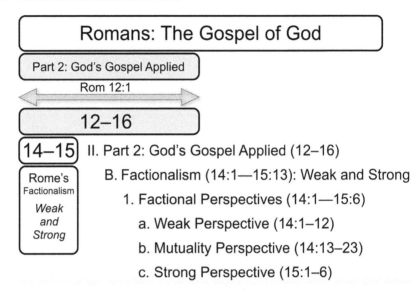

FIGURE 11.2. Outline: Romans 14–15 (Factionalism). Rome's factionalism is engaged.

The structure of this material is difficult to discern. Our units follow the UBS5 and NA28 texts. English translations tend to multiply divisions, which is not necessarily helpful. This disagreement on outlining is due to spiraling discussion that leaves a point only to come back around. Redundancy might be the rhetorical strategy. Unknown to these assemblies, Paul is disadvantaged to appeal more forthrightly (as with the Corinthians, for example). He walks an impartiality tightrope addressing both groups—a challenge, since he seems to identify with the strong.

Lack of agreement on the precise microstructure of these verses should not obscure the elephant in the room: Rome has a serious problem with factionalism, serious enough in Paul's estimation to fracture the unity of the assemblies if not addressed, and apparently leadership in Rome has not stepped up to the plate to solve the problem. Paul had encouraged those with the gift of leadership in Rome that they needed to add "diligence" (σπουδή, *spoudē*) to their expression of this gift (12:8). We already have seen Paul immediately engage this stipulation in his exhortation to love in 12:10. He implicitly does so again in this unit on the weak and strong. Paul is having to do the work of leadership in Rome that Rome's own leaders themselves should be doing, and he is being much more "diligent" about the responsibility by daring to take up this sensitive matter in the very first letter he ever has composed to these saints in Rome. Of course, to cut the leaders in Rome some slack, we need to recognize that from the Corinthian crisis he barely survived only recently, Paul is much more acutely aware of the devastating effects of factionalism inspired by arrogance among believers. The unusual "weak" and "strong" designations probably are Rome's labels, not Paul's. They seem to reflect Roman imperial ideology of superiority and dominance through world conquest and subjugation, as memorialized in the brutalizing blood sport of gladiatorial combat.

FACTIONAL PERSPECTIVES (14:1—15:6)

Weak Perspective (14:1–12)

Paul addresses the matter of the weak perspective first.[1] The context is lost to us. The internal context itself does not provide sufficient clues for a detailed understanding.[2] The debate circulates around diet and days. Some elements sound Jewish, such as the observance of ritual days and reference to the category of "unclean" (κοινός, *koinos*). Other elements simply do not. (Jews were not vegetarians.) The ambiguity therefore raises issues of the social mix. Do the issues come from Jewish believers, gentile believers, or even from some pagan influence in the culturally diverse population of Rome?[3] Many commentaries capitulate to the Jewish background, but without agreement exactly how. The background may be shrouded in local peculiarities. Worlds are colliding in Rome like nowhere else. Both Jewish and gentile ideas seem represented, and perhaps pagan custom or observance might be present (accounting for the vegetarian emphasis). Some admixture of all of the above even could have its hat in the ring. Once again, the Roman church is a wild card in early Christianity.

Paul begins his discussion with the expression "weak in faith." Why Paul even would phrase the matter this way is unclear. Just who

---

[1] For one of the better detailed discussions of the strong and weak, see Schreiner, *Romans*, 726–42. His approach is balanced, concise, and well argued.

[2] Not even agreement on whether the food and drink setting is internal, that is, the observance of the early Christian "love-feast" (Jewett, *Romans*, 860), or external in the pagan setting (Käsemann, *Romans*, 367–68).

[3] For a rundown of the six main options, see Moo, *Romans*, 828–31. He argued for Jewish believers with continued loyalty to Mosaic law. The distinctive use of "unclean" (κοινός, *koinos*) in 14:14 strongly favors this view.

would respond positively to being labeled "weak in faith"? Such an expression hardly could come off as anything but offensive and publicly humiliating. In such an infelicity, Paul would have lost his exhortation before he even got started. The odd nature of the phrasing rhetorically leaves the impression the expression is not Paul's. The labels are local to the factions using them. Hence, they are instantly recognizable to the local factions involved, but certainly not to later readers. In any case they are one of the two factions at each other's throats in Rome.

Those of the "weak in faith" faction are to be "welcomed" (προσλαμβάνεσθε, *proslambanesthe*), apparently by the other faction (**14:1**). The idea for "welcome" in this Pauline context is to receive in fellowship in the union of the faith. The best exegesis is Phlm 17: "Therefore if you have fellowship with me, receive him as me," Paul wrote to Philemon about Onesimus. Roman reception, however, should show diligence not to do so just to gain a grandstand for quarreling opinions (διακρίσεις διαλογισμῶν, *diakriseis dialogismōn*). Apparently, such a tactic already seems to have been employed by the strong faction, so they only feigned fellowship as pretense to argue, and Paul is exposing that hypocrisy for its reality.

The issue is diet (**14:2**). Again, Paul is labeling as "weak" only by force of the labels already applied locally. Vegetarianism is not Jewish, so something else is in the mix here. Trying to say what exactly is just guessing. The problem is not the diet, but the *attitude* to the dieter: "let him not despise" (ἐξουθενείτω, *exoutheneitō*, **14:3**). The idea is to regard such a person as not even having merit or worth, to disdain in such a way as *to malign their character*. Yet, the attitude problem is mutual. To show no partiality, Paul immediately turns right around and says back to the vegetarian that they are not to judge the meat eater either. We should avoid reading this ancient Roman issue through the lens of contemporary debates between carnivores and vegetarians. Such debates are environmental, medical, or otherwise, but certainly not religious.

The Roman issue is fundamentally religious, as Paul's next point makes transparent. A judgmental attitude is used *in order to reject*. In context, rejection would be deciding not acceptable for fellowship. Paul counters with cold truth for the vegetarian: "God has accepted him." No believer has right or authority to veto God's vote in establishing the composition of the fellowship of messianic Israel. The attitudes of

Romans 9–11 surface again. By noting the issue of divine acceptance, Paul makes clear the idea not only is religious, but seriously religious. Someone is declaring anathema without using the word.[4]

Paul gets after the judgmental attitude using a household servant analogy (**14:4**), immediately recognizable to a Roman audience, since as much as half the population of Italy was slave.[5] One had no right nor ever even assumed to judge another's household servant (οἰκέτην, *oiketēn*). "Before his own master he stands or falls"—and yet again, the opening of Romans lands foresquare: "Paul, slave of Messiah Jesus" (1:1). Then, Paul adds the zinger: "And he *will* stand, because the Lord is able to cause him to stand." God declares a believer able to stand as a legitimate part of the messianic community, and he has the power to enforce that declaration. Be careful whom you think you are resisting when you stand in factional judgment against another.

In a sense, Paul already has set in motion a logic that defies the presuppositions of either group. If the weak *refrain* from doing something to honor the Lord, then why is that not, in fact, "strong"? Surely resisting an action one is tempted to take is harder than taking an action one has no thought about either way. Again, if the strong *indulge* in doing something to honor the Lord, then why is that not, in fact, "weak"? Indulging an action that involves no conscience is the definition of easy. The factional presuppositions are turning topsy-turvey. Paul dismantles the labels even as he uses them. Lordship is the key.

The issue shifts abruptly and awkwardly from diet to days (**14:5**). The change in topic rhetorically is jarring. No inherent connection is known externally in pagan culture nor suggested internally within the immediate context. Connection is simply presumed. We even could be dealing with an idiosyncratic development restricted to just the local assemblies or a charismatic leader within one assembly or several. The position could be entirely syncretistic, an admixture of Jewish, gentile, and pagan elements into one tossed salad. The origin is unclear, but the problem is the same: like different diets are evaluated differently, different days are evaluated differently, and the difference is spawning arrogance or judgmentalism, depending on the faction. All such judg-

---

[4] In traditional evangelical terms, as in the arrogance to say something like, "That person just cannot be saved," when the issue raised truly is inconsequential.

[5] Se discussion, pp. 169–77.

ments, Paul admonishes, are private: "Let each one be fully convinced in his own mind."

Paul now gets down to the one salient principle ignored in all the debate that should constrain all thought on these factionally disputed matters. Whether diet or days, all these convictions are held as part of a vital communion with God (**14:6**). Paul insists that whether weak or strong, "none of us lives for himself, and no one dies for himself" (**14:7**). Both sides are ignoring this crucial piece of personal data. Everyone lives or dies "for the Lord." What is not clear is how death suddenly enters into this equation of diet and days. His rhetorical strategy is subtle but powerful. He subtly is injecting what *actually* counts for discipleship in Rome: not diet or days, but death. When he concluded the exultant celebration of God's love in Messiah at the end of Romans 8, he did so with this quotation of Ps 44:22: "Because of you we are being put to death all day long; we are counted as sheep to be slaughtered" (8:36). At the slaughter house is where you know with whom you can hold hands, not before a plate of food. "Therefore, whether we live or die, we belong to the Lord"—and never forget that gospel truth (**14:8**)! That Paul has the issue of 8:36 and faithful discipleship in mind is revealed by how he instantly at this point brings in the death of Jesus: "For unto this Messiah died and came alive: that he might be Lord over both the dead and the living" (**14:9**). Speaking here is the missionary evangelist who already before writing Romans had compiled the incredibly courageous resume itemized in 2 Cor 11:25. Paul knows how to recognize and genuflect to genuine discipleship. Diet and days is not that kind of discipleship.

So, on such inconsequential matters as diet and days, why does anyone dare to judge another, and what justifies this despising (**14:10**)? With the question on despising, Paul has spiraled back around to 14:3. On the matter of belonging to messianic Israel, which both the weak and strong apparently were presuming that their private opinions on diets and days were deciding, "all will stand before the judgment seat of God." This word of the "judgment seat" (βήματι, *bēmati*) is personal for believers and for Paul himself. Jesus had stood before the *bēma* of Pilate.[6] Paul himself had stood before the *bēma* of the proconsul Gallio in Corinth, falsely accused by synagogue leaders. Gallio threw the case

---

[6] Matt 27:19; John 19:13.

out of court.[7] Not long after writing Romans, Paul would be before the *bēma* of another procurator, Festus in Caesarea, making his appeal to the judgment seat of the emperor himself.[8]

Paul adds scriptural authority to nail down the point of judgment perspective (**14:11**). He compresses Isa 45:23, "As I live, says the Lord, to me every knee will bow and every tongue confess to God."[9] Paul concludes, "So then, each of us will give an account of himself to God" (**14:12**). The import is that we do not give account of our sense of rightly serving the Lord through our convictions about diet and days to another human being who is not our Lord. One has the impression the factionalism had to have been serious when Paul has perceived an attempt to usurp the authority of the eschatological *bēma* of God. Who even would dare do that to the emperor Nero? Note how God's imminent final judgment Paul smartly put at the end of Romans 13 to segue into the immediately following weak and strong discussion. Whatever is behind the factionalism in Rome, its profile of mutually bad attitudes of both arrogance and judgmentalism points to storm clouds of consequences on the horizon that to Paul are ominous and alarming.

Mutuality Perspective (14:13–23)

Before going to the perspective of the strong, Paul makes a move for an attitude of mutuality for both sides. That way, he has better chance of being heard by the weak faction when he later aligns with the strong faction. By then, the matter already has been declared inconsequential.

The problem with judgmentalism is that the bad attitude itself becomes a stumbling stone (πρόσκομμα, *proskomma*) or a hindrance (σκάνδαλον, *skandalon*) for a fellow believer (**14:13**).[10] Paul shows his

---

[7] Acts 18:12, 16.

[8] Acts 25:6, 10, 17.

[9] Cf. Phil 2:10–11.

[10] We need to be clear. Making wise discernment not only is right, such judgment is required (1 John 4:1–2). Paul would be hypocritical in the extreme to pronounce an anathema without making a judgment about the truth of the gospel (Gal 1:8–9). The same is true of Jesus's statement about not judging lest one be judged (Matt 7:1–5). The problem is not the making of a judgment. The problem is making a judgment with a beam in the eye. Such a person is incapable of seeing the truth in the first place. Impartiality is out the window. The problem is judgmentalism, an attitude that pretends to see when really blind. Paul is saying one "blindness beam" is bad attitude.

cards a little by throwing in a parenthetical comment in verse 14.[11] He states his personal conviction that nothing in itself is "unclean" (κοι-νόν, *koinon*, **14:14**).[12] The word *koinon* never is used in Greco-Roman literature for religious ritual, but constantly in Jewish literature discussing regulations in both Leviticus 11 and Deuteronomy 14, which is the strongest indication that the concerns here are Jewish.[13] That both food and wine are mentioned later in 14:21 does not infer the Corinthian question of participation in pagan ritual feasts, since the problem of idolatry never is mentioned throughout Paul's entire discussion here in Romans. In his parenthetical, Paul immediately circumscribes the conviction as no excuse for judgmentalism. His conviction is privately held; he does not require his conviction to be someone else's. He recognizes the spiritual truth that whoever is convicted something is unclean, then the boundary of personal conviction already has been crossed. Paul refuses to violate personal conviction.

The problem is awareness of someone else's conviction and willingness flagrantly to violate that conviction by behavior that offends the conscience of another (**14:15**). The discussion is back to diet, because he mentions food. Paul characterizes the response of the offended person by using the verb λυπέω (*lupeō*), which is to cause grief or pain. Likely, this grief or pain is internal within the conscience.[14] We may have a hard time empathizing with how food conviction can be so deeply felt. Paul, however, is fully aware of this kind of deeply felt conviction or emotion confirmed by conscience. This way of speaking is precisely how he describes his own grief over his fellow Israelites as he testifies "my conscience bearing witness" (9:1). What we have to recognize is, such rhetoric as Paul is using in 14:15 means the matter is felt to be of the utmost gravity by the person bearing the conviction. They may even consider their personal relationship with God is on the line. No believer ever should take flippantly such a concern on the part of another believer. That type of response without doubt is "no longer

---

[11] Parenthetical interruption means the argument logic jumps from 14:13 to 14:15, which situates the grammar of the "for" (γάρ, *gar*) conjunction beginning 14:15.

[12] In this context, "in the Lord Jesus" (14:14) likely means Paul's source is not from his internal relationship with Jesus as codified with his "in Christ" expression as much as he has this conviction directly from the Jesus tradition (Matt 15:11; Mark 17:20).

[13] Note particularly Dunn, *Romans 9–16*, 881–919; cf. Schreiner, *Romans*, 730.

[14] Which may be the significance of the present tense.

walking according to love," and the obligation to owe no one anything except the debt of love has gone bankrupt even within the community of faith (13:8). The gravity of the situation is likely behind the strong exhortation, "Do not destroy (ἀπόλλυε, *apollue*) by your food that one for whom Christ died." We cannot be exactly sure what is meant by "destroy" (or "bring to ruin"), but the verb is devastatingly strong, and we may have to allow that the rhetoric goes beyond metaphor.[15] The reality check is, some in the strong camp were willing to do just that. Factionalism in Rome is on the edge of destroying believers and fracturing the church. From Paul's perspective, church leaders in Rome should be going into triage mode.[16]

"Therefore" (οὖν, *oun*) means on the basis of dire consequences of losing one for whom Christ died (**14:16**). "Therefore, do not blaspheme your good," an odd expression, but likely referring to the good freedom of conscience the strong enjoy.[17] Rights do not trump responsibilities, and insisting on rights could blaspheme the lifestyle of faith.

"For the kingdom of God is not food or drink but righteousness and peace and joy in the Holy Spirit" (**14:17**). Righteousness, peace, and joy are characteristics of the New Aeon brought by Messiah (5:1–11). Further, incorporation of "kingdom of God" language infers that the situation is as dire as Paul has divined. Such language is eschatological by default, for only in the end is the kingdom realized fully (1 Cor 15:20–28). This eschatological kingdom note reframes the issue as one of messianic Israel's destiny to achieve the obedience of faith among

---

[15] In the commentary tradition, a range of ideas are covered, as one might suspect. On occasion, surprisingly, no comment even is offered on such a dramatic statement (Nygren, *Romans*, 448; Hultgren, *Romans*, 518; Longenecker, *Romans*, 1008). Schlatter characterized the situation as "moral vascillation" (*Romans*, 259); "tender conscience" for Achtemeier (*Romans*, 221); or "distressed" conscience for Fitzmyer (*Romans*, 696). Käsemann, however, points out that a severe wounding of conscience is in view, and reference to the death of Christ means,"The aim is to show how severe the danger is" and thus eschatological ruin (*Romans*, 376). Others take this cue as well. For "grieved" as salvation at risk and "destroy" as eschatological ruin, cf. Cranfield, *Romans* 2:714; 715n2; Dunn, *Romans 9–16*, 821; Schreiner, *Romans*, 733–38; Moo, *Romans*, 854–55.

[16] That Roman leaders took initiative and asked Paul to deal with the issue is highly unlikely. He simply does not write Romans with the kind of rhetoric that would attach to having on-going personal communications with leaders in Rome about conduct of general church matters. Arguing the purpose of Romans would be moot. The purpose would be to respond to this prior communication, as with 1 Corinthians (1 Cor 7:1).

[17] Moo, *Romans*, 460.

the nations of the world. Not dealing with this factionalism in Rome will damage the work of messianic Israel, and that damage will deter reaching the eschatological goal for the kingdom of God. Integrating the problem of the weak and the strong into the goal of messianic Israel is an astute move toward resolution by forcefully making the point that the risk at stake transcends the issues of either faction. The issue is messianic Israel realizing its destiny in the world. The threat to messianic Israel of the weak and the strong factions is one of the reasons for Romans.

"For the one who serves Messiah in this is pleasing to God and approved by people" (**14:18**). This follow up statement ("for") confirms the issue is messianic Israel. The matter is lordship (14:4, 6), not really lifestyle. Finding this path to reconciliation, then, is establishing the good, acceptable and complete will of God (12:2), and this person is pleasing to God, and everyone for that matter in tune with God.

Paul now brings in the mutuality principle (**14:19**). He makes a major conclusion with a double conjunction, "Therefore, then," ("Αρα οὖν, *ara oun*). "Let us pursue the things of peace and the things of one another's edification (οἰκοδομῆς, *oikodomēs*)." This word of pursuing peace stands as Paul's fundamental exhortation to all in Rome. Peace in this context is the Jewish shalom, that is, the wholeness of life that is complete from every angle of human experience, physical, emotional, social, spiritual. This Jewish shalom concept of the wholeness of life always circumscribes Pauline letters, because he invariably opens a letter with a grace and peace benediction.[18] Peace, however, especially is featured in Romans, perhaps to aid in establishing the cruciality of this exhortation of 14:19 at this point in the gospel of God applied:

- opening grace and peace benediction (1:7)

- promised glory, honor, and peace to everyone who does good (2:10)

- the warning of those who do not know the path of peace (3:17)

- a major component of the New Aeon in Messiah (5:1)

- the mindset of the Spirit being life and peace (8:6)

---

[18] 1 Cor 1:3; 2 Cor 1:2; Gal 1:3; Eph 1:2; Phil 1:2; Col 1:2; 1 Thess 1:1; 2 Thess 1:2; 1 Tim 1:2; 2 Tim 1:2; Titus 1:4; Phlm 3.

- a major element of the eschatological kingdom (14:17)
- the God of hope filling with all joy and peace (15:13)
- the peace benediction closing the letter (15:33)
- a warning that the God of peace soon will crush Satan (16:20)

Thus, promoting peace is fundamental to the work of God. In this case in Rome, peace promotion in practical terms is through body building, or edification, which is diametrically opposed to destroying someone, which Paul spirals back to restate: "Do not destroy (κατάλυε, *katalue*) for the sake of food the work of God" (**14:20**). Paul uses a compound cognate of the same verb as for destroying the weak in faith. The work of God is messianic Israel. Paul adds what he already testified as his own conviction in 14:14, that everything is clean (καθαρά, *kathara*), but making someone fall by food is flat out wrong, even evil (κακὸν, *kakon*). Making someone fall (προσκόμματος, *proskommatos*) in 14:20 intentionally echoes the stumbling stone (πρόσκομμα, *proskomma*) in 14:13.

Paul flips the coin over from bad conduct (κακός, *kakos*) in 14:20 to good conduct (καλός, *kalos*) by restating the same principle again, the redundancy for rhetorical emphasis (**14:21**). He also picks up on the stumbling idea again. The new element added to eating food is "or drink wine," which has not featured in the discussion to this point.[19] This prohibition is not Jewish, that is, not law, so any connection with "unclean" earlier taken as a clear signal of Jewish concerns (14:14) is out of the question.[20] The wine element in 14:21 is what destabilizes the insistence that the social context of the weak in faith is all about Jewish believers having a hard time getting over their Mosaic consciences. All cultures struggle with inebriation (Prov 20:1; Isa 5:11), but this context is religious conscience that could destroy a faith not cultural excess that

---

[19] A rare word in Paul and the only occurrence of "wine" (οἶνος, *oinos*) in Romans. Otherwise, only four other times (Eph 5:18; 1 Tim 3:8; 5:23; Titus 2:3). For prevalence of wine in Roman society, see p. 174, fig. 5.49, thermopolium, and fig. 5.50, amphorae.

[20] The Aaronite priesthood in service in the temple were forbidden wine (Lev 10:8), but not when otherwise engaged. A Nazirite vow prohibited wine (Num 6:3), but the reason of undistracted devotion to God is obvious. No prohibition of drinking wine for the people of Israel in general was part of the Mosaic code. In fact, Deut 14:23 encouraged spending money gained from capitalizing the agricultural tithe on whatever was desired for a feast before the Lord, including wine.

is a nuisance to society. That the matter is hypothetical to overstate the case about food is, well, hypothetical.[21] Taken together at face value, a vegan, non-alcoholic diet in conjunction with ritual observance of certain but unspecified days, all taken so seriously as potentially to inflict irreparable harm to a viable faith when violated is a setup guaranteed to evade confident historical exegesis. Yet, that is exactly what Roman churches had on their minds, and Paul is walking the tightrope with his balancing bar of the lordship of Messiah and the higher call of messianic Israel.

"The belief which you have, you have to your own self before God" (**14:22**). Paul again applies the lordship principle already injected early into the argument, which is a word to both factions. Jesus is Lord. That messianic lordship is the bottom line for any servant of the household. To Jesus confession is made, and from Jesus conviction is obtained (10:9). Paul again is striving to get both sides to move toward each other by both adopting a mutuality perspective based on respect for personal conviction. God's blessing attends to the person who lives by their convictions. Does messianic Israel have any other way to live? Yet, if you "approve," that is, allow yourself to do, that which you do not really believe, you cannot possibly be living out of faith. Such a contradiction cannot be sustained indefinitely, because the righteous live by faith (1:17). So, Paul concludes succinctly, "But the one who doubts if he eats is condemned, because (eating) is not out of faith. Anything not out of faith is sin" (**14:23**). A maxim for messianic lifestyle.

Strong Perspective (15:1–6)

Paul finally reveals all his cards and takes the strong perspective. He has tried to build a case for why the weak in faith should not be offended by his stance, because he is not offended by theirs. In fact, he has commended them for living their convictions, because the bottom line is, they are living out of faith, testifying to the lordship of Messiah, and giving full evidence of the integrity of their conscience.

"Now, we who are strong" (**15:1**). Whoops. Cat is out of the bag. The general impression is, Paul now is taking sides. Were that really the case, he has wasted a lot of ink and papyrus. Actually, Paul drops a rhetorical bombshell. Read closely, while already identifying with the

---

[21] A possibility suggested by Morris, *Romans*, 491.

strong position on clean or unclean food (14:14), Paul's emphatic first person pronoun, "we" (ἡμεῖς, *hēmeis*), powerfully rejects the attitude of the strong. Paul's "we" is telling Roman believers *to look to him for a definition of what they have been sloganizing as "strong in faith,"* not to factional leaders in Rome. Paul's mutuality perspective that he carefully advanced in 14:13–23 redefines the whole issue, and particularly what "strong in the faith" behavior should look like in Rome. He thereby has been working throughout the discussion to take the leadership of that position right out from under local leadership in Rome. He now opens the gate for the Pauline stampede over the strong bad attitude.

We might recall that Paul already expressed a pastoral attitude at the beginning of Romans. In opening the letter, he had written,

> For I am longing to see you so that I may share with you some spiritual gift to strengthen you—or rather so that we may be encouraged mutually by each other's faith, both yours and mine. I want you to know, brothers and sisters, that I often have intended to come to you (but thus far have been prevented), in order that I may reap some harvest among you as I have among the rest of the gentiles (Rom 1:11–13).

Reaping some harvest now is revealed in part as helping to resolve the tensions of the weak and the strong. He is exerting some leadership authority to this end in the letter after having laid the foundation of explaining the gospel of God, that the righteous by faith will live. He trusts those in Rome will be able to perceive the gospel's pertinence and applicability for this problem.

Note the very first word out of the gate from the new leader of the so-called "strong" position: "We have an obligation (Ὀφείλομεν, *opheilomen*)." What is this new word, "obligation"? No factional leader in Rome spoke like that. That word, however, is the gospel of God let loose in Rome. The first time this verb is used in Romans is in 13:8: "Owe no one anything except to love one another." The only other time the verb is used in Romans is here in 15:1. You sly dog, you, Paul. In dealing with taxes, Paul had extended the idea of paying debt in that one should pay all debts, including those social debts of respect and honor (13:7). Paul now is bringing that principle to bear on the issue of the weak and the strong. He himself in how he has written has shown respect and honor to personal conviction, whether weak or strong. He expects Roman assemblies now to follow his lead.

The obligation in 15:1 is to bear the weaknesses of those without strength. This job description is an entirely new agenda for the strong. This burden will require an effort "not to please ourselves," which the factional leaders have not been doing by allowing their bad attitudes to control correspondingly bad behavior. Instead, Paul exhorts, "each one of us." Once again, the question naturally arises, Who is "us"? Indeed, give that some thought, Paul is advising. If you think you are "strong," consider what that really should mean. By subtly redefining the profile of the strong with this "each one of us," Paul rhetorically is calling for a new kind of membership in the strong. Redefined, the "strong" now *bear* the burdens of others, they do not *add* to them. In this case, what is borne is the conscience of the weak in faith. Paul enhances the idea with, "Each one of us is to please his neighbor for the good" (**15:2**). Again, this behavior obviously is not that which has been modeled in Rome. Otherwise, the factionalism would not have developed. "Good," in this context is defined as community building. Note the explanatory additional phrase, "toward edification" (πρὸς οἰκοδομήν, *pros oikodomēn*). Edifying others rather than pleasing oneself is grounded in appeal to the example of Messiah, who did not please himself during his passion (**15:3**). His action fulfilled Scripture (Ps 69:9), in which insult meant for someone else fell on Messiah. Paul adds after the quotation that this Scripture was "written for our instruction" (**15:4**). He means that this particular Scripture should be taken to heart in Rome. This passage provides the perfect picture for drawing the desired profile of the mindset defining the new "strong in faith" in Rome. Being so perfectly applicable, this passage should offer "hope through the endurance" of exactly how to work through the weak and strong problem in Rome. Reconciliation of the two factions would provide needed "encouragement" for the ministry and witness of all assemblies in Rome.

Anticipating that Scripture could work powerfully in this way in Rome inspires a prayer wish based on these very virtues: "Now may the God of endurance and encouragement give you the same mind to one another according to Messiah Jesus so that together in one voice you might glorify the God and Father of our Lord Jesus Messiah" (**15:5–6**). Paul has been chasing after bad attitude directed specifically at the local assemblies in Rome for some time now in Romans.[22] He

---

[22] Cf. Rom 11:20; 12:2, 3, 16; 15:5.

works to build community harmony that will unify house churches in Rome. Community harmony is crucial to community witness ("one voice glorify God"). Part of the burden of Romans is gaining this harmony, unity, and witness in Roman congregations to enable messianic Israel to achieve her manifest destiny of reaching the nations and their own obedience of faith (1:5). The goal is reversing human rebellion that afflicts humankind in this Old Aeon (1:18—3:20) by transforming even inhabitants of Rome, particularly local, messianic communities.

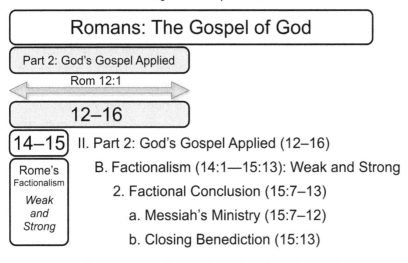

FIGURE 11.3. Outline: Romans 15 (Factional Conclusion). Paul concludes on Messiah.

FACTIONAL CONCLUSION (15:7–13)

The extent of the concluding function of 15:7–13 has some disagreement in the commentaries, whether concluding just the weak and the strong discussion in particular or concluding the whole letter body.[23] The main reason for this impression of concluding the letter body is because some major letter themes are present in 15:7–13, such as Israel's promises, gentile inclusion, and eschatological motifs of hope, joy, peace. However, this reflection may be literary design within the weak and strong unit. The problem of the weak and the strong in Rome is a subset of the larger problem of Jews and gentiles among the nations. That integral connection from microcosm to macrocosm is why Paul needs to resolve the weak and strong factionalism in Rome

---

[23] A good overview is given in Moo, *Romans*, 874.

as a test case showing the power of the gospel to reach the whole world with its call to the obedience of faith. Because Paul has developed the larger discussion in ways that intentionally tie together the two problems and their resolution, the conclusion of the weak and strong discussion in 15:7–13 can evoke the feeling of concluding the letter. An objection to this idea of concluding the whole letter is that other major letter themes are absent, such as justification by faith and victory over Sin. Thus, Moo might be correct that 15:7–13 primarily is meant to conclude the weak and strong in particular, even though reflecting some of the larger themes of the letter.

We still might could wonder about the function as concluding the entire letter body. First, we would point out that an ancient conclusion is not obligated to summarize all themes of the composition. Such an effort even could be perceived as rather boorish. That literary agenda for a conclusion is not ancient literary convention but rather has been assigned by the sensibilities of modern commentators.

Second, rather than insisting on the literary strategy of summary of all themes, we might more productively think an appropriate conclusion for Romans would be found in a concise literary *inclusio*. Paul already has shown use of such a technique on several easily noticeable occasions in Romans. He does mark boundaries this way to designate beginning and ending of units of thought.

How does this *inclusio* idea work with 15:7–13? The unusually laser-focused attention on the ministry of Messiah exclusively throughout these verses stands out in bold relief even on a casual reading. This messianic focus indicates that the topic is not really Jews and gentiles, or any other ideas, as such. Messiah is everything to these concluding verses and, as well, to the gospel of God. Our point is, this exclusive messianic focus in 15:7–13 has every appearance of being a designed *inclusio* on the letter's opening discourse. Note how the premier and controlling motif of the gospel of God to which Paul himself is set apart in the very first verse immediately calls upon the Roman creed to focus that gospel messianically as "concerning his Son, Jesus Messiah our Lord" (1:3). From that messianically centered gospel of God, the entire discourse of Romans flows fluidly through all of its parts until reaching Messiah here again in 15:7–13 in the same way, that is, exclusively focused on what the gospel of God is accomplishing for the obedience of faith among all the nations through Messiah (1:5). Paul in this beautiful *inclusio* in 15:7–13 thus ties the literary bow on that gospel of God ribbon wrapping this whole present to Rome.

We therefore do see the logic of this unit concluding the factionalism discussion. We have no problem with including this unit as part of that outline. However, we have absolutely no objection in seeing this unit as serving double duty for ending the entire letter also. Paul does show a predilection for just such a thing with his unit conclusions.[24]

Messiah's Ministry (15:7–12)

These verses are focused exclusively on Messiah. The material is summarizing. The overall impression is a summary reflection on Messiah's global ministry. Messiah fulfills God's promises to all by creating messianic Israel. He ministers to the circumcised for God's truth (15:7–8). He ministers to the uncircumcised for God's glory (15:9–12).

This unit literarily does double duty. The unit first concludes the discussion of factionalism in Romans 14–15. Simultaneously, the unit forms an *inclusio* that ties off the opening verses of Romans on Paul's apostleship to the gospel of God (1:1–2) focused messianically by the Roman creed (1:3–4).

Messiah's Ministry to Circumcised (15:7–8)

Romans has shown how the Messiah ministers to the circumcised for God's truth. His ministry shows the continuity of God's purposes in Israel. His ministry expresses God's covenant faithfulness to Israel. His ministry reverses Israel's Adamic suppression of the truth intimated in the opening foray into the operation of the wrath of God (1:18–32).

Paul beautifully transitions from the factionalism discussion with a verse that picks up the key verb of his mutuality perspective: "Therefore welcome (προσλαμβάνεσθε, *proslambanesthe*) one another, just as also Messiah has welcomed (προσελάβετο, *proselabeto*) you unto the glory of God" (**15:7**). The present tense of the imperative to the Romans emphasizes their on-going community efforts in working to resolve the grave problem of their factionalism. The aorist tense of Messiah's action focuses on the perspective of the completed whole of the incarnation ministry of Messiah. Thus, Messiah is the pattern of how to behave.

---

[24] Particularly 8:31–38 and 11:33–36, each of which consummate not only their own chapters and subunits, but also their respective major divisions (Romans 1–8, 9–11).

This *proslambanō* verb is used only three times in Romans, all in this unit on factionalism. This verb was key to the opening foray into the discussion (14:1, 3), and Paul has employed another *inclusio* technique with this key verbal idea in this conclusion here at 15:7. The successful work of welcoming one another will be known publically in the result (εἰς, *eis*) that God will be glorified. Indeed, God's glory is the problem of the factionalism: God is not glorified by internecine strife. The gospel, in fact, is contradicted. Roman assemblies unaware are losing their platform for proclamation of the gospel. "Get you grits together," a southern Paul is insinuating, "for the sake of the gospel."

In the macroscale of the gospel, Paul points out, look at how God has worked to reconcile Jews and gentiles (**15:8**). Messiah is a minister to *both* groups, not one or the other. Messiah became a minister to the circumcised for the truth of God. That truth of God is the foundation upon which the entire gospel of God is built, that is, that God keeps (βεβαιῶσαι, *bebaiōsai*) all his promises. God is the original promise keeper. That truth is the whole point of Romans 9–11, that God works through promise and progeny as revealed in the story of the patriarchs to save all Israel. If God is not a promise keeper, so-called good news is anything but, and gentiles should be pitied for believing such a fickle and faithless God.

Messiah's Ministry to Uncircumcised (15:9–12)

The good news is, God has confirmed the promises to the fathers. Messiah has done just that. God presently is working with a remnant to move messianic Israel toward her destiny in the Son. Fully consummated, Israel's destiny will include gentiles, but identified as nations of the world, just as Israel is a nation among the nations.

The ministry of Messiah also is to the uncircumcised, which defines that ministry as global in scope and intent. *Ethnē* is used in **15:9** as "gentile" to counterbalance the explicit use of circumcision in 15:8. Paul accommodates Jewish categorizations of humanity ("Jews," "gentiles"). Yet, he knows circumcision or uncircumcision is nothing in the broad scope of God's work (1 Cor 7:19). Thus, in 15:9 he acquiesces to a Jewish category (*ethnē* as "gentile") only to be rhetorically congruent in counterbalancing reference to the patriarchal promises. He quickly, however, transitions *ethnē* into "nations" in subsequent quotations.[25]

Paul presses the point home, as regularly in Romans, with a series of scriptural quotations. They cover all the bases of the Law, Prophets, and Writings. The first quotation, "Therefore I will praise you among the nations," is from Ps 18:49. This psalm voices the praise of a Jew in the Diaspora determined to worship God ("sing praise") in this alien context. Paul sees this praise of the Diaspora Jew now literally taking place within the multicultural composition of messianic Israel together with its missionary outreach to all the nations, thus unifying all worship of God throughout the world through Messiah.

In **15:10**, Paul calls on Deut 32:43, the last verse of the Song of Moses. The verse is about God avenging the blood of his children and taking vengeance on his adversaries. In that context, the MT reads: "Praise his people, you nations."[26] The object of praise is Israel. Other nations suddenly have to contend with a status reversal of roles. The LXX reads differently: "Rejoice, O heavens, together with him."[27] This opening call to the heavens in the LXX then is doubled, not following the MT, with a second call to the nations: "Rejoice, O nations, with his people."[28] The MT calls nations to praise Israel. The LXX first calls on the heavens (43a) to rejoice with God (in his victory over his enemies) and then calls on the nations (43b) to praise God along with Israel for this victory. Why nations would want to praise God after they just had been defeated by God on behalf of vindicating Israel is unexplained.[29] Paul seems to reflect the second, added phrase of the LXX: "Rejoice, O nations, with his people." His point is similar to the earlier quotation of Ps 18:49: mutual praise of God by all peoples among all the nations.

In **15:11**, Paul calls on Ps 117:1 (LXX 116:1): "Praise the Lord, all you [*ethnē*], let all the peoples praise him!" Most English translations get the semantic domain of *ethnē* wrongly, as the poetically doubled

[25] See discussion of the same issue for translating *ethnē* at Rom 1:5, pp. 226–29.

[26] The text is הַרְנִינוּ גוֹיִם עַמּוֹ (harnînû gôyim ʿammô).

[27] The text is εὐφράνθητε, οὐρανοι, ἅμα αὐτῷ (*euphranthēte ouranoi hama autoi*).

[28] The additional second phrase may not be pure invention on the part of LXX translators. The LXX here may represent an existing Hebrew text for which Qumran provides evidence (4QDeutq); cf. Fitzmyer, *Romans*, 707.

[29] As the old adage goes, something has been lost in translation.

second line of Hebrew poetry using "peoples" (λαοί, *laoi*) to interpret the meaning of *ethnē* makes clear. The term *laos* particularly is used for a body of people united by culture and country as a specific people-group in a specific place, that is, as a *nation*. Paul means, "Praise the Lord all you *nations*," not "praise the Lord all you *gentiles*." And the difference makes a difference. *Otherwise, the prophetic force and import of the connection to Isaiah in the very next quotation is lost entirely.* Again, in 15:11, the thought is the praise of God called for in the Scriptures among all nations. Paul understands messianic Israel in its mission to the nations to be facilitating the response to this call and thereby the fulfillment of Scripture. Rome not only is integral to that fulfillment, but crucial for supporting Paul's mission to extend that fulfillment on to Spain (15:24, 28).

The concluding quotation in **15:12** of Isa 11:10 is the whole point of the entire series of quotations, and the very reason why translating *ethnē* as "nations" throughout this series of quotations is so important.[30] The Davidic (hence, for Paul, messianic) import of Isaiah's prophecy contextualizes Isaiah's definitive prophetic vision of Israel vis-à-vis the nations. The vision is, "The root of Jesse will appear, even the one who arises to rule the nations." The Roman creed as preserved in Rom 1:3–4 essentially interprets this vision, and that is why this use of Isaiah to conclude all these quotations is an intentional *inclusio* with the beginning of Romans. Quoting that creed at the beginning of the letter only to build rapport with the Roman audience would be crass on Paul's part and easily exposed for its superficiality if not genuine to Paul's own thought in the rest of the letter. No doubt Paul did build rapport with his Roman audience by using a Roman creed. But Paul in his genius composition of Romans strategically employed the Roman creed with all due consideration because the creed beautifully captured the messianic focus of the gospel of God for which Paul was apostle of Israel to the nations, but especially because the creed was congruent with his new vision of Israel now reimagined through Isaiah. Paul quoted,

---

[30] Again, we already anticipated this matter at Rom 1:5. As we pointed out already, English traslations regularly are inconsistent, which helps none for accurate exegesis of this Pauline verse. They will translate the quotation of Isaiah here in Rom 15:12 with the word "gentiles," but then turn right around—totally inconsistently—and translate the *original* of Isaiah itself as "nations." See discussion, pp. 226–29.

concerning his Son, born of the seed of David according to the flesh, declared Son of God in power according to the Spirit of holiness by the resurrection from the dead, Jesus Messiah, our Lord (Rom 1:3–4).

Here is the essence of preserving Israelite seed (progeny) for God to be faithful to Israel, an integral part of the theme of Romans 9–11 ("born of the seed of David according to the flesh"). Here is the essence of the dynastic enthronement ritual in the Davidic house that establishes this inherited Davidic throne ("declared Son of God").[31] Here is the "arising" of this ruler to reign ("by the resurrection from the dead").[32] Here is the ruling of the nations ("Jesus Messiah, our Lord"). Paul, in other words, saw the Roman creed as a powerfully effective midrash on the Isaiah prophecy in Isa 11:10 for messianic Israel.[33] He could not agree with Rome more.

FIGURE 11.4. ETHNOUS IOUDAIŌN. "Nation of the Jews" imperial inscription from a series of friezes of conquered nations in Aphrodisias. See p. 146, fig. 9.17 (AMA).

As messianic Israel more and more accomplishes its prophetic destiny, Messiah more and more draws the nations to glorify God for his mercy. Messiah through messianic Israel unifies the nations in the "obedience of faith" (1:5), the nations glorify God in one voice with Israel, and Israel's global mission to the nations envisioned by Isaiah is consummated. The point about "nations" is crucial, because "nations" is a crucial theme of Roman ideology in the imperial Roman gospel.

---

[31] Cf. Psalm 2.

[32] The word "resurrection" in 1:4, ἀνάστασις (*anastasis*), is built off the same verb for "arising" in Isaiah 11:10 (ἀνίστημι, *anistēmi*). Cf. Eph 5:14; 1 Thess 4:14, 16.

[33] Dunn's "an effective recall of the themes of the letter's opening paragraph" (*Romans 9–16*, 853) is suggestive, but misses both the *inclusio* setting and Isaiah's vision.

With his focus on "nations" (not "gentiles"), Paul directly is addressing this key element in the Roman imperial gospel in his letter of Romans.[34] Messiah, not Rome, rules the nations.

Closing Benediction (15:13)

Paul uses benedictions to close major units of the letter, as in 11:36, so here. Following on the heels of the literary *inclusio* in 15:12 going all the way back to the beginning of the letter, the benediction, while closing the factionalism unit by default, also closes the letter body as well.

The God of hope is the language of eschatology. The benediction illustrates how understanding Pauline theology requires constantly incorporating "horizon thinking" into processing anything Paul writes. Paul's mind always is on the horizon of time. Short little benedictions as we meet in **15:13** make this observation ever so true. The benediction takes the reader to the consummation of messianic Israel and the revelation of the children of God, which consummates creation (8:19–21). Paul returns to creation's eschatological future, in which Messiah has reversed the Adamic disaster (5:12–21) and fulfilled all creation's longings (8:18–22). Notable are the words of fullness, such as "all" and "overflow," which function to summon the thought again of God experienced as the all in all, as in the benediction in 11:36. The word of "faith" notably ties back into the theme of Romans at 1:16–17.

The benediction reveals how a vision of the end helps reenvision the present, similar to 5:1–11. Thus, the truth of eschatological destiny inspires present living. Also, consideration of that future destiny instills joy and peace in believing, and hope by the power of the indwelling Spirit. These features ground the ability to push on in spite of present circumstances, which suggests another function for the benediction.

The benediction does double duty not only to close the body but to make a smooth transition to Paul's plans that he will lay out in the next unit of 15:14–33. He makes these plans on the basis of the gospel of God he has presented, entirely encouraged by the horizon he keeps in view at all times of the master plan as expressed in the benediction. In this way, the letter benediction also is Paul's own personal benediction over his planned mission to Spain.

---

[34] See discussion, p. 228, fig 6.4, "*ETHNOUS* in Imperial Inscriptions." For the "Table of Nations" of Genesis 10 as Paul's background, see Scott, *Paul and the Nations.*

12

Pauline Reprise

Paul's Plans and Letter Closing

ROMANS 15–16 TURNS ONCE AGAIN to Paul in a reprise of information about Paul the apostle expressed with an intriguing ambiguity
in the thanksgiving section of Rom 1:8–15. Now, however, the stage is
different. Much dialogue has transpired between there and here, fourteen chapters' worth (longer than anything the long-winded Cicero ever
wrote), and Paul is ready to bring Romans to its apex of purpose.

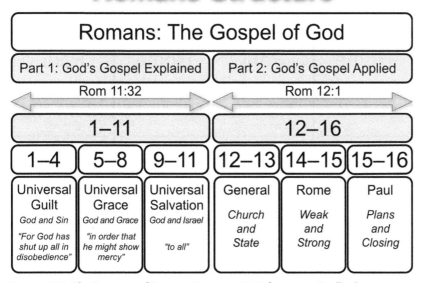

FIGURE 12.1. The Structure of Romans. Romans 15–16 focuses on Paul's plans, again.

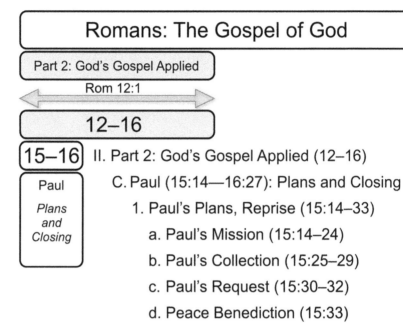

FIGURE 12.2. Outline: Romans 15 (Paul's Plans, Reprise). Paul's plans again, but clearly.

Quite clear in the structure of Romans is a patterned movement in the opening of the letter from addressee to author, Rome to Paul, with the same pattern reflected again from the body of the letter to its closing.

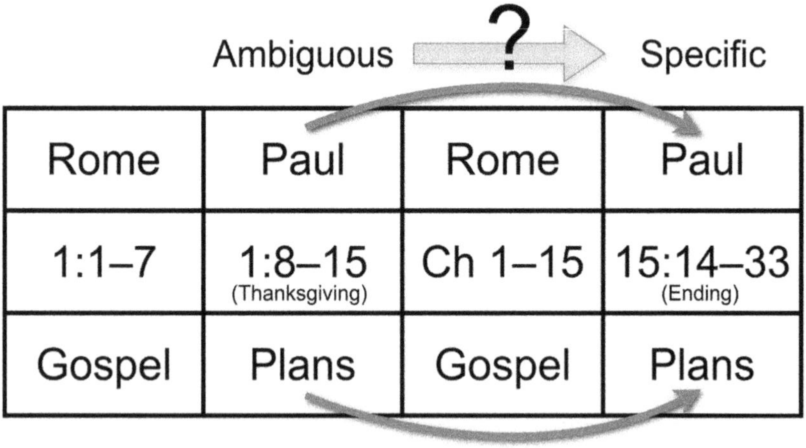

Ambiguous ? Specific			
Rome	Paul	Rome	Paul
1:1–7	1:8–15 (Thanksgiving)	Ch 1–15	15:14–33 (Ending)
Gospel	Plans	Gospel	Plans

FIGURE 12.3. Parallel Movement. Rome and the gospel, Paul and his plans.

This Rome to Paul, Rome to Paul parallel movement within the letter opening and then between the letter body and letter closing likewise is paralleled with the themes of the gospel and Paul's plans echoing in the same way: Rome and the gospel, Paul and his plans. This macro-structure actually is a clue to the purpose of Romans. Romans begins and ends with Paul's plans. So we have Rome and the gospel closely connected to Paul and his plans. Note how these two topics integrally are tied together by Paul into the very structure of Romans.

The question is why is Paul so ambiguous about his plans in the opening of the letter? What he insinuates only vaguely in the opening he says quite forthrightly in the ending. The obvious question is, Why does he wait fifteen chapters to get specific? The answer that seems to be inferred by the structure of the letter is that Paul thinks the gospel explained and applied in the body of the letter is an essential and necessary component for comprehending how his plans involve Rome and represent Rome's best interests in the gospel.

(Beginning)		(Ending)
Paul's Plans	Literary Echoes	Paul's Plans
1:8–15		15:14–33
Text	Terminology	Text
1:1, 9	"serve"	15:16
1:1, 9	"gospel"	15:16
1:5, 8	"obedience of faith"	15:18
1:10, 13	"desire to come"	15:22–23
1:14	"indebted"	15:27

FIGURE 12.4. Literary Echoes. Literary echoes of terminology between the opening thanksgiving section and the ending of Romans on Paul and his plans. For an even more extensive list totaling fifteen items, cf. Kim, *God, Israel, and the Gentiles*, 82–84.

That integral connection between Rome and Paul then ties into the observation of obvious literary echoes of terminology out of the thanksgiving section in 1:8–15 deliberately repeated in the ending unit on Paul's plans in 15:14–33. The repetition is too much and too obvious not to be intentional. Paul is signaling that he deliberately is moving right back to where he started the letter—his plans. Only now, he is ready to become specific, and so he does. What only ambiguously was indicated as "hindered" in the thanksgiving section now is revealed specifically to be the burden of delivering the collection to Jerusalem. What only ambiguously was indicated as a desire to "come" to Rome in the thanksgiving section (What? To set up shop in the pastor's office?) now is revealed specifically to be plans only to go "through" Rome. What only ambigu-

Rhetorical Strategy: General to Specific	
Romans 1	*Romans 15*
"hindered" (1:13)	collection (15:22)
"come" (1:11)	"through" (15:28)
"evangelize" (1:14)	Spain (15:28)

FIGURE 12.5. Rhetorical Strategy. From general and ambigous to specific and clear.

ously was indicated as "evangelize" in the thanksgiving section now is revealed specifically to be a cooperative program for Spain. This moving from general to specific, ambiguous to clear, is rhetorical strategy. Notice that making the wording clear also reveals a planned travel itinerary from Jerusalem to Rome to Spain. The purpose of Romans is tied to accomplishing this itinerary.

FIGURE 12.6. The Pauline Itinerary in Romans.

Paul holds off specificity until the end because the body of the letter is the foundation to Paul's plans. As is typical in a Pauline letter, then, the thanksgiving part of the genre Paul regularly uses to engage main themes, guiding thought, and so forth. A reader always should pay close attention to a Pauline thanksgiving section in any letter. These literary units facilitate exegesis of that writing because this author uses this component of an ancient letter innovatively for literary purposes. Further, here in Romans—on top of all this—the thanksgiving section embeds the actual purpose of the letter. Now, the homing pigeon let loose in Rom 1:8–15 comes home to roost in 15:14–33.

PAUL'S PLANS (15:14–33)

Paul has reached the apex of the purpose of Romans: his personal plans and Rome's participation. We have come back to the opening thanksgiving section of 1:8–15.

Paul's Mission (15:14–24)

Paul begins with a statement of his confidence the Romans are full of goodness, filled with all knowledge, and able to instruct—characteristics he probably has hoped they also have seen of him in his letter to them (**15:14**). The most pertinent characteristic is "instruct," or, more forcefully in context, "admonish," "warn" (νουθετεῖν, *nouthetein*). This is the need of local leadership to take the bull by the horns and deal with the weak and the strong factionalism by adopting the "strong" paradigm Paul has put forward as an alternative to the influence of others with wrong ideas about faith and personal convictions, compounded by bad attitude to boot.

He says this by way of preparing to justify why, if all of the above is true, he should feel the need to write Romans. The practical answer is, because he did not found the church. He wants to make sure they fully are appraised of the gospel he preaches that is foundational to his mission work with pertinent Roman examples of how that gospel applies to daily living to know exactly the stock portfolio in which he will be asking them to invest.

His problem is, the Roman church is a wild card in the early Jesus movement: historically with unknown foundation, unknown teachers, and unknown traditions. Through Prisca and Aquila, Paul has a pretty good idea on some matters, particularly the history and inside story on synagogue disturbances over the preaching of "Chrestus" and its provocation of the Edict of Claudius, and he can be confident at least about that specific house church's understanding of the Pauline gospel through his earlier missionary association with the couple in Corinth and Ephesus. Through them Paul also likely had become aware of a dangerous attitude of arrogance expressed in two different directions simultaneously, one of gentiles toward the divine status of Jews in the story of salvation, a sore spot with the synagogue crowd, and the other of an idiosyncratic factionalism of weak and strong that threatened not only to destroy devoted believers, but also to fracture the fellowship and thereby damage mission and witness. Of other assemblies, however, Paul cannot be sure they would comprehend the full range of implications of his understanding of the gospel of God ("my gospel," 2:16).

So, he admits, "Nevertheless, I have written to remind you more boldly on some points because of the grace given me by God" (**15:15**). He dares, but only to "remind" them what they know, and if anything good comes out of the "reminder," that only would be an expression of God's grace in the first place—the foundation of all God's actions, as explained in the gospel of God (Romans 5–8). Deftly maneuvered.

FIGURE 12.7. Cult Priest Statuary. High status and honor attached to function as cult priest of a patron god or goddess, but particularly of the imperial cult. Left, cult priest 1st–4th cent. AD (IAMI). Right, imperial cult priest, 2nd cent. AD (AAM).

FIGURE 12.8. Provincial Cult Priests. Cult priests of the 1st and 2nd cent. from cities in which Paul established churches. Left, imperial cult priest of Ephesus, 1st cent. AD (EMS). Right, L. Titonus Primus, Isis cult priest of Thessalonica, 120–130 AD (AAM). For other illustrations at Aphrodisias, see p. 134, fig. 9.10, and p. 136, fig. 9.12.

That divine grace in Paul's life, sharpened into Pauline focus, has made him a "servant" (λειτουργὸν, *leitourgon*) of Messiah (**15:16**). The noun form occurs only twice in Romans, here, and in the famous passage about civil authorities being God's "servants" that minister to civic needs (13:6). Paul later will use the verb form to speak of gentiles who have an "obligation" to "minister" to needs of saints in Jerusalem (15:27). Typically unrecognized here is the intense competition among elite provincials in Roman provinces to be granted the extraordinary honor to serve as priest to "minister" in the responsibilities of a local provincial cult. The premier privilege and honor was appointment as an imperial cult priest in the cultic worship of the emperor. Paul is not ashamed of the gospel (1:16), and he regards his "ministry" as servant of Messiah more prestigious than any elite citizen of the empire bearing the signet ring boasting to all high status as imperial cult servant.

Paul's ministry of service for Messiah targets the *ethnē*. English translations often miss the point. His ministry for Messiah targets the "nations," not "gentiles," that is, the defunct Jewish categorization of humankind into "circumcised" and "uncircumcised" that served only to boost pride and boasting in a (presumed well-deserved) election by

God. Ministry to the nations is Isaiah's vision of Israel's global destiny to the nations, just presented so eloquently in the previous unit (15:12). In this work, Paul serves the "gospel of God" as a priest. With "gospel of God," the bow neatly is tied with the first verse of Romans. Paul knew he would arrive here making this concluding statement of his priestly service the moment he dictated the first verse of the letter. The mission purpose ("so that," ἵνα, *hina*) is that the "offering of the nations," the vision of Isaiah, might be "acceptable"—the universal aspiration for any cultic offering by any priest anywhere in the world—having been sanctified by the Holy Spirit, which calls upon the analysis of Rom 8:1–11.

The power of the gospel (1:16) unleashes the righteousness of God through faith (3:21–26), justifying the ungodly (4:1–4), empowering fulfillment of the law through the Spirit (8:1–4), consummating all creation (8:18–25), keeping all the promises of God to Israel (Rom 11:26), and transforming daily living (12:1–2). Yes, that is a long sentence, but then we have the context for Paul's boast and the subsequent rundown of his mission thus far that chronicles the movement toward fulfilling Isaiah's global vision for Israel and the nations in **15:17–19**.

> Therefore, I have a boast in Messiah Jesus the things with respect to God. For I would not dare to speak anything of which Messiah had not accomplished through me unto the obedience of the nations (ἐθνῶν, *ethnōn*), by word and deed, in powerful signs and wonders, in the power of the Spirit of God, so that from Jerusalem circling around up to Illyricum I have fulfilled the gospel of Messiah (Rom 15:17–19).

This word is news, not just for Rome, but for any working with, associating with, or supporting Paul in any way financially or otherwise, past or present. Paul announces in this letter to the Romans that his mission on behalf of Messiah is at a crossroads. Which way he turns will determine everything for accomplishing Isaiah's vision. He wants those in Rome to know assuredly that he has been very careful and deliberative about how to make that decision, so that Rome understands their importance to this decision. Paul has finished the first stage of his messianic mission. He is working the Mediterranean perimeter. He has finished the first third of a circle (κύκλῳ, *kyklōi*, 15:19).[1] The next

---

[1] This κύκλῳ, (*kyklōi*) is a *hapax legomenon* (only once) in the Paulines, and rare in the New Testament (8x; Mark 3:34; 6:6, 36; Luke 9:12; Rom 15:19; Rev 4:6; 5:11; 7:11). This rarity naturally arouses curiosity, especially, why here, particularly?

third would be Italy and west to Spain (15:24), including its notable barbarian populations on the fringes of these Spanish territories (βαρ-βάροις, *barbarois*, 1:14). The last third would be provinces of the north African coastline, and then back to Jerusalem (see fig. 12.6).

His strategy is clear. He has made his ambition to evangelize not where Messiah has been named in order that he not build on another's foundation (**15:20**). Rome can breathe easy. Paul has been wanting to come to Rome for quite some time (1:13), but Rome is not his final destination of his planned mission itinerary. Paul offers Scripture for what has guided his mission compass on this matter. Naturally, he goes straight to Isaiah, because his whole sense of call to the nations has been inspired by his messianic reading of this prophet, particularly in Isaiah's Servant Songs.[2] He quotes again from the fourth song here in **15:21** (as earlier in 10:11): "To those not informed concerning him, they will see, and those who have not heard, they will understand" (Isa 52:15).

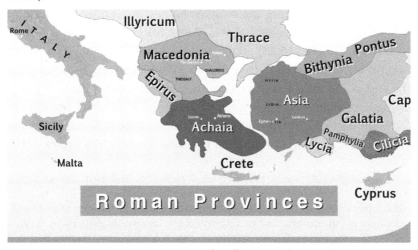

FIGURE 12.9. Roman Provinces. Provinces of Paul's mission thrust to this point.

Paul's faithfulness to this Isaiah-inspired mission has kept him busy in multiple provinces known from Acts, such as Judea, Syria, Cilicia, Cyprus, Lycia-Pamphylia, Galatia, Asia, Macedonia, and Achaia, as well as others unknown from Acts, such as Illyricum. This work, he

---

[2] First: Isa 42:1–4; Second: 49:1–6; Third: 50:4–7; Fourth: 52:13—53:12. He used the second song for his commission as apostle to the nations (1:1, 5; Isa 49:6). He used the fourth song, as here, for the shame motif cropping up multiple times (10:11; Isa 53:1).

now reveals, has been hindering his plans for Rome, making what was expressed ambiguously in 1:13 clear in 15:22. He waited to speak of this mission strategy specifically until he could lay the foundation for grasping its significance within the full narrative of Israel. Paul is making clear to Rome that what is at stake is not simply one more un-circumcised male convert to throw into a big pile just to see how high we can get. That idea never was evangelism for Paul. Paul's vision is for Israel to achieve her destiny among the nations as a light for reve-lation to bring all nations into the worship of the one God in one voice to the glory of the one God who is God of all (3:29–30). Paul was look-ing for the praise of God among all the nations like Rome was looking for the praise of Rome among all the nations. Thus, Paul's mission goal would resonate strongly with a Roman audience, who would perceive instantly the global ramifications for the whole of life for all cultures of such a vision.

Paul now sees no further obstacles in forging ahead, because, for the purposes of reaching the nations, he has "no longer any place in these regions." He sets his sights again on his long-standing ambition to travel to Rome (15:23). This "my work here is done" announce-ment is big news for Paul's sense of his mission strategy at this stage at the end of the third missionary journey writing from Corinth.[3] Inter-esting to contemplate, but impossible to know, is why Paul would have "strongly desired" (ἐπιποθίαν, *epipothian*)[4] to come to Rome for "many years." Though often unremarked by commentators, the source of the

---

[3] According to Luke, Paul at this point is in a pickle. In a pragmatic way, his work is done anyway. He already had lost his mission base of Antioch over his fight with Bar-nabas (Acts 15:36–39). Then, only recently, he just has lost his mission base of Ephe-sus due to the silversmiths' riot (Acts 19:23–40). A lot more is going on in the Acts narrative for these passages than typically is realized. See Stevens, *Acts*, for a narrative analysis of how crucial these events are and the negative frame for the characterization of Paul Luke is putting on them. Paul is without a mission base of support, and he needs Rome to step into that gap on his behalf. Morris noted, "It would be a very great help to Paul if the Christians at Rome could see their way clear to acting as his home church." (*Romans*, 518).

[4] The noun "strongly desire" (ἐπιποθίαν, *epipothian*) is *extremely* rare. Rom 15:23 is its only occurrence in the New Testament (*hapax legomenon*), and the word never occurs in the LXX, Philo, Josephus, or Greek Pseudepigrapha (*1 Enoch, 4 Esdras, Esdras, 2 Baruch, 3 Baruch*, etc.). BDAG *has no information* for the entry, other than to quote this verse in Romans and one appearance in a variant reading at 2 Cor 7:11. The sense of the noun, therefore, has to be pulled from its cognate verb, ἐπιποθέω, (*epipotheō*).

desire likely came from encountering Prisca and Aquila some six years before in Corinth.[5]

The sentence Paul has been writing is broken off unfinished at the end of 15:23 (grammatical anacolouthon). He first chases a rabbit giving the necessary connection between his visit to Rome and a mission to Spain. Yet, outlining his Rome then Spain itinerary provokes chasing yet another rabbit why either itinerary cannot be now. All of this rabbit chasing creates 15:24–27. By then, the grammar of 15:23 is a lost cause, so he has to start all over again at 15:28 to resume the idea of 15:23.[6] For this reason, the beginning of **15:24** is awkward. A translation, for example, may use a long dash (NASB) or a parenthetical (RV) to try to compensate this convoluted thought. Paul means to say his trip to Rome was integral to his plans for Spain. The question why exactly Paul specifically would want to go to Spain, however, is unanswered.[7] We could speculate that prioritizing the Mediterranean basin seemed the best strategy for penetrating the entire empire as quickly and efficiently as possible, but without necessarily suggesting a timeframe for reaching barbarian populations in outer regions, such as the Germanic tribes in the west and Parthian tribes in the east.[8]

"For I hoped while passing through," Paul wrote, and suddenly the expressed desire to come to them (1:11) becomes clear as meaning only coming "through" them. But that passing "through" is not just to wave hello: "and to be assisted (προπεμφθῆναι, *propemphthēnai*) by you for my journey there." Boom! Out on the table. Paul needs assistance from Rome for his mission to Spain—whether financial, personnel, or otherwise. The verb "assist" regularly means missionary support.[9] We are hovering around the purpose of Romans again. Since the ambiguity of 1:11, Paul has taken almost fifteen chapters to lay out fully the portfolio for their investment and the anticipated payment dividends. Paul does expect to "enjoy their company" for a while, which almost leans into an assumption expecting they will join in with his endeavor.

---

[5] Obvious from Acts 18. Noted long ago by Hort, *Rom. and Eph.*, 11 who is quoted by way of agreement by Sanday and Headlam, *Romans*, 411.

[6] Sanday and Headlam, *Romans*, 411.

[7] See discussion, pp. 189–92.

[8] Not to be confused with Munck's theory of completing the so-called "circle of the gentiles" prophetic scheme from Isa 66:19.

[9] Acts 15:3; 20:38; 21:5; 1 Cor 16:6, 11; 2 Cor 1:16; Titus 3:13; 3 John 6.

Paul's Collection (15:25–29)

He explains yet further delay, one more interruption, hopefully brief, of a trip first to Jerusalem to deliver a collection for the poor of the saints in Jerusalem from his churches in other provinces of the empire (**15:25–26**). This one task had taken Paul years to get ready.[10] Macedonia and Achaia were "pleased" to do so (**15:27**), Paul says plainly to signal volition. The offering is not a tithe or tribute payment like an inferior vassal state to its overlord. Instead, the offering expresses paradigmatically the olive tree analogy of Israel as the root and gentiles as wild olive branches grafted into the root (11:17–24). The resources of the root have supplied spiritual blessings through fulfillment of the promise to Abraham that he would bless all families of the earth. Now, in a time of financial need, gentile believers likewise themselves can be a return blessing to the root source of the original blessing. A sense of mutuality expresses the unity of the faith among Jews and gentiles. The collection symbolically represented this critical unity for Paul, and its acceptance in Jerusalem of the Pauline congregations from out in the Diaspora for that very reason crucial to Paul's sense of the full acceptance of his mission by Jerusalem.

Paul's mission churches were pleased because they felt a sense of "obligation." Paul has circled back around to "owe no one anything except to love one another" (13:8), but with a quite strategic purpose. If this financial contribution to Jerusalem is this "obligation" to show love to others on the part of churches of Macedonia and Achaia, what about churches of Italy? Where is their "obligation of love"? Can they participate in the Jerusalem collection? No. Paul is on his way now with those funds as he writes Romans. But Spain still is out in the future, and Paul just has asked for help from Rome for the mission to Spain. Thus, in a rhetorically astute turn of thought by inference, the Roman congregations, if they are listening carefully as the letter has been read to them, should infer they too have their own "obligation of love." In fact, in their own way, they can participate in the giving spirit of the collection as showing the unity of the faith by making their own "collection," if the idea is redirected to Spain as the pertinent application in their own context in distinction from Macedonia and Achaia. Well played, Paul.

---

[10] We can trace the ups and downs of the effort in the Corinthian correspondence.

When the task of delivering the collection is completed safely, Paul will visit Rome on the way to Spain (**15:28**). He already has made clear he needs their help for this further itinerary west (15:24). Yet, he already is making plans for Rome. Without even knowing their yes or no, he is walking by faith that the requested help will be forthcoming: "I know that when I come to you, I will come in the full blessing of Messiah" (**15:29**). "Full blessing" at one level already made explicit early in the letter means mutual encouragement through mutually shared faith (1:11–12). Yet, in this later context surrounded by the details of the collection to Jerusalem integrated into announcing the mission to Spain, then "full blessing" of Messiah would include a positive response to the need for assistance in that effort westward. Notice the confident future tenses in the two elements involving Rome. I *will* set out by way of you to Spain (15:28), and I *will* come in the full blessing of Messiah (15:29). Paul's rhetoric is signaling his faith. He has confidence Rome both will affirm his own gospel of God as explained carefully and fully in his letter as in harmony with their own creedal traditions and, therefore, will become his future mission base, even though he himself did not found this great church, the news of whose faith is being reported in all the world (1:8). We are at the apex of the purpose of Romans—Rome and the gospel, Paul and his plans.

Paul's rhetoric about the collection in 15:25–29 is sophisticated, nuanced carefully, and almost as brilliantly executed as the letter of Philemon—the most stunningly perfect piece of literature Paul ever wrote, and simultaneously his shortest, adding to its perfection. That sophistication is making a request without making a request. In the case of Philemon, requesting the manumission of a slave by an unreconciled slave owner. In the case of Romans, requesting the sponsorship of a mission by an unrelated church body.

Paul's Request (15:30–32)

What Paul does specifically request is prayer. He first appeals to the familial connection, the common uniting bond among all members of messianic Israel and using his strong verb of appeal, Παρακαλῶ (*Parakalō*) in **15:30**.[11] Paul works to establish a bond with Rome. He

---

[11] Only four times in Romans, all in exhortations in part 2, three times signaling a major transition of thought (12:1, 8; 15:30; 16:17).

actually knows some of the house church and tenement assembly members (Romans 16), so the appeal is not minus any relationship at all to Roman believers. The appeal is "through our Lord Jesus Messiah and through the love of the Spirit." He directly reflects the nomenclature of the Roman creed ("Jesus Messiah, our Lord," 1:4) and the reality of the presence of the Spirit generating a sense of God's love (5:5), as well as empowering prayer when we do not know exactly how to pray (8:26–27). In this vein, Paul asks them "to strive together (συναγωνίσασθαι, *synagōnisasthai*) with me in prayers to God on my behalf." Josephus tells of Aristeas in preparation to petitioning his king to set free captive Jews in the kingdom, first went to the captains of the king's guard to get them to "strive together" (συναγωνίσασθαι, *synagōnisasthai*) with him for this intercessory purpose.[12] Paul appeals similarly to the Romans.

He has a three-fold request. He first seeks rescue from "unbelievers in Judea" (**15:31**). He does not say Jewish unbelievers, but likely, that is his meaning. He had to encourage the Thessalonian believers in a similar pattern themselves to remain steadfast in persecution even from their own countrymen as did the churches in Judea from theirs (1 Thess 2:14–15). All such opposition is the downside of "but the rest were hardened" in 11:7.[13]

Paul's second request was that the "ministry" (collection) might be acceptable to the saints. One might be tempted to ask, Why? Who would turn down free money in the first place? Free money is one thing, but this offering is not free. That is, this offering comes at a price. The cost is its symbolism. For Paul, the collection was not just a collection of funds. The collection was a symbol of the unity of Jew and gentile in Messiah.[14] That unity, however, in Pauline terms comes sans circumcision, and that price was too steep for some for whom this very issue was not settled, no matter how many Jerusalem conferences on the matter you might call.[15] This issue is the burden of "according to my gospel"

---

[12] Josephus, *Ant.* 12.18 (12.2.2).

[13] Paul likely was caught off-guard by James's advice that even Jewish *believers* were so strongly against him that his presence in Jerusalem was a quite serious and thoroughly unpredictable burden on the unity of the church in Jerusalem (Acts 21:20–22).

[14] 2 Cor 9:13–15.

[15] You know a problem still seethes under the surface when all you are told is that the "circumcision party" opposition to Peter only becomes "silent" (Acts 11:2; 18), but quite bluntly that those who were scattered from Jerusalem persecution were making pro-

in Rom 2:16. Paul may think he has been persuasive on the issue in Romans 2, and perhaps he was to an already sympathetic audience. Yet, his continuing struggle in synagogue after synagogue among those zealous for the law showed they simply heard with different ears. After writing Romans, his problems when he did arrive in Jerusalem with the Jerusalem church were clear, even if James and the others immediately around him themselves received Paul warmly.[16] Thus, his concern was not misplaced, whether the opposition is Jewish or Jewish believer.

Paul's third request was about coming to Rome after a necessary stop in Jerusalem: "and that after coming to you through the will of God, I might relax together with you in your company" (**15:32**). This idea deliberately runs full circle with the opening of the letter, "asking that by God's will I somehow at last may succeed in coming to you" (1:10) and "So that we may be encouraged mutually by each other's faith, both yours and mine" (1:12).

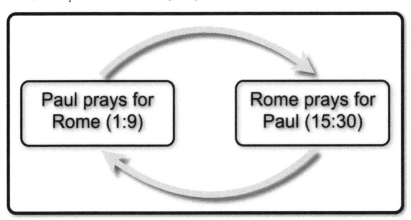

FIGURE 12.10. Prayer *Inclusio*. Paul binds together thanksgiving and conclusion.

This prayer request, then, functions as another literary *inclusio* in the effort to build spiritual bonds between Paul and this unfamiliar group of believers with whom he had no foundational relationship.

clamation "to Jews only" (11:19). Thus, such "silence" after Peter and Cornelius does not mean agreement, because they stirred up trouble again in Antioch, and the Jerusalem Conference had to be called later (15:1). Note the issue still is alive and well in James's tacit admission that he cannot guarantee controlling those "zealous for the law" within the Jerusalem church (Acts 21:20). For more on these issues and Luke's narrative development of them, see Stevens, *Acts*, 261–64; 328–31; 453–54.

[16] Acts 21:17, 20.

Early in the letter, Paul spiritually joins the Romans in prayer in his opening thanksgiving section (1:9–10). Paul now asks the Romans spiritually to join with him in prayer in this concluding section of the letter. Prayer is the final act of mutual consecration between writer and recipient. Paul has worked to secure the Roman church, his future mission, and his spiritual legacy.

Paul acknowledged that the will of God would be necessary for a successful venture in Jerusalem in order to be able then to travel on to Rome, but therein was the rub.[17] In fact, he never did get to "relax together with you in your company"—at least, not exactly like he was anticipating when he dictated those words.

Peace Benediction (15:33)

Paul concludes this earnest prayer request with his own peace benediction. "May the God of peace be with all of you. Amen." (**15:33**). A peace benediction is common to Paul, because the Jewish concept of peace has such rich tradition in its range of meaning and in Jewish culture. At the same time, in a letter to believers in Rome, one hardly can ignore the central significance in imperial propaganda of the virtue of peace brought about by the new age of Augustus for the exhausted and war-weary Roman Republic and people from centuries of civil war. Paul's peace benediction is a subtle but powerful redirect of that propaganda to the true source of peace in the truly New Aeon.[18] The "amen" is proper Jewish conclusion to prayer, a strong affirmation of what has been stated. A beautiful expression of this liturgy comes from the psalm King David assigned to Asaph and his relatives to give thanks to the Lord. After twenty-eight verses comes this final verse with a response of the people: "'Blessed be the Lord, the God of Israel, from everlasting even to everlasting.' Then all the people said, 'Amen,' and praised the Lord" (1 Chr 16:36, NRSV). Paul is inviting the same corporate response from the recipients of this letter.

This peace benediction also closes the letter. Paul has adapted the formulaic "farewell" of a standard Greco-Roman letter into his own

---

[17] And the absence of the will of God regarding Paul's presence in Jerusalem was precisely what interrupted the itinerary he planned in Romans. That divine action, of course, is another book, called Acts. See Stevens, *Acts*, 475–76, for a quick summary.

[18] See discussion, pp. 234–35.

distinctive Pauline letter element, typically labeled the Pauline "peace benediction." Again, as throughout most of the discussion in Romans 15, everything is resonating with Romans 1. We have at 1:7 a peace benediction folded into a grace benediction that creates another standard Pauline formula for beginning a letter. So, with 1:7 and 15:33 we are confronted with yet another *inclusio* technique. Romans leaves a clear impression as one reviews all the material in chapter 15 that Paul never worked harder to "tie things together" on such a macroscale so thoroughly. If you are tired of hearing *inclusio*, talk to the manager.

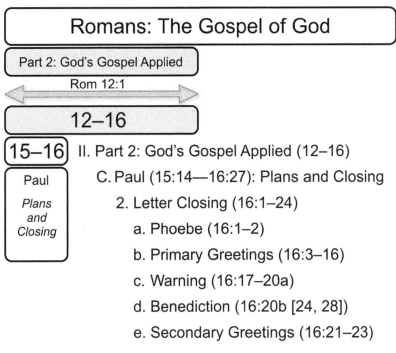

FIGURE 12.11. Outline: Romans 16 (Letter Closing). Letter closing begins the autograph.

LETTER CLOSING (16:1–24)

The letter closing is the autograph. The one who has been dictating the material takes the reed pen from the hand of the professional scribe and writes in their own hand to certify the letter as their own or to personalize the final greetings and farewell.[19] Paul actually refers to his

---

[19] For a superb overview of the complex process of writing an ancient letter, cf. Richards, *Paul and First-Century Letter Writing*; also, Reese, *Paul's Large Letters*.

autograph in Gal 6:11 with his "see what large letters I write in my own hand."[20] We would presume the autograph would register at 16:1 in the original manuscript due to the transition to common letter closing activity, such as recommendations and greetings.

Phoebe Recommendation (16:1–2)

This recommendation stands out for its formality, length, and effusiveness to place high status in a society studiously built on observing its honor-shame codes. Paul offers his formal, high recommendation including a commendation of Phoebe (**16:1**).[21] She is "our sister" (τὴν ἀδελφὴν ἡμῶν, *tēn adelphēn hēmōn*), sensible in a corporate context of churches at Corinth and Cenchreae in Achaia. The "our," however, at the same time nuances outward to Rome, since Paul will ask Romans to show Phoebe hospitality (food, lodging).

FIGURE 12.12. Deaconess *Agathē*. Funerary stele in Philippi of *Agathē*, a deaconess (ΑΓΑΘΗCΔΙΑ/ΚΟΝΟΥ, 3rd/4th lines), and Ioannis, a cashier of the public treasury and a producer and trader of linen (PAM).

Phoebe is a διάκονον (*diakonon*). The descriptor is first in this list accumulating status qualifications requisite of the function of a formal recommendation in the honor-shame codes of the ancient world. This immediate literary context suggests proper translation as higher status ("deacon"), not demotion to lower status of only a function ("servant").[22] Hence, "deacon" is a reasonable and

---

[20] Cf. 1 Cor 16:21; 2 Thess 3:17; Col 4:18; Phlm 19.

[21] Cf. 1 Macc 12:43 for a similar status-setting role of a recommendation.

[22] The matter historically is ambiguous, but not yet do we have the established office of the deaconate (authority and succession), which is the second-century church. We have the gift of "service" in the Roman church (12:7), which is habited or vocational

appropriate translation, as well as a better indication of actual status in the contextual setting of a formal recommendation. Her very high social status becomes even more obvious as we read further.

FIGURE 12.13. Cenchreae Map. Corinth was on an isthmus served by two ports with access to both the Corinthian Gulf on the west through the port at Lechaion and the Saronic Gulf on the east through the port of Cenchreae. To avoid the time and danger of going around the Peloponnese peninsula of southern Greece, cargo was off-loaded and ships dragged across the isthmus along the Diolkos, a paved trackway, and cargo then reloaded on the other gulf—much effort, but faster, cheaper, and safer.

Phoebe's city is Cenchreae, the eastern port of Corinth.[23] Cenchreae is where Paul shaved his head under an unspecified Jewish vow, which again illustrates his own sense of his Jewishness.[24] Corinth was a

acts of ministry, but this idea is more διακονία (*diakonia*), and often expressed as the verb διακονέω (*diakoneō*). The function is defined on the venue of service, as governmental for civil servants (13:4). This *diakonia* role, for example, is the description of Stephanas, who also was at Corinth (1 Cor 16:15). Even so, that the role already is a constituent part of a list of "gifts" to the corporate body in Rome (12:7) already indicates a growing recognition of certain functions having characteristic place in the life of messianic Israel. That valuation already would be starting down the road to common, necessary, and formal responsibilities that eventually develop into offices. Formulation patterns may receive a hint in Phil 1:1 in the reference in the salutation to "elders and deacons" (ἐπισκόποις καὶ διακόνοις, *episkopois kai diakonois*), and in 1 Tim 3:8–13, where office seems clear. For a good discussion, see Fee, *Philippians*, 69.

[23] Strabo, *Geog.* 8.6.22; Philo, *Flacc.* 155.

[24] Acts 18:18; see Stevens, *Acts*, 394.

commercial powerhouse in the first century due to the good fortune of supreme location serviced by two port cities linking shipping both east and west. The city had an active market, much trade, and many artisan shops. Cenchreae likewise was commercially prosperous. We do not know the source of Phoebe's wealth. She could have been landed aristocracy, or, she could have been part of the new class in Roman society, the "new rich," a businessmen's class resulting from Roman conquest. If so, she would function in a similar role in Paul's ministry as did Lydia in Philippi, a dealer in the lucrative and imperially controlled purple-dye trade.[25] Cenchreae is only about seven miles from Corinth.

Phoebe is a member of the church (ἐκκλησίας, *ekklēsias*) in Cenchreae. Luke does not inform of every stop Paul made nor every church Paul founded. The high likelihood, however, is that this congregation owed its existence as a satellite of Paul's eighteen-month ministry at Corinth, similar to the tri-city churches of Laodicea, Hierapolis, and Colossae in the Lycus valley work of Epaphras, an associate of Paul's mission in Ephesus.[26] Thus, the two cities of Cenchreae and Corinth have close connections geographically, commercially, and religiously. Paul is writing Romans from Corinth at the end of the third missionary journey.[27] His contacts with Cenchreae during this time would have been frequent, Phoebe being the most explicit example.

Most readers are caught off-guard to hear that 16:1 is the first use of the word "church" (*ekklēsia*) in Romans. The word *ekklēsia* is found only *three times* in all the Gospels, in only two verses, in only Matthew (Matt 16:18; 18:17). The word occurs only *six times* in all the General Epistles.[28] Revelation has twenty occurrences, but clearly because of the letters to the seven churches in Revelation 2–3. Acts has twenty-three occurrences, but distribution is critical: Only *one* of those twenty-three times is in the first five chapters centered in Jerusalem. In other words, the awkward truth is, the word so ubiquitous today to describe the Jesus movement is actually rare in the New Testament, with one exception. The word *ekklēsia* occurs *sixty-three* times in Paul. The most probable

---

[25] Acts 16:14. Obtaining the dye from the secretions of the snails in the Muricidae family ("Murex") on the Phoenician coast was difficult and expensive.

[26] On Corinth, cf. Acts 18:1–18. On Epaphras and the Lycus valley, cf. Col 1:6; 4:13.

[27] See discussion, pp. 123–24.

[28] Heb 2:12; 12:23; Jas 5:14; 3 John 6, 9 (2x).

explanation is that Paul himself singlehandedly imposed the term onto traditional Christian vocabulary. Paul may have gravitated to this term through the LXX. This *ekklēsia* is the favored word for the assembly of Yahweh.[29] In the Greek world, *ekklēsia* originally was the political assembly of a Greek city-state open to all citizens for self-governance, the most famous being Athens. In the Hellenistic world, the word became common for any assembly, usually a called meeting, often political, but also other groups. Thus, the concept was cross-cultural, flexible, and socially neutral. Paul's use for meetings in private residences in Rome, then, was unremarkable (16:5, 23).

So, Paul commends Phoebe with two purposes in mind.[30] First, "you should welcome (προσδέξησθε, *prosdexesthe*) her in the Lord" (**16:2**). "Welcome" means receive or accept in a beneficial way.[31] The benefit here is "in the Lord," that is, for the sake of the Lord's work, of which, of course, Paul himself is engaged. More solemnity is added by connecting the request to obligation as the community of messianic Israel in Rome: "in a manner worthy of the saints." Since Rome is a part of this group of "saints" (1:7), then they are to receive Phoebe as one of their own. Hospitality is a premier virtue and social skill in the ancient world and in the early church, so here is their opportunity to "share with the saints in their needs" that Paul already had encouraged (12:13). Phoebe is one specific target of that exhortation.[32]

Second, "you should assist (παραστῆτε, *parastēte*) her in whatever matter she should have need of you." This request is benefaction and will assume first-century expectations of the patron-client relationship. The request is founded on a reciprocal basis (16:2b), which means that on behalf of Paul, the Romans already are obligated. They already have been exhorted to pay obligations where due, including respect and hon-

[29] Deut 23:1–2; 1 Chr 28:8; Neh 13:1; Mic 2:5

[30] The "in order that" (ἵνα, *hina*) conjuction often expresses result, but here, the less common purpose. The compounded verbs ("and," καί, *kai*) produce two purposes.

[31] Josephus, *Ant.* 6.255 (6.12.5), records Saul remonstrating with the high priest for "receiving" David, that is, supplying him with weapons and food, but the high priest did not know Saul in his own mind had made David an adversary, not an ally.

[32] See discussion, pp. 470–71.

or (13:7), and Phoebe now is presented formally as one person in particular to whom respect and honor are due.[33]

The reciprocal nature of the benefaction is explained in the "for" explanatory clause that follows. "For even she has been a benefactress (προστάτις, *prostatis*) of many." The term *prostatis* became technical in Roman life for the supportive role of a patron benefactor. Most of society was built on benefaction—literally. Roads, bridges, aqueducts, buildings, temples, monuments, statues and more were financed by a benefactor, some wealthy citizen, who, upon assuming political office paid for these benefits to cities and societies, or, outside political office, insured by these benefactions continuing favorable business enterprises or other advantageous social connections. One of the great aspirations Herod the Great as a client-king of Rome had was to be known across the Mediterranean as a benefactor of Hellenistic culture to the cities. The list of his public works outside of Judea is astounding.[34]

Patronage was not limited exclusively to men. Some women obtained outstanding credentials and reputation. One of these was Plancia Magna, native of Perge, the coastal city in Pamphylia Paul visited twice on the first missionary journey.[35] She had royal blood, high family status, and great power and influence in early second-century Asia. Her father was the Roman senator and proconsul Marcus Plancius Varus, and her mother the Herodian princess Julia. Her brother, Gaius Plancius Varus, also was a Roman senator. Her maternal grandfather was King Tigranes of Armenia. Earlier maternal ancestors included King Archelaus of Cappadocia and Herod the Great of Judea through

[33] Dunn (*Romans 9–16*, 888) indicated "matter" (*pragmati*) included a domain of lawsuit or dispute, pointing to 1 Cor 6:1, noting women could be litigants (Meeks, *Urban Christians*, 24), and suggesting this inference possible here. Judicial burden behind a first introduction is extremely unlikely socially—both inappropriate and offensively presumptive. Further, a contentious legal matter would be so counterproductive to smooth introduction to the assemblies in Rome as to make the effort illogical.

[34] Josephus, *J.W.* 1.422–28 (1.21.11–12); *Ant.* 15.326–30 (15.9.5); 16.18–19, 24–26 (16.2.2). These included palaces, walls, temples, market places, theaters, aqueducts, baths, fountains, land donations, financial donations and more, even paying debts and tributes. Benefactions were made everywhere: Tripoli, Damascus, Ptolemais, Byblus, Berytus, Tyre, Sidon, Damascus, Ascalon, Cos, Rhodes, Lycia, Samnia, Ionia, Athens, Pergamum, Antioch of Syria, and more.

[35] Acts 13:13; 14:25. See the author's on-site video overviewing Plancia Magna at https://drkoine.com/paul/journeys/1mj/south-galatia/index.html.

his Hasmonean princess wife, Mariamne. Her mother was priestess of Artemis in Perge. Plancia herself rose to high priestess there times over, not only of Artemis, but of the imperial cult and of the mother of the gods. Plancia Magna and her brother and maternal cousins are the last known descendants of the Herodian dynasty. The story of Plancia and her family is told in inscriptions. They were notably civic minded, charitable, and generous.[36] The family gave so extravagantly they earned the high status of "second founders" of Perge, expressed in inscriptions by the honorific title *Ktistēs* ("creator," "founder").

FIGURE 12.14. Perge: Hellenistic Gate Courtyard. Renovated by Plancia Magna about 119–122. The niches held honorific statuary on bases with dedicatory inscriptions.

One of her most stunning benefactions was completely renovating the Hellenistic Gate complex leading into Perge. She restored the side towers and courtyard with a two-tiered triumphal arch with statuary to Greek gods and goddesses, as well as to the Roman imperial family. The inscriptions in the complex refer to Plancia without any reference to her husband or son, which suggests her individuality and independent status in the civic arena.[37] The Boule, Demos, and Gerousia gave her the honorific title of "Demiourgos," which was the highest public office in government. The title was a great honor, one among many, and obligated her to sponsor the local games held in Perge, a significant expense, but with which she had no difficulty.

[36] The quality of "euergetism" in inscriptions.
[37] Cf. Caceres-Cerda, "The Exceptional Case of Plancia Magna."

FIGURE 12.15. Plancia Magna Honorific Statue. The inscription on the base emphasizes her family, civic status, and imperial connections. The crown on her head is ringed with busts of significant members of the imperial family (AAM).

FIGURE 12.16. Plancia Magna Inscription. Bi-lingual, two-line inscription, Latin, then Greek. Plancia's name is in the second and fourth lines (Latin, Greek). The first and third lines mention Sabina Augusta, Roman empress of Hadrian, daughter of suffect consul Lucious Vibius Sabinus. Sabina was the only other imperial woman honored in the empire as much as Augustus's wife, Livia. Her image was the first woman ever to appear on coins minted at Rome. She was the most traveled and known empress of her time. She was known to Plancia Magna, illustrating Plancia's high status in imperial society. Sabina was awarded the title Augusta in 128, dating the inscription this year or later.

FIGURE 12.17. Plancia Magna Statue Base. Closeup of the base inscription. The last line provides the important overall life summary: ΤΗΝΠΑΤΡΩΝΙΣ, τὴν πατρώνις, (tēn patrōnis), "the patroness" (AAM).

We have a first-century illustration from Corinth in Achaia of a patroness role similar to that of Plancia Magna at Perge in Pamphylia. Her name was Junia Theodora. She was a citizen of Corinth and a Roman citizen active somewhere in the 40s or 50s, that is, at almost exactly the same time as Phoebe. An inscription documenting her patronage was discovered in 1954. The monument preserves five different formal letters of recommendation written for Junia over the years collected together to create this honorific in Junia's name. She is lauded for her faithful, tireless, and effective representation of the businesses of her native territory of Lycia, right next door to Plancia's Pamphylia.[38] Her role was crucial for providing direct representation of the commercial interests of Lycia to the administrators and civic authorities in the busy port city of Corinth, a major gateway to trade and travel east and west in the Roman empire. Junia's family was Greek (Theodora). The Latin name, Junia, probably was added related to Roman citizenship.

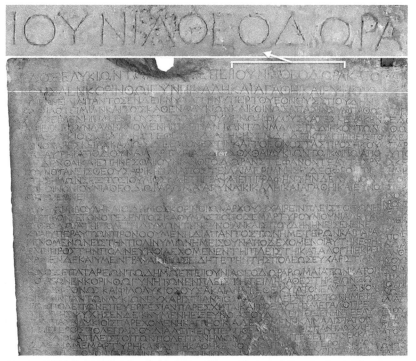

FIGURE 12.18. Junia Theodora Inscription. Honorific inscription for Junia Theodora, a patroness from Corinth at the same time as Phoebe next door at Cenchreae. Her name occurs in the top line as ΙΟΥΝΙΑΘΕΟΔΩΡΑ, Ἰουνία θεοδώρα, *Iounia Theodōra* (AMAC).

The fifth letter in the inscription comprising lines 72–77 preserves a decree of Telmessos in Lycia. The inscription reads in part as follows.

[38] See map of Roman provinces, p. 521, fig. 12.9.

> Since Junia Theodora, a Roman woman, a benefactress having the greatest loyalty to the Lycian federation and our city has completed many benefits for the federation and our city, and dwelling in the city of the Corinthians welcomes in her own home Lycian travellers and our citizens . . . supplying them with everything . . .; displaying her patronage (προστασίαν, *prostasian*) of those who are present . . .[39]

In a similar way, Phoebe also was a woman of means, whose home, like Junia's in Corinth, or Lydia's in Philippi, would have been open to travelers for lodging whom she could assist in various ways according to her finances, as well as by offering information, advice, and political and governmental connections locally in both Cenchreae and Corinth.

The reciprocal nature of the benefaction is that Phoebe already has assisted Paul in some way during his winter stay in Corinth about 57–58. After indicating her patroness role to others, Paul adds, "and of me myself." At that point, he is signaling with this calculated added phrase that Roman assemblies can assist him with his "obligation" to Phoebe for her benefaction to him by accommodating her in Rome. The nature of this recommendation as leading the list of final items to cover in the letter closing indicates the importance of this recommendation and that Phoebe's travel to Rome is not a whimsical leisure trip. The literary character and placement of this recommendation likely infers two realities, and perhaps a third: (1) Phoebe officially bears the letter of Romans to Rome. (2) Phoebe is authorized on behalf of Paul to interpret the letter after its audition by each assembly. (3) Phoebe has funded the writing of Romans and likely has provided her own scribe, Tertius, for the task. The composition of Romans would have taken several months to write, two to three days to make one copy, and cost approximately $3200 in today's currency to produce.[40]

Primary Greetings (16:3–16)

The greetings inspire curiosity immediately. They are not typical. They have quite distinctive characteristics. They are anything but of the nature of "tell so-and-so hi for me." First, they are long. Individuals are

---

[39] The Greek text is available online at the *Bulletin de Correspondence Hellenique, 1959*, Text 500. Charitonidis, Pallas, and Vénencie, *Inscriptions Lyciennes Trouvées A Solômos Près de Corinthe*, 496–508.

[40] Richards, *Paul and First-Century Letter Writing*, 169 (adjusted for inflation).

singled out with great intentionality, specificity, and detail. Second, they have unusual style. Way more effort is being expended here than simply just naming names of people saying hi. Individuals are highly honored. Christian service is noted. Virtuous character is emphasized. Third, these greetings are not really greetings, though rhetorically embedded as greetings. The greetings function as recommendations.

That they serve as recommendations explains a curious common denominator among the names. They reveal heavy emphasis on direct relationship to Paul. This emphasis on relationship to Paul may be a clue as to their function to explain the overall peculiar nature of these greetings. The greetings go beyond greetings. Their rhetorical force seems to be to identify locally in Rome those members of local Roman assemblies who know Paul and can vouch for Paul. They can affirm the letter of Romans in Rome. This connection and knowledge of the author of the letter would be important in a church Paul did not found and never had visited.

These observations that profile the unusual nature of these greetings here suggest the hypothesis that the greetings are being used to single out particular house church leaders in Rome known to Paul as he writes to an unknown church to establish a beachhead of relationship with the assemblies in Rome. These leaders either have been associated with or know about Paul and his previous mission work. For example, connection to one of the names in this list may explain why Illyricum in particular is singled out when Paul earlier in the previous chapter mentioned the orbit of his preaching mission reaching all the way to Illyricum (15:19). Someone in Rome in particular is familiar in some way with that work. Thus, these individuals in particular can vouch for Paul, his mission, and his gospel there in Rome. They also can vouch for the content of the letter as a solid indication of what Paul means when he says the gospel of God.

These greetings and their associated names also provide a window into the social setting of the churches in Rome.[41] The prevalence of Greco-Roman names and minority of Jewish names silently testifies to the social shift from synagogue to house church triggered by the Edict of Claudius. The very character of the fellowship is changing toward a more multiethnic, multicultural blend. The social location is

---

[41] See discussion, "Slavery and Housing," pp. 169–179.

no longer the synagogue, but private associations on private or rental property. This rental property likely would have been of the *insula* type of the poorer sections of Rome, and the resultant tenement churches would have had different social dynamics than those of a house church based on patronage. Several expressions throughout the greetings suggest house churches or assemblies in private and rental residences, such as "the church that meets in their house" (16:5); "those who belong to the household of" (16:11), "and the brother and sisters with them" (16:14); "and all the Lord's people who are with them" (16:15). Further, one should note that the composition indicated by the names evidences the prominent role of women and the significant presence of typical slave names. How the gospel sounds to a slave is different than how the gospel sounds to a slave owner.[42] Thus, entire studies could be pursued on just what the names alone portend.[43]

These names, their social setting, and the very profile of messianic faith inferred in Rome by Paul's letter has an unrecognized implication: *The Roman church has become a prime example of the whole point of Romans as the gospel of God explained and applied. The nations are being reached even as Isaiah had prophesied, and the central exhibit of the gospel explained and applied is turning to Rome.*[44]

Prisca and Aquila (16:3–5a)

Almost all our narrative information on this couple comes from Acts.[45] Paul encounters them in Corinth on the second missionary journey freshly arrived from Rome due to the Edict of Claudius, and they share a joint business venture (σκηνοποιοί, *skēnopoioi*). Aquila is a Jew and native of Pontus. Therefore, they are Paul's fellow kinsmen (*syngenēs*, 9:3) that constitute the remnant Israel of which Paul is part (11:5). They

---

[42] As Oakes, *Reading Romans in Pompeii*, has tried to alert us. See previous discussion, pp. 173–75.

[43] Thirty-three names, twenty-four in Rome. Of those in Rome, seventeen are men, seven are women, with two households and two unnamed women, (mother of Rufus and sister of Nerues), and other unnamed persons. Consult critical commentaries for analysis, which mostly depend on Lampe, *From Paul to Valentinus*.

[44] Luke would add, according to his literary design, "and away from Jerusalem."

[45] Acts 18:2, 18, 26; Rom 16:3; 1 Cor 16:19; 2 Tim 4:19. Luke uses the diminutive "Priscilla," but Paul always "Prisca." See Sanday and Headlam, *Romans*, 418–20 for an extensive excursus with details about this couple.

had a house in Corinth, and apparently later in Ephesus too, where they already hosted a house church before getting back to Rome to sponsor another one.[46] Thus, they evidence business means, some wealth, but not necessarily aristocracy. Evocative of this couple is the Pompeii portrait of the lawyer, Terentius Neo, and his wife, tragically killed by the cataclysmic eruption of Mount Vesuvius in AD 79.[47]

FIGURE 12.19. Terentius Neo Portrait. Portrait of the lawyer, Terentius Neo, and his wife, residents of Pompeii killed by the eruption of Mt. Vesuvius AD 79 (NNAM).

The portrait itself is social commentary. His papyrus scroll with wax seal is wound on a wooden rod (*rotulus*) and could be a marriage contract or some other document. The style is realism. His features are

[46] 1 Cor 16:19; Rom 16:5.

[47] The title is confused. The structure adjoining the house was a bakery, giving the rise to the name, "The Baker and his Wife." The art wrongly was associated with the Pompeii house belonging to a Paquius Proculus, so "Paquius Proculus and his Wife."

not flattering. Though he wears a toga with fashionable cropped hair, his features are rough: brow creases, scraggly facial hair, big ears, and bony features. He is tanned heavily, showing sun exposure. In contrast, his wife is sophisticated. The red ribbon indicates a married woman. She styles a red/purple dress, indicating aristocracy. She is holding a hinged, wooden writing tablet, a portrait convention, but still might indicate education and literacy. Fair skin denotes the culturally elite (i.e., not a field hand). Her fine and delicate hair curls took hours for a slave to achieve in the dressing room. Her stylish head band, fine lips, manicured nails, fine dress, and writing stylus with wax tablet all sign wealth. Socially mismatched, they are rendered pleasantly paired.

Prisca and Aquila are back in Rome in a similar role as at Ephesus, that is, sponsoring an assembly of believers in their home (16:3–4).[48] Prisca mentioned first indicates social standing, similar to the conventions in the Terentius Neo portrait. They obviously travelled widely and easily owned multiple properties of sufficient size to host groups of people. They were quite generous, regularly opening their homes to host Paul (Acts 18:2–3), Apollos (Acts 18:26), the Ephesians (1 Cor 16:19), and the Romans (Rom 16:5). They became notable leaders in every location and some of Paul's closest and most faithful associates ("my coworkers in Messiah Jesus"). We do not know what historical reference is behind "who for my life risked their own necks," but the expression could imply mortal danger. They clearly represented Paul's interests as his patrons in some way to their own potential jeopardy, whether of reputation, finances, or physical harm. Paul then indicates that his gratitude is not his alone but of "all the churches of the gentiles."[49] Never noted in the commentaries is that the expression is a *hapax legomenon* (once only) in Paul.[50] So why here? The context is

---

[48] Edicts expired with the death of the emperor. Claudius died in AD 54. We are assuming sometime then or shortly thereafter, Prisca and Aquila returned to their home in Rome, perhaps maintained during their absence by household slaves, or perhaps purchasing a different residence, likely in the Campus Martius or Adventinus areas of the city. See map of the city of Rome, p. 161, fig. 9.20.

[49] One might argue *ethnōn* either way as "gentiles" or "nations," but "gentiles" seems best in this context in which Paul is adjulating Jewish leaders.

[50] Paul uses the plural of churches in the absolute (no qualifier), or of Messiah or God, or of the saints, or of a province, but never "of the gentiles," except here. *Absolute*: 1 Cor 7:17; 2 Cor 8:18, 23, 24; 11:8, 28; 12:13; *Messiah/God*: Rom 16:16; 1 Cor 11:16;

greeting *Jewish* members of the Roman *ekklēsiai* who have insured the *gentile* presence in messianic Israel, personally offering even their own private residences in any location as a place of assembly for all. Cranfield likely is correct, then, that gentiles, because of widespread impact of this couple through their travels and association with Paul, knew of the "risking their necks" business in particular and even beyond that had many reasons for a general, deep-seated respect and appreciation for their work everywhere.[51] Paul then adds, "and the church (ἐκκλησίαν, *ekklēsian*) in their house" (**16:5a**).[52] Their leadership role literally everywhere they go is obvious. This assembly would be more along the lines of a house church with a patron couple, not a tenement church. Early churches in Rome in some cases were built on the sites of these residential assemblies, as with the famous St. Clement Church.

FIGURE 12.20. Basilica San Clemente, Rome. The basilica is dedicated to Clement I of Rome (92–99), the first of the Apostolic Fathers of the church. The history of the building is well known and documented from a Roman nobleman's home to a house church, to the later two basilicas built on the same spot. The present 11th cent. basilica is built on top of a 4th cent. basilica. Earlier levels of construction underneath reveal a Roman nobleman's home that later served as a church in the 1st cent. Thus, this basilica's history takes us all the way back to the 1st cent. and helps illustrate how early Christians met in homes of wealthy patron sponsors. Use of "church" in that context really was not about a building at all, but a body of believers.

1 Thess 2:14; 2 Thess 1:4; *saints*: 1 Cor 14:33; *province*: 1 Cor 16:1, 19; 2 Cor 8:1; Gal 1:2, 22. Thus, this unique use of chuches in the plual of gentiles in Paul captures attention.

[51] Cranfield, *Romans*, 2:786.

[52] The verse division is minus any sensibility whatsoever.

FIGURE 12.21. Basilica San Clemente: Apse Mosaic. Closeup of the apse mosaic using a Byzantine arabesque motif embellished with scrolled acanthus tendrils, c 1200.

FIGURE 12.22. Basilica San Clemente: First-Century Level. Distinctive first-century herringbone floor and *opera reticulata* wall of a governmental building partially preserved from the AD 64 fire of Rome. A Roman estate later was built on top of this surviving structure, then later was used as a church upon which basilicas were built.

One could conjecture from this Prisca and Aquila leadership picture that emerges so quickly about them that they played a significant role in provoking the Claudius Edict when the early church in Rome had a decided synagogue profile. They certainly were involved as part of the expulsion in any case.

Epaenetus, Mary (16:5b–6)

Unknown outside this verse, Epaenetus has two leading features. First, he is "beloved" (**16:5b**). Paul is affectionate. He uses this "beloved" adjective thirty-seven times in his writing.[53] Paul is sincere. Second, Epaenetus also is the "first convert ("firstfruit," ἀπαρχὴ, *aparchē*) of Asia unto Messiah." The distinction makes him most memorable to Paul.[54] The "unto Messiah" is the crucial prophetic theme of Romans. Epaenetus represents realization for Paul of Israel's destiny of light to the nations through Messiah. Epaenetus is the signal post pointing the way to messianic Israel's future.

Paul greets Mary (**16:6**). She has" toiled much for you." The verb for "toil" is ἐκοπίασεν, *ekopiasen*. The idea is weary work, labor, the common lot of a field hand. This expression is interesting, because the four times Paul employs this expression in this list of greetings, only women carry the honor (Mary, Tryphena, Tryphosa, and Persis).

Andronicus and Junia (16:7)

Paul greets Andronicus and Junia (**16:7**).[55] The Greek name Adronicus is frequent among Jews of the Diaspora. Junia most likely is the wife of Andronicus.[56] The first descriptor is that they are "fellow Jews" (συγ-

---

[53] NRSV translation for English students. See comments, p. 444 and note 112.

[54] The "of Asia" is slightly ambiguous. Whether he is the first Asian convert, or the first convert during the time Paul is in Asia is not clear.

[55] The variant "Julia" in a few Greek manuscripts likely is assimilation to 16:15.

[56] More ink than deserves has been wasted on the gender of Junia. On how the gender identity schizophrenia affected even modern editions of the Greek New Testament after the first quarter of the twentieth century, note the documentation by Epp, *Junia: The First Woman Apostle*. Ancient Greek manuscripts have few accents, but a modern editor by changing the *presumed* accent from acute to circumflex (Ἰουνίαν to Ἰουνιᾶν) can invent a masculine gender (pretend) name "Junias"—a complete fiction, because no such known Roman male name exists. The error is compounded by presuming this fictional male name "Junias," with no historical evidence in support, is a contraction of an actual known Roman male name, Junianus (RSV, NEB, NIV). Lampe (*From Paul to Valentinus*, 139–40, 147) documents the feminine Junia over 250 times in Roman inscriptions, with not even one example of a male Junias. Further, patristic church fathers universally took the name as feminine (Origen, *Rom.* 10.21; Chrysostom, *Rom.* 31.2; Jerome, *Rom.* 16.7). Whereas earlier editions of the Greek New Testament caved

γενεῖς, *syngeneis*). They are the subject of Romans 9–11 (9:3). They now are part of remnant Israel, as Paul (9:27; 11:5). Given the tensions with the synagogues in Rome already endured, as well as the Roman prejudice to Jews in general, their presence in the church could have been problematic. They even may have been targets of the arrogant attitudes of gentiles Paul called out in 11:20 simply on guilt by association. Again, this couple may have figured into the weak and strong controversy in Romans 14–15, whether as part of the weak (less likely) or the strong (more likely, since they seem to be part of the Pauline circle). In any case, they also carry the distinction as "fellow prisoners" (συναιχμαλώτους, *synaichmalōtous*). Paul thus identifies Aristarchus in Col 4:10 and Epaphas in Phlm 23. The term is exceedingly rare.[57] No occurences in the LXX, Josephus, Philo, and elsewhere render the *multiple* uses by Paul quite distinctive, almost functioning as a social identity marker or occupational profile. We necessarily do not need to presume that they were in prison with Paul, only that they suffered imprisonment for the same reason as we know did Paul—for the sake of the gospel. The note on imprisonment would hold great significance for Paul in the social dimension of imprisonment in the first-century world, which was one of shame and dishonoring. This social factor is why the episode at Philippi was such a serious setback for Paul and his reputation as an itinerant preacher and his message.[58] Turning from the social angle to the theological, Andronicus and Junia "get it." They are at the heart of suffering discipleship so core to Paul's entire frame for messianic lifestyle as a "living sacrifice" (12:1). Their discipleship reflects the passion of Messiah, and nothing could be more core to showing that one is "in Messiah." Gentile believers in Rome subtly are admonished to take full note of the witness of Andronicus and Junia before they jump cavalierly and abusively to dismiss their contribution to the quality and profile of messianic Israel.

to pressure for the masculine form, the tide dramatically has shifted to the historical evidence for the feminine (note UBS5, NA28, NRSV). Cf. Fitzmyer, *Romans*, 737–38; Moo, *Romans*, 921–23; Schreiner, *Romans*, 795–96; Longenecker, *Romans*, 1060–61. Quite the story behind this interesting tidbit in translation history.

[57] BDAG lists only a handful of references, none easily knowable or accessible.

[58] Acts 16:23–24. Paul got the best of the honor-shame contest by demanding civic officials publicly come and apologize rather than trying to shoo him off privately with no apology for their illegal actions under Roman law (Acts 16:35–39). See Stevens, *Acts*, 357.

The next phrase is highly controversial: "which ones are well-known ['among' or 'to/by'] the apostles" (οἵτινές εἰσιν ἐπίσημοι ἐν τοῖς ἀποστόλοις, *hoitines eisin episēmoi en tois apostolois*). The word "well known" (ἐπίσημοι, *episēmoi*) has the general sense of having an exceptional quality, being splendid, or prominently standing out in a crowd, that is, outstanding. The sense of the simple preposition (ἐν, *en*) is the headache. If distributive, the preposition means "among" and infers belonging to the group (KJV, NASB, NIV, NRSV). If location, the preposition means "to" (ESV) or "in the eyes of" (CSB), and infers not belonging to the group. So, their roles are radically different on the reading of the preposition alone. They either are outstanding as apostles or they are only well known to the apostles.

The sensitive issue for this phrase is whether a woman could be an apostle. Depends on the meaning of apostle, of course. The answer automatically is (duh) no if the meaning is the twelve men called and discipled by Jesus in the days of his flesh who together constituted the expression, "the twelve apostles," in later tradition. Luke provides the classic definition of that band of brothers known in the early church in describing the selection of Matthias to replace Judas after the ascension of Jesus (Acts 1:21–26). They followed and ministered with Jesus from the time of the inauguration of his public ministry (John's baptism) to its conclusion in his death, resurrection and ascension. That is, they provide historical testimony to the truth of the incarnation of the heavenly Son of God. Though most in the early church disagreed with him rather strongly, Paul insisted he was an apostle in that classic sense, particularly because he had seen the risen Lord.[59] Paul conveniently had to ignore the first part of the classic definition of being with Jesus, discipled by Jesus from the time of John's baptism forward. Ignoring that point is precisely why Paul never could square away with the church on the matter.[60]

The same author who gives us the classic definition of what makes the twelve the Twelve also provides evidence that other definitions of

[59] 1 Cor 9:1–2, 5–6.

[60] Paul suggests his understanding of "apostle" is fixed on having "seen the Lord"—as did he—in his remarks in 1 Cor 15:5–8. In these remarks he distinguishes "the Twelve" as a group (1 Cor 15:5), but then immediately refers to "all the apostles" as *another* group in contradistinction from "the Twelve" (1 Cor 15:7). That larger group of "apostles" is the group of which he considers himself a member (1 Cor 15:9).

"apostle" were floating in the early church, probably more associated with the Hellenist wing of the movement than the Jerusalem-centric element. This evidence is in Acs 14:4, when Luke lets slip that Paul and Barnabas are considered "apostles" by someone. Likely, the someone is the church at Antioch who had commissioned this missionary journey (Acts 13:1–3). The implicit definition here is delegation or representation on behalf of gospel expansion, "sent out" ones. Modern parlance would tend toward the word "missionary."[61]

So, "apostle" can be nuanced. Causing alarm among hierarchial or patriarchal hermeneutical persuasions is unnecessary on that point. At the same time, the grammar of the preposition as "to," while an option at the pure level of grammar, is just not your exegetical best play of the cards you have been dealt. First, "well known *to* the apostles" has no logical sense. Why make the point that they are well known *to* the apostles? *Many* people were well known to the apostles, even Caiaphas for that matter. Second, "well known *to* the apostles" has no rhetorical sense. How would this Jewish emphasis persuade gentiles in Rome? They already show arrogant attitude to things Jewish (Rom 11:20). So, for many reasons, "to" is just not the exegetical strong hand here. The option "among" has much more to recommend itself exegetically, outside the unintended consequence of alarming dogmatic positions.

Even if we go for the sense of "among" for translating the prepostion, we simply cannot presume immediately what Paul means by "apostles." He does not have to mean an association with the Twelve of Jerusalem fame. He could mean little more than the typical Hellenist perspective that would reflect delegated work with the gospel. He also could mean Andronicus and Junia are a part of that larger group in which he includes himself in 1 Cor 15:7. That inclusion would infer the couple had had the supreme privilege of seeing the risen Lord. Such an experience would be incredible in anyone's book.

The crucial point for exegesis is that they are "outstanding." That superlative is the whole point of the rhetoric here. This supreme honor stands out regardless the group to whom they are assigned. The take away here is, *in whatever group*, they are "outstanding." Who would not want to have that gold star on their report card? One could

---

[61] Even in the Apostolic Fathers the term is used for itinerant evangelists; cf. Did. 11.3–6.

turn a whole sermon on the idea of making anything a person does for the Messiah "outstanding," even if you wind up in jail for your faith.

Finally, notable about this couple is that they were "in Messiah" before Paul. Some tend in the direction of tying the couple to the early Jerusalem church.[62] While this Jerusalem connection is possible, since Paul's vision of the risen Lord is early, the connection still is speculation. First, Paul does not make any Jerusalem connection explicitly, and if that was his point, he missed his point. Second, the Pentecost event suggests that Jewish faith in Jesus as Messiah from the beginning launched from Jerusalem immediately out into the world, since many of those saved were pilgrims from all over the world, including Rome (Acts 2:10). So, Jerusalem may not be the point at all. Still, Paul's observation is interesting. Why should this sequence of coming to faith before Paul be any point in particular? Many had that distinction. But not as apostles specially tasked with gospel proclamation. Paul may be claiming innocence by association. Perhaps the following is Paul's flow of thought in the greeting to Andronicus and Junia and its descriptors.

> The gospel of God Andronicus and Junia already have been proclaiming in Rome for some time now that you already accept and support is the gospel of God I am proclaiming. I may be the new kid on the block, but my gospel is not really new. As comfortable as you are with Andronicus and Junia you should be with me. Andronicus, Junia, and I share in suffering imprisonment for the Messiah because we share in the same message about Messiah that we preach.

Compressed Series (16:8–15)

After the first three major sets of Phoebe and the two couples, Prisca and Aquila, and Andronicus and Junia, the greetings pick up pace. Descriptions are shorter, but have no less important function.

- Ampilatus is "beloved" a favorite Pauline term of affection (**16:8**). The name was common in the imperial household, likely a slave.

---

[62] Cf. Longenecker, *Romans*, 1069–70. Longenecker, of course, tendentially needs this association to build his case for the hypothetical construct that the early Jerusalem church thoroughly dominated and controlled the early Roman church, resulting in too much law emphasis in early Roman Christianity. Paul writes Romans to counter this legalism. Some in making a Jerusalem connection go for the Hellenist wing of the early Jerusalem church; cf. Cranfield, *Romans*, 790; Moo, *Romans*, 924.

- Urbanus is a "co-worker in Messiah" (**16:9**). This name also is common in the imperial household; again, likely a slave.

- Stachys is "beloved" as well; perhaps a slave.

- Apelles is "approved (δόκιμον, *dokimon*) in Messiah" (**16:10**). This description echoes closely 14:18, in which Paul describes the person who bridges the gap between the weak and the strong by not destroying by what is eaten the person for whom Messiah died. This greeting puts Apelles forward as the example to follow in particular in working through this issue in Rome. Apelles, that is, is a good example of someone who is able to "approve (δοκιμάζειν, *dokimazein*) the good, pleasing, and complete will of God" (12:2).

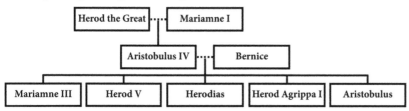

FIGURE 12.23. Herodian Family. A (greatly) simplified Herodian family chart to follow the Aristobulus family of the Hasmonean lineage through the princess Mariamne I.

- Aristobulus family. An arresting family name for one familiar with the Herods. Aristobulus (Minor) was a grandson of Herod through his father Aristobulus IV, Herod's son by the Hasmonean princess, Mariamne I. His brother was Herod Agrippa I, who ruled as king over Judea from 41–44. Along with his older brothers Agrippa I and Herod V of Chalcis, he schooled in Rome and became friends with the future emperor, Claudius. He later died in Rome, leaving only a deaf and mute daughter, so his slaves presumably passed over to the imperial household, thus preserving the "those of Aristobulus" identifier in later generations, which Paul may employ in that sense. We cannot absolutely know this connection, since the Aristobulus name was common, but the possibility is intriguing.[63]

- Herodion is another "fellow Jew" (συγγενῆ, *syngenē*) like Andronicus and Junia (**16:11**).[64] His name would suggest a possible freedman

[63] Cf. Josephus, *J.W.* 2.221 (2.11.6); *Ant.* 20.13.

[64] The term does not specifically mean "relative" in this context (contra NRSV). The meaning is simply kinsman, countryman, fellow Jew, similar to Andronicus and Junia.

of the Herodian family. We do know that the aristocratic elements of this family always had connections with Rome, as the discussion of Aristobulus indicates. These connections persisted even during and after the Jewish War, as with Josephus the historian, and Herod Agrippa II and his sister, Bernice, who was Titus's mistress both in Judea and in Rome until he became emperor.[65]

- Narcissus household, specifically those "in the Lord." Another common slave name, so confidence in historical connections is difficult, but, again, an interesting possibility presents itself. A freedman by this name served emperor Claudius closely.[66] Claudius suspiciously came to an untimely end, Agrippina highly suspicioned for murder to obtain the throne for her young son, Nero. Narcissus similarly came to his end as well.[67] After that, his household would have been assimilated into the imperial estate.

- Tryphaena and Tryphosa (16:12), specifically given as a pair, with the odd linguistic feature of the same root for both names (Tryph-). Both names are common in inscriptions. Alliterated names or same root names often indicated calling attention to family connection, and some family connection might be possible here.[68] Notably, they too "labor strenuously in the Lord," as does Mary (16:6).

- Persis is a quite common female slave name. She has two features. She is "beloved," but, as noted by Dunn, not "my beloved," perhaps to indicate a widely-shared opinion among many.[69] Also, she has "labored much in the Lord," completing the set of four women so identified (Mary, Tryphaena, Tryphosa, Persis).

- Rufus is Latin, often a slave name (16:13). An interesting possible New Testament connection is Mark 15:21, which indicates a Simon of Cyrene was conscripted into carrying Jesus's cross, and oddly adds that Simon was the father of two sons, Alexander and Rufus, a

---

[65] Bernice's story is documented in Josephus, *J.W.* 2.11.6; 15.1; 17.1; *Ant.* 19.9.1; 15.1; 20.1.3; Tacitus, *Hist.* 2.2; Suetonius, *Titus* 7; Cassius Dio, *Hist.* 65.15; 66:18; Juvenal, *Sat.* 61.156–57.

[66] Tacitus, *Ann.* 13.1; Cassius Dio, *Hist.* 60.34; Juvenal, *Sat.* 14.329–31.

[67] Tacitus, *Ann.* 13.1.

[68] Suggesting they were twins is without necessary attestation in the literature.

[69] Dunn, *Romans 9–16*, 897; Contrast the expressions in 16:5, 8, 9.

detail completely superfluous for the narrative action. One possibility is that this Gospel's connection to Peter and Rome is the context for mentioning names that would be familiar to believers in Rome. Possible, but as Evans points out, is little more than speculation.[70] He is described by Paul as "the elect in the Lord." The expression echoes resoundingly throughout Romans 9–11, including the preparatory question about who can make a charge against "God's elect" (8:33), then on into God's purpose of election in the story of the patriarchs (9:11), followed by the remnant at the present time who are "chosen" by grace (11:5) who also obtained what Mosaic Israel missed (11:7), and concluded by the grace that keeps election viable even for the disobedient (11:28). Rufus is part of that story.

- Rufus's mother, who was in Rome at the time of the letter's composition. Paul adds, "and mine," a fictive family metaphor of which he was prone to express throughout his communications with others, but which reveals another undocumented Pauline close relationship that had developed somehow, somewhere, yet, frustratingly, of which Paul elsewhere nor Luke anywhere says anything.

- Asyncritus, Phlegon, Hermes, Patrobas, Hermas (**16:14**). The first two are attested in inscriptions (meaning common), both typical names for slaves and freedmen. Hermes is likely a slave, since naming slaves after gods was common. Patrobas is short for Patrobius, and raises the issue of the infamous freedman of Nero.[71] Identification is unlikely in the extreme. Connection to the household name might be a possibility for the one named here. Hermas was quite a common slave name. Paul adds, "and the brothers and sisters with them." Comment usually is offered that this expression alludes to a "house church." The case of a series of names as in 16:14, however, may be a prime example of the necessary distinction for which Jewett lobbied between "house church" of the patron(ess) style, as with Phoebe, Prisca and Aquila, and Andronicus and Junia, and the "tenement church" within the framework of the crowded *insula* apartments of the lower-class quarters of Rome that would function at

---

[70] Evans, *Mark 8:27—16:20*, 500.

[71] Reputed to be quite greedy and self-indulgent; cf. Tacitus, *Hist.* 1.49; 2.95.

the social level on shared leadership by default.[72] The same may be said for the following series of names.

- Philologus, Julia, Nereus, his sister, and Olympas (**16:15**). Philologus is a common slave and freedman name. Julia was one of the most popular Roman names. Julia had imperial associations because of the daughter of Augustus. The name, therefore, was used often for female slaves, particularly of the imperial household. Since the two names of Philologus and Julia are joined by a conjunction, they may either be husband and wife, or brother and sister. They may both have been imperial slaves. Nereus, again, is a common slave name itself often found in the imperial domain. Whether Nereus "and his sister"[73] were children belonging to Philologus and Julia is simply unknowable. Olympas also was a much used name everywhere. Paul adds, "and all the saints with them." Again, another local church assembly seems in play with this expression. The conjunctions joining the names make two pairs, plus Olympas. Family relationships or otherwise cannot be known, but the likely social context, especially given the predominance of slave or freedmen domains of the names, strongly suggests another tenement style church of the lower-class areas of the city.

Obvious in this list of names is how slave status likely is in the background of so many. Their slave station in life made difficult their effort to follow Jesus.[74] The message of future hope and redemption of the body (Romans 8) would have been quite pertinent and most poignantly felt, resonating strongly with their social identity.

We should remind ourselves here at the very end how Paul began this letter: "Paul, slave of Messiah Jesus" (1:1). Paul identifies as a slave for three reasons. First and foremost, Paul identified as a slave primarily to identify with Israel in her history. Israel's story at its heart is a story of slavery, and that story is not over yet (Romans 6). Even after return from exile, Ezra in dismay confessed, "Behold, we are slaves today" (Neh 9:36). Postexilic Israel could not shake the feeling that its redemption from slavery was yet to be realized.

---

[72] See discussion, pp. 177–79.

[73] Why Paul does not name her is another natural but unanswerable question.

[74] See discussion, pp. 173–77.

Second, Paul also identified as a slave at the beginning of Romans to make a fundamental theological statement of the condition of the human experience as a lordship relationship with a higher power (Romans 1). Real freedom is a question of the right lordship. Ezra's program of "just try harder" by legislating obedience in postexilic Israel was a naïve illusion. Sin is a relationship to a power, not a ticklist of problems to resolve (Romans 5, 7).

Third, Paul identified as a slave at the beginning of Romans to identify with so many members of the various house churches in Rome (Romans 16). Cruel and inhuman as the institution of slavery was in the first century, no other human being better could understand what happened at the cross. Further, no other human being better could say "Jesus is Lord" (10:9) with more sincerity, integrity, and authenticity. Such a person with such a faith Paul knew was the strength of messianic Israel. Patrons may have been necessary for the life of the church, but slaves were essential to telling the story of Israel and to serve as witnesses to the true power of the gospel.

Thus, when Paul wrote the first four words of this letter, he knew he would be here, writing greetings to these house churches with so many slave members. They were his trump card for the gospel of God.

Concluding Exhortation(16:16)

Paul is finished. He signals closure of his greetings section with a call to "greet one another with a holy kiss" (**16:16**). The expression is almost formulaic for Paul.[75] Investigation into first-century Jewish and Greco-Roman practice reveals a complex set of mores and attitudes to public kissing.[76] In the New Testament, the noun *philēma* (φιλήμα) occurs just seven times, four in Paul in contexts of formal greetings.[77] The compounded verb form *kataphileō* (καταφιλέω) adds only six others.[78] Judaism recognized the kiss of reverence, reunion, reconciliation, and farewell. Greco-Roman society was reticent to express a public kiss, but did so for reunions and reconciliation. The holy kiss seems to have been emerging in communities of disciples following Jesus, but Paul may

---

[75] 1 Cor 16:20; 2 Cor 13:12; 1 Thess 5:26.

[76] Note especially, Klassen, "Kiss (NT)," AYBD, 4:89–92.

[77] Luke 7:45; 22:48; Rom 16:16; 1 Cor 16:20; 2 Cor 13:12; 1 Thess 5:26; 1 Pet 5:14.

[78] Matt 26:49; Mark 14:45; Luke 7:38, 45; 15:20; Acts 20:37.

have been setting precedent to encourage a greeting of a kiss in gender mixed social groups. Adding the adjective "holy" is unique to Paul and sets parameters on its meaning, as well as presumes an expected context of public assembly ("greet one another").

In reciprocal relationship, Paul relays greetings presumably from his own churches, those in Galatia, Asia, Macedonia, and Achaia: "all the churches of Messiah greet you." The context would seem to be his own constant contact with them through correspondence and associates, as indicated richly in his letter openings and closings, as well as biographical notations throughout. Indeed, the church from which he probably was writing Romans, Corinth, is one of the best examples of this type of constant contact in letters we have (1–2 Corinthians) and those mentioned but which we do not have ("previous letter" in 1 Cor 5:9 and a "sorrowful letter" in 2 Cor 7:8), not to mention a Corinthian letter to Paul (1 Cor 7:1), as well as private communications, such as Chloe (1 Cor 1:11) and delegations, such as Stephanus, Fortunatus, and Achaicus (1 Cor 16:17). The theological point of adding greetings from his own churches to Rome is to call for the unity of the faith that is so important to his sense of the essence of the gospel message and thereby axiomatically the integrity of gospel witness. Even here, Paul labors to integrate Rome into the Pauline universe of networked churches mutually engaged in the task of fulfilling messianic Israel's call to the nations.

Warning (16:17–20a)

The abruptness of this unit raises eyebrows, but the abruptness can be overplayed. Paul is known to insert warnings into conclusions. A good example is Gal 6:17: "From now on, let no one make trouble for me; for I carry the marks of Jesus branded on my body." Although the interruption into the ending of Romans is more extensive, this literary element is within the range of Pauline literary activity. A letter is a living production in the ancient world, not a static LCD screen with a blinking cursor mark. Further, the letter of Romans took a month or more to compose. Communications by word or letter do not shut down during that process, if the Corinthian material is any indication.

The nature of the danger only can be surmised. We are listening to one end of a phone conversation, so we are missing half the story.

The character is defined by dissension, flattering words, and deception. Paul interprets the activity as the work of Satan. He is confident the "God of peace" will crush this development.

The degree of danger is a question. Is this danger only possible, or is this danger already at work? The distinction is hard to make on the basis of what is said. The easy shift back to a positive tone in the following verses seems to suggests the danger is not of grave concern at the moment, so perhaps only a possible problem to be on the alert to guard against.

The language breathes the air of apocalyptic discourse. The terminology is eschatological. The warning draws on the sense of an apocalyptic imminence of the parousia, or "second coming," but the ideas seem to draw upon the whole complex of thought related to the last judgment. We can compare this sense of imminence in this warning to a similar tone in Rom 13:11.

"Now I beseech you brothers," Paul suddenly transitions out of the greetings (**16:17**). This verb beseech, Παρακαλῶ (*Parakalō*), is a standard way Paul moves to exhortation, which appears here out of sequence, since we long ago left the exhortations that initiated part 2 with the same verb in 12:1. Something has come to Paul's attention as he is trying to finish this exhaustive letter. He inserts an exhortation to cover the matter without having to write an additional letter just for this purpose. He urges them to "watch out for" (σκοπεῖν, *skopein*), the root of our word "scope," like "scope out the place." The idea is to scan the perimeter to investigate. The idea is to get out the spy glass and see what you can see on the horizon. Paul wants them to scan for "dissensions and obstacles," which is ambiguous, so without clear profile. However, the "feel" is something on the order of the dissensions of the weak and the strong, with the obstacles of priding freedom over conscience of other believers that could cause them to stumble. Clearer is that sound apostolic teaching is at stake: "contrary to the teaching which you learned." From whom they learned is unspecified, but the "teaching" would be the traditions of messianic Israel based on the Jesus tradition encoded into the Gospels as interpreted by the Twelve in Jerusalem and continued by other early church leadership in Rome, such as Prisca and Aquila and Adronicus and Junia, and others. The faithful in Rome should turn away from whomever is contradicting the apostolic teaching. What may be in play here is a rogue assembly going off on a tangent due to a charismatic leader who has asserted leadership. This type of problem plagued the Johannine community, for example, especially with the shocking actions of Diotrephes, who unilaterally was throwing out of the church emissaries representing the interests of the elder (3 John 9–10). Naturally, we cannot know this rogue assembly leader problem pertains to the situation in Rome, but the scenario shows one way such a warning would be reasonable.

The reason to avoid such individuals is that the proof is in the pudding (**16:18**). These characters "do not serve our Lord Messiah, but their own appetites (κοιλίᾳ, *koilia*, "stomach," "womb")." We perchance have an allusion to the weak and strong issue on diet manifesting itself, but that cannot be known, and Phil 3:18–19 seems to run a similar track. "Through smooth talk and flattery they deceive the hearts of the naïve." Clearly, the implication is that rhetoric is their strength. Rhetorical flourish always has been able to disguise error. Truth, however, is in the pudding, not the marvelously worded recipe. Some people just have a hard time vetting their sources or anticipating the true deadend of the road of smooth talk to which they are giving too much attention.

Paul is upbeat, however. This positive tone that suddenly inserts itself into the exhortation at **16:19** is what lends to the idea the problem is not acute at the moment, but worrisome if unattended, like that small brown spot on the skin that ignored becomes a melanoma. In contrast to the naïve who might succumb to smooth talk, "the report of your obedience has reached unto all," which, of course, echoes 1:8 that the news of their faith had reached the whole world. So, Paul is able to rejoice over their strongly-grounded faith and tradition. Still, he wants them to be vigilant, "wise unto the good but innocent unto the evil." This wisdom and innocence for the congregation fundamentally is due to the presence of the Holy Spirit of the New Aeon brought about by Messiah, whose effectual working of the obedience of the law (8:1–4) is the proof in the pudding, the result of helping the mind to discern the good, acceptable, and complete will of God (12:2).

Because of these dynamics already in place in the New Aeon, the gospel is the power of God unto salvation to everyone who believes (1:16). The victory already is guaranteed by the historical reality of resurrection (1:3–4). Satan truly is crushed under the feet of those who proclaim the gospel (10:15). The peace that offers "wholeness" (shalom) now (5:1) is prelude to the perfection of consummation to come (8:21).

FIGURE 12.24. Augustus Caesar. General Octavian won the battle of Actium in 31 BC, merging east and west territories of the old Roman Republic into a world empire (LP).

Paul concludes with a potent formula that not only summarizes these theological trajectories of Romans but also could function as a benediction concluding worship: "The God of peace soon will crush Satan under your feet" (**16:20a**). This is Pauline eschatology beautifully expressed in both its present and future dimensions at once.

This word, however, also is counterpropaganda to Rome's gospel about Octavian after his victory at the battle of Actium, when all of Asia Minor was in hot pursuit of coming to terms with the new ruler after a sudden lordship exchange from Antony to Octavian. He made himself the "one who crushes his opponents" but then magnanimously unexpectedly becomes the "reconciler," the "one who brings peace to the world." These are the core themes that became hardwired into all imperial propaganda thereafter. Romans were bred and fed on these themes.[79] As far as Paul was concerned, Jesus and the cross was a new battle of Actium for the whole world, a new age that had dawned.

Grace Benediction (16:20b [24, 28])

Functionally, the grace benediction here in 16:20b is much different than the peace benediction at 15:33. The grace benediction invariably concludes a Pauline letter.[80] Paul's intent when this line is composed is to blow the ink dry and dispatch the letter. This formula ties off with an *inclusio* the opening statement of grace (1:7). In this articulate way, grace begins, ends, and *is* the letter of Romans.[81]

Because of disturbances in the surviving Greek manuscripts, the textual position of the grace benediction is unclear. Greek manuscripts witness three places (20b, 24, 28). These occur at the end of the warning, at the end of a secondary set of greetings, and at the end of the doxology. These variations naturally create versification problems in the English translations. The Authorized Version (KJV) just kicks the can down the road by including the benediction at all three places! Most

---

[79] See discussion at 3:25 (p. 307), 5:1 (p. 326), 8:38 (p. 378), 14:19 (p. 502), and 15:33 (p. 530).

[80] Rom 16:20b; 1 Cor 16:23; 2 Cor 13:13; Gal 6:18; Eph 6:24; Phil 4:23; Col 4:18; 1 Thess 5:28; 2 Thess 3:18; 1 Tim 6:21; 2 Tim 4:22; Titus 3:15; Phlm 25. See discussion, p. 208. The absence of a verse division for the grace benediction at 16:20 has no sense.

[81] Major division (universal grace, Romans 5–8); major theme summary ("therefore God has shut up all in disobedience in order that he might show mercy to all," 11:32); major exhortation transition ("I beg you by the mercies of God," 12:1).

translations omit the last two occurrences at verses 24 and 28, which means they have no verse 24 and no verse 28. All scholars pretty much agree that the benediction inclusion at verse 28 (the end) is spurious based on the weak Greek evidence. But what about at verse 24?

Gamble's study suggested the benediction at verse 24 might be authentic, even though textual evidence is weak.[82] Gamble argued the following hypothetical scenario. Paul was finished, or so he thought at 16:20. Unexpectedly, he was asked by his associates around him at the time in Corinth to send greetings to Rome on their behalf as well. Paul acceded, creating a secondary list of casual and informal greetings of 16:21–23. Since his invariable habit was to conclude his letters with a grace benediction, he dictated a *second* grace benediction to end the letter once again, though redundant. Thus, *both* benedictions at verses 20 and 24 are original, but not really what Paul originally had planned. Gamble's plausible hypothetical reconstruction still has not persuaded most. Arguments against 16:24 that presume an authentic doxology are not persuasive for the majority regarding the doxology as spurious.[83]

Secondary Greetings (16:21–23)

This set of greetings is very unlike the ponderous, formal greetings of the first set and actually more like a standard greeting in a Greco-Roman letter of the first century. These are typical, short, informal, and rather *ad hoc*. They clearly are secondary, intrude on the letter conclusion as planned by the author, and basically have little literary weight, that is, exegetical significance, in contrast to the first set. They are, however, informative. They add specific, historical color to Paul's context in Corinth. Some noteworthy names are on the list.

Timothy (16:21)

Timothy is first, a "co-worker" (16:21). His dominance in the Pauline universe of workers is easily documented both in letters and by letters. He actually, however, is significant here more for his absence. That is, Timothy is *not* included in the opening of the letter of Romans as in numerous other letters.[84] Inclusion in the opening usually has some

---

[82] Gamble, *The Textual History of the Letter to the Romans.*

[83] E.g., Schreiner, *Romans*, 809.

[84] 2 Corinthians, Philippians, Colossians, 1–2 Thessalonians, Philemon.

significance as making some contribution to the letter that is being recognized by the author by including another name in the spot where the author of the letter is identified to the audience. This absence from Romans means Romans is all Paul and nothing but Paul.

Lucius, Jason, and Sosipater (16:21)

All three are identified as "my fellow countrymen" (συγγενεῖς, *syngeneis*). This occurrence is the fourth and last time for this term in Romans. Once again, as with Andronicus and Junia (16:3) and Herodion (16:11), these three Jews sending greetings to Rome are the target of Romans 9–11 (9:3). We simply cannot ignore these names because they were Jews, as if to suggest messianic Israel is done with that. Jews such as Andronicus, Junia, Herodion, Lucius, Jason, and Sosipater (and even Paul himself for that matter) are the very hope Paul has in his mind when he writes about remnant Israel as alive and well and God as at work to save all Israel. Gentiles, indeed, are part of Israel, but *syngeneis* imperatively are part if gentile hope is not going to be flapping in an illusory wind that God keeps his promises.

Lucius (Λούκιος, *Loukios*) is unknown.[85] Since *Loukios* is an alternate form of *Loukas*,[86] the suggestion long has been made this could be Luke of the Gospel and Acts. Surprising here is that Acts is ignored. Luke is not in Corinth at this time. Luke actually does not join up with the Pauline ensemble on the way to Jerusalem until the return through Macedonia at Philippi, where the second "we section" in the Acts text picks up (Acts 20:3).

Jason possibly could be the patron who served as Paul's host during the second missionary journey while Paul was in Thessalonica.[87] He could have joined Paul as Paul passed through Macedonia on the third missionary journey after leaving Ephesus on his way down to "Greece" (Acts 20:2, presumably Corinth). Paul originally had planned to sail straight from Corinth to Syria, but a plot on his life dissuaded him of a sea route, and he took the safer but much longer land journey (Acts 20:3). Thus, the delegates from his churches from Macedonia he likely would have picked up on his way through Macedonia. Those del-

---

[85] The Antiochene leader is unlikely (Acts 13:1).

[86] Deissmann, *Light*, 435–38.

[87] Acts 17:5–7, 9.

egates from Macedonia persumably would have spent the winter with him in Greece before sailing season reopened in March, making them available for sending greetings in Romans. Of course, we cannot know for sure who this person was, so we are forced to speculate.

Sosipater likewise is unknown. Again, potential connection to the collection for Jerusalem would depend on whether this form of the name is a longer form of the name Sopater. A Sopater suddenly shows up in a list of Paul's traveling companions in Acts 20:4. This Sopater is from Berea.[88] Possibly, the Sosipater here in 16:21 is the same as this Sopater of the collection delegation, but, again, we cannot be sure.

Tertius (16:22)

Tertius gains instant fame as the only named scribe of one of Paul's letters, though we know Paul used scribes constantly (**16:22**). Tertius may have earned his right for a greeting just by the arduous task of the composition itself. Yet, he could have been known personally to individuals in Rome. Or, some other life circumstance could have set up this special greeting from the scribe of the letter.

One of those possible life circumstances might be a connection with Paul's patroness, Phoebe. The production of Romans would have been a mammoth undertaking, requiring at least a month to produce, maybe more, and certainly days to produce one, clean copy. A scribe with opportunity to send a greeting otherwise is unknown in a Pauline letter, so stands out. This situation may reflect that Tertius is in the employ of Phoebe, either contracted specially for this project, or on a permanent retainer for Phoebe's business or governmental pursuits on the pattern of Junia Theodora in neighboring Corinth.[89]

The natural question is the amount of involvement Tertius had in the composition of Romans. Ancient scribes had great latitude in their work, on a continuum all the way from word-by-word dictation to free composition following just a suggested idea. Because the language and style of Pauline letters is consistent among them, the inference is that Paul dictated his letters. Ancient scribes did have their own shorthand. One possibility is that Tertius could record shorthand

---

[88] For the significance of this list, see Stevens, *Acts*, 425–26.

[89] See pp. 537–39, for images and discussion of Junia Theodora in Corinth.

what Paul dictated in brief thought units, and pause to write out the fully composed sentences while Paul contemplated his next thought.[90]

The prepositional phrase "in the Lord" at the end is ambiguous for exactly what is modified. Though completely separated from the verb, most take the preposition phrase adverbially ("I greet you in the Lord"). The longer participial phrase ("the one who wrote this letter"), used to identify the person "Tertius," grammatically has displaced the prepositional phrase from its verbal connection. The phrase generally is taken to mean Tertius is a believer.

Gaius, Erastus, Quartus (16:23)

Whether intended for some particular effect is doubtful, but we have a pattern of a single name followed by a series of three names twice in this series of informal greetings. This set is the second of a series of three.

Gaius is host to Paul and "the whole church" (16:23). Whether the work at Corinth had only one assembly or had multiple assemblies as did Rome is unknown. Emphasis on the "whole church," however, may speak to more than one assembly in Corinth. If so, that setting would make Gaius a "super-patron," so to speak. Perhaps individual assemblies gathered together as a whole for infrequent special occasions, such as reading a Pauline letter, and Gaius had accommodations sufficient for this larger meeting. A group of forty to fifty people may have met in the atrium of Gaius's home, somewhat crowded, but meeting the purposes. In any case, he was a person of some financial means in Corinth and important to supporting the life of the church.

Gaius is host to Paul, which puts Paul under social obligation to Gaius along the lines that he advised the Romans to "pay your obligations to everyone" (13:7). Patrons are investing in Paul and his work, so how would Paul repay? Paul's payback to Gaius (and to Phoebe) in return for their investment in him would be threefold: (1) his long ministry at Corinth, (2) in his representative ministry on their behalf in Jerusalem and Rome, and (3) his mission to the nations, particularly

---

[90] For shorthand capabilities, cf. Seneca, *Ep.* 90.25. Again, one of the most informative studies is Richards, *Paul and First-Century Letter Writing*. Richards covers all the salient topics of tools, secretaries, preparation, and dispatch.

the upcoming work in Spain. They already are contributing to this new mission thrust to Spain even now as Paul composes Romans.

The high likelihood is that this Gaius is the one mentioned in 1 Cor 1:14. Paul personally had baptized him, apparently uncommon activity for Paul in his mission work. Gaius likely is the person with the longer name of Titius Justus who early on sponsored the meetings Paul was conducting after Paul was banned from the synagogue there in Corinth (Acts 18:7).

FIGURE 12.25. Erastus Inscription. The seven-inch tall letters originally were capped with bronze. The inscription reads, ERASTVS PROAEDILITATE S P STRAVIT, which abbreviates *Erastus pro aedilitate sua percunia stravit*, "Erastus in return for his aedileship laid [the street] at his own expense." Erastus donated the funds for paving this street that ran by the theater in ancient Corinth. The *aedile* was a public office in Republican Rome for the supervision of public works highly sought after by career-minded politicians. Augustus, however, reduced its importance, diminishing its powers, but imperial Roman colonies and cities continued to use the *aedile* term for their own civic financial operations in the provinces. Credit: Jean M. Stevens.

"Erastus, the city treasurer greets you" (16:23). This Erastus is not likely the same as Paul's assistant mentioned in Acts 19:22 and 1 Tim 4:20, since that Erastus traveled as a companion of Paul, but an official holding major public office and otherwise engaged in important civic duties, including other patron obligations, would not be free to travel.[91] He is, in any case, a Roman citizen (required to hold public office) of this Roman colony, of some wealth and status. Even if a freedman, he could rise in the ranks of money and influence. The question is if the "Erastus Inscription" at Corinth is related to the Erastus of Rom 16:23.

The expression for "city treasurer" that Paul uses is ὁ οἰκονόμος τῆς πόλεως (*ho oikonomos tēs poleōs*). The problem in this wording is that the occupation of an *oikonomos* varied widely, depending on the setting and context. The term *oikonomos* could be no more than a slave

---

[91] *Contra* Goodrich ("Erastus of Corinth," 591, n37), who underplayed the social setting demands and social engagement expectations attending a municipal patron.

or freedman tasked with financial responsibilities, whether residential or governmental. The title could be used for persons of high rank in government. Even a freedman could accumulate significant wealth and status.[92] The question, then, is whether Paul's Greek term, *oikonomos*, is intended to represent the social status as high as the Roman *aedile* (ἀγορανόμος, *agoranomos*), the governmental office in Corinth held by the "inscription Erastus." Why Paul would not have used the Greek term more appropriate to this Roman *aedile* role of *agoranomos* if his Erastus and the "inscription Erastus" were the same is unclear. Literary ambiguity, however, does not impede speculation.

Kent, for example, reasoned the following. *Aediles* in the provinces had three major responsibilities. They functioned as city managers, litigation judges, and public games overseers. However, the internationally famous Isthmian Games at Corinth were so important that these games in particular, unlike anywhere else for cities sponsoring games, required a dedicated set of officials to administrate. Thus, Corinthian *aediles* in particular had only two roles to perform, that is, city manager and litigation judge. That reduced set of responsibilities for Corinthian *aediles* Kent seized upon, "It is possible for this reason that St. Paul does not use the customary word ἀγορανόμος to describe a Corinthian aedile, but calls him οἰκονόμος (*Romans*, XVI, 23)."[93] McRay was sold on Kent's speculation.[94]

However, the reasoning is specious. First, and telling, literary evidence for adjustments to use of the word *agoranomos* in *aedile* contexts is not given for any reason, much less the superficial two, not three, management duties at Corinth. Second, the evidence of first-century authors that we do have does not confirm this linguistic speculation but reveals the opposite. Josephus particularly is careful to associate the Greek term *agoranomos* with the Latin civic office of *aedile*.[95] Friesen's article against equating Erastus in Rom 16:23 with the Corinth inscription should be weighed carefully, even after Goodrich's response.[96]

---

[92] Cf. House of the Freedman, Herculaneum, pp. 172–73, as well as fig. 5.48, p. 172.

[93] Kent, *Inscriptions*, 27.

[94] McRay, *Archeology and the New Testament*, 332.

[95] Josephus, *Ant.* 14.261 (14.10.24): τοῖς τῆς πόλεως ἀγορανόμοις, *tois tēs poleōs agoranomois*.

[96] Friesen, "The Wrong Erastus"; Goodrich, "Erastus of Corinth." Goodrich (584, 588) argued for a *quaestor* translation of *oikonomos*, but presumed that equates to *aedile* level.

The original mid first-century date (ca. 50) perhaps is wrong,[97] but the rarity of the name Erastus holds interest, so discussion should remain open. The question is more than academic. The social picture of early Christianity is impacted. In the end, the ambiguity of Paul's term *oikonomos* and other questions resist conclusions. The Erastus of Rom 16:23 *may* be the Erastus of the Corinthian road inscription, but not enough *literary* evidence is available to take that *historical* conclusion to the bank. You would be just so ambiguous, Paul. Thanks a lot.

Lastly, "Quartus the brother" sends along his greeting. "The brother" likely is an instance of the Greek article used as substantive substitution, that is, in this case, standing in for a personal pronoun, so "our brother."[98] The name of Erastus and that of Quartus are joined by the conjunction "and" (καί, *kai*), which could be insignificant. Yet, the name Quartus is common among slaves and freedmen, so, on an outside chance, he may have been in civic service somehow related to the work of Erastus.

Verse 24 exists because some Greek manuscripts have the benediction of 16:20 repeated here again. The repetition embellishes more on the name Messiah and includes the adjective "all." The position in Greek manuscripts varies. Some have this verse solo, and some have a combination (16:24 or 16:20+24). While the great majority of translations do not include the verse 24 grace benediction, its history might be interesting.

One could argue everything goes back to a non-original doxology. The intrusion of the non-original doxology (16:25–27) displaced this original second grace benediction from verse 24 to verse 28 in order to make room for the doxology but still close the letter with the formulaic Pauline grace benediction. Thus, the doxology disturbance early in the manuscript traditions gave rise to some early manuscripts not having a verse 24. This hypothesis would presume verse 24 was original. Gamble argued for its originality. He conjectured the scenario of an unexpected interruption of associates requesting their own personal greetings. The request rendered Paul's intended conclusion to the letter at 16:20 pre-

---

[97] Based on the circular reasoning of the original proposal; second century seems as likely as the first (Friesen, "The Wrong Erastus," 285).

[98] Cf. Stevens, *Greek Primer*, 69–70; Stevens, *Greek Intermediate*, 63–64. English translations seem about evenly divided.

mature. Accommodating the additional informal greetings required a unique, second grace benediction after they were concluded.[99]

In any case, the grace benediction inserted at the end of this doxology (verse 28) without doubt is not original. This grace benediction entirely is the result of the intrusion of the doxology.

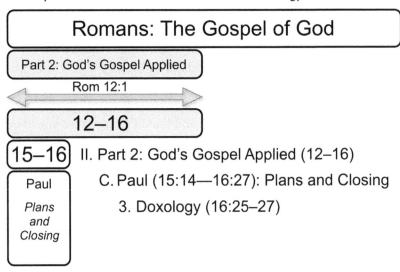

FIGURE 12.26. Outline: Doxology (Rom 16:25–27).

DOXOLOGY (16:25–27)

Introduction

Most scholars conclude the doxology is spurious. The style is overly cumbersome, as if working too hard to imitate Paul by pedantically repeating his phrases almost verbatim without a convincing sense of the context that defines each phrase within Romans.[100] Again, the material blatantly is just attempting to summarize the letter's content, which is passing strange within the letter genre at the very end. Worse, such a summary functionally is quite unnecessary. A concluding doxology is totally unlike Paul in the first place for any letter, even one of the nature of Romans. Even worse, its presence violates Paul's known epis-

---

[99] See discussion at Rom 16:20, pp. 561–62.

[100] As in, "The lady protests too much, methinks," observed by Queen Gertrude of a character overacting in a play in scene 5 of William Shakespeare's *Hamlet*.

tolary style for ending a letter with a grace benediction. Finally, we also have problems in the Greek manuscript traditions that themselves pose significant questions on the doxology's originality. To be sure, in spite of all this, some scholars argue for authenticity, but their arguments simply are not found persuasive to overcome the major problems of this unit.[101]

The likely historical origin of the doxology would be second-century scribes producing this unit for liturgical purposes in the life of the church. A liturgical doxology in that worship setting, which was the main use of Scripture in the church, would make perfect sense. Once created, however, the copying activity of scribes began to include this text as integral to the letter of Romans.

One other hypothesis is that the heretic Marcion was responsible for creating a Romans 1–14 edition of Romans.[102] He cut off these chapters for whatever reasons. The doxology, similar to the idea above, was a scribal effort to conclude a truncated version of Romans to have an ending appropriate for liturgical use in church worship. Whether just by chance or because of Marcion, these multiple editions of Romans happen early, because the manuscript evidence shows all the multiple editions of Romans already circulating in the second century. The interesting evidence of codex 𝔓46 figures into this story.[103]

The doxology summarizes the text of Romans, somewhat. Some major themes are passed over or purposefully ignored. A major theme obviously ignored in a church already anti-Semitic by the second century is Israel. Not one word. Sad that only a century after composition, Paul's Jewish voice already has been scrubbed from church conscience. The doxology stands as silent witness offering poignant evidence that the gentilization of Paul already has gained a full head of steam in the church's worship and theology.

Comment

Dunn pointed out that "the structure is clearly liturgical in character."[104] He then laid out the following balanced lines of phrasing and sounds.[105]

---

[101] See discussion, p. 198.

[102] The accusation made by Origen. See discussion, pp. 196–97.

[103] See discussion, p. 195 and fig. 5.60.

[104] Dunn, *Romans 9–16*, 913.

1. Now to him who is able to strengthen you (Eph 3:20)
2. according to my gospel (Rom 1:1; 2:16)
3. and the proclamation about Jesus Christ (1 Cor 1:21)
4. according to the revelation of the mystery (Rom 11:25)
5. having been kept silent for aeons of time (2 Tim 1:9)
6. but now having been revealed (Rom 3:21)
7. through the Scriptures of the prophets (Rom 1:2)
8. according to the command of the eternal God (1 Tim 1:1)
9. unto the obedience of faith (Rom 1:5)
10. unto all the gentiles (Rom 1:5)
11. having been made known (Rom 9:23)
12. to the only wise God
13. through Jesus Christ
14. to whom be glory unto the ages, amen[106]

The main structure is built on two ideas. The first idea is that of strengthening (line 1) with its associated "according to" in line 2. The second idea is "having been made known" (line 11) with its associated double "according to" in lines 4 and 8.

The poetic structure inverts the normal prose patten of adverbial modifiers and verbs. Note that the participle in line 11 ("having been made known") is set climactically at the end. The two "according to" conjunctions (κατά, *kata*) that work with this verb are set *prior* to the verb in lines 4 and 8. This arrangement conforms to a balanced liturgical delivery of these poetically compressed lines of thought.

Finally the dative case ("to") structures that typically begin or end a doxology break the grammar at line 12, repeated appositively at line 14. Some translations show this broken construction with dash marks before each "to" phrase. While grammatical structure of the sentence is broken (anacoluthon), the ending is stylistic in liturgical practice. The focus of the dative expressions is monotheism, always appropriate to counter the impact of a pagan environment.

Line 8 stands out strongly for its odd wording and a phrase that is alien to Paul. The word "command" is ἐπιταγήν (*epitagēn*). This word, while occurring elsewhere in Paul, is used nowhere else in Romans, so

---

[105] As seen in the Greek text. Not as obvious, however, in English translation.

[106] Dunn then systematically pointed out the liturgical elements easily evident in the structured lines of the Greek text (*Romans 9–16*, 913–14).

seems quite strange positioned in a *summary* whose whole purpose is supposed to be echoing the *main* themes, thoughts, ideas, and words of Romans.[107] In a similar vein, the expression "of the eternal God" (τοῦ αἰωνίου θεοῦ, *tou aiōniou theou*) is found nowhere else in Paul, much less in Romans.[108]

The prophetic function of *ethnē* as "nations" according to the vision of Isaiah has disappeared. These lines of the doxology with their exlusive focus on "gentiles" make obvious that the idea of the Pauline *ethnē* has been reduced to "gentiles" exclusively. The gentiles now exclusively own the gospel, which no longer has anything to do with the Jews. They were judged by God in the First Jewish War and thereafter abandoned. The entire motif of "to the Jew first" has been relegated to a curious artifact of history, a matter only disclosed by excavating a few Old Testament texts. With or without awareness, thus blinded by a myopic gentile view, these scribes have turned Paul's assurance to Israel on its head by tacitly admitting the Word of God *has* failed. The gifts and calling of God are *not* irrevocable.

The significance of "mystery" has changed dramatically as well. In Romans, *mystery is all about Israel*. Mystery is revealing that Israel's hardening is neither total nor final. Further, Paul tactically deploys his revelation of this mystery in order to mitigate gentile conceit in the churches in Rome. The very existence of this doxology says he lost his gambit. In this supposed "Pauline" rewriting, touted as summarizing Romans, mystery is turned on its head entirely. Mystery no longer has anything to do with Israel. Mystery is now gentiles only (lines 10, 11).

Quite obvious in all this is how several key lines are taken from *other* Pauline texts and not from Romans. Also obvious is how several themes important to Romans simply receive no coverage at all. One of the most strikingly absent themes, besides Israel already mentioned, is the Holy Spirit. Again, not one word. This means that nothing from Romans 5 has figured into this supposed summary of Romans, and, almost unbelievably, nothing from the climactic Romans 8, one of the most universally quoted chapters of Romans.

---

[107] In this sense, only in the Pastorals (1 Tim 1:1; Titus 1:3; 2:15). With an entirely different sense, note 1 Cor 7:6, 25; 2 Cor 8:8.

[108] That the concept itself is not antithetical to Pauline thinking is not the point. The point is to reflect Paul. Something patently heretical would not do in the first place.

13

Epilogue

Where Do We Go from Here?

DAUNTING IS THE TASK OF WRITING anything on Paul. "There be dragons out there!" Prodigious minds across the ages and still today have been applied to this piece of literature. Why should my thoughts matter at all? My students, however, kept asking me to write.

To be sure, this book is not really a traditional commentary. The effort is more of a midrash for my students. I would make a comment in class, they would cock their heads in great interest, and then observe, "Well, I did not read *that* in a commentary last night!" I know. So, I wanted just to stay off the radar and not get into trouble. But my students would not let me. With some trepidation, I capitulated to their insistence that getting my thoughts "out there" would be good for discussion sake alone, even if I convinced no one. Thank you, Allyson Presswood Nance, for not giving me any peace on the matter and sparing no quarter from your persistence. You won.

I would like to give a short retrospect of the content of this midrash related to its central thesis. I will summarize the main thesis and its implications and include bullet points of how this is pursued in each chapter of Romans. This will allow the perspective to be apprehended in précis fashion. After the retrospect, I then move to prospect to discuss the question that always is burning in the minds of my students about the time we get to this point in the study of Romans: "So where do we go from here?" To be honest, the short answer is, I do not know. I invite you, the reader, to help me think about that really good question.

RETROSPECT

The thesis of the book is Romans is all about Israel. The category of Israel is the hermeneutical key to all of Romans, and particularly to contested passages (e.g., Romans 7). Paul's gospel of God is guided by Isaiah's vision of Israel's destiny to the "nations," which needs careful distinction to maintain its prophetic character from the separate issue of "gentiles" as uncircumcised males, an overemphasis characteristic of postexilic Israel, not Isaiah. The proper translation of *ethnē* in the pertinent passages, then, is crucial. English translations in general are not helpful here. They reveal category confusion about gentiles versus nations. Isaiah's vision is obscured by this confusion; therefore, exactly what makes Israel, Israel as a child of destiny among the nations also is lost. "Apostle to the gentiles" totally needs to be reconfigured as to what that meant to Paul. For Paul, that was a *diakonos* ministry on *behalf* of Israel, sublimated to Israel, and meaningless without Israel. "Apostle to the gentiles," then, is only on behalf of, and in service to, being apostle to Israel ("to the Jew first"). Two thousand years of repeating the mantra "apostle to the gentiles" over and over in a totally "gentilized Christianity" context obliterates the category Israel and has lost what Paul actually meant calling himself apostle to the gentiles.

The Two Israels

In the context of Paul's own life, "Israel" has two perspectives. Israel in Paul is defined by the two Israels Paul experienced in his life. One was the Israel of Saul of Tarsus. This Israel Paul experienced through the synagogue, defined by the traditions of the Great Assembly arising from the work of Ezra after the exile, exemplified in the Pharisee movement. This was Mosaic Israel. The other was the Israel of Paul of the Damascus Road. This Israel was experienced through the early church, defined by the traditions of the apostles arising from the work of Jesus after John the Baptist, exemplified in the Hellenist movement. This was messianic Israel. Thus, Paul experienced two Israels, one centered in Moses, the other in Messiah. Paul could conceive both Israels to be congruent within Paul's Pharisaic universe, but Moses would have to be understood rightly. The law has to be sublimated to the promise to Abraham and righteousness by faith. The law of Moses was the will of God, rightly taken seriously by the Pharisees, but missing its spirit. The gift of

the Spirit in messianic Israel empowered the spirit of the law's fulfillment within the heart, inaugurating the New Aeon through the death
and resurrection of Jesus Messiah, forgiving sin through righteousness
by faith, overcoming the power of Sin, reaching the nations in the
obedience of faith, and pointing to the renewal of all creation in the
kingdom of God consummated by the final judgment. Therefore, Messiah is the fulfillment of the law.

The Romans Synthesis

Romans is the synthesis of these two Israels in Paul's experience into
one integrative whole, "all Israel." All Israel is messianic Israel, the
Israel Messiah has inaugurated, which fulfills every promise God ever
made, in Abraham, in Moses, in the prophets, including to the two
kingdoms of Israel and Judah, as well as the destiny of Israel as a
nation among the nations, the holy nation Moses prescribed, and the
nation of blessing to all nations as envisioned by Isaiah. That blessing
includes breaking the curse of Adam that impacts not only the entire
human race but all creation as well. God as creator will consummate
all his creative purposes. Along the way to that global and cosmic destiny, messianic Israel fulfills Moses in as much as the law expresses the
will of God.

Thesis Development

The development of the thesis as a heuristic category can provide an
overview of the progress of the chapters of Romans. Whereas more is
covered in each chapter, their significance according to the development of the thesis would keep the following in view.

- Romans 1:1–7 introduces Israel's gospel of God (1:1) and its destiny
  to the nations (1:5).

- Romans 1:8–15 is Paul's plans as central to Israel and the purpose of
  Romans (presently stated ambiguously until having completed explaining and applying the gospel of God).

- Romans 1:18–32 targets Israel as much as gentiles in a subtly handled rhetorical stealth attack.

- Romans 2 targets Abraham as paradigmatic gentile of the nations, Israel's destiny.

- Romans 3 is Israel's righteousness in the promised Messiah through faith, which facilitates Israel's destiny to the nations in Abraham.

- Romans 4 is Abraham as Israel in nuce, in both promise and progeny, targeting the nations.

- Romans 5 is the promise of the New Aeon in Messiah, which is the triumph of messianic Israel, but also the problem of the Old Aeon in Adam, which entangles Mosaic Israel and provokes the present eschatological crisis in the encounter with Messiah.

- Romans 6 is not about individual believers but rather about Israel. Paul reframes the exodus story as experienced in Moses and in the Messiah, Mosaic Israel versus messianic Israel. He uses major exodus/Sinai motifs recognizable to synagogue Jews (baptism, slavery, marriage, law).

- Romans 7 is all about Israel again. Paul reframes the crisis of Mosaic Israel from the perspective of the Old Aeon of Adam. Moses is only subverted by Sin, and certainly not the answer to sin.

- Romans 8 is the crisis of Mosaic Israel resolved by Messiah through the Spirit, and more (flesh, resurrection, creation, celebration).

- Romans 9–11 is "all Israel" as the point and climax of all of Romans 1–11.

- Romans 12–13 is messianic Israel's new society in church and state on the way to being light to the nations fulfilling Isaiah's vision.

- Romans 14:1–15:13 is the crisis of factionalism in Rome's assemblies that jeopardizes Israel's witness and destiny to the nations.

- Romans 15:14–33 is a reprise of Paul's plans from Romans 1. These plans are central to Israel's destiny and vivify the purpose of Romans (now stated clearly after explaining and applying the gospel of God).

- Romans 16 addresses local leadership in Rome known to Paul by way of entree to other assemblies. Prominent among them are Israelites, the focus of Romans 9–11. The various individuals can interpret Paul's gospel of God and reflect the profile of messianic Israel according to Paul's gospel to the local assemblies in Rome. Phoebe is the patroness who paid for the letter, bears the letter, and has the distinct privilege to be its first interpreter.

The Purpose of Romans

The Roman Christians are being asked to participate in the Jerusalem collection in a real way. In effect, they are being asked to cast their lot with Paul and his understanding of the gospel. But how can they do this? In two ways.

First, they can model in their congregations what the collection symbolizes—the unity of Jews and gentiles in Messiah in messianic Israel's quest to fulfill Isaiah's vision of Israel's destiny to the nations. Thus, solving the problems of Jews and gentiles, including the "weak" and "strong" in Rome, is important to Paul. Second, they can "give" to the collection—not by sending money to Jerusalem, since that deadline already has passed. Paul is on his way to Jerusalem now. However, they learn in this letter that Paul plans to pass through Rome on his way to Spain. So, they can give by helping send Paul on his mission to Spain. Thus, Paul in Romans wants to introduce himself and the gospel he preaches as a legitimate apostle to a church he did not establish.

Yet, more than gaining financial support for the Spanish mission is at stake for Paul. At this stage in his life, winning Rome is crucial to Paul, because he no longer has a mission base. Paul first lost Antioch in his fight with Barnabas, and he lost Ephesus in the catastrophic silversmiths' riot. His entire mission is jeopardized and in serious need of a sponsor in the west. Paul conceives Roman support for his own gospel his golden parachute for a new mission west, because he does not know what will happen in Jerusalem in receiving or rejecting the collection. He considers the collection a symbol of acceptance of Pauline churches and the Pauline gospel, but matters may not go well in Jerusalem. Thus, Paul hopes to win Rome's support through this crucial letter. The letter of Romans stands as silent witness that Paul considered Rome the future of the church, particularly in helping move messianic Israel to realize her destiny. In some ways he was correct. However, unintended consequences can present troubling problems. History just has a way of upsetting the apple cart no matter how carefully you stack the apples or try to push the cart down the road.

PROSPECT

As a result of these thoughts, students are trying to digest the thesis that Romans is all about Israel. They have felt the cogency of the argument and are trying to build inferences. The first inference is intuitive, not so much deductive, and worrisome. Something dramatically is wrong with our Pauline hermeneutic of this letter when you survey the literature, and the problem is not just arguing "new perspective," "radical new perspective," etc. till the cows come home, even though this present publication is within the loop of that discussion. The problem is bigger. The problem is coming to terms with history—two-thousand years of history, to be more exact.

Hermeneutical Maneuvers

The elephant in the room is that Paul's expectations did not pan out. In order to see this, however, we have to disabuse ourselves of two hermeneutical maneuvers that are like card tricks, sleight of hand deals that ease the conscience but do not actually address the problem. Interpreting Paul with the advantage of a perspective of two thousand years is not exegesis. That process, plain and simple, is isogesis. That is capitulating to what we *need* Paul to mean for our system to remain intact, not what Paul meant. What two maneuvers are made?

Scrubbing Imminence

The first maneuver is to scrub imminence from Paul's thought. In spite of what Paul says in 1 Thess 4:18, or Rom 13:7, or Rom 16:20, we go merrily on our way. By circumventing the obvious, the load of two thousand years of subsequent church history is not so burdensome. We create the luxury of no felt need to double-check the reality. Even more convenient, we have no need to digest that Paul was overly optimistic. As a reminder for some, talking about prognostication on a sense of imminence is not talking about inspiration.[1]

---

[1] Saying what Paul hoped for did not happen is not saying Paul was not inspired when he wrote authoritative text for the church. Recall that Peter was wrong, not only before the resurrection in the Garden of Gethsemane when he cut off the ear of the high priest's servant, but even after the resurrection when he withdrew from gentile fellowship at Antioch. Barnabas made clear to Paul he was being bull-headed about John Mark prior to the second missionary journey, and Paul wrongly insisted on personally delivering the collection to Jerusalem. See Stevens, *Acts*, pp. 337–47 and 475–77.

Scrubbing Israel

The second maneuver to alleviate the problem of two-thousand years of church history is to scrub Israel from Paul's thought. We have two major options on scrubbing Israel in Paul's thought as witnessed in the ensuing years after Paul. One option is injurious to the health and well-being of Jews for all time. The other option is less harmful to Jews, but no less devastating to grasping Pauline thought.

FIGURE 13.1. Domitian's *Damnatio Memoriae*. Inscription at Ephesus from the imperial temple complex. Originally erected in Domitian's reign (81–96), his name subsequently was erased from the left end of the first line. The formal decree by the Roman Senate was *abolitio nominis*, abolishing a person's name, and the related term *damnatio memoriae*, which is shaming the memory of an individual by erasing their name from public buidlings and monuments. The result was shaming even the memory of the person. Cf. Suetonius, *Domitian* 23.

The first option is to participate in, or give credence to, anti-Semitism. That attitude for sure will guarantee Israel is erased from Paul's thought. Such an "Israel erasure" is uncannily like a *damnatio memoriae* declaration of the Roman senate, in which all reference to a person's name literally is erased from every inscription bearing his name across the empire. A similar result can be achieved socially and religiously for Jews and Judaism. Anything even approaching Jewish sensibility or emphasis is suspect of heresy by default theologically and to be avoided like a pandemic virus. The attitude would be, "After all, they crucified Jesus. They had their chance." Thus, accusations of being a "Judaizer" or perverting salvation with "works salvation" are effective rhetorical shaming devices to keep the Jewish lid on Paul shut tight.

The second option is not as in your face as anti-Semitism, but the process of scrubbing Israel out of the Pauline discourse is just as effective, to the point that not hearing the word Israel does not even raise

582 ROMANS: THE GOSPEL OF GOD

an eyebrow. This option is *to make remnant Israel all Israel.* This is a "what you see is what you get" option, that is, what you see historically is what you get exegetically. Whatever actually happened in history is what Paul meant, by default, right? Thus, taking a cue from the catastrophe of the First Jewish War, this attitude would be "Jews are out, gentiles are in, and that is just the way things turned out." Like an ostrich with our head in the sand, even though we *know* what Paul said in Romans 9–11, because his words are clear (that he concluded with "and thus all Israel will be saved"), we now have to deal with what really happened in history, and that Paul's expectation of all Israel being saved just did not pan out. Simply put, exegetically, we cannot afford to let "all" be "all." The defense would be to misconstrue Paul: "You know, Paul himself said 'not all Israel is Israel.'" The misconstrual is that Paul said that as if to eliminate progeny from the equation. Two-thousand years of church history conveniently becomes more tolerable. Forget about the unintended consequence that such a hermeneutic is built on the false premise that the "Israelite" conundrum with which Paul started Romans 9–11 was not his *real* focus after "all." Such a system "works" if you want a "works" hermeneutic.

Doxology as Witness

Both problems of anti-Semitism and of making gentiles "all Israel" is what turns the doxology tacked onto the end of Romans by second-century scribes into the poster child of the problem with our Pauline hermeneutic. That is, the problem with understanding Paul is quite ancient, even before Augustine or Luther. Of course, we already know this. The admission in 2 Peter is surprising for its transparency: "His letters contain some things that are hard to understand" (2 Pet 3:16). The doxology themes are at the very heart of misunderstanding Paul. In this way, the doxology *needs* to be studied by students of Romans because this configuration of Paul becomes a potent pedagogical tool for getting a grip on what is *not* Paul. The "gentile Israel" the doxology promotes and that has eventuated after two-thousand years of church history de facto is allowed quietly to become exegesis of "all Israel." This slick maneuver is coded into the card trick that Paul's "remnant Israel" within Romans 9–11 equals the "all Israel" of Rom 11:26. Such a hermeneutic is powerful. History is on its side. What you see is what you get. What *is* has to be what Paul *meant.* In fact, this hermeneutic is essential to supersessionism. This take on Paul, then, is the obvious choice for both Catholics and Protestants, since such supersessionism has been cemented into our hermeneutic on Romans 9–11 ever since the composition of the doxology. Because we have two-thousand years of church history under our belts to "confirm" the exegesis, we think we have no other choice.

Hermeneutical Recovery

Actually, we do. We can go with what Paul actually said. We can let the chips of history fall where they may.

Instead, we have argued that Romans is all about Israel, that Romans 9–11 has a progeny component, and that when Paul said "all" he meant "all." Further, what Paul meant by remnant Israel was not what some hermeneutical card tricks have dealt. Remnant Israel most certainly was not "all Israel." Remnant Israel, was, well, remnant Israel, only the *firstfruits* of a later fuller harvest of Israel. This fuller harvest of Israel is facilitated by gentile fullness as one of its components, but *gentile fullness does not consummate Israel's fullness.* Gentile fullness is only *prelude* to "all Israel." Gentile fullness provokes Israel's jealousy, and Israel's jealousy provokes Israel's fullness.[2]

---

[2] We have argued Paul kept Jew and gentile cagtegories distinct. We reject, therefore, Garroway's argument, using Bhabha's "social hybridity" theory, suggesting that Paul inadvertently created a hybrid "gentile-Jew" social construct in which believing gentiles were both Jews but not Jews, gentiles but not gentiles—a social identity so inherently conflicted and unstable as quickly to collapse into an amorphous, non-ethnic "Christian" identity in the next generation of believers (*Paul's Gentile-Jews*, 9). We also reject Perriman's simultaneously engaging but flawed study, *The Future of the People of God*. Perriman had to deconstruct the very essence of eschatology. He converted "last things" to "cyclical things," transforming so-called "eschatology" into nothing more than prophetic discourse about recurring decisive moments of divine judgment in history. Here, a Greek, cyclical philosophy of history surreptitiously is substituted for the linear two aeons of Jewish thought. Perriman proposed the divine wrath Paul predicated to Israel in fact was realized in AD 70, but the remnant people of God by their faithful, martyrological living—just as challenged by Habbakkuk and by Paul—conquered the beast in Constantine's edict. Christ subdued the nations. After 1700 years, though, that hegemony now is dissolving in the post-modern assault on the church. The church no longer can live out Paul's first-century narrative, whose story coherency has fallen apart. The church faces a new, decisive judgment moment, needing to find its new Phoenix rising from these judgment ashes. For Perriman, the church has outlived the NT narrative and must reconstruct a new one. Perriman's grand construct, however, ostensibly of Paul's Romans, is another example of exegesis by historical hindsight.

Hermeneutical Conundrum

So, what happened? The Jewish War. The Jewish War not only changed Judaism forever. The Jewish War changed the Jesus movement forever too. After that catastrophe, all cards were off the table for the Pauline universe. Paul was aware that war with Rome potentially was out there as a growing possibility. That prospect did not take much scanning of the morning newspapers to read the tea leaves. But Paul also believed the appearing of Jesus was imminent. What turned those messianic tumblers in his Pharisaic world was not a well-argued essay on why believing Jesus is the Messiah is reasonable for Jews. What rocked Paul's world was Jesus. The revelation of a risen Lord was Paul's own visionary epiphany into a career of messianic hermeneutic based on Jesus of Nazareth. Even though the law said anyone hung on a tree was cursed, the resurrection forced Paul to rethink the curse of the law. His epiphanic theology brought him to the essence of *both* gentile fullness *and* all Israel simultaneously. Since that vision was Paul's moment of faith, and he realized that that vision was the only thing that would have worked for him, perhaps he could envision some type of epiphany for all Israelites on a global, national scale, like at the foot of a mountain or something. Such an epiphany might be the only thing that would work for other Israelites as well. Preaching in the synagogue, while harvesting a few, such as Crispus, Gaius, Apollos, Andronicus and Junia, Prisca and Aquila, and others, still was not even close to the promise of Pentecost abundance in Israel.

Whether such an epiphanic vision could be presumed to be the parousia of Jesus might be a stretch, even though this is the very solution that dispensational thinking has championed.[3] Yet, this thought experiment is offered only to illustrate possible potential hopes Paul could have harbored as he wrote, "and thus all Israel will be saved." Paul calculated easily that God's present mercy to gentiles would come to consummation soon by being able to reach the nations in a way doable, even in Paul's own ministry. His imminence thinking strongly suggests whatever he was conceptualizing he was expecting to happen

---

[3] Not to be read as an endorsement for dispensational eschatology. The system inherently has too many flaws to be hermeneutically viable. Further, the complex issues of Zionism, the secular state of Israel, and global politics with which such eschatological views can be associated are problematic. See Stevens, *Revelation*, 84–96.

soon. That means when he spoke of the jealousy of Israel, he likely was speaking of some reality he thought he was going to experience. But he did not have much time. The Jewish War was barreling down the tracks like a locomotive stoked as high as her boilers could stand. Then, he was incarcerated and martyred. Then, the war broke out, and those Pauline days of writing Romans were gone with the wind.

Bibliography

Abasciano, Brian J. *Paul's Use of the Old Testament in Romans 9.1–9: An Intertextual and Theological Exegesis*, LNTS. Vol. 301. Edited by Mark Goodacre. London, New York: T&T Clark, 2005.

Abbott, Frank Frost. *The Common People of Ancient Rome: Studies in Roman Life and Literature*. New York: Biblo and Tannen, 1965.

Abegg Jr., Martin G., ed. *Qumran Non-biblical Manuscripts*. Accordance. OakTree Software: Altamonte Springs, FL. Version 3.3. 2009.

'*Abodah Zarah*. Translated by A. Mishcon and A. Cohen. In *The Babylonian Talmud*. Translated and ed. by Isidore Epstein. 2 vols. London: Soncino Press, 1935.

Accordance, Version 13. OakTree Software Specialists, Altamonte Springs, Fla., 2013.

Achtemeier, Paul J. *Romans*. Interpretation. Atlanta: John Knox, 1985.

Ad C. Herennium: De Ratione Dicendi (Rhetorica Ad Herennium). [Cicero]. Translated by Harry Caplan. Cambridge, MA: Harvard University Press; London: William Heinemann Ltd., 1954.

Aeschylus. Translated by Herbert Weir Smyth. LCL. London: William Heinemann; New York: G. P. Putnam's Sons, 1922–26.

Aland, Kurt, ed. *Kurzgefasste Liste der griechischen Handschriften des neuen Testaments*. 2nd ed. Arbeiten zur neutestamentlichen Textforschung 1. Berlin: Walter de Gruyter, 1994.

Aland, Kurt and Barbara Aland. *The Text of the New Testament*. 2nd ed. Translated by Erroll F. Rhodes. Grand Rapids: Eerdmans, 1989.

Aland, Barbara, Kurt Aland, Johannes Karavidopoulos, Carlo M. Martini, and Bruce M. Metzger, eds. *The Greek New Testament*. 5th rev. ed. Stuttgart: United Bible Societies, 2014.

Aland, Barbara, Kurt Aland, Johannes Karavidopoulos, Carlo M. Martini, and Bruce M. Metzger, eds. *Novum Testamentum Graece*. 28th ed. Stuttgart: German Bible Society, 2012.

Allison, Penelope M. *The Insula of Menander at Pompeii, Volume III: The Finds, A Contextual Study*. Oxford: Oxford University Press, 2007.

Anderson Jr., R. Dean. *Ancient Rhetorical Theory and Paul: Revised Edition*. Contributions to Biblical Exegesis and Theology, 18, Edited by Tj. Baarda, A. van der Kooij, and A. S. van der Woude. Leuven: Peeters, 1998.

_____. *Glossary of Greek Rhetorical Terms: Connected to Methods of Argumentation, Figures and Tropes, from Anaximenes to Quintilian*. CBET 24. Leuven: Peters, 2000.

Aratus, *Phaenomena*. John Hopkins New Translations from Antiquity. Translated by Aaron Poochigian. Baltimore, MD: John Hopkins University Press, 2010.

Aristeas. *The Old Testament Pseudepigrapha*. Accordance, Version 10.1.7. 2013. Print ed.: In vol. 1 of *Old Testament Pseudepigrapha*. Edited by R. H. Charles. 1913. 3 vols. Oxford: Clarendon.

Aristides, Aelius. *The Complete Works: Orations 1–16*. Leiden: Brill, 1997.

Aristotle. *Ars Rhetorica*. Edited by W. D. Ross. Oxford: Clarendon, 1959.

———. *On Rhetoric: A Theory of Civic Discourse, Newly translated with Introduction, Notes, and Appendixes*. Translated by George A. Kennedy. Oxford: Oxford University Press, 1991.

Athenagoras. *The Ante-Nicene Fathers* on CD-ROM. Logos Research Systems Version 2.0. 1997. Print ed.: Athenagoras. In vol. 2 of *The Ante-Nicene Fathers*. Alexander Roberts, James Donaldson, and A. Cleveland Coxe, eds. 1885–1896. 10 vols. New York: Christian Literature Company.

Augustine. *The Nicene and Post-Nicene Fathers of the Christian Church* on CD-ROM. Accordance Bible Software Version 10.1.5, 2013. Print ed.: Augustine. In vol. 1 of *The Nicene and Post-Nicene Fathers of the Christian Church*. Series 2. 1886–1889. Philip Schaff and Henry Wace, eds. 14 vols. New York: Christian Literature Company.

Augustus. *Res Gestae Divi Augusti: The Achievements of the Divine Augustus*, with an introduction and commentary by P. A. Brunt and J. M. Moore. Oxford, New York: Oxford University Press, 1967.

Aune, David Edward. *The Cultic Setting of Realized Eschatology in Early Christianity*. Supplements to Novum Testamentum, no. 28. Leiden: Brill, 1972.

———. "Romans as a Logos Protreptikos in the Context of Ancient Religious and Philosophical Propaganda." *Paulus und das antike Judentum: Tübingen-Durham-Symposium im Gedenken an den 50. Todestag Adolf Schlatters*. Edited by Martin Hengel and Ulrich Heckel. Tübingen: J.C.B. Mohr, Paul Siebeck, 1991.

Aurelius, Marcus. *The Communings with Himself of Marcus Aurelius Antoninus, Emperor of Rome, Together with His Speeches and Sayings*. Translated and revised by Charles Reginald Haines. LCL. London: William Heinemann; New York: G. P. Putnam's Sons, 1930.

Aurelius Victor: De Caesaribus. Translated with an Introduction and Commentary by H. W. Bird. Translated Texts for Historians LUP (Book 17). Liverpool: Liverpool University Press, 1994.

Aus, Roger D. "Paul's Travel Plans to Spain and the 'Full Number of the Gentiles' of Rom. XI 25." NT. Vol. 21, no. 3 (Jan 1979), 232–62. doi https://doi.org/10.1163/156853679X00154.

The Babylonian Talmud. Translated and ed. by Isidore Epstein. 2 vols. London: Soncino Press, 1948.

Badenas, Robert. *Christ the End of the Law: Romans 10.4 in Pauline Pespective*. JSNTSup 10. Sheffield: JSOT, 1985.

Barclay, John M. G. *Jews In The Mediterranean Diaspora: From Alexander to Trajan (323 BCE–117 CE)*. Edinburgh: T&T Clark, 1996.

Barr, George K. *Scalometry and the Pauline Epistles*. JSNTSS 261. London, New York: T&T Clark, 2004.

Barr, James. *Old and New in Interpretation: A Study of the Two Testaments*. 2nd ed. London: SCM, 1982.

Barrett, C. K. *A Commentary on the Epistle to the Romans.* HNTC. New York, Evanston, London: Harper and Row, 1957.

Bartchy, S. Scott. "Slavery (Greco-Roman)." *The Anchor Bible Dictionary.* Edited by David Noel Freedman. 6 vols. New York: Doubleday & Co., 1992. 6:66–67.

Barth, Karl. *A Shorter Commentary on Romans.* Translated by D. H. van Daalen. London: SCM, 1959.

Bartlett, Bruce. "How Excessive Government Killed Ancient Rome." *Cato Journal.* Vol. 14, no. 2 (Fall 1994), 287–303.

Barton, William Eleazar. *The Samaritan Pentateuch: The Story of a Survival among the Sects.* Oberlin, OH: Bibliotheca Sacra Co., 1903.

Beard, Mary, et al. *Religions of Rome.* Vol. 1: *A History.* Cambridge: Cambridge University Press, 1998.

Becker, Jürgen. *Paul: Apostle to the Gentiles.* Translated by O. C. Dean Jr. Foreword by Marion L. Soards, Louisville: Westminster John Knox, 1993.

Beker, J. Christiaan. *Paul the Apostle: The Triumph of God in Life and Thought.* Philadelphia: Fortress, 1980.

Biblia Hebraica. Edited by Rudolf Kittel. Stuttgart: Wurttembergische Bibelandstalt, 1937.

Bingham, Sandra. *The Praetorian Guard: A History of Rome's Elite Special Forces.* Waco, TX: Baylor University Press, 2013.

Blackwell, Ben C., John K. Goodrich, and Jason Maston, eds. *Reading Romans in Context: Paul and Second Temple Judaism.* Grand Rapids: Zondervan, 2015.

Boccaccini, Gabriele and Carlos A. Segovia, eds. *Paul the Jew: Rereading the Apostle as a Figure of Second Temple Judaism.* Minneapolis: Fortress, 2016.

Bockmuehl, Markus. *Jewish Law in Gentile Churches: Halakhah and the Beginning of Christian Public Ethics.* New York: T & T Clark, 2000; paperback, Grand Rapids: Baker, 2003.

Borgen, Peder. *Early Christianity and Hellenistic Judaism.* Edinburgh: T&T Clark, 1996.

Bornkamm, Günther. "The Letter to the Romans as Paul's Last Will and Testament," *AusBR* 11 (1963–64), 2–14.

Bowers, W. P. "Jewish Communities in Spain in the Time of Paul the Apostle." *Journal of Theological Studies.* N. S. 26(2)(1975), 395–402.

Bowman, John. *The Samaritan Problem: Studies in the Relationships of Samaritanism, Judaism, and Early Christianity.* Franz Delitzch Lectures 1959. Translated by Alfred M. Johnson Jr. Pittsburgh: Pickwick, 1975.

Boyarin, Daniel. *A Radical Jew: Paul and the Politics of Identity.* Berkeley, Los Angeles, London: University of California Press, 1994.

Brawley, Robert A. "Multivocality in Romans 4." *Reading Israel in Romans: Legitimacy and Plausibility of Divergent Interpretations.* Christina Grenholm and Daniel Pate, eds. Romans through History and Culture Series. Christina Grenholm and Daniel Pate, eds. Harrisburg, PA: Trinity Press International, 2000, 74–95.

Bray, Gerald, ed. *Ancient Christian Commentary on Scripture, New Testament VI: Romans.* Downers Grove, IL: InterVarsity, 1998.

Brown, Raymond E. and Joseph P. Meier. *Antioch and Rome: New Testament Cradles of Catholic Christianity.* New York and Ramsey, NJ: Paulist Press, 1983.

Browning, Benjamin. *Facing the Mob: Rome, the Crowd, and the New Testament.* Eugene, OR: Pickwick (forthcoming).

Bruce, F. F. *The Epistle of Paul to the Romans: An Introduction and Commentary.* TNNC. Grand Rapids: Eerdmans, 1963.

_____. *The Epistles to the Colossians, to Philemon, and to the Ephesians.* 2nd rev. ed. NICNT. Grand Rapids: Eerdmans, 1984.

_____. *Paul: Apostle of the Heart Set Free.* Grand Rapids: Eerdmans, 1977.

Bultmann Rudolf. *Theologie des Neuen Testaments.* Tübingen: Mohr, 1984.

_____. *Theology of the New Testament.* With a New Introduction by Robert Morgan. Waco, TX: Baylor Press, 2007.

Burge, Gary M. *Jesus and the Land: The New Testament Challenge to "Holy Land" Theology.* Grand Rapids: Baker Academic, 2010.

Caceres-Cerda, Barbara F. "The Exceptional Case of Plancia Magna: (Re)analyzing the Role of a Roman Benefactress." *CUNY Academic Works,* 2018. Available online at https://academicworks.cuny.edu/gc_etds/2634. Accessed April 27, 2021.

Calvin, John, *Institutes of the Christian Religion.* Translated by Henry Beveridge. Peabody, MA: Hendrickson, 2008.

Campbell, Constantine R. *Paul and the Hope of Glory: An Exegetical and Theological Study.* Grand Rapids: Zondervan, 2020.

Campbell, Douglas A. *The Deliverance of God: An Apocalyptic Rereading of Justification in Paul.* Grand Rapids: William B. Eerdmans, 2009.

_____. *The Rhetoric of Righteousness in Romans 3.21–26.* JSNTSS 65. Sheffield: JSOT Press, 1992.

Campbell, William S. "Divergent Images of Paul and His Mission," 187–211. *Reading Israel in Romans: Legitimacy and Plausibility of Divergent Interpretations.* Christina Grenholm and Daniel Pate, eds. Romans through History and Culture Series. Christina Grenholm and Daniel Pate, eds. Harrisburg, Penn.: Trinity Press International, 2000.

_____. "Romans 3 as a Key to the Structure and Thought of Romans," 252–64. *The Romans Debate: Revised and Expanded Edition.* Edited by Karl P. Donfried. Edinburgh: T & T Clark, 1991.

Capes, David B., Rodney Reeves, and E. Randolf Richards. *Rediscovering Paul: An Introduction to His World, Letters and Theology.* 2nd ed. Downers Grove, IL: InterVarsity, 2017.

Carter, Warren. "Roman Imperial Power: A New Testament Perspective." *Rome and Religion: A Cross-Disciplinary Dialogue on the Imperial Cult,* 137–51. Jeffrey Brodd and Jonathan L. Reed, eds. WGRWSS. No. 5. Atlanta: Society of Biblical Literature, 2011.

Cary, M. and H. H. Scullard. *A History of Rome: Down to the Reign of Constantine.* 3rd ed. Bedford: St. Martin's, 1976.

Cassius Dio, Cocceianus. *Dio's Roman History.* Translated by Ernest Carey. LCL. London: William Heinemann; New York: G. P. Putnam's Sons, 1914–1927.

Cate, James Jeffrey. "How Green Was John's World? Ecology and Revelation." In *Essays on Revelation: Appropriating Yesterday's Apocalypse in Today's World.* Edited by Gerald L. Stevens. Eugene, OR: Pickwick, 2011.

Chaniotis, Angelos. "The Jews of Aphrodisias: New Evidence and Old Problems." *Scripta Classica Israelica* 21 (2002), 209–42.

Charitonidis, Séraphin, Demetrios I Pallas, and Jacques Vénencie, *Inscriptions Lyciennes Trouvées A Solômos Près de Corinthe,* 496–508.

Charles, R. H. *A Critical History of the Doctrine of the Future Life in Judaism, and in Early Christianity, or Hebrew, Jewish and Christian Eschatology from Pre-prophetic Times til the Close of the New Testament Canon*. London: Adam and Charles Black, 1913.

Charlesworth, James H., ed. *The Messiah: Developments in Earliest Judaism and Christianity*. Minneapolis: Fortress, 1992.

Chilton, Bruce. *Rabbi Paul: An Intellectual Biography*. New York: Doubleday, 2004.

_____. *Resurrection Logic: How Jesus' First Followers Believed God Raised Him from the Dead*. Waco, TX: Baylor University Press, 2020.

Christiansen, Ellen Juhl. *The Covenant in Judaism and Paul: A Study of Ritual Boundaries as Identity Markers*. Leiden: Brill, 1995.

Chrysostom, John. *John Chrysostom: On the Priesthood, Ascetic Treatises, Homilies and Letters*. Edited by Philip Schaff. Grand Rapids: Eerdmans, 1975.

Ciampa, Roy E. and Brian S. Rosner. *The First Letter to the Corinthians*. PNTC. Grand Rapids: Eerdmans, 2010.

Cicero, M. Tullius. *De Natura Deorum, Academica*. Translated by H. Rackham. LCL. London: William Heinemann; Cambridge: Harvard University Press, 1933.

_____. *De Officiis*. Translated by Walter Millar. LCL. London: William Heinemann; Cambridge: Harvard University Press, 1913.

_____. *De Re Publica, De Legibus*. Translated by Clinton Walker Keyes. LCL. London: William Heinemann; Cambridge: Harvard University Press, 1928.

_____. *Epistulae ad familiares*; URL: http://www.perseus.tufts.edu/hopper/text?doc=Cic.+Fam.+2.8.1&fromdoc=Perseus%3Atext%3A1999.02.0009; accessed 08 April 2015.

_____. *The Speeches*. Translated by John Henry Freese, R. Gardner, and N. H. Watts. LCL. London: William Heinemann; Cambridge: Harvard University Press, 1931.

_____. *Tusculan Disputations*. Translated by J. E. King. LCL. Vol. 141. Cambridge: Harvard University Press, 1927.

Clement of Alexandria. *The Ante-Nicene Fathers* on CD-ROM. Accordance Bible Software Version 10.1.5, 2013. Print ed.: Clement of Alexandria. In vol. 2 of *The Ante-Nicene Fathers*. Alexander Roberts, James Donaldson, and A. Cleveland Coxe, eds. 1885–1896. 10 vols. New York: Christian Literature Company.

Clement of Rome. *The Ante-Nicene Fathers* on CD-ROM. Logos Research Systems Version 2.0. 1997. Print ed.: Clement of Rome. In vol. 1 of *The Ante-Nicene Fathers*. Alexander Roberts, James Donaldson, and A. Cleveland Coxe, eds. 1885–1896. 10 vols. New York: Christian Literature Company.

Coffey, David M. "Natural Knowledge of God; Reflections on Romans 1:18–32." TS 31 (1970), 674–91.

Collingwood, R. G. and J. N. L. Myres. *Roman Britain and the English Settlements*. 2nd ed. OHE. Oxford: Oxford University Press, 1937.

Collins, John J. "Jewish Apocalyptic Against Its Hellenistic Near Eastern Environment." ASOR 220 (1975), 27–36.

Conybeare, W. J. and J. S. Howson. *The Life and Epistles of St. Paul*. Hartford: S. S. Scranton Company, 1893.

Cooper, Mark Dwain. "The Intertextual Link between Parazēloō and Leimma in Rom 11:1–15." Unpublished PhD dissertation, New Orleans Baptist Theological Seminary, 2018.

Cranfield, C. E. B. *The Epistle to the Romans*. ICC, 2 Vols. Edinburgh: T&T Clark, 1979.

Cranford, Michael. "Abraham in Romans 4: The Father of All Who Believe." *NTS* 41, no. 1 (1995), 71–88. doi:10.1017/S0028688500022955.

Cullmann, Oscar. *Christ and Time: The Primitive Christian Conception of Time and History*. 3rd ed. Eugene, OR: Wipf and Stock, 2018.

Cyril of Jerusalem. *The Nicene and Post-Nicene Fathers of the Christian Church* on CD-ROM. Accordance Bible Software Version 10.1.5, 2013. Print ed.: Cyril of Jerusalem. In vol. 7 of *The Nicene and Post-Nicene Fathers of the Christian Church*. Series 2. 1886–1889. Philip Schaff and Henry Wace, eds. 14 vols. New York: Christian Literature Company.

Dahlberg, B. T. "Wrath of God," *IDB* 4:903–08.

Danker, Frederick W. *Benefactor: Epigraphic Study of a Graeco-Roman and New Testament Semantic Field*. St. Louis, MO: Clayton, 1982.

Das, A. Andrew. *Paul, the Law, and the Covenant*. Peabody, MA: Hendrickson, 2001.

Daube, David. *The New Testament and Rabbinic Judaism*. Jordan Lectures in Comparative Religion, no. 2 (1952). London: Athlon Press, 1956.

Davies, J. G. "Genesis of Belief in an Imminent Parousia." *JTS* 14 (1963), 104–07.

Davies, W. D. "Apocalyptic and Pharisaism." *ET* 59 (1948), 233–37.

_____. *Paul and Rabbinic Judaism: Some Rabbinic Elements in Pauline Theology*. 2nd ed. London: SPCK, 1962.

Deissmann, Adolf. *Light from the Ancient East: The New Testament Illustrated by Recently Discovered Texts of the Graeco Roman World*. Translated by Lionel R. M. Strachan. Eugene, OR: Wipf and Stock, 2004.

Delling, Gerhard. "τάσσω," *TDNT* 8:27–48.

DelRio, Delio. *Paul and the Synagogue: Romans and the Isaiah Targum*. Eugene, OR: Wipf and Stock, 2013.

Demosthenes. Translated by C. A. Vince, J. H. Vince, Norman W. DeWitt, and Norman J. DeWitt. LCL. London: William Heinemann; Cambridge: Harvard University Press, 1953–1962.

deSilva, David A. *Honor, Patronage, Kinship, and Purity: Unlocking New Testament Culture*. Downers Grove, IL: InterVarsity, 2000.

_____. *An Introduction to the New Testament: Contexts, Methods and Ministry Formation*. Downers Grove, IL: InterVarsity, 2004.

Dicke, John. "Christian," in *The International Standard Bible Encyclopedia*. Fully Revised, Illustrated, in Four Volumes. Edited by Geoffrey W. Bromiley. Vol. 1. Grand Rapids: Eerdmans, 1979.

Diodorus Siculus. *Complete Works of Diodorus Siculus*. Delphi Ancient Classics. Vol. 32. Delphi Classics, Kindle Edition, 2014.

Diogenes Laertius. *Delphi Complete Works of Diogenes Laertius (Illustrated)*. Translated by R. D. Hicks. Delphi Ancient Classics. Vol. 47. Delphi Classics, Kindle Edition, 2015.

Dittenberger, Wilhelmus. *Orientis Graecae Inscriptiones Selectae, Supplementum Sylloges inscriptionum graecarum*. Lipsiae: S. Hirzel, 1903.

Dodd, Brian. *Paul's Paradigmatic "I": Personal Example as Literary Strategy*. Library of New Testament Studies. JSNTSS, No. 177. Sheffield Academic Press, 1999.

Dodd, Charles H. *The Epistle of Paul to the Romans*. MNTC. London: Hodder and Stoughton, 1936.

Donaldson, Terence L. "Israelite, Convert, Apostle to the Gentiles: The Origin of Paul's Gentile Mission." *The Road from Damascus: The Impact of Paul's Conversion on*

His Life, Thought, and Ministry. Edited by Richard N. Longenecker. Grand Rapids: Eerdmans, 1997, 62–84.

_____. *Paul and the Gentiles: Remapping the Apostle's Convictional World*. Minneapolis: Fortress, 1997.

Donfried, Karl P. "Justification and Last Judgment in Paul." *Interpretation* 30 (1976), 140–52.

Donfried, Karl P., ed. *The Romans Debate: Revised and Expanded Edition*. Peabody, MA: Hendrickson, 2001.

Doty, William G. *Letters in Primitive Christianity*. Guides to Biblical Scholarship, New Testament Series. Edited by Dan O. Via Jr. Philadelphia: Fortress, 1973.

Dreyer, Boris, and Helmut Engelmann. "Augustus und Germanicus im ionischen Metropolis." *Zeitschrift für Papyrologie und Epigraphik* 158: 175–182.

Dunn, James D. G. *The Partings of the Ways: Between Christianity and Judaism and Their Significance for Christianity*. Norwich, UK: SCM, 1991.

_____. *Romans*. WBC, Vols. 38a, 38b. Dallas: Word, 1988.

_____. *The Theology of Paul the Apostle*. Grand Rapids, Cambridge: Eerdmans, 1998.

Earl, Donald. *Age of Augustus*. New York: Crown, 1968.

Earle, Ralph. "Inn; Lodge; Lodging." *International Standard Bible Encyclopedia, Revised*. Edited by Geoffrey W. Bromiley. Grand Rapids: Eerdmans, 1988. 2:826–27.

Eastman, David L. *The Ancient Martyrdom Accounts of Peter and Paul*. Writings from the Greco-Roman World. Vol. 39. Atlanta: SBL Press, 2015.

_____. *Paul the Martyr: The Cult of the Apostle in the Latin West*, WGRW-Sup 4. Atlanta: Society of Biblical Literature, 2011.

Edmundson, George. *The Church in Rome in the First Century: An Examination of Various Controverted Questions Relating to Its History, Chronology, Literature, and Traditions; Eight Lectures Preached before the University of Oxford in the Year 1913 on the Foundation of the Late Rev. John Bampton*. Oxford, 1913; reprint, CreateSpace Independent Publishing Platform, 2016.

Eisenbaum, Pamela. *Paul Was Not a Christian: The Original Message of a Misunderstood Apostle*. San Francisco: HarperOne, 2009.

Eisenstadt, S. N. and L. Roniger. *Patrons, Clients and Friends: Interpersonal Relations and the Structure of Trust in Society*. Cambridge: Cambridge University Press, 1984.

Elliot, J. K. *The Apocryphal New Testament*. Oxford: Clarendon, 1993.

Elliott, Neil. *The Arrogance of Nations: Reading Romans in the Shadow of Empire*. PCCS. Minneapolis: Fortress, 2008.

_____. *The Rhetoric of Romans: Argumentative Constraint and Strategy and Paul's Dialogue with Judaism*. JSNTSS, No. 45. Edited by David Hill. Sheffield: JSOT Press, 1990.

Ellis, E. Earle. *Paul's Use of the Old Testament*. Grand Rapids: Eerdmans, 1957.

Epictetus. *The Discourses as Reported by Arrian, the Manual and Fragments*. Vol. 2. Translated by W. A. Oldfather. LCL. Vol. 218. 1926–28. Cambridge: Harvard University Press, 1969.

Epicurus. *Letters, Principle Doctrines, and Vatican Sayings*. Translated with an Introduction and Notes by Russell M. Geer. In *Library of Liberal Arts*. Indianapolis: Bobbs-Merrill Co., 1964.

Epiphanius. *The Panarion of Epiphanius of Salamis, Book I (Sects 1–46)*. 2nd Revised and Expanded Edition. Translated by Frank Williams. Nag Hammadi and Manichean Studies (Book 63). Leiden: Brill Academic, 2008.

Epp, Eldon J. *Junia: The First Woman Apostle*. Foreword by Beverly Roberts Gaventa. Minneapolis: Fortress, 2005.

Esler, Philip F. "Ancient Oleiculture and Ethnic Differentiation: The Meaning of the Olive-tree Image in Romans 11." JSNT 26.1 (2003), 103–24.

Euripides. Translated by Arthur S. Way. LCL. London: William Heinemann; Cambridge: Harvard University Press, 1950.

Eusebius. *The Nicene and Post-Nicene Fathers of the Christian Church* on CD-ROM. Accordance Bible Software Version 10.1.5, 2013. Print ed.: Eusebius. In vol. 1 of *The Nicene and Post-Nicene Fathers of the Christian Church*. Series 2. 1886–1889. Philip Schaff, Henry Wace, eds. 14 vols. New York: Christian Literature Company.

Evans, Craig A. *Mark 8:27—16:20*. WBC. Vol. 34B, Rev. ed. Grand Rapids: Zondervan, 2015.

_____. "Mark's Incipit and the Priene Calendar Inscription: From Jewish Gospel to Greco-Roman Gospel," JGRCJ, No. 1 (2000), 67–81.

_____. "Paul and the Prophets: Prophetic Criticism in the Epistle to the Romans (with special reference to Romans 9–11)." *Romans and the People of God: Essays in Honor of Gordon D. Fee on the Occasion of His 65th Birthday*. Sven K. Soderlund and N. T. Wright. Grand Rapids, Cambridge: Eerdmans, 1999, 115–28.

Evans, Craig A. and James A. Sanders, eds. *Paul and the Scriptures of Israel*. JSNTSup 83. Sheffield: Sheffield Academic Press, 1993.

Fanning, Bruce M. *Verbal Aspect in New Testament Greek*. Oxford: Clarendon, 1990.

Farrar, Frederic. W. *The Life and Work of St. Paul*. New York: Dutton, 1880.

Fee, Gordon D. *The First Epistle to the Corinthians*. NICNT. Grand Rapids: Eerdmans, 1987.

_____. *God's Empowering Presence: The Holy Spirit in the Letters of Paul*. Peabody, MA: Hendrickson, 1994.

_____. "Paul's Conversion as Key to His Understanding of the Spirit." *The Road from Damascus: The Impact of Paul's Conversion on His Life, Thought, and Ministry*. Edited by Richard N. Longenecker. Grand Rapids: Eerdmans, 1997, 166–83.

_____. *Paul's Letter to the Philippians*. NICNT. Grand Rapids: Eerdmans, 1995.

Fee, Gordon D. and Douglas Stuart. *How to Read the Bible for All Its Worth*. Grand Rapids: Zondervan, 2003.

Feldman, Louis H. "Financing the Colosseum," *Biblical Archeology Review*, July-August 2001.

Ferguson, Everett. *Backgrounds of Early Christianity*. 3rd ed. Grand Rapids: Eerdmans, 2003.

Ferrero, Guglielmo. *The Greatness and Decline of Rome*. Vol 5. *The Republic of Augustus*. Translated by H. J. Chaytor. New York: Putnam's Sons, 1909. Kessenger Legacy Reprints. Whitefish, MT: Kessenger, 2010.

Fine, Steven. "Non-Jews in the Synagogues of Late-Antique Palestine: Rabbinic and Archeological Evidence." *Jews, Christians, and Polytheists in the Ancient Synagogue: Cultural Interaction during the Greco-Roman Period*, 224–42. Edited by Steven Fine. Baltimore Studies in the History of Judaism. London, New York: Routledge, 1999.

Fischer, Avraham. "My Jewish Learning," on Lev 16:1–20:27. Accessed April 27, 2021. https://www.myjewishlearning.com/article/constructive-criticism.

Fitzmyer, Joseph A. *Romans: A New Translation with Introduction and Commentary.* AB. Vol. 33. New York: Doubleday, 1993.

Flesher, Paul V. M. and Bruce Chilton. *The Targums: A Critical Introduction.* Waco, TX: Baylor University Press, 2011.

Fox, Robert Lane. *Pagans and Christians.* New York: HarperCollins, 1986.

Fredriksen, Paula. *Paul: The Pagans' Apostle.* New Haven, London: Yale University Press, 2017.

Freedman, David Noel. "The Flowering of Apocalyptic." JTC 6 (1969), 166–74.

Frier, Bruce W. *Landlords and Tenants in Imperial Rome.* Princeton: Princeton University Press, 1980.

Friesen, Steven J. "The Wrong Erastus: Ideology, Archeology, and Exegesis." In *Corinth in Context: Comparative Studies on Religion and Society.* Steven J Friesen, Dan Schowalter, and James Walters, eds. *Novum Testamentum, Supplements* 134. Leiden: Brill, 2010, 224–49.

Funk, Robert W. "The Apostolic Parousia: Form and Significance" in *Christian History and Interpretation: Studies Presented to John Knox.* Edited by W. R. Farmer, C. F. D. Moule, and R. R. Niebuhr. Cambridge: University Press, 1967.

Furnish, Victor Paul. *Theology and Ethics in Paul.* Nashville: Abingdon, 1968.

Gager, John G. "Functional Diversity in Paul's Use of End-Time Language." JBL 89 (1970), 325–37.

_____. *Reinventing Paul.* Oxford: Oxford University Press, 2002.

_____. *Who Made Early Christianity?: The Jewish Lives of the Apostle Paul.* American Lectures on the History of Religions. New York: Columbia University Press, 2015.

Galinsky, Karl. *Augustan Culture: An Interpretive Introduction.* Princeton: Princeton University Press, 1996.

_____. "The Cult of the Roman Emperor: Uniter or Divider?" *Rome and Religion: A Cross-Disciplinary Dialogue on the Imperial Cult,* 1–21. Jeffrey Brodd and Jonathan L. Reed, eds. WGRWSS. No. 5. Atlanta: Society of Biblical Literature, 2011.

Gamble Jr., Harry. *The Textual History of the Letter to the Romans.* Studies and Documents 42. Edited by Irving Alan Sparks. Grand Rapids: Eerdmans, 1977.

Garlington, Don B. "The Obedience of Faith in the Letter of Romans—Part I: The Meaning of ὑπακοὴ πίστεως (Rom 1:5; 16:26)." WTJ 52 (1990), 47–72.

_____. "The Obedience of Faith in the Letter of Romans— Part II: The Obedience of Faith and Judgment by Works." WTJ 53 (1991), 47–72.

_____. "The Obedience of Faith in the Letter of Romans—Part III: The Obedience of Christ and The Obedience of the Christian." WTJ 55 (1993), 87–112.

Garroway, Joshua D. *Paul's Gentile-Jews: Neither Jew nor Gentile, but Both.* New York: Palgrave MacMillan, 2012.

Gaston, Lloyd. *Paul and the Torah.* Vancouver, BC: University of British Columbia Press, 1987.

Gates, Charles. *Ancient Cities: The Archaeology of Urban Life in the Ancient Near East and Egypt, Greece, and Rome.* London: Routledge, 2003.

Gathercole, Simon J. *Where Is Boasting? Early Jewish Soteriology and Paul's Response in Romans 1–5.* Grand Rapids, Cambridge: Eerdmans, 2002.

Geller, Stephen A. *Parallelism in Early Hebrew Poetry.* Harvard Semitic Monographs. Leiden: Brill, 1979.

Glancey, Jennifer A. *Slavery in Early Christianity.* Oxford: Oxford University Press, 2002.

Goodrich, John K. "Erastus of Corinth (Romans 16.23): Responding to Recent Proposals on His Rank, Status, and Faith." *New Testament Studies* 57, no. 4 (2011), 583–93. doi:10.1017/S0028688511000063.

Grenholm, Christina, and Daniel Patte, eds. *Reading Israel in Romans: Legitimacy and Plausibility of Divergent Interpretations.* Romans through History and Culture Series, Christina Grenholm and Daniel Patte, eds. Harrisburg, PA: Trinity Press, 2000.

Griffin, Miriam. "Urbs Roma, Plebs, and Princeps," in *Images of Empire.* Edited by Loveday Alexander. Sheffield: Sheffield Academic, 1991.

Gruber, Daniel. *Rabbi Akiba's Messiah: The Origins of Rabbinic Authority.* Kindle Edition. Elijah Publishing, 2012.

Grundmann, Walter. "δόκιμος." *TDNT* 2:255–60.

_____. "Χρίω κτλ." *TDNT* 9: 228–43.

Gutmann, J., ed. *Ancient Synagogues: The State of Research.* Brown Judaic Studies 22. Chico, CA: Scholars Press, 1981.

Haney, Herbert M. *The Wrath of God in the Former Prophets.* New York: Vantage, 1960.

Hanson, Anthony T. *The Wrath of the Lamb.* London: SPCK, 1957.

Hanson, Kenneth C. and Douglas E. Oakman, *Palestine in the Time of Jesus: Social Structures and Social Conflicts.* Minneapolis: Augsburg Fortress, 1998.

Harland, Philip A. *Associations, Synagogues and Congregations: Claiming a Place in Ancient Mediterranean Society.* Minneapolis: Fortress, 2003.

Harrill, J. Albert. *Paul the Apostle: His Life and Legacy in Their Roman Context.* Cambridge: Cambridge University Press, 2012.

_____. *Slaves in the New Testament: Literary, Social, and Moral Dimensions.* Minneapolis: Fortress, 2006.

Hayes, Richard B. *Echoes of Scripture in the Letters of Paul.* New Haven, London: Yale University Press, 1989.

_____. *First Corinthians.* Interpretation. Louisville: John Knox, 1997.

Heemstra, Marius. *How Rome's Administration of the Fiscus Judaicus Accelerated the Parting of the Ways Between Judaism and Christianity: Rereading 1 Peter, Revelation, the Letter to the Hebrews, and the Gospel of John in Their Roman and Jewish Contexts.* Doctoral Dissertation, September 2009, Rijksuniversiteit Groningen. Veenendal, the Netherlands: Universal, 2009.

Heilig, Christoph, Thomas Hewitt, and Michael F. Bird, eds. *God and the Faithfulness of Paul: A Critical Examination of the Pauline Theology of N. T. Wright.* Minneapolis: Fortress, 2017.

Hengel, Martin. *Judaism and Hellenism: Studies in Their Encounter in Palestine in the Early Hellenistic Period.* Translated by John Bowden. 2 Vols. Minneapolis: Fortress, 1981.

Hengel, Martin and Anna Maria Schwemer. *Paul Between Damascus and Antioch: The Unknown Years.* Translated by John Bowden. Louisville: Westminster John Knox, 1997.

Hennecke, Edgar and William Schneemelcher, eds. *New Testament Apocrypha.* Translated by R. McL. Wilson. 5th ed. Vol. 2. Louisville: Westminster John Knox, 1992.

Herodotus. *The Persian Wars*. Translated by A. D. Godley. 2 vols. LCL. Cambridge: Harvard University Press, 1921–1925.

Hesiod. *The Homeric Hymns and Homerica*. Translated by Hugh G. Evelyn-White. LCL. London: William Heinemann; Cambridge: Harvard University Press, 1954.

Hill, Duncan. *Ancient Rome: From the Republic to the Empire*. Bath, UK: Parragon, 2007.

Holland, Glenn S. "The Self against the Self in Romans 7.7–25." *The Rhetorical Interpretation of Scripture: Essays from the 1996 Malibu Conference*. Edited by Stanley E. Porter and Dennis L. Stamps. JSNTSS, No. 180. Edited by Stanley E. Porter. Sheffield: Sheffield Academic Press, 1999, pp. 260–71.

Holland, Tom. *Contours of Pauline Theology: A Radical New Survey of the Influences on Paul's Biblical Witness*. Scotland, UK: Mentor, 2004.

———. *Romans: The Divine Marriage, A Biblical Theological Commentary*. 2 Vols. London: Apiary Publishing, 2011, rev. 2020.

Holmes, Michael W. *The Apostolic Fathers: Greek Texts and English Translations*. Updated ed. Grand Rapids: Baker, 2007.

Holum, Kenneth G. "Building Power: The Politics of Architecture." BAR 30, No. 5 (Sept–Oct 2004), 36–45, 57.

Homer. *The Iliad*. Translated by A. T. Murray. LCL. London: William Heinemann; Cambridge: Harvard University Press, 1924–1925.

———. *The Odyssey*. Translated by A. T. Murray. LCL. London: William Heinemann;

Hood, Renate Viveen. "A Socio-Anthropological Analysis of Gentile-Jew Relationships in Rome and Antioch." Ph.D. diss., New Orleans Baptist Theological Seminary, 2002.

Hooker, Morna D. "Adam in Romans I," *NTS* 6 (1959–60), 297–307.

———. "Further Notes on Romans I," *NTS* 13 (1967), 181–83.

Horace. *Satires, Epistles, and Ars poetica*. Translated by H. Rushton Fairclough, LCL. Vol. 194. Cambridge: Harvard University Press, 1926, 1960.

Horsley, Richard A., ed. *Paul and Empire: Religion and Power in Roman Imperial Society*. Harrisburg, PA: Trinity Press International, 1997.

———. *Paul and the Roman Imperial Order*. Harrisburg, PA: Trinity Press International, 2004.

Hort, Fenton J. A. *Prolegomena to St. Paul's Epistles to the Romans and the Ephesians*. London: Macmillan, 1895.

Hübner, Hans. *Law in Paul's Thought: A Contribution to the Development of Pauline Theology*. Studies of the New Testament and Its World. Edited by John Riches, Edinbugh: T&T Clark, 1984.

Hultgren, Arland J. *Paul's Letter to the Romans: A Commentary*. Grand Rapids: Eerdmans, 2011.

Humphrey, Edith M. "Why Bring the Word Down? The Rhetoric of Demonstration and Disclosure in Romans 9:30—10:21." *Romans and the People of God: Essays in Honor of Gordon D. Fee on the Occasion of His 65th Birthday*. Sven K. Soderlund and N. T. Wright. Grand Rapids, Cambridge: Eerdmans, 1999, 129–48.

Hunter, A. M. *The Epistle to the Romans*. TBC. London: SCM Press, 1955.

Hurtado, Larry W. "The Doxology at the End of Romans," in *New Testament Textual Criticism: Its Significance for Exegesis (Essays in Honor of Bruce M. Metzger)*. Edited by E. J. Epp and G. D. Fee. Oxford: Clarendon, 1981, 185–99.

Huttner, Ulrich. *Early Christianity in the Lycus Valley*. Translated by David Green. Ancient Judaism and Early Christianity. Leiden: Brill, 2013.

Hyldahl, Niels. "Reminiscence of the Old Testament at Romans 1:23," NTS 2 (May 1956), 285–88.

Ignatius. *Apostolic Fathers: English Translation* on CD-ROM. Accordance Bible Software Version 10.1.5, 2013. Print ed.: Ignatius. *The Apostolic Fathers: English Translation*. Translated by Michael W. Holmes. Grand Rapids: Baker, 1992, 1999.

Irenaeus. *The Ante-Nicene Fathers* in *Accordance Bible Software*, Version 10.1.5. 2013. Print ed.: Irenaeus. In vol. 1 of *The Ante-Nicene Fathers*. Alexander Roberts, James Donaldson, and A. Cleveland Coxe, eds. 1885–1896. 10 vols. New York: Christian Literature Company.

Jeffers, James S. *The Greco-Roman World of the New Testament Era: Exploring the Background of Early Christianity*. Downers Grove, IL: InterVarsity, 1999.

Jerome. *The Nicene and Post-Nicene Fathers of the Christian Church* on CD-ROM. Accordance Bible Software Version 10.1.5, 2013. Print ed.: Jerome. In vol. 1 of *The Nicene and Post-Nicene Fathers of the Christian Church*. Series 2. 1886–1889. Philip Schaff and Henry Wace, eds. 14 vols. New York: Christian Literature Company.

The Jerusalem Talmud: A Translation and Commentary on CD. Edited by Jacob Neusner. Translated by Jacob Neusner and Tzvee Zahavy. Peabody, MA.: Hendrickson, 2010.

Jervell, Jacob. "The Letter to Jerusalem." *The Romans Debate: Revised and Expanded Edition*. Edited by Karl P. Donfried. Peabody, MA: Hendrickson, 1991.

Jervis, L. Ann. *The Purpose of Romans: A Comparative Letter Structure Investigation*. JSNTSS 55. Sheffield: JSOT Press, 1991.

Jewett, Robert. *A Chronology of Paul's Life*. Philadelphia: Fortress, 1979.

———. "Following the Argument of Romans." *The Romans Debate: Revised and Expanded Edition*. Edited by Karl P. Donfried. Peabody, MA: Hendrickson, 1991.

———. *Romans: A Commentary*. Hermeneia. Minneapolis: Fortress, 2007.

Johnson, Richard Warren. "Confronting the Beast: The Imperial Cult in the Book of Revelation." In *Essays on Revelation: Appropriating Yesterday's Apocalypse in Today's World*. Edited by Gerald L. Stevens. Eugene, OR: Pickwick, 2011.

Jones, Brian W. *The Emperor Domitian*. Reprint edition. London: Routledge, 1993.

———. *Suetonius: Domitian*. Bristol: Bristol Classic, 1996.

Josephus. Modules on CD-ROM. Accordance Bible Software. OakTree Software, Inc., Altamonte Springs, Fla. Greek text, ver. 1.5. 2005. Based on 1890 Niese edition, public domain. English text, ver. 1.3. 2005. Print ed.: *The Works of Flavius Josephus, Complete and Unabridged*. Updated edition. Translated by William Whiston. Peabody, MA: Hendrickson, 1987.

———. Translated by H. St. J. Thackeray et al. 10 vols. LCL. Cambridge: Harvard University Press, 1926–1965; reprint 1968.

———. *The Works of Josephus: Complete and Unabridged*. Updated edition. Translated by William Whiston. Peabody: Hendrickson, 1987.

Justin's History of the World. In *Justin's Epitome of The History of Pompeius Trogus, Literally Translated, with Notes and a General Index*. Translated by John Selby Watson. London: George Bell and Sons, 1886.

Justin Martyr. *The Ante-Nicene Fathers* on CD-ROM. in *Accordance Bible Software*, Version 10.1.5. 2013. Print ed.: Justin Martyr. In vol. 1 of *The Ante-Nicene Fathers*. Alexander Roberts, James Donaldson, and A. Cleveland Coxe, eds. 1885–1896. 10 vols. New York: Christian Literature Company.

Juvenal. *Juvenal and Perseus*. LCL. Vol. 91. Translated by Susanna Morton Braund. Cambridge: Harvard University Press, 2004.

Kalimi, Isaac. "The Hiding of the Temple Vessels in Jewish and Samaritan Literature." In *Fighting Over the Bible: Jewish Interpretation, Sectarianism and Polemic from Temple to Talmud and Beyond*. BRLJ 54. The Netherlands: Brill, 2017, 208–216.

Kallas, James. "Romans XIII:1–7; an Interpolation." NTS 11 (July 1965), 365–74.

Käsemann, Ernst. *Commentary on Romans*. Translated and edited by Geoffrey W. Bromiley. Grand Rapids: Eerdmans, 1980.

_____. "'The Righteousness of God' in Paul." *New Testament Questions of Today*. London: SCM-Canterbury Press Ltd, 1969, 168–82.

Kasher, Aryeh. *Jews, Idumeans, and Ancient Arabs*. Tübingen: J. C. B. Mohr, 1988.

Kaylor, R. David. *Paul's Covenant Community: Jew and Gentile in Romans*. Atlanta: John Knox, 1988.

Kebede, Aschalew. *How Can the Concepts of Universalism and Nationalism in the Book of Isaiah Be Reconciled?* Ann Arbor: UMI, 1988.

Keener, Craig S. *Acts: An Exegetical Commentary*. Vol. 1: Introduction and 1:1—2:47; Vol. 2: 3:1—14:28; Vol. 3: 15:1—23:35; Vol. 4: 24:1—28:31. Grand Rapids: Baker Academic, 2012-2015.

_____. *IVP Bible Background Commentary: New Testament*. Downers Grove, IL: InterVarsity, 1993.

_____. *Paul, Women and Wives: Marriage and Women's Ministry in the Letters of Paul*. Peabody, MA: Hendrickson, 1992.

Kennedy, George A. *New Testament Interpretation Through Rhetorical Criticism*. Studies in Religion. Edited by Charles H. Long. Chapel Hill and London: University of North Carolina Press: 1984.

Kent, John Harvey. *The Inscriptions, 1926-1950*. Vol. 8, part 3 of *Corinth: Results of Excavations Conducted by The American School of Classical Studies at Athens*. Princeton, NJ: The American School of Classical Studies at Athens, 1966.

Kim, Johann D. *God, Israel, and the Gentiles: Rhetoric and Situation in Romans 9-11*. SBL Dissertation Series 176. Atlanta: Society of Biblical Literature, 2000.

Kim, Seyoon. *Paul and the New Perspective: Second Thoughts on the Origin of Paul's Gospel*. Grand Rapids, Cambridge: Eerdmans, 2002.

Klassen, William. "Kiss (NT)." AYBD 4:89–92.

Klein, William, Craig Blomberg, and Robert Hubbard. *Introduction to Biblical Interpretation*. Rev. ed. Downers Grove, IL: InterVarsity, 2004.

Koch, Klaus. *The Rediscovery of Apocalyptic: A Polemical Work on a Neglected Area of Biblical Studies and Its Damaging Effects on Theology and Philosophy*. Translated by Margaret Kohl. London: SCM, 1972.

Koenig, John. "Hospitality." In *Anchor Yale Bible Dictionary*. Edited by John J. Collins. New Haven, CT: Yale University Press, 1992, 3:299–301.

Koester, Helmut. *Introduction to the New Testament. Volume 1: History, Culture, and Religion of the Hellenistic Age*, 2nd ed. 2 Vols. New York: Walter de Gruyter, 1995.

_____. "τέμνω," *TDNT* 8:106–12.

Konkel, August H. "What Is the Future of Israel in Romans 9–11?" In *The Letter to the Romans: Exegesis and Application*. Stanley E. Porter and Francis G. H. Pang, eds. McMaster NTS. Vol. 7. Eugene, OR: Pickwick, 2018, 115–26.

Kraemer, Ross S. "Typical and Atypical Jewish Family Dynamics: The Cases of Babatha and Berenice," in *Early Christian Families in Context: An Interdisciplinary*

Dialogue. Edited by David L. Balch and Carolyn Osiek, Religion, Marriage, and Family. Edited by Don S. Browning and David Clairmont. Grand Rapids: Eerdmans, 2003.

Kruse, Colin G. *Paul's Letter to the Romans*. PNTC. Grand Rapids, Cambridge: Eerdmans, 2012.

Kümmel, Helmut. *Introduction to the New Testament: Revised English Edition*. Translated by Howard Clark Kee. Nashville: Abingdon, 1975.

Lactantius. *The Ante-Nicene Fathers* in Accordance Bible Software, Version 10.1.5. 2013. Print ed.: Lactantius. In vol. 7 of *The Ante-Nicene Fathers*. Alexander Roberts, James Donaldson, and A. Cleveland Coxe, eds. 1885–1896. 10 vols. New York: Christian Literature Company.

Ladd, George E. *A Theology of the New Testament*. Grand Rapids: Eerdmans, 1974.

Lampe, Peter. *Die stadtrömischen Christen in den ersten beiden Jahrhunderten: Studien zur Sozialgeschichte*. WUNT 18. Tübingen: Mohr-Siebeck, 1987; 2nd ed. 1989.

_____. *From Paul to Valentinus: Christians at Rome in the First Two Centuries*. Minneapolis: Fortress, 2003.

Lauterbach, Jacob Z. *Mekilta de-Rabbi Ishmael: A Critical Edition on the Basis of the Manuscripts and Early Editions with an English Translation, Introduction, and Notes*. Philadelphia: Jewish Publication Society, 1961 (original, 1933).

Lawlor, H. J. "St. Paul's Quotations from Epimenides." *The Irish Church Quarterly*. Vol. 9, no. 35 (July 1916), 180–93.

Leach, James. *Creative Land: Place and Procreation on the Rai Coast of Papua Guinea*. New York: Berghahn Books, 2003.

Leeman, A. D. *Orationis Ratio: The Stylistic Theories and Practice of the Roman Orators Historians and Philosophers*. Vols. 1–2. Amsterdam: Adolf M. Hakkert, 2001; reprint of the 1963 edition in one volume.

Leenhardt, Franz J. *The Epistle to the Romans*. London: Lutterworth, 1961.

Leon, H. J. *The Jews of Ancient Rome*. Updated Edition. Introduction by Carolyn Osiek. Peabody, MA: Hendrickson, 1995.

Levine, Lee I. *The Ancient Synagogue: The First Thousand Years*. 2nd ed. New Haven, CT: Yale University Press, 2005.

Lewis, Robert Brian. *Paul's 'Spirit of Adoption' in Its Roman Imperial Context*. LNTS. Vol. 545. New York: Bloomsbury, 2016.

Liao, Paul Shang-hsin. "The Place of Covenant in the Theology of the Apostle Paul." PhD thesis, Hartford Seminary Foundation, 1973.

Liberati, Anna Maria and Fabio Bourbon. *Ancient Rome: History of a Civilization that Ruled the World*. New York: Barnes and Noble, 2000, arrangement with original publishers, White Star, Vercelli, Italy, 1996.

Licht, Jacob. "Taxo, or the Apocalyptic Doctrine of Vengeance." JJS 12 (1961), 95–103.

Lindsay, Hugh. *Adoption in the Roman World*. Oxford: Cambridge, 2009.

Linebaugh, Jonathan A. "Wisdom of Solomon and Romans 1:18—2:5: God's Wrath against *All*." In *Reading Romans in Context: Paul and Second Temple Judaism*. Ben C. Blackwell, John K. Goodrich, and Jason Maston, eds. Grand Rapids: Zondervan, 2015, 38–45.

Ling, Roger. *Roman Painting*. Oxford: Cambridge, 1991.

Ling, Roger, *et al. The Insula of the Menander at Pompeii, Volume I: The Structures*. Oxford: Clarendon, 1997.

Ling, Roger and Lesley Ling. *The Insula of the Menander at Pompeii, Volume II: The Decorations.* Oxford: Clarendon, 2005.

Livy. *History of Rome.* Translated by Frank Gardner Moore et al. 14 vols. LCL. Cambridge: Harvard University Press, 1919–1959; reprint 1965.

Ljungmen, Henrik. *Pistis: A Study of Its Presuppositions and Its Meaning in Pauline Use.* Lund: C. W. K. Gleerup, 1964.

Longenecker, Bruce W., ed. *Narrative Dynamics in Paul: A Critical Assessment.* Louisville, London: Westminster John Knox, 2002.

Longenecker, Richard N. *The Epistle to the Romans: A Commentary on the Greek Text.* NIGTC. Grand Rapids: Eerdmans, 2016.

Louw, Johannes P. and Eugene A. Nida, eds. *Greek English Lexicon of the New Testament Based on Semantic Domains, Second Edition.* Vol. 1: Introduction and Domains. New York: United Bible Societies, 1988, 1989.

Lucretius Carus, Titus. *De Rerum Natura.* Translated by W. H. D. Rouse. LCL. London: William Heinemann; Cambridge: Harvard University Press, 1924–1937.

Lüdemann, Gerd. *Opposition to Paul in Jewish Christianity.* Translated by M. Eugene Boring. Minneapolis: Fortress, 1989.

———. *Paul, Apostle to the Gentiles: Studies in Chronology.* Foreword by John Knox. Translated by F. Stanley Jones. Minneapolis: Fortress, 1984.

Lyall, Francis. "Roman Law in the Writings of Paul—Adoption." *Journal of Biblical Literature* 88 (1969), 458–66.

Lycurgas. *Minor Attic Orators.* Translated by K. J. Maidment and J. O. Burtt. LCL. London: William Heinemann; Cambridge: Harvard University Press, 1953–1954.

Maas, Michael. *Readings in Late Antiquity: A Sourcebook.* Routledge Sourcebooks for the Ancient World. Vol. 10. 2nd ed. Philadelphia: Routledge, 2010.

MacDonald, Dennis R. "Apocryphal and Canonical Narratives about Paul." *Paul and the Legacies of Paul,* 55–70. Edited by William S. Babcock. Dallas: Southern Methodist University Press, 1990.

Macdonald, John. *The Theology of the Samaritans.* NTL. London: SCM, 1964.

MacMullan, Ramsay. *Enemies of the Roman Order: Treason, Unrest, and Alienation in the Empire.* Cambridge: Harvard University Press, 1966.

Macpherson, John. "Was There a Second Imprisonment of Paul in Rome?" *The American Journal of Theology.* Vol. 4, no 1 (Jan 1900), 33–35.

Malherbe, Abraham J. *Paul and the Popular Philosophers.* Minneapolis: Fortress, 1989.

Malina, Bruce J. *Christian Origins and Cultural Anthropology: Practical Models for Biblical Interpretation.* Louisville: Westminster John Knox, 1986.

———. *The New Testament World: Insights from Cultural Anthropology.* 3rd ed. Louisville: Westminster John Knox, 2001.

Malina, Bruce J. and John J. Pilch. *Social-Science Commentary on the Letters of Paul.* Minneapolis: Fortress, 2006.

Mann, Jacob. *The Bible as Read and Preached in the Old Synagogue: A Study in the Cycles of the Readings from Torah and Prophets, as well as from Psalms, and in the Structure of the Midrashic Homilies.* Vol 1: The Palestinian Triennial Cycle: Genesis and Exodus. Prolegomenon by Ben Zion Wacholder. LBS. New York: KTAV, 1971.

Manson, Steve. "For I Am Not Ashamed of the Gospel (Rom. 1:16), The Gospel and the First Readers of Romans." *Gospel in Paul: Studies on Corinthians, Galatians and Romans for Richard N. Longenecker.* JSNTSS, No. 108. Edited by by L. Ann Jervis and Peter Richardson. Sheffield: Sheffield Academic Press, 1994.

Manson, T. W. "St. Paul's Letter to the Romans—and Others." Pages 3–15 in *The Romans Debate*. Rev. and expanded. Edited by Karl P. Donfried. Peabody, MA: Hendrickson, 1991.

Marshall, I. Howard. *New Testament Theology: Many Witnesses, One Gospel*. Downers Grove, IL: InterVarsity, 2004.

_____. "Rom 16:25–27—An Apt Conclusion" in *Romans and the People of God: Essays in Honor of Gordon D. Fee on the Occasion of His 65th Birthday*. Edited by S. K. Soderlund and N. T. Wright. Grand Rapids: Eerdmans, 1999, 36–48.

Massey, Gerald. *Ancient Egypt: The Light of the World, A Work of Reclamation and Restitution in Twelve Books*. London: T. Fisher Unwin, Adelphi Terrace, 1907.

Matlock, R. Barry. *Unveiling the Apocalyptic Paul: Paul's Interpreters and the Rhetoric of Criticism*. JSNTSS 127. Sheffield: Sheffield Academic Press, 1996.

McKay, K. L. *A New Syntax of the Verb in New Testament Greek: An Aspectual Approach*. SBG, Vol. 5. New York: Peter Lang, 1994.

McNamara, Martin. *The New Testament and the Palestinian Targum to the Pentateuch*. AnBib 27a. Rome: Biblical Institute Press, 1978.

_____. *Targum and Testament Revisited: Aramaic Paraphrases of the Hebrew Bible*. 2nd ed. Grand Rapids: Eerdmans, 2010.

McRay, John. *Archeology and the New Testament*. Grand Rapids: Baker, 1991.

Meeks, Wayne. *The First Urban Christians: The Social World of the Apostle Paul*. 2nd ed. New Haven and London: Yale University Press, 2003.

Memar Marqah: The Teaching of Marqah, 2 vols. Translated and ed. by John Mac-Donald. Beihefte zur Zeitschrift für die altertestamentliche Wissenschaft, no. 84. Edited by Georg Fohrer. Berlin: Verlag Alfred Töpelmann, 1963.

Menander, The Principal Fragments. Translated by Francis G. Allinson. LCL. London: William Heinemann; Cambridge: Harvard University Press, 1930.

Merrill, Elmer Truesdell. "The Expulsion of Jews from Rome under Tiberius." *Classical Philology* 14/4 (October 1919), 365–72.

Metzger, Bruce M. "The Redemption of Our Body: The Riddle of Romans 8:19–22." *Romans and the People of God: Essays in Honor of Gordon D. Fee on the Occasion of His 65th Birthday*. Sven K. Soderlund and N. T. Wright. Grand Rapids, Cambridge: Eerdmans, 1999, 92–114.

_____. *The Text of the New Testament: Its Transmission, Corruption, and Restoration*. 2nd ed. New York and Oxford: Oxford University Press, 1968.

_____. *A Textual Commentary on the Greek New Testament: A Companion Volume to the United Bible Societies' Greek New Testament (Fourth Revised Edition)*. 2nd ed. Stuttgart: German Bible Society, 1994.

Meyer, Heinrich August Wilhelm. *Critical and Exegetical Commentary to the Epistle to the Romans*, 2 vols. CECNT. London: T&T Clark, 1881.

Migne, Jacques-Paul. *Patrologiae cursus completes, series graeca. Fathers of the Church*. 1862. Charleston, SC: Nabu Press (BiblioLabs), 2010.

Minucius Felix, Marcus. *Minucius Felix*. Translated by Gerald R. Rendall based on an unfinished version by W. C. A. Kerr. LCL. London: William Heinemann; Cambridge: Harvard University Press, 1931.

The Mishnah, Translated from the Hebrew with Introduction and Brief Explanatory Notes. Translated by Herbert Danby. Oxford: Oxford University Press, 1933.

Mommsen, Theodor and U. von Wilamowitz-Moellendorff. "Die Einführung des asianischen Kalenders." In *Mittheilungen des Kaiserlich Deutschen Archäologischen Instituts, Athenische Abtheilung.* 24: 275–293. Berlin: Gebr. Mann, 1899.

Montgomery, James Alan. *The Samaritans, The Earliest Jewish Sect: Their History, Theology and Literature.* Introduction by Abraham S. Halkin. New York: KTAV, 1968.

Moo, Douglas J. *The Epistle to the Romans.* Grand Rapids, Cambridge: Eerdmans, 1996.

_____. "Israel and Paul in Romans 7.7–12," New Testament Studies 32, 1986, 122–35. Accessed April 28, 2021. DOI: https://doi.org/10.1017/S0028688500013540.

Moody, Dale. "Romans." BBC. Nashville: Broadman, 1970.

Morris, Leon *The Epistle to the Romans.* PNTC. Grand Rapids: Eerdmans, 1988.

Moule, C. F. D. "The Influence of Circumstances on the Use of Eschatological Terms." JTS, n.s. 15 (1964), 1–15.

_____. "The Judgment Theme in the Sacraments." *In The Background of the New Testament and Its Eschatology.* W. D. Davies and David Daube, eds. Cambridge: Cambridge University Press, 1956, 464–81.

Moule, H. C. G. *The Epistle of Paul the Apostle to the Romans, with Introduction and Notes.* CBSC. Cambridge: Cambridge University Press, 1952.

Moxnes, Halvor. "Honor and Shame." *The Social Sciences and New Testament Interpretation,* 19–40. Edited by Richard Rohrbaugh. Peabody, MA: Hendrickson, 1996.

Munck, Johannes. *Paulus und die Heilsgeschichte.* Acta Jutlandica 26:1; Tellogisk serie 6. Aarhus: Aarhus University Press, 1954.

_____. *Paul and the Salvation of Mankind.* Translated by Frank Clarke. Atlanta: John Knox, 1959; paperback, 1997.

Murphy-O'Connor, Jerome. *St. Paul's Corinth: Texts and Archeology.* Third revised and expanded edition. Collegeville, MN: Liturgical Press, 1983, 2002.

Murray, John. *The Epistle to the Romans: The English Text with Introduction, Exposition and Notes.* NICNT. Grand Rapids: Eerdmans, 1959, 1965.

Nanos, Mark D. *The Mystery of Romans: The Jewish Context of Paul's Letter.* Minneapolis: Fortress, 1996.

Nanos, Mark D. and Magnus Zetterholm. *Paul within Judaism: Restoring the First-Century Context to the Apostle.* Minneapolis: Fortress, 2015.

Nedarim. Translated by H. Freedman. In *The Babylonian Talmud.* Edited by Isidore Epstein. London: Soncino Press, 1936.

Newman, Barclay M. and Eugene A. Nida. *A Translator's Handbook on Paul's Letter to the Romans.* New York: United Bible Societies, 1973.

Neyrey, Jerome H. "The Idea and the System of Purity." *The Social Sciences and New Testament Interpretation,* 80–106. Edited by Richard Rohrbaugh. Peabody, MA: Hendrickson, 1996.

_____. *The Social World of Luke-Acts: Models for Interpretation.* Peabody, MA: Hendrickson, 1991.

Nygren, Anders. *Commentary on Romans.* Translated by Carl Rasmussen. Philadelphia: Fortress, 1949.

Oakes, Peter. *Reading Romans in Pompeii: Paul's Letter at Ground Level.* Minneapolis: Fortress; London: SPCK, 2009.

O'Conner, J. Murphy and James H. Charlesworth, eds. *Paul and the Dead Sea Scrolls.* New York: Crossroad, 1990.

Origen. *The Nicene and Post-Nicene Fathers of the Christian Church* on CD-ROM. Accordance Bible Software Version 10.1.5, 2013. Print ed.: Origen. In vol. 1 of

The Nicene and Post-Nicene Fathers of the Christian Church. Series 2. 1886–1889. Philip Schaff and Henry Wace, eds. 14 vols. New York: Christian Literature Company.

Orlando, Robert. *Apostle Paul: A Polite Bribe.* Foreword by Gert Lüdemann. Eugene, OR: Wipf and Stock, 2014.

O'Rourke, J. J. "Romans 1:20 and Natural Revelation." CBQ 23 (1961), 301–6.

Osborne, Grant. *Romans.* IVP NTCS. Downers Grove, IL: InterVarsity, 2004.

Osiek, Carolyn and Margaret Y. MacDonald, with Janet H. Tulloch. *A Woman's Place: House Churches in Earliest Christianity.* Minneapolis: Fortress, 2006.

Packer, James E. *The Insulae of Imperial Ostia.* MAAR 31. Rome: American Academy in Rome, 1971.

Packer, J. I. "The 'Wretched Man' Revisited: Another Look at Romans 7:24–25." *Romans and the People of God: Essays in Honor of Gordon D. Fee on the Occasion of His 65th Birthday.* Edited by Sven K. Soderlund and N. T. Wright. Grand Rapids, Cambridge: Eerdmans, 1999, 70–81.

Parker, Robert. *Miasma: Pollution and Purification in Early Greek Religion.* New York: Oxford University Press, 1983.

Pate, C. Marvin, J. Scott Duvall, J. Daniel Hayes, E. Randolph Richards, W. Dennis Tucker Jr., and Preben Young. *The Story of Israel: A Biblical Theology.* Downers Grove, IL: InterVarsity, 2004.

Pausanias. *Description of Greece.* Translated by W. H. S. Jones. LCL. Companion volume arranged by R. E. Wycherley. London: William Heinemann; Cambridge: Harvard University Press, 1918–1935; rev. ed., 1955.

Perriman, Andrew. *The Future of the People of God: Reading Romans Before and After Western Christendom.* Eugene, OR: Cascade, 2010.

Petersen, Norman R. *Rediscovering Paul: Philemon and the Sociology of Paul's Narrative World.* Philadelphia: Fortress Press, 1985.

Petronius. Translated by W. H. D. Rouse and E. H. Warmington. LCL. Cambridge: Harvard University Press, 1913; updated by Michael Heseltine 1987.

Philo. *Philo, With an English Translation by F. H. Colson,* 9 vols. LCL. London: William Heinemann Ltd.; Cambridge: Harvard University Press, 1937.

_____. *The Works of Philo, Completed and Unabridged.* New Updated Edition. Translated by C. D. Yonge. (Peabody, MA: Hendrickson, 1993). Oaktree Software module, ver. 1.2.

Pitre, Brandt, Michael P. Barber, and John A. Kincaid. *Paul, A New Covenant Jew: Rethinking Pauline Theology.* Grand Rapids: Eerdmans, 2019.

Plato. *Laws.* Translated by R. G. Bury. LCL. London: William Heinemann; Cambridge: Harvard University Press, 1926.

Plevnik, Joseph. "Honor/Shame." *Handbook of Biblical Social Values,* 106–15. John J. Pilch and Bruce J. Malina, eds. Peabody, MA: Hendrickson, 1998.

Pliny the Elder. Translated by John Bostock and Henry T. Riley. Sydney: Wentworth, 2016.

Pliny the Younger. Translated by Betty Radice. 2 vols. LCL. Cambridge: Harvard University Press, 1969.

Plummer, Robert L. "Melanchthon as Interpreter of the New Testament." *Westminster Theological Journal.* Vol. 62 (Fall 2002), 257–65.

Plutarch. *The Parallel Lives.* Translated by Bernadotte Perrin et al. 28 vols. LCL. Cambridge: Harvard University Press, 1914–1969.

Polhill, John B. *Paul and His Letters*. Nashville: Broadman and Holman, 1999.

Polybius. *The Histories*. Translated by W. R. Paton, LCL. Vol. 6. Cambridge: Harvard University Press; London: William Heinemann, 1925; reprinted 1954.

Porter, Stanley E. "Ancient Rhetorical Analysis and Discourse Analysis of the Pauline Corpus" in *The Rhetorical Analysis of Scripture: Essays from the 1995 London Conference*, Journal for the Study of the New Testament Series, no. 146, Edited by Stanley E. Porter and Thomas H. Olbricht. Sheffield: Sheffield Academic Press, 1997.

_____. *The Apostle Paul: His Life, Thought, and Letters*. Grand Rapids: Eerdmans, 2016.

_____. *Verbal Aspect in the Greek of the New Testament, with Reference to Tense and Mood*. SBG. Vol. 1. New York: Peter Lang, 1989, 1993.

Porter, Stanley E., ed. *The Pauline Canon*. Pauline Studies. Vol. 1. Leiden, Boston: Brill, 2004.

Postell, Seth D. *Adam as Israel: Genesis 1–3 as the Introduction to the Torah and Tanakh*. Eugene, OR: Pickwick, 2011.

Price, S. R. F. *Rituals and Power: The Roman Imperial Cult in Asia Minor*. Cambridge: Cambridge University Press, 1984.

Pummer, Reinhard. *The Samaritans: A Profile*. Grand Rapids: Eerdmans, 2016.

Purvis, James D. *The Samaritan Pentateuch and the Origin of the Samaritan Sect*. Harvard Semitic Monographs, no. 2. Cambridge: Harvard University Press, 1968.

Quintilian, *Institutio Oratoria*. Translated by H. E. Butler. Cambridge, MA; London: Harvard University Press, 1921.

_____. *The Orator's Education*. Translated and ed. by Donald A. Russell. LCL. Vol. 3. Cambridge: Harvard University Press, 2001.

Räisänen, Heikki. *Paul and the Law*. Philadelphia: Fortress, 1983.

_____. *Jesus, Paul and Torah: Collected Essays*. Translated by by David E. Orton. JSNTSS 43. Sheffield: JSOT Press, 1992.

Rajak, Tessa. "The Synagogue within the Greco-Roman City," *Jews, Christians, and Polytheists in the Ancient Synagogue: Cultural Interaction during the Greco-Roman Period*, 161–73. Edited by Steven Fine. Baltimore Studies in the History of Judaism. London, New York: Routledge, 1999.

Reese, Steve. *Paul's Large Letters: Paul's Autographic Subscriptions in the Light of Ancient Epistolary Conventions*. LNTS. Vol. 561. New York: Bloomsbury, 2017.

Reicke, Bo. *Re-examining Paul's Letters: The History of the Pauline Correspondence*. Edited by David P. Moessner and Ingalisa Reicke. Harrisburg, PA: Trinity Press Inter-national, 2001.

Reid, Marty L. "Paul's Rhetoric of Mutuality: A Rhetorical Reading of Romans." SBL 1995 Seminar Papers: Society of Biblical Literature Annual Meeting 1995. Edited by Eugene H. Lovering Jr. Atlanta: Scholars Press, 1995.

Reinhardt, Wolfgang. "The Population Size of Jerusalem and the Numerical Growth of the Jerusalem Church," *The Book of Acts in its First Century Setting*. Edited by Bruce W. Winter, *Volume 4: Palestinian Setting*. Edited by Richard Bauckham. Grand Rapids: Eerdmans; Carlisle: Paternoster, 1995.

Reynolds, J. and R. Tannenbaum, *Jews and God-fearers at Aphrodisias: Greek Inscriptions with Commentary*, Proceedings of the Cambridge Philological Association Supp. 12. Cambridge Philological Society 1987.

Richards, E. Randolph. *Paul and First-Century Letter Writing: Secretaries, Composition and Collection*. Downers Grove, IL: InterVarsity, 2004.

Richards, E. Randolph and Brandon J. O'Brien. *Misreading Scripture with Western Eyes: Removing Cultural Blinders to Better Understanding the Bible.* Downers Grove, IL: InterVarsity, 2012

Richardson, Peter. *Herod: King of the Jews and Friend of the Romans.* SPNT. Edited by D. Moody Smith. Columbia, SC: University of South Carolina Press, 1996.

Riesner, Rainer. *Paul's Early Period: Chronology, Mission Strategy, Theology.* Translated by Doug Stott. Grand Rapids, Cambridge, U.K.: Eerdmans, 1998.

Robinson, D. W. B. "The Priesthood of Paul in the Gospel of Hope," in *Reconciliation and Hope: New Testament Essays on Atonement and Eschatology presented to L. L. Morris on His 60th Birthday.* Edited by Robert Banks. Grand Rapids: Eerdmans, 1974.

Rock, Ian E. *Paul's Letter to the Romans and Roman Imperialism: An Ideological Analysis of the Exordium (Romans 1:1–17).* Foreword by John W. D. Holder. Eugene, OR: Pickwick, 2012.

Rodriguez, Rafael and Matthew Thiessen, eds. *The So-Called Jew in Paul's Letter to the Romans.* Minneapolis: Fortress, 2016.

Roetzel, Calvin J. "The Judgment Form in Paul's Letters." JBL 88 (1969), 305–12.

_____. *Judgment in the Community: A Study of the Relationship between Eschatology and Ecclesiology in Paul.* Leiden: Brill, 1972.

_____. *The Letters of Paul: Conversations in Context.* Louisville: Westminster/John Knox, 1991.

Rollins, Wayne G. "New Testament and Apocalyptic." NTS 17 (1971), 454–76.

Rowley, H. H. *The Relevance of Apocalyptic: A Study of Jewish and Christian Apocalypses from Daniel to the Revelation.* 2nd ed. London: Lutterworth, 1963.

Runesson, Anders, Donald D. Binder, and Birger Olsson. *The Ancient Synagogue from its Origins to 200 C.E.: A Source Book.* Ancient Judaism and Early Christianity 72. Leiden: Brill, 2008.

Russell, D. S. *The Method and Message of Jewish Apocalyptic, 200 BC–AD 100.* OTL. Philadelphia: Westminster, 1964.

Safrai, Shmuel. "The Synagogue." In *The Jewish People in the First Century: Historical Geography, Political History, Social, Cultural and Religious Life and Institutions.* Shmuel Safrai and M. Stern, eds. Vol 2. CRINT. Assen/Maastricht: Van Gorcum; Philadelphia: Fortress, 1974, 1987, 908–44.

Safrai, Shmuel and M. Stern, eds. *The Jewish People in the First Century: Historical Geography, Political History, Social, Cultural and Religious Life and Institutions.* 2 Vols. CRINT. Assen/Maastricht: Van Gorcum; Philadelphia: Fortress, 1974, 1987.

The Samaritan Chronicle No. II (or: Sepher Ha-Yamim), From Joshua to Nebuchadnezzar. Translated and ed. by John Macdonald. Beifhefte zur Zeitschrift für die alttestamentliche Wissenschaft, no. 107. Edited by Georg Fohrer. Berlin: Walter de Gruyter, 1969.

Sanday, William and Arthur C. Headlam. *A Critical and Exegetical Commentary on the Epistle to the Romans.* 5th ed. ICC. Edinburgh: T&T Clark, 1902.

Sanders, E. P. *Judaism: Practice and Belief, 63 BCE–66 C.* London: SCM; Philadelphia: Trinity Press International, 1992.

_____. *Paul and Palestinian Judaism: A Comparison of Patterns of Religion.* Minneapolis: Fortress, 1977.

Sanhedrin. Translated by H. Freedman. In *The Babylonian Talmud.* Translated and ed. by Isidore Epstein. 2 vols. London: Soncino Press, 1935.

Saxby, Alan. *James, Brother of Jesus, and the Jerusalem Church: A Radical Exploration of Christian Origins.* Foreword by James Crossley. Eugene, OR: Wipf and Stock, 2015.

Schlatter, Adolf. *Gottes Gerechtigkeit: Ein Kommentar zum Römerbrief.* 2nd ed. Stuttgart: Calwer Verlag, 1952.

_____. *Romans: The Righteousness of God.* Translated by Siegfried S. Schatzmann. Foreword by Peter Stuhlmacher. Peabody, MA.: Hendrickson, 1995.

Schmithals, Walter. *The Apocalyptic Movement: Introduction and Interpretation.* Translated by John E. Steely. Nashville: Abingdon, 1975.

Schneemelcher, Wilhelm. "Apocalyptic Prophecy of the Early Church: Introduction." Translated by David Hill. In *New Testament Apocrypha.* Edited by Edgar Hennecke and Wilhelm Schneemelcher. English translation ed. by R. McL. Wilson. 2 vols. Philadelphia: Westminster, 1959 and 1964, 2:684–89.

Schoeps, H. J. *Paul, the Theology of the Apostle in the Light of Jewish-Religious History.* Translated by Harold Knight. Philadelphia: Westminster, 1961.

Schonweiss, H. and H. C. Hahn. "Anger, Wrath," NIDNTT 1:105–13.

Schreiner, Thomas R. *The Law and Its Fulfillment: A Pauline Theology of the Law.* Grand Rapids: Baker, 1993.

_____. *Romans.* BECNT. Edited by Moises Silva. Grand Rapids: Baker, 1998.

Schweitzer, Albert. *The Mysticism of Paul the Apostle.* Translated by William Montgomery. London: A. & C. Black, 1931.

Scott, James M. *Paul and the Nations: The Old Testament and Jewish Background of Paul's Mission to the Nations with Special Reference to the Destination of Galatians.* WUNT 48. Tübingen: Mohr, 1995.

Scroggs, Robin. "Paul as Rhetorician: Two Homilies in Romans 1–11." *Jews, Greeks and Christians: Religious Cultures in Late Antiquity. Essays in Honor of William David Davies.* Edited by Robert Hamerton-Kelly and Robin Scroggs. Leiden: E. J. Brill, 1976.

Segal, Alan F. *Paul the Convert: The Apostolate and Apostasy of Saul the Pharisee.* New Haven and London: Yale University Press, 1990.

Seneca, Lucius Annaeus. *Epistolae morales ad Lucilium. Seneca: Epistles 66–92.* Translated by Tichard M. Gummere. LCL. 3 vols. Cambridge, MA: Harvard University Press, 1920.

Septuaginta. Edited by Alfred Rahlfs. Editio altera by Robert Hanhart. Stuttgart: Deutsche Bibelgesellschaft, 2006. Accordance module, Ver. 11, Oaktree Software.

Sevenster, J. N. *Paul and Seneca.* Supplements to Novum Testamentum, no. 4. Leiden: Brill, 1961.

Shabbath. Translated by H. Freedman. In *The Babylonian Talmud.* Translated and ed. by Isidore Epstein. 2 vols. London: Soncino Press, 1938.

Shakespeare, William. *Hamlet: Deluxe Edition (Illustrated).* n. p. Golden Classics, 2020.

Shear, Theodore L. "Excavations in the Theatre District and Tombs of Corinth in 1929." *American Journal of Archeology* 33.4 (1929), 515–46.

Sherwin-White, A. N. *Roman Society and Roman Law in the New Testament.* Oxford: Oxford University Press, 1963; reprint, Grand Rapids: Baker, 1978.

Sibylline Oracles. The Sibylline Oracles: Translated from the Greek into English Blank Verse. Translated by Terry Milton. Geneva: IPA, 2008.

Sifre: A Tannaitic Commentary on the Book of Deuteronomy. Translated from the Hebrew with Introduction and Notes by Reuven Hammer. Yale Judaica Series.

Edited by Leon Nemoy. Vol. XXIV: Sifre on Deuteronomy. London: Yale University Press, 1986.

Skipper, Ben. "Echoes of Eden: An Intertextual Analysis of Edenic Language in Romans 1:18–32." Unpublished PhD dissertation. New Orleans Baptist Theological Seminary, 2017.

Smith, Dennis E. and Joseph B. Tyson, eds. *Acts and Christian Beginnings: The Acts Seminar Report.* Salem, OR: Polebridge, 2013.

Smith, Taylor Clarence. "The Meaning of ὀργὴ θεοῦ [sic] in the Pauline Epistles." Unpublished ThD thesis, Southern Baptist Theological Seminary, 1944.

Son, Sang-Won (Aaron). *Corporate Elements in Pauline Anthropology. A Study of Selected Terms, Idioms, and Concepts in the Light of Paul's Usage and Background.* Analecta Biblica 148. Rome: Pontifical Biblical Institute, 2001.

Sophocles. Translated by F. Storr. LCL. London: William Heinemann; Cambridge: Harvard University Press, 1912–1913.

Sourvinou-Inwood, Christine. *'Reading' Greek Death: To the End of the Classical Period.* Oxford: Oxford University Press, 1995.

Spencer, Aída Besançon. *Paul's Literary Style: A Stylistic and Historical Comparison of II Corinthians 11:16–12:13, Romans 8:9–39, and Philippians 3:2–4:13.* ETSM. Jackson, MS: Evangelical Theological Society, 1984.

Stanley, Christopher D. *Arguing with Scripture: The Rhetoric of Quotation in the Letters of Paul.* New York, London: T&T Clark, 2004.

_____. *Paul and the Language of Scripture: Citation Technique in the Pauline Epistles and Contemporary Literature.* SNTS 74. Cambridge: Cambridge University Press, 1992.

Stendahl, Krister. *Paul Among Jews and Gentiles.* Philadelphia: Fortress, 1976.

Stevens, Gerald L. *Acts: A New Vision of the People of God.* Second Edition. Eugene, OR: Pickwick, 2019.

_____. "Capital Crimes in the Roman Empire" *Biblical Illustrator.* Vol. 26, no. 2, (Winter 1999–2000), 60–63.

_____. *Divine Wrath in Paul: An Exegetical Study.* Eugene, OR: Pickwick, 2020.

_____. *New Testament Greek Intermediate: From Morphology to Translation.* Eugene, OR: Pickwick, 2008.

_____. *New Testament Greek Primer: From Morphology to Grammar.* 3rd ed. Eugene, OR: Pickwick, 2014.

_____. *Revelation: The Past and Future of John's Apocalypse.* Eugene, OR: Pickwick, 2014.

_____. *Stevens Greek Workbook: A Companion to the Accordance Module.* Eugene, OR: Cascade, 2017.

Stewart, James S. *A Man in Christ: The Vital Elements of St. Paul's Religion.* Grand Rapids: Baker, 1975.

Stirewalt Jr., M. Luther. *Paul, the Letter Writer.* Grand Rapids, Cambridge: Eerdmans, 2003.

Stoicorum Veterum Fragmenta. Edited by Hans F. A. von Arnim. Stuttgart: B. G. Teubner Verlagsgesellschaft, 1964.

Stowers, Stanley Kent. "On the Comparison of Blood in Greek and Israelite Ritual." *Hesed Ve-Emet: Studies in Honor of Ernest S. Frerichs,* 179–96. BJS. Jodi Magness and Seymour Gitin, eds. Atlanta: Scholars, 1998.

_____. *A Rereading of Romans: Justice, Jews, and Gentiles.* New Haven: Yale University Press, 1994.

Strabo. *The Geography of Strabo.* Vol. 2. Translated by Horace Leonard Jones. LCL. Vol. 50, 1923. Cambridge, MA: Harvard University Press, 1988.

Suetonius. *The Lives of the Caesars.* Translated by J. C. Rolfe. 2 vols. LCL. Cambridge: Harvard University Press, 1914; reprint 1965.

Tacitus. Translated by M. Hutton et al. 5 vols. LCL. Cambridge: Harvard University Press, 1914–1937.

Tajra, Harry W. *The Martyrdom of St. Paul: Historical and Judicial Context, Traditions, and Legends.* WUNT 2/67. Tübingen: Mohr, 1994; reprint, Wipf and Stock, 2010.

The Targums of Onkelos and Jonathan Ben Uzziel on the Pentateuch, with the Fragments of the Jerusalem Targum, from the Chaldee. Translated by J. W. Etheridge. 2 vols. in 1. New York: KTAV, 1968.

Tasker, R. V. G. *The Biblical Doctrine of the Wrath of God.* London: Tyndale, 1951.

Taylor, Nicholas. *Paul, Antioch and Jerusalem: A Study in Relationships and Authority in Earliest Christianity.* JSNTSS 66. Sheffield: JSOT Press, 1992.

Teeple, Howard M. *The Mosaic Eschatological Prophet.* JBLMS. Philadelphia: Society of Biblical Literature, 1957.

Tertullian. *The Ante-Nicene Fathers* on CD-ROM. Accordance Bible Software Version 10.1.5, 2013. Print ed.: Tertullian. In vol. 3 of *The Ante-Nicene Fathers.* 1885–1896. 10 vols. Alexander Roberts, James Donaldson, and A. Cleveland Coxe, eds. New York: Christian Literature Company.

Testamenta XII Patriarcharum, Edited According to Cambridge University Library MS Ff 1.24 fol. 203a–262b. With short notes by M. De Jonge. Pseudepigrapha Veteris Testamenti Graece, no. 1, A. M. Denis and M. De Jonge, eds. Leiden: Brill, 1964.

Testamentum Iobi. Edited by S. P. Brock. Pseudepigrapha Veteris Testamenti Graece, no. 2. Edited by A. M. Denis and M. De Jonge. Leiden: Brill, 1967.

Theophilus. *Ad Autolycum.* Translated and ed. Robert M. Grant. Oxford Early Christian Texts. New York: Oxford University Press, 1970.

Thielman, Frank. *Paul and the Law: A Contextual Approach.* Downers Grove, IL: InterVarsity, 1994.

Thiselton, Anthony C. *The First Epistle to the Corinthians.* NIGTC. Grand Rapids: Eerdmans, 2000.

Thompson, Marianne Meye. "'Mercy upon All': God as Father in the Epistle to the Romans" in *Romans and the People of God: Essays in Honor of Gordon D. Fee on the Occasion of His 65th Birthday.* Edited by S. K. Soderlund and N. T. Wright. Grand Rapids: Eerdmans, 1999, 203–216.

Thornhill, A. Chadwick. *The Chosen People: Election, Paul and Second Temple Judaism.* Downers Grove, IL: InterVarsity, 2015.

Thornton, M. K. and R. L. Thornton, *Julio-Claudian Building Programs: A Quantitative Study in Political Management.* Mundelein, IL: Bolchazy-Carducci, 1989.

Thornton, T. C. G. "St. Paul's Missionary Intention in Spain." *Expository Times* 86(4) (1975), 120.

Thucydides. *History of the Peloponnesian War.* Translated by Charles Forster Smith. LCL. Vol. 1. Cambridge: Harvard University Press, 1923, rev., reprinted 1935.

Tobin, Thomas H. *Paul's Rhetoric in Its Context: The Argument of Romans.* Peabody, MA: Hendrickson, 2004.

Tomson, Peter J. *Paul and the Jewish Law: Halakha in the Letters of the Apostle to the Gentiles.* CRINT. Section 3: Jewish Traditions in Early Christian Literature. Assen/Maastricht: Van Gorcum; Minneapolis: Fortress, 1990.

Towner, Philip H. "1,2 Tim, Titus." NICNT. Grand Rapids: Eerdmans, 2006.

Trebilco, Paul. *The Early Christians in Ephesus from Paul to Ignatius.* Grand Rapids: Eerdmans, 2007.

Valerius Maximus. *Memorable Doings and Sayings, Volume I: Books 1–5.* Translated and ed. by D. R. Shackleton Bailey. LCL. Vol. 492. Cambridge: Harvard University Press, 2000.

VanHorn, Nathan W. "Arguing from Abraham: Remembrance as Rhetorical Warrant in Romans 1–4." Unpublished PhD dissertation, New Orleans Baptist Theological Seminary, 2016.

Vielhauer, Philip. "Apocalypses and Related Subjects: Introduction." Translated by David Hill. In *New Testament Apocrypha.* Edgar Hennecke and Wilhelm Schneemelcher, eds. English translation ed. by R. McL. Wilson. 2 vols. Philadelphia: Westminster, 1959 and 1964, 2:582–600.

_____. "Apocalyptic in Early Christianity: Introduction." Translated by David Hill. In *New Testament Apocrypha.* Edited by Edgar Hennecke and Wilhelm Schneemelcher. English translation ed. by R. McL. Wilson. 2 vols. Philadelphia: Westminster, 1959 and 1964, 2:608–42.

Virgil. Translated by H. Rushton Fairclough. 2 vols. LCL. Cambridge: Harvard University Press, 1916.

Vos, Geerhardus. *The Pauline Eschatology.* Grand Rapids: Eerdmans, 1953.

Wallace, David R. *Election of the Lesser Son: Paul's Lament-Midrash in Rom 9–11.* Minneapolis: Fortress, 2014.

Wallace-Hadrill, Andrew. "*Domus* and *Insulae* in Rome: Families and Households." In David L. Balch and Carolyn Osiek, eds. *Early Christian Families in Context: An Interdisciplinary Dialogue.* Grand Rapids: Eerdmans, 2003, 3–18.

Watson, Duane F. "The Contributions and Limitations of Greco-Roman Rhetorical Theory for Constructing the Rhetorical and Historical Situations of a Pauline Epistle." *The Rhetorical Interpretation of Scripture: Essays from the 1996 Malibu Conference.* Edited by Stanley E. Porter and Dennis L. Stamps. JSNTSS, No. 180, Edited by Stanley E. Porter. Sheffield: Sheffield Academic Press, 1999, 125–51.

Watson, Francis. *Paul and the Hermeneutics of Faith.* London, New York: T&T Clark, 2004.

Wedderburn, Alexander J. M. "Adam in Paul's Letter to the Romans." JSNTSup 3 (1980), 413–30.

_____. *The Reasons for Romans.* Minneapolis: Fortress, 1991.

Weima, Jeffrey A. D. *Neglected Endings: The Significance of the Pauline Letter Closings.* JSNT.SS 101; Sheffield: Sheffield Academic, 1994.

_____. *Paul the Ancient Letter Writer: An Introduction to Epistolary Analysis.* Grand Rapids: Baker, 2016.

Weitzman, Steven. "Forced Circumcision and the Shifting Roles of Gentiles in Hasmonean Ideology." HTR. Vol. 92, Issue 1 (January 1999), 37–59.

Westerholm, Stephen. *Israel's Law and the Church's Faith: Paul and His Recent Interpreters.* Grand Rapids: Eerdmans, 1988.

_____. *Perspectives Old and New on Paul: The "Lutheran" Paul and His Critics.* Grand Rapids, Cambridge: Eerdmans, 2004.

White, L. Michael. "Capitalizing on the Imperial Cult: Some Jewish Perspectives." *Rome and Religion: A Cross-Disciplinary Dialogue on the Imperial Cult*, 173–214. Jeffrey Brodd and Jonathan L. Reed, eds. WGRWSS, No. 5. Atlanta: Society of Biblical Literature, 2011.

Wiefel, Wolfgang. "The Jewish Community in Ancient Rome and the Origins of Roman Christianity." *The Romans Debate: Revised and Expanded Edition*. Edited by Karl P. Donfried. Peabody, PA: Hendrickson, 1991, 85–101.

Wilken, Robert L. *The Christians as the Romans Saw Them*. New Haven and London: Yale University Press, 1984.

Wilson, Mark. "*Hilasterion* and Imperial Ideology: A New Reading of Romans 3:25." HTS. Vol. 73, no. 3 (2017), 1–9. Online, https://doi.org/10.4102/hts.v73i3.4067. Accessed April 27, 2021.

Wilson, Robert McL. *Gnosis and the New Testament*. London: Blackwell, 1967.

Winter, Bruce W. *Divine Honours for the Caesars: The First Christians' Responses*. Grand Rapids, Cambridge: Eerdmans, 2015.

_____. *The Paul Quest: The Renewed Search for the Jew of Tarsus*. Grand Rapids, Downers Grove, IL: InterVarsity, 1998.

_____. *Roman Wives, Roman Widows: The Appearance of New Women and the Pauline Communities*. Grand Rapids, Cambridge: Eerdmans, 2003.

Wise, Michael O. *The First Messiah: Investigating the Savior Before Christ*. New York: HarperSanFrancisco, 1999.

Wright, Nicholas Thomas. *The Climax of the Covenant: Christ and the Law in Pauline Theology*. Minneapolis: Fortress, 1991.

_____. *Jesus and the Victory of God* in Christian Origins and the Question of God. Vol. 2. Minneapolis: Fortress, 1996.

_____. *The New Testament and the People of God* in Christian Origins and the Question of God. Vol. 1. Minneapolis: Fortress, 1992.

_____. *Paul and the Faithfulness of God*. Christian Origins and the Faithfulness of God. Vol. 4. Minneapolis: Fortress, 2013.

_____. *Paul and His Recent Interpreters*. Minneapolis: Fortress, 2015.

_____. *The Paul Debate: Critical Questions for Understanding the Apostle*. Waco, TX: Baylor University Press, 2015.

_____. *The Resurrection of the Son of God* in Christian Origins and the Question of God. Vol. 3. Minneapolis: Fortress, 2003.

_____. *Surprised by Hope: Rethinking Heaven, the Resurrection, and the Mission of the Church*. New York: HarperCollins, 2008.

Wuellner, Wilhelm. "Paul's Rhetoric of Argumentation in Romans: An Alternative to the Donfried-Karris Debate Over Romans." *The Romans Debate: Revised and Expanded Edition*. Edited by Karl P. Donfried. Peabody: Hendrickson, 1991, 128–146.

Zanker, Paul. *The Power of Images in the Age of Augustus*. Ann Arbor, MI: University of Michigan Press, 1990.

Zebabim. Translated by H. Freedman. In *The Babylonian Talmud*. Translated and ed. by Isidore Epstein. 2 vols. London: Soncino Press, 1948.

Scripture Index

Ancient Documents Index

Modern Authors Index

Subject Index

CPSIA information can be obtained
at www.ICGtesting.com
Printed in the USA
LVHW111615171121
703615LV00005B/210